Frommer's®   Gillis

S0-CFQ-760

Washington, D.C.

with Kids

8th Edition

by Beth Rubin

WILEY

Wiley Publishing, Inc.

About the Author

Beth Rubin has lived in the Washington, D.C. area since 1963. Having played tour guide for 40-plus years to her own two children (and friends and relatives she had not previously known), she now visits the sights with her inquisitive, fun-loving grandchildren. Her byline appears on features and essays in *The Washington Post, Roll Call, The Star Ledger, Art & Antiques* magazine, and the *Washingtonian*. Besides turning out eight editions of this guidebook, she is also the author of an award-winning novel, *Split Ends*.

Published by:

Wiley Publishing, Inc.

111 River St.
Hoboken, NJ 07030-5774

ISBN-13: 978-0-471-77344-3
ISBN-10: 0-471-77344-1

Editor: Jennifer Reilly
Production Editor: Michael Brumitt
Cartographer: Roberta Stockwell
Photo Editor: Richard Fox
Production by Wiley Indianapolis Composition Services

Front cover photo: Panda sleeping on rock at National Zoo
Back cover photo: Cherry blossoms in front of Washington Monument

For information on our other products and services or to obtain technical support, please contact our Customer Care Department within the U.S. at 800/762-2974, outside the U.S. at 317/572-3993 or fax 317/572-4002.

Wiley also publishes its books in a variety of electronic formats. Some content that appears in print may not be available in electronic formats.

Manufactured in the United States of America

5 4 3 2 1

Contents

List of Maps

For the fab 4: Joshua, Jaymie, Dustin, and Caitlin

Acknowledgments

I want to thank the many individuals—inside the Beltway and beyond—whose expertise and input made this book possible. I could not have completed this book without your help. To the visitors who took the time to write about their own experiences in the nation's capital, thank you for your valuable feedback. Thank you Rachel Lightbourne and Judy Colbert for your research assistance. Thanks to my family and friends for sticking by me when I was near deadline and at my crankiest, and to my editors, Jennifer Reilly and Melissa Klurman, for their encouragement, professionalism, and sharp eyes (all four of them).

An Invitation to the Reader

In researching this book, we discovered many wonderful places—hotels, restaurants, shops, and more. We're sure you'll find others. Please tell us about them, so we can share the information with your fellow travelers in upcoming editions. If you were disappointed with a recommendation, we'd love to know that, too. Please write to:

Frommer's Washington, D.C. with Kids, 8th Edition
Wiley Publishing, Inc. • 111 River St. • Hoboken, NJ 07030-5774

An Additional Note

Please be advised that travel information is subject to change at any time—and this is especially true of prices. We therefore suggest that you write or call ahead for confirmation when making your travel plans. The authors, editors, and publisher cannot be held responsible for the experiences of readers while traveling. Your safety is important to us, however, so we encourage you to stay alert and be aware of your surroundings. Keep a close eye on cameras, purses, and wallets, all favorite targets of thieves and pickpockets.

Other Great Guides for Your Trip:

Frommer's Washington, D.C.

Frommer's Washington, D.C. from $80 a Day

Frommer's Portable Washington, D.C.

Frommer's Memorable Walks in Washington, D.C.

Washington, D.C. For Dummies

Frommer's Virginia

Frommer's Maryland & Delaware

Frommer's Star Ratings, Icons & Abbreviations

Every hotel, restaurant, and attraction listing in this guide has been ranked for quality, value, service, amenities, and special features using a **star-rating system.** In country, state, and regional guides, we also rate towns and regions to help you narrow down your choices and budget your time accordingly. Hotels and restaurants are rated on a scale of zero (recommended) to three stars (exceptional). Attractions, shopping, nightlife, towns, and regions are rated according to the following scale: zero stars (recommended), one star (highly recommended), two stars (very highly recommended), and three stars (must-see).

In addition to the star-rating system, we also use **six feature icons** that point you to the great deals, in-the-know advice, and unique experiences that separate travelers from tourists. Throughout the book, look for:

Finds	Special finds—those places only insiders know about
Fun Fact	Fun facts—details that make travelers more informed and their trips more fun
Moments	Special moments—those experiences that memories are made of
Overrated	Places or experiences not worth your time or money
Tips	Insider tips—great ways to save time and money
Value	Great values—where to get the best deals

The following **abbreviations** are used for credit cards:

AE	American Express	DISC	Discover	V	Visa
DC	Diners Club	MC	MasterCard		

Frommers.com

Now that you have the guidebook to a great trip, visit our website at **www.frommers.com** for travel information on more than 3,000 destinations. With features updated regularly, we give you instant access to the most current trip-planning information available. At Frommers.com, you'll also find the best prices on airfares, accommodations, and car rentals—and you can even book travel online through our travel booking partners. At Frommers.com, you'll also find the following:

- Online updates to our most popular guidebooks
- Vacation sweepstakes and contest giveaways
- Newsletter highlighting the hottest travel trends
- Online travel message boards with featured travel discussions

How to Feel Like a Washington, D.C. Family

I moved to Washington, D.C. as a dewy-eyed college student—before the Kennedy Center or Metro; before Watergate, Iran-Contragate, Monicagate, or Iraqgate; and probably before you were born. I grabbed a B.A. from George Washington University in Foggy Bottom and a Mrs. (I actually married a native), and then found a job with a trade association—a polite term for lobbying groups. After a few years, I traded downtown traffic and bureaucracy for suburban diaper duty and freelancing. Raising two children a dozen miles from the National Mall had its perks. Whenever the kids grew restless with Play-Doh and Mr. Rogers—and in later years during school vacations—I bundled them into the car, and we headed to D.C. Back then, there were few resources targeted to families visiting the nation's capital. So we were trailblazers in a way, discovering the wonders of Washington, D.C. by the seat of our pants (and, sometimes, diapers). Armed with a map and a Frommer's guidebook, we found out which museum exhibits had the most kid appeal and where to let off steam. We learned the best and worst times to visit the popular attractions and where to get a quick and cheap meal. An inveterate note-taker, I amassed a lot of information—information that I shared with local friends and out-of-town visitors. Little did I know that I had sown the seeds for a guidebook. With the kids in school full time and bored with baking brownies for PTA functions, I began writing travel features in 1980. A decade later I parlayed my knowledge and our family's experiences into *Frommer's Washington, D.C. with Kids,* here in its 8th edition.

Since I first set foot on a D.C. street more than 40 years ago, I've lived through more scandals than I can count, endured Potomac Fever and worsening D.C. traffic, and survived 12 administrations of nine presidents. I was at one of the Washington Senators' final baseball games in 1971 and at one of the Washington Nationals' first games in 2005. The kids are now grown and are parents themselves. In the blink of an eye, I morphed into the grandmother of four munchkins whom I delight in introducing to the wonders of the nation's capital. Heaven knows my step is a bit slower, and I have more silver in my hair than in my jewelry box. Restaurants, hotels, dress codes—and many of the major players—have come and gone. But some things haven't changed. I still get a thrill on Capitol Hill. And when I walk past the White House. Or visit the newest zoo babies at the National Zoo. Or take in a world-class exhibition at one of the myriad museums or galleries. And whenever I'm downtown with the family, if you dig into my backpack, you'll still find—tucked beneath the tissues and snacks and crayons—my notepad and pen.

There's no doubt that living in or visiting the Center of the Free World can be an exciting and educational experience. Washington produces and employs more spin-doctors

Washington, D.C. Area

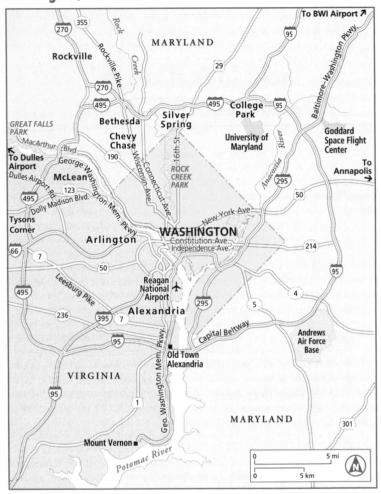

than anywhere else on the planet. This is not only the nation's capital, but also the *world* capital of security leaks. This is where congressional investigations, protests, spies, filibusters, motorcades, and national debts in the zillions are as commonplace as crabs in the Chesapeake Bay—or corn in Iowa. It's a place where our presidents take the oath of office outside the Capitol and subsequently lie in state in its Rotunda. D.C. is where protestors and special-interest groups converge to exercise their rights to free speech and assembly. Washington is where today's rumors bump noses with tomorrow's headlines—and cover-ups. What better place for children to learn the inner workings of our unique, if at times, confounding, form of government?

If you scratch the District's grimy bureaucratic surface, you'll uncover a cosmopolitan city that is rich in history—a microcosm of the American Experience and a living classroom. No wonder it's a top travel destination for families. For most of us who live in the Washington metropolitan area, D.C. is less about executive privilege, multibillion-dollar budgets, and votes than it is *home*—a vibrant multicultural city where we work, play, and raise our kids. A place where families fly kites on the Mall or listen to free concerts from front-row blankets on the Capitol lawn. Where we pause, in awe, to watch the president's motorcade pass by, even if we dislike the current president's policies. Or the president. Frequently we spot—on city streets, in restaurants, shops, and theaters—legislators, media moguls, and Hollywood celebs. We never tire of visiting the city's magnificent landmarks, sights, and diverse neighborhoods, whether on foot or via Metro, bicycle, open-air tram, cruise boat, and kayak.

Washington, D.C. is just another place on the map. And it's like nowhere else.

Kids and Washington, D.C. go together like peanut butter and jelly. Little wonder, then, that children of all ages come to know and love the fascinating international playground that is the nation's capital. Washington has broad tree-lined boulevards, numerous parks and recreational areas, and multiethnic shops and restaurants, not to mention its host of attractions (historic and new), waiting to be discovered and rediscovered. The nation's capital is a natural as a family vacation destination. Not bad for a 69¼-square-mile parcel of former swampland!

For those of us living in or near "the District" or "D.C.," it's not surprising that visiting families flock to Washington in huge numbers. In fact, nearly 19 million visitors came to Washington in 2004 when D.C. was named the 4th-most-visited U.S. destination (after Orlando, Las Vegas, and New York). Rest assured, the District pulls out all the stops to extend a friendly hand to families. Local hotels bend over backward to cater to families by offering special rates and perks to those with kids in tow. And restaurants go out of their way to please pint-size patrons with kids' menus, half portions, crayons—and sometimes free food. It's no accident that thousands of buses and planeloads of schoolchildren arrive annually from all over the world. Where else can kids visit the president's house, touch a moon rock, view the city from atop a 555-foot obelisk, and cruise the Potomac on a luxury yacht or the C&O Canal on a mule-drawn boat—all within minutes of the U.S. Capitol? And that's just for openers!

Despite the staggering number of museums and federal buildings, much of downtown Washington resembles an enormous park. First-time visitors are quick to note the abundance of greenery cozying up to all the marble and granite. In fact, gardens, fountains, and parks hug most major sightseeing attractions. The area known as the National Mall (stretching for 2 miles from the U.S. Capitol to the Lincoln Memorial) is the perfect site for chasing pigeons or flying a kite. Anyone with kids knows that they have short attention spans and typically get bored and antsy after an hour in a museum. These same kids, cranky from being cooped up and longing for physical activity, can exit almost any museum in D.C. onto a glorified yard and let loose.

Compared to other urban areas, both in the United States and abroad, Washington's skyline is surprisingly and refreshingly uncluttered. You can thank the founding fathers for that: Because the original city planners declared that no building could be higher than the dome of the U.S. Capitol, the height of commercial buildings is strictly regulated to 110 feet. And if you've visited other major cities recently, you'll be pleased to discover that Washington's foremost tourist areas are clean and safe.

Getting around D.C. is a breeze. All major attractions are accessible by the Metro, the public rail/bus system. Despite signs of aging that may occasionally cause delays and frustration, the subways are clean, safe, and surprisingly graffiti free. They're also quiet. It's easy to navigate the city with kids on the Metro, even if they're in strollers. Some stations are at hotels, shops, and food courts listed in this book. Most are within a couple of blocks of your destination. And except for a few neighborhoods, where you're not apt to be in the first place, you can unleash older children to wander on their own. Teenagers will enjoy exploring areas such as Georgetown and Old Town Alexandria, which are uniquely appealing to this age group.

You don't need a degree in accounting to budget for a D.C. vacation. Or a huge budget! Prices for food, lodging, and entertainment compare favorably with those of other tourist meccas around the United States and around the world. If you've recently been to New York, London, Los Angeles, or Rome, you'll find Washington a relative bargain—even if you can't sleep for free in the White House. Families also find that they can eat well in a wide variety of kid-friendly Washington restaurants without breaking the bank. Best of all, almost all the major attractions are free. Try that in New York or Paris!

Tourism is the second-largest industry in D.C. The first, as you might have guessed, is the federal government. The "natives" (sort of an inside joke, because so many residents come from somewhere else) are friendly, helpful, and eager to make visitors feel at home. Washington is, after all, everyone's home, and it tends to engender a sense of belonging to short-term guests as well as longtime residents.

Although D.C.'s citizens enjoy many perks, they have suffered, one way or another, because of local politics. Here's why. According to the Constitution, Congress has the power to "exercise exclusive legislation . . . over the seat of the Government of the United States." Believe it or not, before 1961 and the passage of the 23rd Amendment, residents of the District could not vote in national elections. Under the Reorganization of 1967, the president appointed a mayor and nine-member council to govern the District.

In 1970, Congress okayed legislation for a delegate to represent the District in the House of Representatives, but here's the catch: This rep can vote on committees but not on legislation on the House floor. And although Washington has had an elected mayor and city council since 1975, Congress continues its tight reign over the D.C. budget. It must be true that adversity builds character, because those who live and work in the District share an immense feeling of pride. Chances are, it will rub off on you and yours during your visit.

Kids who snooze their way through American History in school wake up when they tour the Capitol, White House, and other federal buildings. Being there and seeing for themselves where laws are enacted, where the president lives, and where the government works leave a mark on young minds—one that won't soon be erased.

1 Frommer's Favorite Washington, D.C. Family Experiences

Watching the Fourth of July Fireworks on the Mall. You can't beat the setting of the Washington Monument grounds, National Mall, or west front of the Capitol for observing the nation's birthday. A concert by the National Symphony Orchestra, culminating in the *1812 Overture,* accompanies the magnificent pyrotechnic display. See p. 119 for a map of the Mall.

Seeing the Sunset Behind the Lincoln Memorial. Make sure your camera is primed and ready to snap for one of Mother Nature's better shows. The west front section of the Capitol is the best vantage point for a sweeping view across the Mall to the Lincoln Memorial and beyond.

Catching a Free Concert on the Capitol Lawn. Memorial Day and Labor Day weekends and July 4th, local families toting blankets and chairs camp on the Capitol lawn to hear a free concert by the National Symphony Orchestra and songs by a megastar or two, and then join in the traditional sing-along. See "Calendar of Kids' Favorite Events" in chapter 2 for more information.

Row, Row, Rowing Your Boat on the Potomac. Don't go home without viewing Washington's waterfront and several major sights from an appropriate conveyance: rowboat, canoe, or kayak. Or let someone else play captain on a river cruise. Equally fun is pedaling a 2- or 4-seater around the Tidal Basin before visiting the Jefferson and FDR memorials. See "Boating" under "Outdoor Activities" in chapter 8.

Picnicking on the Mall. Have your hotel pack a picnic, or get carryout from a food court or restaurant to enjoy on the Mall. There's plenty of room on the 2-mile lawn between the Capitol and Lincoln Memorial.

Looking up Your Congressional Representative or Senator. Stop and say hello to the folks who partake in those lengthy and boring filibusters, battle the pigheaded opposition, and work long days (and often nights). Tell him/her how you feel—how you *really feel*—about important issues. Be prepared: You may end up shaking hands with an administrative assistant who looks about 12. Research your representatives or senators at www.senate.gov or www.house.gov, or call © **202/224-3121.** See p. 153 for more information on visiting the U.S. Capitol.

Spying on the Giant Pandas at the National Zoo. Visit the baby panda, born July 9, 2005, to Mei Xiang. Plan your visit to arrive early in the day when the pandas are most active. For an even more up-close-and-personal look, you can use the pandacam. See p. 135.

Taking Pictures of the Cherry Blossoms. Forget about buying those touched-up postcards. Make your own. Photos of the cherry blossoms, the White House, or other famous D.C. sights make stunning cards to mail or email to friends and family. They're also one-of-a-kind souvenirs of your visit.

Listening to a Military Band Concert. March yourselves over to a free military band concert, and salute the red, white, and blue. The concerts are held two or three evenings a week in summer at several D.C. venues and Arlington Memorial Cemetery. See "Military Band Concerts" under "Music" in chapter 10.

Seeing a Free Movie on the Mall. Families blanket the Washington Monument grounds summer evenings for "Screen on the Green," free screenings of classics such as *Casablanca* and *The Graduate* under the stars. See p. 248.

Getting a Bird's-Eye View from the Washington Monument. Come here at off times for a shorter wait, and thrill to a panorama of downtown D.C.; Arlington, Virginia; and beyond. Yes, it is touristy, and yes, it is usually crowded. Go anyway. If you've been during the day, go at night. You may not recognize the sights, but it is a spectacular view! See p. 145.

Reading the Charters of Freedom at the Archives. A moving experience awaits visitors, especially first-timers, regardless of their hailing port. The Declaration of Independence, Constitution, and Bill of Rights have been much more reader-friendly (especially to youngsters and those with disabilities) since the Archives' building renovation and charters restoration a few years ago. See p. 164.

Experiencing America the Beautiful in *To Fly* **at the Air and Space Museum's IMAX Theater.** What is it about this movie? Thirty years after its debut, crowds still line up to view it. My eyes still mist over at the breathtaking photography—and I've seen it at least a dozen times. See p. 125.

2 Best Hotel Bets

Most Family-Friendly near the Mall: The **J.W. Marriott,** 1331 Pennsylvania Ave. NW (✆ **202/626-6991**), and **L'Enfant Plaza,** 480 L'Enfant Plaza SW (✆ **202/484-1000**), are each less than a 10-minute walk to the Mall. Both offer plenty of family perks, along with nearby sightseeing, dining, and shopping opportunities. And both have direct access to the Metro, so no raindrops need fall on your heads. See p. 64.

Most Child-Pampering Hotel: The Four Seasons, 2800 Pennsylvania Ave. NW (✆ **800/332-3442** or 202/342-0444), does not discriminate, pampering children every bit as much as their parents. Some of the hotel's kid-spoiling tactics include gifts at check-in, brownies and milkshakes at tea, videos to borrow, kid-size terry robes, and milk and cookies at evening turndown. See p. 69.

Most Fun for Kids 5 and Older: The Helix, 1430 Rhode Island Ave. NW (✆ **800/706-1202** or 202/462-9001), knows how to create the right atmosphere for young-at-heart fun-seekers. When was the last time you had a pillow fight? Well, get on the stick! Request the Family Bunk Room for four, with a king and double-decker bed (top single, bottom double), and battle it out for the top berth. See p. 67.

Best Views: L'Enfant Plaza, 480 L'Enfant Plaza SW (✆ **202/484-1000**), has rooms that enjoy views of the Potomac River; Arlington, Virginia; and Georgetown. See p. 65. Some top-floor rooms of the **Omni Shoreham,** 2500 Calvert St. NW (✆ **202/234-0700**), overlook Rock Creek Park and/or downtown. See p. 73.

Best Value for Families: Holiday Inn on the Hill, 415 New Jersey Ave. NW (✆ **800/638-1116**), has a convenient Capitol Hill address, a rooftop pool with sundeck and snack bar, and a Family Fun Package with lots of perks. At all times, kids 18 and under stay free with parents, and best of all, kids 12 and under eat free in the Senators Grille. See p. 60.

Best Suite Deals: Washington Suites Georgetown, 2500 Pennsylvania Ave. NW (✆ **877/736-2500** or 202/333-8060), is a short walk from the Foggy Bottom Metro and has lots more to recommend it—kids 18 and under free in the same suite (with a separate bedroom), and complimentary cribs, strollers, and expanded continental breakfast daily. Pets are welcome too. You'll find a grocery store and slew of neighborhood restaurants within a few blocks. See p. 71.

Best Bargain for Families: Hosteling International–Washington, D.C., 1009 11th St. NW, at K St. (✆ **202/737-2333**). If you don't mind roughing it a bit, staying here is a bargain and makes for a super family experience not far from the action. Kids 3 to 11 (with a parent) pay only $10 per night, those 2 and under are free,; and special family activities are gratis. See p. 62.

Hippest Bathrooms: Helix, 1430 Rhode Island Ave. NW (✆ **800/706-1202** or 202/462-9001). Better than a jolt of java in the morning are the Helix's minimalist, crayon-colored bathrooms. What? A bathroom without a traditional vanity?

Where does the water go? And how does it get there? This could be the most fun your family have ever had brushing their teeth. See p. 67.

Most Peace and Quiet: Morrison–Clark, 1015 L St. NW (between 11th St. and Massachusetts Ave.; © 800/332-7898 or 202/898-1200). If your kids are out of diapers and well behaved—there are lots of antiques here ripe for breaking—opt for a room with a porch or balcony overlooking the garden courtyard. Stay here for a genteel experience a tad off the beaten path yet convenient to the Metro and the sights. Kids 16 and under stay free with parents, and weekend breakfast is complimentary. See p. 80.

Coolest Decor: Helix, 1430 Rhode Island Ave. NW (© 800/706-1202 or 202/462-9001). In a town that takes itself too seriously, here are royal blue and orange countertops, curtained platform beds, floating entertainment centers, lava lamps, and Pop Rocks in the honor bar. This is hotel as entertainment. See p. 67.

Best Pool: L'Enfant Plaza, 480 L'Enfant Plaza (© 202/484-1000). The attractive outdoor pool (covered in the winter) is surrounded by potted flowering plants and has plenty of seating and, best of all, a snack bar. Many families opt for a room off the pool. (This is also a primo place to watch the Fourth of July fireworks!) See p. 65.

Best Hotel Food Deal for Kids, Coffee Shop: At the **Holiday Inn on the Hill,** 415 New Jersey Ave. NW (© 800/638-1116), guests 12 and under eat free in the on-site Senators Grille restaurant, where they can order their faves (pancakes, hot dogs, pizza, and the like) off the kids' menu at breakfast, lunch, and dinner. See p. 60. At the **Grand Hyatt at Washington Convention Center,** 1000 H St. NW (© 202/582-1234 or 800/233-1234), kids 3 and under eat for free in the Grand Cafe; kids 12 and under can order from the kids' menu or half portions from the regular menu. See p. 63.

Most Welcoming to Pets: From April to October, **The Holiday Inn Select in Old Town,** 480 King St., Alexandria, Virginia (© 703/549-6080), hosts Doggy Happy Hour every Tuesday and Thursday from 5 to 8pm. Bring Fido for water and biscuits while you enjoy free hors d'oeuvres in the brick courtyard. See p. 261.

Best for Athletic Families: The jocks and jockettes in your family will love the **Omni Shoreham,** 2500 Calvert St. NW (© 202/234-0700), for its oversize outdoor pool and extensive grounds for power walks or jogs. Exit the hotel's back door to Rock Creek Park's 10 miles of hiking and biking trails and its 1½-mile fitness course with 18 exercise stations. You can also walk to the zoo. See p. 73.

3 Best Dining Bets

Best Burgers: Houston's, 7715 Woodmont Ave., Bethesda, MD (© 301/656-9755), and 12256 Rockville Pike, Rockville, MD (© 301/463-3535), consistently serves the best burgers in the area. I mourn the day Houston's closed its Georgetown location. Go at off times or bring a copy of *War and Peace* to read while you wait. Runner-up award goes to **Fuddruckers,** 734 7th St. NW (© 202/628-3361) or 18th St. and Jefferson Place

NW, just off Connecticut Ave. (© 202/659-1660).

Best Hot Dogs: Nathan's, the top dawgs introduced almost 90 years ago in NYC, get my vote. But outside of some D.C.-area supermarkets, you will have to travel to Pier C at either Reagan National Airport or BWI Airport to get one. Word has it that Nathan's will be more readily available in our area in the coming years. Runner-up goes to the much-easier-to-find

Sabrett's. Just look for the carts with the blue and yellow umbrellas downtown and near the Mall. See p. 87.

Best Kids' Menu: Senators Grille at the Holiday Inn on the Hill serves free food to kids 12 and under (with an adult) at breakfast, lunch, and dinner. The portions may not be huge, but hey, who's complaining? Youngsters can choose among a bunch of well-prepared kid faves—pancakes, hamburgers, pizza, and the like—on the kids' menu. See p. 60.

Best Place for Politicking: Head for the exclusive **Senators' Dining Room** (✆ 202/224-2350) in the U.S. Capitol to rub elbows with U.S. senators and order a tureen of famous Senate Bean Soup, which, after many years, still costs only $4.50. You'll need a "request letter," and men must wear a suit and tie to experience this D.C. moment. See the introduction to the "Capitol Hill" section of chapter 5 for more information.

Best Pizza: Pizzeria Paradiso, at 2029 P St. NW (✆ 202/223-1245) and 3282 M St. NW (✆ 202/337-1245), is *the* place for wood-oven-baked classic pizza. I usually stick to the basic Margherita or Quattro Formaggi (four cheeses). Pizza this good doesn't need extra toppings. See p. 104.

Best Tex-Mex: Austin Grill, 750 E St. NW, between 7th and 8th streets (✆ 202/393-3776); 2404 Wisconsin Ave. NW (just north of Georgetown; ✆ 202/337-8080); and in the Maryland and Virginia 'burbs, has a varied menu of *deliciosa* Tex-Mex favorites and Margaritas for Mom and Dad. *Muy bueno!* See p. 92.

Best Food Court: The **Food Court at the Ronald Reagan Building and International Trade Center,** 1300 Pennsylvania Ave. NW (✆ 202/312-1300), is in a primo location for hungry downtown sightseers. Belly up to one of the stands for hamburgers, chicken, salads, deli, Cajun, wraps, and ethnic fare (pizza, sushi, dim sum, and filled pita). On Capitol Hill, you will find similar fare with even more selections (plus all those trains and shops) at **Union Station,** 50 Massachusetts Ave. NE (✆ 202/371-9441). See p. 87.

Best Restaurant for Teens: A trip to the **Hard Rock Cafe,** 999 E St. NW, next to Ford's Theatre (✆ 202/737-ROCK), will make you a hero to your kids. Here, you can ogle (depending on your age) Britney Spears' costume, an autographed Stones photo, or one of Chuck Berry's guitars. This will take your mind off the food, which is okay but nothing to write a song about. See p. 93.

Best Ice Cream: Gifford's, 7237 Woodmont Ave., Bethesda, MD (✆ 301/907-3436), has been pleasing generations of area ice cream lovers for decades with its rich ice cream treats. Try the Hot Fudge or Swiss sundaes or double-dip cone. See p. 110. If you can't make it to Bethesda, head for one of **Ben & Jerry's** six D.C. locations. See p. 90.

Best Ice Cream Parlor: Thomas Sweet ("Sweet's" to locals), 3214 P St. NW (at Wisconsin Ave.; ✆ 202/337-0616), reminds me of my youth and the Malt Shoppe in Archie comics. The ice cream is made on the premises, and a single-dip ice cream cone is $2.15; a double, $2.75. Quite a deal in this day and age. See p. 100.

Best Milkshake: Chick and Ruth's Delly, 165 Main St., Annapolis, MD (✆ 410/269-6737), makes the kind of thick shakes and malts of which poetry is writ. If you have to ask how much ice cream goes into these monsters, you shouldn't go here. You could nurse one of these too-thick-to-sip-through-a-straw babies for an hour. See p. 272.

Best Breakfast: The Market Lunch (in Eastern Market), 225 7th St. SE (✆ 202/547-8444), is the place for blueberry pancakes and local Capitol Hill ambience. You may have to wait, but that's part of the experience. See p. 87. For hearty breakfast platters—bacon and eggs, omelets, and the like—head to **Afterwords Café,** 1517 Connecticut Ave. NW (© **202/387-1462;** p. 102), or **Luna Grill and Diner,** 1301 Connecticut Ave. NW (© **202/835-2280;** p. 102). If you want more formal trappings (for example, tablecloths), make a reservation at the **Old Ebbitt Grill,** 675 15th St. NW (© **202/347-4801**). See p. 94.

Best Place for a Picnic: Tote that hamper or brown bag to the **National Mall,** between 4th and 7th streets NW. For picnicking alfresco, you can't beat the lawn between the Washington Monument and the Capitol. (Aren't you glad you don't have to cut the grass?) When in Georgetown, go to **Washington Harbour Park,** foot of 31st (below M Street).

Best Waterfront Dining: Friends, we have a three-way tie here. **Sequoia,** 3000 K St. (© **202/944-4200**), perched on the Potomac in Georgetown, has a drop-dead view of the riverfront and pretty good food. At the **Chart House,** 1 Cameron St., Alexandria, VA (© **703/684-5080**), on another part of the Potomac, you can drool over the yachts along with your coconut shrimp. **Cantler's Riverside Inn,** 458 Forest Beach Rd., Annapolis, MD (© **410/757-1311**), is situated on picturesque Mill Creek and is *the* place to go for steamed Maryland blue crabs. See p. 264 and 272, respectively.

Best Selection: America, 50 Massachusetts Ave. NE at Union Station (© **202/685-9555**), serves tasty takes on regional favorites and comfort food (meatloaf, steak, pizza, pork chops, ribs, burgers, wraps, soups, and sandwiches). Few, other than linebackers, can finish the oversize portions here. Let the kids split an order, or doggy-bag the leftovers. See p. 86.

Best Romantic Restaurant (for Night When You Hire a Sitter): The **Sea Catch Restaurant and Raw Bar,** at Canal Square, 1054 31st St. NW, Georgetown (© **202/337-8855**), has seating overlooking the picturesque C&O Canal. Many think the restaurant serves the best seafood in D.C. Make a reservation for a coveted outdoor table as soon as you plan your escape. See p. 97.

4 Best of the Best

Best Place to Run Around: Head for the **National Mall** (you can't miss it—just step outside almost any Smithsonian museum). If you have time, go to **Rock Creek Park** at 5200 Glover Rd. NW (© **202/426-6829**), where you may also ride bikes or horses, play tennis or golf, gaze at the stars, swing, slide, hike, or rent a boat on the C&O Canal or Potomac. See p. 200.

Best Views: The Washington Monument, 15th Street and Constitution Avenue NW (© **202/426-6841**), can't be beat, but you need passes spring and summer. See p. 145. You'll rarely have a wait at the **Old Post Office,** 1100 Pennsylvania Ave. NW (© **202/289-4224**). Take the elevator to the clock tower for a panoramic view of downtown and beyond. See p. 163. The **National Cathedral,** Massachusetts and Wisconsin aves. NW (© **202/537-6200**), is a bit out of the way, but the view from the Pilgrim Observation Gallery is spectacular. See p. 150.

Best Ride for Kids: Both the **Carousel on the Mall,** 1000 Jefferson Dr. SW (on the Mall outside the Smithsonian "Castle"; © **202/357-2700**), and the **Dentzel Carousel** at Glen Echo Park, MacArthur Boulevard at Goldsborough Road, Glen Echo, MD (© **301/492-6282**), get my vote. See "Carousels" under "Rides for Children" in chapter 8.

Best Souvenirs: Souvenir City, 1001 K St. NW (between 10th and 11th streets; © **202/638-1836**), sells shirts, books, paperweights, mugs, and other D.C.-inspired mementos. See p. 235.

Best Toy Store: Barston's Child's Play, 5536 Connecticut Ave. (© **202/244-3602**), and **Sullivan's,** 3412 Wisconsin Ave. NW (© **202/362-1343**), get my vote and have stood the test of time. Both are in the Friendship Heights neighborhood, because that's where a large number of affluent D.C. families live. Though they're a bit out of the way if you're staying in downtown D.C., the stores are well stocked and excel at giving their young customers one-on-one attention. (For this toy shopper, they are a refreshing alternative to the large, impersonal toy "factories" where customer service is far from the numero-uno concern.) See p. 234.

Best History Lesson: For older kids, sitting in the **House or Senate galleries at the U.S. Capitol,** East Capitol Street and 1st Street NE (© **202/225-6827** or 202/224-3121), when either is in session is to view history in the making. Bear in mind that the House and Senate are not in session all the time. You can check the local papers or the Capitol website to see what is on the docket. See p. 153.

Most Unusual Tour: D.C. Ducks, Union Station, 50 Massachusetts Ave. NE (© **202/966-DUCK**), departs Union Station to tour various Washington, D.C. sights on land and sea (the Potomac River) in refurbished World War II amphibious vehicles. See p. 213.

2

Planning a Family Trip to Washington, D.C.

Logistics take on a whole new meaning when you're dealing with a group—nothing is simple when the needs of the many must be taken into account, as happens with most (successful) family vacations. Happily, I've trouped all over Washington, D.C. on your behalf, and thought long and hard about the details so that you won't have to work too hard to devise a terrific trip to suit your own entourage.

1 Visitor Information

Nothing beats careful planning for a smooth-running, fun-filled vacation, especially when traveling with kids. I think familiarizing yourself with your destination is always helpful. Because you're traveling to the nation's capital, why not practice the precepts of a democracy and include your children in the planning process? Encourage your kids to borrow books from the library and surf the net for information. Then gather everyone at the dinner table, and share what you've learned along with your mac and cheese. Discuss your priorities, and before you know it, you have a working itinerary.

Our family likes to list "must-sees," followed by backups we can live without. I've found that it's wise not to leave anything but the weather (and, if you're not fussy, where to eat) to chance. Make any necessary reservations before you arrive. Then allow those unrehearsed magic moments to filter in. Speaking of planning: If you want to eat lunch in the members' dining room or to take VIP tours of the Capitol, White House (groups of 10 or more only), Kennedy Center, Bureau of Engraving and Printing, or FBI (when it reopens), contact your congressional representatives. You don't have to be very important; this will allow you to tour with a smaller group. Passes are limited, and 6 months before your visit is not too soon to write. Send your request, with the dates of your trip, names of people in your party, your phone number, and mailing address, to your senator, C/O U.S. Senate, Washington, DC 20510, or your representative, C/O U.S. House of Representatives, Washington, DC 20515. If you're not sure whom you should write to, call the Capitol switchboard (© 202/224-3121), or visit www.house.gov or www.senate.gov.

Besides combing the travel shelves of your local library and bookstores, you can order brochures from the following sources: **Washington, D.C. Convention and Tourism Corporation,** 901 7th St. NW, 4th Floor, Washington, DC 20001 (© 202/789-7000 or 800/422-8644; www.washington.org); the **Washington, D.C. Chamber of Commerce,** Visitor Information Center in Ronald Reagan Building, 1300 Pennsylvania Ave. NW

(℃ **202/866-DCISFUN** [347-7386]; www. dcchamber.org); **Washington, D.C. Accommodations** (℃ **202/289-2220** or 800-503-3330; www.wdcahotels.com); **Capitol Reservations** (℃ **202/452-1270**

or **800/847-4832;** www.visitdc.com); and **Bed and Breakfast Accommodations, Ltd.** (℃ **877/893-3233;** www.bedand breakfastdc.com).

2 Money

ATMS

The easiest and best way to get cash away from home is from an ATM (automated teller machine). The Cirrus (℃ **800/424-7787;** www.mastercard.com) and PLUS (℃ **800/843-7587;** www.visa.com) networks span the globe; look at the back of your bank card to see which network you're on, and then call or check online for ATM locations at your destination. Be sure you know your personal identification number (PIN) and daily withdrawal limit before you depart. *Note:* Remember that many banks impose a fee every time you use a card at another bank's ATM; that fee can be higher for international transactions (up to $5 or more) than for domestic ones (where they're rarely more than $2). In addition, the bank from which you withdraw cash may charge its own fee. To compare banks' ATM fees within the United States, use www.bankrate.com.

You can use your credit card to receive cash advances at ATMs. Keep in mind that credit card companies protect themselves from theft by limiting maximum withdrawals outside their home country, so call your credit card company before you leave home. And keep in mind that you'll pay interest from the moment of your withdrawal, even if you pay your monthly bills on time.

TRAVELER'S CHECKS

Traveler's checks are something of an anachronism from the days before the ATM made cash accessible at any time. Given the fees you'll pay for ATM use at banks other than your own, however, you might be better off with traveler's checks if you're withdrawing money often.

You can buy traveler's checks at most banks. **American Express** offers denominations of $20, $50, $100, $500, and (for cardholders only) $1,000. You'll pay a service charge ranging from 1% to 4%. By phone, you can buy traveler's checks by calling ℃ **800/807-6233.** American Express cardholders should dial ℃ **800/ 221-7282;** this number accepts collect calls, offers service in several foreign languages, and exempts Amex gold and platinum cardholders from the 1% fee.

Visa offers traveler's checks at Citibank locations nationwide, as well as at several other banks. The service charge ranges between 1.5% and 2%; checks come in denominations of $20, $50, $100, $500, and $1,000. Call ℃ **800/732-1322** for information. AAA members can obtain Visa checks for a $9.95 fee (for checks up to $1,500) at most AAA offices or by calling ℃ **866/339-3378. MasterCard** also offers traveler's checks. Call ℃ **800/223-9920** for a location near you.

Foreign-currency traveler's checks are useful if you're traveling to one country or to the Euro zone; they're accepted at locations where dollar checks may not be, such as bed and breakfasts, and they minimize the currency conversions you'll have to perform while you're on the go. **American Express, Thomas Cook, Visa,** and **MasterCard** offer foreign-currency traveler's checks. You'll pay the rate of exchange at the time of your purchase (so it's a good idea to monitor the rate before you buy), and most companies charge a transaction fee per order (and a shipping fee if you order online).

If you do choose to carry traveler's checks, keep a record of their serial numbers

What Things Cost in Washington, D.C.

Taxi from National Airport to J.W. Marriott	$15
Taxi from Dulles Airport (Virginia) to J.W. Marriott	$45
Taxi from BWI Airport to J.W. Marriott	$60
Super Shuttle from Dulles Airport (Virginia) Downtown Hotel	$52 (family of 4)
Local telephone call	35¢
Metro ride	$1.35 –$3.90
Taxi	$4 (within same zone) and up
Double room at J.W. Marriott (very expensive)	$369–$429
Double room at the Carlyle Suites (moderate)	$153–$269
Double room at the Best Western Capital Beltway (inexpensive)	$119
Lunch for one at Hard Rock Cafe (moderate)	$20
Lunch for one at the Air and Space Museum (inexpensive)	$8–10
Lunch (hot dog, soda, and potato chips) from street vendor	$3–$4
Dinner for one at America (moderate)	$25
Dinner for one at Bullfeathers (inexpensive)	$16
Medium soft drink in a restaurant	$1.50–$2
Ice-cream cone	$2.25–$2.75
Roll of Kodak 100 film, 36 exposures	$6
Admission to National Zoological Park	Free
Movie ticket (adult)	$6.50 (matinee before 6pm) or $8.50 (evening)
Movie ticket (child)	$5.50

separate from your checks in the event that they are stolen or lost. You'll get a refund faster if you know the numbers.

CREDIT CARDS

Credit cards are another safe way to carry money. They also provide a convenient record of all your expenses, and they generally offer relatively good exchange rates. You can also withdraw cash advances from your credit cards at banks or ATMs, provided you know your PIN. If you don't know yours, call the number on the back of your credit card, and ask the bank to send it to you. It usually takes 5 to 7 business days, though some banks will provide the number over the phone if you tell them your mother's maiden name or some other personal information.

3 When to Go

THE CLIMATE For obvious reasons, you'll probably plan your visit for spring or summer, when the kids are out of school. That's fine, but understand that the warm-weather months are when Washington is most crowded. Although summer is the best time to take advantage of numerous free outdoor events and reduced hotel rates, the heat and humidity can wilt a cactus. However, if you dress appropriately and sightsee early or late in the day, you'll fare well.

July and August are the warmest months, with average highs in the mid-80s. This is not to say that it won't heat up to the mid-90s—it does with disturbing regularity and oppressively high humidity. Fortunately, all the public buildings, restaurants, and hotels in Washington are air-conditioned, and many hotels have swimming pools.

If your kids are preschoolers or budding geniuses who can afford to miss school, fall is a lovely time to visit. The weather is usually pleasant and mild, and you can enjoy the city while the rest of the world is at home, work, or school. In winter, hotel prices usually dip around the Christmas holidays, and lines at attractions are shorter.

Highs in December, January, and February are in the mid-40s, with lows around 30°F. Again, these are averages. The rainfall is evenly distributed throughout the year, so don't leave home without a raincoat.

Average Monthly Temperatures

	Jan	Feb	Mar	Apr	May	June	July	Aug	Sept	Oct	Nov	Dec
Avg. High (°F)	45	44	53	64	75	83	87	84	78	68	55	45
Avg. High (°C)	7	7	12	18	24	28	31	29	26	20	13	7
Avg. Low (°F)	27	28	35	44	55	63	68	66	60	48	38	30
Avg. Low (°C)	-3	-2	2	7	13	17	20	19	16	9	3	-1

HOLIDAYS On the following legal national holidays, banks, government offices, and post offices are closed. Subways (Metrorail) and buses (Metrobus) operate less frequently, usually on a Saturday or Sunday schedule (✆ **202/637-7000;** www.mata.com for information). Museums, stores, and restaurants vary widely in their open/closed policies. To avoid disappointment, call before you go.

National holidays are January 1 (New Year's Day), third Monday in January (Martin Luther King, Jr.'s Birthday), third Monday in February (Presidents' Day), last Monday in May (Memorial Day), July 4th (Independence Day), first Monday in September (Labor Day), second Monday in October (Columbus Day), November 11 (Veterans' Day/Armistice Day), fourth Thursday in November (Thanksgiving Day), and December 25 (Christmas Day).

The Tuesday following the first Monday in November is Election Day. It is a legal holiday in presidential-election years (2008, 2012, and so on).

If you're planning to visit during the **National Cherry Blossom Festival,** which runs for 2 weeks from late March into April, write for a schedule of events to National Cherry Blossom Festival, P.O. Box 33224, Washington, DC 20033-0224, or call the hot line (✆ **202/547-1500;** www.nps.gov/nacc/cherry).

Internet surfers can obtain information on all museums that are part of the **Smithsonian Institution** at www.si.edu.

For information on **Metrorail** service, contact the **Washington Metropolitan Area Transit Authority,** 600 5th St. NW,

Washington, DC 20001 (© **202/637-7000;** www.wmata.com), and request the free "Metro Pocket Ride Guide."

CALENDAR OF KIDS' FAVORITE EVENTS

Whether you decide to visit Washington in June or in January, or any time in between, you'll find a wide range of special events to enhance your sightseeing. Most are free. For the latest information before you leave home, contact the **Washington, D.C. Convention and Tourism Corporation,** 1212 New York Ave. NW, Suite 600, Washington, DC 20005 (© **202/789-7000;** www.washington.org), and request the quarterly "Calendar of Events" brochure.

The Washington, D.C. Visitor Center, in the Ronald Reagan Building, 1300 Pennsylvania Ave., is a one-stop shop for brochures and information (© **800/DCISFUN** [324-7386]; www.dc visit.com or www.dcchamber.org).

The **White House Visitors Center,** on the southeast corner of 15th and E streets NW, is open daily from 7:30am to 4pm. Stop in to view the 30-minute video and see the exhibits about the home's architecture, history, and first families (© **202/208-1631;** www.whitehouse.gov). Also consult the "Weekend" magazine of *The Washington Post* every Friday. Before you attend a special event, it's smart to call and verify the time and location. Some changes and cancellations are inevitable.

January

Martin Luther King, Jr.'s Birthday. This national holiday is celebrated the third Monday in January with speeches, dance performances, and choral presentations citywide, as well as a wreath-laying ceremony at the Lincoln Memorial. Check local newspapers for free commemorative events, or call © **202/619-7222.**

Robert E. Lee's Birthday Bash. Lee's birthday is observed January 19 at Arlington House in Arlington National Cemetery, and the celebration features 19th-century music, food, and memorabilia (© **703/557-0613**). Free. You can also visit the Lee–Fendall House at 614 Oronoco

St. in Old Town Alexandria (© **703/548-1789**).

Inauguration Day. This monumental event is held on January 20 of every fourth year when the president is sworn in at the West Front of the Capitol. The next presidential inauguration will be January 20, 2009. A colorful and *very* lengthy parade follows the ceremony from the Capitol to the White House along Pennsylvania Avenue. Free.

February

Black History Month. This is observed by museums, libraries, and recreation centers with special exhibits, events, and performances to celebrate African-American contributions to American life. Check local newspapers and magazines for events, or call © **202/357-2700.**

Abraham Lincoln's Birthday. A moving wreath-laying ceremony and reading of the Gettysburg Address at the Lincoln Memorial on February 12 commemorate the birthday of the 16th U.S. president. It's truly inspiring (© **202/619-7222**).

Chinese New Year Parade. Although younger kids might be frightened by the firecrackers, the colorful street parade of lions and dragons, dancers, and music-makers through Chinatown (H St. NW, between 5th and 7th sts.) is great family fun. After the parade, fill up on dumplings and duck (Peking, of course) at one of Chinatown's many restaurants. *Note:* Sometimes the Chinese New Year is in early March. Blame it on the moon.

George Washington's Birthday. The father of our country's birthday is celebrated with a parade through Old Town Alexandria's historic district on the Saturday closest to his February 22 birthday. The parade begins at Wilkes and St. Asaph streets. Wear your finest white stockings and a powdered wig (© **703/838-5005**). Free. On February 22, a ceremony is held at the Washington Monument and is cosponsored by the National Park Service and Washington National Monument Society (© **202/619-7222**). Free. George Washington's Mount Vernon estate features a family celebration on Presidents' Day, on the third Monday of the month (© **703/780-2000**). Free.

March

St. Patrick's Day Parades. On the Sunday before St. Paddy's Day (on March 17 when it falls on a Sunday), it's top o' the mornin' at the festive afternoon parade down Constitution Avenue, from 7th to 17th streets NW, with floats, bagpipes, bands, and dancers (© **202/637-2474**; www.dcst patsparade.com). Old Town Alexandria also celebrates the wearin' of the green with a procession down King Street (© **703/549-4535**; www.fun side.com).

Ringling Bros. and Barnum & Bailey Circus. The world's only three-ring circus pitches its tent at the D.C. Armory for 2 weeks of thrills and chills extending into April. Treat your kids, if they've never been. It's still the greatest show on Earth (© **703/448-4000**; www.ringling.com).

Smithsonian Kite Festival. Breeze on down to the Washington Monument grounds for this annual event that draws kite makers from all over the country. Prizes and trophies are awarded for homemade kites, but you must register between 10am and noon (© **202/357-2700**; www.kitefestival.org). Free.

National Cherry Blossom Festival. If you hit this right—no snow, no gale winds, no August-in-spring weather—the vision of thousands of cherry trees blooming around the Tidal Basin will take your breath away. There are a parade of floats with cherry-blossom princesses from each state, free concerts, a marathon, a Japanese lantern-lighting ceremony, and fireworks (© **202/619-7222**; www.nps.gov/nacc/cherry). Late March to early April. See "Parks, Gardens & Other Wide-Open Spaces" in chapter 8 for more about the famed trees.

April

White House Easter Egg Roll. Children 8 and under, accompanied by an adult, are invited on Easter Monday to the South Lawn of the White House, where free eggs and entertainment are dished out. Although there's a crunch of people and eggshells, your kids might find the event "egg-citing." No yolk! Line up early at the southeast gate of the White House on East Executive Avenue. Because of tightened security following the September 11, 2001, terrorist attacks and the ongoing war in Iraq, this event is sometimes limited to White House staff and their families. Call © **202/456-7041** (www.whitehouse.gov) for the latest information before putting on your bunny ears. Free.

Thomas Jefferson's Birthday. On April 13, gather at the Jefferson Memorial to honor the birthday of this Renaissance man and third U.S. president with military drills and a wreath-laying ceremony (© **202/619-7222**; www.nps.gov/jeff). Free.

White House Garden Tour. Tour the Children's Garden, with its bronze impressions of the hands and feet of White House children and grandchildren among the tulips and azaleas, and the executive mansion's public rooms. Line up at least an hour before this weekend event. Call © **202/456-7041** (www.whitehouse.gov) for information before going. Free.

William Shakespeare's Birthday. The bard's birthday is celebrated the Saturday closest to April 23 at the Folger Shakespeare Library, 201 E. Capitol St. SE, with music, theater, children's events, and food (© **202/544-7077;** www.folger.edu). Free.

May

Eastern Market Street Festival. On the first Sunday in May, the streets around Eastern Market, 7th and C streets SE, are filled with vendors selling clothes, jewelry, and artifacts to benefit a local charity. Enjoy carnival rides, crafts, music, and food while you browse (© **703/ 534-7612;** www.easternmarket.net). Free.

National Cathedral Flower Mart. Children's games, flower booths, entertainment, and food spring up on the grounds of the majestic National Cathedral, Wisconsin Avenue and Woodley Road NW, during the first weekend of the month. There's also an extensive selection of herbs for sale (© **202/537-6200;** www.cathedral. org). Free.

Air Show at Andrews AFB. Go ballistic over the Army's Golden Knights parachute team and an aerial show by the Air Force Thunderbirds in their F-16s at this weekend open house at Andrews Air Force Base in Camp Springs, Maryland. Kids can climb aboard aircraft and tanks. Go early, allow plenty of driving time, and bring earplugs (© **301/ 981-1110;** www.andrews.am.af.mil). Free.

Memorial Day Concert. The Sunday of Memorial Day weekend, Washington's own National Symphony Orchestra serenades you on the West Lawn of the Capitol (© **202/416-8100;** www. nps.gov). Bring a blanket. Free.

Memorial Day Ceremonies. Witness wreath-laying ceremonies in Arlington Cemetery at the Kennedy grave site and the Tomb of the Unknowns, and services at the Memorial Amphitheater accompanied by military bands (© **202/ 685-2851**). Free.

More Wreath-Laying Ceremonies. These ceremonies also take place at the Vietnam and Korean War Veterans memorials, just south of 21st Street and Constitution Avenue NW (© **202/ 619-7222;** www.nps.gov), and at the Navy Memorial, Pennsylvania Avenue between 7th and 9th streets NW (© **202/737-2300,** ext. 768). Free.

June

Civil War Living History Day. Take a torchlight tour of Union and Confederate camps, and watch "soldiers" in Civil War uniforms reenact a battle and perform drill competitions at Fort Ward Museum and Park, 4301 W. Braddock Rd., Alexandria, Virginia (© **703/838-4848;** www.funside. com). Free.

Alexandria Red Cross Waterfront Festival. Tall ships berth at Alexandria's historical waterfront during this family-oriented weekend (usually the second weekend of June), featuring games, refreshments, entertainment, arts and crafts, and the blessing of the fleet (© **703/549-8300;** www.water frontfestival.org).Adults $10; children 2 to 12 $5; under 2 free.

Juneteenth Jubilee. Storytellers, infantry-reenactment groups, clowns, and magicians commemorate the day Texas slaves learned of the Emancipation Proclamation. Call for the festival location, which changes from year to year (© **202/287-2060;** www.19thof june.com). Free.

Festival of American Folklife. One of the most popular annual events in the nation's capital, the 10-day folklife festival on the Mall is filled with music, crafts, and ethnic foods reflecting America's rich multicultural heritage (© **202/357-2700;** www.folklike.si. edu). Free. *Note:* The festival spills over into July.

National Capital Barbecue Battle. Bring your appetites to the grandest pork barrel of them all (June 24–25, 2006). Local restaurants pit their pork against each other for a rib-roaring good time sauced with cooking demonstrations and music. Third weekend of the month at Pennsylvania Avenue NW between 9th and 14th streets (© **202/ 828-3099;** www.barbecuebattle.com). Adults $10; children 6 to 12 $5; under 6 free.

Greater Washington Soap Box Derby. Drivers between 9 and 16 years old coast down Capitol Hill in their aerodynamic vehicles at the traffic-stopping event that has taken place annually for more than 50 years (www. dcsoapboxderby.org). Free.

July

Independence Day Celebration. The nation's capital celebrates its birthday in grand style, beginning with a 12:30pm parade along Constitution Avenue from 7th to 17th streets NW (© **202/619-7222;** www.july4th parade.com). Enjoy entertainment all afternoon at the Sylvan Theatre on the Washington Monument grounds (© **202/426-6841**). At 8pm, the National Symphony plays on the Capitol's West Lawn (© **202/416-8100**), and a fantastic fireworks display starts at about 9:20pm (© **202/619-7222**). Bring something to sit on. Check newspapers July 3 and 4 for details. Free.

Virginia Scottish Games. One of the largest Scottish festivals in the United States features Highland dancing, fiddling competitions, a heptathlon, animal events (sheep shearing and other activities), and plenty of long-winded bagpipers. It's usually held the third weekend of the month at Episcopal High School, 3901 W. Braddock Rd., Alexandria, Virginia (© **703/912-1943;** www.vascottishgames.org). Adults $15; children 5 to 12 $5; under 5 free.

Latin American Festival. A parade along Constitution Avenue caps the weekend celebration (fourth weekend of the month), featuring entertainment, arts and crafts, and delicious international snacks. The festival radiates in all directions from Freedom Plaza at 14th Street and Constitution Avenue NW. For more information, you can write to: Festival Latino Americano de Washington, D.C., 1807 Belmont Rd. NW No. 208, Washington, DC 20009, or call © **202/328-3040** (www.dclatino.com). Free.

Farm Tours. About 15 Montgomery County, Maryland, farms open their doors and stalls to visitors during the third or fourth weekend of this month. If your kids think eggs hatch in little corrugated cartons, bring them here. Some farms offer hayrides, pony rides, and other special activities. For information call © **301/590-2823;** www. montgomerycountymd.gov. Free.

August

Renaissance Festival. Crownsville, Maryland (about 30 miles from downtown), is the site of a 16th-century fair with jousting matches, magicians, wandering minstrels, and crafts. A special children's area has pony rides, a zoo, and Tudor-era amusements. Armor up on weekends from late August to mid-October (© **800/296-7304;** www.rennfest.com). Free for kids under 12 on Children's Weekend; always free for kids under 7. Otherwise, $17 adults; $15 seniors; $8 children (ages 7 to 15).

U.S. Army Band's *1812 Overture.* The Salute Gun Platoon of the 3rd U.S. Infantry provides the noisy finale to this patriotic concert by the U.S. Army Band at the Sylvan Theatre, Washington Monument grounds (℡ 202/619-7222; www.usarmyband. com). Free.

Labor Day Concert. The National Symphony bids adieu to summer, even though it's usually still hot as blazes, with a concert on the West Lawn of the Capitol (℡ 202/619-7222; www. kennedy-center.org/nso). Free.

International Children's Festival. Rain or shine, the sun will be out at Wolf Trap Farm Park in Vienna, Virginia, where craft, music, and dance workshops, and performances delight families (℡ 703/642-0862; www. wolf-trap.org). $10 adults/teens; $8 kids 3 to 12 and seniors.

College Park Airport Open House and Air Fair. Fly over here with your crew for airplane and helicopter rides, an air show, and exhibits at the area's oldest airport, at 1909 Corporal Frank Scott Dr., College Park, Maryland (℡ 301/864-5844; www.pgparks. com). Free.

Constitution Day Commemoration. On September 17 at the National Archives, Constitution Avenue at 8th Street NW, pay your respects to the Constitution on the anniversary of its signing. A naturalization program and honor-guard ceremonies are part of the day's events (℡ 202/501-5000; www. archives.gov). Free.

Rock Creek Park Day. Children's activities, environmental and recreational exhibits, foods, crafts, and music highlight the celebration of Washington's largest park, which reached the ripe old age of 115 in 2005. The event is usually held on the Saturday closest to September 25, the park's birthday (℡ 202/426-6829; www.nps.gov/rocr). Free.

Folger Open House. Here's a chance to go behind the scenes in a theater. Inspect costumes and scenery, and watch a rehearsal in the Shakespeare Theatre (an authentic model of an Elizabethan theater) at the Folger Library, 201 E. Capitol St. SE (℡ 202/544-7077; www.folger.edu). Free.

Kennedy Center Open House Arts Festival. Treat your senses to a musical celebration by more than 40 entertainers (musicians, musical groups, vocalists, choral groups, mimes, and dancers) who appear in every nook and cranny of the "Ken Cen" (℡ 202/467-4600; www.kennedy-center.org). Free.

Black Family Reunion Celebration. Gospel music, ethnic treats, dancing, and craft demonstrations enliven the Washington Monument grounds (℡ 202/619-7222; www.nps.gov). Free.

Greek Fall Festival. Games for kids, a Greek buffet, arts and crafts, jewelry, and Oriental rugs are featured at this lively bazaar at Saint Sophia Cathedral, 36th Street and Massachusetts Avenue NW (℡ 202/333-4730; www.saint sophiawashington.org). Music and dancing after 5pm. Free.

October

D.C. Open House. On the first Saturday and Sunday of the month, about 50 sites in 12 neighborhoods offer free walking tours and free admission to museums and performances (no phone; www.culturaltourismdc.org).

U.S. Navy Birthday Concert. Wear your dress blues to the DAR Constitution Hall, 1776 D St. NW, for the concert celebrating the Navy's birthday (231 years young in 2006) (℡ 202/433-6090; www.navyband.navy.mil). Free, but tickets must be ordered in

September. Send a self-addressed, stamped envelope to Navy Birthday Tickets, U.S. Navy Band, Building 105, Washington Navy Yard, Washington, DC 20374-5054.

White House Fall Garden Tour. One weekend this month (all day Sat, Sun afternoon only), the public is invited to visit the Rose Garden, South Lawn, and beautiful beds of multihued chrysanthemums, as well as some of the White House's public rooms, while enjoying the upbeat sounds of military bands. Line up at the southeast gate, E Street and East Executive Avenue, an hour before the tour starts (© 202/456-7041; www.whitehouse.gov). Free.

Corcoran Gallery of Art's Fall Family Day. Films, storytellers, mimes, and dancers highlight the fall celebration at the Corcoran, 17th Street and New York Avenue NW (© 202/639-1700; www.corcoran.org). Free.

Theodore Roosevelt's Birthday. Even if you forgot to send a card, on the Saturday closest to T. R.'s birthday (Oct 27), you can celebrate on the island named after him with nature programs, island tours, and special kids' entertainment. No food is available on the island, but you can picnic outside. The island is off the G. W. Parkway, north of Roosevelt Bridge (© 703/289-2500; www.nps.gov). Free.

November

Veterans' Day Ceremonies. Military music accompanies a solemn ceremony honoring the nation's war dead. The Memorial Amphitheater at Arlington National Cemetery is the service site, where the president or another high-ranking official lays a wreath at the Tomb of the Unknown Soldier (© 202/619-7222; www.nps.gov). Free.

Sugarloaf's Autumn Crafts Festival. Puppet shows, storytelling, and a petting zoo will keep the youngsters happy while grownups shop for holiday gifts and souvenirs sold by 400 artists and craftspeople at the Montgomery County Fairgrounds in Gaithersburg, Maryland (© 301/963-3247; www.sugarloaf crafts.com).

December

Festival of Music and Lights. More than 200,000 twinkling bulbs sparkle and gleam on the greenery at the Washington Mormon Temple in Kensington, Maryland, through Twelfth Night. Concerts are held nightly until New Year's Eve (© 301/587-0144; www.lds.org). Free.

Scottish Christmas Walk. A parade through historic Old Town Alexandria, Virginia, includes Celtic activities for children, tartan-clad bagpipers and Highland dancers, and house tours (© 703/549-0111; www.campagna center.org). Free.

Old Town Christmas Candlelight Tours. Several historic homes, dressed up with period decorations, open their doors to visitors. Music, colonial dancing, and refreshments add to the festive atmosphere (© 703/838-5005; http://oha.ci.alexandria.va.us).

Holiday Celebration. Decorated Christmas trees, holiday crafts, ethnic food, stories, and music at the Smithsonian's National Museum of American History demonstrate how Americans celebrate Christmas, Hanukkah, Kwanzaa, and the New Year. Join the holiday fun at the Smithsonian (© 202/357-2700; www.si.edu). Free.

People's Christmas Tree Lighting. The People's Christmas Tree, towering some 60 feet, is lighted each year on the west side of the Capitol to herald the holiday season. There's music, too (© 202/224-3069; www.capitol holidaytree.org). Free.

National Christmas Tree Lighting and Pageant of Peace. Every year on the Ellipse (between the White House and Constitution Avenue), one or more members of the First Family throw the switch that lights the nation's blue spruce Christmas tree and 57 Scotch pine siblings, representing the 50 states, the District of Columbia, and the six U.S. territories. Musical and choral performances take place every evening from 6 to 9pm, except Christmas, through December 30 (© 202/619-7222; www.nps.gov). Free.

U.S. Navy Band Holiday Concert. A free concert awaits all holiday revelers at DAR Constitution Hall, 1776 D St. NW (© 202/433-6090; www.navy band.navy.mil). Free, but reservations are required.

Kennedy Center Holiday Celebrations. Since its opening in 1971, the Kennedy Center has been celebrating the holidays in grand style. The festivities include a *Messiah* Sing-Along, Hanukkah Festival, Christmas Eve and New Year's Eve programs, and concerts by local children's choruses (© 202/467-4600; www.kennedy-center.org). Many events are free.

4 What to Pack

You can leave your tux and gown at home unless you're attending a state occasion at the White House. Casual attire—jeans, sweat suits, and your most comfortable walking shoes—is recommended for sightseeing. If you're planning on dining in an elegant restaurant, pack one dressier outfit. A few of the fancier places require men to wear jackets.

It's easy to pack for summer: Bring the lightest clothing you own (preferably in a breathable, natural fiber like cotton), and double the number of T-shirts, sport shirts, or blouses you normally wear on a summer day. Washingtonians measure the heat by the number of shirts they soak, as in "Yesterday was a real scorcher—a three-shirter!"

Fall, winter, and spring frequently blur, so prudent packing means bringing clothing that can be layered. In fall, mild weather is the rule, often lingering well into October or November. But every rule has an exception, so don't forget a jacket. In the winter, you'll need a heavy topcoat or lined raincoat. Some years, spring sneaks by while everyone is asleep; sometimes it lasts several weeks. Be prepared, and bring a mix of winter and summer things.

Be sure to include a sweater or sweatshirt, no matter what the season. In summer, the overly air-conditioned public buildings and restaurants can shock your overheated system. Because precipitation is spread fairly evenly throughout the year, always take a raincoat.

Layering is the name of the game when it comes to packing for children. Unless you're traveling with an infant or toddler, packing for them is the same as packing for you, except that their stuff takes up less space. Remind teenagers that nobody in Washington has seen their clothes before, so they don't have to pack every stitch they own.

A raincoat and rain hat make sense in any season, but I'm not a fan of umbrellas. I think they're a hazard, obstruct one's vision, and are too easy to lose. Waterproof boots, warm gloves, and a hat with earflaps are wintertime necessities.

As every parent knows, the younger the child is, the more clothes he or she will mess up. Because a washer and dryer might not be handy, plan two outfits per day for kids under 5, and throw in a few extra shirts for good measure. Take at least one extra outfit for little ones in a carry-on bag. If all their gear is stowed in the cargo hold, overhead rack, or trunk, you won't be a happy parent if you have to change their wet, smelly clothing in a hurry. Include enough diapers—and then some—to keep the baby's bottom dry until you can get to your suitcase or a store.

If your kids are flying alone, contact the individual airline or request a copy of **"Kids and Teens in Flight"** from the U.S. Department of Transportation, I-25, Washington, DC 20590. When traveling by plane, make sure everyone has a sweatshirt or sweater. It can get downright chilly once you're airborne, and airline blankets disappear quickly. Ask your pediatrician about oral decongestants and

nasal sprays, especially if your kids have colds. Changes in cabin pressure, especially during takeoffs and landings, can cause excruciating inner-ear pain in some kids. Give older kids hard candy to suck during takeoffs and landings.

Don't forget two laundry bags or a couple of pillowcases or plastic bags for dirty clothes. Most hotels have laundry and/or dry cleaning services, but they can be costly. There are few laundromats in D.C., and they might not be convenient to where you're staying. Pack liquid detergent in a small plastic bottle, or fill a couple of small resealable plastic bags with powdered laundry soap so that you can do emergency washing in the sink.

5 Health, Insurance & Safety

HEALTH If you or your children require **medication,** pack plenty in a carry-on bag. You'll also want a **first-aid kit**—small basic kits are available at most pharmacies and supermarkets, or call your physician or local Red Cross chapter for a recommendation.

In addition, remember grownup and children's-strength aspirin, a thermometer, cough syrup, a plastic cup, flexible straws, baby wipes, a plastic spoon, a nightlight, and pacifiers. In addition, be prepared for **motion sickness.** Make sure you have a bottle of liquid Dramamine close at hand when traveling. Kids who are fine in a car could get sick on a boat, plane, or train, and vice versa.

If you or the kids wear **eyeglasses,** by all means bring backups. If extra pairs are unavailable, bring the prescriptions. You can't sightsee if you can't see!

Before you leave, get a list of your **kids' inoculations** and the dates they were administered from your pediatrician. In an emergency, you're not apt to remember this information.

If possible, before you leave home, obtain the name of a **Washington, D.C.**

pediatrician from your hometown physician or relatives or friends in the Washington area. I hope this never happens. But if your child spikes a fever of 102°F (39°C) in the middle of the night, you won't feel like flipping through a couple of hundred unfamiliar names in the Yellow Pages.

If you are caring for someone else's child, make sure that the child's parent or guardian has filled out and signed a **notarized letter** giving you the legal right to authorize medical and surgical treatment. Basically, it should say, "So-and-So has the right to authorize medical/surgical treatment after all attempts to reach parents fail." According to one hospital spokesman, though, "No invasive treatment will be done unless a parent can be notified; in case of a life-threatening emergency, doctors will take responsibility until the parent can be notified." Doctors and lawyers say that these forms will "facilitate treatment," even though they might not be legally binding. If you have custodial care of a child with divorced parents, it's wise to get forms from both parents.

If you've never taken a first-aid course or earned a Boy Scout or Girl Scout first-aid badge, pick up a copy of *A Sigh of Relief*, by Martin I. Green (Bantam Books). It'll tell you everything you need to know about the most common childhood emergencies and how to treat them.

MEDICAL INSURANCE   Most health insurance policies cover you if you get sick away from home—but verify that you're covered before you depart, particularly if you're insured by an HMO.

SAFETY   A welcome presence on D.C. streets is the group of friendly and helpful goodwill ambassadors dressed in bright red jackets with the SAM (Safety and Maintenance) insignia and/or "Downtown D.C." logo on their caps. Known as **SAMs,** they give directions; advise on dining, shopping, and sights; and will walk you to your Metro station, hotel, or car. Equipped with walkie-talkies, they work closely with the Metropolitan Police. Should you see any suspicious behavior, report it to them. For more information, check the Business Improvement District website (www.downtowndc.org).

Discuss with your kids what they should do if they get separated from you during the trip. Some parents dress their kids in bright colors when they're sightseeing. You might want to take a tip from preschool groups on field trips and have your very young ones wear a name tag that includes the name and phone number of your hotel and your cellphone number.

When you check into your room, give the kids a little time to settle in before rushing off to an activity. Find the nearest fire exits, and discuss the do's and don'ts of fire safety. If there isn't a card in the room describing emergency procedures, ask for one at the front desk. Before turning in, some families pack a small bag or sack with emergency items: a flashlight, an extra room key, wallets, and the like. If there's a fire drill in the middle of the night, you'll be good to go in a matter of seconds.

6 Words of Wisdom & Helpful Resources

FAMILY TRAVEL RESOURCES
How to Take Great Trips with Your Kids (The Harvard Common Press) is full of good general advice that can apply to travel anywhere.

You can find good family-oriented vacation advice on the Internet from sites like the **Family Travel Network** (www.familytravelnetwork.com); **Traveling Internationally with Your Kids** (www.travelwithyourkids.com), a comprehensive site offering sound advice for long-distance and international travel with children; and **Family Travel Files** (www.thefamilytravelfiles.com), which offers an online magazine and a directory of off-the-beaten-path tours and tour operators for families.

If you'd like to join a tour, **Familyhostel** (© **800/733-9753;** www.learn.unh.edu/familyhostel) takes the whole family, including kids ages 8 to 15, on moderately priced domestic and international learning vacations. Lectures, fields trips, and sightseeing are guided by a team of academics.

FOR GRANDPARENTS
Mention the fact that you're a senior citizen when you make your travel reservations. Check with your airline (especially America West, Continental, and American) to see whether it offers senior discounts; many hotels also offer discounts for seniors. In most cities, people over the age of 60 qualify for reduced admission to theaters, museums, and other attractions, as well as discounted fares on public transportation.

One reliable agency that targets traveling grandparents is **Elderhostel** (© **877/426-8056;** www.elderhostel.org), which

Take Note
Travel information is always subject to change, but never more so than following the September 11, 2001, terrorist attacks. Therefore, I strongly recommend that you verify all information included in these pages before you leave home and again when you arrive in Washington. I warn you that some of the tours, sites, and areas of interest listed in this book might not be open during your visit to Washington, D.C. For the latest news and a free Visitors Guide, check with the **Washington, D.C. Convention and Tourism Corporation** at ℂ **800/422-8644** or 202/789-7000, or www.washington.org.

arranges study programs for those age 55 and over in the United States and in more than 80 other countries. Of particular interest are the "Intergenerational" programs, which include Grand Canyon adventures and a Harry Potter–themed trip to Oxford, England. Most courses last 5 to 7 days in the United States (2–4 weeks abroad), and many include airfare, accommodations in university dormitories or modest inns, meals, and tuition.

FOR FAMILIES WITH SPECIAL NEEDS

Washington welcomes visitors with physical disabilities with open arms and relatively few obstacles. Most of the museums, monuments, and public buildings—as well as many theaters and restaurants—are accessible to travelers with disabilities. The Metro, the public transportation system, is rated among the nation's best for accommodating those with disabilities. The **Washington Metropolitan Transit Authority** publishes a free guide on the Metro's bus and rail system accessibility (ℂ **202/962-6464;** TDD 202/638-3780; www.wmata.com). Each Metro station is equipped with an elevator (complete with Braille number plates) to train platforms, and rail cars are fully accessible. Punctuated rubber tiles lead up to the granite-lined platform edge to warn visually impaired Metro riders that they are nearing the tracks. Train operators make station and onboard announcements of train destinations and stops.

The Washington, D.C. Convention and Tourism Corporation publishes a fact sheet detailing general accessibility around town. For a free copy, call (ℂ **202/789-7000;** www.washington.org), or write to WCTC, 901 7th St. NW, 4th Floor, Washington, DC 20001.

Regular **Tourmobile** trams (see "Organized Tours" in chapter 6) are accessible to visitors with disabilities. The company also operates special vans for immobile travelers, complete with wheelchair lifts. Call a day ahead to ensure that the van is available for you when you arrive. For information, call ℂ **202/554-5100.**

All Smithsonian museum buildings are accessible to visitors in wheelchairs. A free, comprehensive publication called "Smithsonian Access" lists all services available to visitors with disabilities, including parking, building access, sign-language interpreters, and more. To obtain a copy, call ℂ **202/357-2700** or TTY 202/357-1729.

Dial the local number to speak to a real person. The Lincoln, Jefferson, and Vietnam memorials and the Washington Monument are equipped to accommodate visitors with disabilities and they keep wheelchairs on the premises. Call ahead to other sightseeing attractions for accessibility information and special services (ℂ **202/426-6841**).

Call your senator or representative to arrange wheelchair-accessible tours of the Capitol; special tours for the hearing- and seeing-impaired can also be arranged. If you need further information on these tours, call ✆ **202/224-4048.**

Most of the large performing-arts venues in town offer special services for special-needs audience members, ranging from headphones for the hearing-impaired to large-print programs to wheelchair-accessible seats. Most also offer specially priced tickets for patrons with physical disabilities.

7 The 21st-Century Traveler

PLANNING YOUR TRIP ONLINE
SURFING FOR AIRFARES

The "big three" online travel agencies— **Expedia.com, Travelocity.com,** and **Orbitz.com**—sell most of the air tickets bought on the Internet. (Canadian travelers should try expedia.ca and Travelocity.ca; U.K. residents can go for expedia.co.uk and opodo.co.uk.) **Kayak.com** is also gaining popularity and uses a sophisticated search engine (developed at MIT). Each has different business deals with the airlines, and all may offer different fares on the same flights, so it's wise to shop around. Expedia, Kayak, and Travelocity will also send you **e-mail notification** when a cheap fare becomes available to your favorite destination. Of the smaller travel-agency websites, **SideStep** (www.sidestep.com) has gotten the best reviews from Frommer's authors. The website (with optional browser add-on) purports to "search 140 sites at once" but in reality beats competitors' fares only as often as other sites do.

Also remember to check **airline websites**—especially those for low-fare carriers such as Southwest, JetBlue, AirTran, West-Jet, or Ryanair, whose fares are often misreported or simply missing from travel agency websites. Even with major airlines, you can often shave a few bucks from a fare by booking directly through the airline and avoiding a travel agency's transaction fee. But you'll get these discounts only by **booking online:** Most airlines now offer online-only fares that even their phone agents know nothing about. For the websites of airlines that fly to and from your destination, go to "Getting There," p. 29.

The airlines frequently offer special family fares as well. Children under 2 who do not occupy a seat usually travel free, and depending on the airline, various discounts apply to kids between the ages of 2 and 12. If you will be traveling with an infant, toddler, or active preschooler, when you make your reservation, request the seats behind the bulkhead, where you'll have more legroom and they'll have more play room. Many planes have special fittings for bassinets, and some will allow you to use your child's car seat. To find out if your particular brand of car seat is approved by the Federal Aviation Administration, read **"Child/Infant Safety Seats Acceptable for Use in Aircraft"** (www.faa.gov). Also ask about special meals for your kids. Better yet, bring a sandwich from home.

Great **last-minute deals** are available through free weekly e-mail services provided directly by the airlines. Most of these are announced on Tuesday or Wednesday and must be purchased online. Most are valid only for travel that weekend, but some (such as Southwest's) can be booked weeks or months in advance. Sign up for weekly e-mail alerts at airline websites, or check megasites that compile comprehensive lists of last-minute specials, such as **Smarter Travel** (smartertravel.com). For last-minute trips, **site59.com** and **lastminutetravel.com** in the United States and **lastminute.com** in Europe often have better air-and-hotel package deals than the major-label sites.

If you're willing to give up some control over your flight details, use what is called an **"opaque" fare service** like **Priceline** (www.priceline.com; www. priceline.co.uk for Europeans) or its smaller competitor **Hotwire** (www.hotwire. com). Both offer rock-bottom prices in exchange for travel on a "mystery airline" at a mysterious time of day, often with a mysterious change of planes en route. The mystery airlines are all major, well-known carriers—and the possibility of being sent from Philadelphia to Chicago via Tampa is remote; the airlines' routing computers have gotten a lot better than they used to be. Your chances of getting a 6am or 11pm flight, however, are still pretty high. Hotwire tells you flight prices before you buy; Priceline usually has better deals than Hotwire, but you have to play its "name our price" game. If you're new at this, the helpful folks at **BiddingForTravel** (www.biddingfor travel.com) do a good job of demystifying Priceline's prices and strategies. Priceline and Hotwire are great for flights within North America and between the United States and Europe. But for flights to other parts of the world, consolidators will almost always beat their fares. *Note:* In 2004, Priceline added nonopaque service to its roster. You now have the option to pick exact flights, times, and airlines from a list of offers—or opt to bid on opaque fares as before.

SURFING FOR HOTELS

Shopping online for hotels is generally done one of two ways: by booking through the hotel's own website or through an independent booking agency (or a fare-service agency like Priceline; see below). These Internet hotel agencies have multiplied in mind-boggling numbers of late, competing for the business of millions of consumers surfing for accommodations around the world. This competitiveness can be a boon to consumers who have the patience and time to shop and compare the online sites for good deals—but shop they must, for prices can vary considerably from site to site. And keep in mind that hotels at the top of a site's listing may be there for no other reason than that they paid money to get the placement.

Of the "big three" sites, **Expedia** offers a long list of special deals and "virtual tours" or photos of available rooms so you can see what you're paying for (a feature that helps counter the claims that the best rooms are often held back from bargain booking websites). **Travelocity** posts unvarnished customer reviews and ranks its properties according to the AAA rating system. **Trip Advisor** (www.tripadvisor) is another excellent source of unbiased user reviews of hotels around the world. Although even the finest hotels can inspire a misleadingly poor review from a picky or crabby traveler, the body of user opinions, when taken as a whole, is usually a reliable indicator.

Other reliable online booking agencies include **Hotels.com** and **Quikbook. com**. An excellent free program, **Travel-Axe** (www.travelaxe.net), can help you search multiple hotel sites at once, even ones you may never have heard of—and conveniently lists the total price of the room, including the taxes and service charges. Another booking site, **Travelweb** (www.travelweb.com), is partly owned by the hotels it represents (including the Hilton, Hyatt, and Starwood chains) and therefore is plugged directly into the hotels' reservations systems—unlike independent online agencies, which have to fax or e-mail reservation requests to the hotel, a good portion of which get misplaced in the shuffle. More than once, travelers have arrived at the hotel only to be told that they have no reservation. To be fair, many of the major sites are undergoing improvements in service and ease of use, and Expedia will soon be able to plug directly into the reservations systems of many hotel chains—none of which can be bad news for consumers. In the meantime, it's a good idea to **get a confirmation number** and **make a printout** of any online booking transaction.

In the opaque website category, **Priceline** and **Hotwire** are even better for hotels than for airfares; through both, you're allowed to pick the neighborhood and quality level of your hotel before paying. Priceline's hotel product even covers Europe and Asia, though it's much better at getting five-star lodging for three-star prices than at finding anything at the bottom of the scale. On the down side, many hotels stick Priceline guests in their least desirable rooms. Be sure to go to the BiddingforTravel website (see above) before bidding on a hotel room on Priceline; it features a fairly up-to-date list of hotels that Priceline uses in major cities. For both Priceline and Hotwire, you pay upfront, and the fee is nonrefundable. *Note:* Some hotels do not provide loyalty-program credits or points or other frequent-stay amenities when you book a room through opaque online services.

SURFING FOR RENTAL CARS

For booking rental cars online, the best deals are usually found at rental-car company websites, although all the major online travel agencies also offer rental-car reservations services. Priceline and Hotwire work well for rental cars, too; the only "mystery" is which major rental company you get, and for most travelers the difference among Hertz, Avis, and Budget is negligible.

INTERNET ACCESS AWAY FROM HOME

Travelers have any number of ways to check their e-mail and access the Internet on the road. Of course, using your own laptop—or even a PDA (personal digital assistant) or electronic organizer with a modem—gives you the most flexibility. But even if you don't have a computer, you can access your e-mail and even your office computer from cybercafes.

WITHOUT YOUR OWN COMPUTER

It's hard nowadays to find a city that *doesn't* have a few cybercafes. Although there's no definitive directory for cybercafes—these are independent businesses, after all—two places to start looking are **www.cyber captive.com** and **www.cybercafe.com**.

Aside from formal cybercafes, most **youth hostels** have at least one computer with Internet access. And most **public libraries** across the world offer access free or for a small charge. Avoid **hotel business centers** unless you're willing to pay exorbitant rates.

Most major airports now have **Internet kiosks** scattered throughout their gates. These kiosks, which you'll also see in shopping malls, hotel lobbies, and tourist information offices around the world, give you basic Web access for a per-minute fee that's usually higher than cybercafe prices. The kiosks' clunkiness and high price, however, mean you should avoid them whenever possible.

WITH YOUR OWN COMPUTER

More and more hotels, cafes, and retailers are signing on as Wi-Fi (wireless fidelity) "hotspots," from where you can get high-speed connection without cable wires, networking hardware, or a phone line (see below). You can get a Wi-Fi connection in several ways. Many laptops sold in the past year have built-in Wi-Fi capability (an 802.11b wireless Ethernet connection). Mac owners have their own networking technology, Apple AirPort. For those with older computers, you can plug in an 802.11b/**Wi-Fi card** (around $50). You sign up for wireless access service much as you do for cellphone service, through a plan offered by one of several commercial companies that have made wireless service available in airports, hotel lobbies, and coffee shops, primarily in the

United States (followed by the U.K. and Japan). **T-Mobile Hotspot** (www.t-mobile. com/hotspot) serves up wireless connections at more than 1,000 Starbucks coffee shops nationwide. **Boingo** (www.boingo. com) and **Wayport** (www.wayport.com) have set up networks in airports and high-class hotel lobbies. iPass providers (see below) also give you access to a few hundred wireless hotel lobby setups. Best of all, you don't need to be staying at the Four Seasons to use the hotel's network; just set yourself up on a nice couch in the lobby. (Pricing policies can be byzantine, but in general you pay around $30 a month for unlimited access, and prices are dropping as Wi-Fi access becomes more common.) To locate other hotspots that provide **free wireless networks** in cities around the world, go to **www. personaltelco.net/index.cgi/Wireless Communities**.

For dial-up access, most business-class hotels throughout the world offer dataports for laptop modems, and a few thousand hotels in the United States and Europe now offer free high-speed Internet access via an Ethernet network cable. You can bring your own cables, but most hotels rent them for around $10. **Call your hotel in advance** to see what your options are.

In addition, major Internet Service Providers (ISPs) have **local access numbers** around the world, allowing you to go online by placing a local call. Check your ISP's website or call its toll-free number and ask how you can use your current account away from home, and how much it will cost.

The **iPass** network also has dial-up numbers around the world. You'll have to sign up with an iPass provider, which will then tell you how to set up your computer for your destination(s). For a list of iPass providers, go to www.ipass.com and click "Individuals Buy Now." One solid provider is **i2roam** (www.i2roam.com; © **866/811-6209** or 920/235-0475).

Wherever you go, bring a **connection kit** of the right power and phone adapters, a spare phone cord, and a spare Ethernet network cable—or find out whether your hotel supplies them to guests.

USING A CELLPHONE ACROSS THE U.S.

Just because your cellphone works at home doesn't mean it'll work elsewhere in the country (thanks to our nation's fragmented cellphone system). It's a good bet that your phone will work in major cities, but take a look at your wireless company's coverage map on its website before heading out; T-Mobile, Sprint, and Nextel are particularly weak in rural areas. If you need to stay in touch at a destination where you know your phone won't work, **rent** a phone that does from **InTouch USA** (© 800/872-7626; www.intouch global.com) or a rental car location, but be aware that you'll pay $1 a minute or more for airtime.

If you're venturing deep into national parks, you may want to consider renting a **satellite phone ("satphone"),** which is different from a cellphone in that it connects to satellites rather than ground-based towers. A satphone is more costly than a cellphone but works in the absence of cellular signal and towers. Unfortunately, you'll pay at least $2 per minute to use the phone, and it works only where you can see the horizon (usually not indoors). In North America, you can rent Iridium satellite phones from **RoadPost** (www.roadpost.com; © **888/290-1606** or 905/272-5665). InTouch USA (see above) offers a wider range of satphones but at higher rates.

If you're not from the United States, you'll be appalled by the poor reach of our GSM (Global System for Mobiles) wireless network. Your phone will probably work in most major U.S. cities; it definitely won't work in many rural areas. (To see where GSM phones work in the

U.S., check out www.t-mobile.com/coverage/national_popup.asp.) And you may or may not be able to send SMS (text messaging) home—something Americans tend not to do anyway, for various cultural and technological reasons. (International budget travelers like to send text messages home because it's much cheaper than making international calls.) Assume nothing—call your wireless provider, and get the full scoop. In a worst-case scenario, you can always rent a phone; InTouch USA delivers to hotels.

8 Getting There

BY PLANE
THE MAJOR AIRLINES
Scheduled domestic airlines flying into Washington's three airports include **Air-Tran** (✆ 800/825-8538), **America West** (✆ 800/235-9292), **American** (✆ 800/433-7300), **Continental** (✆ 800/525-0280), **Delta** (✆ 800/221-1212), **Northwest** (✆ 800/225-2525), **Southwest** (✆ 800/435-9792), **US Airways and US Airways Shuttle** (✆ 800/428-4322), and **United** (✆ 800/241-6522).

For a quarterly guide to flights in and out of National and Dulles, write to **Metropolitan Washington Airports Authority,** P.O. Box 17045, Washington Dulles International Airport, Washington, DC 20041; www.metwashairports.com. To receive a similar guide for BWI, write to **Maryland Aviation Administration,** Marketing and Development, P.O. Box 8766, BWI Airport, MD 21240-0766; www.bwiairport.com.

Note: Late in 2005, US Airways and Delta cut their round-trip shuttle fares to New York to as low as $138. The fares must be booked at least 21 days in advance on the Internet.

SHUTTLES TO & FROM NEW YORK
The shuttles are convenient because you can just show up, buy a ticket, and hop on the next plane out. But to save money, if you will be traveling at least one-way on a Saturday or Sunday, book at least 3 days ahead.

The **Delta Shuttle** (✆ **800/221-1212**), which flies out of La Guardia's Marine Terminal in New York and Reagan National Airport, has 15 flights a day Monday through Friday, 7 flights Saturday, and 13

Security
The fluctuations in security at the White House, U.S. Capitol, Pentagon, and presidential monuments and memorials since September 11, 2001, and our invasion of Iraq bear watching. As of late 2005, self-guided tours of the **White House** were open *only* to groups of 10 or more, arranged well in advance through a congressional representative. The **U.S. Capitol** was open to visitors with only a few restrictions. The **Pentagon** was closed to all but select groups; the **Washington Monument** and **Bureau of Engraving and Printing** were open to individuals with timed, same-day passes. Be sure to bring a bona fide photo ID; many sights require adults (16 and over) to have them for admission. Leave your Swiss army knife and any other suspect items at home or in your hotel room. Guaranteed, they will be confiscated before you will be allowed into any government building. For the latest security information and restrictions, check individual attractions' websites or the Washington, D.C. Convention and Tourism Corporation at www.washington.org.

on Sunday. Please call for the latest information.

As this book goes to press, the lowest shuttle fare is about $150 round-trip. From there, the fares escalate. Before you book your ticket, ask about special advance-purchase, student, and promotional fares. Most airlines added fuel surcharges following hurricane Katrina, so past bargains are harder to come by.

The **US Airways Shuttle** (℡ 800/428-4322) runs from a separate terminal at La Guardia Airport in New York to Reagan National Airport. Ask about student (12–24 years old) and senior (age 62 and over) discounts. Frequency of departures and prices are similar to those on Delta.

THE D.C. AREA'S AIRPORTS

If you're arriving by commercial airline, you will land at one of Washington's three major airports: **Reagan National, Dulles, or Baltimore–Washington International (BWI).**

Several shuttle services serve D.C.'s airports. All require reservations, usually 24 hours in advance, for transit to the airport. Departures from the airports run about every 20 minutes or as needed. Payment is by cash or credit card.

The **"Super Shuttle"** (℡ 202/296-6662 or 800/258-3826; or 410/859-0800 in Baltimore; www.supershuttle.com) offers door-to-door service between Dulles, Reagan National, and BWI airports and the Metropolitan D.C. area 24 hours a day. Call for pricing, which is based on ZIP code. To give you an example, the fare from Reagan National Airport to the White House ZIP code is $12, plus a $1 fuel surcharge; $8 for second passenger and kids 3 and older. Kids 2 and under ride for free. On arrival, board the Super Shuttle blue van at the airport. Reservations are required 24 hours ahead for transit to the airport.

The **Maryland Shuttle and Sedan** (℡ 800/590-0000 or 301/230-0000;

www.marylandshuttle.com) serves all three airports 24 hours a day. The fare from Bethesda to Reagan National Airport is $23; from Bethesda to Dulles, $23; Bethesda to BWI, $29.

RONALD REAGAN WASHINGTON NATIONAL AIRPORT (REAGAN NATIONAL OR "NATIONAL") Just across the Potomac River in Virginia, National Airport is about a 15- to 30-minute taxi ride from downtown in non–rush-hour traffic and costs about $15; it's much less via the Metro, depending on where you're staying, and you'll have to do some walking. This is the most convenient airport to downtown (less than 5 miles), but it's also the most congested. Following the September 11, 2001, terrorist attacks, heightened security dictates arriving at the airport 1½ hours before your departing flight (2 hr. for international). Be sure to carry a photo ID. Without it, you will be denied boarding for your flight. You will probably be required to remove your shoes when passing through the scanner, so you may want to wear slip-ons. (For what it's worth, I've found the security checkpoints at D.C.-area airports to run much more smoothly than others in the nation.) The stunning glass-and-steel main terminal designed by Cesar Pelli has 54 skylighted domes and a five-story glass wall overlooking the Potomac River. If you've got time to kill, the view from Gate 43 is primo.

Covered pedestrian bridges connect the Metro station and the terminal. Of course, the best parking spaces—112 of them right next to the terminal—are reserved for VIPs—senators, congressional reps, and local politicians. That's right—we pay their salaries *and* for their optimum parking spaces!

In the vast commercial space, 40 shops, 25 eateries, and 30 retail carts vie for travelers' wallets. There's even a meditation room near the baggage claim area so that you can compose yourself if your flight out is canceled or delayed.

For airport information, call ☎ **703/417-8000; www.mwaa.com.**

Shuttle service is provided by some hotels. Check to see if yours is one of them. A taxi from National to downtown Washington, D.C. costs about $15 for the first person, plus various charges depending on time of day, number of passengers, and pieces of luggage (www.dctaxi.dc.gov). Trains on **Metro's Blue and Yellow lines** stop at National. The **Metro** is the quickest way to get to many locations in the District and beyond because local roads are notoriously bottle-necked. Count on a 15- to 20-minute ride into D.C. To help you, maps, fares, and traveling times are posted at every stop. Trains run Sunday through Thursday 5am to midnight, Friday 5am to 3am, and Saturday 7am to 3am (☎ **202/637-7000;** phone line open Mon–Fri 6am–10:30pm, Sat–Sun 8am–10:30pm).

The **Super Shuttle** (☎ **800/258-3826**) departs Reagan National every 20 to 30 minutes for D.C. hotels. The fare to central D.C. is $12 for the first person, plus a $1 fuel surcharge; $8 for the second passenger and kids 3 and older; free for kids 2 and under. You must make a reservation, however, for the return trip to the airport.

WASHINGTON DULLES INTERNA-TIONAL AIRPORT (DULLES) This airport is located in Chantilly, Virginia, about 30 miles and a 35- to 45-minute ride to downtown D.C. in non–rush-hour traffic. The main Eero Saarinen–designed terminal is an architectural marvel. It is also huge. There is a second mid-field terminal, and a third is on its way sometime this decade. For airport information, call ☎ **703/572-2700;** www.mwaa.com.

A **taxi** from Dulles to downtown Washington costs about $50 for the first passenger, $5 for each additional.

The **Super Shuttle** (☎ **800/258-3826;** www.supershuttle.com) serves downtown D.C. from Dulles (also Reagan National). The fare from Dulles to the J. W. Marriott, for example, is $22 for the first person, plus a $1 fuel surcharge; and $10 for each additional person and kids 3 and older (free for kids 2 and under). Vans hold up to seven people. With a big group, ask about a special rate for renting an entire van. Vans depart the airport on demand, about every 20 to 30 minutes. Make reservations for your return to the airport via phone or online: reservations@supershuttle.com

Metrobus makes hourly runs to the L'Enfant Plaza Metro Station for only $2.50. The ride takes about 50 minutes (☎ **202/637-7000;** www.wmata.com).

The **Washington Flyer Shuttle** (☎ **703/685-1400;** www.washfly.com) provides daily express bus service between the West Falls Church (Virginia) Metro station and Dulles. Buy tickets at the Arrivals level, Ground Transportation Center. The fare between the West Falls Church Metro and Dulles is $8 one-way, $14 round-trip.

BALTIMORE–WASHINGTON INTERNATIONAL AIRPORT (BWI)
One of the nation's fastest-growing airports, BWI is a few miles south of Baltimore, Maryland, 34 miles to the heart of downtown D.C., and about a 45-minute ride. Despite some growing pains, it is the most user-friendly of the three airports serving Washington. BWI is a hub for Southwest (with more than 160 flights daily to 35 nonstop U.S. destinations), the best airline on the planet, in my opinion. The new A/B concourse, completed in 2005, is home to umpteen Southwest ticket counters, a food court, and retail shops.

BWI sports a two-level observation gallery, with computerized interactive displays and a Smithsonian Museum Shop. If you have time to kill, sink into one of the comfortable leatherette chairs in front of the 147-foot-wide window, where you can marvel at the takeoffs and landings. By punching a flight number into one of the computer displays, your kids can learn the altitude, speed, and location of the plane of their choice. For airport information, visit www.bwiairport.com.

Taxi fare from BWI to downtown Washington is about $60 per family.

The **BWI Express/B30 bus** goes to the Greenbelt Metro station on Metro's Green line, about a 20-minute ride. From Greenbelt, it is about a 20-minute ride to downtown D.C. There are 25 departures weekdays, 21 on weekends, and it's only $3. Go to the lower level of the International Pier/Concourse E, and follow signs to Public Transportation. For more information, call © **202/637-7000;** www.wmata.com.

Train service is available daily on **Amtrak** (© **800/USA-RAIL**) and weekdays on **MARC** (© **800/325-RAIL**) at the BWI Airport Station, 5 minutes from the airport. A **courtesy shuttle** runs every 15 to 20 minutes between the airport and the train station weekdays between 6am and midnight. Weekend service tends to be less regular.

INTERAIRPORT TRANSFERS

The three area airports are far apart. For convenience, people saddled with luggage and children would be better served, even though it would cost more, to take a taxi.

Atlas Airport Sedan (© **202/800/574-2852** or 703/644-5009; http://atlasairportsedan.com) carries passengers between airports. The lower fare is for three passengers plus luggage; the higher, for a stretch-limo for up to six passengers plus luggage: Dulles to National, $55/ $125; BWI to Dulles, $85/$210; BWI to National, $70/ $175.

The **Washington Flyer** (© **703/685-1400;** www.washfly.com) operates daily between Dulles and the West Falls Church Metro. Daily departures from

Dulles are every 30 minutes from 5:45am weekdays, 7:45am weekends, until 10:45pm. Depart from Door 4 on the arrivals level of the main terminal. Note, however, that this is not the fastest or more efficient shuttle service available.

From West Falls Church Metro to Dulles, the Flyer leaves every 30 minutes from 6:15am weekdays; 8:15am weekends until 10:45pm daily.

BY CAR

Most visitors arrive in Washington by car. Although a car is helpful if you want to take excursions to many points outside the city, it can be a real liability in the downtown area. You might want to consider leaving the car at home and renting one for day trips outside the city.

Washington's streets are congested, and its drivers—many of whom learned to drive elsewhere or not at all—follow many different rules of the road. The result can be less than pleasant. In addition, **parking** in most sectors is expensive or nonexistent. (At some hotels, parking is included in the room rate. Find out in advance, or you might be unpleasantly surprised by having to shell out up to $30 a day. It cost me $15 recently for 2 hours. You should also ask if there is a reparking charge every time you use the car.) If your sightseeing plans are restricted to the city and close-in environs, leave the family buggy at home; you'll have a far better time. The District's efficient subway system will transport your brood to within a short walk of all the major attractions.

Like it or not, whether you are arriving from the north (I-270, I-95, I-295), south (I-95, Rte. 1, Rte. 301), east (Rte. 50/301, Rte. 450), or west (Rte. 7, Rte. 50, I-66, Rte. 29/211), you will run into the **Capital Beltway** (hereinafter known as the **Beltway**). This 66-mile road encircles Washington, D.C. (some think like a noose) and has 56 interchanges that intersect with all the major approach routes to the city. Sometimes more than 600,000 cars per day travel the Beltway, and gridlock is not uncommon, especially between 6 and 9am and 3 and 7pm. The eastern segment of the Beltway is part of I-95, which joins Baltimore, Maryland, to the north and Richmond, Virginia, to the south.

To confuse you, the rest is designated I-495, but mercifully dual I-495/I-95 signs are posted. Before you leave home, study a map; make sure you have directions from the intersection of the Beltway and whichever interstate or road you will be traveling to your destination.

To further challenge those driving into the D.C. metropolitan area, Maryland's exits correspond to the nearest milepost. Virginia's are numbered consecutively. Go figure. People have been known to drive the entire 66 miles of the Beltway before realizing that they've missed their exit. You don't want to spend your vacation this way; there's no room service and not much of a view.

North of the city, I-270 links the Maryland suburbs with I-70 at Frederick. To the southwest, I-66 and U.S. 50 connect with the Virginia segment of I-495. If you're a member of **AAA,** request a Trip-Tik and other pertinent information (© **800/222-4357** or 703/222-6000) before you depart.

BY TRAIN

Amtrak (© **800/872-7245;** www. amtrak.com) offers daily service to Washington from several East Coast, Midwest, and West Coast cities. Travelers from the far West change trains in Chicago or New Orleans. Amtrak's high-speed Acela trains travel as fast as 150 miles per hour along the Northeast Corridor, linking Boston, New York, and Washington. The Acela cuts about 15 to 30 minutes off the usual 3¾-hour ride between New York and Washington, and as much as an hour off the trip between Boston and Washington.

Although Amtrak is the most efficient way to get to D.C. from New York and points in between, it has had some problems in recent years, probably owing to financial woes, aging equipment, and cutbacks. Fares went up appreciably in the fall of 2005, due in part to hurricane Katrina and the subsequent rising fuel prices. On a Regional train, the round-trip fare between New York and Washington ranges from $152 (unreserved, which means you could stand if the train is full) to $290 (reserved at peak times). The price rises from there to $304 for the Acela Express, which is about 15 to 20 minutes faster. Children get a discount, especially in summer. Bear in mind that some weekend and holiday blackouts might apply, so check when you call. Between Boston and Washington, the round-trip unreserved fares begin at $208, a bargain if you don't mind sitting for 7 to 8 hours. The fare on the Acela Express ranges from $302 to $376. It's cheaper to fly, but I'd rather walk than contend with Boston Logan Airport. Kids up to 15 pay half the adult rate when accompanied by a fare-paying passenger 18 or older. Every adult passenger is allowed two children's-fare tickets. **Seniors** 62 and older are entitled to a 15% discount. **AAA** members get a 10% discount. Also ask about special fares and promotions, especially in summer. There is a 5% discount for booking online. Passengers with disabilities are entitled to a 15% reduction on regular one-way coach fares. Children with disabilities between the ages of 2 and 15 can travel for 50% of the fare for adults with disabilities. The discount does not apply to the Metroliner.

If you arrive by Amtrak, your first glimpse of Washington will be **Union Station,** at Massachusetts Avenue NE and North Capitol Street, a stone's throw from the U.S. Capitol. The grand scale of Union Station does much to heighten the excitement of arrival, and the kids might want to spend their entire vacation here, among the food court, movies, shops, and restaurants. There's **Metro** service right in the building, and **taxis** are plentiful. **MARC** (Maryland Rural Commuter System) and **Virginia Railway Express** arrive and depart from here, too. Many Amtrak trains also stop at the **New Carrollton Station** in Lanham, Maryland, about 15 to 20 minutes by rail and 20 minutes by car from Union Station. Long-term parking is more readily available at New Carrollton, but be advised it may still fill early on weekday mornings. If you're staying in the Maryland suburbs, taking Amtrak to New Carrollton is more convenient than Union Station.

Kids usually enjoy train travel because it's less confining than a car or plane, and it's fun visiting the snack bar. You might want to consider giving your children a food allowance to last the entire trip so that they don't bug you every few minutes. Also, Amtrak is not known for its snack-bar cuisine. When I take my grandkids on the train, I bring sandwiches from home and let them buy drinks and snacks.

Maryland Rural Commuter System (MARC) operates trains between Union Station in Washington, BWI Airport, and downtown Baltimore Monday through Friday (✆ **800/325-RAIL**).

9 Show & Tell: Getting the Kids Interested in D.C.

Successful family vacations don't just happen serendipitously. If you follow these simple guidelines, your family should have a good time and will fill several scrapbooks with happy memories:

- Help your children gather information about the nation's capital.
- Plan ahead and allow them input in organizing your sightseeing schedule.
- Think small. Prioritize your sightseeing objectives, leaving time for recreational and spontaneous activities such as chasing squirrels and eating ice cream.

Supplement your kids' knowledge of D.C. by borrowing from the library or purchasing a basic book about the city and reading it with them nightly before your trip.

SPECIAL PROJECTS   Of course, as a family vacation destination, Washington is anything but boring and yucky. Your mission, should you decide to accept it, is to get your kids so fired up about the impending trip that they probably won't sleep the night before you leave home.

Here are some suggestions to get them involved and excited for your trip. Ask them to jot down everything they see or hear about Washington, D.C. or its residents. If they listen to the radio, watch TV, or pick up a newspaper occasionally for something other than the comics (or to line the birdcage), this will be a snap. You can discuss their lists at mealtime and "fill in the blanks." They might shock you and learn the details of the latest government scandal completely on their own.

Again, I suggest that you borrow from your local library or purchase one or more of the many books on Washington to help familiarize your kids with the city. Then they'll be better able to participate in planning the family's sightseeing activities. If they have a say in what they see and do, everyone will have a more enjoyable vacation.

Encourage older children to write to the **Washington, D.C. Convention and Tourism Corporation,** 901 7th St. NW, Washington, DC 20001, or at www.washington.org, for free brochures and maps. Invite them to read chapter 6 of this guide and write down the attractions that most interest them. They can request information about any of the **Smithsonian's** museums by writing to the Public Affairs Office, Smithsonian Institution, Washington, DC 20560 (Attention: *Name of specific museum*), or by visiting www.si.edu.

Under your supervision, your children can also send away for maps and guidebooks—you know that kids love to receive mail.

Washington, D.C.: A Capital Adventure, part of the Video Visits series, is a marvelous 50-minute tape with gorgeous photography and informative narration. The tape gives a wonderful overview of the city's history and major sightseeing highlights while delivering a sugarcoated lesson in U.S. history. It's available for rent at many video stores or online, new and used, at several websites. If this doesn't whet your family's travel appetite, nothing will.

3

Getting to Know
Washington, D.C.

Welcome! You and your family are about to embark on an adventure in one of the most inspiring and captivating cities in the world. The nation's capital is distinguished by an eclectic style: Old South mixes with high-tech, marble and granite blend with cherry blossoms and magnolias, ethnic festivals meld with presidential inaugurals, and the nation's history bumps noses with tomorrow's headlines. With so much to see and do, there is little doubt that you and your children will have fun discovering the many facets of this enchanting and enigmatic city.

1 Orientation

IMPORTANT INFORMATION RESOURCES

The White House Visitor Center, at the southeast corner of 15th and E streets NW (© 202/456-7041; www.whitehouse.gov), has information about the White House (and restrooms, too). When or if the security restriction is lifted, the center will also distribute tickets for White House tours. Currently, the White House is open only to groups with reservations provided by their congressional representative or senator. Meanwhile, you can watch the video "Within These Walls," which some find more satisfying than an actual visit to the presidential home. The Visitor Center, open daily from 7:30am to 4pm, sometimes with extended summer hours until 4:30, is closed Thanksgiving, December 25, and January 1. For general information about Washington attractions, visit the **D.C. Visitor Information Center** run by the D.C. Chamber of Commerce in the **Ronald Reagan Building,** 1300 Pennsylvania Ave. NW (© 866/DCISFUN [324-7386]). It's conveniently located right at the Federal Triangle metro stop. Also check the front section of the Bell Atlantic **Yellow Pages,** available at most (if not all) hotels. The more than 30 pages of valuable information and maps will help you get your bearings. For information on **Maryland attractions,** call © 866/639-3526 or visit www.mdisfun.org. For information on **sights in Virginia,** call © 800/847-4882 or visit www.virginia.org.

If you need help sorting out mixed-up tickets, retrieving lost baggage, or locating lost family members, the **Travelers Aid Society** will come to the rescue. Besides maintaining desks at Dulles Airport (© 703/572-8296) and Reagan National (© 703/417-3975), the society has a booth next to the McDonald's in Union Station, 50 Massachusetts Ave. NE at North Capitol Street (© 202/371-1937; www.traveler-said.org). In Baltimore, Travelers Aid operates out of the Samaritan Center, 19 W. Franklin St, (© 410/468-4627).

To find out what's going on day by day, see Washington's two daily newspapers, *The Washington Post* (the Thursday "Weekly" section and Friday "Weekend" magazine are especially helpful) and the **Washington Times.** The spirited weekly **City Paper** is published every Thursday and is available at all Metro stations and 1,300 D.C. shops and restaurants. **Jewish Week** comes out every Thursday. If you're staying in the suburbs, look for the Friday edition of the **Journal** newspapers (no relation to the *Wall Street Journal*), which are chockablock with things to do and see. The **Washingtonian,** a popular monthly magazine, lists area events, previews major happenings, and reviews restaurants; also look for **Washington Flyer** magazine (available free at the airports) and **Here!** (available at downtown hotels and newsstands).

For a free copy of the Smithsonian's **"Planning Your Smithsonian Visit,"** which is full of valuable tips, write to or stop by the Smithsonian Information Center, 1000 Jefferson Dr. SW, Washington, DC 20560 (© **202/357-2700;** www.si.edu). The Information Center is open from 9am to 5:30pm daily. A listing of Smithsonian exhibits and activities appears every Friday in the "Weekend" magazine of *The Washington Post.*

CITY LAYOUT

The District of Columbia is shaped like a baseball diamond—but with a chunk missing, as if someone took a big bite out of the field between third base and home.

The District was originally laid out on a grid, and if you pay attention to a few general rules, you should have little difficulty finding your way around. It will help enormously if you consult the "Washington, D.C. at a Glance" map in this chapter while digesting the following.

The U.S. Capitol marks the center of the city, which is divided into quadrants: **Northeast (NE), Northwest (NW), Southeast (SE),** and **Southwest (SW).** All addresses are followed by one of the four designations. *Pay attention to them:* The same address can (and often does) appear in all four quadrants of the city. Most tourist attractions are in either the NW or SW quadrant.

MAIN ARTERIES & STREETS **North Capitol Street** and **South Capitol Street** run north and south, respectively, from the Capitol. **East Capitol Street**—you guessed it—divides the city into north and south. Easy, right? Unfortunately, it's here that the plot thickens: Where you would logically expect to find West Capitol Street, you actually find the area known as the **National Mall.** The north side of the Mall is **Constitution Avenue;** the south side is **Independence Avenue.**

Lettered streets above and below (north and south, if you prefer) East Capitol Street run east and west and are named **alphabetically,** beginning with A Street. Just to keep things interesting, there is no B or J Street, although Constitution Avenue on the north side of the Mall and Independence Avenue on the south side are the equivalent of B Street. I understand that Pierre L'Enfant, who laid out the city, omitted J Street because the "I" and "J" too closely resembled each other in old-style printing.

Numbered streets run north and south, so theoretically at least, there's a 1st Street (NE and SE; NW and SW) on either side of the Capitol.

State-named avenues (now we're getting to the fun part!) radiate from the Capitol, like a lot of wheel spokes, all bearing state names. They slice diagonally through the numbered and lettered streets, creating a host of circles and sometimes havoc. If you're new in town, it is possible to drive several times around these circles before finding the continuation of the street you were on.

The primary artery is **Pennsylvania Avenue,** scene of parades, inaugurations, and other splashy events. Pennsylvania Avenue runs between the Capitol and the White House and then continues on a northwest trajectory from the White House to

Washington, D.C. at a Glance

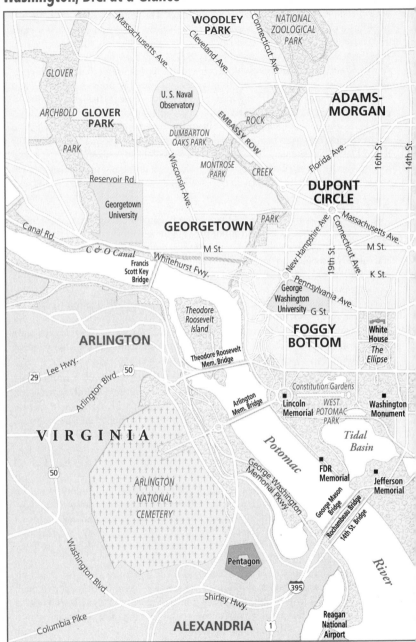

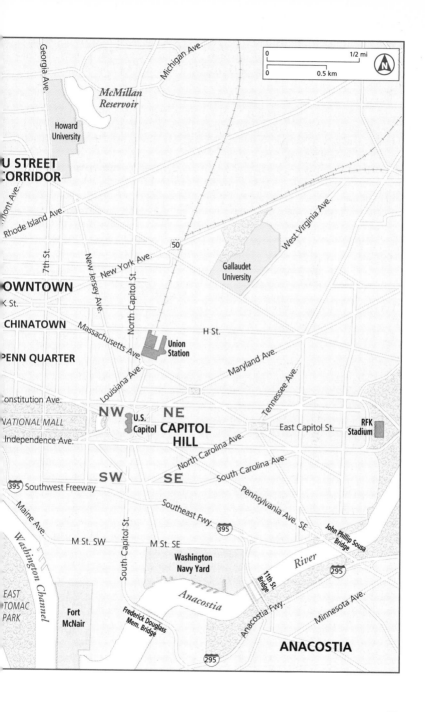

McMillan
Reservoir

Howard
University

Georgia Ave.

Michigan Ave.

U STREET
CORRIDOR

mont Ave.

Rhode Island Ave.

7th St.

New Jersey Ave.

New York Ave.

North Capitol St.

West Virginia Ave.

50

Gallaudet
University

DOWNTOWN

K St.

CHINATOWN

PENN QUARTER

Massachusetts Ave.

Louisiana Ave.

H St.

Union
Station

Maryland Ave.

Constitution Ave.

NATIONAL MALL

Independence Ave.

NW
U.S.
Capitol

NE
CAPITOL
HILL

Tennessee Ave.

East Capitol St.

RFK
Stadium

SW

SE

North Carolina Ave.

South Carolina Ave.

395 Southwest Freeway

Maine Ave.

M St. SW

South Capitol St.

M St. SE

Washington
Navy Yard

Southeast Fwy.

395

Pennsylvania Ave. SE

John Phillip Sousa
Bridge

River

295

Washington Channel

EAST
POTOMAC
PARK

Fort
McNair

Frederick Douglass
Mem. Bridge

Anacostia

11th St.
Bridge

Anacostia Fwy.

Minnesota Ave.

ANACOSTIA

295

0   1/2 mi

0   0.5 km

39

Georgetown. In the original plan, the president was supposed to have an uninter-rupted view of the Capitol Building from the White House. But Andrew Jackson placed the Treasury Building between the White House and the Capitol, blocking off the presidential vista.

Pennsylvania Avenue between 15th and 17th streets NW, fronting the White House, is closed to cars for security reasons. To handle the traffic snarls caused by this 2-block closing, H Street is one-way eastbound between 13th and 19th streets NW; I Street is one-way westbound between 11th and 21st streets NW. If you're driving, good luck—you'll need it.

Constitution Avenue is north of and parallels **Independence Avenue.** It runs east–west, flanking the U.S. Capitol and the Mall with its many major museums (and important government buildings to the north and south), the Washington Monu-ment, the Ellipse, and the White House (to the north), and continues past the Reflect-ing Pool to the Lincoln Memorial and the Potomac River. Until the late 1800s, when Tiber Creek ran through town (down what is now Constitution Avenue) to meet the Potomac, the entire area was a malaria-infested swamp. You can be sure D.C. had trouble drawing tourists then. In fact, it had trouble drawing anyone, and D.C. was considered a hard-luck post. For many politicians, it still is.

Washington's longest avenue, **Massachusetts Avenue,** runs north of and parallel to Pennsylvania Avenue. Along this street, heading northwest, you'll find Union Station, Dupont Circle, and Embassy Row. Farther still, you'll see the Naval Observatory (the vice president's residence is on the premises), Washington National Cathedral, and American University. Then Massachusetts Avenue just keeps going, right into Maryland.

Connecticut Avenue, running more directly north, starts at Lafayette Square near the White House. Heading north, it cuts through Dupont Circle and Rock Creek Park, past the National Zoo's main entrance, through a mostly residential neighbor-hood and then well into suburban Maryland. Between K Street and Dupont Circle, it's lined with both casual and elegant eateries, shops, and high-rise office and apart-ment buildings, a bit like New York's Fifth Avenue. **Wisconsin Avenue,** from the point where it crosses M Street, creates Georgetown's main intersection. Antiques shops, trendy boutiques, restaurants, and pubs all vie for attention. Yet on the side streets, lined with lovely Georgian and Federal homes, Georgetown manages to main-tain its almost-European charm. Wisconsin Avenue continues into Chevy Chase and Bethesda, Maryland. In Rockville, it becomes Rockville Pike/Route 355. Farther north, it is Frederick Avenue/Route 355.

FINDING AN ADDRESS   Finding an address in Washington, D.C. is easy—once you get the hang of it. In any four-digit address, the first two digits indicate the near-est lower-numbered cross street. For example, 1750 K St. NW is between 17th and 18th streets in the northwest quadrant of the city. In a three-digit address, look at the first digit. A restaurant at 620 H St. NW would be between 6th and 7th streets.

The digits of state-named avenues refer to the nearest numbered street. For exam-ple, 1600 Pennsylvania Ave. NW is on Pennsylvania Avenue at 16th Street.

Finding an address on a numbered street is a little stickier. First, assume that the addresses between A and B streets are numbered in the 100s, between B and C in the 200s, between C and D in the 300s, and so on. Now suppose that you're looking for 808 17th St. NW. Following this line of reasoning, the first digit in 808 signifies eight letters or blocks away from A Street, so start counting! If you come up with H, you're a winner: 808 17th St. is between H and I streets. This will become a game to your kids, who will find your destination while you're still deciding whether you're in SW or NW, although they might want to remove their socks when they run out of fingers in this exercise!

THE NEIGHBORHOODS IN BRIEF

To help you get acquainted with the city, the following alphabetical rundown will give you a preview of Washington's major sightseeing areas.

Adams–Morgan Centered around 18th Street and Columbia Road NW, colorful, vibrant, multiethnic Adams–Morgan is host to many international shops, restaurants, and music clubs. Whether you hunger for Ethiopian, Italian, Latin American, or any other cuisine that comes to mind, family appetites will be well satisfied. You'll encounter fewer briefcases and buttoned-down shirts and minds here than in any other sector of the city. Parking, however, is a problem, especially on weekends. Although the 15- to 20-minute walk from the nearest Metro is fine in nice weather, I don't recommend it after dark. Be safe, and take the shuttle from the Woodley Park–Zoo/Adams–Morgan Metro station (6pm–midnight weekdays, later on weekends); the no. 98 Metrobus ("U Street/Woodley Park Metro") for 35¢, no transfer necessary; or a taxi.

Capitol Hill Known affectionately as "the Hill," this area encompasses much more than just the awe-inspiring U.S. Capitol. Bounded by the western side of the Capitol to the west, H Street NE to the north, RFK Stadium to the east, and the Southwest Freeway (I-395) to the south, it is home to the Library of Congress, the Folger Shakespeare Library, Union Station, the U.S. Botanic Garden, and the Capital Children's Museum. You'll also find that the restaurants in this part of town are especially kid-friendly.

Convention Center/Penn Quarter Until a few years ago, this was one of D.C.'s least attractive areas. That was then, as the saying goes. The neighborhood has come back with many new hotels and restaurants and with a decidedly prettier face. Credit the 1997 opening of the MCI Center (for sports events and concerts by major stars) and the April 2003 opening of D.C.'s new Convention Center at 8th Street and Mt. Vernon Place NW— 2.3 million square feet on six levels, making it the sixth largest in the country. For business travelers and vacationers alike, it is convenient to Metro Center (the transfer station for Metro's Red, Orange, and Blue lines). It is also within walking distance of the FBI Building, International Spy Museum, Old Patent Office Building (home of the National Museum of American Art and National Portrait Gallery, both scheduled to reopen July 4, 2006), Chinatown, Ford's Theatre, and restaurants to accommodate all those conventioneers. Hotels catering to business travelers offer great weekend rates and perks for families.

Downtown Critics used to argue that Washington lacks a vibrant downtown. See for yourself. Geographically spread out, the area is centered on Connecticut Avenue and K Street NW, and extends east to 7th Street, west to 22nd Street, north to P Street, and south to Pennsylvania Avenue. The heart of the business community beats here. Although the White House and most of historic Pennsylvania Avenue are here, there are fewer attractions than in other sectors. However, it is four or fewer Metro stops to the sights on the National Mall and Capitol Hill.

You'll find in this cosmopolitan area many of the city's finest restaurants, national retail chains (Ann Taylor, Banana Republic, The Gap), and street vendors hawking everything from soft pretzels to designer knockoffs.

Dupont Circle   Dupont Circle (the neighborhood) surrounds Dupont Circle (the traffic circle and park). The park—and, by extension, the neighborhood—is distinguished by an abundance of squirrels and pigeons, young people with multipierced body parts, and ongoing chess games between seniors. Radiating from the intersection of Connecticut and Massachusetts avenues NW lies an area colored by the many artistic types and free spirits who reside there. One of my favorite art museums, the Phillips Collection, is here, along with many smaller galleries, diverse restaurants, boutiques, and bookstores. It's a great place for browsing and people-watching.

Foggy Bottom   An industrial center in the 18th century, Foggy Bottom lies west of the White House and stretches about 10 blocks to the foot of Georgetown. Pennsylvania Avenue and Constitution Avenue are its northern and southern perimeters. The area is villagelike, with row houses and postage-stamp-size gardens fronting brick-walked, tree-lined streets. Foggy Bottom derives much of its panache and international flavor from the State Department, International Monetary Fund, the Kennedy Center for the Performing Arts, and George Washington University.

Georgetown   Long a favorite tourist draw, this bustling area, once a prosperous tobacco port, radiates from the intersection of Wisconsin Avenue and M Street NW. Georgetown's riverfront setting, Federal and Victorian architecture, boutiques, and wealth of restaurants draw visitors of all ages. Sightseeing attractions include the C&O Canal, the pre-Revolutionary Old Stone House, and the magnificent Dumbarton Oaks Gardens and Museum. On this picturesque parcel, you'll find the Washington Harbor Complex with restaurants and a scenic promenade. The Georgetown University campus perches on a hill in the western corner of this vibrant neighborhood. Dining outdoors, walking, biking, or renting a boat on the canal are all popular warm-weather respites. Georgetown is always packed on weekends.

The Mall   Your kids will think you're crazy when you tell them they can't buy clothing at this "Mall." They can, however, visit most of the Smithsonian museums and galleries, the Lincoln Memorial, the Washington Monument, and the Vietnam, Korean War Veterans, and WWII memorials, *and* shop for souvenirs. You also can take a ride on an antique carousel, watch the Fourth of July fireworks, or catch a free outdoor summertime concert or movie. This lush, parklike rectangle between the Capitol and Lincoln Memorial attracts kite fliers, joggers, Frisbee-tossers, inline skaters, and picnickers.

2 Getting Around

BY PUBLIC TRANSPORTATION

Because Washington's Metrorail subway system is generally reliable, efficient, clean, and quiet (it's even carpeted!), your kids might want to spend their whole visit riding underground.

DISCOUNT PASSES   Metro offers a **One-Day Pass,** which is a good deal at $6.50 per person. It can be used after 9:30am weekdays and all day Saturday, Sunday, and

Getting to Georgetown

The Georgetown Metro Connection (© **202/625-RIDE**; www.georgetown dc.com), a privately run shuttle service, buses visitors (via two lines) between the Foggy Bottom, Dupont Circle, and Rosslyn Metro stations and various stops in Georgetown, a distance of 10 or more blocks, depending on your destination. You can catch a Metrobus (30, 32, 34, or 36) near the Foggy Bottom Metro station, but it usually takes longer. The Wisconsin Avenue Line of the Georgetown shuttle goes between Georgetown and Foggy Bottom Metro by way of Wisconsin Avenue, the Georgetown waterfront, and K Street NW. The M Street Line of the Georgetown shuttle travels between the Rosslyn Metro station (Arlington, Virginia), Georgetown, and Dupont Circle Metro station via Key Bridge, M Street, Pennsylvania Avenue, L Street, and New Hampshire Avenue NW. Ask the driver for the stop nearest your destination. Hours of operation are Mon–Thurs 7am–midnight; Fri 7am–2am; Sat 8am–2am; Sun 8am–midnight. The fare is $1 one-way, or just 35¢ if you have a Metro transfer (ticket machine near the escalator).

federal holidays. If you're stickin' around for a while, the **7-Day Fast Pass** is $32.50. Metrobus offers passes for commuters and other frequent riders, but D.C. isn't a bus riding–friendly city like New York. You can purchase the passes at any station or at the **Washington Metropolitan Area Transit Authority,** 600 5th St. NW (© **202/637-7000;** www.wmata.com). Kids 4 and under always ride free on the Metro. Senior citizens (65 and older) and handicapped people with valid proof ride the Metrorail and the Metrobus for a reduced fare.

BY SUBWAY   Metrorail (Metro), Washington's subway system, opened in 1976. The system's more than 100 miles of track blanket the metropolitan area, reaching deeply into the Maryland and Virginia suburbs. The cars are graffiti free, streamlined, and attractive, with air-conditioning and comfortable, upholstered seats. Signs at both ends of the cars tell the name of the next station. Kids can sit in the first seat of the first car, and note the train's speed and eye the control panel in the operator's compartment.

Forget the shrill, grinding noises you might have endured in other cities' subways. The Metro is relatively quiet. With most stations just 2 or 3 minutes apart, you're never more than a short walk from all the major attractions. Designed with safety in mind, the system has few dark nooks and crannies in the stations to shelter criminals, and Metro Transit Police (MTPD) constantly monitor and patrol the trains and stations.

Most cars have been replaced over the years, but the escalators and elevators have been showing the aches and pains of old age. If the escalators are "sick" at your station, and you're not up to walking, ride the elevator. When riding the escalator with a small child, stand to the right, hold your child's hand, and don't allow your youngster to sit on the step. Unfortunately, accidents occasionally do happen.

Pick up a **Pocket Guide** in any station, and tuck it in your bag or use it as a bookmark for easy retrieval. Call © **202/637-7000** with your questions, or go to www. metroopensdoors.com. The five Metro lines—Red, Blue, Orange, Yellow, and Green—operate Sunday through Thursday from 5am to midnight, Friday from 5am

Metro Stops

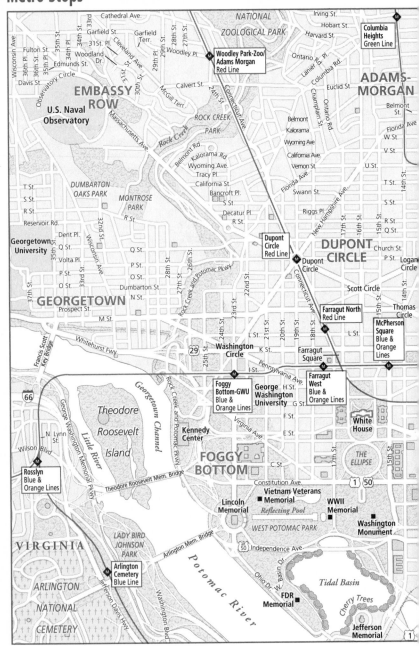

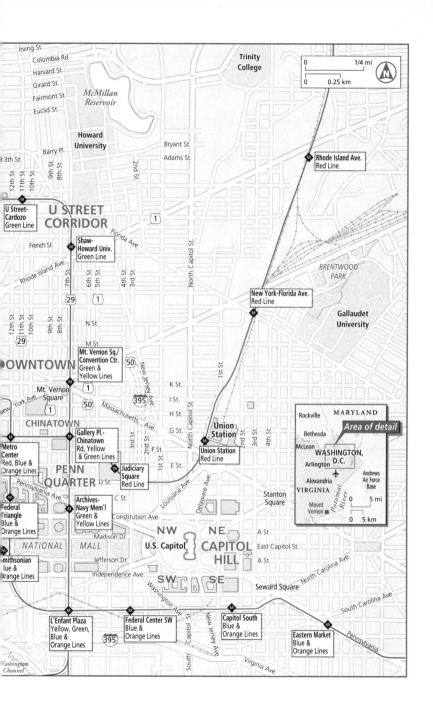

Irving St.
Columbia Rd.
Harvard St.
Girard St.
Fairmont St.
Euclid St.

McMillan
Reservoir

Trinity
College

0   1/4 mi
0   0.25 km

Howard
University

Bryant St.
Adams St.

13th St.

Rhode Island Ave.
Red Line

U Street-
Cardozo
Green Line

**U STREET
CORRIDOR**

Florida Ave.

French St.

Shaw-
Howard Univ.
Green Line

Rhode Island Ave.

7th St.
6th St.
5th St.
4th St.
3rd St.

2nd St.

North Capitol St.

BRENTWOOD
PARK

New York-Florida Ave.
Red Line

Gallaudet
University

12th St.
11th St.
10th St.
9th St.
8th St.

(29)

(29)

(1)

N St.

M St.

Mt. Vernon Sq./
Convention Ctr.
Green &
Yellow Lines

DOWNTOWN

Mt. Vernon
Square

(1)

(50)

New Jersey Ave.

50

395

Massachusetts
Ave.

New York Ave.

CHINATOWN

K St.

I St.

H St.

G St.

F St.

North Capitol St.

1st St.

2nd St.
3rd St.
4th St.

MARYLAND

Rockville

Area of detail

Bethesda

McLean

**WASHINGTON,
D.C.**

Arlington

Alexandria

VIRGINIA

Andrews
Air Force
Base

Mount
Vernon

Potomac River

0   5 mi

0   5 km

Metro
Center
Red, Blue &
Orange Lines

Gallery Pl.-
Chinatown
Rd, Yellow
& Green Lines

3rd St.
2nd St.
1st St.

E St.

Union
Station

Union Station
Red Line

Stanton
Square

**PENN
QUARTER**

Judiciary
Square
Red Line

D St.

Pennsylvania Ave.

Federal
Triangle
Blue &
Orange Lines

Archives-
Navy Mem'l
Green &
Yellow Lines

C St.

Constitution Ave.

Louisiana Ave.

Delaware Ave.

Madison Dr.

NW   NE

A St.

East Capitol St.

NATIONAL   MALL

Jefferson Dr.

U.S. Capitol

**CAPITOL
HILL**

A St.

Smithsonian
Blue &
Orange Lines

Independence Ave.

SW   SE

Seward Square

North Carolina Ave.

South Carolina Ave.

Washington
Channel

Washington Ave.

L'Enfant Plaza
Yellow, Green,
Blue &
Orange Lines

395

Federal Center SW
Blue &
Orange Lines

Capitol St.

New Jersey Ave.

Capitol South
Blue &
Orange Lines

Eastern Market
Blue &
Orange Lines

Pennsylvania

South

Virginia Ave.

Taxi Zones

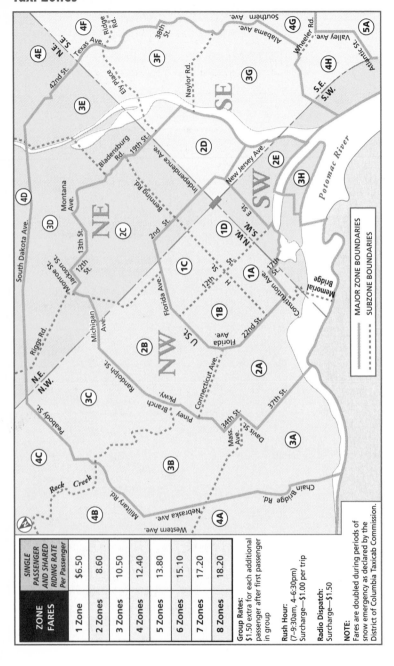

ZONE FARES	SINGLE PASSENGER AND SHARED RIDING RATE Per Passenger
1 Zone	$6.50
2 Zones	8.60
3 Zones	10.50
4 Zones	12.40
5 Zones	13.80
6 Zones	15.10
7 Zones	17.20
8 Zones	18.20

Group Rates:
$1.50 extra for each additional passenger after first passenger in group

Rush Hour:
(7–9:30am, 4–6:30pm)
Surcharge—$1.00 per trip

Radio Dispatch:
Surcharge—$1.50

NOTE:
Fares are doubled during periods of snow emergency as declared by the District of Columbia Taxicab Commission.

MAJOR ZONE BOUNDARIES

SUBZONE BOUNDARIES

Tourmobile

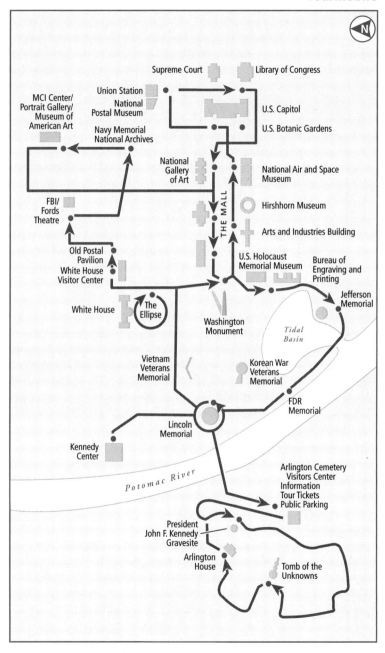

Supreme Court
Library of Congress

MCI Center/
Portrait Gallery/
Museum of
American Art

Union Station
National
Postal Museum

U.S. Capitol

Navy Memorial
National Archives

U.S. Botanic Gardens

National
Gallery
of Art

National Air and Space
Museum

FBI/
Fords
Theatre

THE MALL

Hirshhorn Museum

Arts and Industries Building

Old Postal
Pavilion
White House
Visitor Center

U.S. Holocaust
Memorial Museum

Bureau of
Engraving and
Printing

Jefferson
Memorial

White House

The
Ellipse

Washington
Monument

Tidal
Basin

Vietnam
Veterans
Memorial

Korean War
Veterans
Memorial

Lincoln
Memorial

FDR
Memorial

Kennedy
Center

Potomac River

Arlington Cemetery
Visitors Center
Information
Tour Tickets
Public Parking

President
John F. Kennedy
Gravesite

Arlington
House

Tomb of the
Unknowns

to 3am, Saturday from 7am to 3am, and Sunday from 7am to midnight. A weekend schedule is usually adopted on holidays, and evening hours are sometimes extended for special events such as the Fourth of July festivities on the Mall. Trains run about every 6 to 12 minutes, more frequently during rush hour, and less so after 8pm. Marking the entrance to every Metro station is a narrow brown column inscribed with the letter "M." Below the "M" is a colored stripe or stripes that tell you which line or lines operate there. Station names also appear in Braille on the columns at all Metro stops. The stationmaster will answer any routing or fare-card questions you might have.

Your ticket to ride is a computerized fare card from the intimidating-looking machines near the entrance. (If it takes you a while to figure out the system, welcome to the club.) You may also purchase a fare card—in $10, $15, or $20 denominations—online. Under the distance-based fare system, you pay the minimum, $1.35 to $2.35 ("Reduced Fare") during nonrush hours (9:30am–3pm and after 7pm weekdays; all day Sat, Sun, and holidays up to 2am), and the "Regular Fare" during rush hours (5–9:30am and 3–7pm weekdays, 2am–closing weekends). The minimum fare is $1.35; the maximum is $3.90. Fares are posted beneath the large colored map or the stationmaster's window. The machines take nickels, dimes, quarters, bills up to $20, and credit and debit cards. **Warning:** Change is returned in coins up to $5. If you feed the machine a $10 bill for a $1.20 fare, you'll be walking around with $3.80 in coins. You can buy multiple fare cards of the same value with one transaction. If you arrive at a destination and your fare card comes up short, add what's necessary at an Exitfare machine near the exit gate.

Because you need a fare card to enter and exit each station, keep it handy for reinsertion at your destination. If you will be transferring to a Metrobus, pick up a transfer on the mezzanine level when you enter the system (*not* your destination station). With the transfer ticket, it will cost you only 35¢ when boarding the Metrobus. Otherwise, you'll pay the full fare of $1.25. Purchase a round-trip fare card, when possible, to save time. On your last day in D.C., plan carefully. There are no cash refunds on amounts showing on your fare card.

BY BUS   You don't have to be a genius to figure out the **Metrobus** system, but it helps. For complete information, be sure to visit www.metroopensdoors.com.

The 13,000 stops on the 1,500-square-mile route (operating on all major D.C. arteries and in the Virginia and Maryland suburbs) are indicated by red, white, and blue signs. However, the signs—at best—just tell you what buses pull into a given stop, not where they go. For routing information, call ℰ **202/637-7000.** Using a computer, a transit-information agent can tell you the most efficient route from where

---

Get Smart

If you plan to park in a Metro station lot, you will need a **SmarTrip** card to get out. SmarTrip is a rechargeable card that can also be used for Metro fares, bus fares, and transfers. The cost is $30 (includes $25 in value on the card and a $5 processing fee) if you order one via snail mail *before* you leave home (ℰ **888/762-7874;** www.wmata.com). You can also purchase one from a Metrorail vending machine (next to the fare-card machines; no service fees) or at the Metro Sales Facility at 12th and F St. NW. (Are you having fun yet?) You can add up to $300 value with a credit card. To gain access to Metro, just swipe the SmarTrip card over the SmarTrip icon on the turnstile.

---

you are to where you want to go (using bus and/or subway) almost instantly. Calls are taken daily between 6am and 10:30pm, but the line is often busy. A voice-response information system is available at the same number 24 hours a day. You can also get routing and fare information online at www.wmata.com. All you have to do is key in where you are coming from, your destination, and the time you want to go or arrive.

If you travel the same route frequently and would like a free map and time schedule, ask the bus driver, or call ☎ **202/637-7000** and request one. Information about free parking in Metrobus fringe lots is also available from this number.

The fare on regular routes is $1.25 ($3 for express routes), and transferring from Metrorail to Metrobus costs 35¢. (*Note:* You will pay the going fare when transferring from bus to rail—no special deals here.) There are additional charges for travel into the Maryland and Virginia suburbs. Bus drivers are not equipped to make change, so be sure to carry exact change or use a SmarTrip card, which looks like a credit card. If you'll be riding a lot in one day, purchase a one-day regional bus pass from the bus driver. The pass costs $3 and is good on most buses in the D.C. area. Other passes include zones in Virginia or Maryland.

Most buses operate daily around the clock. Service is very frequent on weekdays (especially during rush hours), but less so on weekends and late at night. There's a full bus-information center (the **Metro Sales Facility**) at the Metro Center Station (12th and F streets), where tokens and special bus tickets are available.

Up to two children 4 and under ride free with a paying passenger on both the Metrorail and the Metrobus, and there are reduced fares for senior citizens (☎ **202/962-1245**) and those with disabilities (☎ **202/962-1245**). Finally, if you leave something on a bus, on a train, or in a station, call **Lost and Found** (☎ **202/962-1195**; www.metroopensdoors.com).

The **Georgetown Metro Connection** shuttle is operated by a collective of Georgetown businesses. Blue buses run from the Foggy Bottom, Dupont Circle (19th St. at Sunderland Place), and Rosslyn (VA) Metro stations to various stops along M Street and Wisconsin Avenue. The fare is 35¢ if you remember to pick up a transfer near the escalator as you exit Metro. Otherwise, it is $1 one-way.

The **Circulator** (☎ **202/962-1423**; www.dccirculator.com) shuttle bus was introduced to alleviate downtown congestion. Although it looks good on paper, I have my doubts about its efficacy. The large buses (with three doors) run every 5 minutes weekdays and every 10 minutes Saturday and Sunday, from 7am to 9pm, on two east–west routes between Union Station and Georgetown and two north–south routes between the Convention Center and southwest waterfront. There is no formal schedule. The fare is $1 one-way, free with a Metrobus transfer. Pay with exact change, Metro transfers, or a SmarTrip card. Purchase tickets at the sidewalk fare meters along the routes. All-day passes should be available by the time you read this.

BY CAR

Unless you absolutely have to, **don't drive in D.C.** If you don't swallow anything else in this guidebook, please accept on blind faith (and my more than 40 years of living in the area) that you'll waste precious time crawling through Washington's heavily trafficked downtown streets. Unless you're going to see the attractions in Virginia and Maryland (many of which require wheels to get to), you'll be better served using the comprehensive public transportation system and walking. D.C.'s many one-way streets and circles habitually confound motorists. Driving a car is especially nightmarish during rush hour (weekdays from about 6–10am and 3–7pm) and in the spring and summer seasons, when traffic jams are the norm—and only a smidge better at other times of the day and year. At *all times,* street parking is very limited, and parking lots are ruinously expensive. If you're driving into D.C. for the day, you might want to park in Union Station's ample garage and then board the Metro or take a taxi to your destination.

All the major car-rental companies, however, are represented here. Some handy phone numbers are: **Budget** (© 800/527-0700), **Hertz** (© 800/654-3131), **Thrifty** (© 800/367-2277), **Avis** (© 800/331-1212), and **Alamo** (© 800/327-9633).

BY TAXI

District cabs work on a zone system. Fares went up in 2005, and then a $1.50-per-ride fuel surcharge was added. (Another good reason to ride Metro or walk.) If you ride within one zone, the fare is $6.50. A two-zone trip costs $8.60; three zones cost $10.50. The maximum, eight zones, costs $18.20. I have rarely been able to reach the office on the phone, so for more information, I suggest going to the website, **www. dctaxi.dc.gov.** For as long as I can recall, the D.C. Taxicab Commission has been reviewing the zone system. If the taxicab commission ever gives the green light to a meter system, it would be a boon to visitors, because short rides would become cheaper. But at this point, it's still just talk. And where the D.C. government is concerned, the prevailing logic is usually "difficult is better."

If you want to hire a taxi for an hour or more, the hourly rate is $20 for the first hour and $5 for each additional quarter hour. Bear in mind that you're unlikely to travel more than three zones unless you're staying in some remote section of town. The driver's identification card must, by law, be displayed on the cab's right-side sun visor.

Be careful: Fare supplements can add up. There's a rush-hour surcharge of $1 between 7 and 9:30am and 4 and 6:30pm. Also, there's a $1.50 charge for each additional passenger after the first. If you want to stop en route, it'll cost you $1 for under 5 minutes, and the stop can't be more than 5 blocks from your destination (honest). The baggage-handling rate for one piece of luggage is 50¢. Trunks and large articles cost $2. Tipping is up to you, but the going rate is 10% to 15% of the fare.

Believe it or not, if you exit or enter the cab at a zone boundary, your fare could jump to the next level, depending on which side of the street you are on (the zone line goes down the middle of some streets). If you think this sounds confusing, that's because it is—even to those of us who have been living here for a long time. A few years ago, a friend and I took a cab *6 blocks* to make a curtain at the Kennedy Center. The cost: $9.40 without a tip. Absurd. The not-so-hidden message: Unless it's late at night, or you're in an iffy neighborhood, walk whenever possible or take the Metro.

The zone system is not used when your destination is an out-of-district address (such as the airport); the fare is then based on mileage covered—$2 for the first mile or part of a mile, and 70¢ for each additional half mile or part. You can call © 202/ 331-1671 to find out what the rate should be between any point in D.C. and an address in Virginia or Maryland. If you decide to go for broke, it's generally easy to hail a taxi; there are about 9,000 cabs, and drivers are allowed to pick up as many passengers as can comfortably fit (provided that the new passenger doesn't take the first passenger more than 5 blocks out of the way). In bad weather or when I'm in a hurry, I walk to the nearest hotel or museum where cabs are usually lined up. If your group is small, you can count on sharing the taxi. You can also call a taxi, although there is a charge for doing so. Try **Diamond Cab Company** (© 202/387-6200), **Yellow Cab**

(© 202/544-1212), or **Capitol Cab** (© 202/546-2400). They're three of the oldest and most reputable companies. If you have a complaint, note the driver's name and cab number, and call the **Taxicab Complaint Office** (© 202/727-5401).

BY TOURMOBILE

If you're visiting Washington for the first time, consider the Tourmobile, a National Park Service concession. It's an ideal way to get an overview of the major attractions. The open-air, blue-and-white sightseeing trams run on routes along the Mall and as far out as Arlington Cemetery and even (with coach service) Mount Vernon.

The full-day **American Heritage Tour** (Washington and Arlington Cemetery) visits 17 sites on or near the Mall and 4 sites at Arlington Cemetery: the Visitor Center, the grave sites of John and Robert Kennedy and Jacqueline Kennedy Onassis, the Tomb of the Unknowns, and Arlington House. One fare allows you to use the trams for a full day. The cost is $20 for age 12 and older; $10 for children 3 to 11. A 2-day pass is $30 for 12 and older, and $15 for ages 3 to 11. For Arlington Cemetery only, adults pay $6; children ages 3 to 11, $3. You may order American Heritage Tour tickets a day ahead at Ticketmaster (www.ticketmaster.com). The price is the same, but you'll have to pay a service fee of $2.50. You may board vehicles at any of 23 popular locations. If you wish to pay by credit card, ticket kiosks are located at the Washington Monument (1401 Jefferson Dr. NW), Arlington Cemetery, and Union Station (50 Massachusetts Ave. NE, in the main hall). Otherwise, you pay the driver with cash or traveler's checks only when you board. Along the route, you may get off at any stop to visit monuments or buildings. When you finish exploring each area, you step aboard the next Tourmobile that comes along. The trams travel in a loop, serving each stop about every 20 to 30 minutes. Trams follow "figure-8" circuits from the Capitol to Arlington and back. Children under 3 ride free. If you're traveling with very young children, the 2-day pass makes a lot of sense.

Along the route, the savvy guides regale visitors with colorful commentary. They will also answer your questions. It might seem like a lot of money to plunk down at one time, but I think it's well spent. With kids in tow, you can cover a lot of ground with comfort and ease.

Tourmobiles operate year-round, daily from approximately 9am to 4:30pm. Summer hours are usually extended to 6:30pm, but you can expect seasonal and year-to-year variations. For further Tourmobile information, including a full list of stops, call © 202/554-5100 or visit the website www.tourmobile.com.

Tourmobile also runs seasonal round-trip tours (lasting about 4 hours) to **Mount Vernon** (mid-June through Labor Day). Coaches depart from the Arlington National Cemetery Visitor Center and the Washington Monument at 10am, noon, and 2pm. The price is $25 for those 12 and older, $12 for children 3 to 11, and includes admission to Mount Vernon. Make a reservation at least half an hour before departure time at the Washington Monument Tourmobile stop or Arlington Cemetery Visitor Center. The **Frederick Douglass Tour** is another seasonal offering (mid-June to Labor Day). It includes a guided tour of Frederick Douglass's home, Cedar Hill. Call for reservations and departure times. The adult fare is $7; children ages 3 to 11 pay $3.50, which includes admission. The seasonal (mid-June to Labor Day) **Washington by Night** tour of the presidential monuments, war memorials, and Capitol is $20 for adults, $10 for kids 3 to 11. Purchase tickets at the Tourmobile kiosk in Union Station (50 Massachusetts Ave. NE), also the departure point for the tour.

BY OLD TOWN TROLLEY TOURS

Similar to Tourmobile, and very competitive in terms of price and quality, is the **Old Town Trolley** (② 202/832-9800; www.historictours.com). For a fixed price, you can get on and off these green-and-orange open-air vehicles as many times as you like at 17 locations in the District, including Union Station, the Old Post Office, the White House, National Cathedral, and other popular sites. The trolley is not licensed to stop directly on the Mall, and that is the primary difference between it and Tourmobile. The trolleys operate daily between 9am and 4:30pm, later in summer. Cost is $28 for riders 12 and older, $14 for kids 4 to 11, and free for children 3 and under. There is a 10% discount if you book online. The full narrated tour takes about 2¼ hours, and trolleys come by every 20 to 30 minutes beginning at 9am.

Tickets can be purchased in Union Station (50 Massachusetts Ave. NE, in the main hall). Or book online, save 10%, and present your e-ticket when you board.

For additional tour information, see chapter 6.

FAST FACTS: Washington, D.C.

American Express   There is one American Express Travel Service office downtown at 1150 Connecticut Ave. NW (② 202/457-1300) and several in the Maryland/Virginia suburbs. Call ② 800/528-4800 for exact locations.

Area Codes   If you are calling a D.C. number from somewhere outside the District, dial 202 before the last seven numbers. If you are in D.C. and are calling D.C., no area code is needed. In D.C., dial 301 or 240 for the close-by Maryland suburbs; 410 for Baltimore, Annapolis, and the Eastern Shore of Maryland; and 703 for suburban Virginia.

Babysitters   Most hotels will secure a bonded sitter for your brood. **weeSIT**, operating out of Burke, Virginia, has been providing hotel child care to visiting families for over 20 years. weeSIT charges $15 per hour (each extra child costs $1), with a 4-hour minimum plus a $15 travel charge (② 703/764-1542; www.weesit.net).

Dentist   Call ② 800/DOCTORS or the **D.C. Dental Society** at ② 202/547-7613, Monday through Friday from 8am to 4pm. Pediatric dentists are listed in the Yellow Pages under "Dentists, Grouped by Practice."

Doctor   Call ② 800/362-8677 for a referral service, ask your hotel's concierge, or call your hometown physician for a referral.

Drugstores   For free same-day delivery (provided medicine is in stock), call **Tschiffely Pharmacy,** 1330 Connecticut Ave. NW (② 202/331-7176), or **Union Station** (② 202/408-5178). The **CVS** chain has two 24-hour locations: 7 Dupont Circle NW (② 202/785-1466) and 1211 Vermont Ave. NW (② 202/628-0720). Two of CVS's suburban all-night stores are at Bradley Boulevard and Arlington Road, Bethesda, Maryland (② 301/656-2522); and Lyon Village Shopping Center, 3133 Lee Hwy., Arlington, Virginia (② 703/522-0260).

Emergencies   Call ② 911 for fire, police, or ambulance. For poison control, call ② 202/625-3333. Also see "Health, Insurance & Safety," in chapter 2.

Hospitals   In case of a life-threatening emergency, call ② 911. For emergencies not requiring immediate ambulance transportation but requiring emergency-room treatment, call one of the following hospitals. To save time and aggravation, call first and get directions; you or your taxi driver might need them.

- **Children's Hospital National Medical Center,** 111 Michigan Ave. NW (✆ **202/ 884-5000** for emergency room and general information).
- **George Washington University Hospital,** 901 23rd St. NW (✆ **202/715-4911** for emergency room; 202/715-4000 for general information).
- **Georgetown University Hospital,** 3800 Reservoir Rd. NW (✆ **202/444-2119** for emergency room; 202/444-2000 for general information).
- **Sibley Memorial Hospital,** 5255 Loughboro Rd. NW (✆ **202/537-4080** for emergency room; 202/537-4000 for general information).
- **Washington Hospital Center,** 110 Irving St. NW (✆ **202/877-7234** for emergency room; 202/877-7000 for general information).

Laundry & Dry Cleaning   If you are looking for a self-service, coin-operated laundry, try **Washtub Laundromat,** 1511 17th St. (at P St.) NW (✆ **202/332-9455**). For complete laundry and dry-cleaning services with pickup and delivery, contact **Bergmann's** (✆ **800/544-7413** or 703/247-7600). For same-day dry-cleaning service, try **MacDee Quality Cleaners** at 1639 L St. NW (✆ **202/296-6100**); and at 1822 N St. NW (✆ **202/457-0555**), open Monday through Saturday. Most hotels provide laundry and dry-cleaning services and/or have coin-operated laundry facilities.

Liquor Laws   The minimum drinking age is 21. Establishments can serve alcoholic beverages Monday through Thursday from 8am to 2am, Friday and Saturday until 3am, and Sunday from 10am to 2am. Liquor stores are closed on Sunday.

Police   In an emergency, dial ✆ **911.** For a nonemergency, call ✆ **202/727-4326.** For the location of the nearest district headquarters, call ✆ **202/727-1000.**

Post Office   The **National Capital Post Office** (next to Union Station), at North Capitol Street and Massachusetts Avenue NE (✆ **800/275-8777**), is open Monday through Friday from 7am to midnight and Saturday and Sunday from 7am to 8pm. For the location of the post office nearest your hotel, ask at the front desk. For **ZIP code information,** call ✆ **202/682-9595.**

Safety   I wish I could tell you that there is no crime in Washington, but I'd be lying. Although the number of violent crimes has declined dramatically in recent years, the adverse media hype (outside D.C.) continues. Rest assured that the areas in which you'll be spending most, if not all, of your time are relatively safe. To help ensure that your family has a safe visit, stay out of dark and deserted areas, and don't wander aimlessly. Criminals are known to prey on those who appear defenseless, so be alert to what's going on around you, and walk purposefully. If your children are young, hold their hands. Make sure your family has a plan if you are separated. Kids old enough to understand should know the name and address of their hotel.

Always lock your hotel room, car doors, and trunk. Wear a money belt under your clothes, and keep a close eye on your pocketbook, camera, and wallet. Hold on to your purse in a restaurant; don't drape it over a chair back or put it on an empty seat. When you buy something, put your money and credit cards away, and secure your wallet before you go out on the street. Leave expensive jewelry at home; what you do bring, don't flash. Do not make eye contact with suspect-looking individuals. If approached by a panhandler, say "No" or "Sorry" and keep walking.

When you're downtown—anywhere between the White House and Capitol, Massachusetts Avenue and the Convention Center to the Mall—and want an escort to your hotel, the Metro, or your car, or if you need directions, look for the friendly, helpful men and women in bright red jackets with the **SAM** (safety and maintenance) insignia on their shirts/jackets and "Downtown D.C." on their hats. If you can't find one, call the dispatcher at ☎ **202/624-1550.** They provide "At-Your-Side Service" Monday to Friday until 7:30pm from October to March, and until 9:30pm from April to October. They claim a response time of 10 minutes or less. Employed by the Downtown D.C. Business Improvement District (BID) and in close cahoots with the Metropolitan Police Department, they are ambassadors of goodwill and safety. And they carry walkie-talkies. For more info, go to their website: www.downtowndc.org.

Taxes The sales tax on merchandise is 5.75% in D.C., 5% in Maryland, and 4.5% in Virginia. The restaurant tax is 10% in D.C., 5% in Maryland, and 4.5% in Virginia. The hotel sales tax is 14.5% in D.C., 5% (plus 5%–7% local or city tax) in Maryland, and 10% in Virginia.

Time Washington, D.C. is on **Eastern Standard Time,** except when daylight saving time (DST) is in effect from the first Sunday in April (clocks are moved ahead 1 hr.) to the last Sunday in October (clocks are moved back 1 hr.). Beginning in 2007, DST will begin on the second Sunday of March and end the first Sunday of November. When it's noon in Washington, it's 11am in Chicago, 10am in Denver, and 9am in Los Angeles. To find out the local time, dial ☎ **202/844-2525.**

Useful Telephone Numbers Local calls cost 35¢. You might find the following telephone numbers useful during your stay (*Note:* Washington's 202 area code is not needed if you are calling from within D.C.):

Amtrak ☎ **800/872-7245**
Daily Calendar of Events ☎ **202/789-7000**
Dental Referrals ☎ **202/547-7613**
Dial-a-Museum ☎ **202/357-2020**
Dial-a-Park ☎ **202/619-7275**
D.C. Convention and Tourism Corp. ☎ **202/789-7000**
D.C. Rape Crisis Center ☎ **202/333-7273**
Medical Referrals ☎ **800/362-8677**
Metro Information ☎ **202/637-7000**
Metro Visitors with Physical Disabilities Information ☎ **202/962-1245**
Poison Control ☎ **202/625-3333**
Smithsonian Information Center ☎ **202/357-2700**
Travelers Aid Society (Union Station) ☎ **202/371-1937**
Visitors Information Association ☎ **202/789-7000**

Weather For the local weather forecast, call ☎ **202/936-1212.** If you want the extended outlook for the area and the air quality, call ☎ **703/260-0107.**

4

Family-Friendly Accommodations

When it comes to choosing a place to stay with your kids, look for a hotel that is convenient to the Metro, sightseeing attractions, restaurants, and amusements. A complimentary terrycloth robe and 24-hour room service might turn you on, but such amenities are of little consequence to youngsters. What's important to them is that they're close to food and fun: If there's a refrigerator, restaurant, snack machine, pool, or shopping nearby, your kids will be happy staying almost anywhere.

Many of the District's large hotel chains offer budget-minded traveling families, who occasionally opt to enjoy a light bite in their rooms rather than dine in a restaurant, the options of coffee bars, fast-food kiosks, or shops that carry snacks and light fare right in their lobbies.

Make sure your kids know the difference between food taken *into* the rooms and food taken out of them. Guests pay dearly for taking snacks and beverages from stocked refrigerators and minibars. If there's no lock on yours, tell your kids that the contents are off limits unless they clear it with you first.

Many D.C. hotels have an indoor or outdoor pool (covered in winter for year-round swimming) with a poolside beverage or snack bar. And nearly all hotels have on-site or nearby fitness clubs. Some are complimentary; some charge a fee. Of course, kids must be accompanied by an adult at the pool or health/fitness club. Many guest rooms offer complimentary premium channels or charge a small fee for pay-per-view movies and/or video games, so there should be enough to keep your tot entertained when you're not out and about in the city.

Depending on your budget, the selection of places to stay in Washington, D.C. is wide indeed. For those who prefer to leave the city at night, I've included several hotels in the Maryland and Virginia suburbs. The following suggestions cover a broad spectrum, from super-duper luxury hotels to budget alternatives. All, with a few exceptions, are within easy walking distance of the Metro, and all have something (in most cases, several somethings) that makes them attractive to kids. If you can't swing a $3,000-a-night Presidential Suite or room with a view of the Capitol, don't despair. You won't be spending that much time in your room anyway. At day's end, flopping into a bed—even one with a few lumps—will spell relief.

GETTING THE MOST FOR YOUR DOLLAR

To get the best value for your travel dollar, stay away from the District during the high season, which runs from late March to mid-June, when prices are at their highest. To save the most, visit between mid-June and Labor Day, when Congress and your kids are on vacation. The trade-off for a summer visit is Washington's notorious heat and humidity. In 2005, most hotels offered family incentive packages and summer savings. These hotel packages included accommodations, admission to a private museum and/ or tickets to a performance, and a welcome gift for the kiddies. Rates started at $99 per night. History—and 15 years penning this book—has taught me that great deals will be in effect during subsequent summers. Call ℂ **202/789-7000** or go to www. washington.org for information on this or other bargains. The months of January and February are usually slow, and rates typically fall. The trade-off for lower prices and fewer tourists: cold, damp weather. If you can live without cherry blossoms, definitely avoid the 2-week festival in late March and early April; it's an expensive and crowded time to visit D.C. And owing to Mother Nature's quirkiness, the blossoms often peak before or after the festival anyway.

Weekday rates can drop 30% to 50% on weekends; depending on occupancy, you might be able to cash in on weekdays as well. Hotels sometimes run unadvertised special promotions, but you won't find out about them if you don't ask. So speak up when you make a reservation.

Many experienced travelers believe you'll be quoted a better rate if you call a hotel directly instead of reserving through its toll-free number or at the website. While the Web is fantastic for research, I've been burned a few times when I've made a reservation at a hotel's Web site and there was no record of it when I showed up (usually hungry and cranky). It's always a good idea to print out your confirmation page and bring it with you in case you need proof of your reservation. When quoted a price, don't be afraid to ask if anything else is available for less. There's probably no point trying this around cherry-blossom time, but it's amazing what reservations clerks will come up with when you tell them you're going to shop around.

It's no secret that in most cases accommodations in the suburbs are less expensive than in D.C. But as usual, there's a trade-off for the lower prices. Many disagree, but I think there's a lot to be said for waking up in a city and having the attractions at your fingertips (maybe even a view of the Potomac or U.S. Capitol from your hotel) instead of having to commute into the city and getting stuck with a view of a highway or shopping mall.

HELPING HANDS

For information on accommodations, try the **Washington, D.C. Convention and Tourism Corporation,** 901 7th St. NW, 4th Floor, Washington, DC 20001 (ℂ **202/ 789-7000;** www.washington.org). **Washington D.C. Accommodations,** 1201 Wisconsin Ave., NW, Washington, DC 20007 (ℂ **800/503-3330;** www.dcaccommodations. com), offers free advice and reservations. If you're more comfortable with someone else doing the negotiating for you, write or call **Capitol Reservations,** 1730 Rhode Island Ave. NW, Suite 302, Washington, DC 20036 (ℂ **800/847-4832;** www.visit dc.com). They handle hotels in all price ranges and are privy to discounts because of their high-volume business. Additionally, they screen all the hotels they use for cleanliness and to make sure they're in safe neighborhoods.

Take Time to Total Taxes
When you're budgeting for your vacation, remember the hefty hotel-room tax: it's 14.5% in the District. On a $200 room, that's an extra $29 per night.

Groups who will occupy 10 or more rooms should know about **U.S.A. Groups** (© 800/872-4777; www.usagroups.net). This free service represents hotel rooms at almost every property in the Washington, D.C. and suburban Virginia/Maryland region and will work hard to find the best accommodations at the rates you request, saving your group valuable time and money.

1 Capitol Hill

After living in the D.C. area for more than 40 years, I still get a thrill every time I see the Capitol, especially when it is lit like a beacon at night. If you stay here, you, too, can find your thrill on Capitol Hill and be close to the area's many attractions and family-friendly restaurants. *A word of warning:* Although my "Hill" friends accuse me of being overly cautious, I maintain that walking on side streets in this neighborhood after dark is not a smart idea. However, walking near the hotels and restaurants listed in this book should be fine if it's not too late at night. Kids like to stay in this area because of its proximity to Union Station, bustling Eastern Market, and all of the Mall attractions.

EXPENSIVE

Hotel George 𝒜𝒜 *(Finds)*   Two blocks from the Capitol and Union Station, the eight-story Hotel George occupies a pre–Depression era building, but there's nothing depressing about the accommodations or service. Contemporary-style posters of G. W. hang in the hip two-story glass, chrome, and limestone lobby and uncluttered guest rooms. Floor-to-ceiling cherry cabinets conceal dresser drawers, closet space, and a refreshment center. The rooms, spare but soothing in tone, are done in shades of tasteful beige. The upholstered lounge chairs with ottomans and armchairs do much to soften the decor's hard edges. Business types can use the T1 lines for Internet access. Unwind with a choice movie on one of the complimentary premium stations (Nintendo is extra). Bathrooms (most with tub and shower; eight with shower only) are a symphony of gray-and-white marble and black granite.

Families can spread out by booking an adjoining parlor room (the hotel has two) with a double-size Murphy bed. The George Suite is a one-bedroom suite with separate living room, wet bar, powder room, dressing area, Jacuzzi, and shower.

Award-winning chef Jeffrey Buben whisks up delectable French bistro fare at Bistro Bis, which, like the hotel, sports a clean, contemporary look. Open for breakfast, lunch, and dinner, Bis is a grownup kind of place, with such items as escargots, steak tartare, sweetbreads, and sea scallops regularly on the lunch and dinner menu. The food is exquisite; the setting, romantic. Although the kitchen will gladly prepare "child-friendly" food for your tots, I suggest trying Bis with youngsters only at breakfast and lunch. At dinner, you'd do better to feed the kids in Union Station, with its myriad restaurants and multiple-choices Food Court. Then you could hire a sitter and slip downstairs for a romantic meal.

Where to Stay in Washington, D.C.

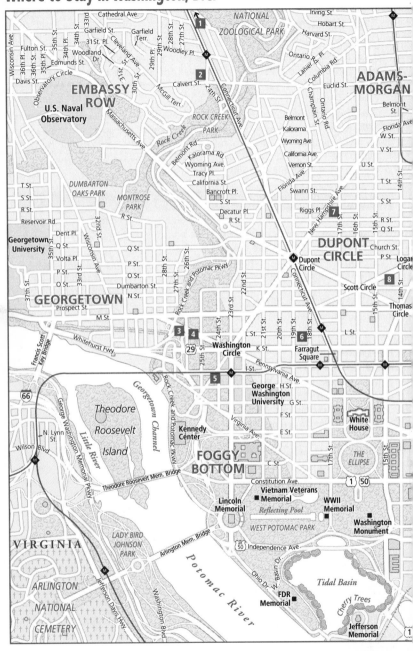

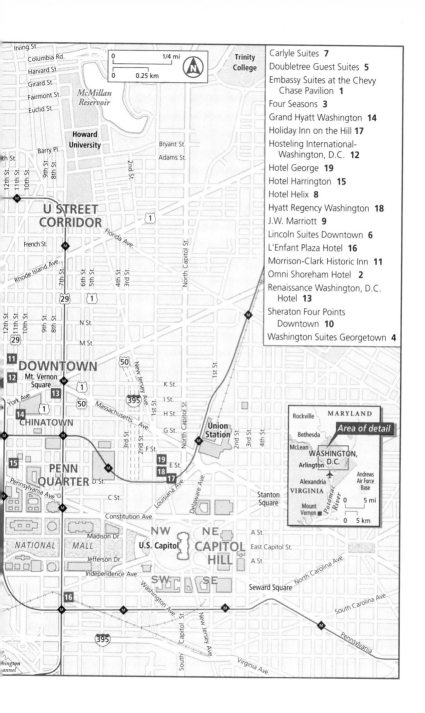

Carlyle Suites **7**
Doubletree Guest Suites **5**
Embassy Suites at the Chevy
    Chase Pavilion **1**
Four Seasons **3**
Grand Hyatt Washington **14**
Holiday Inn on the Hill **17**
Hosteling International-
    Washington, D.C. **12**
Hotel George **19**
Hotel Harrington **15**
Hotel Helix **8**
Hyatt Regency Washington **18**
J.W. Marriott **9**
Lincoln Suites Downtown **6**
L'Enfant Plaza Hotel **16**
Morrison-Clark Historic Inn **11**
Omni Shoreham Hotel **2**
Renaissance Washington, D.C.
    Hotel **13**
Sheraton Four Points
    Downtown **10**
Washington Suites Georgetown **4**

15 E St. NW, Washington, DC 20001. ℂ **800/576-8331** or 202/347-4200. Fax 202/347-4213. www.hotelgeorge.com. 139 units. $149 (summer weekends)–$350 (midweek in the fall). Weekend/seasonal specials. Kids 16 and under stay free. Crib free, rollaway $25. AE, DISC, MC, V. Valet garage parking $24 overnight with in-and-out privileges. Metro: Union Station. **Amenities:** Restaurant; fitness center; secretarial services; room service. *In room:* A/C, TV/VCR, fax, dataport, minibar, coffeemaker, iron, safe, dual-line phone system.

Hyatt Regency Washington 🏵🏵   A convenient Capitol Hill location and special perks make the Hyatt a perennial favorite for families. You can book a second room for the kids at half price, and the restaurants and room service have special kids' menus. All rooms and suites benefited from a $13 million renovation in 2004, with new bedding, furniture, carpeting, wall coverings, wireless Internet access, and enhanced lighting fixtures.

The hotel is within walking distance of the Metro, the U.S. Capitol, and other Hill attractions. However, it's a little farther (10–30 min. walking, depending on where you're going) to the Mall and Smithsonian museums.

The five-story atrium lobby and luxurious rooms were front-page news when the hotel opened during the Bicentennial. Now the oft-imitated style is as fresh as last year's scandal. But it's still attractive. Some rooms have showers only, so if you're a bubble-bath fan, be sure to state your preference.

The large, heated indoor pool (in a two-story glass atrium) is sure to attract your kids' attention; here as well as in the health club, children of any age are welcome, although those under 16 must be accompanied by a parent. There's a $12 daily fee (per room) to use the pool and fitness center.

The sunny **Park Promenade** is a 200-seat atrium restaurant for breakfast, lunch (weekday themed buffet), and dinner, with seasonal dishes at reasonable prices. Head to **NetWorks,** the lobby bar with four TV sets, which serves appetizers from 3pm to 2am. **Perks, Coffee & More** opens at 6am daily and features Starbucks coffee, Krispy Kreme donuts, sandwiches, salads, and the Pizza Factory until 10pm or so.

If you want, you can join the Regency Club, for which you pay more but get placed on a club-designated floor and get perks such as free continental breakfast, hors d'oeuvres, desserts/cordials in the evening, a private lounge (for the entire floor), and a special concierge (just for Regency Club guests). Little ones here can partake in all the same goodies as grownups, except for alcoholic beverages.

400 New Jersey Ave. NW, Washington, DC 20001. ℂ **800/233-1234** or 202/737-1234. Fax 202/737-5773. www.washington.hyatt.com. 834 units. $139–$429, Regency Club $35 extra; weekends from $139 single or double. Children under 18 stay free in parents' room. Crib free. Weekend and seasonal specials; AAA discounts. AE, DISC, MC, V. Valet parking $30 (overnight with in-and-out access). Metro: Union Station. **Amenities:** Restaurant; coffee shop; bar; indoor pool; fitness center; concierge; business center; room service 6am–midnight weekends (mornings and evenings weekdays); babysitting; laundry/dry cleaning service. *In room:* A/C, TV, Wi-Fi Internet (fee), fax, dataport, coffeemaker, hair dryer, iron, ADA equipment for guests with disabilities.

MODERATE

Holiday Inn on the Hill 🏵🏵 *Finds*   At this prime Capitol Hill location—the Capitol is only 2 blocks away, and Union Station is just a 5-minute walk—the Holiday Inn is a find, especially on weekends, when the rates sometimes dip as low as $139. Kids 12 and under always eat free in Senators Grille, the on-site restaurant, open for breakfast, lunch, and dinner. Can you beat that?

The whole place had a $10 million renovation in 2003 that included the lobby and guest rooms and looks mighty spiffy—pared down and sophisticated with animal prints and luxe furnishings, black granite vanities, 27-inch TV, workstations with ergonomic mesh chairs, free high-speed Internet access, and Nintendo. The rooms have always been large (for a big-city hotel). Now they seem even larger because they are uncluttered. For more space (and more money), request a room with an adjoining parlor—a large TV/sitting room. The four King Executive rooms have a small refrigerator, microwave, and sink.

In summer, take the young ones swimming in the rooftop pool—one of the largest in the city. The pool, with its adjacent sundeck and Skybox snack bar, is a place your whole family can relax while also enjoying a sandwich or hamburger and a cold drink. **Senators Grille** has a special kids' menu with games and pictures to color, and the chef has upgraded the grownup menu. The ambience is still casual, with old Washington Senators memorabilia (Washington's former baseball team that left in 1971) and wide-screen TVs. The all-you-can-eat breakfast buffet, from 6 to 10:30am, could be your main meal for the day. The kids' breakfast menu includes pancakes, French toast, cereal, and fruit, and bacon and eggs. At lunch and dinner, kids can order a hamburger, cheeseburger, hot dog, or pizza with a side of applesauce and a beverage. In the cocktail lounge, snacks cost $1 to $2 during Happy Hour.

415 New Jersey Ave. NW, Washington, DC 20001. ✆ **800/638-1116** or 202/638-1616. Fax 202/638-0707. www.hi onthehilldc.com. 343 units. $109–$269. Ask about the special Family Fun Package. Kids 18 and under stay free in parents' room. Crib free, rollaway $20. AE, DC, DISC, MC, V. Self-parking $20 per day, underground parking available. Metro: Union Station. **Amenities:** Restaurant (kids 12 and under eat free with an adult); rooftop outdoor pool; room service (6am–11pm). *In room:* A/C, TV, coffeemaker, hair dryer, iron.

2 Convention Center

This area has come back with a bang and a boom, as in building boom. The opening in 1997 of the MCI Center (which hosts sports events and concerts) and Convention Center in 2003 at 8th Street and Mt. Vernon Place NW have spawned new office and residential complexes, hotels, and restaurants. Once an eyesore, this neighborhood is wearing a much prettier face. And it is within walking distance of many attractions—among them Ford's Theatre, the Spy Museum, and the FBI. Hearty souls hoof it 7 or 8 blocks to the Mall attractions, but you can catch a train at the nearby Metro Center (12th and G sts. NW).

VERY EXPENSIVE

Sheraton Four Points Downtown 🎗🎗   The Sheraton is convenient to the Convention Center (about 2½ blocks) and within walking distance of many downtown attractions. A minifridge, two-phone dataports and high-speed Internet access, and a view of something more pleasing than an elevator shaft are by request only—unless you book a suite. The hotel installed new For Comfort Beds in 2005, and a renovation of the guest rooms, lobby, fitness room, and pool area is scheduled for an early 2006 completion. Ask when making a reservation. If the renovation is still ongoing when you're traveling, request a room far from the work.

Although this may not be the most picturesque block in the city, it's definitely "coming back." And the location is primo. It's 3 blocks to the Metro Center, where you can hop a train on three of Metro's five lines. Walk to Ford's Theatre, the FBI, the Shops at National Place, the Mall, the MCI Center for a sports event or rock concert, and downtown shopping. A small indoor rooftop swimming pool with a sundeck (but no lifeguard) is more than adequate for cooling off after pounding the pavement.

Kids can watch free movies on TV or the channel airing tourism information. **Corduroy Restaurant and Lounge** serves American cuisine, breakfast, lunch, and dinner daily. Many favorite family-friendly restaurants—Hard Rock Cafe, T.G.I. Friday's, Capitol City Brewing Co.—are within a few blocks. You can call room service when the spirit moves you.

1201 K St. NW, Washington, DC 20005. © **202/289-7600.** Fax 202/349-2215. www.fourpointswashingtondc.com. 265 units. $109–$249. Children under 18 stay free in parents' room. Crib free. AE, DC, DISC, MC, V. Valet parking $26 overnight (in-and-out privileges; maximum height 6′ 8″). Metro: Metro Center or McPherson Square. **Amenities:** Restaurant; small indoor pool; 24-hour fitness center; concierge; business center, secretarial services; room service (7am–midnight); laundry service; dry cleaning service. *In room:* A/C, TV, coffeemaker, iron, free high-speed Internet service.

EXPENSIVE
Renaissance Washington, D.C. Hotel ✦   Personally, I could do without the hustle and bustle weekdays at the Renaissance, which serves mainly conventioneers. But the Renaissance is centrally located, convenient to the White House area (about 8 blocks west), and the Mall. On weekends, the place is relatively quiet. That's when families can take advantage of huge savings and enjoy all the extras on a shoestring.

A $16 million renovation project in 2003 updated the lobby, guest rooms, and restaurant. Additional renovations to the guest rooms in the main tower were completed in 2004. An entire six-story tower with 146 rooms constitutes the **Renaissance Club,** where guests are pampered with extra amenities (for a price). Club guests also have a private concierge-staffed lounge, a cozy domain where you can enjoy sharing a complimentary continental breakfast with the kids from 6:30 to 10am. Afternoon hors d'oeuvres are available from 5 to 7pm for grownups.

Adjacent to the third-floor health club are a 60-foot pool and juice machines. The large atrium lobby is broken up into small sitting areas—ideal for kids who want to get out of the room, if only to play cards or checkers. Public areas and several guest rooms are ADA-compliant for guests with disabilities.

The **Florentine** is an upscale gourmet restaurant featuring American regional cuisine. Florentine welcomes children and has high chairs but no boosters. There are no kids' menus, but kids can share their parent's entrees or order an appetizer, soup, or salad if they're not up to an adult-size dinner portion. The **President's Sport Bar** has 12 plasma-screen televisions and serves all kinds of imported and domestic beers. The **Lobby Bar** offers a pleasing modern, boutique-type setting. **Espresso/Starbucks** coffeehouse is open from 6:30am until 10pm.

999 9th St. NW, at K St. NW, Washington, DC 20001. © **800/228-9898** or 202/898-9000. Fax 202/789-4213. www. Renaissancehotels.com. 807 units. $249–$369 double. Children 18 and under stay free in parents' room. Crib and rollaways free. Seasonal/weekend packages. AE, DISC, MC, V. Parking $27 valet (in-and-out privileges), $22 self-parking. Metro: Gallery Place or Metro Center. **Amenities:** 2 restaurants; 2 bars; indoor pool; fully equipped health club; concierge; 24-hour room service; massage; babysitting; laundry/dry cleaning service. *In room:* A/C, TV, coffeemaker, hair dryer, video message retrieval, T1 computer and wireless Internet connection (daily fee includes local and long-distance phone calls and high-speed Internet access).

INEXPENSIVE
Hosteling International–Washington, D.C. ✦ *Value*   With the money you save by staying here, you can fund a return visit next year! Hosteling International (HI)

A Room-Service Alternative
Too tired to dine out? Families staying near the convention center can order a pie from **Domino's Pizza** at 1300 L St. NW (© **202/639-8700**).

offers dorm-style rooms in a renovated downtown building. All the guest rooms and hallways were redone as of July 2005, with new mattresses and bunk beds. The lobby also received a fresh coat of paint and new carpet in the fall of 2005. High-speed modem lines (fee) and free Wi-Fi were also added. Lodging is strictly no-frills, but the area is teeming with new office buildings and trendy condos. The location, just 3 blocks north of the Metro Center stop, is extremely convenient. The big question is: Can your family survive without an in-room TV? The good news: There's a 60-inch big-screen TV in the television room.

The dorm-style rooms—all air-conditioned—have 4 to 12 beds; clean, recently renovated bathrooms are down the hall. Although some of the dorm rooms are coed, most are for men or women, so couples are separated, with sons sleeping in the same dorm as fathers and daughters with their mothers. There are also five family rooms that can sleep up to six people.

The hostel provides linens, pillows, blankets, towels, soap, and shampoo/conditioner. All you have to do is bring your clothes, toothpaste and toothbrush, and this guidebook. A gift shop sells toiletries and souvenirs in case you forgot something essential.

Upon registering, you'll be given a calendar of free events and activities around town. The HI also offers free special activities for guests—walking tours, concerts, movies, and more. And the knowledgeable staff at the information desk is available to help you with sightseeing and other travel questions. Free movies are shown every evening at 8pm. The hostel also has a comfortable lounge, storage lockers, indoor parking for bicycles, and a self-service laundromat. All public areas and rooms are accessible to travelers with disabilities. All guest rooms are nonsmoking. Checkout is 11am.

To cut costs further, you can shop for groceries at the Giant supermarket at 9th and O streets NW, prepare your meals in the huge self-service kitchen, and eat in the shared dining room. Ideally, your kids will meet some interesting international visitors who will spark their interest in learning about other countries.

1009 11th St. NW, at K St., Washington, DC 20001. © 202/737-2333. Fax 202/737-1508. www.HIWashingtondc.org. 270 beds. $29 HI members; $32 nonmembers (yearly membership is $28 per adult). Children 3–11 (with a parent) pay $15 per night, 2 and under free (if they sleep in the same bed), includes free continental breakfast. No cribs. MC. V. No parking; public lots, some street parking in area. Metro: Metro Center, McPherson Square, Gallery Place. **Amenities:** Tour desk; coin-op laundry.

3 Downtown

If you stay in this area, you can roll out of bed and onto the White House lawn. Well, *almost.* Most of the top sights (such as the Smithsonian museums, presidential memorials, and U.S. Capitol) are within walking distance or just a few stops away on the Metro. You'll be in the thick of things and also have your pick of restaurants and shopping. You'll usually pay top dollar for accommodations at a downtown hotel, but you can't beat the convenience. And if your time is limited, wouldn't you rather spend it *in* rather than traveling *to* a museum?

VERY EXPENSIVE

Grand Hyatt Washington ✦✦   The Grand Hyatt is within walking distance of the Spy Museum, National Portrait Gallery, the White House, the National Mall, the FBI, Ford's Theatre, Chinatown, the MCI Center, and lots of shopping. Large, well-appointed rooms surround a stunning 12-story, glass-enclosed atrium filled with light and greenery. A major renovation was completed in 2004. Direct underground access to the Metro Center is a huge plus in nasty weather, and the **Old Town Trolley** (p. 52) stops right outside.

As part of the weekend family program, kids 18 and under (traveling with a parent or guardian) get their own room at half price, as well as special room service and restaurant menus. After a tough day of sightseeing, they can unwind in the indoor pool (kids must be accompanied by an adult, and there is a $7 per-room, per-day admission charge to the pool only, $14 if adults use the newly renovated fitness center). Kids can also play arcade games and shoot pool in the **Grand Slam** sports bar (with a parent or guardian) or watch an in-room movie. Another family-travel enhancing aspect of the hotel is that it has implemented a total nonsmoking policy that extends to all guest rooms and suites, elevator landings, and the Regency Club.

You can breakfast or lunch on American fare in the airy **Grand Café** (open daily 6:30am–2pm) surrounding the lagoon. Kids 3 and under eat free; those 12 and under can order smaller portions for half price or items from the children's menu. Relax while the pianist at the white baby grand piano (atop a glass-and-stone "lily pad") sends soothing sounds your way.

Sharing is encouraged, and children are welcome at dinner in the **Via Pacifica** restaurant. Fusion cooking highlights an eclectic but very down-to-earth menu. Enjoy drinks and light fare at the **Via Bar,** overlooking the lagoon, daily from 4pm to midnight.

The **Zephyr Deli** is open for breakfast, lunch (sandwiches, pizza, salads), and snacks weekdays from 6:30am to 2:30pm and weekends from 6:30am to 1:30pm. Pick up sandwiches and picnic on the Mall or in your room if you return for a mid-day siesta. Kids can accompany their parents to the **Grand Slam** to watch their favorite teams on large-screen TVs while downing tapas, burgers, hot dogs, chicken wings, potato skins, and nachos. Because this is primarily a bar, please don't send your kids here unaccompanied. **Butler's** is the Hyatt's Martini and Tapas bar, good for a martini your way—shaken or stirred. Enjoy jazz on four large plasma TVs. Although this isn't suitable for small children, teens might enjoy the tapas and atmosphere.

1000 H St. NW, Washington, DC 20001. ✆ **800/233-1234** or 202/582-1234. Fax 202/637-4781. www.grandwashington. hyatt.com 888 units. $149–$340. Children under 18 stay free in parents' room or get their own room for half price on weekends. Crib free. Special family weekend rates, Regency Club, Business Plan available; AAA discounts. AE, DISC, MC, V. Self-parking $20, valet parking $26 (each 24-hour period with in-and-out privileges for valet service). Metro: Metro Center. **Amenities:** 4 restaurants; 3 bars; indoor pool; on-site health club with steam and sauna; bike rental; concierge; tours; car rental; business center, secretarial services; room service (6:30am–midnight); in-room massage by appointment; babysitting (outside company); laundry service; same-day dry cleaning. *In room:* A/C, TV, dataport, minibar (in some suites), coffeemaker, hairdryer, iron, safe.

EXPENSIVE

J. W. Marriott 👫👫   One look at the large, opulent lobby and you know the Marriott family has come a *long* way since opening a root-beer stand on 14th Street in 1927. A $25 million renovation of the guest rooms, including flat-screen TVs, was due to be completed in the first quarter of 2006. When making a reservation, ask if the work has been finished. If not, ask for a room away from the dust and noise. Attractive as the Marriott is, it's easy to become disoriented. One end of the lobby flows into Eat at National Place (a convenient 575-seat food court with Quizno's, Five Guys, and other eateries), making things a bit more confusing, so keep a sharp eye on younger kids.

The hotel boasts a great location; the Metro Center, with trains on the Blue, Orange, and Red lines, is just 1 block away, and there are plenty of sights, restaurants, and shopping nearby as well. The pool and health club will keep kids occupied when you're not out sightseeing. The rooms are light and bright, with a king or two double beds, a good-size dresser, a desk and chair, two phones, and a TV with cable and premium movie channels. Suites have kitchenettes. Bathrooms are generous in size, with plenty of amenities. Kids can get OnDemand for a fee. (For this, you traveled to Washington?) A limited number of rooms have a view of the Washington Monument or Pennsylvania Avenue rather than a courtyard. (Be a squeaky wheel if you want one.)

Weekend visitors should ask about special packages, which can include full complimentary breakfasts and late checkouts. Kids stay free, and those 5 and under eat free from the special kids' menu in the hotel restaurants.

The bar, **1331,** open for lunch and dinner, features Continental/Asian fusion cuisine and high prices. Older kids with sophisticated taste buds might like it, but younger ones will consider it a punishment (and so might your wallet). The tech-connected will appreciate the sports events on the nine high-definition TV screens and the tableside laptop jacks. A working fireplace warms up diners during winter months. Watch the Pennsylvania Avenue traffic from **The Avenue Grill,** on the lower level. Serving American cuisine in a casual setting, the restaurant's emphasis is on Angus steaks and fresh seafood; it's open for breakfast, lunch, and dinner. **The Lobby Coffee Cart** opens at 6am and features Starbucks coffee, pastries, fruits, and fresh juices. At lunch or dinner, young kids might be better served at Eat at National Place (next door) or the Reagan Building food court (a block away). A host of good restaurants are also within a short walk or Metro ride.

1331 Pennsylvania Ave. NW at E St., Washington, DC 20004. © **800/228-9290** or 202/393-2000. Fax 202/626-6991. www.marriotthotels.com. 772 units. Weekdays $129–$389; ask about weekend/special rates. Children under 16 stay free in parents' room. Crib/rollaway free. AE, DC, DISC, MC, V. Valet garage parking $28 (with in-and-out privileges). Metro: Metro Center, F Street exit. **Amenities:** 2 restaurants and bars; coffee shop; indoor swimming pool; health club with hot tub and sauna; concierge; tours; business center, secretarial services; connecting mall with shops and restaurants; 24-hour room service, in-room massage; babysitting; laundry service. *In room:* A/C, TV, minibar, hair dryer.

L'Enfant Plaza Hotel ⭑⭑⭑ This hotel is great for families with children, for many reasons. First of all, it's less than a 10-minute walk to the National Air and Space Museum and other Smithsonian museums on the National Mall. Don't feel like walking? The steps off the lobby lead to a Metro station; the Smithsonian station is just a stop away.

The lobby is quiet, elegant, and European in tone; the staff is professional, gracious, and courteous. As part of the "We Love Kids!" program, children receive a cool welcome gift on arrival, and there's Nintendo available in guest rooms. Family board games are available for free at the front desk. Children can also order from a special kids' menu in the restaurant.

Cushy guest rooms with elegant furnishings contain either two doubles or a king. Suites come with kitchenettes. Rooms take up the top four floors of the 15-story office building. The 14th- and 15th-floor rooms have balconies. Great views here range from the Washington Monument to the Washington Cathedral.

The outdoor pool is a knockout, as nice as those at resorts, with plenty of chaises and chairs. In winter, the pool area is covered with a bubble. A lifeguard is on duty from 9am to 8pm.

A 5-minute walk over a pedestrian-only bridge will lead you to the waterfront, where you can board the *Spirit of Washington* cruise to Mount Vernon, inspect the seafood stands along Maine Avenue, eat in one of several riverside restaurants, or ogle the pleasure craft in the marina. This neighborhood, although convenient to the Mall, is less than ideal for after-dark strolling. I suggest taking the Metro or a taxi back to the hotel at night.

The **American Sea Grill,** which serves breakfast, lunch, and dinner on the lobby level, features fresh seafood with Pacific Rim flair. Appetizers and tasting plates star here. A kids' menu for 12 and under has items for $4 to $6 and comes with a coloring and activity book. Next to the grill, business types frequent the Foggy Bottom Brew Pub, with tap beers and pub fare. On Wednesday and Thursday from 5 to 8pm, a yakitori (Japanese grill) station serves up grilled beef, shrimp, and chicken on skewers: a winning combination for about $1.50 a skewer. The Lobby offers more than 50 types of martinis for those 21 and over.

480 L'Enfant Plaza SW, Washington, DC 20024. ℂ 800/635-5065 or 202/484-1000. Fax 202/646-4456. www.lenfant plazahotel.com. 370 units. $299 single/double weekdays; $475 suite. Weekend specials from $139; ask about special packages. Children under 18 stay free in parents' room. Crib free, rollaway $20. AE, DC, DISC, MC, V. Valet garage parking $25 (in-and-out privileges); self-parking $16. Metro: L'Enfant Plaza. Pets accepted. **Amenities:** Restaurant; 2 bars; outdoor pool (covered Sept–May) with snack bar (seasonally); fully equipped health club complimentary to adults (Nautilus equipment, weights, aerobic classes, and on-call masseuse); concierge; secretarial services; room service (6:30am–midnight); laundry service. *In room:* A/C, TV w/pay movies, coffeemaker, dual phone lines, high-speed Wi-Fi, hair dryer, safe, iron.

MODERATE

Lincoln Suites Downtown 🄵 *Value*   Visitors enjoy the comforts of home here in a hip setting just four Metro stops from the Smithsonian museums. Don't be fooled by a name, though: The spacious efficiency "suites" are one room. King studio suites have a desk, two phones, and a computer jack. Two rooms are wheelchair-accessible, and one has a roll-in shower. The small, sterile lobby—all chrome and marble—is a minimalist's dream that's given a nice human touch by the warm cookies and milk served every evening. A free continental breakfast is served daily. A $4 million renovation is scheduled for late 2006. Be sure to ask for a room away from dust and noise if you visit between late 2006 and the first half of 2007.

You can walk to the White House, National Geographic Society Explorers Hall, and the Renwick and Corcoran galleries within 15 minutes. Another 10, and you can be on the Mall. Upscale dining and shopping establishments line Connecticut Avenue 2 blocks away. Vendors hawk fast food, clothing, and souvenirs outside Connecticut Avenue/K Street office buildings.

Mackey's Public House serves Irish fare in a setting befitting its name. Youngsters are welcome anytime, but the pub can become a bit rowdy and the floor gets sticky Friday and Saturday nights. **Recessions II** has a Mediterranean and Continental menu and is open for (American-style) breakfast, lunch, and dinner 6 days a week (closed Sun).

1823 L St. NW, Washington, DC 20036. ℂ 800/424-2970 or 202/223-4320. Fax 202/223-8546. www.lincolnhotels.com. 99 studio suites. Weekdays $169–$239 single or double; weekends $149–$199 single or double. Children under 16 stay free in parents' room. Extra person $10. Crib free, rollaway $10. Weekend packages available. AE, DC, DISC, MC, V. Parking $20 (valet, with in-and-out privileges), free on street Fri night–Sun. Metro: Farragut North or Farragut West. Pets (under 25 lb.) allowed, $20 per day. **Amenities:** 2 restaurants; free passes to the nearby Bally's Total Fitness; tour desk; room service (lunch and dinner); coin-op laundry; same-day dry cleaning service. *In room:* A/C, TV w/pay movies, kitchenette or kitchen (full kitchen with 4-burner stove, microwave, and full-size refrigerator in 28 of the 99 suites [$10 extra]), wet bar, coffeemaker, iron.

INEXPENSIVE

Hotel Harrington *Value*   Little wonder that this old-timer is still truckin' after so many years. The price is right, and the location is prime. It's 5 blocks from the White House, and an easy walk to the FBI, Ford's Theatre, Eat at National Place, the Old Post Office Pavilion (with a food court), the National Aquarium, and several Smithsonian museums. The Metro Center, with three of the five Metrorail lines (Red, Blue, and Orange), is 2 blocks away. The Harrington has been family owned since 1914 and is still one of the best deals around. Note, though, that due to the great prices, this hotel is often filled with school groups.

Make no mistake, you'll know you're in an older hotel, but the high-ceilinged rooms are clean and are updated annually with new carpets and drapes. Closets and bathrooms are small; some bathrooms have a shower only. Most rooms have a desk and chair, and all rooms have a TV with complimentary CNN and HBO. Request a refrigerator, and stock it with snacks from the CVS Pharmacy at 13th Street and Pennsylvania Avenue NW. Triples and quads are ideal for families, with different bed configurations (queen and twin) and two bathrooms. Large family rooms sleep up to six people. Three restaurants (one a cafeteria) offer reasonably priced fare on site, or you can take the money you're saving by staying here and go splurge at the nearby Hard Rock Cafe. Board games (free) and movies are available for family entertainment. Have the kids ask for a souvenir paper airplane Harrington Hawk. (The owner of the hotel is a plane buff.)

The **Blue Plate Café,** a no-frills cafeteria, is open daily for breakfast and lunch. If the line is out the door at lunch, try **Ollie's Trolley,** a bargain for a quick burger, fries, and shake. **Harry's Pub,** with sidewalk tables in good weather, is open from lunchtime until 1am for drinks, sandwiches, and snacks.

11th and E sts. NW, Washington, DC 20004. (C) **800/424-8532** or 202/628-8140. Fax 202/347-3924. www.hotel-harrington.com. 245 units. Weekdays from $99 for 1 to 4 people single or double; triples and quads from $109. Family discounts available. Crib free. AE, DC, DISC, MC, V. Garage self-parking (4 blocks from hotel), $10 (with in-and-out privileges) per 24 hours (cars and minivans only). Metro: Metro Center. **Amenities:** 3 restaurants; nearby health club; gift shop with tour desk; coin-op laundry (tokens and soap in the gift shop). *In room:* A/C, TV.

4 Dupont Circle

Dupont Circle has a free-spirited, residential feel to it and a real sense of neighborhood. Dupont Circle (the park) lends itself to people-watching and pigeon-chasing. The neighborhood is less uptight and more colorful than most of "official" Washington. Also, you'll find great "local" restaurants around here. The area east of Dupont Circle around 14th and P streets, considered a low-rent district a decade ago, has made quite a comeback in recent years.

Stay here if your kids are older and interested in browsing boutiques and art galleries (the Phillips is a gem), and if you don't mind a few extra minutes on the Metro to the Mall attractions. Most of the hotels are less pricey than their closer-in counterparts.

EXPENSIVE

Hotel Helix *★*   This sophisticated boutique hotel, part of the popular Kimpton Group, attracts people in the arts, lobbyists, and sybarites.

Standard guest rooms are a blend of funk, minimalist, pop art, and psychedelic decor. Think orange bathroom vanities, electric blue and lime green built-in room accessories, a freestanding entertainment center, sheer fabric that pulls around platform beds covered in faux fur, and Pop Rocks and Bugles in the honor bar.

A Room-Service Alternative

Dupont Circle has become so yuppified that the Whole Foods supermarket (4 blocks east of Dupont Circle) does a bang-up business. You can pick up a rotisserie chicken, salads, imported cheeses, and bread, and have a feast in your room. You'll find Whole Foods at 1440 P St. NW (℃ **202/332-4300**). Open daily from 8am to 10pm. The Jamba juice–coffee bar opens daily at 7am.

Specialty rooms include Zone Rooms, which include a separate curtained space with an amazingly comfortable Euro-style chair and ottoman and lava lamp—all very conducive to "zoning" out. Eats Rooms have a small fridge, sink, and microwave. Bunk Rooms, ideal for a family of four, are intended for fun-seekers, such as those into post-midnight pillow fights. The top bunk is a twin; the bottom opens up to a full-size bed. There's also a 27-inch TV in the bunk room with a DVD player and Nintendo 64. Across the room is a king-size bed.

To the right of the lobby (where complimentary champagne is served to adult guests from 5 to 6pm every afternoon) is the **Helix Lounge** for cocktails and American-style light fare kicked up a notch. The upholstered chairs light up when you sit down, and alcove banquettes are covered in patent leather. (Do stick your head in here after dark. It's a scene.) The menu is limited to about a dozen items, but nearly everything is kid-friendly, especially the Angus burger ($11). Brunch is served weekends. With younger children, I strongly suggest vacating the lounge by 8pm. On weekends, the room rocks with an attractive and diverse bouquet of young people. To ensure your beauty sleep, ask for a room on one of the higher floors (the Helix has 10).

The "Bring 'em Along" family package in a bunk room is priced at $219 and includes board games, a pizza party with two large pizzas, two pints of Häagen-Dazs ice cream, and more. The only drawback I see here is the 15-minute walk to the Metro at MacPherson Square or Dupont Circle. Those who have trouble getting around should plan on using a taxi or consider staying in a hotel closer to a Metro station. Otherwise, the neighborhood is a walker's and voyeur's delight.

1430 Rhode Island Ave. NW, Washington, DC 20005. ℃ **800/706-1202** or 202/462-9001. Fax 202/332-3519. www.hotelhelix.com. 178 units. $119–$189. Weekend/seasonal specials. Kids 17 and under are free with parents. Crib free, rollaway free. AE, MC, V. Valet garage parking $26 overnight with in-and-out privileges. Metro: McPherson Square or Dupont Circle. Pets accepted (no charge). **Amenities:** Helix Lounge (bar/restaurant); on-site workout room (complimentary passes to the YMCA and its pool are available); complimentary business center with printing and Internet access. *In room:* A/C, TV/VCR, fax, dataports, complimentary wireless Internet access, minibar, coffeemaker, iron, safe, robe.

MODERATE

Carlyle Suites   This eight-story, all-suites hotel, 3 blocks from the Dupont Circle Metro, sits on a residential street (by D.C. standards) near restaurants, shops, and galleries. One of the district's top family attractions, the National Geographic Society Explorers Hall, is 6 blocks away.

The Carlyle Suites, distinguished by its Art Deco exterior and lobby, has lots going for it besides its location. The 170 suites underwent a $5 million renovation in late 2004. Rooms now have two double beds and a sofa bed, or a king and sofa bed. Suites are average in size, with large closets, a dining and sitting area, and well-equipped kitchenettes. Each suite is custom-designed, combining classic Art Deco finishes and impressive features like fully equipped kitchens, workspaces with cordless phones, complimentary high-speed Internet access, and bath and living areas with accents in granite and stainless steel. Kids under 18 stay free with their parents, and pets are welcome (no Burmese pythons, please), but please let the hotel know you're bringing a pet when you make your reservation. A small Safeway market is 2 blocks away. Load up on supplies, and your family can eat meals in the room, if you choose, or snack while enjoying a movie on complimentary cable with 66 channels, including HBO and Showtime. Tables and chairs are set in a courtyard off the lobby for relaxing or writing postcards.

The **Lillies** restaurant, on a glass-enclosed patio, offers year-round outdoor dining, whatever the weather. On mild days, the roof retracts to "let the sunshine in." The ample breakfast buffet will fortify your family before you set out. Light fare is served at lunch, and the dinner menu includes a wide range of creative main dishes as well as home-style favorites. Alex, the chef, is happy to cut adult portions to child size, and pizza and hamburgers are staples at lunch and dinner. If you prefer to relax and eat in your room, all items can be packed "to go," but there is no room service. A separate area of the Carlyle Café serves light fare and cocktails from 4pm until midnight.

1731 New Hampshire Ave. NW, between R and S sts., Washington, DC 20009. (✆) 202/234-3200. Fax 202/387-0085. www.carlylesuites.com. 170 efficiency suites. $129 (weekends)–$299. Children under 18 stay free in parents' room. Crib and rollaway free. Extra person $10. Weekend packages available. AE, DC, MC, V. Parking free but limited. Metro: Dupont Circle (Q St. exit). Pets (75 lb. or under) accepted (no charge). **Amenities:** Restaurant; food-shopping service; free access to the nearby (5 blocks) adults-only Washington Sports Club; babysitting can be arranged, but requests must be made in advance. *In room:* A/C, TV, hair dryer, iron, complimentary high-speed Internet access.

5 Georgetown

A small, sophisticated riverfront town within the city, Georgetown draws locals and out-of-towners with its fine Georgian architecture, hundreds of restaurants and shops, and party atmosphere (especially evenings and weekends). Younger kids seem to enjoy the activity (people, cars, lots to look at). Of all D.C.'s neighborhoods, however, it is the least accessible to the Metro. For that reason, I am recommending only one hotel in Georgetown—because it is so special. There are several others, if you don't mind the inconvenience. The nearest Metro station is Foggy Bottom; from there, you can take the Georgetown Metro Connection shuttle (✆ **202/625-RIDE;** www.georgetown dc.com/shuttle.php), which runs every 10 to 15 minutes and makes numerous stops between the Foggy Bottom, Dupont Circle, and Rosslyn (Arlington, VA) Metro stations. See chapter 3 for travel details.

Four Seasons ⚜⚜⚜   I'm surprised that the management of this elegantly appointed yet unpretentious hotel can coax guests to leave after experiencing the TLC that the Four Seasons is famous for worldwide. The hotel's staff-to-guest room ratio is 2:1, and the concierge staff alone fills as many as several hundred requests a day—everything from 30 dozen long-stemmed red roses to Super Bowl tickets. Some visitors have

A Room-Service Alternative

Whole Foods, at 2323 Wisconsin Ave. NW (✆ **202/333-5393**), about half a mile *uphill* (or a short cab ride) from Wisconsin Avenue and R Street, is well stocked with plenty of healthy eats, gourmet items, and takeout fare. There's also a small convenience store at 20th and P streets that carries the essentials.

checked in empty-handed (I don't suggest it) and been outfitted within hours—even at night. The hotel's credo: "You want; we get." A $25 million enhancement designed by famed interior designer Pierre Yves Rochon was completed in late 2005. The entire East Wing was reconfigured, making two rooms out of three, so now the majority of the rooms are 50% larger.

The hotel, overlooking Rock Creek Park and the C&O Canal at the east end of Georgetown, with its historic homes and concentration of fine restaurants and shops, is only a few blocks away from Washington Harbor, with more restaurants on the Potomac and a lovely park. A complimentary Four Seasons VW Phaeton sedan is sometimes available on request. But don't hold your breath.

Some recent guests you might have heard of include Sheryl Crow, Nicholas Cage, Tom Hanks, and Val Kilmer. While business and entertainment types, heads of state, and royalty have frequented the hotel regularly since it opened in 1979; families who choose to stay here will enjoy the same service afforded sultans and silver-screen stars.

A lavish attention to details distinguishes the Four Seasons. Traveling with an infant? In addition to bottles and a bottle warmer, a change of diapers, and a diaper pail, cribs come furnished with bumpers and a colorful mobile. Children can borrow a video, board game, or Nintendo at the concierge desk, perhaps after taking tea (finger sandwiches, brownies, and milkshakes) in the **Garden Terrace.** Families checking into a suite receive "the works": snacks, sodas, balloons, stuffed toys, games, books, and video games. Kids under 13 receive a game or activity book (squeeze toys for babies) and their own menu in **Seasons** restaurant or in the Garden Terrace. Guests may borrow a wireless PC or portable DVD player with headphones. Kids also get milk and cookies at evening turndown (there'll be no living with them when you get home!), so you won't have to feel guilty about asking the concierge to secure a bonded babysitter and enjoying nearby Georgetown nightlife without them.

The health club is 12,500 square feet of state-of-the-art luxury. In addition to the lap pool, whirlpool, steam, sauna, Nautilus equipment, and weights, you'll find a Vichy shower, hydrotherapy, an aerobics studio, "quiet rooms," and complimentary juices, coffee, and fruit. Water toys are kept poolside for little squirts. While you work out, they can amuse themselves at the computer. Children under 16 must be accompanied by an adult at the pool, in the whirlpool, and at the fitness club.

The **Garden Terrace** lounge, with overstuffed couches and large floral displays, overlooks Rock Creek Park. It's open for cocktails throughout the afternoon and evening and for tea 3 to 5pm daily. A pianist plays most afternoons and evenings. There's a spectacular (and expensive) Sunday Jazz Brunch (10:30am–2pm) featuring a jazz guitarist. The brunch costs $63 for adults and $38 for kids 12 and under; reservations are strongly recommended. You may want to try it for a special occasion. **Seasons** features contemporary American fare at breakfast, lunch, and dinner. The eclectic menu changes seasonally and offers alternative cuisine (low-calorie, low-sodium, and low-cholesterol) selections in addition to fish, seafood, chicken, and various combinations thereof. Its wine cellar has long been regarded as one of the country's best. The children's menu consists of more basic fare.

2800 Pennsylvania Ave. NW, Washington, DC 20007. ℭ **800/332-3442** or 202/342-0444. Fax 202/944-2076. www. fourseasons.com. 211 units including 51 suites. From $575 for a king premiere room to $6,400 for the 3-bedroom Presidential Suite, per night. Children under 16 stay free in parents' room; crib and rollaway free. Ask about weekend, special, and seasonal packages. AE, DC, DISC, MC, V. Valet parking $29, self-parking complimentary with some packages. Metro: Foggy Bottom and then Georgetown Connection shuttle. Pets (under 15 lb.) accepted. **Amenities:** Restaurant;

bar; indoor heated pool and whirlpool; sauna; fully equipped state-of-the-art fitness club; children's programs; video-tape and compact disc library; concierge; tours; car rental; business center, secretarial services; salon; 24-hour room service; in-room massage; babysitting; laundry/dry cleaning service. *In room:* A/C, TV, minibar, hair dryer, safe.

6 Foggy Bottom

In the West End of the city between Georgetown and the White House, Foggy Bottom is distinguished by its relatively quiet tree-lined streets and Lilliputian row houses. The sophisticated international/cultural/college-town air is generated by the State Department, the Kennedy Center, and George Washington University. Stay here, and you'll be able to walk to concerts and plays, as well as free performances (daily at 6pm) on the Millennium Stage of the Kennedy Center. Pinstripers, students, artistic types, and old-timers populate the neighborhood after dark. Charming Foggy Bottom is within walking distance of Georgetown and accessible to D.C.'s sights via the Metro station at 23rd and I streets NW.

EXPENSIVE

Doubletree Guest Suites–New Hampshire Avenue ✮ A warm bag of chocolate chip cookies welcomes visitors to the Doubletree. Nice touch! The hotel is less than a block from the Foggy Bottom Metro. The suites, renovated in July 2005, have a separate living room with a sofa bed, a bedroom with king or two queen beds, two phone lines, a walk-in closet, and wireless Internet connection.

In addition, suites have full kitchens with a microwave, full-size refrigerator, stove, cookware, toaster, coffeemaker, and service (silverware) for four. Stock up on snacks at the Safeway in the Watergate, 2½ blocks away. A complimentary continental breakfast is served in the lobby weekends only. Room service is available 6:30 to 10:30am and 5 to 10pm. Cool off in the small rooftop pool and relax on the sundeck, open seasonally from Memorial Day through Labor Day. It's too small to do laps, but it's big enough for a cooling dunk. If you're combining business with pleasure, the voice mail, dataports, and wireless Internet will come in handy. The big pluses at Doubletree Guest Suites (in addition to those yummy cookies) are space and privacy.

801 New Hampshire Ave. NW, Washington, DC 20037. © **800/424-2900** or 202/785-2000. Fax 202/785-9485. www.doubletree.com. 103 suites. $109–$269. Children under 18 stay free in parents' room. Crib free, rollaway $20. 3rd and 4th extra person $20 each. Weekend and special packages available. Monthly rates. AE, DC, DISC, MC, V. Valet parking $25 per day. Metro: Foggy Bottom, then walk 1 block south on New Hampshire Ave. (toward the Kennedy Center). Pets accepted up to 75 lbs. ($20 per day). **Amenities:** Continental breakfast weekends; pool; room service (6:30–10:30am and 5–10pm); coin-operated laundry; laundry and dry cleaning service. *In room:* A/C, TV, hair dryer, iron.

Washington Suites Georgetown ✮ Walk to the heart of Georgetown, the Kennedy Center, and the White House, from this kid-friendly hotel. In 2005, the spacious suites received new bedding, carpeting, and drapes. The lobby and public areas were refurbished in 2003. Units are over 600 square feet, with a living/dining area with pullout sofa, separate bedroom/vanity area, full kitchen (refrigerator, stove, dishwasher, microwave, coffeemaker, dishes, pots and pans, and utensils), and bathroom. The freebies include warm, freshly baked cookies upon check-in, high-speed Internet access, deluxe continental breakfast (daily), use of cribs and strollers, and a daily newspaper. Guests are invited to the weekly managers' reception Tuesdays from 6 to 7pm for free snacks and beverages. Veg out and watch a movie on one of the premium channels, or let the kids play Nintendo until they fall asleep.

There's a pleasant tree-lined patio off the rear of the lobby, and dozens of restaurants are within a few blocks. **Johnny Rockets,** a perfect family treat, is just 5 blocks away on M Street in Georgetown. **Kinkead's,** one of the best restaurants in the entire city, is a short walk (not recommended for very young children at dinner). And who can resist **T.G.I. Friday's,** also nearby, for satisfying family fare? **Marshall's Restaurant,** a casual neighborhood drop-in kind of place, is just three doors away at 2524 L St. NW. There are a Ben & Jerry's and a Häagen-Dazs a few blocks away in Georgetown to satisfy your sweet tooth (or teeth). If you're taking your kids to look at colleges, the hotel is just a 5-minute stroll to George Washington University (you're practically on campus) and about a mile east of Georgetown University.

2500 Pennsylvania Ave. NW, Washington, DC 20037. ℂ 877/736-2500 or 202/333-8060. Fax 202/338-3818. www. washingtonsuiteshotel.com. 124 units (suites). $149–$309 (seasonal). Children under 18 stay free in parents' room. Crib, stroller free. Extra person $20. Special weekend and Family Fun packages are available on the hotel's website. Extended stay rates available. AE, DISC, MC, V. Valet parking $25 per day. Metro: Foggy Bottom, then walk north on 23rd St 1½ blocks, left at Pennsylvania Ave. 2 blocks. Pets accepted ($20 per day). **Amenities:** Complimentary high-speed Internet access, complimentary continental breakfast daily; daily newspaper, fitness room (adults only); coin-op laundry; laundry/dry cleaning service. *In room:* A/C, TV, full kitchen, coffeemaker.

7 Upper Northwest

The northwest pocket of the city borders Chevy Chase, Maryland. Like Neverland, it's not on any map and is more a state of mind. The neighborhood is largely residential, with many of the District's most expensive homes, and shopping and restaurants that cater to a sophisticated and discriminating clientele. Stay here, and you'll have a 20-minute Metro ride to the Mall. But you'll be only a Metro station or two away (in some cases, a walk) from the National Zoo, a must-see with kids.

EXPENSIVE

Embassy Suites at the Chevy Chase Pavilion ⋆⋆ At this property in the Chevy Chase Pavilion, guests enjoy a full, free, cooked-to-order, delicious breakfast, which is sufficient enough reason to relocate, in my opinion. Renovation of the spacious suites is in the planning stages. Be sure to ask when you make a reservation. Suites consist of a bedroom with a king bed or two doubles and a separate living room with a sofa bed. There are two TVs with HBO, pay-per-view movies, and Nintendo; high-speed Internet access (daily fee); and a wet bar and refrigerator, so the munchkins need never go hungry.

Stay dry with underground access to the Friendship Heights Metro station. From there, it's only a 15-minute ride to downtown. Enjoy shopping downstairs in the multi-level Chevy Chase Pavilion with 25 shops (World Market, Pottery Barn, Stein Mart, Talbots, J. Crew, and Ann Taylor Loft), as well as a Washington Sports Club (hotel guests receive complimentary admission) and food court with 10 eateries. The hotel is within walking distance of scores of restaurants and more excellent shopping at Mazza Gallerie (with Neiman Marcus and Filene's Basement), Lord & Taylor, Saks, and Tiffany & Co.

After a tough day of sightseeing, swim in the rooftop indoor pool, unwind in the Jacuzzi, or work out in the fully equipped health club (kids must be accompanied by an adult). Then unwind with a complimentary cocktail.

Within the Chevy Chase Pavilion is the **Cheesecake Factory,** with California cuisine and 35 varieties of cheesecake, plus specialty pastas and gourmet pizza baked in a wood-burning oven. **Maggiano's,** half a block away on Wisconsin Avenue, has super

Italian fare and huge portions. The front room is down-home casual for a quick bite with little ones. Several other restaurants are within easy walking distance.

4300 Military Rd. NW, at Wisconsin Ave., Washington, DC 20015. (C) 800/EMBASSY or 202/362-9300. Fax 202/686-3405. www.embassysuitesdc.com. 198 suites. Weekdays $239–$309; weekends $149–$209. Rates include breakfast and cocktails. Children 18 and under stay free in parents' room. Crib free, rollaway $10. Ask about the Georgette Klinger spa special (guests already receive a 15% discount). Weekend, AAA, family, and seasonal packages available. AE, DC, DISC, MC, V. Garage self-parking $15 per day. Metro: Friendship Heights (Western Ave. exit). **Amenities:** Restaurant; indoor pool; health club; Jacuzzi; room service (6:30am–11pm); coin-op laundry. *In room:* A/C, TV, dataport, refrigerator, coffeemaker, hair dryer, iron, microwave.

Omni Shoreham Hotel 🌟🌟   The dowager queen of D.C. hotels—a member of Historic Hotels of America and Great Resorts and Hotels—celebrated its 75th birthday in 2005. When this hotel was just the plain-old Shoreham, it provided the setting for Perle Mesta's celebrated parties, numerous inaugural balls, and Harry Truman's poker games. The cavernous lobby is usually filled with conventioneers weekdays. If you think bigger is better, and if yours is a family of fitness freaks, look no further. Adjacent to Rock Creek Park, the Omni Shoreham is a self-contained 11-acre resort in a residential neighborhood off Connecticut Avenue, about 100 yards from the Metro and less than 15 minutes from downtown. At day's end, cool off in the large outdoor pool (open Apr–Oct), work out in the health club ($7 per day or $13 for length of stay per person over 16 years of age), or stroll through the gardens. If you crave more exercise, head out the hotel's back door into Rock Creek Park, with hiking, biking, and jogging trails, and a fitness course.

The guest rooms are some of the largest in the city and elegantly furnished. Marble-floored bathrooms and myriad amenities aside, the best thing about the Omni Shoreham is its location—you can walk to the National Zoo.

Please note that prices here vary widely depending on availability, the season, and whether you stay on a weekday or a weekend. So you could pay anything from a bargain rate ($129 when the hotel runs a weekend special) to top dollar ($450 for a suite).

Robert's restaurant is casually elegant (reminds me of Versailles) and serves American Continental cuisine at breakfast, lunch, and dinner. Try a yummy salad, sandwich, or a Mexican-inspired dish along with very good service in the mirrored, high-ceilinged room. There are highchairs and booster seats, as well as an all-day kids' menu with such standbys as grilled cheese, mac and cheese, PB&J, hot dog, hamburger, and chicken fingers. The breakfast buffet is $5.95 for kids. Stop at **A Little Something Gourmet,** a European gourmet carry-out in the lobby, for a little something to tide you over to the next big meal. Enjoy your light bite at an outdoor table or in your room. The adults-only **Marquee Bar and Lounge** is a martini-and-cigar bar serving imported beers on tap. A pool bar, located on the pool deck, is open seasonally and features light fare and beverage service.

2500 Calvert St. NW at Connecticut Ave., Washington, DC 20008. (C) 800/THE-OMNI or 202/234-0700. Fax 202/265-7972. www.omnihotels.com. 834 units. $129 (weekend specials)–$309 (weekdays); $229–$450 suite. Children under 18 stay free in parents' room. Crib free, rollaway $25. Extra person $25. Family and weekend packages available. AE, DC, DISC, MC, V. Garage self-parking $22; valet $26 (in-and-out privileges). Metro: Woodley Park–Zoo/Adams Morgan; then walk south 1½ blocks and cross Calvert Street. **Amenities:** 2 restaurants; bar; outdoor pool; 1½-mile fitness course with 18 exercise stations (in Rock Creek Park); 10 miles of jogging, hiking, and bicycle trails; spacious health club/spa with sauna, Cybex equipment; video checkout; concierge (6:30am–11pm); 24-hour room service; massage; babysitting; laundry service. *In room:* A/C, TV, coffeemaker, iron, complimentary high-speed wireless Internet.

8 Suburban Maryland

The Montgomery County suburbs of Chevy Chase and Bethesda are largely residential and well known for their fine shopping, restaurants, kid-filled vans, and gridlock. The Metro ride into D.C. is 20 to 30 minutes, depending on where you stay in Chevy Chase (closer in) or Bethesda. Don't even think of driving into the District if you stay in Maryland. You could fly to Europe faster. Due east, in Prince George's County, is Lanham, a commercial/industrial area with numerous hotels and family-friendly restaurants. Stay here, and you'll be 1 mile from Amtrak (20 min. to Union Station) and the New Carrollton Metro (20 min. to the Smithsonian station).

BETHESDA

Not too long ago, Bethesda was a sleepy suburban village. These days, however, the area is overbuilt and overpopulated with people, office buildings, and cars. The once-bucolic small town is now a traffic-choked minimegalopolis. The big draws in Bethesda are its excellent restaurants (ethnic and American) in all price ranges, almost all of which are within walking distance of the hotels listed below. The Metro ride to downtown D.C. is about 30 minutes.

EXPENSIVE

Hyatt Regency Bethesda ⚓   Providing top-notch facilities at a convenient suburban location next to the Bethesda Metro, the Hyatt knows how to deliver the goods to vacationing families.

As Yogi Berra used to say, you'll get "déjà vu all over again" when you enter the large, plant-filled, open-atrium lobby, with its requisite bar. There is a definite tendency, obviously intentional, toward repetition among Hyatts, and this location is no exception. You have to admit, though, that it's eye-catching.

The guest rooms, redecorated in 2002 and enhanced with new duvets, throws, decorative pillows and bolsters in late 2005, are large and sumptuous, with a king or two double beds, plenty of closet and drawer space, and marble bathrooms. When making reservations, ask for the best family rate available.

Some rooms have balconies/terraces. Don't be surprised, though, if your view is of commercial downtown Bethesda—not the pretty picture it once was.

Your kids will spend nary a dull moment here. There are a large, glass-enclosed, heated rooftop indoor pool (open weekdays from 6am to 10pm and weekends and holidays from 7am to 10pm), a fully equipped health club (you'll have to go with them), and a family-style restaurant. An 11-screen movie theater is within walking distance, as are more than 150 restaurants and Gifford's ice cream parlor. Imagination Stage, producing children's theatrical events, is about 5 blocks from the hotel (at 4908 Auburn Ave.). Check with the concierge for details.

The hotel's family-friendly **Daily Grill** is open for breakfast, lunch, dinner, and Sunday brunch. **Morton's** (steakhouse) is open for dinner nightly, featuring the finest USDA prime aged steaks, seafood, and fine wines, for which the chain in known. Reservations are highly recommended. The **Concourse Lobby Lounge** is located in the spectacular atrium, with coffee-bar service every morning from 6am and beverage and appetizers from 2pm until closing. Adjacent to the hotel at Bethesda Metro Center is a food court selling a variety of fast food and snacks. Bethesda has more restaurants than you can shake a stick at, representing just about every ethnic persuasion. And the nearby Tastee Diner is open 24/7. Ask the concierge for suggestions. Mazza

Gallerie, Chevy Chase Pavilion, and White Flint Mall (with Bloomies, Lord & Taylor, Border's, and numerous specialty shops) are about equidistant by car or Metro.

One Bethesda Metro Center (Wisconsin Ave. and Old Georgetown Rd.), Bethesda, MD 20814. ℂ **800/233-1234** or 301/657-1234. Fax 301/657-6453. www.bethesda.hyatt.com. 390 units. Weekdays $215–$299 single, second person is $25 more, $150 additional for an executive suite; weekends from $99 single and $25 for each additional person. Children 18 and under stay free in parents' room. Crib and rollaway free. Special weekend, family, AAA, and senior packages available. AE, DC, DISC, MC, V. Self-parking $12 for weekend self-parking; $15 weeknight self-parking; $20 and $17 for weekend and weeknight valet parking, each per day with unlimited in-and-out privileges. Metro: Bethesda. **Amenities:** 2 restaurants; bar; heated indoor pool; fully equipped health club with hot tub, sauna, and workout area; concierge; business center, secretarial services; room service (6:30am–11pm); babysitting; laundry service. *In room:* A/C, TV, coffeemaker, hair dryer, iron, high-speed Internet connection (fee), Ethernet cards available at front desk.

CHEVY CHASE

Chevy Chase is synonymous with *upscale*. Well-heeled professionals and their families live in the affluent bedroom community full of large, older homes. Kid-friendly restaurants and shopping—quality department and specialty stores, and designer boutiques—serve discerning residents and visitors alike.

MODERATE

Holiday Inn Chevy Chase   This Holiday Inn is ideal for families that want to mix heavy doses of shopping with their sightseeing. Stroll over to Chevy Chase Pavilion, Saks Fifth Avenue, Lord & Taylor, Gucci, Brooks Brothers, Yves St. Laurent, and Mazza Gallerie (with Neiman Marcus and many upscale boutiques and specialty stores). When you run out of money and want to head downtown for some free sightseeing, the Friendship Heights Metro is only 2 blocks away.

If you're a light sleeper, traffic from Wisconsin Avenue may disturb you. Inquire about a quiet room away from the street and/or on an upper floor when you make a reservation. A lifeguard watches over the third-floor outdoor pool Memorial Day to Labor Day, and guests have use of the on-site fitness center. While you're working out, the younger kids can enjoy an in-room movie on Showtime or HBO, or watch their favorite sports on ESPN: Premium channels are free.

There are a slew of family restaurants within walking distance, too. Clyde's, the Cheesecake Factory, and Chadwick's all welcome families. And if you don't want to leave the hotel, you can always try the **Avenue Deli,** which is open for breakfast and lunch, and has a children's menu with plenty of good things to eat, as well as an adult menu for those footing the bills. At **Julian's** (an upscale steak, pasta, and seafood restaurant), families can enjoy lunch and dinner specials such as grilled salmon and prime rib in a more formal dining-room setting. Older kids are welcome here; preschoolers are not.

5520 Wisconsin Ave., Chevy Chase, MD 20815. ℂ **800/HOLIDAY** or 301/656-1500. Fax 301/656-5045. www.holiday-inn. com/chevychasemd. 213 units, including 11 suites. Weekday and weekend rates from $169 single or double. Crib $15 per night, rollaway $15 per night. Children 18 and under stay free in parents' room. "Great Rates" and "Best Breaks" packages available through toll-free reservation number. AE, DC, MC, V. Free parking. Metro: Friendship Heights. **Amenities:** 2 restaurants; outdoor pool; fitness center. *In room:* A/C, TV.

LANHAM

Lanham is commercial, with businesses, office parks, and lots of reasonably priced restaurants. It's a bit off the beaten path, yet only 1 mile from the New Carrollton Metro/Amtrak station. From there, it's a 20-minute ride on the Marc commuter train (weekdays only) to Union Station or 25 minutes to the Smithsonian Metro station on the Mall. For many families, the low hotel rates outweigh any inconvenience and the lackluster neighborhood. You might want a car if you stay here. Without it, you'll be limited to the hotel restaurant once you return from D.C. Of course, you can always take a taxi to a nearby restaurant.

INEXPENSIVE

Best Western Capital Beltway *(Value* Located in Prince George's County, near the intersection of Route 450 and the Beltway (495), the Best Western provides complimentary van service (2 or more times per hour, 8am–9pm) to the New Carrollton Metro station, just 1 mile away. There, you can board a train and be in the heart of downtown D.C. in 20 minutes or head to Six Flags, just 5 miles away. The hotel is equidistant (20 miles) from BWI and Reagan National airports and 2 miles from NASA's Goddard Space Flight Center, with a Visitor Center, exhibits, a gift shop, model rocket launches, and other family events.

The spacious two-story lobby is comfortably and attractively furnished, accented with stained-glass panels. A small gift shop is off the lobby. A heated indoor pool with a retractable roof is open year-round. The roof is open from Memorial Day weekend to early September. Refurbishment of all guest rooms was completed in 2004. Each room has a 25-inch TV; microwaves and refrigerators are available on request for a small charge. Telephones have free local calls and long-distance access. Sixth-floor rooms have king beds; other floors have two doubles each—perfect for a family of four whose kids have not yet had a growth spurt. Traffic noise from the Beltway is a dull hum. At these prices, it's worth investing in earplugs. The quietest quarters are poolside and odd-numbered rooms.

Neptune's on the lobby level serves a free breakfast buffet daily from 7 to 10am. The **Bay Street Nightclub** is a large wood-accented space (kind of clubby in appearance) that caters to those 25 and older. Within a 5-minute drive are oodles of fast-food and sit-down restaurants such as Red Lobster. Less than a mile away in Greenbelt are dozens more. Because this is, for the most part, a nonresidential neighborhood, I don't suggest a walk after dark.

5910 Princess Garden Pkwy., Lanham, MD 20708. © **800/866-4458** or 301/459-1000. Fax 301/459-1526. www.bestwestern.com/capitalbeltway. 169 units. From $89–$109 double (2 double beds). Children 17 and under stay free in parents' room. Crib $10, rollaway $10. Ask about spring and summer family specials. AE, DC, DISC, MC, V. Free parking. Shuttle service to Metro. Metro: New Carrollton. **Amenities:** Restaurant; bar; indoor pool; fitness room; game room; coin-op laundry. *In room:* A/C, TV, coffeemaker, hair dryer, iron and board, dataport, free DSL high-speed Internet access.

9 Suburban Virginia

The Virginia suburbs are marked by fine shopping, restaurants, and gridlock. If you travel into the District on Metro—a 10- to 30-minute ride, depending on where you're staying (Rosslyn is closest, Vienna is farthest)—you won't have to fight the traffic. Maryland and Virginia residents continue to trade barbs over the up- and downsides of living in their respective states. I break out in hives when I cross the border into Virginia. It reminds me of L.A. without the palm trees and the Pacific. But don't let that deter you.

ARLINGTON

Arlington National Cemetery and the Pentagon are in Arlington, which extends westward from the Potomac River between McLean (north) and Alexandria (south). With easy access to D.C. via Metro and the Key, Roosevelt, and Memorial bridges, the area is attractive to visitors and residents alike. The closest of D.C.'s bedroom communities, Arlington consists of older, established neighborhoods, high-rise condos and office buildings, and shopping center after shopping center. Area shopaholics favor Fashion Centre at Pentagon City, with 160 stores (including Macy's and Nordstrom), a multiplex theater, and several restaurants.

EXPENSIVE

Embassy Suites Crystal City *⋒*   Except on weekends and in summer, business types account for most of this hotel's clientele. I'm surprised that more families don't stay here year-round. If you stay in Crystal City—a future world of multistoried offices, residences, restaurants, and shopping—you'll be able to board a train and be downtown (Yellow or Blue lines) or at Arlington Cemetery (Blue line) within 10 minutes, depending on the day's agenda. The hotel's free shuttle can take you to Reagan National Airport (very convenient with kids and luggage), the Pentagon City Metro station, or Fashion Centre at Pentagon City (four stories of shopping, with Macy's, Nordstrom, Gymboree, The Children's Place, Discovery Channel Store, and Gap Kids, among others, plus 13 eateries in the Food Court and a number of "proper" sit-down restaurants).

Comfortable and attractive furnishings and a spacious bathroom distinguish suites. Not enough can be said about the merits of having the kids sleep in a separate room with their own TV—worth twice the price, in my mind.

After a full day downtown, relax on the sundeck, or watch the kids swim in the indoor pool. Breakfast and late-afternoon cocktails are complimentary. The Crystal Grille, nestled in a tropical setting off the atrium, is open for (complimentary) breakfast, as well as lunch and dinner. At lunch and dinner, the kids' menu has five items to choose from, ranging from $5 to $10.

1300 Jefferson Davis Hwy., Arlington, VA 22202. ℭ **703/979-9799.** www.embassysuitesdcmetro.com. 267 suites. Weekdays $150–230; weekends $110 and up. Rates include full breakfast and cocktails daily. Children 18 and under stay free in parents' room. Crib free, rollaway $30. Special weekend packages (from $110); ask about AAA, AARP rates. AE, DC, DISC, MC, V. Garage self-parking $5–$15. Transportation to Reagan National Airport and nearby shopping. Metro: Crystal City or Pentagon City. **Amenities:** Restaurant; indoor pool; exercise equipment; hot tub; sauna; laundry service. *In room:* A/C, TV, dataports, microwave, fridge, coffeemaker, hair dryer, iron.

MODERATE

Radisson Hotel Reagan National Airport *Value*   Price and accessibility to the major sights are the drawing cards at this comfortable Radisson close to Reagan National Airport. Walk 1½ blocks to Crystal City Metro station or take advantage of the complimentary shuttle service to Metro, local shopping and dining, and the airport.

In 2004, the hotel's guest rooms had a complete makeover and morphed from a Days Inn to a Radisson. Rooms are sumptuously furnished, with high-thread-count linens, goose-down comforters, plenty of pillows and bolsters, and oversized towels. Small refrigerators and microwaves are handy for chilling snacks and drinks and heating leftovers—or popcorn. If you can't live without e-mail, there is high-speed Internet access (fee). A small lobby shop stocks snacks and sundries. The **2020 Bistro & Lounge** lacks natural light, but it is open for breakfast, lunch, and dinner. Rather lackluster to my taste, it is convenient and has a children's menu at lunch and dinner for kids 10 and under. In the area are scores of restaurants—Legal Seafood, McCormick & Schmick's, Chili's, and Charlie Chang's, to name a few. Generous George's, a local family favorite for pizza and such is 5 miles away in Alexandria. Ask the concierge if the shuttle driver will take you. A lifeguard is on duty at the rooftop outdoor pool (open Memorial Day–Labor Day). You may spot some planes taking off or landing at Reagan. For sure, you will hear them. Get your fill of shopping and eating at Crystal

City Underground (within walking distance) and the Fashion Centre at Pentagon City (a quick Metro or complimentary shuttle ride). All the downtown sights and Old Town Alexandria are 10 to 15 minutes away via the Metro. You can also get off at the Rosslyn stop and walk over the Key Bridge to Georgetown. Ask about Hot Deals or check the website. Rates have sometimes dipped as low as $76.

2020 Jefferson Davis Hwy. (U.S. 1), Arlington, VA 22202. ☎ **800/333-3333** or 703/920-8600. 245 rooms, 6 suites. Weekdays $160–$250; weekends $76–$229 (suite). Children under 18 stay free in parents' room. Weekend and seasonal packages available. AE, DC, DISC, MC, V. $10 per day parking. Complimentary shuttle service to Reagan National Airport, Metro, shopping/dining. Metro: Crystal City. **Amenities:** Restaurant; outdoor pool; business center; fitness center; concierge; Enterprise car-rental desk; room service (6am–10pm); same-day laundry/dry cleaning service; executive-level rooms. *In room:* A/C, TV, refrigerator, microwave, coffeemaker, hair dryer, iron.

VIENNA

Vienna, despite its lovely residential neighborhoods, is better known as a landscape of shopping (malls, strip shopping centers, and stand-alones), restaurants, and dawn-to-dawn gridlock. It's about 15 minutes by car from Wolf Trap Park for the Performing Arts, which features great live entertainment and family activities spring to fall. Stay here, and you'll have a half-hour ride on Metro into the city yet be just minutes from world-class shopping. Families flock to Tysons Corner Center for their kids' clothes, shoes, electronics, videos, music, games, and toys. It's one of the most successful malls in the country and has, as you might expect, several restaurants and a multiplex movie theater. You could easily spend a day here. Many do.

EXPENSIVE

Embassy Suites Tysons Corner   Let Embassy Suites be your chauffeur. About 12 miles from the heart of D.C., this hotel has a shuttle that will ferry you to restaurants and shopping within 2 miles of the hotel. The shuttle is available from 7am to 11pm. If you return from sightseeing hungry or want to shop with your kids, you can leave the buggy in the lot and just sit back and relax—navigating suburban Virginia roads is not for amateurs.

If you stay at an Embassy Suites, you and your kids won't be tripping over one another. There's a lot to be said for that, especially when you're spending every waking moment in one another's company. Each suite, all of which were renovated in 2004, has a king bed in the bedroom and a queen sleeper sofa in the living room; they all overlook the lushly landscaped atrium. The bedroom and living room each has a TV with free HBO and cable, and On Command video. Every morning, your family can look forward to a full, cooked-to-order American breakfast; evenings, wind down at the complimentary 2-hour manager's reception (drinks and munchies) in the Atrium Lounge. Please note that the weekend rate is sometimes half the weekday rate, putting the hotel in the "Inexpensive" category if you arrive on Friday and depart on Sunday.

The Metro is not within walking distance, but the hotel provides free transportation to the Dunn Loring station. It's about a 10-minute ride to the Metro station and a 20- to 30-minute ride to the Mall. Serious shoppers will want to visit nearby Tysons Corner Center and Tysons II. Drivers will find plenty of on-site complimentary parking.

Carnevale Cafe serves American fare in a casual setting, and there's a kids' menu.

8517 Leesburg Pike, Vienna, VA 22182. ☎ **800/EMBASSY** or 703/883-0707. Fax 703/760-9842. www.tysons corner.embassysuites.com. 234 suites. Weekdays $189–$289; weekends $99–$149. Children 12 and under stay free in parents' room. Crib free, rollaway $25. Extra person $10. Several packages available. AE, DC, DISC, MC, V. Free self-parking. Complimentary shuttle to Metro. Metro: Dunn Loring. **Amenities:** Restaurant, complimentary cooked-to-order breakfast and evening cocktails; heated indoor pool; on-site health club; large hot tub; sauna; room service

(11am–11pm); coin-op laundry; laundry service/dry cleaning service. *In room:* A/C, TV, minibar, fridge, coffeemaker, hair dryer, iron.

MODERATE

Sheraton Premiere at Tysons Corner   The Sheraton Premiere offers luxury accommodations with all the frills. Located 12 miles from Washington (at I-495, I-66, and Dulles Toll Road), Dulles Airport is about 8 miles away; Reagan is 15 miles. The facilities, service, and food are all first class. Eighteen suites, including the presidential suite, overlook Virginia's Blue Ridge Mountains and have a working fireplace.

The location is convenient to kid magnets: Wolf Trap Center for the Performing Arts, Tysons Corner and Tysons II, Toys R Us, 18 movie theaters, and numerous restaurants. Complimentary transportation to the Dunn Loring Metro is provided every hour (on the hour) from 7am to 10pm. From Dunn Loring to the hotel, service is every hour (on the half hour) from 7:30am to 10:30pm. Please note that this schedule can and does change frequently, so be sure to ask when you check in.

A restaurant and a bar are on the premises to serve you, along with great recreational facilities. The weekend package includes free continental breakfast.

Ashgrove's is the Sheraton's family-friendly restaurant for informal dining. Kids are welcome anytime. At lunch, they can order from their own menu, which includes grilled cheese, chicken tenders, pizza, hamburgers, and peanut butter and jelly with a banana happy face. All items are priced between $3 and $5. **First Impressions** is a lobby bar serving light fare.

8661 Leesburg Pike, Vienna, VA 22182. © **800/325-3535** or 703/448-1234. Fax 703/893-8193. www.sheraton.com. 437 units. Weekdays $169–$249 single or double, $250–$400 suite; weekends $89 and up. Children under 12 stay free in parents' room. Crib free, rollaway $15. Extra person $15. Weekly rates; promotional packages. AE, DC, DISC, MC, V. Free parking. Metro: Dunn Loring or West Falls Church. **Amenities:** Restaurant; lobby bar; Budget Car Rental office; indoor (open all year) and outdoor pools (open seasonally, approximately Memorial Day until after Labor Day) with lifeguard; 18-hole golf privileges; 2 racquetball courts; fitness center with exercise equipment, weights, hot tub, sauna, and Lifecycles; salon; room service (6am–midnight); massage; laundry service. *In room:* A/C, TV, minibar, coffeemaker, hair dryer, high-speed Internet connection

10 Bed & Breakfasts

Staying in a B&B can enhance your family's visit if you like personalized service and meeting and greeting other visitors in an intimate setting. The downside is that you might not be near a Metro station and will have to rely more on taxis and buses. I personally love B&Bs but think families with young children are better served by staying in a hotel. Having said that, rooms in B&Bs run the gamut from pint-size rooms (with the john down the hall) to suites accessorized with antiques in historic buildings.

In addition to my specific B&B recommendation, I've listed two reservations services. Reserve as early as possible to get the best selection of locations and lowest rates, and do specify your needs and preferences: For instance, discuss children, pets, smoking policy, preferred locations (do you require convenient public transportation?), parking, availability of TV and/or phone, preferred breakfast, and choice of payment.

B&B RESERVATION SERVICES

The **Bed and Breakfast League/Sweet Dreams & Toast,** P.O. Box 9490, Washington, DC 20016–9490 (© **202/363-7767** or 202/363-8396; bedandbreakfast-washington dc@erols.com), represents more than 85 B&B accommodations in the District. Through this service, you might find a room in a mid-1800s Federal-style Capitol Hill mansion, a Georgetown home with a lovely garden, or a turn-of-the-century Dupont

Circle town house filled with Victorian furnishings. Accommodations are all screened, and guest reports are taken seriously. Hosts are encouraged, although not required, to offer such niceties as fresh-baked muffins at breakfast. All listings are convenient to public transportation. Rates for most range from $55 to $155 single and from $80 to $165 double, plus tax, and from $10 to $25 per additional person. There are a 2-night minimum-stay requirement and a booking fee of $10 (per reservation, not per night). Most credit cards are accepted.

Bed & Breakfast Accommodations Ltd., P.O. Box 12011, Washington, DC 20005 (*©* **202/328-3510;** Fax 202/332-3885; www.bedandbreakfastdc.com), has about 80 homes, inns, guesthouses, and furnished apartments in its files. Its current roster offers, among many others, a Georgian-style colonial brick home on a tree-lined avenue near the Tenleytown Metro, an 1887 restored Victorian home with a fenced-in yard in the heart of downtown, and a charming suburban home in Chevy Chase, Maryland. Rates are from $65 to $200 double in private homes, $15 for an extra person, and from $65 for a full apartment. At guesthouses and inns, rates run the gamut from $65 to $265. Ask about off-season or longer-stay discounts. Most major credit cards are accepted.

A DOWNTOWN B&B RECOMMENDATION

Morrison–Clark Historic Inn *★★★* *(Finds* The Morrison–Clark Historic Inn, the only inn in the nation's capital to be listed on the National Register of Historic Places, is a top choice if you appreciate charm and ambience. It's also the home of one of the city's finest restaurants.

The original twin buildings were erected in the 1860s, and the interior is worthy of an *Architectural Digest* spread, from the Victorian entry parlor to the beautifully decorated guest rooms, individualized with wicker, antiques, original art, and fresh bouquets. All 54 Victorian rooms (some of which have an Italian Carrera marble nonworking fireplace) have one queen or two double beds, and some accommodations have bougainvillea-draped trellised balconies or private porches surrounding a courtyard garden with a fountain. Most of the parlor suites are done in French country with down duvets and have a separate living area with a sofa bed.

A complimentary continental breakfast of fresh-baked breads, muffins, croissants, brioches, and pastries is served in the Drawing Room daily. After the pastries and croissants, step (or waddle) into the complimentary on-site fitness center for damage control. Gratis daily newspapers, twice-a-day maid service with Belgian chocolates at bed turndown, and complimentary overnight shoeshines are but a few of the extras at the Morrison Clark, which raise the B&B concept to new heights of luxury. The management is gracious about accepting children of all ages, but because there are so many pretty things to break, consider staying here only if your kids are at least 8 or 9—or behave as such.

The hotel's noted restaurant serves Southern cuisine and is open Tuesday through Saturday for dinner. The chefs shop for the freshest ingredients from the Eastern Market (farmers' market) on Capitol Hill. Frequently voted one of the 100 best restaurants in the Washington, D.C. area by *Washingtonian* magazine, it's one of my favorite places to dine. In pleasant weather, reserve a table in the brick courtyard (table umbrella provided for the pale at heart). Reservations are a must. Although the management encourages parents to bring their children, I'd think twice—not because they're not welcome, but because it's not fair to the other diners if your kids aren't on their best behavior.

1015 L St. NW. (between 11th St. and Massachusetts Ave.), Washington, DC 20001. © **800/332-7898** or 202/898-1200. Fax 202/ 289-8579 www.morrisonclark.com. (check for Internet specials). Weekdays $159–$269 single ($20 extra per person); weekends from $139–$159 single or double. Rates include continental breakfast daily. Children 16 and under stay free in parents' room. Crib $20, rollaway $20. Extra person $20. Group rates available. AE, DC, DISC, MC, V. Valet parking $24. Metro: Mount Vernon and Metro Center stations, walk east 1 block on F or G St. NW to left at 11th St., continue 4 blocks, and cross Mass. Ave.; take a taxi at night. **Amenities:** Restaurant, complimentary continental breakfast daily; fitness club; concierge; business center and secretarial services; room service; babysitting; laundry/dry cleaning service. *In room:* A/C, TV, minibar, hair dryer.

11 Campgrounds

If you're an outdoorsy family, consider staying in one of Maryland or Virginia's many campgrounds. Here are two of the closest and best equipped.

Aquia Pines Camp Resort ⭐ (*Value*)   The heavily wooded Aquia Pines lies 1 mile from Exit 143a off I-95, about 35 miles south of D.C. and 10 miles north of George Washington's boyhood home, Fredericksburg. It's the Virginia campground most convenient to D.C.'s sights. The bathrooms are so clean that the National Campground Association once photographed them for a training film. Now that's clean!

For those who want to rough it less, consider renting one of the 30 deluxe campsites with instant phone hookup and cable TV, or a modest cabin consisting of one room with a double bed, two bunk beds, and a porch. You'll have to use the campground restrooms, and linen service is strictly BYO. Or you can opt for one of three deluxe cabins with a full bathroom, air-conditioning, and a kitchenette.

In season, there are nightly orientation programs on Washington and historic Virginia, as well as special summertime and weekend family activities. A Wal-Mart and two supermarkets are 1 mile from the campground (a third is 2 miles away) and there's an on-site store with the essentials. So if you forgot the marshmallows, your stay won't be spoiled. Pets are welcome, but *not* in the cabins. Because the nearest Metro station is 25 miles, Mount Vernon is about 30 miles, and Washington is 35 miles away, the Aquia Pines owner recommends driving to D.C. and parking in a lot. Another option (in season): Visit Mount Vernon, with plenty of free parking; take a cruise to Georgetown, spend time there, and return to Mount Vernon late in the day. Two Virginia Rail Express stations, with ample parking, are each 6 miles from Aquia Pines. Trains on the Fredericksburg Line run weekdays only, with stops at L'Enfant Plaza and Union Station (25–30 min.). The fare to D.C. is $14.50 round-trip. (For more information, see chapter 3, "Getting to Know Washington, D.C.")

3071 Jefferson Davis Hwy., Stafford, VA 22554. © **800/726-1710** or 540/659-3447. www.aquiapines.com. Rates for 4 persons, unless otherwise noted. $36.50 tent, no hookup ($5 each additional guest); $36.50 water and electricity; $40 water, electricity, sewer; $47 campsites with cable/phone hookup; $49 rustic cabin; $108 luxury cabin (1–5 persons; 2 parents and their 3 children). Extra cabin guests $8 each, per night. DISC, MC, V. Pets accepted except in cabins. Metro: Franconia/Springfield (also Virginia Rail Express train). **Amenities:** Large heated pool; minigolf; playground; game room; car-rental desk; general store, shopping arcade; coin-op laundry; hot showers; picnic tables; free firewood; basketball court.

Cherry Hill Park ⭐ (*Value*)   This 58-acre campground lies just 10 miles from downtown Washington, with easy access via I-95. Be warned that purists searching for Walden Pond will hardly consider staying here a back-to-nature experience once they see all the amenities.

First off, unlike many campgrounds that are open only in the summer, this one is open year-round. In season, April through October, a certified master RV technician is on site for repairs and advice. During the same period, food service is available at the poolside cafe. And when was the last time you "roughed it" with a walk-in beach-style pool, separate kids' pool, basketball court, play areas with age-appropriate equipment, nature trails, fishing ponds (catch and release), hot tub, sauna, sundeck, large-screen TV lounge with fireplace, game rooms, 30-plus washers and dryers, and tour options? Hey, there's even a concierge onboard to serve you, and dog walkers are available to take Poochy on his midnight bathroom run. The Gurevich family runs the place like a Southern-style Borscht Belt resort, and you can enjoy line dancing (for a fee unless you're just watching) every Wednesday night in the conference center. And it's just 20 minutes from Six Flags America. The site's 58 acres with trees and natural floral landscaping help absorb the traffic drone from the nearby Beltway, but if you're light sleepers, it might be a good idea to pack earplugs.

Starlight Theatre offers free family-fare movies in season. Grab a bench or bring your chairs and be surrounded by six Bose speakers.

If you don't want to drive into D.C., the Greenbelt Metro station is only 3 miles away. Or catch the 83 Metrobus at the campground entrance (Cherry Hill Road) to the College Park Metro station. The bus runs daily with service more frequent week-days than Saturday and Sunday.

9800 Cherry Hill Rd., College Park, MD 20740. ℂ **800/801-6449** or 301/937-7116. Fax 301/937-3110. www.cherry hillpark.com. 400 RV and tenting campsites. $50 per recreational vehicle, which includes 2 persons; $5 each additional person age 6 and over; $55 for pull-through sites; $65 for premium campsite with instant phone service. $36 tent camping (2 persons). $2 fee for each additional vehicle (1 car is included with each RV). Five air-conditioned and heated trailers (2 trailers have 3 bedrooms for 6 people; the other 3 have 1 bedroom and a large living room that also can sleep a total 6), 2 air-conditioned cabins (12' × 20' for 5 people), and 1 yurt are available for rental. Trailers are $95 per night for the first 4 people; cabins and the yurt are $60 a night with a 2-night minimum stay (bring your own bedding). Pets not allowed. Hookups include electric (20/30/50 amps), cable TV, water, and sewer. Ask about discounts. DISC, MC, V. **Amenities:** 2 pools; miniature golf; fitness classes; hot tub; sauna; play areas; game rooms; tour options; coin-op laundry; propane refills; firewood; dog walkers; fishing pond; basketball court; nature trails. High-speed wireless Internet service (fee).

5

Family-Friendly Restaurants

At last count, Washington and environs had more than 2,500 restaurants to choose from—everything from burgers, pizza, and USDA Prime aged beef to cuisine of just about every ethnic persuasion you can think of. So finding a place to eat is never a problem in Washington. The hard part is choosing. Be adventurous; your family's education doesn't end when you leave the Smithsonian. If you're raising your children in a meat-and-potatoes environment, expand their gustatory horizons and try a Thai or Greek restaurant (check out the "Restaurants by Cuisine" listing below). And if your family has never tasted fresh crabmeat, here's your opportunity to savor this delicious local specialty that's harvested from nearby Chesapeake Bay from late spring through fall (Aug and Sept are prime).

Because space prohibits listing every family restaurant, consider this chapter a sampling. Well-behaved kids who like to dine rather than eat and run are welcome at just about any restaurant in the city. However, when deciding where to dine with a very young child, please consider the appropriateness of your choice. Kids who would rather blow bubbles into their drinks than eat a square meal are served better by casual restaurants, fast food, or takeout. Nobody wants to dress up and pay a lot of money in a fine restaurant to play peek-a-boo with an antsy tot at the next table. Consider what shape your kids are in, too. (They might not be on their best behavior after 14 museums in 2 days.)

The drinking age in D.C. is 21. No exceptions are made for almost-21-year-olds dining with adults, so don't even think of offering your offspring a sip of your cocktail. A single violation could close the restaurant for good.

To save time on days when you want to pack in as much downtown sightseeing as possible, eat in a museum or federal-building restaurant or cafeteria. When you want simple, walk-away fare—hot dogs, chips, ice cream, and sodas—look for the pagoda-style roofs of the free-standing food-service kiosks nestled among the elms on the Mall. Or head for a food court in one of D.C.'s enclosed malls. Hey, this is Washington, so everyone should exercise their freedom of choice at these popular eateries. The selections are consistent and inexpensive. On a beautiful day, get it to go and picnic on the grass or on a park bench.

Nothing can ruin an otherwise pleasant day faster than an interminable wait in a mobbed restaurant. Because sometimes service might be less than speedy, especially during peak times, you could bring along some crayons, scrap paper, and a few playthings. Of course, it's always a good idea to have crackers or other snacks in your bag to pacify impatient little ones. If you don't have reservations and you want attentive service, try to get seated before noon or after 2pm for lunch and no later than 6 or 6:30pm for dinner.

The tax on restaurant meals is a hefty 10% in the District.

NOTE ON PRICES The following reviews include a range of specific menu prices as often as possible. I've also categorized the restaurants as expensive, moderate, or inexpensive, based on rough estimates of what it would cost to feed a family of four: two parents and two children, assuming that one of the kids is young enough to be satisfied with either a kids' meal or a half portion or just an appetizer. If this mythical family would have to spend $120 or more for dinner (excluding any bar tab), I've classed that restaurant as **very expensive;** $75 to $120 as **expensive;** between $50 and $75, **moderate;** and under $50, **inexpensive.**

1 Restaurants by Cuisine

AFTERNOON TEA

Four Seasons 🏵🏵 (Georgetown; $$$, p. 101)

Renaissance Mayflower Hotel (Downtown; $$$, p. 95)

Washington National Cathedral 🏵🏵 (Upper Northwest; $$$, p. 107)

AMERICAN

Afterwords Café at Kramerbooks (Dupont Circle; $, p. 102)

America 🏵🏵 (Capitol Hill; $–$$, p. 86)

Brickskeller 🏵 (Dupont Circle; $–$$, p. 102)

Bullfeathers 🏵 (Capitol Hill; $–$$, p. 87)

Capitol City Brewing Co. (Convention Center; Capitol Hill; $–$$, p. 84)

Chadwicks (Upper Northwest; Alexandria, Virginia; $–$$, p. 106)

Cheesecake Factory 🏵 (N. Bethesda, Maryland; Upper Northwest; $–$$, p. 106)

Chili's Grill & Bar 🏵 (Vienna, Virginia; $, p. 112)

Clyde's 🏵 (Georgetown; Vienna, Virginia; $$, p. 97)

Fuddruckers 🏵 (Convention Center; Downtown; Dupont Circle; Rockville, Maryland; $, p. 93)

Garrett's (Georgetown; $$, p. 98)

Georgetown Bagelry 🏵🏵 (Georgetown; $, p. 100)

Hamburger Hamlet 🏵 (Bethesda, Maryland; $–$$, p. 108)

Hard Rock Cafe 🏵 (Convention Center; $$, p. 93)

Houston's 🏵🏵 (Bethesda, Maryland; Rockville, Maryland; $–$$, p. 108)

Kinkead's 🏵🏵🏵 (Foggy Bottom; $$$–$$$$, p. 96)

Luna Grill & Diner 🏵 (Dupont Circle; $–$$, p. 102)

Mackey's Public House (Downtown; $–$$, p. 93)

Market Lunch (Capitol Hill; $, p. 87)

Morton's 🏵🏵🏵 (Downtown; Georgetown; Vienna, Virginia; $$$–$$$$, p. 97)

Old Ebbitt Grill 🏵 (Downtown; $$, p. 94)

Philadelphia Mike's (Bethesda, Maryland; $, p. 109)

Tastee Diner 🏵 (Bethesda, Maryland; $, p. 109)

T.G.I. Friday's (Downtown; Foggy Bottom; Vienna, Virginia; $, p. 96)

BAKERY

Bread & Chocolate (Downtown; p. 95)

CAJUN/CREOLE

Louisiana Express 🏵 (Bethesda, Maryland; $–$$, p. 109)

CANDIES

Chocolate Chocolate (Downtown; p. 95)

Kron Chocolatier 🏵🏵 (Upper Northwest; p. 107)

Key to Abbreviations: $$$$ = Very Expensive $$$ = Expensive $$ = Moderate $ = Inexpensive

CHINESE

Foong Lin ☞ (Bethesda, Maryland; $$, p. 107)

Tony Cheng's Seafood and Mongolian Barbecue (Convention Center; $$, p. 91)

COOKIES

Bread & Chocolate (Downtown; p. 95)

Larry's Cookies (Capitol Hill; Downtown; p. 90)

Mrs. Field's (Georgetown; p. 100)

EAST ASIAN

Pan Asian Noodles & Grill ☞ (Dupont Circle; $, p. 101)

ECLECTIC/FOOD COURTS

National Place (Downtown; $, p. 95)

Food Court at the Old Post Office (Downtown; $, p. 92)

Food Court at the Ronald Reagan Building and International Trade Center (Downtown; $, p. 94)

Food Court at Union Station ☞☞ (Capitol Hill; $, p. 87)

Market Lunch (Capitol Hill; $, p. 87)

GERMAN

Cafe Mozart (Convention Center; $$, p. 91)

GREEK

Athenian Plaka ☞ (Bethesda, Maryland; $$, p. 107)

ICE CREAM

Baskin-Robbins (Upper Northwest; p. 106)

Ben & Jerry's ☞ (Adams Morgan; Capitol Hill; Downtown; Dupont Circle; Georgetown; Upper Northwest; p. 90)

Cold Stone Creamery (Upper Northwest; p. 106)

Cone E' Island (Foggy Bottom; Vienna, Virginia; p. 96)

Gifford's ☞ (Bethesda, Maryland; p. 110)

Häagen-Dazs (Capitol Hill; Georgetown; p. 90)

Thomas Sweet ☞ (Georgetown; p. 100)

IRISH

Mackey's Public House (Downtown; $–$$, p. 93)

ITALIAN

Adams–Morgan Spaghetti Garden ☞ (Adams–Morgan; $–$$, p. 104)

A.V. ☞ (Convention Center; $–$$, p. 91)

Filomena's Ristorante ☞ (Georgetown; $$–$$$, p. 98)

Otello ☞ (Dupont Circle; $$, p. 101)

Paolo's ☞ (Georgetown; $$, p. 100)

Pizzeria Paradiso ☞ (Dupont Circle; Georgetown; $, p. 104)

LIGHT FARE

Sky Terrace (Downtown; $$, p. 95) (Also see "Eclectic/Food Courts" above)

MEXICAN

El Tamarindo ☞ (Adams–Morgan; $–$$, p. 104)

Rio Grande Café (Bethesda, Gaithersburg, Maryland; Ballston, Reston, Virginia; $–$$, p. 108)

MOROCCAN

Marrakesh ☞ (Convention Center; $$, p. 90)

PIZZA

Il Forno ☞ (Bethesda, Maryland; $, p. 109)

Pizzeria Paradiso ☞ (Dupont Circle; Georgetown; $, p. 104)

RIBS/BARBECUE

Houston's ☞☞ (Bethesda, Maryland; Rockville, Maryland, $–$$, p. 108)

O'Brien's Pit Barbecue ☞☞ (Rockville, Maryland; $–$$, p. 110)

Red, Hot & Blue (Arlington,
Virginia; $–$$, p. 86)

SALVADORAN
El Tamarindo 🍴 (Adams–Morgan;
$–$$, p. 104)

SANDWICHES
Roy's Place 🍴🍴 (Gaithersburg,
Maryland; $–$$, p. 110)

SEAFOOD
Crisfield Seafood Restaurant 🍴 (Silver
Spring, Maryland; $$, p. 111)
Kinkead's 🍴🍴🍴 (Foggy Bottom;
$$$–$$$$, p. 96)
Sea Catch Restaurant and Raw Bar 🍴🍴
(Georgetown; $$$–$$$$, p. 97)

SOUTHWESTERN
Chili's Grill & Bar 🍴 (Vienna,
Virginia; $, p. 112)

STEAKHOUSES
Morton's 🍴🍴🍴 (Downtown;
Georgetown; Vienna, Virginia;
$$$–$$$$, p. 97)

TEX-MEX
Austin Grill 🍴🍴 (Convention Center;
Glover Park (north of Georgetown);
Bethesda, Maryland; Alexandria
and Springfield, Virginia; $$,
p. 92)
Cactus Cantina 🍴 (Upper Northwest;
$$, p. 105)

THAI
Jandara (Upper Northwest; $$,
p. 105)

VIENNESE
Cafe Mozart (Convention Center; $$,
p. 85)

2 Capitol Hill

Capitol Hill is surprisingly kid-friendly, probably because so many politicians, lobbyists, and their staffs live here with their families. If your stomach starts growling while you're touring the Capitol, Supreme Court, or Library of Congress, try one of their dining rooms or cafeterias for a quick meal or snack; you'll find listings for these in chapter 6.

Your family can slurp famed Senate bean soup (the recipe is more than 100 years old!) alongside legislators weekdays between 11:30am and 3pm. A tureen of soup still costs $4.50 in the exclusive **Senators' Dining Room** 🍴 in the U.S. Capitol. There are two hitches: (1) You must first secure a "request letter" from your senator, which you can pick up and bring to the dining room, or the senator's office can forward it directly to the dining room, and (2) men (ages 12 and older) are required to wear a suit and tie (no hair rollers or flip-flops for women). For more information, contact the Senators' Dining Room at ⏰ **202/224-2350.** If these rules are too stringent, stop by the Capitol's basement snack bar (Room SB10; ⏰ **202/224-5340**) for breakfast and lunch between 7:30am and 3pm. Soups, sandwiches, and specials cost $3.95 to $4.95. (How come they can keep the prices low here, but the sky is the limit with government spending elsewhere?)

INEXPENSIVE TO MODERATE

America 🍴🍴 ⟨Value⟩ AMERICAN   Look no further than the Navaho Fried Bread & Spicy Chicken (deep-fried dough filled with grilled chicken, guacamole, tomato, onion, lettuce, and salsa). If that doesn't sound good, there are still options galore to choose

On the Run

In a hurry? For a quick bite when you're on the go, grab a snack from a street vendor. My kids were raised on hot dogs, soft pretzels, and ice cream without ill effect. They even graduated from college and are gainfully employed. Some vendors sell such upscale treats as filled croissants and Chipwiches (ice cream sandwiched between chocolate chip cookies). The pizza and egg rolls are usually substandard. My personal favorite is a Sabrett's hot dog with "the works." Look for a pushcart with the blue-and-yellow Sabrett's logo umbrella.

from. How about sautéed lemon-pepper chicken, red beans and rice, a burger, soup, salad, sandwich, pasta, or a fish or vegetarian dish? Or maybe you'd prefer some comfort food along the lines of meatloaf, pork chops, or chicken pot pie? This cavernous, multilevel Union Station restaurant tries (and usually succeeds) to be all things to all diners. Kids can order chicken tenders, pizza, a hot dog, or spaghetti for $6.95 (which includes a drink). Opt for a balcony table for a view of the spectacular Main Hall.

Union Station, 50 Massachusetts Ave. NE. © 202/682-9555. www.arkrestaurants.com. High chairs, booster seats, kids' menu, crayons. Reservations recommended at dinner. Most items at lunch and dinner $6–$15; kids' meal $6.95. AE, DC, DISC, MC, V. Sun–Thurs 11:30am–last seating at 9:30pm; Fri–Sat 11:30am–last seating at 10pm. Metro: Union Station.

Bullfeathers ⚓ AMERICAN   Hamburgers, nachos, soups, sandwiches, and salads make this a popular spot for sippers and suppers of all ages. Just stick to the basics, and you won't be disappointed. If you are, let me know. Suits and Hill wanna-be's of all ages fill the place for happy hour, which can stretch well into the evening. Dining outdoors is a delight on a summer's eve. The bargain children's menu includes peanut butter-and-jelly sandwiches, chicken, hot dogs, spaghetti, and a 3½-ounce kiddie burger, half the size of the Bullfeathers signature burger. Light fare and nightly beer specials are served in the saloon.

410 1st St. SE. © 202/543-5005. www.bullfeatherscapitolhill.com. High chairs, booster seats, kids' menu. Reservations recommended, particularly at lunch. Main courses $6.59–$11 lunch, $6.59–$21 dinner, kids' menu $2.95–$5.25. AE, DC, DISC, MC, V. Mon–Sat 11:15am–midnight. Metro: Capitol South.

Food Court at Union Station ⚓⚓ *Value* ECLECTIC   It's fun to case the myriad stands before making a selection at this bustling food court. Some of the best bets for youngsters are the all-beef European kosher hot dog at Frank & Stein, the deep-dish pizza at Ilardo's, and the charbroiled hamburger at Flamer's. There are also BBQ, deli, Tex-Mex, sushi, and wraps. Top off your visit to Union Station with some ice cream from Häagen-Dazs or Ben & Jerry's, or a cannoli or other mouthwatering pastry at Vacarro's. Hey, have 'em all. I won't tell.

50 Massachusetts Ave. NE. © 202/371-9441. Reservations not accepted. Most items $4–$10. No credit cards. Mon–Sat 10am–9pm; Sun noon–6pm.

Market Lunch *Value* ECLECTIC/AMERICAN   Try the mouthwatering blueberry buckwheat pancakes, egg platters, or French toast for breakfast at this tiny eatery inside historic Eastern Market. If you want breakfast on Saturday, you must be in line before noon. After that, it's lunch only. The soft-shell crab (seasonal) sandwich on homemade bread is a lunchtime specialty, with the crab cake a close second. Weather permitting, there's outdoor seating. Weekends, the place jumps with hordes of shoppers hunting for arts and crafts bargains Saturday and the outdoor flea market Sunday.

Where to Dine in Central Washington, D.C.

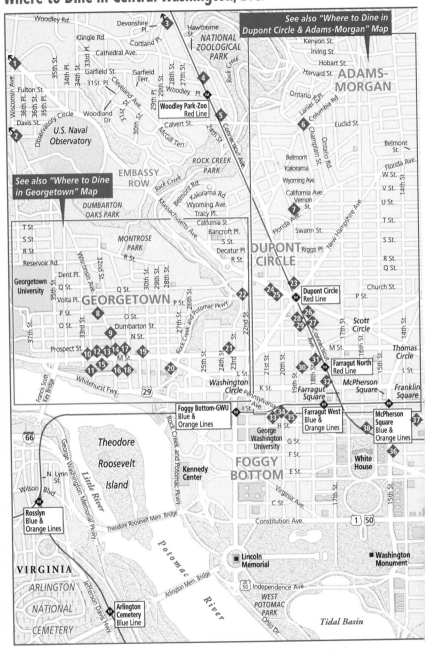

See also "Where to Dine in Dupont Circle & Adams-Morgan" Map

See also "Where to Dine in Georgetown" Map

NATIONAL ZOOLOGICAL PARK

ADAMS-MORGAN

Woodley Park-Zoo
Red Line

ROCK CREEK PARK

EMBASSY ROW

DUMBARTON OAKS PARK

MONTROSE PARK

DUPONT CIRCLE

Dupont Circle
Red Line

Georgetown University

GEORGETOWN

Scott Circle

Thomas Circle

Franklin Square

Farragut North
Red Line

McPherson Square

Farragut Square

Washington Circle

Foggy Bottom-GWU
Blue & Orange Lines

George Washington University

Farragut West
Blue & Orange Lines

McPherson Square
Blue & Orange Lines

FOGGY BOTTOM

White House

Theodore Roosevelt Island

Kennedy Center

Rosslyn
Blue & Orange Lines

VIRGINIA

ARLINGTON NATIONAL CEMETERY

Arlington Cemetery
Blue Line

Potomac River

Lincoln Memorial

Washington Monument

WEST POTOMAC PARK

Tidal Basin

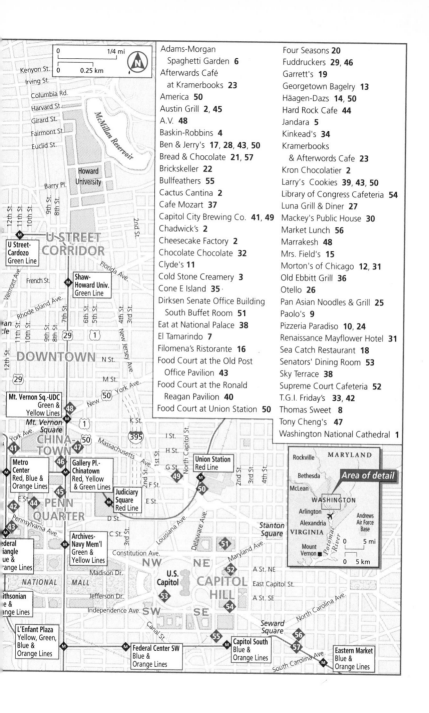

225 7th St. SE. (€) 202/547-8444. High chairs. Reservations not accepted. Breakfast $3–$6; lunch $4–$12. No credit cards. Tues–Sat 7:30am–3pm; Sun 11am–3:30pm (lunch only). Metro: Eastern Market.

COOKIES, CANDY & ICE CREAM

Ben & Jerry's ICE CREAM   Who'd have thought that two young men dishing it out at a stand in Burlington, Vermont, would've created such an empire? Sample this rich, environmentally correct product, and you'll know why Ben and Jerry are mooing all the way to the bank. It's expensive, but you get what you pay for. After lunch at Union Station or on your way to the Capitol, stop at the street-level counter and grab some Cookie Dough or Chunky Monkey in a waffle cone or dish. Ice cream doesn't get much better than this. Also at the Old Post Office, 1100 Pennsylvania Ave. ((€) **202/842-5882**); 1350 Connecticut Ave. (rear of building facing 19th St. at N), near Dupont Circle ((€) **202/785-4882**); and 3135 M St. NW in Georgetown ((€) **202/ 965-2222**).

Union Station, 50 Massachusetts Ave. NE. (€) 202/842-2887. www.benjerry.com. Most treats $3–$6. AE, DISC, MC, V. Daily 10am–10pm.

Häagen-Dazs ICE CREAM   Häagen-Dazs certainly rates up there with the best commercially produced ice cream anywhere. But it's pricey. I like to think of it as designer ice cream. The shop also has sundaes, shakes, smoothies, sorbets, and low-fat ice creams. There are other locations at 3120 M Street in Georgetown ((€) **202/333- 3433**) and 703 7th St. in Gallery Place ((€) 202/783-4711).

Union Station, 50 Massachusetts Ave. NE. (€) 202/789-0953. Most treats $2.95–$6.35. AE, DISC, MC, V. Daily 10am–10pm.

Larry's Cookies COOKIES   Of the various cookie–brownie bars sold here, the "Special" is particularly heavenly because it marries brownie to chocolate chip cookie. These treats are sold by weight and will set you back about $2 apiece.

Union Station, 50 Massachusetts Ave. NE. (€) 202/289-7586. Also at the Old P.O. Pavilion, 1100 Pennsylvania Ave. NW ((€) 202/682-1018). Cookies and brownies about $2 each. AE, MC, V. Mon–Fri 6:30am–9pm; Sat 7am–9pm; Sun 7am–7pm.

3 Convention Center

If you're staying in this area, visiting the Spy Museum, have tickets to an event at the MCI Center, or just want to eat on 7th Street with its multitude of restaurants, shops, and action, this is a logical neighborhood in which to dine. The choices are varied, and Chinatown, with the greatest concentration of Asian restaurants in the city, is here. You'll also find many other ethnic restaurants, hotel dining rooms, and coffee shops, and the favorite of many kids: the Hard Rock Cafe.

EXPENSIVE

Marrakesh ⍟ *(Finds)* MOROCCAN   Dining at this lively, colorful oasis is an evening's entertainment and a fitting place to celebrate a special event. Sink into the pillowed banquettes and partake of the seven-course fixed-price dinner built around entrees of lamb, chicken, beef, and vegetarian dishes. At Marrakesh, eating is strictly a hands-on experience, accompanied by Moroccan music and belly dancing. Don't be surprised if someone in your party becomes part of the entertainment. It's a lot of fun and good value for the money (provided you don't order a lot of wine). If your kids need a high chair or a booster seat, they're too young to dine here. Plan on spending 3 hours for dinner. Valet parking costs $5.

617 New York Ave. NW. Ⓒ 202/393-9393. www.marrakeshwashington.com. Reservations required. Fixed-price dinner $27 per person; kids 12 and under half price Sun–Thurs. No credit cards; checks accepted. Daily 6–11pm. Metro: Gallery Place–Chinatown.

MODERATE

A.V. *Ⓕ* ITALIAN   Since sliding its first pizza from the oven more than half a century ago, A.V. has spawned numerous spin-offs in the D.C. area. The lack of pretense in decor might not win your approval, but this ristorante still reigns supreme if you like hearty orders of pasta smothered in no-nonsense sauces or simply prepped fish. Noteworthy are the linguine sauced with clams and garlic and the eggplant parmesan. Your kids can share a single portion, enough for two adults in many cases. Start with the white pizza (with or without cheese), originally introduced in the United States right here in 1949. The thin-crust, New York–style pizza brightens the smiles of die-hard tomato pie lovers. If you skip the specials and share, you can dine like a don for less than $15 a head. Feed your loose change into the jukebox, and enjoy your favorite opera aria. There's free parking in lots adjacent to the restaurant—a rarity.

607 New York Ave. Ⓒ 202/737-0550. High chairs, booster seats. Reservations not accepted. Appetizers $2.95–$8.95; main courses $6.50–$17.95. AE, DC, DISC, MC, V. Mon–Thurs 11:30am–10pm; Fri 11:30am–midnight; Sat 5pm–midnight. Closed Sun. and the first 3 weeks of August. Metro: Mt. Vernon Square/U. D.C. or Gallery Place (3 blocks).

Cafe Mozart GERMAN/VIENNESE   You could do a lot "wurst" than to dine at this gemütlich restaurant tucked behind a deli where the *sauerbraten* (sweet-and-sour braised pot roast) and *wiener schnitzel* (breaded veal cutlet) are almost as good as my grandmother's. Try the *unsere wuerste* (sausage) platters served with potato salad and sauerkraut or red cabbage. The food is robust and tasty, and the service is warm and friendly. On the menu for *kinder* (children) are hamburger, hot dog, sandwiches, and linguine (!)—all with a side dish. Most are under $6. They offer takeout and delivery service too. Some nights, there is live music. The monthly Opera Night is fun if your progeny are so inclined. Complimentary parking weeknights is available after 6pm at the garage next door.

1331 H St. NW. Ⓒ 202/347-5732. www.cafemozartgermandeli.com. High chairs, booster seats, kids' menu. Reservations recommended at dinner. Breakfast $3–$5; lunch $6.95–$20; dinner $17–$22 (small portions $13–$16). Kids' menu items $5.50–$7. AE, DC, DISC, MC, V. Mon–Fri 7am–10pm; Sat 9am–10pm; Sun 11am–10pm. Closed Thanksgiving, Dec 25, Jan 1. Metro: Metro Center or McPherson Square.

Tony Cheng's Seafood and Mongolian Barbecue CHINESE   It might take a while to choose from the extensive menu (more than 200 items) of Szechuan, Cantonese, and Hunan dishes in this tablecloth—but unpretentious—restaurant. The dim sum alone, served upstairs every day at lunch, merit a visit. I've yet to meet the child who didn't cotton to dumplings. If you're on a budget, come at lunch and stick to the dim sum. Some of the signature dishes served here are stir-fried crabs with ginger and scallions, and whole steamed sea bass. The kids can practice their prowess with chopsticks on the fish and other appetizers and entrees. If they grow bored, they can make faces at the fish in the large tanks. On the first floor is a buffet-style Mongolian barbecue. Kids over 4 or 5 enjoy choosing the ingredients (meats, vegetables, sauces) for their meal and then watching the cook stir-fry the concoction on the giant grill. Frankly, I prefer to leave it to the pros in the kitchen, but that's your call.

619 H St. NW. Ⓒ 202/371-8669. High chairs and boosters. Reservations recommended. Main courses $6–$13 lunch, $8–$30 dinner. AE, MC, V. Mon–Thurs & Sun 11am–11pm, Fri–Sat 11am–midnight. Metro: Gallery Place/Chinatown.

INEXPENSIVE TO MODERATE

Austin Grill 🏵🏵 TEX-MEX   This place has a partylike atmosphere, with inexpensive, extensive Tex-Mex fare served in an unpretentious setting reminiscent of a Texas roadhouse. Try the house-braised *carnitas* (pork) fajitas or one of the popular combo plates that include a mix of enchiladas, tacos, or tamales. You'll also find Texas chili, fajitas, and a selection of margaritas.

From the children's menu (with puzzles and a map and flag of Texas to color), kids can order a single taco, enchilada, quesadilla, nachos, burger, or PB&J (that old Tex-Mex favorite!). All come with soda and choice of potato chips, red beans and rice, or applesauce for only $5. A scoop of ice cream is $1; a glass of juice, 75¢. Spiciness is noted on the menu to assist you when ordering for tender palates. Things can get lively—some would say boisterous—with the mostly under-30 crowd. Although your children will probably love it, *you* might end up with a headache. The restaurant is convenient to the FBI, Ford's Theatre, the Spy Museum, and the Convention Center. In season, there's outside dining shaded by awnings and trees.

The original Austin Grill is at 2404 Wisconsin Ave. NW, above Georgetown (✆ 202/337-8080). In Alexandria, Virginia, visit its location at 801 King St. (✆ 703/684-8969). In Springfield, Virginia, there's one at 8430-A Old Keene Mill Rd. (✆ 703/644-3111). The Bethesda, Maryland, location is at 7278 Woodmont Ave. (✆ 301/656-1366). In Baltimore, there's one at 2400 Boston St. (Canton, near Fells Point; ✆ 410/534-0606.)

750 E St. NW, between 7th and 8th sts. ✆ **202/393-3776**. www.austingrill.com. High chairs, booster seats, kids' menu, crayons. Reservations for 15 or more. Lunch entrees $6–$17; dinner $8–$18; kids' meal $5. AE, DC, DISC, MC, V. Mon–Thurs 11am–10pm; Fri–Sat 11am–11pm; Sun 11am–9:30pm. Metro: Gallery Place or Archives.

Capitol City Brewing Co. AMERICAN   The first brew pub in D.C., Capitol City is noisy, fun, and reasonable—three good reasons to bring your half-pints and try one of *theirs*. Beer lovers will want to try one of the microbrews made on the premises (I favor the amber). Children seem fascinated by the beer-making equipment upstairs. This is not the spot for an intimate conversation, but it's warm and welcoming to kids.

The basket of pretzels and mustard is a nice touch and—aren't they clever?—makes you *very* thirsty. The generous hamburgers are yummy and served with seasoned fries. Barbecued ribs have a strong following. The menu has expanded to include seafood, jambalaya, and other Cajun/Creole favorites. The kids can order a hot dog, hamburger, chicken tenders, mac and cheese, or grilled cheese, $4 each with applesauce, fries, and a juice box. A wait is not unusual at dinner and on weekends. Capitol City has another location at 2 Massachusetts Ave. NE (at the Postal Square Building; ✆ 202/842-BEER) and 2700 Quincy St. in Arlington, Virginia (✆ 703/578-3888). When you're in Baltimore, raise a mug at the Light Street Pavilion at the Inner Harbor (✆ 410/539-7468).

1100 New York Ave. NW (corner of H and 11th sts.). ✆ **202/628-2222**. www.capcitybrew.com. High chairs, booster seats, kids' menu. Reservations for 15 or more. Lunch and dinner $6.95–$19; kids' menu items $4. AE, DC, DISC, MC, V. Mon–Sat 11am–2am; Sun 11am–midnight. Metro: Metro Center.

INEXPENSIVE

Food Court at the Old Post Office *Value* ECLECTIC   If you're sightseeing on the Mall or along Pennsylvania or Constitution avenues, duck in here for a quick meal or a snack in the International Food Court. You'll find everything from Indian and Asian fare to burgers and fries at the 11 food stands. Also save room for Ben & Jerry's ice cream. Enjoy free entertainment weekdays during lunch, and weekend afternoons, starting either at 1 or 2pm and ending either at 4 or 5pm.

1100 Pennsylvania Ave. NW. ☎ 202/289-4224. Most items $3–$8. No credit cards. Mon–Sat 10am–7pm. Metro: Federal Triangle.

Fuddruckers ☞ AMERICAN   On bustling 7th Street, in the Penn Quarter near the Convention Center, Fudd's is a logical spot for lunch or dinner before or after visiting the Spy Museum or attending an event at the MCI Center. Part of a national chain, Fudd's consistently dishes up tasty, reasonable family fare if you don't mind ordering at the counter and a little noise. The excellent hamburgers come in four sizes and are cooked to order. Personalize your burger with the many selections—everything from salsa to melted cheese—at the fixings bar. With a side of fries or onion rings and a thick shake, you should be good to go until the following day. The hot dogs are just so-so. The oversize salads are fair to middlin' and oh so filling. I can live without the desserts, but my grandchildren won't leave without a brownie or cookie for the road. There's also a Fuddruckers in Dupont Circle at 18th St. NW and Jefferson Place, between Connecticut Ave. and M St. (☎ 202/659-1660), and at 1592 A Rockville Pike in Rockville, MD (☎ 301/468-3501).

734 Seventh St. ☎ 202/628-3361. www.fuddruckers.com. High chairs, kids' menu. Reservations not accepted. All main courses less than $10; kids' menu items (with fries) $4.05–$4.40. AE, DC, DISC, MC, V. Mon–Thurs 11am–10pm; Fri–Sat 11am–11pm; Sun 10am–10pm. Metro: Gallery Place–Chinatown.

Hard Rock Cafe ☞ AMERICAN   Let the good times roll as you ogle costumes worn by Britney Spears (not while she was pregnant) and No Doubt's Gwen Stefani, an autographed Stones photo, and one of Chuck Berry's guitars. Nobody comes here just for the food, so stick to the basics: burger platters (real beef or veggie), sandwiches, and chicken salads. The jumbo combo appetizer (spring rolls, chicken wings, onion rings, potato skins, and chicken fingers with four dipping sauces) will feed little ones—for about a week. Save room for the hot-fudge brownie sundae—it'll make you feel like dancin'. So will the 29 video monitors strategically placed throughout the restaurant. Go at off times unless you like lines. You'll be a hero to your kids for bringing them here. (If you're sensitive to noise, bring earplugs.)

999 E St. NW, next to Ford's Theatre. ☎ 202/737-ROCK. www.hardrock.com. High chairs, booster seats, kids' menu. Reservations not accepted; arrange preferred seating 24 hours in advance online. (You'll go to the head of the line when you arrive.) Main courses $8.95–$23. AE, DC DISC, MC, V. Sun–Thurs 11am–11pm; Fri–Sat 11am–midnight. Metro: Metro Center or Gallery Place/Chinatown.

4 Downtown

Visiting the Corcoran or Renwick late in the day? Celebrating a special occasion? With older kids, slip into one of the upscale restaurants on K Street NW, Washington's restaurant row, for a heady (and expensive) dining experience. If you have tickets to a show at the Warner or National, try one of the many restaurants that have sprouted up in recent years on and around 7th Street (near the Convention Center and MCI Center). *Please note:* Downtown covers a large area, and the boundaries blur, so also see the "Convention Center" recommendations, above.

MODERATE

Mackey's Public House IRISH/AMERICAN   Where can you be in Washington and Dublin at the same time? Head to Mackey's and snuggle up in a "snug" (tables separated by glass partitions for a modicum of privacy). For a taste of the Emerald Isle, try the fish and chips or corned beef and cabbage ($9.95 each). Or go for a burger, sandwich, salad, appetizer, or soup. Do try a side of mashed potatoes with roasted garlic or braised cabbage, and wash it down with one of Ireland's finest beers, including Guinness, Harp, and Smithwick's. An order of chicken tenders or buffalo wings—perhaps with a side of homemade chips (fries)—will more than fill a wee one.

Avoid Mackey's Friday nights, especially with young children. That's when business types and students let down their hair, and things can get a bit rowdy. Outdoor seating is available, weather permitting.

1823 L St. NW. ℂ 202/331-7667. www.mackeyspub.com. High chairs. Sandwiches and entrees range from $7.95–$13. AE, MC, V. Mon 11:30am–midnight; Tues–Thurs 11:30am–2am; Sat noon–3am. Metro: Farragut North.

Old Ebbitt Grill ⊛ AMERICAN   Around the corner from the White House, the Ebbitt is consistently good and open almost 'round the clock. This is a primo power-breakfast scene. There could be more deals sealed here over eggs Benedict than behind closed doors in the Capitol. Lunch features overstuffed sandwiches and huge salads. The location is convenient if you have tickets to a show. The staff is known to go overboard to please munchkins. The kids' menu has eight choices; all include milk or soda and ice cream or fruit for dessert. (Wonder how many orders they get for fruit?) The large saloon appeals with its polished wood, brass, and gaslights. Much of the menu changes daily, relying on local fresh goods (like fish and seafood) and produce. You can keep your tab in the inexpensive-to-moderate range with something from the raw bar, a sandwich or a hamburger, or a sumptuous dessert—how about a chocolate layer cake with raspberry sauce and whipped cream? The **Ebbitt Express,** a fast-food takeout deli on site, is open for breakfast and lunch Monday through Friday from 7:30am to 5pm (and you can order online!).

675 15th St. NW, between F and G sts. ℂ 202/347-4801. www.ebbitt.com. High chairs, booster seats, kids' menu, crayons. Reservations recommended. Breakfast (most items) $8.95–$9.95; Brunch (Sat–Sun) $10–$16.95; lunch (most items) $9.95–$13.95; dinner (most main dishes) $14.95–$15.95. Kids' menu items $5. AE, DC, DISC, MC, V. Mon–Fri 7:30am–1am; Sat–Sun 8:30am–1am. Closed Dec 25. Metro: Metro Center.

INEXPENSIVE
Food Court at the Ronald Reagan Building and International Trade Center
⟨Value⟩ ECLECTIC/FOOD COURTS   Conveniently located near the White House Visitor Center, Ford's Theater, and the Museum of American History, and just a short stroll from the Mall, this food court, with 18 eateries, has seating for close to 1,000 and is in the same building as the Chamber of Commerce's D.C. Visitor Information Center. You'll find the usual selection of fast foods (hamburgers, chicken, salads, deli, wraps) and ethnic fare (pizza, Cajun, sushi, dim sum) in pleasing surroundings. (I'm surprised they don't serve ketchup sandwiches. Remember when Ronnie was in the White House and he recommended ketchup as a vegetable?) *Take note:* There are no high chairs or booster seats, but I'm campaigning! Before or after your meal, you may want to tour (on your own any time; with a guide Mon, Wed, and Fri at 11am) the vast glass, steel, and stone building—a stunning architectural feat. Do check out the hunk of the Berlin Wall at the Woodrow Wilson Memorial Plaza entrance (at Pennsylvania Ave.). Also, there's free entertainment daily in summer noon to 1:30pm on Woodrow Wilson Plaza. Friday and Saturday evenings (year-round) at 7:30pm, you can catch the irreverent political satire of the Capitol Steps in the building's amphitheater. On a nasty day, this is a good choice, as the Metro entrance is accessible from the building.

1300 Pennsylvania Ave. NW. ℂ 202/312-1300. www.itcdc.com. Mon–Fri 7am–7pm, Sat 11am–6pm; Mar–Aug Sun noon–5pm (closed Sun Sept–Feb). Metro: Federal Triangle.

National Place *Value* ECLECTIC/FOOD COURTS   Nibble your way through Five Guys (hamburgers, hot dogs, fries), Kabuki (Japanese), Quizno's (sandwiches), Slice of Italy (pizza), Naan and Beyond (Indian), and Mei Wah Express (Chinese). Just 1 block from the Metro Center, this is a good spot for a quick meal or snack when sightseeing near the White House. There's plenty of seating, but you'll have to improvise a booster seat.

1331 Pennsylvania Ave. NW (enter at 13th and F sts.). ℂ 202/662-1250. High chairs. Most items $2–$7. No credit cards. Open Mon–Sat 11am–7pm. Closed Sun. Metro: Metro Center or Federal Triangle.

Sky Terrace LIGHT FARE   The extraordinary view of downtown and the environs is feast enough for most souls. Go anytime in good weather. *Note:* The prices match the location; both are high. The menu has expanded, so you can graze on an appetizer ($5–$10); eat a burger ($8.50), sandwich, salad, or cheese and fruit plate ($10); order an entree ($14–$16); or just have dessert ($6–$7) and/or drinks (smoothies, beer, wine, cocktails) on this very special rooftop. You can almost touch the planes landing and taking off from National Airport. It might be fun to ask your kids how many buildings they can identify from this vantage point.

Hotel Washington, 15th St. and Pennsylvania Ave. NW. ℂ 202/638-5900. High chairs. Reservations not accepted. All items $5–$18. AE, DC, DISC, MC, V. Daily 11:30am–12:30am. Metro: Metro Center.

COOKIES, CANDY & ICE CREAM

Bread & Chocolate BAKERY/COOKIES   Don't limit yourself to cookies here. Go ahead—sample the just-out-of-the-oven croissants and pastries, or enjoy a salad, sandwich, or hot entree in the dining area. Bread & Chocolate is open for breakfast, lunch, and dinner. Eat in or take out.

There are other branches at 666 Pennsylvania Ave. SE on Capitol Hill (ℂ **202/ 547-2875**) and 5542 Connecticut Ave. NW (ℂ **202/966-7413**).

2301 M St. NW. ℂ **202/833-8360**. High chairs, booster seats. Menu items $2.15 (croissant)–$6.95 (chicken salad sandwich). AE, DISC, MC, V. Mon–Thurs 7am–6pm; Fri–Sat 7am–7pm; Sun 8am–6pm. Metro: Foggy Bottom, and then 3-block walk.

Chocolate Chocolate CANDIES   Chocolate Chocolate: my two favorite words in the English language. The shop carries a sweet selection of imported and locally made candy. Among the goodies: local and imported hand-dipped chocolates.

1050 Connecticut Ave. NW. ℂ **202/466-2190**. Items 50¢ and up (1 piece of chocolate)–$52 (pound of imported Neuhaus chocolates). AE, DISC, MC, V. Mon–Fri 10am–6pm. Metro: Farragut North.l

AFTERNOON TEA

Renaissance Mayflower Hotel   The soothing setting of the elegant Café Promenade is the scene for full tea (finger sandwiches, scones, biscuits, pastries, tea) daily. The price is $24 per person, with no discounts for youngsters. Try this with mature preteens or older kids for a special grownup treat.

1127 Connecticut Ave. NW. ℂ **202/347-3000**. AE, DISC, DC, MC, V. Mon–Sat 3–5pm; Sun 3:30–5:30pm. Metro: Farragut North.

5 Foggy Bottom

Row houses fronted by brick sidewalks and postage-stamp-size gardens make Foggy Bottom one of the most attractive and distinctive neighborhoods in the city. If you have business at the State Department or are attending a Kennedy Center or Lisner Auditorium performance, you've come to the right place.

EXPENSIVE TO VERY EXPENSIVE

Kinkead's ✷✷✷ AMERICAN/SEAFOOD   This is a dining establishment for those who know and enjoy fine food. Kinkead's welcomes children, but frankly, it is not appropriate for kids under 8 or 10. And it is pricey. If you're ready to splurge, you're in for a treat. Chef Bob Kinkead has won several awards, among them the James Beard Award for best chef in the mid-Atlantic region. The kitchen makes everything from scratch, even the mayonnaise, and depends on fresh and locally grown produce. The menu is heavy on seafood and fresh fish. I can personally vouch for the pepita-crusted grilled salmon with shrimp, crab, and chiles. For dessert, try the crème brûlée. Downstairs, in the cafe/raw-bar area, you can graze on soups, salads, and appetizer-size portions (many with seafood in one form or another). The New England clam chowder and fried Ipswich clams rival any I've sampled in New England. A tinkling piano adds atmosphere during the evening. With young children, I think you'll feel more comfortable (and so will other diners) if you sit here or in the enclosed court-yard. The clientele is comprised largely of locals, pols (the White House is 5 blocks away), and business types. After 5:30pm, there's valet parking for $5.

2000 Pennsylvania Ave. NW (entrance on I St. between 20th and 21st sts.). ✆ **202/296-7700.** www.kinkead.com. High chairs, booster seats. Reservations recommended. Main courses $16–$24 lunch, $24–$30 dinner. AE, DC, DISC, MC, V. Lunch Sun–Fri 11:30am–2:30pm; dinner daily 5:30–10 pm. Metro: Foggy Bottom.

INEXPENSIVE

T.G.I. Friday's AMERICAN   The servers are enthusiastic and young. The decor is garage-sale chic, with Tiffany lamps, hanging plants, antiques, and photos everywhere. I'll go out on a limb and say Friday's serves the best food of the many chains I've tried. Those 12 and under can choose from standbys such as pizza, hamburgers, ribs, spaghetti, and hot dogs on the kids' menu (drinks included). The appetizers are among the tastiest items and enough for a small meal. Try the pot stickers (dumplings) or Jack Daniels Tower (ribs, shrimp, sesame chicken strips). Friday's salads and chicken dishes are consistently good. Save room for the Brownie Obsession (a brownie covered with fudge sauce, vanilla ice cream, caramel sauce, and pecans), and be sure to ask for extra spoons.

Try Friday's any day of the week, including the branches at 1201 Pennsylvania Ave. NW and in Maryland and Virginia.

2100 Pennsylvania Ave. NW (entrance on 21st St. at I St.). ✆ **202/872-4344.** www.tgifridays.com. High chairs, booster seats, kids' menu, crayons. Main courses $7–$20; kids' menu $3.85 (pizza), $6.60 (ribs). AE, DC, DISC, MC, V. Sun–Thurs 11am–midnight; Fri–Sat 11am–1am. Metro: Foggy Bottom.

ICE CREAM

Cone E' Island   Kids of all ages love the waffle cones, loaded with ice cream (Jack and Jill's and Hershey brands), hot fudge, and whipped cream. What's not to like? Loyal fans will tell you that it's well worth the cost and calories.

2000 Pennsylvania Ave. NW. ✆ **202/822-8460.** $2.75–$5 (3 scoops). No credit cards. Daily noon–midnight. Metro: Foggy Bottom, and then north on 23rd St; right at Pennsylvania Ave. 3 blocks.

6 Georgetown

Georgetown is one of Washington's most sophisticated neighborhoods and oft-visited tourist areas, so quite a few restaurants are there. I seriously doubt that you'll have trouble finding one that serves your favorite ethnic cuisine. The Metro does not run into Georgetown, but you can take the Georgetown Connection Shuttle (🕐 **202/ 625-RIDE;** www.georgetowndc.com/shuttle.php) from the following Metro stations: Foggy Bottom, Dupont Circle, and Rosslyn (Virginia). Each bus makes several stops. When you board, tell the driver where you're going, and ask for the stop closest to your destination. For more details, see chapter 3.

If you're out past 11pm, I suggest taking a taxi to your Metro station of choice or to your hotel. Call me a worrywart, but it's better to play it safe.

VERY EXPENSIVE

Morton's 🍴🍴🍴 AMERICAN/STEAKHOUSE   Come here for one of the best steaks in town—maybe in the country. While some Morton's fans prefer the veal chop, oversize lobsters, or prime rib, I'm a sucker for the steak and side orders of hash browns and fresh vegetables—enough for two or three servings. Soups, salads, and pastas are available for the less carnivorous and, along with daily specials, are a bit easier on the wallet than the main entrees. Well-mannered kids over 10 are welcome; no strollers are allowed in the restaurant, and two kids may want to share a portion. Be forewarned that lobster is market price (usually over $20 a pound). It may be cheaper to drive to Maine. Check out the permanent collection of Leroy Neiman paintings while you're here. Valet parking is $5.

There are a downtown Morton's at 1050 Connecticut Ave. NW (at L St.; 🕐 202/ 955-5997) and branches in Tysons Corner, Virginia (🕐 703/883-0800); Arlington/ Crystal City at 1631 Crystal Square Arcade (🕐 703/4181444); Reston, at 11956 Market St. (🕐 703/796-0128); and Baltimore at the Sheraton Hotel, 300 S. Charles St. (🕐 410/547-8255).

3251 Prospect St. NW, off Wisconsin Ave. 🕐 **202/342-6258.** www.mortons.com. Reservations recommended. Main courses $24 (chicken)–$42 (porterhouse). AE, DC, MC, V. Mon–Sat 5–11pm; Sun 5–10pm. Reston, Tysons, and Connecticut Ave. restaurants also serve lunch Mon–Fri, 11:30am–2:30pm. Closed most major holidays. Metro: Foggy Bottom; then 20-min. walk or Georgetown Metro Connection shuttle.

Sea Catch Restaurant and Raw Bar 🍴🍴 SEAFOOD   When you're in the mood to linger over exquisite seafood dishes, reserve a canalside table at this attractive stone-and-brick historic landmark, once a warehouse for goods transported on the C&O Canal. Pop some oysters or clams at the 40-foot marble raw bar to whet your appetite for seasonal specialties such as Dover sole, soft-shell crabs, crab cakes, or lobster. A handful of meat and chicken entrees are also listed. Key lime pie, "triple X" decadent chocolate cake (one of my fave desserts *anywhere*), or cheesecake is a fitting finale. Well-behaved kids over 6 are welcome. There's free parking (3 hrs.) at Constitution Parking Lot, 1054 31st St.

Canal Square, 1054 31st St. NW, at M St. 🕐 **202/337-8855.** www.seacatchrestaurant.com. High chairs. Reservations recommended. Main courses $7.25–$17 lunch (including sandwiches), $18–$32 dinner. AE, DC, DISC, MC, V. Mon–Sat noon–3pm and 5:30–10pm. Closed Sun. Metro: Foggy Bottom; then 20-minute walk or Georgetown Metro Connection shuttle.

MODERATE

Clyde's 🍴 AMERICAN   The first Clyde's opened in 1963, shortly after the wheel was invented. Now the Clyde's family has grown to seven. Have brunch in the sunny

Omelette Room, or head for the cheery Patio Room for a burger, sandwich, salad, or something more substantial from the menu that changes daily and features seasonal favorites. At dinner, you can opt for bar food (burgers and such).

All items on the kids' menu are $5 (burgers, chicken fingers, and pasta, plus a few other choices) and include juice, milk or a soft drink, and a sundae. Each child receives a Busy Bag of small toys, crayons, and puzzle and coloring pages. Stay out of the bar area if you bring the children—or if you want to retain your hearing and sanity.

The 4-to-7pm "Afternoon Delights" snack menu at the bar was inspired by the Starland Vocal Band's hit song of the same name (maybe before you were born). Look for the gold record in the Patio Room. After visiting the Washington Dolls' House and Toy Museum or shopping at Mazza Gallery, Lord & Taylor, or Saks, stop at the Clyde's at 70 Wisconsin Circle, Chevy Chase, Maryland, near the Friendship Heights Metro station (🕿 301/951-9600). You'll also find Clyde's at 707 7th St. NW, at H St. (🕿 202/349-3700), in Alexandria (🕿 703/820-8300), at the Mark Center in Reston (🕿 703/787-6601), and near Tyson's Corner in Vienna, Virginia (🕿 703/734-1901).

3236 M St. NW. 🕿 **202/333-9180.** www.clydes.com. High chairs, booster seats, kids' menu. Reservations strongly recommended. Bar food and lunch $7.95–$16; dinner main courses $14–$23. AE, DC, DISC, MC, V. Mon–Fri 11:30am–midnight; Sat 10am–1am; Sun 9am–midnight. Metro: Foggy Bottom; then 20-minute walk or Georgetown Metro Connection shuttle.

Filomena's Ristorante 🅕 ITALIAN   Even with a reservation, on Friday and Saturday nights you might have to wait, so eat early or go on a weeknight. At dinner, Filomena's is appropriate for well-behaved kids 8 and older. At lunch, the restaurant is fine for most kids; try the panini (sandwich on a large roll). My fave: sausage, peppers, onions, and provolone. Or design your own calzone. Filomena's is fun and serves delicious fresh house-made pasta. Choose one of the many delicious sauces. The Linguine Cardinale (lobster sauce) is *molto bene.* Or opt for one of the seafood, chicken, or veal entrees. Everybody's friendly, and it's not unusual to hear your neighbor's life story before the espresso arrives. Sandra Bullock, Harrison Ford, and Tom Cruise have dined here. Let's face it; they can afford to eat anywhere. Don't miss the home-baked desserts. The kitchen will prepare half orders of pasta for bambinos.

1063 Wisconsin Ave. NW, below M St. 🕿 **202/338-8800.** www.filomenadc.com. High chairs. Reservations recommended. Main courses $6.95–$14.95 lunch ($9.95 buffet lunch Fri–Sat); $8.95–$32.95 dinner; Sun brunch $13.95. AE, DC, DISC, MC, V. Daily 11:30am–11pm. Closed Jan 1, Thanksgiving, Dec 24 (evening), Dec 25. Metro: Foggy Bottom; then Georgetown Connection shuttle.

Garrett's AMERICAN   Congratulations to Garrett's on its 25th anniversary in 2005. Thomas Sim Lee, the second governor of Maryland, built this tavern in what is now a National Historic Trust building. Locals belly up to the three copper-topped bars and feed one of the hottest jukeboxes around. Bypass the noisy bar scene downstairs, decorated with vintage train memorabilia, for a table on the glass-enclosed second-floor terrace. Kids under 10 can order a hot dog and fries, chicken fingers, spaghetti, grilled cheese, or a PB&J sandwich, or parents can make kitchen requests for their kids. The "All Aboard Appetizers" include potato skins, buffalo wings, nachos, and quesadillas—enough for a meal for small appetites. Soups, chili, burgers, and sandwiches are tasty alternatives. Or select a pasta and choose a sauce (parmesan, white wine–garlic, marinara). Also check out the seafood chowder, other seafood dishes, and delectable salads. The kitchen is flexible in this neighborhood watering hole and has been a longtime favorite of local families.

Where to Dine in Georgetown

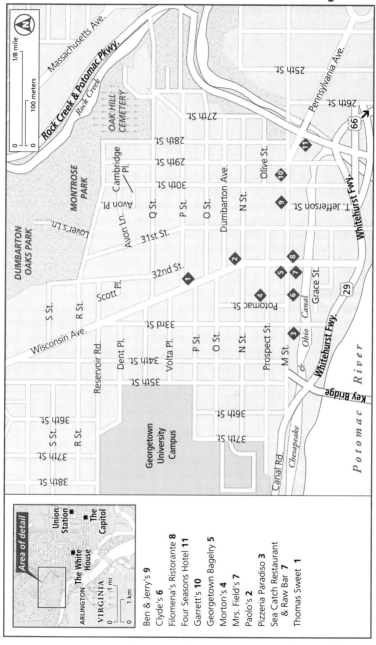

Ben & Jerry's **9**
Clyde's **6**
Filomena's Ristorante **8**
Four Seasons Hotel **11**
Garrett's **10**
Georgetown Bagelry **5**
Morton's **4**
Mrs. Field's **7**
Paolo's **2**
Pizzeria Paradiso **3**
Sea Catch Restaurant & Raw Bar **7**
Thomas Sweet **1**

3003 M St. NW. ✆ **202/333-1033.** www.garrettsdc.com. High chairs, booster seats, kids' menu, crayons. Reservations recommended for 10 or more. Appetizers $3.95–$6.95; sandwiches $5.75–$9.25; main courses $6.95–$11 lunch, $10.25–$22 dinner; kids' menu $4.25. AE, DC, DISC, MC, V. Mon–Thurs 11:30am–10pm; Fri 11:30am–11pm; Sat noon–11pm; Sun noon–10:30pm. Metro: Foggy Bottom; then 15-min. walk or Georgetown Metro Connection shuttle.

Paolo's ✮ ITALIAN   Paolo's is a looker, and its beauty is more than skin deep. Munch the breadsticks with tapenade while deciding on one of the California-style pastas, signature pizzas cooked in a wood-burning oven, chicken or fish dishes, or a salad—all well seasoned and attractively served. House specialties are the shrimp scampi and roasted chicken served with grilled veggies and roasted potatoes. Because Paolo's is a hot spot, especially on weekends, try it at off times. Among the items on the kids' menu are grilled chicken breast, pizza, and grilled cheese. The average price is $3.95 and includes a beverage.

There are Paolo's branches in Reston, Virginia (✆ 703/318-8920); Baltimore's Inner Harbor (✆ 410/539-7060); and farther afield in Towson, Maryland (✆ 410/ 321-7000)—check them out if you are in the neighborhood.

1303 Wisconsin Ave. NW, between N and Dumbarton sts. ✆ **202/333-7353.** www.paolosristorante.com. High chairs, booster seats, kids' menu, crayons and paper. Reservations recommended. Main courses $12–$24. AE, DC, DISC, MC, V. Mon–Thurs 11:30am–11:30pm, late-night pizza menu until 12:30am; Fri–Sat 11:30am–12:30am, pizza menu until 1:30. Sun brunch 11am–3pm; dinner until 11:30pm. Metro: Foggy Bottom; then 15-min. walk or Georgetown Metro Connection shuttle.

INEXPENSIVE

Georgetown Bagelry ✮✮ AMERICAN   Now here's an oxymoron—a truly inexpensive Georgetown restaurant! A few years back, the bagels here won a blind tasting of six bagel shops by unbiased *Washington Post* staff. Near the busy crossroads of Wisconsin Avenue and M Street, Georgetown Bagelry offers counter seating for about 20 bagel noshers. Try my favorite, an ET (everything) bagel with Nova Scotia salmon and cream cheese ($6.55). Chase it with freshly squeezed OJ, and finish with a dish of fresh fruit salad. In nice weather, get it and go to the canal or riverfront. How many places can you buy lunch and walk away with change from $10? A second location, at 5227 River Rd., Bethesda, Maryland (✆ **301/657-4442**), is open Monday through Friday 6am to 5pm, Saturday 7am to 4pm, and Sunday 7am to 3pm.

3245 M St. NW, off Wisconsin Ave. ✆ **202/965-1011.** Bagels plain 80¢ each, or $1.95–$6.55 dressed. MC, V. Mon–Fri 6am–8pm; Sat 7am–8pm; Sun 7am–6pm. Metro: Foggy Bottom; then Georgetown Connection shuttle.

COOKIES, CANDY & ICE CREAM

In addition to the places listed below, there's a Ben & Jerry's at 2135 M St. NW (✆ **202/965-2222**) and a Häagen-Dazs. See the full review on p. 90.

Mrs. Field's   These soft, chewy, chip-laden cookies are nearly as good as homemade, and the muffins are also excellent. They make the perfect bribe when you need one (with kids, that's about every 30 sec.).

Shops at Georgetown Park, Wisconsin Ave. and M St. NW. (3222 M St. NW). ✆ **202/337-5117.** $1.50 per cookie. Mon–Sat 10am–9pm, Sun noon–6pm. MC, V. Metro: Foggy Bottom; then 15-min. walk or Georgetown Metro Connection shuttle.

Thomas Sweet ✮ *(Finds)*   This old-style ice cream parlor is a reincarnation of the "malt shoppe" in the Archie comics. The ice-cream-making operation (135 flavors!) is located in the store, where it handles the large demand from area restaurants and some of the Smithsonian museums. The best seller is the "Blend In," a customized mix of up to three toppings (fresh fruit, cookies, and candies) with any flavor of ice cream or yogurt. The bittersweet chocolate is said to be the best in the world. Open for breakfast (eggs with ham or bacon, croissants, and muffins served all day) and ice cream. Period. Get your sugar rush while enjoying the passing parade of students, tourists, Brooks Brothers suits, and blue-haired ladies.

3214 P St. NW (at Wisconsin Ave.). © **202/337-0616**. Single scoop $2.15; banana split $4.95. No credit cards. Sun–Thurs 8am–11pm; Fri–Sat 8am–midnight; Sun 9am–midnight. Metro: Foggy Bottom; then 15-min. walk or Georgetown Metro Connection shuttle.

AFTERNOON TEA

Four Seasons *ﾒﾒ*   Enjoy tea, served daily, in the beautiful Garden Terrace overlooking Rock Creek Park. A children's tea menu features mini peanut butter-and-jelly sandwiches, milkshakes, brownies, and chocolate chip cookies. Full tea costs $29 per adult, $18 for kids 5–12. For me (at these prices), tea is a special-occasion splurge.

2800 M St. NW. © **202/342-0444**. Reservations required. AE, DC, DISC, MC, V. Daily 2–5pm. Metro: Foggy Bottom; then 15-min. walk.

7 Dupont Circle

Dupont Circle and Adams–Morgan lend themselves to people-watching, shopping, and dining—often at the same time. The restaurants reflect both neighborhoods' unzipped, diverse natures. Besides fine-dining establishments, you'll find bistro, diner, and pub fare, sandwiches, pizza, wraps, and ice cream. There's also plenty of eye candy. What kid can turn down an opportunity to ogle pink hair and multipierced body parts? Dupont Circle (the park in the center of the rotary) is a good place to let the little darlings run around and create havoc (under supervision) and then fall into one of the many family-friendly restaurants within a few blocks of the park (and Metro stop).

In addition to the restaurants listed below, there's a Ben & Jerry's branch near Dupont Circle, at 1350 Connecticut Ave. (rear of building facing 19th St. at N). See p. 90 for a full review.

MODERATE

Otello *ﾒ* ITALIAN   Otello is a friendly, family-operated neighborhood trattoria, more typical of those in New York than in D.C. The sauces taste freshly made and pack the right amount of punch. Seafood and veal are as fine as you'll find south of Baltimore's Little Italy. Have your favorite pasta, served with a variety of sauces. The osso bucco (veal shanks in a well-seasoned sauce) is a house specialty. This restaurant is not suitable for bambinos under 8, although half portions are available for kids at half price.

1329 Connecticut Ave. NW. © **202/429-0209**. www.otellodc.com. Booster seats. Reservations recommended. Main courses $9.50–$12 lunch, $12–$16 dinner. AE, DISC, DC, MC, V. Mon–Fri noon–2:30pm; Mon–Sat 5:30–10:30pm. Metro: Dupont Circle.

Pan Asian Noodles & Grill *ﾒ Value* EAST ASIAN   Because it's very good and very reasonable, Pan Asian is also very crowded, especially at lunchtime. Go early or late for a quick, inexpensive meal of soup (the wonton is especially worthwhile), noodles, and grilled dishes derived from various Asian cuisines, real and imagined. The Pad Thai is a winner and enough for two little ones to share. Create your own soup from the many broths, noodles, and meats on the menu. Fancy it's not—you order at the counter and carry your food to a table—but the service is as crisp as a fried noodle.

2020 P St. NW. © **202/872-8889**. High chairs, booster seats. Main courses $5.25–$7.95 lunch, $7.75–$17 dinner. AE, DISC, MC, V. Mon–Sat 11:30am–2:30pm; Sun–Thurs 5–10pm; Fri–Sat 5–11pm. Metro: Dupont Circle.

INEXPENSIVE TO MODERATE

Luna Grill & Diner ℛ AMERICAN   Slide into a booth at the hip, retro Luna for delicious diner food with a funky-chic 'tude. Sip fresh-squeezed OJ with your bagel, cream cheese, and lox; granola and fruit; or steak and eggs at breakfast. (There's plenty of traditional breakfast fare, too.) Lunch and dinner entrees include salads, pasta, burgers, sides of mashed potatoes and gravy, nachos, and chicken wings. We're talking major comfort food: tasty, warm, and satisfying. The kitchen fills more orders for its roast turkey and meatloaf than anything else. Half-price pasta nights are Sunday and Monday. Although there's no kids' menu, burgers, salads, sandwiches, and pastas are under $10. Luna has a second location at 4024 28th St., Arlington, Virginia (℃ **703/ 379-7173**).

1301 Connecticut Ave. NW (at N St.). ℃ **202/835-2280**. www.lunagrillanddiner.com. High chairs, booster seats. Reservations not accepted. Breakfast $2.95–$7.95; lunch $5.95–$8.95; dinner main course $9.95–$15; Sat–Sun brunch $7.95–$9.95. AE, DC, DISC, MC, V. Mon–Thurs 8am–11pm; Fri–Sat, 8am–1am; Sun 8am–10pm. Metro: Dupont Circle (1 block) or Farragut North (3 blocks).

INEXPENSIVE

Afterwords Café at Kramerbooks AMERICAN   After browsing at Kramerbooks, stop for a meal or snack at Afterwords, where the atmosphere is as bohemian as Washington allows itself to get, and you can devour a book or newspaper until your food comes. The menu changes seasonally, but the OJ is always freshly squeezed, and it seems to me that the food has improved over the years. Try a delicious omelet served with potatoes and fresh fruit garnish, muffins, coffee or tea, and complimentary Bloody Mary or Strawberry Mimosa at brunch Saturday (mimosa on Sunday). I can't think of a more civilized way to decompress on the weekend. At other times, you'll find everything from salads, soup, sandwiches, pasta (always a safe bet), and vegetarian dishes to calorie-packed desserts such as sour cream blackout cake and banana splits. For $15, you can order any 3 items to share off an extensive "Sharezies" (lite fare) menu. And there is a Kids at the Café menu ("for folks under 4 feet") with favorites such as mac and cheese, grilled cheese, spaghetti, and hamburgers. If they're not up for a full breakfast, they can get a bagel and cream cheese ($1.50) or yogurt ($2). Wednesday through Saturday evenings, there's live music—folk, jazz, or blues. Grownups could indulge in 1 of the 10 martinis or a large pitcher of margaritas ($18) while the children enjoy ice-cream treats.

1517 Connecticut Ave. NW., between Dupont Circle and Q St. ℃ **202/387-1462**. High chairs, kids' menu. Reservations accepted for 6 or more. Appetizers $3.95–$7.75; lunch and dinner main courses $7–$16; Sat–Sun breakfast/brunch $8.50–$17; kid's menu $6–$6.75. AE, MC, V. Mon–Thurs 7:30am–1am; continuously Fri 8am–Sun 1am. Metro: Dupont Circle.

Brickskeller ℛ AMERICAN   At the corner of 22nd and P streets, the Brick serves pub fare in a setting reminiscent of Cheers. Dartboards on weekends and video games accessorize the place. When I visit the Brick, it's like going home. During my college days in D.C., I spent some time here when my parents thought I was at the library. More than 1,000 kinds of beer (making this the *Guinness Book of World Records* holder for most different kinds of beer commercially available—who says D.C. is dull?) and an oldies-filled jukebox will nurture your nostalgia trip. Your underagers can play electronic games and munch on chicken wings, burgers, and other light fare. Vegetarians won't starve. Try the tempura vegetables, onion rings (made in-house), french fries, and salads. The Brickskeller has been pleasing patrons for more than 45 years. Add your name to the list with a visit.

Where to Dine in Dupont Circle & Adams–Morgan

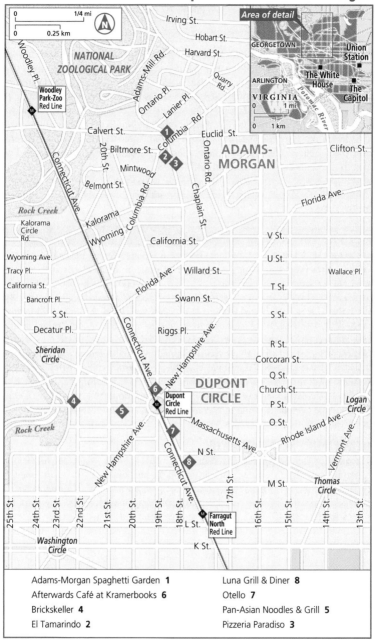

Adams-Morgan Spaghetti Garden **1**
Afterwards Café at Kramerbooks **6**
Brickskeller **4**
El Tamarindo **2**

Luna Grill & Diner **8**
Otello **7**
Pan-Asian Noodles & Grill **5**
Pizzeria Paradiso **3**

1523 22nd St. NW. © 202/293-1885. www.thebrickskeller.com. High chairs, booster seats. Reservations accepted for 8 or more. Most items $3.95–$12. AE, DC, DISC, MC, V. Mon–Thurs 11:30–2am; Fri 11:30–3am; Sat 6pm–3am; Sun 6pm–2am. Kitchen closes 1 hour before restaurant closes. Metro: Dupont Circle.

Pizzeria Paradiso ⊛ ITALIAN/PIZZA   Pizzeria Paradiso serves authentic, wood-oven–baked classic pizza. Stick to the basic Margherita or Quattro Formaggi (four cheeses) if your arteries can handle it. On pizza this good, you don't need extra toppings. Stop here for a quick bite when you're browsing Dupont Circle or visiting the Phillips Collection. There's seating for 40 and a couple of high chairs but no booster seats. Hey, stand if you have to. The pizza is worth it. Not in the mood? Try a calzone or sandwich on really good bread. There's a second, equally good location in Georgetown at 3282 M St. NW (a stone's throw from the Shops at Georgetown Park and two doors from Dean and Deluca; © **202/337-1245**).

2029 P St. NW. © 202/223-1245. High chairs. Reservations not accepted. $7.95 (8″ plain)–$16 (12″ with seafood). DC, DISC, MC, V. Mon–Thurs 11:30am–11pm; Fri–Sat 11:30am–midnight; Sun noon–10pm. Metro: Dupont Circle; then walk 1½ blocks.

8 Adams–Morgan

Like most kids, I love Adams–Morgan because it is colorful, vibrant, and edgy. I must warn you, however, that parking is next to impossible in the area, especially on weekends. The good news: You can take the Metro to the Woodley Park–Zoo/Adams–Morgan station and walk 10 minutes across the Calvert Street Bridge (at Connecticut Ave. and Calvert St.) to 18th and Columbia Rd. NW, or board the Adams Morgan–U Street Link, a shuttle that runs from the station to 18th Street and Columbia Road weekday and Sunday evenings and all day Saturday. The Link runs every 10 to 15 minutes Monday to Thursday and Sunday 6pm to midnight; Friday 6pm to 1am; Saturday 10am to 1am. Get a transfer at your Metro *departure* station before you board the train. Give it to the shuttle driver along with 25¢. If you forget the transfer, the cost is $1.10. If you miss the last shuttle (with kids, I doubt it!), take a taxi. Do not walk. See the "Where to Dine in Dupont Circle & Adams–Morgan," map (p. 103) for locations of restaurants in this section.

INEXPENSIVE TO MODERATE

Adams–Morgan Spaghetti Garden ⊛ ITALIAN   This might not be *Gourmet* magazine fare, but most of the hearty, large-portioned pasta dishes—lasagna, spaghetti, ravioli, and the like—are priced between $8 and $12. Chicken, veal, and shrimp are served with a side of spaghetti marinara for under $13. The pizza puttanesca is adorned with black olives, tomato, capers, and plenty of garlic. *Bellissima!* This could be the last place in the city where you can get a glass of wine for $3. The second-floor rooftop affords a view of one of the city's more interesting neighborhoods, although it's not open full time. Try the outside deck on the lower level for open-air dining. The restaurant has a genuine family-friendly attitude and even modifies menu items for kids and prices accordingly.

2317 18th St. NW, near Columbia Rd. © 202/265-6665. High chairs, booster seats, children's portions. Reservations for groups of 8 or more. Appetizers $2–$5.95; pasta main courses $6.45–$9.95; meat main courses $8.95–$14; children's spaghetti portions $3.95. AE, DISC, DC, MC, V. Tues–Sun noon–midnight. Closed Thanksgiving, Dec 25, Jan 1. Metro: Woodley Park–Zoo/Adams–Morgan or Dupont Circle.

El Tamarindo ⊛ SALVADORAN/MEXICAN   This neighborhood spot serves authentic Mexican and Salvadoran cooking that is hearty, authentic, and reasonable.

You can't go wrong with the chicken, beef, or shrimp fajitas. Kids can order a la carte items such as burritos, pupusas, tamales, tostadas, chimichangas, and tacos. I've never been here when there were not kids in abundance, and the prices are ridiculously low. The congenial atmosphere is gratis. The restaurant is open until the wee small hours—perfect for quelling your teenagers' late-night munchies. If you're here late, take a cab back to your hotel. If you're already in Adams–Morgan, walk south on 18th St. (from Columbia Rd.) 4 blocks to Florida Ave.

1785 Florida Ave. NW (near intersection of 18th and U sts.). *C* 202/328-3660. High chairs, booster seats. Reservations for 20 or more. Appetizers $4.95–$7.95; main courses $5.95 (quesadilla)–$13 (steak and shrimp fajitas). AE, DISC, MC, V. Mon–Thurs 11am–3am; Fri–Sat 10am–5am, Sun 10am–3am. Metro: Woodley Park–Zoo/Adams–Morgan and then Metrobus no. 98 to 18th St. and Columbia Rd. and walk south 4 blocks to Florida Ave.; or U Street–Cardozo and then walk west on U St. 4 blocks.

9 Upper Northwest

Oodles of D.C. kids call this largely residential neighborhood home, so it's no surprise that the local restaurants cater to them (and the folks who pay for their french fries and braces). You'll find plenty of family-pleasing fare, especially in the burger, over-stuffed-sandwich, and dessert categories.

MODERATE

Cactus Cantina *⟡* TEX-MEX   This cozy cantina, decorated with twinkling lights and other tacky touches, is on busy Wisconsin Avenue (1 block from the National Cathedral and a short drive from the National Zoo). Except for the traffic hum, you could be on a dusty plain south of the border. Tex-Mex lovers drool at the mention of mesquite-grilled fajitas. The generous combination platters ($9.50) appease large appetites. Many applaud the Camarones Brochette, broiled cheese- and jalapeño-stuffed shrimp wrapped in bacon. The kids' menu offers five items (taco, quesadilla, and so on) served with rice and beans for $3.95. Sunday brunch features half a dozen entrees in the $6.95 to $11 range, such as huevos rancheros. Toast Cactus Cantina's ever-popular tortilla chips with a margarita or a glass of sangria. Show up before 6pm for dinner, especially on weekends. Try to sit near the glassed-in tortilla-making machine. Kids like to watch as the dough is fed into the top and then cooked while being pulled through the machine. Imagine a giant tortilla toaster.

3300 Wisconsin Ave. NW. *C* 202/686-7222. www.cactuscantina.com. High chairs, booster seats, kids' menu, crayons. Reservations for lunch for 10 or more Mon–Thurs, 15 or more lunch Fri–Sun. Appetizers $4.95–$9.95; main courses $7.95–$17; kids' menu, $3.95. AE, DC, DISC, MC, V. Mon–Thurs 11am–11pm; Fri–Sat 11am–midnight; Sun 10:30am–11pm (brunch 10:30am–3pm). Metro: Tenleytown; then take any no. 30 bus south (15 min. walk from Metro).

Jandara THAI   Appetizers such as barbecued chicken in peanut sauce, spring rolls, and coconut chicken soup will keep you busy while deciding among the many fish, chicken, and pork main dishes. If your innards are heat-sensitive, ask your server to recommend some of the milder dishes. For kids, consider a satay, spring rolls, or dumplings. And if you don't mind bus fumes, dine at a sidewalk table in nice weather. Jandara is convenient to the National Zoo.

2606 Connecticut Ave. NW, at Calvert St. *C* 202/387-8876. High chairs, booster seats. Appetizers $3.95–$6.95; main courses $6.95–$25. AE, DC, DISC, MC, V. Mon–Thurs 11am–10:30pm; Fri–Sat 11am–11pm; Sun 11am–10:30pm. Metro: Woodley Park–Zoo/Adams–Morgan.

INEXPENSIVE TO MODERATE

Chadwicks AMERICAN   Going to Chadwicks is like visiting an old friend. Children are greeted with crayons and their own menus to color. The service is friendly and prompt, and the cocktails are generous. The hamburgers and sandwiches are ample and tasty, and Sunday brunch is a bargain, with most entrees in the $8 to $11 range. A shaded outdoor patio is pleasant and somewhat sheltered from automobile fumes.

I've been receiving good reports on the seafood and pasta, as well as the $6.95 super deal lunch: a burger with fries, onion rings, coleslaw or potato salad. It includes a soft drink, coffee or tea, and is available Monday through Saturday. If you're visiting Georgetown or Alexandria, Virginia, Chadwicks is there, too, at 3205 K St. NW (✆ 202/333-2565) and 203 S. Strand St., Old Town (✆ 703/836-4422), respectively.

5247 Wisconsin Ave. NW, at Jenifer St. ✆ 202/362-8040. High chairs, booster seats, kids' menu, crayons. Main courses $6.50–$12 lunch, $6.50–$19 dinner; kids' menu items $2.95. AE, DISC, MC, V. Mon–Sat 11:30am–midnight; Sun 10am–midnight. Metro: Friendship Heights.

The Cheesecake Factory ✇ AMERICAN   The California-based Cheesecake Factory blew in like a Santa Ana wind when the restaurant opened in 1991, the first location outside California. Judging by the lines, this is no ill wind. The first-class fries are crunchy and greaseless, and the salads and chicken dishes are tasty and oversized. In fact, I rarely leave without a doggy bag. The extensive menu is worthy of framing. Many complain about the noise and the wait. I'll keep saying it until I'm blue in the face: Go early, especially with easily tired young 'uns. Don't forget the real reason you came: to try at least 1 of the 35 kinds of cheesecake. Be sure to save some room. There's no kids' menu, but the lengthy appetizer menu offers kid-pleasing taquitos, mini-crab cakes, pot stickers (dumplings), and Roadside Sliders (minihamburgers on Lilliputian buns). Outside D.C., try the Cheesecake Factory at White Flint Mall in North Bethesda, Maryland (✆ 301/770-0999), at Tyson's Galleria Northern Virginia (✆ 703/506-9311), or at the Inner Harbor in Baltimore (✆ 410/234-3990).

5345 Wisconsin Ave. NW (Chevy Chase Pavilion). ✆ 202/364-0500. cheesecakefactory.com. High chairs, booster seats. Appetizers $5.95–9.50; Main courses $7.95–$25. Desserts $3.95–$6.95. AE, DISC, MC, V. Mon–Thurs 11:30am–11:30pm; Fri–Sat 11:30am–12:30am; Sun 10am–11pm. Metro: Friendship Heights.

ICE CREAM & CANDY

Baskin-Robbins   They must be doing something right, because this brand sells more ice cream than any other retail dealer in the country. The franchises are institutional, but like an old friend, they're there when you need them.

2604 Connecticut Ave. ✆ 202/483-4820. www.baskinrobbins.com. Single dip $1.95; double dip $3.35. AE, MC, V. Daily 11am–10pm. Metro: Woodley Park–Zoo/Adams–Morgan; then a 5-min. walk.

Cold Stone Creamery   My family of experts (related by blood and a love of the cool, sweet stuff) have this to say about the national chain's first D.C. location: The portions are generous, and the ice cream is creamy. The draw here is the mix-in toppings from a selection that includes everything from fresh brownies to Heath Bars. The chocolate is not as flavorful as some other brands we revere but definitely above average. Try the "Germanchokolatecake" (chocolate ice cream with mix-ins of coconut, brownies, caramel. and pecans). More locations are sprouting in the suburbs.

3508 Connecticut Ave. NW (3 blocks north of zoo). ✆ 202/237-2605. www.coldstonecreamery.com. Single scoop with 1 mix-in (candy, cake, or nuts) $3.20; banana split $5. Daily 11am—11pm. Metro: Woodley Park–Zoo/Adams–Morgan; then a 7-min. walk.

Kron Chocolatier ✿✿   In a recurring dream, I fall into a vat of Kron's melted bittersweet chocolate and live happily ever after. Try the Budapest cream truffles and chocolate-dipped strawberries, and you, too, will have sweet dreams. Kids will find their own favorites. Underground parking is free with ticket validation.

Mazza Galleria, 5300 Wisconsin Ave. NW. © 202/966-4946. www.krondc.com. Most chocolates $17 per ½ pound; truffles $25 per ½ pound, almond toffee butter crunch $17 per pound. AE, MC, V. Mon–Fri 10am–8pm; Sat 10am–6pm; Sun noon–5pm; extended hours around Christmas. Metro: Friendship Heights.

AFTERNOON TEA
Washington National Cathedral ✿✿ (Finds)   What a lovely setting in which to enjoy tea. The Tour and Tea is every Tuesday and Wednesday, with the tour departing from the nave at 1:30, followed by the tea at 3pm. Tea can be taken only in conjunction with the tour. The cost is $22, regardless of age. I recommend this for patient, well-behaved kids 8 and older. Finger sandwiches, scones, and a variety of sweets are served on linen napery in the Cathedral tower gallery, with its wonderful view of the city. The teas are immensely popular and must be booked well in advance (often months). There is, however, a wait list, and last-minute cancellations sometimes occur.

Massachusetts and Wisconsin aves. NW. © 202/537-8993. www.cathedral.org/cathedral. MC, V. Tues–Wed at 1:30pm. Metro: Dupont Circle; then any northbound Mass. Ave. bus to Wisconsin Ave.

10 Suburban Maryland

Years ago, if you lived in the suburbs and wanted a decent meal, you had to venture downtown. Now there are so many restaurants ringing the Beltway that many diners prefer to stay put—as well they should. In addition to the places listed below, there's a Fuddruckers in Rockville at 1592A Rockville Pike (© **301/468-3535**); see the full review on p. 93.

BETHESDA
MODERATE
Athenian Plaka ✿ GREEK   Consistency is what you'll get at this suburban restaurant. The portions are generous and well prepared; the servers are pleasant; and the restaurant has old-world charm. Daily specials at lunch and dinner are a good value. Try any of the fork-tender roasted lamb dishes (or kebabs), the moussaka, or grilled rockfish (in season). If your kids are not up to a full meal, they can order a bowl of egg-lemon soup or an appetizer portion of stuffed grape leaves, hot or cold. If they make faces, tell them that *dolmas* are Greek egg rolls. The *melitzanosalata* (I can't pronounce it either; ask for the eggplant dip with garlic and lemon juice) and a large Greek salad are a satisfying meal. The rice pudding is as good as my grandmother's. Opt for a table on the patio in good weather. There's live music Friday evenings.

7833 Woodmont Ave., Bethesda, MD. © 301/986-1337. High chairs, booster seats. Main courses $6.95 –$11 lunch, $12.95–$22 dinner. AE, DC, DISC, MC, V. Sun–Thurs 10am–10pm; Fri 11am–11pm; Sat noon–midnight; Sun noon–11pm (brunch 11am–3pm). Metro: Bethesda.

Foong Lin ✿ CHINESE   This neighborhood restaurant has a friendly waitstaff that is especially considerate to young families. Foong Lin consistently turns out delicious Cantonese, Hunan, and Szechuan favorites. It may take you a while to digest the lengthy menu of appetizers, soups, specialties, and a la carte beef, pork, chicken, seafood, and noodles in scores of permutations. Don't overlook the seasonal specialties ($11–$18). There are scores of items to tempt the kids. How about some tasty finger foods such as egg rolls and spring rolls, dumplings, chicken wings, or shrimp toast? If you're staying in Bethesda or Chevy Chase, delivery service is available within 3 miles from 4:30 to 10pm with a $15 minimum order. The crispy whole fish is exceptional. See if you can talk the kids into trying it.

7710 Norfolk Ave., Bethesda, MD. ✆ **301/656-3427**. High chairs, booster seats. Main courses $5.95–$8.95 lunch, $7.95–$18 dinner. AE, MC, V. Mon–Thurs 11am–10:30pm; Fri–Sat 11am–11pm; Sun noon–10pm. Closed Thanksgiving. Metro: Bethesda.

INEXPENSIVE TO MODERATE

Hamburger Hamlet 🦆 AMERICAN   Despite the sometimes-inconsistent service and the lines, Hamburger Hamlet has been attracting families since 1979. Children can amuse themselves with the restaurant-supplied crayons to draw on the white paper tablecloths until the grub comes. Portions are large, especially the side dishes. I recommend sticking with the burgers (15 "styles," including turkey and vegetarian), sandwiches, fish tacos, and fajitas. And then there's the Ultimate Hot Fudge Cake (fudgey layer cake with vanilla ice cream, hot fudge, and whipped cream). Be prepared to wait 15 minutes or longer at prime time. In Gaithersburg, there's a branch in the Rio Center at 9811 Washington Blvd. (✆ **301/417-0773**). In Virginia, you'll find one at Crystal City Underground (✆ **703/413-0422**) and one in Old Town Alexandria at 109 S. St. Asaph St. (✆ **703/683-1776**).

10400 Old Georgetown Rd., Bethesda, MD. ✆ **301/897-5350**. www.hamburgerhamlet.com. High chairs, booster seats, kids' menu, crayons. Reservations accepted for 8 or more. Main courses $6.50–$17 (most under $11); kids' menu items $4.50 (includes drink). AE, DC, DISC, MC, V. Mon–Thurs 11am–10:30pm; Fri–Sat 11am–11pm; Sun 11am–10pm (brunch until 2pm).

Houston's 🦆🦆 AMERICAN/RIBS/BARBECUE   Absolutely and positively, Houston's serves the best hickory-grilled hamburgers in the D.C. area (for $10). Many of us mourn the closing of the Georgetown location, but the Metro stops in Bethesda, just 2 blocks from Houston's. When the line is long (at peak lunch and dinner hours), put your name on the list and take a walk—to Outer Mongolia. Or solve the problem by eating early or late. The barbecued ribs ($21 for a full rack with fries and coleslaw) and salads are outstanding; wash them down with a shake or a frosty mug of beer. As of late 2005, there was not a printed kids' menu. Just ask for a kid's grilled cheese, hamburger, cheeseburger, or chicken tenders. A beverage and scoop of ice cream are included—all for $5. This clubby-looking restaurant is part of a chain extending from Atlanta to Phoenix to Chicago. Its popularity is easily understood: Houston's ambience is welcoming to all ages, and the food is fresh and first quality. Also in Rockville, at 12256 Rockville Pike (✆ **301/468-3535**).

7715 Woodmont Ave., Bethesda, MD. ✆ **301/656-9755**. High chairs, booster seats. Reservations not accepted. Main courses $10–$25 (most under $14). AE, MC, V. Tues–Sat 11am–11pm; Sun–Mon 11am–10pm.

Il Forno 🦆 PIZZA   You can't get pizzas like these delivered. No cardboard residue here! They're baked in huge wood-burning ovens so that the thin New York–style crust has just the right amount of bite and doesn't collapse under the weight of the very fresh toppings. The garlic bread and calzones are worth trying, too. Space is tight indoors, so opt for a seat outside in favorable weather.

Il Forno is also at 8941 N. Westland Dr., Gaithersburg (✆ **301/977-5900**).

4926 Cordell Ave., Bethesda, MD. ✆ **301/652-7757**. High chairs, booster seats. Reservations suggested. Pies $11.25 (large plain)–$17 (large with everything). AE, DISC, MC, V. Tues–Fri 11:30am–3pm and 5–10pm. Sat–Sun 5–11pm. Metro: Bethesda.

Louisiana Express ✿ CAJUN/CREOLE   Cajun, casual, and cheap, Louisiana Express excels at New Orleans–style po' boys (aka subs, hoagies, and grinders), fish fritters, and gumbos. Wash it down with a Dixie or Blackened Voodoo beer. For the kiddies' more sensitive palates, there are unspicy chicken, french fries, calas (fried rice balls), and crab balls (small crab cakes). Try one of the breakfast sandwiches or omelets served from 7:30am to 2:30pm daily. The a la carte Saturday and Sunday brunch (9am–2:30pm) features pastries and pancakes, along with traditional N'awlins egg dishes like Eggs Sardou (poached eggs with spinach and artichoke hearts on an English muffin with hollandaise sauce) or *pain perdu* (French toast). You can stuff your craws with some mighty good eats for less than $10 in most instances. There's a garage a block away.

4921 Bethesda Ave., Bethesda, MD. ✆ 301/652-6945. www.louisianaexpresscompany.com. High chairs, booster seats. Reservations not accepted. Sandwiches and main dishes $4.50–$14; breakfast and Sat–Sun brunch $5–$10. MC, V. Mon–Thurs 7:30am–10pm; Fri–Sat 7:30am–11pm; Sun 9am–9pm (brunch until 2:30pm). Metro: Bethesda.

Philadelphia Mike's AMERICAN   You'll have to order at the counter and share an oilcloth-covered table with strangers—but that's a small price to pay for the best cheese steak sandwich (on warm, baked-on-the premises bread) this side of South Philly. Most subs are $5 to $6 and come small, medium, and large (5-inch, 7-inch, and 12-inch). Try one of the variations of a cheese steak (grilled paper-thin steak slices and melted cheese with lettuce, tomato, fried onions, hot peppers, and oil dressing), but please don't taint it with mayonnaise. In Philadelphia, that's a capital offense. For kids, there's also burgers, hot dogs, or grilled cheese sandwiches. There's free parking in the rear of the building. Enter on Woodmont Avenue.

7732 Wisconsin Ave., Bethesda, MD. ✆ 301/656-0103. www.philadelphiamikes.com. High chairs, booster seats. All items under $8. AE, MC, V. Mon–Fri 8am–9pm; Sat 9am–9pm; Sun 9am–4pm. Metro: Bethesda.

Rio Grande Café MEXICAN   Build a better burrito, and the world will beat a path to your door. Order a margarita, and dig into the warm tortilla chips and chunky salsa while the kids watch the Rube Goldberg contraption that produces around 400 tortillas an hour. The Fajitas Al Carbon are numero uno for big appetites. On the kids' menu for *los niños* are nachos, tacos, and enchiladas. All items are $5.25 (drink extra). Or maybe they would prefer an appetizer or an a la carte taco or burrito. Finish with honey-drenched sopapillas. *¡Que bueno!* Go at off times, especially on weekends or holidays.

There are branches in Gaithersburg, Maryland (✆ 240/632-2150); Ballston, Virginia (✆ 703/528-3131); and Reston, Virginia (✆ 703/904-0703).

4870 Bethesda Ave., Bethesda, MD. ✆ 301/656-2981. High chairs, booster seats, kids' menu. Reservations not accepted. Appetizers $4.50–$13 (fajitas); most main courses $8.95–$19; Sun brunch $8.50–$9.95. AE, DC, DISC, MC, V. Mon–Thurs, Sun 11am–10:30pm; Fri–Sat 11am–11:30pm. Metro: Bethesda.

Tastee Diner ✿ *Value* AMERICAN   'Round the clock, 7 days a week, 364 days a year (closed Christmas) are the hours of the Tastee Diner. None of the new neon-and-chrome-plated establishments calling themselves diners holds a candle to the Tastee, which served its first creamed chipped beef on toast in 1942. Come here for the hearty breakfasts, homemade chili and soups, sandwiches, and desserts. At breakfast, the Kiddie Special consists of one large pancake or one egg with a strip of bacon for $2.95. I'm in love with the Diner Home Fries (with onion, bacon, and melted cheese). I didn't say it was healthful, but it is delish. The kids' menu, for kids 12 and under, is served all day and includes the one egg, one pancake, strip of bacon combo; mini pancakes (plain, blueberry, chocolate chip); hamburger; grilled cheese; spaghetti; and chicken tenders. The tired leatherette booths, individual jukeboxes, colorful regulars, chatty short-order cooks, and beehived waitresses spell *Happy Days*.

Elsewhere in Maryland, there are Tastee Diners in Silver Spring, at 8601 Cameron St. (✆ **301/589-8171**), and in Laurel at 118 Washington Blvd. (U.S. 1; ✆ **301/953-7567**).

7731 Woodmont Ave., Bethesda, MD. ✆ **301/652-3970**. www.tasteediner.com. High chairs, booster seats, kids' menu, crayons. Reservations not accepted. Breakfast $2.95–$8.25; lunch $2.95–$6.95; dinner $3.95–$15. MC, V. Daily 24 hours. Closed Dec 25. Metro: Bethesda.

ICE CREAM

There's a branch of **Ben & Jerry's** in Bethesda at 4901-B Fairmont Avenue (✆ **301/652-2233**). See the full review on p. 90.

Gifford's 🍦   The family-owned Gifford's chain had a corner on the market before dying out in the 1970s and 1980s. Many of us went into prolonged mourning. Then along came Dolly Hunt. Bearing the original recipes, she reopened Gifford's on July 4, 1989. Hello, Dolly! And thank you. The Swiss chocolate and hot fudge sundaes are worth the trip (a short walk from the Bethesda Metro station) from wherever you are. You may want to stop at an ATM on the way. If you're tired of cups and regulation-size sugar cones, try the generous waffle cone. Space is limited to nine tables, but there's always the curb (or car, if you drove).

7237 Woodmont Ave., Bethesda, MD. ✆ **301/907-3436**. Single-dip cone $3.80; Super Banana Split $7.50. MC, V. Sun–Thurs 11:30am–10pm; Fri–Sat 11am–11pm (open until midnight during summer). Metro: Bethesda; then 7-min. walk.

GAITHERSBURG
INEXPENSIVE

Roy's Place 🍴🍴 *Finds* SANDWICHES   Granted, it's a trip from downtown D.C., but if you have the time or are staying in suburban Maryland, it's worth it. The Dagwood-style sandwiches are delish and satisfying, and range in price from $6.45 for brisket to $22 for the 5-decker Bender Schmender (with almost everything but the kitchen sink). The average sandwich price is $9 to $10. Roy's is fun, funky, and great for the frugally inclined. The decor is grandma's-attic chic. Allow time to digest the 18-page menu of zany sandwich combinations and permutations, such as The Nothing Burger (a plain hard roll with butter), The Katherine of Tarragon (roast turkey breast, Swiss cheese, tomato, and tarragon mayo), and The Real Gasser (broiled knockwurst, cheese, onions, and relish on French bread). You may also order a hamburger, full dinner, meal-size salad, vegetarian 'wich, or 1 of 18 plain sandwiches for "chicken eaters" and "little chicken eaters" (kids). Several imported beers are offered on tap.

2 E. Diamond Ave., Gaithersburg, MD. ✆ **301/948-5548**. www.roysplacerestaurant.com. High chairs, booster seats. 65¢ (ice-cube sandwich)–$22; most sandwiches are $9–$10. AE, DC, DISC, MC, V. Mon–Sat 11:30am–10 or 10:30pm; Sun 11:30am–9pm. Route 355 north (the extension of Wisconsin Ave. and Rockville Pike) into Gaithersburg. Cross the bridge; go left at Chestnut, and turn left on East Diamond to Roy's on left. Plenty of free parking in Roy's lot.

ROCKVILLE
INEXPENSIVE

O'Brien's Pit Barbecue 🍴🍴 RIBS/BARBECUE   Texas ribs and barbecued beef brisket are top draws in this award-winning Western-style cafeteria and carryout, family owned for 30 years. In my opinion, O'Brien's very best offering is the chopped pork sandwich with plenty of barbecue sauce and side dishes of smoky baked beans and coleslaw. Other top sandwich choices are the pit ham or sausage. Add two vegetables and Texas toast for a meal that's hard to finish.

If you're not into pork, try the smoked turkey or chicken breast. For kids, there are a hot dog ($2.75), chicken filet sandwich ($4.75), and lots of homey sides such as potato salad. The friendly waitstaff makes junior cowpokes feel right at home. There's plenty of free on-site parking.

387 E. Gude Dr., Rockville, MD. © **301/340-8596**. www.obrienspitbarbecue.com. High chairs. Reservations not accepted. Most items $5.75–$10. AE, DISC, MC, V. Sun–Thurs 11am–9pm; Fri–Sat 11am–9:30pm. Closed Thanksgiving, Christmas, Easter. Not convenient to Metro.

SILVER SPRING
MODERATE
Crisfield Seafood Restaurant ⚜ SEAFOOD   The decor might be early restroom, but don't let it turn you off. There is charm in the checkered floor and worn wooden countertop where lone diners belly up for raw oysters and fried shrimp. Crisfield's serves some of the freshest seafood west of the Chesapeake Bay. The cold seafood platter, fried combo platters, crab cakes, and baked stuffed fish and shrimp have been pleasing patrons for 60 years. A personal favorite, if you can handle the butter: crab Norfolk. The sinfully rich and delicious seafood bisque of shrimp, lobster, and crabmeat in a tomato-cream base is a steal at $6.25. Kids under 12 can order a crab cake, fried shrimp, or fried fish platter for $8. Avoid dinnertime on weekends or go early. Metered street parking is available; there's parking in an adjacent lot after 6pm.

8012 Georgia Ave., Silver Spring, MD. © **301/589-1306**. High chairs, booster seats, kids' menu. Reservations not accepted. Main courses $4.75–$40; kids' menu entrees $5, platters $8. AE, MC, V. Tues–Thurs 11am–10pm; Fri–Sat 11am–11pm; Sun noon–9:30pm. Metro: Silver Spring.

11 Suburban Virginia

A generation ago, the area near and beyond the Beltway was considered the "boonies." Those days are long past. The number of fast-food, pizza, pub, ethnic, and fine dining establishments continues to grow with the population and urban sprawl. Stay in this area, and you'll have as many restaurants from which to choose as if you'd stayed in downtown D.C. In addition to the restaurants listed below, there's a **Rio Grande Café** in Ballston at 4301 N. Fairfax Dr. (© **703/528-3131**) and one in Reston at 1827 Library St. (© **703/904-0703**). See the full review on p. 108. There are a bunch of **T.G.I. Friday's** restaurants in suburban Virginia (see p. 96 for a full review), including one in Vienna at 2070 Chain Bridge Rd. (© **703/556-6173**). There's also a **Morton's** steakhouse in Vienna (© **703/883-0800**); see p. 97.

ALEXANDRIA
See the "Old Town Alexandria" section in chapter 11.

ARLINGTON
MODERATE
Red, Hot & Blue ⚜ RIBS/BARBECUE   Some think it's easier to get into heaven than to snare a table at Red, Hot & Blue at peak time. The Memphis ribs, pulled-pig sandwiches, and onion loaf have a large following in these parts. A good buy is the rack of ribs for two with two side dishes for $22 (single rack is $19) Those 10 and under can order a pulled-pork, brisket, or chicken sandwich; mini–corn dogs; grilled

cheese; or chicken nuggets (Love Me Tenders) from the children's menu. All are served with fries or applesauce and a beverage. Your bill will fall in the inexpensive category if you skip the ribs and stick with the sandwiches, all under $8. The place is nothing to look at. If you want beauty, go to the National Gallery. If you want great ribs, wet (with sauce) or dry, come here. Take home a souvenir bottle of the tangy barbecue sauce. Avoid a wait by arriving before 6pm.

There is an RH&B Express at 3014 Wilson Blvd., Clarendon (Arlington), Virginia (© **703/243-1510**), and there are branch restaurants in several towns in Virginia and Maryland (see the website for a full list).

1600 Wilson Blvd., Arlington, VA. © **703/276-7427**. www.redhotandblue.com. High chairs, booster seats, kids' menu, crayons. Reservations not accepted. Main courses (other than ribs) $9–$15; kids' dinner $4–$5. AE, DC, DISC, MC, V. Sun–Thurs 11am–10pm; Fri–Sat 11am–11pm. Closed Thanksgiving, Dec 25. Metro: Rosslyn or Court House.

VIENNA
MODERATE

Clyde's ☆ AMERICAN   The burgers (I'm partial to the blue-cheese-and-bacon variety), ribs, pasta dishes, and salads are delish. The menu sometimes changes daily so the chef can utilize the freshest produce and seasonal items, such as locally caught seafood. Monthly specials bear watching. In September 2005, single-lobster dinners were $18, two for $28. There's a full range of chicken, beef, fish, and pasta items, as well as seasonal specialties such as crab cakes on the grownup menu. The grilled chicken salad is a best seller. Big, brassy, and divided into several dining areas, Clyde's merits a look around on your way in or out. In the main dining room, kids might have questions about the naked ladies—excuse me, nudes—in the paintings.

8332 Leesburg Pike, Vienna, VA. © **703/734-1901**. www.clydes.com. High chairs, booster seats, kids' menu, crayons. Reservations recommended. Main courses $7.25–$18; kids' menu items $5. AE, DC, DISC, MC, V. Mon–Sat 11am–11pm; Sun 10am–11pm; Sun brunch 10am–4pm.

INEXPENSIVE TO MODERATE

Chili's Grill & Bar ☆ SOUTHWESTERN/AMERICAN   Elegant it's not, but Chili's serves good food and loves families, which is probably why so many families love it. It's the kind of place where you don't have to keep reminding your kids to keep their voices down. Fajitas freaks, young and old, say that these are among the best in town. The burgers, well-seasoned fries, and salads are all tasty and generous, and many rate the barbecued ribs a 10. The kids' menu has 11 choices—the usual suspects (hamburgers and hot dogs, mac and cheese). All come with a choice of sides and beverage. A zillion Chili's locations can be found throughout Washington, D.C. and Virginia suburbs. Among them: in Rockville, Maryland, at 11428-A Rockville Pike, (© **301/881-8588**). If you're staying in Virginia's Vienna/Tysons Corner area, this is a good choice. Ask the concierge/front desk for directions.

8051 Leesburg Pike, Vienna, VA. © **703/734-9512**. www.chilis.com. High chairs, booster seats, kids' menu, crayons. Reservations not accepted. Main courses $9–$17; kids' menu items $3–$6.70 (most under $5). AE, DISC, MC, V. Mon–Thurs 11am–11pm; Fri–Sat 11am–midnight; Sun 11am–10pm.

Exploring Washington, D.C. with Your Kids

You could spend an entire lifetime discovering the wonders of Washington, D.C., but you probably have other things to do as well, such as working, eating, and paying bills. So be realistic and scale down your expectations. It's better to spend quality time on a few attractions than to dash through a multitude. (I am one of those type A's who sometimes bites off more than she can chew. Please do as I say, not as I do.)

Look to your children when planning your itinerary, and be sure to factor in time for relaxing. Visit a few well-chosen sites and then let off steam in one of the city's many parks and recreational areas. Dunk in the hotel pool, or if shopping is your favorite sport, browse in one of the museum shops or glitzy indoor malls. Remember, this is a vacation, not an endurance contest!

The night before a museum visit, some parents read their kids a relevant story. Others buy postcards on entering a museum or gallery and accompany their youngsters on a scavenger hunt to find the pictured object or work of art. You probably have your own preferred ways of getting your youngsters psyched for sightseeing. If you're new at this, the best advice I can offer is don't overschedule. Young children have short attention spans. Catch a movie, puppet show, or theater presentation for a change of pace. Preschoolers often get antsy after 20 minutes in a museum. When they do, it's fruitless to push them further. Stop for a snack, rest, or get some fresh air. Then try again. You'll know when they've had it!

Here's a tip from a savvy friend of mine. In museums, let the kids stop in the museum store *first* to look around and buy a souvenir. If logic prevails, you'll avoid the unpleasantness of having them bug you while you're viewing the exhibits.

When you're on a tight schedule, concentrate your sightseeing in and around the downtown area known as the National Mall (see map on p. 119). Here, you will find the presidential monuments, most of the Smithsonian museums, the U.S. Capitol, the White House, and numerous other attractions—all free and within walking distance of each other.

SUGGESTED ITINERARIES

For Toddlers

Day 1 Run, don't walk, to the zoo. Go early, especially in the summer and on weekends. There's plenty to keep everyone occupied for several hours. Pack a picnic or buy lunch at one of the snack bars or the cafeteria/restaurant on the premises.

Day 2 Visit the animal exhibits and O. Orkin Insect Zoo in the National Museum of Natural History. Cross the Mall to the Smithsonian Castle. Ride the carousel. Then grab lunch in one of the museum eateries or from a street

Washington, D.C. Attractions

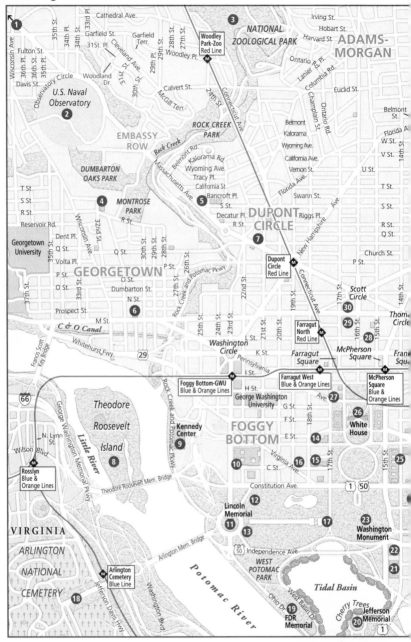

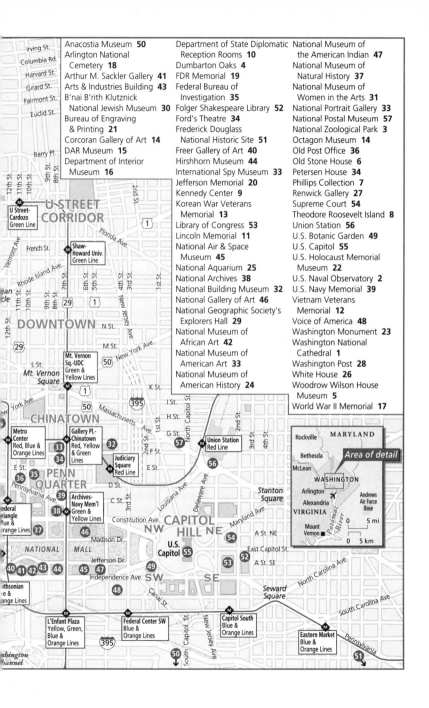

Anacostia Museum **50**
Arlington National
  Cemetery **18**
Arthur M. Sackler Gallery **41**
Arts & Industries Building **43**
B'nai B'rith Klutznick
  National Jewish Museum **30**
Bureau of Engraving
  & Printing **21**
Corcoran Gallery of Art **14**
DAR Museum **15**
Department of Interior
  Museum **16**

Department of State Diplomatic
  Reception Rooms **10**
Dumbarton Oaks **4**
FDR Memorial **19**
Federal Bureau of
  Investigation **35**
Folger Shakespeare Library **52**
Ford's Theatre **34**
Frederick Douglass
  National Historic Site **51**
Freer Gallery of Art **40**
Hirshhorn Museum **44**
International Spy Museum **33**
Jefferson Memorial **20**
Kennedy Center **9**
Korean War Veterans
  Memorial **13**
Library of Congress **53**
Lincoln Memorial **11**
National Air & Space
  Museum **45**
National Aquarium **25**
National Archives **38**
National Building Museum **32**
National Gallery of Art **46**
National Geographic Society's
  Explorers Hall **29**
National Museum of
  African Art **42**
National Museum of
  American Art **33**
National Museum of
  American History **24**

National Museum of
  the American Indian **47**
National Museum of
  Natural History **37**
National Museum of
  Women in the Arts **31**
National Portrait Gallery **33**
National Postal Museum **57**
National Zoological Park **3**
Octagon Museum **14**
Old Post Office **36**
Old Stone House **6**
Petersen House **34**
Phillips Collection **7**
Renwick Gallery **27**
Supreme Court **54**
Theodore Roosevelt Island **8**
Union Station **56**
U.S. Botanic Garden **49**
U.S. Capitol **55**
U.S. Holocaust Memorial
  Museum **22**
U.S. Naval Observatory **2**
U.S. Navy Memorial **39**
Vietnam Veterans
  Memorial **12**
Voice of America **48**
Washington Monument **23**
Washington National
  Cathedral **1**
Washington Post **28**
White House **26**
Woodrow Wilson House
  Museum **5**
World War II Memorial **17**

vendor. Eat outside, weather permitting. A pleasant dining alternative is the Food Court at the Ronald Reagan Building and International Trade Center, where there's often family entertainment. In the afternoon, visit the Aquarium in the Commerce Department. If you're not too tired, cross the street to the National Museum of American History and single out one or two exhibits.

Day 3 Start out at one of the Smithsonian museums you've missed, such as the Air and Space Museum, where little airplane fans will be in their element. In fair weather, pick up something yummy from the Food Hall at Union Station or the Food Court at the Ronald Reagan Building and picnic on the museum's grounds. Tuck in a siesta after lunch and then visit another Smithsonian museum. Mature 4- and 5-year-olds and older siblings will enjoy seeing a movie in the Air and Space Museum, but don't sit too close to the screen. The larger-than-life images and booming soundtrack might frighten younger kids. If time permits, and they are still upright, spend a half-hour or so looking around; that's about all kids this age can take. Have dinner near your hotel (or spring for room service or order in a pizza) and turn in early.

For 6- to 8-Year-Olds

Day 1 Hop on a Tourmobile tram, and after you've completed the loop and listened to the narrator's spiel, spend the afternoon visiting one or two sights that interested you most on the tour.

Day 2 Visit the Air and Space Museum in the morning and then have lunch at one of the museum eateries on the Mall. In the afternoon, tour the Hirshhorn, especially the outdoor sculpture garden, and then ride the carousel nearby. Cross the Mall to the Museum of Natural History or the Museum of American History, or cast an eye (but not a fishing line) into the tanks of the Commerce Department's Aquarium. Have dessert at the Old Post Office or the Ronald Reagan Building and International Trade Center—both close by. Or go back to your room and rest. You deserve it.

Day 3 At the Bureau of Engraving and Printing, see how money is made—literally. Pool your pennies for lunch and then visit the past at the DAR Museum's Children's Attic. If you're still rarin' to go, visit one of the presidential memorials: the Washington Monument or the Lincoln, Jefferson, and Roosevelt memorials. You might want to include, or substitute, the Vietnam and Korean War Veterans memorials. In the warm-weather months, rent a boat or bicycle, and paddle or pedal away the afternoon. In winter, ice-skate at the National Sculpture Garden or Pershing Park rink, or warm up in the U.S. Botanic Garden. Or cool down in your hotel pool. When Washington is at its steamiest, chill in your room and watch a movie. After dark, take a taxi to see the illuminated presidential memorials.

For 8- to 10-Year-Olds

Day 1 Start early and spend the morning at the Spy Museum, one of the most popular sites in all D.C. Splurge on lunch at the Hard Rock Cafe or grab a hot dog or slice of pizza from a street vendor. Visit Ford's Theatre National Historical Site and the Petersen House across the street, where Lincoln died. Go back to your hotel for a swim, or hop on the Metro and choose one of the following: Interact with the displays at the National Geographic Society's Explorers Hall or U.S. Postal Museum, or stroll through

Highlights for Kids: The Top Attractions by Age Group

Picking Washington's top 10 attractions for kids of different ages is next to impossible. Depending on your kids' ages and interests, your family's top 10 will probably include a mix of some of the following, along with selections listed in this chapter under "For Kids with Special Interests."

2 to 4   National Zoo, FDR Memorial, National Museum of Natural History (dinosaurs, O. Orkin Insect Zoo), National Aquarium, DAR Museum, National Museum of American History (first-floor machinery), National Air and Space Museum (planes suspended from ceiling, space station, and space capsule), Hains Point playground (East Potomac Park), carousel on the Mall, Hirshhorn Sculpture Garden, National Gallery Sculpture Garden, Constitution Gardens.

4 to 6   National Zoo, American Museum of Natural History, FDR Memorial, DAR Museum, National Air and Space Museum, National Gallery Sculpture Garden, National Museum of American History, Bureau of Engraving and Printing, National Gallery of Art Sculpture Garden or Hirshhorn Sculpture Garden, Oxon Hill Farm (Maryland), Hains Point playground (East Potomac Park), Rock Creek Park.

6 to 8   National Zoo, American Museum of Natural History, National Air and Space Museum, National Museum of American History, presidential monuments (Washington Monument, and Lincoln, Jefferson, and Franklin Delano Roosevelt memorials), Bureau of Engraving and Printing, DAR Museum, U.S. Postal Museum.

8 to 10   National Zoo, American Museum of Natural History, National Air and Space Museum, National Museum of American History, presidential monuments, the International Spy Museum, the Capitol, National Geographic Society, Bureau of Engraving and Printing, National Museum of the American Indian.

10 and older   National Zoo, National Museum of American History, American Museum of Natural History, National Air and Space Museum, presidential monuments, Mount Vernon, the National Museum of the American Indian, the Capitol, International Spy Museum, National Geographic Society, Bureau of Engraving and Printing.

Georgetown or Dupont Circle, stopping for dessert along the way.

Day 2   Time for a Mall crawl. Start at the Air and Space Museum (be sure to buy movie tickets first). Have lunch on the Mall. In the afternoon, go to the American History Museum or the National Museum of the American Indian. Pick up a map at each information desk and concentrate on a few exhibits. In between, take pictures on the Mall or fly a kite (you can buy one in the Air and Space Museum's gift shop). Have dinner in or near your hotel or have dinner delivered and watch an in-room movie.

Day 3   Begin at the Museum of Natural History, O. Orkin Insect Zoo (feeding times are 10:30am, 11:30am, and 1:30pm during the week, an hour later on weekends), and then visit the dinosaurs. Lunch in the museum or Old Post Office Pavilion food court. Check out the nearby Aquarium and/or American History Museum. If you're tired or the weather is crummy, see the sights on a Tourmobile or Jolly Trolley tour. Have dinner at Union Station and shop or see a movie. Or take a taxi to view the presidential monuments after dark.

For Preteens

Day 1   Same as Day 1 for 8- to 10-year-olds. Stroll around Georgetown or Union Station after dinner, see a movie (both places have multiplex theaters) and indulge in a yummy dessert, or catch a theater performance.

Day 2   Same as Day 2 for 8- to 10-year-olds. You might want to skip a museum or two and substitute Arlington National Cemetery. Or maybe your crew's idea of a good time is cruisin' Georgetown or an indoor mall

for souvenirs. Or go to the Air and Space museum in the morning and then take the bus to the new Udvar-Hazy facility at Dulles Airport to see two huge hangars full of vintage flying machines. Take a nighttime tour of the major sights, or visit the Washington Monument or Lincoln Memorial on your own.

Day 3   Same as Day 3 for 8- to 10-year-olds. After lunch, ride a bike, take a hike, or pick out something else you like. A visit to Arlington National Cemetery, Mount Vernon (by boat in nice weather), or Alexandria's Old Town is in order. In the evening, see free entertainment (nightly at 6pm on the Kennedy Center Millennium Stage), catch a theater performance, or go to a sporting event (depending on the season—pro football, soccer, basketball, or baseball) or a concert at the MCI Center, where there are also interactive games where you can test your sports skills. Too pooped to peep? Snuggle in bed with pizza and a cable movie.

1 The Smithsonian Institution ⟨★⟩⟨★⟩⟨★⟩

According to the Greater Washington Board of Trade, "If all the treasures of the Smithsonian Institution were lined up in one long exhibit, and you spent 1 second looking at each item, it would take you more than 2½ years of around-the-clock touring to see them all." I haven't double-checked their computations, but you have to admit, the statistics are impressive. According to one poll, 40% of all Americans have visited the Smithsonian, the largest museum/research complex in the world.

Like other cultural institutions adversely affected by cutbacks, the Smithsonian has, in recent years, sought funding from corporations and individuals—hence, the O. Orkin Insect Zoo and Janet Annenberg Hooker GGM (geology, gems, and minerals) Hall at the Museum of Natural History. Currently, the federal government supplies about 75% of the Smithsonian's revenues.

In 1846, when English scientist James Smithson's (he died in 1929) willed funds were sent to the United States (105 bags of gold sovereigns, equal to about $500,000) to establish an institution "for the increase and diffusion of knowledge among men," he probably never imagined that today the Smithsonian conglomerate would house some 13 million artifacts, encompass numerous buildings, and have become one of the world's major tourist attractions.

For a full page of Smithsonian special events for the coming month, residents can turn to the "Smithsonian Sampler" in *The Washington Post Weekend* magazine, published the

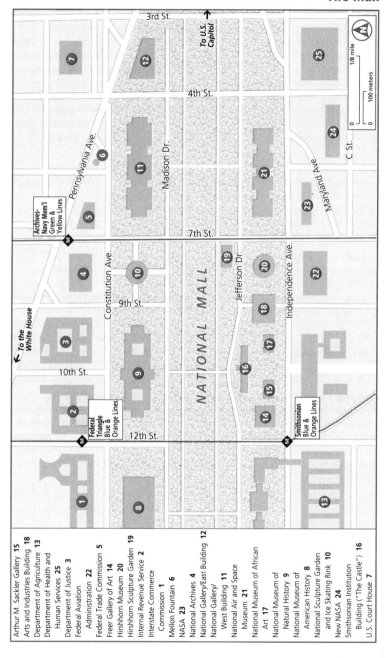

Arthur M. Sackler Gallery **15**
Arts and Industries Building **18**
Department of Agriculture **13**
Department of Health and
  Human Services **25**
Department of Justice **3**
Federal Aviation
  Administration **22**
Federal Trade Commission **5**
Freer Gallery of Art **14**
Hirshhorn Museum **20**
Hirshhorn Sculpture Garden **19**
Internal Revenue Service **2**
Interstate Commerce
  Commission **1**
Mellon Fountain **6**
NASA **23**
National Archives **4**
National Gallery/East Building **12**
National Gallery/
  West Building **11**
National Air and Space
  Museum **21**
National Museum of African
  Art **17**
National Museum of
  Natural History **9**
National Museum of
  American History **8**
National Sculpture Garden
  and Ice Skating Rink **10**
New NASA **24**
Smithsonian Institution
  Building ("The Castle") **16**
U.S. Court House **7**

third Friday of every month. The Smithsonian museums are open from 10am to 5:30pm daily except December 25. "The Castle," with its visitor information center, is open from 9am to 5:30pm. Every year Congress votes whether to extend hours in spring and summer. From late May to September 4, 2005, the Smithsonian museums remained open until 7:30pm. Call ahead or check the website to avoid disappointment (© 202/357-2700; www.si.edu).

Because one-third of the approximately 15 million people who visit the Smithsonian annually do so in June, July, and August, you might want to schedule your visit for any other month. Or arrive when the doors open or late in the afternoon. Bear in mind that Mondays are the quietest and Saturdays and Sundays are the busiest; early morning and late afternoon are the least crowded. Tuck these Smithsonian phone numbers in your wallet: Information: © 202/357-2700; Dial-A-Museum: © 202/357-2020, for daily activities and special events; and TDD: © 202/357-1729. You can also visit the website at www.si.edu.

Smithsonian Institution Building ("the Castle")   Ages 4 and up. As I mentioned earlier, the Smithsonian information center in the Castle is a good place to begin your tour of D.C. Press a button on one of the video-display monitors to get information on the Smithsonian and more than 100 other attractions. About a dozen pages are devoted to kid-pleasing things to see and do. You might have trouble prying your progeny away from the monitors' highly imaginative and colorful graphics. Two electronic wall maps will help you get your bearing and plan your day. Information specialists are on hand to assist visitors daily from 9am to 4pm.

Also check the video screens mounted on the information desk where "Today at the Smithsonian" lists events and exhibits, and ask for **"10 Tips for Visiting the Smithsonian with Children,"** which includes a map, family highlights, and a quiz for kids—all free. In the gift shop, you can purchase a "Guide to the Nation's Capital," a detailed map with brief descriptions of the major museums and attractions. Not only is the map immensely helpful, but it also makes a nice souvenir.

In two orientation theaters, a 20-minute video is shown throughout the day, giving a Smithsonian overview. Guides printed in seven languages are available for foreign visitors. While you're at the Castle, you might want to inquire about the **Smithsonian Young Associate Program,** which offers workshops, films, and live performances for children throughout the year (© 202/357-3030).

If you enter the Castle from Jefferson Drive (on the Mall), you'll find, on the left, the crypt bearing the remains of James Smithson. Although he died in Genoa, Italy, on June 26, 1829, he was brought to this spot—ironically, his first time on U.S. soil and his final resting place—in 1904.

Before you leave the Castle, make a quick sweep of the **Children's Room,** open daily from 10am to 5:30pm. The trompe l'oeil fantasy garden and skylights have been

---

Break Time

If you find yourself on the Mall before the museums open, and you haven't had your cup of joe, slip into the Seattle's Best Coffee Shop in the Castle, south entrance (Independence Ave., © 202/357-2700), for coffee and a muffin. The cafe is open daily from 8:30am to 5pm. The menu is limited, but it includes sandwiches, salads, and snacks. Prices are $1.50 to $6.

Arts and Industries Building Closure

The distinctive Victorian-style red brick–and–sandstone building on the south side of the Mall opened in time for President Garfield's first inaugural ball in March 1881. Better known to visitors as the home of the Discovery Theater, a venue for top-notch children's theater, it will be closed to the public for several years while it undergoes renovation.

restored to their original state in the cozy, light-filled space. From here, you can exit to the Mall's **Enid A. Haupt Victorian Garden,** enchanting spring through fall and with benches for weary visitors.

1000 Jefferson Dr. SW. ✆ **202/357-2700;** 202/359-2900 for a recording. www.si.edu. Free admission. Daily 9am–5:30pm. Closed Dec 25. Metro: Smithsonian.

Anacostia Museum and Center for African-American History and Culture

Ages 4 and up. You have to cross Washington's lesser-known river, the Anacostia, to get to this Smithsonian facility that focuses on African-American art, culture, and history. Augmenting its permanent collection and changing exhibits, the Anacostia offers free family workshops and events several times a month. Past examples include a slide show, "Origins of Islamic Calligraphy," a hands-on workshop to create henna, and a tour of public art related to the African-American experience. Call the museum's education department (✆ **202/633-4870**) to find out about upcoming family activities and guided tours offered Monday through Friday.

Visitors with reservations can take a guided walk along the George Washington Carver nature trail on the museum grounds. It's less than a third of a mile long, so even the youngest scouts in your party should be able to keep up the pace. You might want to tote snacks or lunch to eat in the picnic area, because there's no onsite restaurant, and the neighborhood surrounding the museum is not recommended for casual strolling.

1901 Fort Place SE. ✆ **202/633-4820.** www.anacostia.si.edu. Free admission. Daily 10am–5:30pm. Closed Dec 25. Metro: Anacostia, local exit, left to Howard St., and take the W-2 or W-3 bus to the museum entrance. By car, take I-395 north to I-295 south to Martin Luther King, Jr. Ave. Left on Morris Ave., which becomes Erie St., and then Fort Place.

Freer Gallery of Art 🎨   **Ages 8 and up.** It is nearly impossible to visit the Freer and not be taken with the beauty of the museum itself, as well as its contents. As you emerge from the Mall exit of the Smithsonian Metro station, the stunning Renaissance-style facade and colorful banners of the Freer will greet you. In a concerted effort to draw young people, the museum has added a number of colorful workbooks that challenge youngsters to examine what they see and to think critically and creatively.

The museum is named for Detroit industrialist and art connoisseur Charles Lang Freer, who made a bundle from manufacturing the first railroad cars in the Midwest and became James McNeill Whistler's chief patron; this is where you'll find the world's largest Whistler collection—more than 1,200 pieces. The museum is recognized internationally for its collection of Asian art spanning 6,000 years. To give you an idea of the breadth of the riches of the Freer, at any given time, 10% or less of the museum's permanent collection is on view.

Among the treasures, and hands-down the best-known work, is Whistler's *Harmony in Blue and Gold: The Peacock Room.* The actual dining room you'll see was painted by Whistler between 1876 and 1877 for the British businessman Frederick Leyland, who

Activities That Don't Cost a Penny

- Watch the sun set behind the Lincoln Memorial.
- Ride to the top of the Washington Monument after dark.
- Warm up in the National Zoo's Amazonia rain forest exhibit or U.S. Botanic Garden.
- Attend a summertime concert on the Ellipse (behind the White House), at the Capitol (West Lawn), or at Navy Memorial Plaza (Pennsylvania Ave. between 7th and 9th sts.)
- Redesign the FBI Building.
- See who, or what, is buried in the crypt under the Capitol.
- Guess the weight of the globe in the National Geographic Society's Explorers Hall.
- Imagine how you'd spend the money printed in 1 day at the Bureau of Engraving and Printing.
- Find world heavyweight champion Joe Louis's grave at Arlington National Cemetery.
- Discover your favorite work of art in the Corcoran Gallery.
- Ask a Native American docent at the National Museum of the American Indian about his or her ancestry.
- Rename the works in the Hirshhorn Museum's or National Gallery's Sculpture Garden.
- Count the crystals in the Kennedy Center Opera House chandelier.
- Visit Kermit the Frog at the Smithsonian Museum of American History.
- Trace the origins of your family tree at the National Archives.
- Go inline skating in front of the White House.

engaged Whistler to redecorate his dining room around the artist's painting, *The Princess from the Land of the Porcelain,* and a large collection of blue-and-white Oriental porcelain. Whistler's feelings about Leyland's failure to pay what he felt the job was worth are reflected in the mural of two peacocks over the sideboard.

Children over 10 are usually intrigued to learn the story behind this extraordinary dining room, which has been moved, piece by piece, from London to Detroit to Washington, D.C. See if your children can find Whistler's trademark butterfly signature. (He left his imprint in four places in the room.)

When you arrive, be sure to pick up one or more of the free family guides tied to individual exhibits, such as "Animal Hunt." This is a painless way to introduce children to the treasures here and stimulate their imagination. **ImaginAsia** is a free, ongoing program of art-related activities for children 6 to 14 and their adult companions. After touring the collections with a guide, participants express themselves in their own works of art to take home. ImaginAsia is held Saturday and Sunday during the school year and on Tuesday, Wednesday, and Thursday in summer. Call to verify times

- Make up a story about Fragonard's *Young Girl Reading* in the National Gallery's West Building.
- Skip rocks in the Tidal Basin.
- Find out what "Star Route" means in the National Postal Museum.
- Picnic along the Potomac River or behind the Old Stone House in Georgetown.
- See how long it takes to walk the length of the National Mall.
- Feed the ducks in Constitution Gardens.
- Hear a case before the Supreme Court (Oct–April).
- Enjoy the vista from the Washington National Cathedral's Pilgrim Observatory Gallery.
- Fly a kite on the Mall.
- Write a letter to the president.
- View downtown from the tower in the Old Post Office.
- Sit in Albert Einstein's lap (2101 Constitution Ave. NW).
- Wish on a star at the Naval Observatory.
- Dip your toes in the Reflecting Pool.
- Explore the 2-mile nature trail in Glover Archbold Park.
- Identify the birds and planes over Theodore Roosevelt Island.
- Stroll along the Maine Avenue/Water Street SW waterfront, and choose your dream boat.
- Watch a polo match in West Potomac Park (Sun afternoon, late Apr–Oct, excluding Aug).

(℃ 202/357-2700). Group tours are offered from 10am to noon on Saturday in the Sackler Gallery classroom on the second floor. Reservations are required (℃ 202/357-4880, ext. 422).

Docent-led tours are offered every day but Wednesday at 12:15pm, departing from the information desk. Reservations for group tours must be made in writing at least 4 weeks in advance. The Freer is joined by an exhibition gallery to the adjacent Arthur M. Sackler Gallery.

Jefferson Dr. at 12th St. SW, on the south side of the Mall. ℃ 202/357-2104. www.asia.si.edu. Free admission. Daily 10am–5:30pm. Closed Dec 25. Metro: Smithsonian (Mall or Independence Ave. exits).

Hirshhorn Museum and Sculpture Garden ✧✧   **Ages 2 and up.** While other teenage boys were hanging out on the front stoop or getting into mischief, a young Latvian immigrant, Joseph Hirshhorn (1899–1981), was buying etchings in New York. The rest, as they say, is history. The museum bearing the mining magnate and art collector's name opened in 1974 with his little "gift" of mostly 20th-century art—2,000 pieces of sculpture and 4,000 paintings and drawings. When Hirshhorn died at the age of 82, additional works were bequeathed from his estate. The collection continues to receive gifts from other donors and is the fifth-most-visited art museum in the United States. Seems like yesterday, rather than 32 years ago, that I attended the opening of this incredible museum. (I was 5 years old at the time. *If* you believe that, I have a monument I'd like to sell you.) Even kids who gag at the mention of going to an art museum find something to like at the Hirshhorn. Take preschoolers outside to the sculpture garden. The plaza provides an inviting and soft-edged setting for more than a dozen works, including Calder's black stabile, *Two Discs,* and Claes Oldenberg's *Geometric Mouse.* Your children should have something interesting to say about Lucio Fontana's billiard-ball–like spheres. Lie on the grass or rest on one of the benches amid the greenery and contemplate the scene. It's always the right time to ride the carousel, nearby on the Mall.

Kindergartners on up find the museum's doughnutlike inner space intriguing. They may become disoriented while traversing the concentric rings, but that's part of the fun. Paintings hang in the galleries of the outer circle, while sculptures and plenty of comfortable seating fill the inner circle (known as an ambulatory), where light pours in through floor-to-ceiling windows. If your family takes one mental postcard away from the Hirshhorn, I'll bet it will be Ron Mueck's ultrareal, much-larger-than-life sculpture, *Big Man.* Bearing an uncanny resemblance to Uncle Fester, the husky nude with a bald head looks like he's taking a "time out" on the lower level near the Warhols. On the second floor, look for *Guardian Angel* and works by Rodin and Degas. Ask your kids which of Matisse's *Heads of Jeanette* looks like you in the morning.

Older kids can explore on their own after viewing a short orientation film in the lower-level theater. They might like the portraits by Eakins and Sargent on the third floor before moving on to works by Bellows, Sloane, O'Keeffe, de Kooning, Pollock, and others. Many young people find the more abstract works appealing, even though "they don't look like anything." For a sweeping panorama of the Mall area, peer out the windows of the Abram Lerner Room for a view of the Old Post Office, National Archives, National Gallery (East and West), and U.S. Capitol.

At the information desk, pick up a free self-guided "Family Guide" with activities tied to specific works. Ask about films for families, too. Improv Art is a drop-in program for kids 5–11 and their families. Go to the Lower Level Improv Art Room for an activity sheet. Young at Art, for kids 6–9, takes place on select weekends. Call to preregister at ⓒ **202/633-3382.** Tours are given June through September, Monday through Friday at noon, and Saturday and Sunday at noon and 2pm. October through May tours are Monday through Friday at 10:30am and noon, and Saturday

---

Break Time

At the Hirshhorn's **Full Circle Café,** surrounded by the sculpture garden on the south side of the Mall at Independence Avenue and 8th Street SW, you'll find a self-service outdoor cafe. Featured are hot and cold sandwiches, pizza, and salads ($5–$11), plus sodas, beer, and wine ($3–$5). Desserts include an almond amaretto bar and jumbo chocolate chip cookie. Hot dogs, sandwiches, and pint-size cheese pizzas are always on hand for small fries. Reservations and credit cards are not accepted. It's open daily from late May to early September from 11am to 3pm, weather permitting.

and Sunday at noon and 2pm. Sculpture Garden tours are offered June through September, Monday through Saturday at 10:30am. Special exhibition tour times vary (inquire at the information desk). No tours are given on holidays. In the museum shop, you'll find posters, art books, and prints.

Independence Ave. and 7th St. SW, on the south side of the Mall. © 202/357-2700. www.si.edu/hirshhorn. Free admission. Daily 10am–5:30pm; Thurs May to Labor Day until 8pm; sculpture garden daily dawn–dusk; plaza daily 7am–dusk. Closed Dec 25. Metro: L'Enfant Plaza (Smithsonian exit) or Smithsonian.

National Air and Space Museum 🍿🍿🍿   **Ages 2 and up.** Longer than two football fields, the National Air and Space Museum is a huge pinkish marble monolith that opened July 1, 1976, in time for the U.S. Bicentennial. No, it's not much to look at from the outside; the magic begins when you enter. Inside, major historical and technological feats of air and space flight are documented in 23 exhibit areas.

Almost every specimen in the Air and Space Museum was flown or used to back up a craft, and this triggers excitement and a sense of immediacy in kids of all ages. The planes suspended from the ceiling appear to be in flight, and younger kids (young enough not to be embarrassed) might want to lie down and look straight up for the maximum effect. Before your family flies off in different directions, line up at the (Lockkeed Martin) **IMAX Theater** 🍿🍿 box office, and buy tickets ($8 adults, $6.50 ages 2–12, and $7 age 60 and over) for one of the special flight-related movies shown several times a day on the five-story IMAX screen. If you have time for only one, make it *To Fly,* the museum's inaugural film, which airs daily at least once. I've seen it more times than I can count, and I think it's safe to say that you won't ever forget it. Also on the huge screen: *Fighter Pilot,* where you feel like you're at the stick, guiding the F15-E through high-tech maneuvers. Climb aboard *Space Station 3D* for a glimpse of space 20 miles above Earth, or set off for the landscape of *Magnificent Desolation: Walking on the Moon.* With younger kids, I'd opt for *To Fly,* with a running time of a half-hour; the other two are longer. (See the "Films" section in chapter 10 for details.) *A tip:* The first morning show (10:15am) and the last afternoon show (6pm) almost never sell out. Go early or late, and avoid disappointment. You may **order tickets ahead** at www.smithsonian.org/IMAX or © **202/633-4629** (both with a service fee). Albert Einstein Planetarium show tickets (see below) are available from these outlets as well. Tickets are $8 for adults, $6.50 ages 2 to 11, and $7 for 60 and older.

Next, if you're interested in catching a heavenly show, take an out-of-this-world journey at the **Albert Einstein Planetarium** (see full review on p. 177). I suggest buying your tickets for the planetarium shows before you begin circling the exhibits.

Stop at the information desk for a floor plan and list of events. The museum hosts Family Days, usually Saturdays at 11am, in conjunction with a specific exhibit. Activities may include a film, story time, short talk, and/or actors in period dress. To avoid wasting time and energy—this place is huge—note the exhibits that interest your crew most. Docent-led tours of the museum are held daily at 10:30am and 1pm. Call ahead for information on group tours. With kids under 6, it's best to see the highlights on your own. Tell 2- to 4-year-olds to "look up," because the overhead sights appeal to this age group the most.

Fasten your seat belts—we're ready to blast off. Start on the first floor with **"Milestones of Flight,"** in the two-level gallery at the museum's entrance (Gallery 100). If you view nothing else in this museum, make sure to see this permanent exhibition. There's a good reason why it occupies the museum's center stage. Highlights include the 1903 *Wright Flyer* (the first airplane), Charles Lindbergh's *Spirit of St. Louis, Sputnik I,* John Glenn's *Friendship 7, Gemini 4,* the *Apollo 11* command module *Columbia, Pioneer 10,* Chuck *(The Right Stuff)* Yeager's *Bell X-1,* and *SpaceShipOne.* This remarkable craft is the first privately owned and operated spacecraft to fly more than 62 miles above Earth (it reached an altitude of 70 miles on Oct. 4, 2004!). When the line isn't too long, school-age kids love to walk through the Skylab Orbital Workshop, a backup for America's first space station. Check out the Apollo lunar module on the first floor's east end. "Explore the Universe" answers questions about the origins of the universe through artifacts (astrolabes, globes, and the like), telescopes, and digital technology (wide-field planetary cameras).

Make sure to see what might be the museum's most successful educational project to date, **"How Things Fly"** (Gallery 109). The largely interactive exhibit makes principles of aerodynamics accessible to school-agers on up. The internal workings of a piston engine are revealed in the Continental cutaway. Aspects of lift and drag are provided by wind tunnels and computer activities. Climb into a full-size Cessna 150 and handle the controls regulating the wings and tail; learn about orbits and trajectories via computer. Sometimes docents or local high school or college students are on hand to demystify concepts for younger visitors.

"Looking at Earth" should appeal to the scientific-minded, with its aerial photographs and satellite imagery (Gallery 110). The Surveyor, Lunar Orbiter, and Ranger are hangared in the hall devoted to Lunar Exploration Vehicles (Gallery 112). In **"Rocketry and Space Flight"** (Gallery 113) are the *Vega,* flown by Amelia Earhart on the first transatlantic flight by a woman, and spacesuits. Next door (Gallery 114) is devoted to the space race between the United States and the former Soviet Union. If you're interested in the rocketry and space-flight milestones and missions touched off by the Soviet Union's launching of *Sputnik* on October 4, 1957, **"Space Race"** has your name on it.

Tomorrow's astronauts will learn more about the early years of manned space flight in **"Apollo to the Moon"** (Gallery 210). The 30th anniversary of *Apollo 11* (1999), a major milestone, is still being celebrated at the NASM. While the guidance and navigation aids, maps and charts, and full-size mock-up of a lunar-module cockpit and command module docking target will intrigue many, I found the razor and shave cream, sealed fruitcake, lunar rock, and water gun far more interesting (call me shallow).

Touch down in the Shuttle Shop and Museum Gift Shop 🎁🎁 to pick up some freeze-dried ice cream sandwiches for snackin'. The selection of books, kites, models, posters, and T-shirts is one of the best in the city.

The **Steven F. Udvar–Hazy Center** at Washington Dulles International Airport in suburban Chantilly, Virginia, opened in December 2003 to rave reviews. Humongous hangars house 80% of the national collection *not* displayed at the flagship museum on the Mall. In the 10-story-high aviation hangar that is the length of three football fields are the *Enola Gay,* the space shuttle *Enterprise,* the shark-mouthed *Curtiss P-40 Warhawk* (flown in WWII), the Boeing 307 *Stratoliner* (first pressurized passenger plane), the Boeing 367-80 (first successful commercial jet), an Air France *Concorde,* and the *Blackbird* reconnaissance plane. In addition, there are a large-format theater, flight simulator, restaurants, and gift shops. Among the displayed artifacts are Lindbergh memorabilia and Amelia Earhart's flight suit. Every May, the Center holds a **Space Day** for families, with lots of hands-on stuff, balloon rocket races, stories, and usually visits by astronauts. Hours are 10am to 9pm. Admission and parking are free.

Break Time

The Wright Place (get it?) is perfect for kids. Here fast food has joined fast planes. The food court offers fare from McDonald's, Boston Market (chicken and side dishes), and Donatos Pizzeria (small personal pizzas). Designed especially for the museum, the restaurant resembles a hangar with launching pad–type scaffolding.

The **Flight Fare Cafe,** an outdoor stand on the museum's west side, has hot dogs, a couple of sandwiches and salads, pastries, and cold drinks. It is open daily, weather permitting. Prices at both range from $3 to $10. The hours are the same as the museum's, 10am to 5pm daily.

Perhaps more exciting to the kids is the observation tower for watching Dulles air traffic. You can also catch an IMAX movie: *Fighter Pilot* (filmed from an F15-E), *Space Station,* and *To Fly* for a fee (see details above), or the free film *Stars Tonight.* A shuttle whisks visitors here from the NASM on the Mall in downtown D.C. four times a day for $12 round-trip, $11 seniors (no discounts for kids). Purchase tickets at the IMAX or Einstein box office, or order ahead (a good idea, but with a $2 per-ticket fee; © **202/633-4629** or 877/932-4629). A video of the new facility is shown on the bus so the time passes quickly. Docent-led tours of the facility are held daily at 10:30am and 1pm. Because of heavy commuter traffic, I suggest doing this midday during the week or on a Saturday or Sunday morning. And please wear sturdy shoes. The floors are concrete.

For a free calendar of events, write to Calendar, National Air and Space Museum, Room 3733 MRC 321, Washington, DC 20560.

7th St. and Independence Ave. SW (enter at Independence Ave. or Jefferson Dr.). © 202/357-2700. www.nasm.edu. Free admission. Daily 10am–5:30pm; ask about extended summer hours. Closed Dec 25. Metro: L'Enfant Plaza (Smithsonian Museums exit).

National Museum of African Art ✸ **Ages 4 and up.** Most kids over 5 will find the carved wooden masks and fertility dolls of particular interest here, the only museum in the United States dedicated solely to African art. The bovine gong on the first-floor landing is a hit with youngsters, especially after they discover what happens when they push the button next to it. The collection of mostly 19th- and 20th-century traditional arts and artifacts, formerly housed in cramped Capitol Hill quarters, was relocated here in 1987. The tomblike setting is shared with the Arthur M. Sackler Gallery. More than 6,000 objects in the permanent collection are displayed in rotating exhibits. The museum received a significant collection of artwork in September 2004: the Walt Disney Co.–Tishman Collection (the late real estate magnate Paul Tishman had given his artwork to Disney). The exhibition is slated to open in February 2007. I've heard that Disney used the objects as inspiration for many of the items in *The Lion King.* Only a portion of the art will be on view at any one time. See if the 18th-century bronze mask, festooned with snakes and crocs and capped by an ominous-looking spike, is displayed during your visit. Ouch!

One or two weekends a month (more often in summer), there's storytelling for kids, focused on an individual country or special subject. Inquire at the information desk about the free gallery guide and other children's and family activities. Saturdays at 10:30am, kids 5–10 are invited to "Let's Read About Africa," introducing youngsters to African literature. A story is read and then kids do an art activity. Parents are invited to call ahead for a schedule of family workshops, films, and storytelling (© **202/357-4860**). The **Warren M. Robbins Library** is open to researchers by appointment Monday through Friday from 10am to 5pm (© **202/357-4875**). The museum shop has crafts, artifacts, clothing, and jewelry (© **202/786-2147**).

950 Independence Ave. SW. © **202/357-2700** or 202/357-4600. www.nmafa.si.edu. Free admission. Daily 10am–5:30pm; ask about extended summer hours. Closed Dec 25. Metro: Smithsonian (Mall or Independence Ave. exits).

National Museum of American History ⊛ **Ages 2 and up.** Major aspects of America's cultural, scientific, and technological history come alive here, intriguing kids of all ages. Three floors packed with exhibits that bridge more than 200 years—from the country's early days (the original Star-Spangled Banner that inspired our national anthem) to the present (Archie and Edith Bunker's well-worn chairs, Dorothy's ruby slippers, Muhammad Ali's boxing gloves, and Seinfeld's "puffy shirt")—provide a comprehensive overview of American social history. Don't try to cover it all in one visit. Also, please note that beginning in 2006, the museum will be undergoing renovations. Because some of the exhibitions described below may be affected, call before you visit.

First, pick up one or more of the museum's helpful **brochures for families.** A favorite is "Hunt for History," a self-guided-tour brochure with activities and questions pertaining to selected museum objects for two age groups (6–9 and 10–13) in English and Spanish. The "America on the Move Family Guide" asks, "Where do you want to go first?" as it guides families with questions and activities through this popular exhibition. I think the first-floor of this museum is hot (or "cool," if you prefer), and so do most kids. Rather than presenting an assortment of disparate objects, the museum is making a concerted effort to make connections and to focus on interpreting history.

Old Patent Office to Reopen

The Old Patent Office Building, the third-oldest federal building in D.C., which houses the Smithsonian American Art Museum and the National Portrait Gallery, closed for renovation in 2000. It is scheduled to reopen July 4, 2006, as the Donald W. Reynolds Center for American Art and Portraiture. (Why? Because the Reynolds Foundation donated $45 million toward renovations of the historic building.) You'll understand if I am skeptical. Things usually take longer than people in this town say they will. I hope they prove me wrong. When it reopens, the building that served as an infirmary during the Civil War (poet Walt Whitman was a nurse there) will have, in addition to its stellar collections, a large auditorium, cafe, museum store, and lots of interactives for kids. As part of the exhibit of works from the Smithsonian's American art archives, visitors will be able to watch conservators performing their painstaking work. Less evident but sure to be appreciated by all: updated fire, electrical, and communications systems, and improved access for the handicapped. Until the reopening, some exhibitions and programs of the National Museum of American Art will continue at the Renwick Gallery at 17th Street and Pennsylvania Avenue NW. Some of the exhibitions of the National Portrait Gallery have been on the road, traveling to other institutions in the United States and abroad.

This is best revealed in **"America on the Move"** on the first floor. This exhibit tracks U.S. history through our changing transportation system—from the first railroad to California (1876) to 20th-century modes of getting from Point A to Point B, all of which have left their impact on the present. Among the wheeled vehicles are a Chicago Transit Authority L car, an electric streetcar, and huge steam locomotives, such as the 199-ton "1401" model that chugged through the late 19th and early 20th centuries. All are perennial kid-pleasers, as are the tractors and other farm machinery around the corner in the Hall of Agriculture. (I wouldn't mind parking the 1913 Model-T Ford in my driveway.)

A new permanent exhibition on the third floor, "The Price of Freedom: Americans at War," surveys U.S. military history from Colonial times until the present through interactive stations and multimedia presentations. In the Civil War section, visitors can watch a puppet play ("Give Me Liberty") or learn field maneuvers and drills (with docent assistance). There are loads of interactives throughout this mammoth exhibition. Let me know what you think. Call me sexist, but the guys in your group will probably enjoy seeing the Willy's Jeep from World War II and the UH-H1 Huey helicopter from Vietnam a lot more than the girls will. Pin a medal on the museum for at least trying to show the harrowing effects of war on families and loved ones. So far, there's no word on how the museum will deal with the war in Iraq. Stay tuned.

Also on the third floor, and a respite from war games, is **"The American Presidency: A Glorious Burden."** It is fun, fun, fun, and also highly informative—chockablock with presidential memorabilia, videos, and interactives. Kids can gawk at Amy Carter's dollhouse, Chelsea Clinton's ballet slippers, and other items belonging to presidential offspring. Step up to the podium and deliver (part of) a presidential speech. Ogle Lincoln's office coat, Truman's gaudy sport shirt, photos from the 1945 Yalta Conference, peanut banks (a la Jimmy Carter), and Clinton's sax. This is a must with kids 8 and older.

Curators labored close to a year to catalogue, pack, and reassemble gourmet cooking diva **Julia Child's kitchen**—including utensils, dishes, and the sink. Known as "Bon Appetit! Julia Child's Kitchen at the Smithsonian," the kitchen served for 7 years as the set for Child's successful TV cooking series, *Bon Appetit!* The **Hands On Science Center,** part of the "Science in American Life" exhibition on the first floor, simplifies concepts for kids (according to the entrance sign) from "5 to 105." Don't drop off your kids and disappear. Children ages 5 through 12 must be accompanied by an adult. Under the supervision of docents, kids are invited to don neon safety goggles and take part in various experiments involving dry ice, DNA profiling, and pH levels of liquids—to name a few. Hours are seasonal, so please call ahead, visit the website, or ask when you arrive.

Also on the first floor is "Separate Is Not Equal: Brown v Board of Education," celebrating the 50th anniversary in 2004 of the end of segregation in public schools. Here you'll see a portion of the Woolworth counter from Greensboro, North Carolina, site of the history-making sit-in, and the robe worn by Supreme Court Justice Thurgood Marshall (then a young attorney for the NAACP) when he argued the case before the Supreme Court.

The museum's second floor is devoted to social and cultural history, such as the original **Star-Spangled Banner** (aka Old Glory). It managed to survive the 1814 British attack on Fort McHenry in Baltimore, but it nearly succumbed to the ravages of light, air pollution, and 200 years when it was taken down in the 1990s. The flag

Break Time

Rest your weary feet and grab a snack at the National Museum of American History Palm Court **Coffee and Gelato Bar** on the lower level (📞 **202/633-1000**). Start with something healthful from the brief menu of sandwiches, salads, and soups, or skip straight to 1 of the 24 flavors of gelato. You can also enjoy your favorite sandwich at Subway in the rear of the Palm Court. Most items are $2.50 to $7.25. It's open daily from 10am to 5pm. High chairs and boosters are available.

Growling stomachs and cranky tots can also be appeased in the **Main Street Café** (📞 **202/357-2700**). It, too, is on the lower level across from the museum store. On your way in or out, check out the collection of lunchboxes from 1880 to the present in "Taking America to Lunch." Satisfy your hunger with a large selection of hot and cold items—made-to-order deli-style sandwiches, pizza, hot dogs and hamburgers, desserts, or comfort food (meat, potatoes, and veggies), and more exotic fare such as antipasto, seafood salad, and barbecued chicken (did I say "exotic?"). It's more than adequate, and it's convenient. The spacious refueling spot is open for lunch and snacks. Plenty of high chairs and seating are available, and most major credit cards are accepted. Most items cost $4 to $8. Hours are 11am to 4pm; extended hours in summer are usual.

---

is on view in the conservation lab until its new home is completed. Speaking of flags, you can also view the Pentagon Flag that hung outside the Pentagon after the September 11, 2001, terrorist attacks.

In these enlightened times, peek at the exhibit **"First Ladies: Political Role and Public Image."** In addition to the gowns worn by presidential wives, plenty of First Lady memorabilia—photographs, jewelry, personal effects, and campaign mementos—are displayed, and the exhibit points out the women's public and political roles.

The third floor is for those whose hobbies and interests include popular culture, photography, textiles, and, last but not least, money—an interest all ages seem to share. The items change frequently in the **"Popular Culture"** exhibition, but you are bound to see at least one of the following: Dorothy's ruby slippers, Jim Henson's Kermit the Frog Muppet, Mr. Rogers's sweater, or basketball player Rebecca Lobo's U.S. Olympic team uniform.

Tours of the museum's highlights are at 10:15am and 1pm Tuesday through Saturday, and other times as docents are available. Check with the information desks, inside the Constitution Avenue and mall entrances.

14th St. and Constitution Ave. NW, entrances on Constitution Ave. and Madison Dr. 📞 202/633-1000. www.americanhistory.si.edu. Free admission. Daily 10am–5:30pm. Closed Dec 25. Metro: Smithsonian (Mall exit) or Federal Triangle.

National Museum of the American Indian   **Ages 4 and up.** The NMAI opened on the Mall (between Air and Space and the Capitol) in September 2004. A showcase for the culture, traditions, and history of American Indians from North and South America, the enormous project succeeds on some levels. But the planners may have bitten off more than they could chew. Should you go? Absolutely. For starters, the massive sandstone exterior—situated close to so many ugly institutional federal buildings—is beyond impressive.

Once inside, my reactions—to the artifacts, paintings, and sculptures from two dozen tribes throughout North, Central, and South America—were all over the map.

How best to describe the overall effect? "Uneven" comes to mind. So does "disjointed." I leave it to you whether it satisfies visitors' curiosity about our nation's original forefathers. Blatantly missing, however, is any reference to the near obliteration of these indigenous peoples by the "civilized" white man.

Being the newest kid on the block (er, mall), the NMAI is usually crowded. Go early, when it opens, or late. To gain entrance, queue up in the General Entry line at the east entrance between 10am and 5pm, where there is often a 10-minute or longer wait; pick up a timed Museum Pass between 10am and noon at the (same) east entrance for same-day admission after 1pm; or reserve passes in advance (© 866/400-NMAI [6624]; www.tickets.com). The first two options are free; the third is not. There is a "convenience fee" of $1.75 per ticket plus a one-time "processing" fee of $1.50—some "convenience."

Stop at the welcome desk for info on special events and a **Family Guide,** with suggestions for discussion topics during your visit and postvisit activities. The guide is also available at the website, www.nmai.si.edu, for preplanning. The soaring atrium, when you first enter, is awe-inspiring. It often serves as a performance space. If you're pooped, rest on a bench and let the kids run around.

Once you get your bearings, begin your visit on the fourth floor in the **Lelawi Theater,** where an introductory film is shown in-the-round on four fringed-cloth screens and overhead. Exhibitions on the fourth floor are dedicated to tribes of different areas, including videos, clothing, and artifacts from the Mayans (Yucatan Peninsula), Hoopas (California), Santa Clara pueblo (New Mexico), and Lakotas (South Dakota). The Lakota buffalo headdress is a must-see for kids. Also, point them toward the "projectile points" (politically correct term for arrowheads), colorful weavings, abstract sculptures by Allan Houser, and interactives for identifying pieces of wood, pottery, and baskets.

On the third floor, numerous videos and exhibits attempt to capture the essence of "Our Lives," how various tribes live, work, and preserve their heritage. Except with older kids, I suggest targeting just one or two displays here, such as the colorful and extensive collection of Native American dolls. Also on the third floor is the Learning Center, which is open to the public daily for research (if you want help from a docent for "guided hands-on sessions," you must make an appointment).

Special events, such as films and speakers, including visits by children's authors such as Richard Van Camp of Canada's Dogrib Nation, are held in the first level Rasmuson Theater. Performances are held in the theater, Atrium, and outdoor Welcome Plaza. Performances in 2005 included Navajo dancers, retelling of creation stories by an Amazon tribe from Columbia, the Alaska Native Arts and Culture Festival, and demonstrations of beadwork and basket making.

Mitsitam, the museum cafe, is pleasing to the eye, palate, and pocketbook. The food is well above standard museum fare and offers choices for vegetarians and vegans. Dine on sweet corn tamales, smoked seafood, tortilla soup, smoked turkey sandwich, and other Native American–inspired dishes. Kids can get a fry-bread taco, chili enchilada, or burger. The cafe is open daily from 10am to 5pm. Main dishes are $6 to $15. A buffalo burger with the works is $6.

4th St. and Independence Ave. SW. (between Air and Space and the Capitol). © 202/633-1000. www.nmai.si.edu. Free admission. Daily 10am–5:30pm; ask about extended summer hours. Closed Dec 25. Metro: L'Enfant Plaza or Smithsonian.

National Museum of Natural History 𝕶𝕶𝕶 **Ages 2 and up.** I've always been partial to this museum (the most-visited museum in the world), and so are most kids. In summer, before you enter, I suggest walking around to the 9th Street side of the museum to see the outdoor **Butterfly Garden.**

Go first to the four-story, marble-pillared rotunda on the first floor and pick up a floor plan and calendar of events at the information desk. The child hasn't been born who won't ooh and aah over the 8-ton **African Bush Elephant,** which is more than 13 feet tall!

I urge two-legged mammals to hoof it to the **Mammal Hall,** where mammalian evolution and adaptation are depicted in in-your-face exhibits—a gape-mouthed hippo, a leopard resting on a branch, and a Grevy's zebra at a watering hole are among the 274 specimens in settings akin to their natural habitats. My grandkids like this almost as much as the zoo. And unlike zoo animals, these are always awake (in a manner of speaking). While on safari, Teddy Roosevelt (the old Rough Rider) shot many of the African game animals in the dioramas. This is a hands-on experience with plenty of interactives.

Make like a fly and buzz upstairs to the **O. Orkin Insect Zoo** 𝕶, a living museum exhibit and a favorite with young and old alike. Leave your arachnophobia at the door before meeting the tarantulas. When was the last time you held a hissing cockroach? Well, you can do it here. View bees swarming around their hive, watch ants building a colony, observe millipedes as long as stretch limos, and marvel at the amazing Amazon walking stick (a dead ringer for Tommy Tune).

The insect zoo, with many colorful visual aids, crawls with more than one million visitors annually. In one interactive display, kids can test their knowledge of insect camouflages. The youngest members of your colony are invited to crawl through a replica of an African termites' mound (in the wild, these mounds grow to 25 ft.!). You might go bug-eyed peering inside a model home for common household insects that most likely cohabitate with your family. Touch models of four insect heads in the Adaptation Section, and increase your knowledge of spider strategies and ants' sociability. The rainforest exhibit features giant cockroaches, leaf-cutter ants, and tropical plants.

If you're interested in observing a tarantula's table manners, be here for chow call (Tues–Fri 10:30 and 11:30am and 1:30pm). Weekend meals are served at 11:30am and 12:30 and 1:30pm (they like to sleep late). Docents circulate to answer questions and dispel myths.

Remember *Jurassic Park?* In the **Dinosaur Hall,** get up close and personal with skeletons of the stegosaurus and triceratops, among others, and rare bones of juvenile dinosaurs. If you want to go eyeball to eyeball with quetzalcoatlus, the largest flying reptile (here, suspended from the ceiling), climb the stairs, where you can also examine several oldies but goodies mounted on the wall. In the fossil collection, you'll find

---

Break Time

The Atrium Café (a bright, six-story soaring space; sort of a Hyatt with fast food) is a glorified food court/cafeteria with standard lunch faves: burgers, hot dogs, fries, pizza, sandwiches, and wraps. You know the drill. Not tempted? A short distance away is the **Food Court in the Old Post Office,** 11th Street and Pennsylvania Avenue NW. Of course, there are always the food vendors parked end to end outside the museums.

Fun Fact A Gem of a Story

Talk about romancing the stone. The legendary **Hope Diamond,** once the eye of a Hindu idol in India, was stolen in the 17th century, and as the story goes, the gods put a curse on all future wearers.

The stone was named for British gem collector Henry Philip Hope, who listed the gem in his 1839 catalog. The rock first caught socialite Evalyn Walsh McLean's eye in 1908, when she noticed it in the Constantinople harem of the sultan of the Ottoman Empire. McLean was on a 3-month honeymoon trip with her husband, Ned, whose family owned *The Washington Post.* Before McLean purchased the stone from jeweler Pierre Cartier for $184,000 in 1911, previous owners included Louis XIV, Louis XVI, and Marie Antoinette, who learned the hard way that diamonds aren't necessarily a girl's best friend.

McLean, the last person to wear the celebrated 45½-carat blue diamond, counted presidents and monarchs among her friends, owned several homes, and, on the surface, led a charmed life, once spending $48,000 for a dinner party in 1912. But it was a life marred by tragedy (or perhaps the curse of the Hope Diamond). Her husband went insane, the marriage dissolved, and then her eldest son was killed in an accident. Still, she continued to wear the diamond. She is reported to have said, "I always thought it was garish—until I owned it." Touché! In the wake of the Great Depression, financial ruin followed. In 1933, the *Post* was sold at auction to Eugene Meyer. The curse continued—in 1946, McLean's only daughter died of a drug overdose at the age of 24.

When McLean died in 1947, friends put the diamond in a cigar box. When no bank would accept it, it found a temporary haven in an FBI vault before being sold to jeweler Harry Winston in 1949 to pay McLean's estate taxes. Nine years later, Winston donated the gem to the Smithsonian. It is said that the mailman who delivered the gem to the Smithsonian had his leg crushed in a truck accident. Soon thereafter, his wife and dog died, and his house burned to the ground.

specimens of creatures that swam in the seas 600 million years ago and a 70-million-year-old dinosaur egg. Skeletons of dinosaurs that lived more than 100 million years ago are always big hits.

"African Voices" presents the diversity and influence of the African people, history, and culture—family, work, community, environment—through photos, artifacts, sculpture, pottery, and textiles. Interactive audio and video stations allow you to view a timeline and listen to folk tales, traditional songs, and oral histories. Nearby, and less exciting I think, are the exhibits devoted to Asian cultures and Pacific cultures.

For a hands-on experience, take kids between 2 and 8 to the **Discovery Room,** where they can touch all but a few very fragile items, and explore and learn at their own pace. Among the room's treasures are large boxes of bones, reptile skins, and shells. There's a crocodile head and even a preserved rattlesnake in a jar. Discovery

Room hours in 2005 were Tuesday through Friday, noon to 2:30pm; Saturday and Sunday, 10:30am to 3:30pm. During busy times, get your free passes at the door.

The **Janet Annenberg Hooker Hall of Geology, Gems, and Minerals** ✦✦ dazzles the eye and mind. The hall accommodates visitors in a hurry as well as those wanting to digest the exhibits and scores of interactive stations in depth. The centerpiece is the 45½-carat **Hope Diamond** in the Harry Winston Gallery (named for the esteemed jeweler who purchased the diamond and donated it to the museum in 1958), valued at $100 million. (See the box "A Gem of a Story," above). Many visitors are surprised by its color—and size. What a rock! The most-visited object in all the Smithsonian museums revolves in a freestanding glass case, lit dramatically from above.

Among the other glittering treasures are diamond earrings supposedly worn by Marie Antoinette on her final ride—to the guillotine—and a necklace comprised of 374 diamonds and 15 emeralds. The displays of other gems and minerals, to my mind, upstage the polished gems.

In another section of the hall, a world map records the activity of every volcano and earthquake in the last 40 years, accompanied by sound effects. Kids (and you, too!) can pound the granite mounting of a seismograph that demonstrates the sensitivity of the instrument. In the dimly lit hall where four mines are realistically re-created, watch the video of how gems and minerals are formed and mined; then peek through the window to catch a glimpse of another jewel: the National Mall.

Moon rocks brought back by the Apollo astronauts and a 1,371-pound meteorite are on display in the space devoted to Earth and the solar system. Visitors can access a computer linking various meteorites and craters.

The **Discovery Center** (as in Discovery Channel) encompasses a cafeteria-style restaurant, museum shop, and 500-seat Johnson IMAX Theater. In the **IMAX Theater** ✦, you can view large-scale movies about the natural world. Put on your 3-D glasses to witness the live-action nature dramas. Recent choices have included *Into the Deep, T-Rex: Back to the Cretaceous,* and *Wild Safari: A South Africa Adventure.* Tickets are $8 for adults, $6.50 for kids 2–11, and $7 for seniors 60 and older. I strongly suggest ordering tickets ahead or buying them in the morning when the museum opens. For more information or to purchase tickets ahead, call ℂ **202/633-4629.**

The **Naturalist Center,** a research library/lab for those 10 and older, is located at 741 Miller Dr. SE, Suite G2, Leesburg, Virginia (ℂ **800/729-7725** or 703/779-9712). The center is open Tuesday through Saturday from 10:30am to 4pm; it's closed Sunday, Monday, and federal holidays.

Tours of the museum's highlights are offered Tuesday through Friday at 10:30am and 1:30pm, September through June. No tours July and August. Meet at the information desk in the rotunda.

During your visit, do stop at the museum shops on the ground floor, open from 10am to 5:30pm. Look no further for a wide selection of crafts, jewelry, books, science kits, toys, posters, T-shirts, and more.

Friday nights, you can groove to free live jazz (with well-behaved kids 10 and older) in the **Smithsonian Jazz Cafe** (ℂ **202/633-7400;** www.mnh.si.edu/imax) from 6 to 10pm. Enjoy a buffet from 6 to 9:30pm. All items are a la carte, priced from $4 to $6 for appetizers and desserts to $20 for filet mignon. You can also catch an IMAX movie at 6, 7:15, and 8:15pm; admission is $10 all ages.

10th St. and Constitution Ave. NW (2nd entrance on Madison Dr.). ℂ **202/357-2700.** www.nmnh.si.edu. Free admission. Daily 10am–5:30pm. Closed Dec 25. Metro: Smithsonian or Federal Triangle.

THE SMITHSONIAN INSTITUTION **135**

National Postal Museum 𝕽𝕽   **Ages 6 and up.** A joint project of the Postal Service and the Smithsonian Institution, the Postal Museum has the largest and most comprehensive collection of its kind in the world. It is a must stop for philatelists and anyone interested in postal-service history. A 1924 DeHavilland air-mail plane suspended, along with others, from the ceiling of the 90-foot-high atrium greets visitors descending the escalators from the very ornate lobby entrance. At the information desk, pick up copies of "A Self-Guided Tour for Very Young Visitors" and "Check It Out!"

"Binding the Nation," one of the museum's permanent exhibitions, covers early postal history from pre-Revolutionary days to the late 19th century. Did you know, for example, that Benjamin Franklin served as postmaster for the colonies? Or that he was fired? Find out why and lots more during your visit.

"Moving the Mail" explores the ways the postal service moves 600 million pieces per day. The amazing thing is that most of it is delivered (eventually). Aside from displays of stamps and postal documents, you'll see an 1850s stagecoach and replica of a Southern Railway mail car, complete with mailbags and sorting table. At one time, 32,000 railway mail clerks, considered the elite of the postal system, delivered 95% of the U.S. mail via rail. In the Philatelic Gallery, you can view every stamp since the mid-1800s.

"The Art of Cards and Letters" resonates. The focus here is on the role of personal mail in our daily lives. Think about it: letters home from soldiers, letters from anxious parents to kids at camp, letters from college kids asking for money. **"Customers and Communities"** takes the personal a step further with exhibits on how the mail-delivery system evolved in the 20th century to meet the needs of a growing population.

Half-hour guided tours are offered during normal museum hours; frequency depends on docent availability. Groups (of 10 or more) must call at least 3 weeks ahead to schedule a tour (📞 **202/633-5534**). Family Workshops are held one Saturday or Sunday a month from 1 to 3pm. Additional workshops for teens and adults take place monthly. When you're in the Union Station/Capitol Hill area, squeeze in this museum posthaste. It has my stamp of approval! (Sorry, I couldn't resist.)

2 Massachusetts Ave. NE (Washington City Post Office Building, next to Union Station). 📞 **202/357-2700**, or 202/357-2991 to schedule group tours. www.si.edu/postal. Free admission. Daily 10am–5:30pm. Closed Dec 25. Metro: Union Station (1st St. exit).

National Zoological Park 𝕽𝕽𝕽   **Ages 2 and up.** More than 5,000 animals call the National Zoo home, and your children will probably want to see each and every one of them. Occupying 163 acres a few Metro stops from the White House, the zoo boasts many rare and endangered species. Despite some problems in recent years, it is perennially a premier attraction for families. On weekends, during school vacations, and in the summer, go early in the morning, not only because it's less crowded, but also because the animals are spunkier. Typically, they nap in the middle of the day (sounds good to me). In May and June, when the zoo residents become parents, it's an especially appealing time to bring your little ones. Speaking of babies, did you know that giraffes grow as much as an inch a day, doubling their height in their first year? And they usually stand and take their first steps within 10 minutes after they're born. (So how come it takes human babies 10 *months* or more?)

Olmsted Walk is the zoo's main drag, and more than 3 miles of trails crisscross the park. If you follow the helpful signs along the way, you won't get lost. The terrain is hilly, so leave your flip-flops under the bed and wear your most comfortable nonskid shoes. Be sure to lift up your kids in strollers so that they can see everything. If they

The National Zoological Park

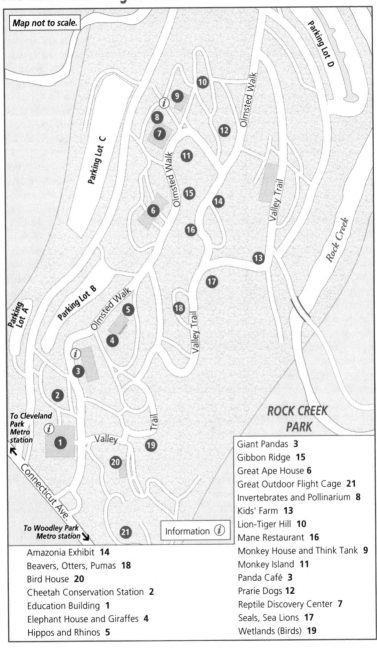

Map not to scale.

Parking Lot D

Olmsted Walk

Rock Creek

Parking Lot C

Parking Lot B

Olmsted Walk

Parking Lot A

Valley Trail

To Cleveland Park Metro station

Connecticut Ave.

Valley Trail

ROCK CREEK PARK

To Woodley Park Metro station

Information *i*

Giant Pandas **3**
Gibbon Ridge **15**
Great Ape House **6**
Great Outdoor Flight Cage **21**
Invertebrates and Pollinarium **8**
Kids' Farm **13**
Lion-Tiger Hill **10**
Mane Restaurant **16**
Monkey House and Think Tank **9**
Monkey Island **11**
Panda Café **3**
Prarie Dogs **12**
Reptile Discovery Center **7**
Seals, Sea Lions **17**
Wetlands (Birds) **19**

Amazonia Exhibit **14**
Beavers, Otters, Pumas **18**
Bird House **20**
Cheetah Conservation Station **2**
Education Building **1**
Elephant House and Giraffes **4**
Hippos and Rhinos **5**

136

don't get cranky along the way, you could easily spend half a day or longer here. Older kids, of course, can go on forever, and you'll probably be the one shouting "Uncle!"

Stop first at the information kiosk near the zoo's Connecticut Avenue entrance to pick up a map and check on any special programs—over a dozen most days that involve the animals' feeding, bathing, or training. In "How Do You Zoo?" kids are invited to role-play in a zookeeper's office, commissary, vet hospital, and animal exhibit. Geared to 5- to 10-year-olds, it's open Saturday and Sunday from 10am to 4pm.

Pandas ☟☟ Mei Xiang (may-SHONG, "beautiful fragrance"), the female, and Tian Tian (t-YEN t-YEN, "more and more"), the male, arrived in December 6, 2000, and live in a 17,500-square-foot habitat, furnished largely with bamboo. Rumors to the contrary that they met over the Internet, they were chosen for their genetic compatibility. And here's proof: A male panda cub, named Tai Shan ("peaceful mountain"), was born July 9, 2005, weighing in at a few ounces. At 1 year, he will weigh about 50 pounds, not reaching "adulthood" and his full weight of 200 to 250 pounds until he is 4 or 5. Because pandas are high-altitude dwellers, they can handle Washington's winter weather with aplomb. Summer's heat and humidity are a different story, so the zoo installed air-conditioned grottos and misting sprays. The pandas' diet consists of about 50 pounds of bamboo a day, nutritious biscuits, carrots, and apples. The Chinese have agreed to loan the pandas for 10 years, so they'll be around until at least 2010.

Almost faster than a speeding bullet are the cheetahs who occasionally race (weather permitting) in the zoo's **Cheetah Conservation Station** next to the visitor center. The station comes mighty close to mirroring the cheetahs' African savanna home. Zazi (Mom) and Ume (Dad) welcomed five little cubs in April 2005, swelling the zoo's cheetah population to five adults and nine young.

Nearby are the large land mammals: rhinos, hippos, giraffes, and elephants. The elephant training delights audiences at 11am most days. From the Elephant House, follow Olmsted Walk to the large and small cats, apes, orangutans, gibbons, and reptiles. Try to catch the seal and sea lions' training demonstration at 11:30am (check first at the information desk), and stop to peek through the window in the otter pool for a close-up of these endearing animals' high jinks.

Bald eagles Sam (female) and Tioga (male) can't fly due to injuries sustained as fledglings, so this awesome pair sticks pretty close to the ground. This exhibit also houses hawks (also birds of prey), videos, and other information about the bald eagles. Take a look at the **American Prairie** exhibit, sure to have you humming "Home on

Tips for Your Zoo Trip

1. Go early, especially if you drive. The parking lots often fill by 9:30am weekends, holidays, school vacations, and May through September. If you take Metro and want to beat the crowds, arrive between 8 to 10am or after 2pm weekdays; weekends, before 10am or after 4pm.
2. Before leaving home, print activity sheets at the Zoo's website and bring them with you. They will help you navigate and add to your child's experience.
3. Wear comfy, nonskid shoes.
4. Cater first to the youngest in your clan. Break frequently to snack, rest, and people-watch.

the Range" in no time flat. Prairie dogs (actually rodents, but cute rodents) prowl the prairie grasses when they're not burrowing to escape the stares of funny-looking tourists. Roaming the range are two American Bison, named Ten Bears (a boy) and Kicking Bird (a girl), who weigh in at close to 2,000 pounds each.

The invertebrate exhibit features tanks of starfish, sponges, and crabs, as well as spiders—all displayed very much out in the open. Although grownups are occasionally turned off, children usually want to inspect the dirt-filled sandbox inhabited by a bunch of creepy-crawlers. Last time I checked, this exhibit was open Wednesday through Sunday only.

You won't find bipeds in pinstripe suits or pantyhose in the **Think Tank** here. Instead, in an awesome spectacle, Thursday through Sunday 10am to 4pm, you can watch orangutans ("orangs") commuting (much as they do in the wild) between the Great Ape House and the Think Tank along cables 45 feet above the main path. Daily demonstrations engage the public in three areas: language, tool use, and sociability. Along with macaques (a genus of chiefly Asian monkeys, including the rhesus), the orangutans demonstrate their problem-solving skills while scientists explain their behavioral-research findings to onlookers. As visitors, you are invited to participate in a variety of activities here.

Ever wonder why flowers are colorful? Or what butterflies eat? Find the answers to these questions and many more in the **Pollinarium,** also part of the zoo's BioPark exhibit.

The **Great Outdoor Flight Cage,** which is 130 feet in diameter, is a sky-high, mesh-enclosed hemisphere that your little chickadees can enjoy. Older kids and adults can carry their featherweight concerns to the Bird Resource Center at the rear of the Bird House and take a guided tour of a room in which eggs incubate and zoo workers examine some of our ailing fine-feathered friends. Watch the flamingoes and other residents on the live webcams. FYI: The bat cave closed. Life will never be the same.

Don't miss **Amazonia,** still being greeted with great fanfare since opening over a decade ago. An ideal cool-day escape—it's plenty steamy inside—the re-created rain forest at the edge of Rock Creek Park lies at the foot of Valley Trail. The exhibit supports a broad array of plants and animals. Enjoy an underwater view of the freshwater fish of the Amazon, some of which are 7 feet long.

For a behind-the-scenes view of Smithsonian research as it happens, step into the **Amazonia Science Gallery,** adjacent to the Rainforest Exhibit, where the biodiversity of the Amazon is re-created. The concept of a cutting-edge working research institute allows visitors to analyze their own voices and compare them to animal vocalizations. Scientists and education specialists are on hand to explain what they do and how they do it. In the **GeoSphere,** projectors, satellite imagery, and computer-generated information provide visual images that illustrate the Earth's geophysical process.

Near Amazonia and the Rock Creek Park entrance lies the **Kids' Farm** 🐾🐾 (geared to kids 3–8), with chickens, cows, donkeys, ducks, and goats—and a fly or two or three. Children can climb atop a giant rubber pizza with movable foam toppings. Depending on staff availability and weather, kids can groom the donkeys and goats in the Caring Corral, typically open for about 1½ hours in the morning and again in the afternoon. For an update, ask at the information kiosk when you arrive.

"What if Adam and Eve were tempted by a fuzzy-tailed squirrel rather than a snake?" This is one of the questions posed in the **Reptile Discovery Center.** You have to admit it's a step up from "snake house." The center, with its many hands-on exhibits, is attempting to raise the biological literacy of zoo visitors and modify negative notions about reptiles and amphibians. The desired effect is nearly achieved by having reptile keepers and docents on hand to answer questions.

Immensely popular is the zoo's take on a slumber party, **"Snore & Roar."** After an animal-house tour and hike with flashlights, the kids (6 and older) bed down in 4-person tents near the lions and tigers. It's $50 to sleep near the animals, one adult for every three kids. (You didn't think you could just drop them off, did you?) The wait list is always long, so if you're interested, sign up early.

Snack bars and ice-cream stands are scattered throughout the park. At the **Panda Cafe,** enjoy a fast-food break at tables with umbrellas. The **Panda Express Grill,** across from the Panda House, serves sandwiches, salads, cotton candy, and ice cream from 10am to 4pm, and accepts most credit cards. The **Mane Restaurant** is at the bottom of the hill if you started at Connecticut Avenue. Hot dogs, hamburgers, and fresh salads are available. But many visitors prefer to bring sandwiches, buy drinks and ice cream, and dine alfresco at one of the zoo's grassy picnic areas.

Across the street from the main Connecticut Avenue entrance are a trio of eateries, open daily, that I recommend as superior to the zoo's food for humans; I can't speak for the elephants and orangutans. **Animal Crackers Cafe** is open for breakfast, lunch, and snacks, with PB&J, hot dogs, and grilled cheese for the kids. **Zoo Market and Deli** has few tables, but you can pick up sandwiches and snacks, and picnic in the zoo. Try the panda-shaped ice cream sandwich. The **Oxford Tavern** (aka the Zoo Bar) features yummy burgers and sandwiches, and a children's menu. Filled with families at noon, at night the local animals take over, so I suggest eating outdoors.

The Zoo Store in the visitor center is open daily and carries a wonderful selection of zoo-related books on several reading levels, stuffed (excuse me, "plush" is the politically correct term) animals, and animal puzzles.

Beginning late June, a free summer concert series, Sunset Serenades, runs for five consecutive Thursdays, 6:30–8:30pm, on Lion/Tiger Hill. You can BYO or get supper to go at the Mane Restaurant and picnic while you listen.

3001 Connecticut Ave. NW. (C) **202/633-4800.** Weekend guided walking tours: (C) 202/633-3025. www.si.edu/nat zoo. Free admission. Buildings: Apr 1–late Oct 10am–6pm; late Oct–late March 10am–4:30pm. Grounds: Apr 1–late Oct 6am–8pm; late Oct–Apr 1 6am–6pm. Closed Dec 25. How Do You Zoo? open Sat–Sun 10am–4pm. Zoo bookstore open daily 9am–5pm. Fee for parking based on length of visit, up to $12. Free parking for FONZ members; parking for visitors with disabilities in Lots A, B, and D; some street parking. Strollers rent for $3 single, $8 double for FONZ members, and $4 single, $11 double for nonmembers plus a paid deposit, driver's license, or military ID. Pets are not allowed in the park. Metro: Cleveland Park (an easier walk) or Woodley Park–Zoo/Adams–Morgan and then northbound L-2 or L-4 bus, or walk 1/3 mile uphill.

Renwick Gallery 🐾 **Ages 6 and up.** Washington's first private art museum was the original home of the Corcoran collection. The Renwick, a department of the National Museum of American Art, celebrated its 30th anniversary in 2002. The gallery, in a stunning 19th-century French Second Empire–style building, is a personal favorite of mine. The first floor exhibits showcasing contemporary crafts and decorative arts appeal to kids because they're 3-D and usually colorful (blown glass, quilts, and so on). The second floor is devoted to works from the permanent collection, exhibited on a rotating basis. Most kids over 6 have at least a fleeting appreciation of the interior space. Especially impressive is the broad carpeted staircase leading to the second floor. You almost expect the trumpets to announce your arrival. The 90-foot **Victorian Grand Salon,** with its 38-foot skylight ceiling and wainscoted plum walls holding scores of paintings, is striking—even if you don't warm to the art.

Where Children Can:

- Crawl through a replica of an African termites' mound—the O. Orkin Insect Zoo in the **National Museum of Natural History.**
- Enjoy free entertainment—**Kennedy Center Millennium Stage, Old Post Office,** and **Ronald Reagan International Trade Building.**
- Gin raw cotton—the Hands-On History Room in the **National Museum of American History.**
- Whisper and be heard clear across the room—the **U.S. Capitol's Statuary Hall.**
- Watch millions of dollars being printed—the **Bureau of Engraving and Printing.**
- Take a simulated orbital flight—Earth Station One in the **National Geographic Society's Explorers Hall.**
- View the model tarantula featured in the James Bond movie *Dr. No*—the **International Spy Museum.**
- Be dazzled by a 45½-carat diamond—the **National Museum of Natural History.**
- Sink their teeth into a freeze-dried ice cream sandwich—the **National Air and Space Museum's** gift shop.
- Pedal a boat next to two presidential monuments—the **Tidal Basin,** next to the Jefferson Memorial and the Franklin Delano Roosevelt Memorial.
- Touch a moon rock—the **National Air and Space Museum.**
- Dress in colonial clothing—the **DAR Museum.**
- Watch a clock that always reads 7:22am—the **Petersen House,** where Lincoln died on April 15, 1865, at 7:22am.
- Ride a carousel in the heart of the city—outside the **Smithsonian's Arts and Industries Building.**
- Peer up at a 15-story ceiling—the **National Building Museum.**
- Pet a crab or fish—the **National Aquarium's** touch tank.
- Explore the oldest house in Washington—the **Old Stone House** in Georgetown.
- Dine with U.S. senators—the **Senate Dining Room** in the Capitol.
- Find the grave of the founder of the Smithsonian Institution—the **Smithsonian "Castle."**

Without a doubt, the most popular work in this museum for young people is Larry Fuente's whimsical *Game Fish,* an eye-catching sailfish trophy whose scales glitter with a colorful array of toys and game pieces. If you can lure the kids away, see if Patti Warashina's *Convertible Car Kiln* is displayed.

The Octagon Gallery was designed for Hiram Powers's nude, *The Greek Slave* (now in the Corcoran). Because of its prurient nature (for the Victorian era), viewing times were once different for men and women. The Octagon Gallery is now home to a remarkable example of trompe l'oeil imagery: Wendell Castle's *Ghost Clock* is actually a solid piece of carved mahogany. Honest!

Walk-in tours are weekdays at noon and Saturday and Sunday at 2pm. Prearranged tours are at 10 and 11am and 1pm (© **202/357-2532**). The merchandise in the intimate museum shop—crafts, books, clothing—is well chosen and unique, a favorite of mine for gift buying, especially the art-inspired children's books.

Pennsylvania Ave. at 17th St. NW. © **202/357-2700**. www.nmaa.si.edu. Free admission. Daily 10am–5:30pm. Closed Dec 25. Metro: Farragut North (K St. exit) or Farragut West (17th St. exit).

Arthur M. Sackler Gallery (of Asian and Near Eastern Art) Ages 6 and up.

The Sackler shares a 4.2-acre underground museum complex with the National Museum of African Art, the International Gallery, and several Smithsonian classrooms and services. While Chinese bronzes, Southeast Asian sculpture, and Persian manuscripts might not appeal to your kids upon entering, they're sure to have a change of heart during their visit.

Children with an interest in archaeology can pursue exhibitions of some of the oldest art ever made. Even the youngest visitors enjoy counting the fanciful animal forms among the intricate designs on 4,500-year-old bronze vessels in **"Arts of China."** You can pick up free family guides at the information desk. **ImaginAsia** is the highly successful program cosponsored by the Sackler and Freer galleries aimed at children from 6 to 14 and their companions. Participants tour with a special activity guide and then create their own works of art based on their impressions of what they've seen. Topics change monthly during the school year, more frequently in summer. ImaginAsia is held on Saturdays and Sundays during the school year and Tuesdays, Wednesdays, and Thursdays in summer. Call for the current schedule of docent-led tours offered daily (© **202/357-2700**). For information about museum programs and temporary exhibits, call © **202/357-3200**, or inquire at the information desk.

On the way out, visit the Victorian-style Enid A. Haupt Garden (p. 196), with its geometric parterre. On one side of the garden, you can enter a moon gate to an Asian garden; on the other, a small waterfall cascades into a smaller pond. The garden is open Memorial Day to Labor Day from 7am to 8pm; the rest of the year, it's open from 7am to 5:45pm.

1050 Independence Ave. SW. © **202/357-2700**. www.asia.si.edu. Free admission. Daily 10am–5:30pm. Tours 11:30am Thurs–Tues. Closed Dec 25. Metro: Smithsonian.

2 Monuments, Memorials & the National Cathedral
PRESIDENTIAL MONUMENTS

Four U.S. presidents have been honored with monuments in the nation's capital: George Washington, Abraham Lincoln, Thomas Jefferson, and Franklin Delano Roosevelt. Try to see them all. I could wax poetic on the feelings elicited by each, but you should find out for yourself.

Park Your Questions with the Rangers

Please note that monuments and memorials are not staffed by park rangers 24/7. Rangers are usually on site to answer questions and give directions from 9 or 9:30am to 5 or 5:30pm; in summer, usually until 7:30pm or later.

Monuments & Memorials

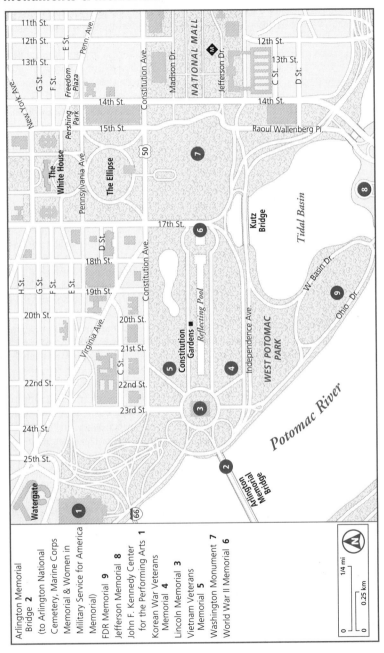

11th St.
12th St.
E St.
Penn. Ave.
13th St.
New York Ave.
NATIONAL MALL
M
12th St.
13th St.
C St.
D St.
G St.
F St.
Constitution Ave.
Madison Dr.
Jefferson Dr.
Freedom Plaza
14th St.
14th St.
Pershing Park
15th St.
Raoul Wallenberg Pl.
Pennsylvania Ave.
The White House
The Ellipse
50
7
8
Tidal Basin
Kutz Bridge
17th St.
6
D St.
18th St.
Constitution Ave.
H St.
G St.
F St.
E St.
19th St.
W. Basin Dr.
9
Ohio Dr.
20th St.
20th St.
Reflecting Pool
Independence Ave.
WEST POTOMAC PARK
Virginia Ave.
21st St.
C St.
Constitution Gardens
5
4
22nd St.
22nd St.
23rd St.
3
24th St.
Potomac River
25th St.
2
Watergate
Arlington Memorial Bridge
1
66

Arlington Memorial
    Bridge **2**
    (to Arlington National
    Cemetery, Marine Corps
    Memorial & Women in
    Military Service for America
    Memorial)
FDR Memorial **9**
Jefferson Memorial **8**
John F. Kennedy Center
    for the Performing Arts **1**
Korean War Veterans
    Memorial **4**
Lincoln Memorial **3**
Vietnam Veterans
    Memorial **5**
Washington Monument **7**
World War II Memorial **6**

N

0   1/4 mi
0   0.25 km

Thomas Jefferson Memorial ✮✮✮ *(Moments*   **Ages 8 and up.** Some students of history think that Jefferson was the Rodney Dangerfield of his time, that he "got no respect." While the memorials to Washington and Lincoln enjoyed prestigious downtown addresses for quite a spell, in accordance with L'Enfant's plan, Mr. Jefferson wasn't appropriately honored until April 13 (his birthday) in 1943, when the Jefferson Memorial was dedicated.

Well, good things come to those who wait. On a parcel reclaimed from the Potomac, on line with the south axis of the White House, a memorial was erected similar to Rome's Pantheon. Jefferson so favored this architectural model that he used its columned rotunda design at the Virginia State Capitol, the University of Virginia, and Monticello, his home in Charlottesville, Virginia.

Above the entrance, he is seen standing before Benjamin Franklin, John Adams, Roger Sherman, and Robert Livingston, members of the committee appointed to write the Declaration of Independence. Engraved on the interior walls are inscriptions from Jefferson's writings that sum up his philosophies on freedom and government. History buffs might note that certain "liberties" were taken with the Declaration of Independence. There are 11 mistakes that can't be blamed on the typing pool. Can your family find them?

The Capitol, White House, Washington Monument, and Lincoln Memorial are visible from the steps, and it's a front-row seat for the Cherry Blossom Festival. After a visit to the memorial, you'll probably agree that Jefferson finally received the respect that he so richly deserved. For high drama, come at night and sit on the steps. If your kids don't think it's awesome, leave them home next time.

Tidal Basin, south end of 15th St. SW, in West Potomac Park. ☎ 202/426-6821. www.nps.gov/jeff. Free admission. Daily 8am–midnight. Closed Dec 25. Transportation: Accessible by car, cab, or Tourmobile. Metro (Smithsonian); then a 15-min. hike.

Lincoln Memorial ✮✮✮   **Ages 4 and up.** I had an English professor who said if you weren't moved by the Lincoln Memorial, your heart had probably stopped.

If the only image that you hold of the 16th U.S. president is on a penny, toss it aside and come see this one. The 19-by-19-foot statue of a seated, contemplative Abraham Lincoln was designed by Daniel French. It took 28 blocks of marble and 4 years of carving to complete, and it is the focal point of the classically inspired monument by Henry Bacon.

A gleam in some politician's eye shortly after Lincoln's death in 1865, this Parthenon look-alike was not completed until 1922. The Doric columns number 36, one for each state in the Union at the time of Lincoln's death. The names are inscribed on the frieze over the colonnade. The names of the 48 states at the time of the memorial's dedication appear near the top of the monument, and a plaque for Alaska and Hawaii was added later.

The stirring words of Lincoln's "Gettysburg Address" and "Second Inaugural Address" are carved into the limestone walls, and above them allegorical murals by Jules Guérin represent North–South unity and the freeing of the slaves.

If you can come here at night, when the crowds thin out, I urge you to do so. From the rear of the memorial, gaze across the Potomac to Arlington National Cemetery and the eternal flame at John F. Kennedy's grave. From the steps, take in the reflecting pool, a nighttime mirror of the memorial, and past it to the Washington Monument, Mall, and Capitol. If the sight doesn't grab you, well, my English professor spoke the truth.

A Little Piece of History

The little stone house on the southwest corner of 17th Street and Constitution Avenue was the lock keeper's house for L'Enfant's "Canal Through Tiber Creek" plan. L'Enfant envisioned a canal meandering along Constitution Avenue from the Potomac River in Georgetown, through the Ellipse, and east through the District before dipping south to the Anacostia River. Believe it or not, the canal was built and used until the coming of the railroads made it obsolete in the 1870s. The lock keeper's house is the only remnant of this piece of D.C. history.

As the result of a project conceived by a group of high school students visiting from Scottsdale, Arizona, a visitor center opened in the once-gloomy basement of the memorial in 1994. Most striking in the minimuseum are photographs and film clips of history-making protests and civil-rights events that took place at the site, such as Marian Anderson's Easter 1939 concert after she, as an African-American woman, was barred from singing at DAR Constitution Hall, and Martin Luther King, Jr.'s 1963 "I Have a Dream" speech. Also on display are 13 marble tablets carved with Lincoln quotations and exhibits detailing the memorial's design and construction. The "Lincoln Legacy" is a permanent exhibition, open from 8am to midnight daily.

The roadway project to enhance security and improve traffic flow is scheduled for completion in late summer 2006. Hallelujah.

West of the Mall at 23rd St. NW, between Constitution and Independence aves. NW. (C) 202/426-6895. www.nps. gov/linc. Free admission. Daily 24 hours. Park staff on duty 8am–midnight. Metro: Foggy Bottom.

Franklin Delano Roosevelt Memorial 🐨🐨🐨 Ages 6 and up. The newest of the presidential monuments was dedicated in May 1997. The length of three football fields, it lies on the western shore of the Tidal Basin, near the Jefferson Memorial. Entrances are at several points from the pathway along the Tidal Basin. It's about a 10-minute walk from the Smithsonian Metro station, longer from the Foggy Bottom station. The Tourmobile trams also stop here. I hesitate to recommend this, but limited street parking is available in front of the memorial. The parklike setting makes this a good place to bring kids.

Anchored by restrooms at both ends, the FDR monument is marked by imposing granite walls; fountains (the most aesthetically pleasing aspect of the monument, in my opinion); meditative areas; and bunkerlike areas evoking Roosevelt's first inauguration, the Great Depression, World War II, postwar optimism, and FDR's accomplishments.

Of interest to younger children, beside the awesome fountains, is the sculpture of FDR's beloved dog Fala (here 3 ft. high), loyally depicted next to the president's feet. A 39-ton statue of Eleanor Roosevelt stands at the entrance of Room Four. Mrs. Roosevelt is the first First Lady to be honored in a presidential memorial. Perhaps the most inspiring aspect of this latest stone homage to U.S. presidents is the view across the Tidal Basin to D.C.

An information center and bookshop (open 9am–9pm) are located at the main entrance (south end). On display in the information center, among the Roosevelt memorabilia, is a replica of FDR's wheelchair, which he designed. A pamphlet containing the quotes etched in the granite walls of the memorial is a meaningful souvenir.

900 Ohio Dr. SW (west side of the Tidal Basin, West Potomac Park). (C) 202/426-6841. www.nps.gov./fdrm. Free admission. Daily 8am–midnight. Closed Dec 25. Metro: Smithsonian.

Washington Monument ⭐⭐   **Ages 6 and up.** If you fly into Reagan National Airport, you will be treated to a supreme view of this monument. Standing 555 feet, 5 inches tall in its stockinged feet, the marble-and-granite obelisk is an engineering marvel with walls that taper from 15 feet at the base to 18 inches at the top.

Nearly half a century passed from its conception to the actual construction between 1848 and 1884—a story and a half, if you have the time and interest to research it. During the Civil War, the unfinished structure was known as Beef Depot Monument because cattle grazed the grounds before they were slaughtered. Another sidelight: The monument is not positioned exactly according to L'Enfant's plan. It had to be shifted eastward a tad because the original site was too marshy. That's a polite way of saying that D.C. was a varmint- and mosquito-infested swamp.

Come on a weekday, if at all possible. Everyone 2 and older must pick up a free timed ticket from the 15th Street kiosk, beginning at 8:30am until they are gone, or order ahead from the U.S. Park Service (📞 **800/967-2283,** between 10am and 10pm). There is a $1.50 per ticket fee plus 50¢ shipping. Visitors used to be able to climb the 897 steps. Now you'll have to take the elevator—faster than in most apartment buildings—and you'll be at the top in a little over a minute. The view is spectacular, especially after dark. For a singular Washington moment, watch the sun set behind the monument from the 14th Street (west) side of the Museum of American History.

Designed by Robert Mills, architect of the Treasury and Old Patent Office buildings, the monument is two-tone, but not by original design. Notice how the stones darken about 150 feet from the base. During the construction of the monument, the Civil War as well as other matters put the building process on hold. When the government resumed the project in the 1870s, the "new" marble, mined from another part of the quarry, was darker. If you've ever tried to match paint, you'll understand the problem.

The monument grounds are often the site of concerts and other special events in summer.

15th St. and Constitution Ave. NW. 📞 **202/426-6841.** www.nps.gov/wamo. Free admission. Daily 9am–4:45pm. Closed July 4th and Dec 25. Metro: Smithsonian.

WAR MEMORIALS

Arlington National Cemetery ⭐⭐ (Moments   **Ages 6 and up.** More than 216,000 American war dead are buried in the 612 acres of hallowed hills overlooking the nation's capital from the Virginia side of the Potomac River. Try to include this in your itinerary, especially if you have school-age children in tow—there is much to feed the mind and the spirit.

Four million visitors enter Arlington National Cemetery annually to watch specially trained members of the 3rd Infantry Regiment from the adjacent Fort Myer guard stand sentinel day and night over the simple but inspiring white marble **Tomb of the Unknowns.** Four unidentified bodies from this century's four wars are interred here. The soldiers who stand guard are part of the nation's oldest military unit, known as the Old Guard; it dates from Colonial times. If you're close enough, you might notice that the soldiers' white gloves are wet. Before standing guard, they soak their gloves to better grip the wood handle of the bayonet-tipped M-14. The changing of the guard takes place every half-hour from April through September and every hour on the hour from October through March.

The **Memorial Amphitheater** is the setting for Memorial Day and Veterans' Day services. Junior historians interested in the Spanish–American War will want to see the

Arlington National Cemetery

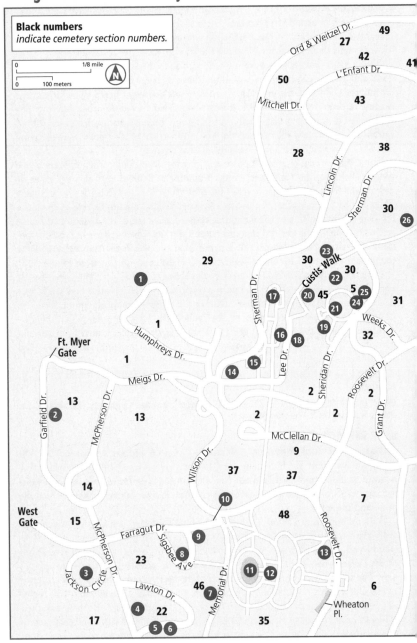

Black numbers
indicate cemetery section numbers.

0 _____ 1/8 mile
0 _____ 100 meters

Ord & Weitzel Dr.   49
27
42
50   L'Enfant Dr.   41
Mitchell Dr.   43

28   38

Lincoln Dr.   Sherman Dr.   30   26

29   30   23   Custis Walk   30
1   17   22   5   25
Sherman Dr.   20   45   24   31
1   16   18   21   Weeks Dr.
Ft. Myer / Gate   Humphreys Dr.   19   32
1   14   15   Lee Dr.   Sheridan Dr.   Roosevelt Dr.
Meigs Dr.   2   2   2
Garfield Dr.   13   2   McClellan Dr.   Grant Dr.
2   13   9
McPherson Dr.   Wilson Dr.   37   37   7
14   10   48
West Gate   15   Farragut Dr.   9   Roosevelt Dr.
McPherson Dr.   Sigsbee Ave.   8   13   6
23   11   12
3   Lawton Dr.   46   Memorial Dr.
Jackson Circle   4   22   7   Wheaton Pl.
17   5   6   35

146

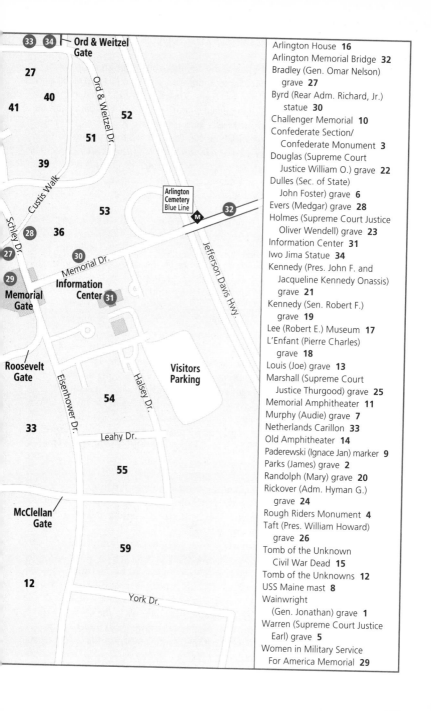

Arlington House **16**
Arlington Memorial Bridge **32**
Bradley (Gen. Omar Nelson)
  grave **27**
Byrd (Rear Adm. Richard, Jr.)
  statue **30**
Challenger Memorial **10**
Confederate Section/
  Confederate Monument **3**
Douglas (Supreme Court
  Justice William O.) grave **22**
Dulles (Sec. of State)
  John Foster) grave **6**
Evers (Medgar) grave **28**
Holmes (Supreme Court Justice
  Oliver Wendell) grave **23**
Information Center **31**
Iwo Jima Statue **34**
Kennedy (Pres. John F. and
  Jacqueline Kennedy Onassis)
  grave **21**
Kennedy (Sen. Robert F.)
  grave **19**
Lee (Robert E.) Museum **17**
L'Enfant (Pierre Charles)
  grave **18**
Louis (Joe) grave **13**
Marshall (Supreme Court
  Justice Thurgood) grave **25**
Memorial Amphitheater **11**
Murphy (Audie) grave **7**
Netherlands Carillon **33**
Old Amphitheater **14**
Paderewski (Ignace Jan) marker **9**
Parks (James) grave **2**
Randolph (Mary) grave **20**
Rickover (Adm. Hyman G.)
  grave **24**
Rough Riders Monument **4**
Taft (Pres. William Howard)
  grave **26**
Tomb of the Unknown
  Civil War Dead **15**
Tomb of the Unknowns **12**
USS Maine mast **8**
Wainwright
  (Gen. Jonathan) grave **1**
Warren (Supreme Court Justice
  Earl) grave **5**
Women in Military Service
  For America Memorial **29**

mast from the USS *Maine* ("Remember the Maine") on the other side of Memorial Drive.

The imposing Greek Revival building at the top of the hill, **Arlington House,** once belonged to Gen. Robert E. Lee and Mary Randolph Curtis, who just happened to be Martha Washington's great-granddaughter. Lee was married here and lived in the neoclassical mansion until 1861 when he resigned from the U.S. Army to command the Northern Virginia Rebel Army. Four weeks later, the house was seized by Union troops. When the Union Army was looking for a burial site for its soldiers, Gen. Montgomery Meigs suggested that the war dead be buried "in Lee's backyard."

The government ultimately bought the property, and since 1933 the National Park Service has been cutting the grass and taking care of the furnishings. Check out the servants' quarters during the free self-guided tour (9:30am–4:30pm Oct–Mar; until 6pm Apr–Sept).

The marble, slate, and Cape Cod fieldstone grave sites of **John F. Kennedy,** 35th U.S. president; his wife, Jacqueline Kennedy Onassis; and two of their infant children lie off Sheridan Drive on the sloping lawn below Arlington House. At night, the Eternal Flame can be seen from the Rooftop Terrace of the Kennedy Center and several other D.C. vantage points. Sen. Robert Kennedy's grave lies close by, marked by a simple cross. The site is best visited early in the morning before the masses arrive. JFK and William Howard Taft are the only U.S. presidents buried in Arlington.

Pierre L'Enfant was moved from a pauper's grave to his final resting place near Arlington House when it finally dawned on those in power that, despite his supposedly cantankerous disposition, L'Enfant did a bang-up job designing the capital city. Many newcomers (and old-timers, too) have trouble finding their way around D.C. and think that L'Enfant should have been left undisturbed in his original burial site.

The **Women in Military Service for America Memorial** (www.womensmemorial. org) honors the 1.8 million American women who have served in the military, from the American Revolution to the present. The memorial, dedicated October 18, 1997, incorporates the spruced-up neoclassical granite retaining/entrance wall designed in the 1920s by McKim, Mead & White. Carved from the hillside behind the semicircular wall are the computer registry, where visitors can access the personal recollections and photographs of over 250,000 U.S. servicewomen, a Hall of Honor, a theater, a conference center, 14 exhibit alcoves, and a gift shop. Kudos to retired Air Force Brig. Gen. Wilma L. Vaught, who oversaw the project for more than a decade, and on-site project manager Margaret Van Voast. The memorial is a fitting and long-overdue answer to "What did you do in the war, Mom?"

The **Marine Corps War Memorial** (www.nps.gov/gwmp/usmc.htm) and the statue of the Marines raising the flag over **Iwo Jima** are near the Orde–Weitzel Gate at the north end of the cemetery. The U.S. Marine Drum and Bugle Corps and Silent Drill team perform at the Iwo Jima Memorial on Tuesday evenings at 7pm early June to mid-August. Bring something to sit on. Free shuttle buses whisk visitors from the visitor center to the parade site (© **703/289-2500**). Nearby is the 49-bell **Netherlands Carillon** (© **703/289-2500**). You can climb the tower (kids under 12 must be with an adult) or tiptoe through 15,000 blooming tulips in the spring. Enjoy a concert by guest carillonneurs on Saturday and holidays during April, May, and September from 2 to 4pm. In years past, the concerts were held on Saturday from 6:30 to 8:30pm, June through August. Just north of Arlington Cemetery at **Fort Myer,** visit the caisson platoon stables of the Old Guard, which counted George Washington as one of its members. The horses, used in processions and presidential funerals, can usually be viewed Monday through Friday from noon to 4pm. Drive here or take a taxi from the Arlington Cemetery Metro or visitor center. Nearby, the **Old Guard Museum** (www.mdw.army.mil/oldguard) contains displays dating from the Revolutionary War era. The museum is open Monday through Saturday from 9am to 4pm and Sunday from 1 to 4pm.

Arlington, VA (west side of Memorial Bridge). © 703/697-2131. www.arlingtoncemetery.org. Free admission. Apr–Sept daily 8am–7pm; until 5pm the rest of year. Metro: Arlington Cemetery. You can also walk across Arlington Memorial Bridge (from near the Lincoln Memorial), or board a Tourmobile downtown or at the cemetery's visitor center.

Korean War Veterans Memorial ⟡ Ages 2 and up.

After years of squabbling and disagreement over its design, the Korean War Veterans Memorial was unveiled in July 1995. Since then, it has been hailed as a tour de force. On a 4-acre parcel southeast of the Lincoln Memorial and across from the Vietnam War Veterans Memorial (with your back to Lincoln, it is to the right of the Reflecting Pool), the stainless-steel statues of 19 poncho-draped soldiers on the march make a powerful statement, drawing the viewer into the action. In the background is a black granite mural wall with the etched faces of support troops. The faces were culled from actual photos of Korean War veterans.

Southeast of Lincoln Memorial, French Dr., and Independence Ave. © 202/426-6841. www.nps.gov/kowa. Free admission. Daily 24 hours. Park staff on duty 8am–7:30pm (summer extended hours). Metro: Smithsonian (Independence Ave. exit) or Foggy Bottom and then walk.

Vietnam Veterans Memorial ⟡⟡ (Moments) Ages 10 and up.

The Wall, 140 panels of polished black granite stretching almost 500 feet, honors the nearly 60,000 men and women who died or remain missing as a result of the Vietnam War. Names are listed chronologically, from the first casualty in 1959 to the last in 1975. Although many leave the site misty-eyed, children too young to know anything of the Vietnam War will probably be bored. Vietnam veteran Jan Scruggs initiated the project in 1979, and since its opening on November 13, 1982, the memorial has been one of the most-visited sites in Washington. Nearby is the Vietnam Women's Memorial, a bronze sculpture of three women and a wounded soldier, which was dedicated in November 1993.

Northeast of the Lincoln Memorial near 21st St. and Constitution Ave. NW. © 202/634-1568. www.nps.gov/vive. Free admission. Daily 24 hours, with rangers on duty 8am–7:30pm (summer extended hours). Metro: Foggy Bottom (walk east on H or I sts., turn right at 21st St., and walk for 6 or 7 blocks).

World War II Memorial Ages 10 and up.

A 7.4-acre parklike setting with fountains and a rainbow pool at the east end of the Reflecting Pool (between the Washington Monument and Lincoln Memorial) honors the 16 million who served in the American armed forces during WWII, those who gave their lives, and those at home who supported the war effort. The granite and bronze bases of the memorial plaza are inscribed with the seals of the armed services. Highlights of the war years are depicted in 24 bas-relief panels. Two pavilions mark the north and south ends of the plaza, which visitors can access via ramps. Granite benches hug the curvilinear walls—a good place to reflect, and also to rest your weary dogs and let the kids romp. The 56 granite pillars, representing each state, territory, and the District of Columbia at the time of the war, are arranged according to the year each entered the Union. Sculpted into the Freedom Wall at the western side of the memorial are 4,000 gold stars. They symbolize the 400,000 American soldiers who died during the war. That's a lot of casualties.

The memorial is pleasing enough, but also a reminder that we have learned little about the idiocy of war in the intervening years.

17th Street NW, between Washington Monument and Reflecting Pool. © 202/426-6841. www.nps.gov/nwwm. Free admission. Daily 24 hours, with rangers on duty 8am–7:30pm (summer extended hours). Metro: Foggy Bottom or Smithsonian; then a 15-min. walk.

NATIONAL CATHEDRAL
Washington National Cathedral *Moments*   **Ages 4 and up.** Because the cathedral (officially named the Cathedral Church of St. Peter and St. Paul) is one of the few sights in Washington not close to a Metro station, I suggest taking a taxi, a Metrobus, or the Old Town Trolley. The sixth-largest religious structure in the world perches on a parcel known as "the close" on Mount St. Alban. The cathedral is visible from several vantage points inside and outside the city. The top of the tower is 676 feet above sea level—that's mighty high, given Washington's zero elevation. Construction began in 1907 on the Gothic-inspired cathedral, but not until 1990, with the completion of the twin west towers, was the cathedral officially consecrated. Pick up an illustrated guide in the Cathedral Museum Store detailing the history and architecture before exploring on your own, or take the 30-minute guided tour Monday through Saturday between 10am and 11:30am and 12:45 and 3:15pm, and Sunday from 12:45 to 2:30pm (© 202/537-6207). Tours begin every 15 to 20 minutes. No tours are given Thanksgiving, Christmas, and Easter.

The **Space Window,** 1 of more than 200 stained-glass windows in the cathedral, is dedicated to the Apollo 11 mission. Can your kids pick out the moon rock? Viewing the **Rose Window** in the North Transept at dusk is a religious experience in itself. The vaulted ceiling above the 518-foot-long nave is 102 feet. But everything is kid size in the charming **Children's Chapel,** with its tiny chairs and pint-size pipe organ, scaled for a 6-year-old.

The **Pilgrim Observation Gallery** has a fantastic view of Washington beyond the flying buttresses and gargoyles. The gallery is open Monday through Saturday from 10am to 4pm and Sunday from noon to 4pm.

Let your youngsters loose to run around, or meander with them, through nearly 60 magnificent acres of beautifully landscaped prime real estate. Enjoy a family picnic, perhaps, and then stop in at the **Bishop's Garden** (open daily during daylight hours) south of the cathedral. It's modeled on a medieval walled garden. Dried herbs, teas, gifts, and books are sold in the **Herb Cottage.** At the **Greenhouse,** on South Road, you can purchase growing herbs and plants. The Museum Shop, Herb Cottage, and Greenhouse are open daily, except December 25 and January 1, from 9:30am to 5pm (© 202/537-6267).

The **Flower Mart,** held the first Friday (10am–6pm) and Saturday (10am–5pm) in May, features plants and garden items along with rides, puppet shows, and other activities for kids. More than 50 vendors sell food items, jewelry, and crafts. Free shuttles run from the Tenleytown Metro both days (© 202/537-3185). **Family Saturdays** refers to a series of workshops that include a tour of the cathedral and an art project. Geared to kids 4 to 12, it's usually held the third Saturday of the month, from 10 to 11:30am and noon to 1:30pm. The cost is $6 per child. Call © 202/537-02184 for reservations. In the **Gargoyle's Den** (for kids 6–12) most Saturdays between 10am and 2pm, docents help kids get a taste of cathedral arts through arts-and-crafts projects (create a gargoyle or carve a stone). The cost is $5 per group of up to four people, $1 for each additional person. For more information, call © 202/537-2934.

Hear the **Cathedral Choir Evensong** most Mondays through Thursdays at 5:30pm during the school year. Demonstrations of the cathedral's 10,650-pipe organ are Monday and Wednesday at 12:30pm, and anyone can attend. The cathedral also hosts special concerts throughout the year. For information on Tour and Tea at the cathedral, see p. 107. At the cathedral's annual open house in September, visitors can tour the bell tower. Special **Behind the Scenes tours** are suitable for kids 12 and older. They're held Monday through Friday at 10:30am and 1:30pm from July through February. *Note:* Includes climbing lots of stairs. For more information, call ℂ **202/537-2934.**

Massachusetts and Wisconsin aves. NW. ℂ **202/537-6200.** www.cathedral.org. Donations $3 for adults, $2 seniors, $1 for children. Worship free. Mon–Fri 10am–5:30pm; Sat. 10am–4pm; Sun 12:30–4:30pm; extended summer hours to 8pm weeknights. Metro: Tenleytown and then no. 32, 34, or 36 bus south on Wisconsin Ave. Bus: N-2, -3, -4 up Massachusetts Ave. from Dupont Circle, or take Old Town Trolley.

3 The White House & Branches of the Government

Some of the sites listed below have suspended or limited their tours since September 11, 2001, and the war with Iraq, and tour details are subject to change based on security concerns. To avoid disappointment, please call any of the federal buildings you'd like to visit before you go.

The White House 🐾🐾   **Ages 10 and up.** Self-guided tours are open to groups of 10 or more only, Tuesday through Saturday (except federal holidays) between 7:30am and 12:30pm. Visitors must make reservations through their congressional representatives (you can look them up at www.senate.gov and www.house.gov). You must submit your name, date of birth, and Social Security number to your U.S. representative or senator, who will submit all names for security screening. Allow several weeks at least. You may make your request up to 6 months in advance. Assuming you pass muster and get your tickets, before your tour, stop first at the **White House Visitor Center,** 15th and E streets, to peruse the exhibits to enhance your visit. A White House spokesperson says that the tour is appropriate for kids 12 and over. (I think that mature 10- and 11-year-olds will get something out of it, too.) For the trivial pursuers among you, the White House has no front door or back door—just a north front and a south front.

Like Aaron Neville, I "tell it like it is." The 20- to 35-minute self-guided tour closely resembles a cattle roundup and takes in the ground and main public floors, including the East, Green, Blue, and Red rooms, the State Dining Room, Cross Hall, North Entrance Hall, and the Oval Room, where Franklin Roosevelt gave his fireside chats. On display, besides presidential portraits and memorabilia, are period furnishings (for the most part reflecting the Greek Revival and Victorian styles), portraits of the First Ladies, and exhibits on the day-to-day operation of the White House and its role as a national symbol.

(Fun Fact Birthday Greetings from the President

If a family member is celebrating an 80th (or higher) birthday, and you'd like the president to send the celebrant a greeting card, send a written request—at least 6 weeks in advance—with Gram's or Gramp's birthday and address to Greeting Office, The White House, Washington, DC 20500.

The White House Area

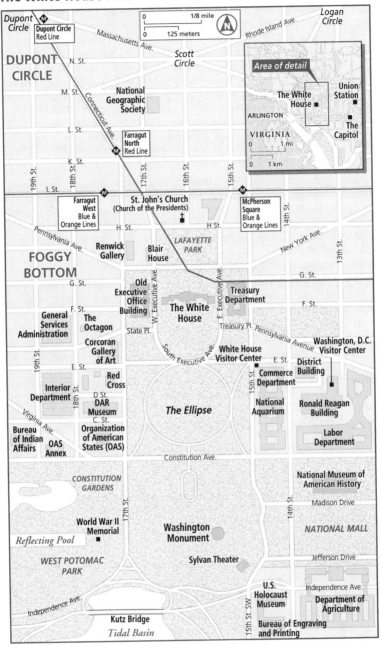

Dupont Circle

Dupont Circle Red Line

Massachusetts Ave.

Rhode Island Ave.

Logan Circle

0   1/8 mile
0   125 meters

DUPONT CIRCLE

N. St.

Scott Circle

M. St.

National Geographic Society

Connecticut Ave.

L. St.

Farragut North Red Line

K. St.

19th St.

18th St.

17th St.

16th St.

15th St.

I. St.

Area of detail

The White House

Union Station

ARLINGTON

VIRGINIA

The Capitol

0   1 mi
0   1 km

Farragut West Blue & Orange Lines

St. John's Church (Church of the Presidents)

H. St.

McPherson Square Blue & Orange Lines

14th St.

H St.

Pennsylvania Ave.

Renwick Gallery

Blair House

LAFAYETTE PARK

New York Ave.

13th St.

FOGGY BOTTOM

G. St.

Old Executive Office Building

G. St.

W. Executive Ave.

The White House

Treasury Department

F. St.

General Services Administration

F. St.

The Octagon

State Pl.

Treasury Pl.

E. Executive Ave.

Pennsylvania Avenue

Washington, D.C. Visitor Center

Corcoran Gallery of Art

South Executive Ave.

White House Visitor Center

E. St.

District Building

19th St.

Interior Department

E. St.

Red Cross

15th St.

Commerce Department

National Aquarium

Ronald Reagan Building

18th St.

D St.

DAR Museum

C. St.

Bureau of Indian Affairs

OAS Annex

Organization of American States (OAS)

The Ellipse

Labor Department

Virginia Ave.

Constitution Ave.

CONSTITUTION GARDENS

17th St.

National Museum of American History

14th St.

Madison Drive

World War II Memorial

Reflecting Pool

Washington Monument

NATIONAL MALL

WEST POTOMAC PARK

Sylvan Theater

Jefferson Drive

U.S. Holocaust Museum

15th St. SW

Independence Ave.

Department of Agriculture

Independence Ave.

Kutz Bridge

Tidal Basin

Bureau of Engraving and Printing

Fun Fact Heads Up

The rotunda's cast-iron dome (which replaced the original one of copper and wood) was begun in 1855 and finished in 1863 during Lincoln's presidency. It has a diameter of nearly 100 feet and weighs 9 million pounds. Don't get nervous: You're safe standing on the rotunda floor, 180 feet beneath it, as more than 5,000 tons of ironwork provide the girding.

Young children do enjoy the annual Easter egg roll and the spring and fall garden tours (see "Calendar of Kids' Favorite Events" in chapter 2 for details). On the west side of the South Lawn lies the Children's Garden, with bronze imprints of the hands and feet of White House children and grandchildren. A word of caution: Waits of more than 2 hours in line for the Easter egg roll are not unusual. My advice: Take plenty of snacks. Call or check the website for the latest info about tickets and security. In 2005, tickets were given out the weekend before the (Monday) event.

1600 Pennsylvania Ave. NW (visitor entrance at East Gate on E. Executive Ave.). ✆ 800/717-1450 or 202/456-7041. www.whitehouse.gov. Free admission. Closed during presidential functions. Metro: McPherson Square, Farragut North, or Farragut West.

U.S. Capitol 🜲🜲🜲   **Ages 6 and up.** Even if your home is outside the United States, the Capitol will give you a sense, more than any other federal building, of what this country is all about. As you face the Capitol's East Front, the Senate side is north (right), and the House side is south (left). Flags fly over the respective sides when either is in session, and night sessions are indicated by a light burning in the dome. Presidential inaugurations have taken place here since 1801. The Rotunda is the site of state funerals for U.S. presidents (beginning with Abraham Lincoln) and heroes, military and otherwise. (In October 2005, Rosa Parks became the first woman, second African American, and 1 of only 30 private citizens to lie in state in the Rotunda. Parks spearheaded the civil rights movement when, in 1955, she refused to give up her bus seat to a white man in Montgomery, Alabama.) The House Chamber is where the president delivers the State of the Union message every January. Information on committee meetings is published weekdays in *The Washington Post*'s "Today in Congress" column. Call ahead if you're interested in a specific bill.

   Free tickets for guided tours (in groups of 40) are first come, first served at the ticket kiosk near the intersection of 1st Street SW and Independence Avenue beginning at 9am daily, Monday through Saturday. Tickets are for same day only. Even the youngest kids need a ticket. Because of heightened security, you will be refused admission if you have any of the following along: aerosol or nonaerosol sprays; cans, bottles, or liquids; oversized suitcases, duffle bags, or backpacks larger than 14 inches wide by 13 inches high and 4 inches deep; knives, razors, or box cutters; Mace or pepper spray; or firearms and explosives (just in case you were wondering). Strollers, cameras, and video recorders are okay. A coatcheck room is available only if you have tickets for the Senate or House galleries. For up-to-date information, call ✆ **202/225-6827.**

   The short but sweet half-hour tour departs every few minutes from the Rotunda every day but Sunday. A word to the wise: The guides say that during peak times (Sat, around major holidays, and Mar–Sept) it is best to visit from noon to 1pm. The guides are so well scrubbed, so smooth, and so knowledgeable that they must be running for

Capitol Hill

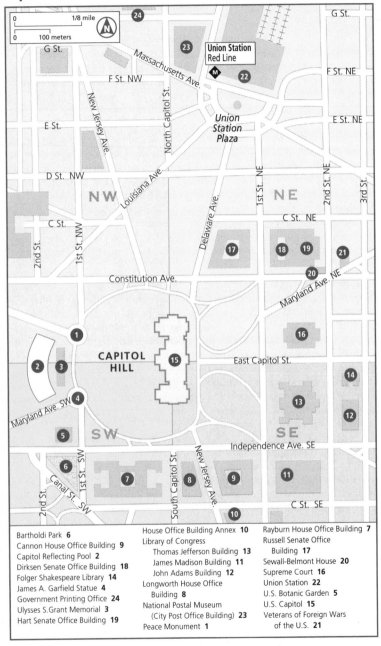

U.S. Capitol Floor Plan

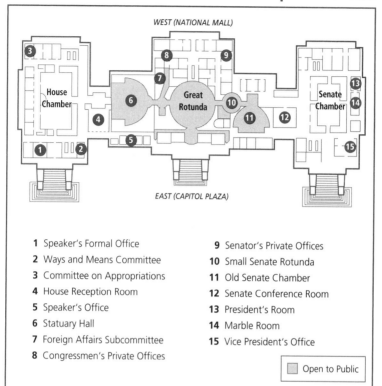

WEST (NATIONAL MALL)

House Chamber

Great Rotunda

Senate Chamber

EAST (CAPITOL PLAZA)

1 Speaker's Formal Office

2 Ways and Means Committee

3 Committee on Appropriations

4 House Reception Room

5 Speaker's Office

6 Statuary Hall

7 Foreign Affairs Subcommittee

8 Congressmen's Private Offices

9 Senator's Private Offices

10 Small Senate Rotunda

11 Old Senate Chamber

12 Senate Conference Room

13 President's Room

14 Marble Room

15 Vice President's Office

☐ Open to Public

office. Encourage older kids to ask questions during the tour and then allow time for wandering around and attending a hearing or committee meeting, usually held in the morning or other times when Congress is not in session. If you have toddlers, quit after the introductory tour.

The guides do a marvelous job describing the history of **Statuary Hall,** where the House met from 1807 to 1857. Here you'll find statues of U.S. presidents, important state figures, statesmen, legislators, Supreme Court justices, and inventors. Note the bronze plaque on the floor where John Quincy Adams collapsed on February 21, 1848. He died in an adjoining room soon thereafter. Due to an acoustical anomaly, whispers can be heard across the room. Usually, the guide will demonstrate this phenomenon, to your kids' delight. If the guide forgets, ask. It's the kind of experience that sticks in a child's memory forever.

To the right of the entrance of Statuary Hall is a painting depicting the signing of the Declaration of Independence. That's Thomas Jefferson stepping on John Adams' foot—no love lost there, according to historians.

Constantino Brumidi's allegorical fresco the *Apotheosis of Washington* lines the very top of the dome and depicts Washington accompanied by Liberty, Victory, and Fame. The 13 figures crowned with stars represent the 13 original states. If your neck stiffens looking up at the masterpiece, pity poor Brumidi, who spent 11 months on his back to complete the painting. More than 25 years of Brumidi's handiwork is also evidenced elsewhere in the Capitol—in the frieze encircling the rotunda, the Senate reception room, the President's Room, and the first-floor Senate corridors.

The Crypt was originally intended as Washington's final resting place, but his relatives insisted on Mount Vernon. (You know how family can be.) So instead of Washington, the Crypt holds changing exhibits that describe the history and construction of the Capitol.

If you visit the **House Gallery,** the Democrats will be seated to the right of the presiding officer and Republicans to the left. Senators have assigned seats, according to seniority, but representatives do not, and a system of bells informs those not in attendance of what is going on. Wouldn't the kids love this when they're absent from school?

The Supreme Court met in the **Old Supreme Court Chamber** from 1800 to 1860. Thomas Jefferson was sworn in as president here in 1801, and in 1844, Samuel F. B. Morse sent the first telegraph message ("What hath God wrought?") to Baltimore from here.

If you visit the handsome **Old Senate Chamber,** built between 1793 and 1800 and in use until 1859, note the mahogany desks with inkwells and sand shakers for blotting the ink, and the handsome red carpet with gold stars. No wonder this was considered the hottest show in town for many years. When crowds overflowed the galleries, it is said that some senators politely gave their seats to ladies. In the new Senate Chamber, they now lose their seats to ladies—14 women members as of 2003.

Led by Sen. Jefferson Davis (later president of the Confederacy), Congress appropriated $100,000 in 1850 for building a Capitol extension to include new House and Senate wings. The Senate moved into its new quarters on January 4, 1859. The House convened for the first time in the new south building on December 16, 1857. Originally, the House met in what is now Statuary Hall.

Before you leave here, do two things:

1. Take your kids down to the basement for a ride on the subway, run by electromagnets, between the Capitol and Dirksen and Hart Senate office buildings. Until the new subway began running in 1994, our representatives rode an antiquated open-air tram. As you're riding, think about the cost: a trifling $18 million of our tax dollars.

2. Stroll around to the West Front for an unbroken view of the Mall, the Washington Monument, and the Lincoln Memorial.

Sometime in early 2007, the first-ever **Capitol Visitor Center** is slated to open in a new three-level, underground addition. When completed, it will have a Great Hall, orientation theater, 600-seat dining room, gift shop (natch!), and skylights for viewing the dome. I've heard that visitors will also be able to watch live video of the House and Senate floors. (Wonder if less-than-scrupulous lawmakers will be chagrined into cleaning up their acts?) Enter from the East Front plaza.

Morning VIP tours, appropriate for kids 10 and up, include admission to the House and Senate galleries. Usually, the House and Senate convene from noon until late afternoon, but exceptions are almost a rule. Whether you want the special tour or just passes to the galleries, you must write your representative or senator far in advance (see "Visitor Information" in chapter 2, or check www.house.gov or www.senate.gov). Last-minute passes are usually available if you stop at your senator's office. Call if you don't know the location (© **202/224-3121**). Passes are given to noncitizens who show their passports to the appointment desk on the Senate side, first floor, or the Door-keeper of the House. In the summer or any other time when Congress is not in session, visitors can enter the Senate and House galleries without a special pass. Groups of more than 15 can schedule a tour up to 6 months in advance (© **202/224-4910**). Remember to call in advance to find out whether the building is open to visitors and what restrictions are in place.

East end of the Mall, entrance on E. Capitol St. and 1st St. NE. © 202/225-6827. www.aoc.gov. Free admission. Sept–Feb daily 9am–4:30pm; Mar–Aug daily 9am–8pm. (Call ahead, because extended hours change from year to year.) Tours every 15–20 min., 9am–4:30pm Mon–Sat. No tours Sunday. Closed Thanksgiving, Dec 25. Metro: Capitol South or Union Station.

Federal Bureau of Investigation (FBI) 𝖆𝖆   **Ages 8 and up.** *Note:* At press time, the FBI building is closed for extensive renovations and was due to reopen in spring/summer 2007. Because speed is seldom a factor in Washington, save yourself time and possible disappointment and call first.

Everyone is fascinated with the evil that men do, and for many, this is the best tour in Washington. If you haven't written to your senator or representative for VIP tickets, arrive by 8:30am, especially in spring and summer, for the hour-long tour conducted every 15 minutes Monday through Friday from 8:45am to 4:15pm.

Don't let your first impression of the hideous concrete bunker—dubbed "Fort Hoover" by locals—put you off. Once inside, well-versed guides will take you past a series of exhibits detailing past and current bureau work. Try to stand close to the guide so you don't miss anything.

A brief introductory film gives a historical overview of the bureau's activities. With any luck, your kids won't recognize a relative among the **Ten Most Wanted,** the famous list begun in 1950. According to FBI legend, two fugitives whose pictures were recognized here by tourists were later apprehended. The late yippie/radical Abbie Hoffman claimed that he took the FBI tour several times while on the lam.

Although they might not recognize Al Capone or Ma Barker in the rogues' gallery, your kids will snap to attention when they see the gangsters' weapons, the U.S. Crime

Did You Know?

- The Capitol cornerstone, misplaced during work on the East Front in the 1950s, is still missing.
- Several years ago, a women's restroom was created closer to the Senate side of the Capitol to accommodate the growing number of women in the Senate. It has two stalls, two sinks, and no glass ceiling.
- The 19½-foot statue *Freedom,* perched atop the dome since 1863, was supposed to be nude. You can imagine what a furor that caused in the mid-1800s, so sculptor Thomas Crawford draped the figure in a flowing robe. Despite the feathers flowing from the eagle-topped helmet, Freedom is not a Native American. All 7 tons of her were lowered from the dome by helicopter on May 9, 1993, for cleaning and restoration, which took several months. (You have to admit, 130 years is a long time to go without a bath.)

Clock as it ticks off the numbers and frequency of violent crimes in this country, devices used by spies for transporting microfilm, and an actual surveillance tape.

A whopping 187 million fingerprints are on file, and they're retained for 83 years before being discarded. Along the way, you'll be shown more than 5,000 confiscated firearms, as well as a room full of furs, jewelry, silverware, and art objects seized in narcotics and tax-evasion cases. Sorry, no souvenirs.

If you happen to see a white-coated technician examining a bloody fabric sample in the **Serology Lab,** be assured that it's the real thing. They don't use props here. Drug samples and related paraphernalia are part of the Drug Enforcement Agency's (DEA) exhibit; a world map shows the routes taken by carriers of illicit substances into this country. You'll also learn how the bureau is waging the battle against illegal drugs.

Older children will particularly enjoy visiting the **Instrumental Analysis Unit,** where a car's make and model can be determined from a paint chip (20,000 samples are on hand from foreign and domestic models), the **Firearms Identification Unit,** and the **Hairs and Fibers Lab.**

What leaves kids gasping, however, is the tour's bang-up finish. In a small auditorium facing a firing range, you'll hear and see a sharp-eyed agent pump several rounds from a 9mm automatic pistol and submachine gun (successor to the notorious Tommy Gun) into several defenseless paper targets, which end up like so many slices of Swiss cheese. What a show!

J. Edgar Hoover FBI Building, Pennsylvania Ave. and 10th St. NW (tour entrance E St. between 9th and 10th sts.). ℭ 202/324-3447. www.fbi.gov. Free admission. Mon–Fri 8:45am–4:15pm. Closed weekends and federal holidays. Metro: Archives/Navy Memorial, Metro Center, or Gallery Place.

Bureau of Engraving and Printing **Ages 6 and up.** You can bet your bottom dollar that the buck starts here. Kids old enough to appreciate money will go gaga over the green stuff.

This 40-minute guided tour is available on a first-come, first-served basis, Monday through Friday from 9am to 2pm. The tour is so popular that you need tickets during the months of March through August. Same-day free tickets are available at the kiosk on Raoul Wallenberg Place (15th Street SW) beginning at 8am. They're usually gone by 9am. September through February, no tickets are required. Congressional/VIP tours are weekdays at 8:15 and 8:45am only. (See chapter 2 for more information on how to get VIP tours.) *Note:* If the Department of Homeland Security announces a Code Orange alert on the day of your visit, the bureau will be closed.

Workers in 'round-the-clock shifts print about 22 million notes per day; that's about $77 billion annually. Each sheet (plain old paper at the start) picks up color from ink-filled lines engraved in the heavy steel plates. The backs are printed first; the faces are printed the next day. At the FBI, you'll learn that counterfeiting at this level is very difficult. The bureau also prints Treasury bonds and White House invitations.

If you think that "pieces of eight" were coined by Robert Louis Stevenson for *Treasure Island,* stop between 8:30am and 3:30pm at the visitor center, where you'll find the real thing as well as electronic games and video displays related to the "root of all evil." You can also purchase a souvenir bag of shredded green. (Incidentally, the life expectancy of a $1 bill is 18 months. Easy come, easy go.)

14th and C sts. SW (enter on 14th St.). ℭ 202/622-2000. www.bep.treas.gov. Free admission. Mon–Fri 9am–2pm. Closed federal holidays and Dec 25–Jan 1. Metro: Smithsonian.

Break Time

The **South Buffet Room** in the Dirksen Senate Office Building is a convenient refueling spot when exploring Capitol Hill (© **202/224-7196**). Getting here is half the fun. Take the free subway that runs under the Capitol to this all-you-can-eat buffet. There's a carvery station featuring ham, roast beef, or turkey, plus several steamer trays with additional hot main courses, side dishes, a full salad and fruit bar, a wide choice of desserts, and (nonalcoholic) beverages included in the price of admission. Finish the feast at the make-your-own sundae bar. The lunch buffet costs $11 for adults and $8.50 for children under 10. Reservations are taken for groups of six or more. American Express, Discover, MasterCard, and Visa are accepted. It's open Monday through Friday from 11:30am to 2:30pm. High chairs and boosters are available.

Department of Interior Museum   **Ages 6 and up.** If you thought that the Department of the Interior was a government decorating firm, do pay a visit here to see what the National Park Service, Fish and Wildlife Service, Geological Survey, Office of Territorial and International Affairs, and bureaus of Land Management, Reclamation, Mines, and Indian Affairs are all about. Many aspects of the department's activities are effectively displayed in the museum's exhibits of Native American artifacts and crafts, mapping techniques, mineral specimens, and early land bounties (grants of land given in lieu of monetary payment for military service).

Children are drawn to the imposing buffalo head, sand paintings, wood carving, birch bark canoe, baskets, pottery, and beadwork. They also enjoy viewing the 1930s-era dioramas, such as the depiction of an Alaskan gold mine. (Some dioramas are in a secure area, so call ahead to see what hoops you will need to jump through to gain access.) Can they identify the tribes in the silhouetted scenes of Native American life? Special tours for kids 5 and older, in groups of three or more, must be made 2 weeks in advance. Across the hall in Room 1023, the **Indian Craft Shop** sells quality American Indian pottery, jewelry, and other crafts Monday through Friday from 8:30am to 4:30pm and the third Saturday of every month from 1 to 4pm. Special family programs are sometimes offered during Saturday hours (© **202/208-4659**).

1849 C St. NW. © **202/208-4743**. www.doi.gov/museum. Free admission. Mon–Fri 8:30am–4:30pm; 3rd Sat. of month 1–4pm. Photo ID (driver's license, student ID, employment card) needed for adults to enter. Closed federal holidays. Metro: Farragut West. Limited metered street parking.

Department of State Diplomatic Reception Rooms   **Ages 12 and up.** Kids over the age of 12 who are interested in seeing a showcase of 18th-century and early 19th-century American furniture and decorative arts can take a fine arts tour of the diplomatic reception rooms on the eighth floor of the State Department. Secretaries of state, VIPs, and cabinet members have all hosted bashes here. The terrace views of the Lincoln Memorial and Potomac River aren't bad. Guided tours (Mon through Fri, 9:30am, 10:30am, 2:45pm) are by reservation only, 4 weeks in advance.

23rd and C sts. NW (enter at 23rd St.). © **202/647-3241**. www.state.gov/m/drr. Free admission. Tours Mon–Fri 9:30am, 10:30am, and 2:45pm by reservation only. Strollers not permitted; leave them and kids under 12 at home. Closed major holidays. Metro: Foggy Bottom

Library of Congress ✦   **Ages 10 and up.** The nation's library is also the world's largest. Established as a research center for Congress in 1800, the library's first collection, then housed in the Capitol, was burned during the War of 1812. The cornerstone for the Thomas Jefferson Building section, a formidable example of Italian Renaissance architecture, was laid in 1890, and construction lasted 11 years until it was complete. (When you're on the Hill, stop to see the exterior and Great Hall of the Thomas Jefferson Building, and enjoy the view of the Capitol from the west steps.)

Anyone over high-school age can do research or browse here, but , you may not borrow the books. More than 500 miles of shelves fill the Thomas Jefferson, James Madison, and John Adams buildings.

To get to the library's **visitor center,** enter from 1st Street SE at Independence Avenue (sidewalk level). The **Main Reading Room,** located in the Jefferson Building, is awesome. Researchers are always welcome; others may gain entry only during the hour-long guided tour. I think you'll agree that the **Great Hall** is a sight to behold, with its soaring arches, ceilings decorated with mosaics, and marble stairways cleaned to a spit-and-polish shine. In the **Southwest Gallery and Pavilion** on the second floor, you'll find "American Treasures of the Library of Congress," a permanent exhibition of maps, rare books, and photographs. Among the treasures is L'Enfant's blueprint for Washington. You'll also see the contents of Lincoln's pockets the night he was assassinated.

But first, catch the video in the theater. Tours are Monday through Friday at 10:30 and 11:30am; 1:30, 2:30, and 3:30pm. Most kids 10 and older should find it interesting; anyone younger (unless they're especially precocious or bookish) will think it's boring. Among the special collections housed in 20 reading rooms are children's literature and genealogy. The recently expanded gift shop invites browsers and souvenir collectors.

The **Gutenberg Bible** and **Giant Bible of Mainz** are displayed on the main floor, along with rotating exhibits of photographs, music manuscripts, prints, and posters. With very young children, skip the Jefferson Building tour and head for the Madison Building next door on 1st Street, between Independence Avenue and C Street SE. The **Copyright Office,** one of the library's departments, is located here. On the fourth

Break Time

You can grab a quick bite to eat at the handsome **Library of Congress Cafeteria** (© **202/554-4114** or 202/707-8300), on the sixth floor of the Madison Building. Inside there's a wall of windows overlooking the city. There's a salad bar at lunch, as well as hot main dishes, carved meats, health food, pizza, fast food (fried chicken, burgers), deli sandwiches, and desserts. Prices for main courses range from $3 to $7. Reservations and credit cards are not accepted. It's open Monday through Friday from 9:30 to 10:30am and from 12:30 to 3pm (snacks and drinks only 2 to 3pm). A coffee shop is open Monday through Friday from 9 to 10:30am and 12:30 to 4pm and Saturday 8:30am to 2pm; a cappuccino bar is open Monday through Friday from 9am to 5pm.

The more formal **Montpelier Room,** adjoining the cafeteria, serves a marvelous $10.50 buffet lunch Monday through Friday between 11:30am and 2pm. Prime rib is featured on Friday. Reservations are required for four or more (© **202/707-8300**). MasterCard and Visa are accepted here. This place is definitely not for very young kids.

floor, the copyright exhibit features one of the original Maltese falcons, masks from *Star Wars,* Bert and Ernie puppets, Barbie dolls, posters, and more. Visit anytime between 8:30am and 5pm.

Capitol Hill, 10 1st St. SE between Independence Ave. and East Capitol St. ℂ **202/707-8000.** www.lcweb.loc.gov. Free admission. Mon–Sat 10am–5pm. Closed Dec 25 and other major holidays. Metro: Capitol South.

The Pentagon   **Ages 8 and up.** The world's largest office building (3.7 million sq. ft.) is the headquarters of the Department of Defense—that's the Army, Navy, Air Force, Marines, Coast Guard, and Joint Chiefs of Staff. Any school kid can tell you that it was named for its five-sided construction. About 23,000 people work here daily, occupying offices along 17.5 miles of corridors.

Since the terrorist attacks on September 11, 2001, the Pentagon has been closed to walk-in visitors (like you and your family). Only school and educational groups and other "select" groups are admitted; then it's by reservation only.

Fund-raising is under way for a memorial to the victims of the attacks, near the west face of the Pentagon (marking the flight path). It will feature 184 illuminated benches, one for each victim. Groundbreaking is expected late in 2006, with the dedication sometime in 2008. The 59 benches facing the Pentagon will represent those who died in the building; 125 benches, representing the passengers on American Airlines Flight 77, will face the opposite direction so that visitors can see the engraved names of the victims against the sky. Each bench will sit above a small reflecting pool. The reflected light will make the memorial visible from far away and from above. For more information on the memorial, see http://memorial.pentagon.mil.

Arlington, VA (across the 14th St. Bridge). ℂ **703/695-1776.** www.defenselink.mil. Free admission. Closed to individuals; group tours only by special advance request. Those 16 and older must have a photo ID. Groups of nine or more must reserve 2 weeks or more ahead. Metro: Pentagon.

Supreme Court 🌟🌟   **Ages 10 and up.** About 150 cases are heard annually by the highest court in the nation, empowered by Article III of the Constitution to ensure that congressional, presidential, and state actions comply with the Constitution.

In this imposing structure of classic Greek design, once thought too grandiose for its intention, the Supreme Court hears cases during about half the weeks from the first Monday in October through April. Only about 50 seats are open to the public, so arrive by 9am. Cases are heard Monday through Wednesday from 10am to 3pm, with a lunch-hour recess from noon to 1pm. Although children are welcome in the courtroom, no disruptions are tolerated. Phone the information office (ℂ **202/479-3211**) or consult the *Washington Post's* "Supreme Court Calendar" for the schedule.

From mid-May to early July, you may attend half-hour sessions on Monday at 10am, when the justices release orders and opinions. The many rituals attendant with the justices' entrance will fascinate older children. You can tell them that "Oyez! Oyez!" is French legalese for "Hear ye, hear ye."

When the court is not in session, you may attend a free lecture (9:30am–3:30pm, every hour on the half-hour) about Court procedure and the building's architecture. Follow up the lecture with a walk through the Great Hall (open Mon–Fri from 9am–4pm) and see the 20-minute film on the workings of the Court (ℂ **202/479-3211**).

On the ground floor, take a look at the imposing spiral staircases and Court-related exhibits. There's also a gift shop on this level, open from 9am to 4:25pm. From the top of the entrance steps, there's a wonderful view of the Capitol.

Break Time

Hear ye, hear ye. The decision is out on the food in the **Supreme Court Cafeteria** (© 202/479-3246): It might not be supreme, but it's appealing. Fresh-baked muffins are featured at breakfast; soup, sandwiches, main courses, salad bar, ice cream, and desserts are available at lunch. Main courses range from $4 to $7. There's also a carryout **snack bar** with homemade cakes and pies selling for $3 or less per slice. Reservations and credit cards are not accepted. The cafeteria is open to the public Monday through Friday from 7:30 to 10:30am, 11:30am to noon, and 1 to 2pm (court employees only noon to 1pm). When the court is in session the snack bar is open Monday through Friday from 10:30am to 12:15pm and 1:15 to 3:30pm (12:15–1:15pm for court employees only).

1st St. and Maryland Ave. NE, opposite the U.S. Capitol. © 202/479-3030. www.supremecourtus.gov. Free admission. Mon–Fri 9am–4pm. Closed Sat., Sun, holidays. Metro: Capitol South or Union Station.

ARCHITECTURE

National Building Museum   **Ages 10 and up.** Once you visit the former Pension Building, which somewhat resembles Rahway Prison on the outside and a Roman bath and Renaissance palace on the inside, you'll know why this museum is dedicated to the building arts. It is the only U.S. institution dedicated solely to architecture, urban planning, design, engineering, and construction, and is one of D.C.'s *ooh* and *ahh* experiences.

Statistics to stick in your suitcase: The exterior measures 400 feet by 200 feet. The interior Corinthian columns are 75 feet high, 8 feet in diameter, and 25 feet in circumference. And 70,000 bricks went into *each* column!

In 1885, Grover Cleveland was the first president to hold an inaugural ball here. In case you're planning a future event and your family room doesn't cut it, the Great Hall is available for events other than presidential social functions. It measures 316 feet by 116 feet, and the ceiling is 159 feet high. That's about 15 stories.

"Washington, Symbol and City," is the museum's signature exhibition, exploring the growth and development of the federal capital. Temporary exhibitions usually change every 6 to 8 months. **"An Architectural Wonder: The U.S. Pension Building"** details the building's history and construction. If your children are over 10 or have an interest in architecture and urban development, this is an excellent introduction to D.C. If they have zero interest, come here anyway for a quick glimpse of the Great Hall.

Tours are conducted Monday through Wednesday at 12:30pm; Thursday through Saturday at 11:30am, 1:30 and 2:30pm; and Sunday at 12:30 and 1:30pm. Saturday and Sunday from 2:30 to 3:30pm, families may drop in for free workshops. Saturday's subject: "Bridging the Gap"; Sunday's, "Arches and Trusses." All ages are welcome. In addition, special family programs are held some weekends throughout the year. The museum also hosts summer family drop-in programs for a nominal fee. Past projects have included making fans in the shape of buildings and decorating mirrors with beads and ornaments. Call for days and times. Three Sundays a year, the museum's Great Hall becomes airspace, as model-plane enthusiasts gather to launch their lightweight balsa and elastic band aircraft. Call or check the website for details.

The Museum Shop, on the ground floor, has a broad selection of arch. design-related books, objects for the home and office, prints, and posters. 272-7706). Hours are Monday through Saturday, 10am to 5pm and Sunday 1, 5pm. The **High Noon Café** is open for sandwiches, soups, salads, desserts, and b. erages Monday through Friday from 8:30am to 4pm, Saturday from 10am to 4pm, and Sunday from 11am to 4pm (© **202/303-0353**).

401 F St. NW, at Judiciary Square, between 4th and 5th sts. NW. © **202/272-2448**. www.nbm.org. Free admission. Mon–Sat 10am–5pm; Sun noon–5pm. Closed major holidays. Metro: Judiciary Square.

The Octagon Museum (the Museum of the American Architectural Foundation) **Ages 12 and up.** Built in 1800 as a summer retreat for a family of wealthy Virginia planters, this Federal-style town house (not really a perfect octagon) was a temporary home for President Madison and the missus after the British burned the White House during the War of 1812. Madison signed the Treaty of Ghent here in 1815. Today the oldest U.S. museum devoted to architecture and design is the head-quarters of the American Institute of Architects, which built offices behind the house several years ago. In addition to changing exhibitions are finds unearthed from a dig during the building's restoration. Walk-in tours, of interest to kids 12 and older, are

Don't Tear It Down

Although the **Old Post Office** ✦ (1100 Pennsylvania Ave. NW, between 10th and 12th sts.; © **202/289-4224**) is no longer a working post office, families love to come here to eat, shop, and enjoy the family entertainment. Do take a few minutes from your chicken wings and peanut butter fudge to inspect the impressive architecture. Built in 1899 as quarters for the federal postal department, it suffered years of neglect. The three-level renovated complex reopened in May 1984, thanks largely to the efforts of Nancy Hanks, a for-mer head of the National Endowment for the Arts in the 1970s. Renovation began in 1978 and took 6 years to complete.

If you do nothing else, tour the **clock tower** ✦✦. The vista, from the equivalent of a high-rise's 12th floor, is astounding, and the windows are covered with thin wires, so you don't have to be nervous about your little ones. On your way to the tower, stop on the 10th floor to check out the **10 Congress bells,** replicas of those at Westminster Abbey. They range from 600 to 3,000 pounds, and each one is about 5 feet in diameter. The order in which the bells are struck changes continuously, and it takes nearly 4 hours to go through all the permutations. A full peal honors the opening and clos-ing of Congress, state occasions, and national holidays. You may attend a practice session Thursday between 7 and 9pm, but I suggest calling first. Tours of the tower are free and are conducted by the National Park Service (© **202/606-8691;** www.nps.gov) from 8am to 11pm in April through August, and 10am to 5:45pm in September through March. Meet your guide in the lower lobby near the 12th Street entrance for a ride up, up, and away in the glass elevator.

sponsors walking and bus tours of local architectural sites
vance reservations (℃ **202/879-7766**).

/638-3105. www.archfoundation.org. Admission $5 adults, $3 students and sen-
-Sun 10am–4pm. Closed major holidays. Metro: Farragut West or Farragut North.

RIES

Library of Congress earlier in this chapter.

ibrary ⊛ **Ages 10 and up.** The 19th-century oil magnate
Henry Clay Folger built this library for his vast collection of original First Folios and
other rare books and manuscripts. Since opening in 1932, the Folger, whose neoclassical white marble facade is decorated with sculpted scenes from Shakespeare's plays,
has been recognized as one of the world's most esteemed research libraries on Will (as
he was known to his Elizabethan friends) and the Renaissance.

Anyone who wants to do research on 16th- or 17th-century European life—social
history, geography, science, and law—need look no further than the more than
300,000 books here. To gain access to the library's materials, you must first become a
"reader" (researcher); call the registrar at ℃ **202/675-0306.**

The library is home to a gem—an authentic Elizabethan theater that is open to visitors when not in use for rehearsals or performances. The highly regarded **Folger Consort** performs here regularly, and Shakespeare's birthday (Apr 23) is celebrated with an
open house every year on the closest Saturday. Free guided tours are given Monday
through Friday at 11am and Saturday at 11am and 1pm; garden tours are offered
every third Saturday at 11am and 1pm April through October.

January through June of 2007, the Folger will play a major role in the city's 6-
month "Shakespeare in Washington" festival. Participants will include museums, theater, opera, and dance companies. Family performance workshops (such as
"Swordplay," stage combat made easy) feature drama and improvisation for kids 8 to
14 some Saturdays from 10am to noon. The charge is $12 per person. Ask about other
Shakespeare-related activities for families. For information, call ℃ **202/544-7077.**

201 E. Capitol St. SE. ℃ **202/544-4600.** www.folger.edu. Free admission. Mon–Sat 10am–4pm. Closed all federal
holidays. Metro: Capitol South or Union Station.

National Archives ⊛ **Ages 6 and up.** If you have any doubts about the inscription
on the statue out front—"What is past is prologue"—step inside the rotunda. The
building is a classical structure with—count 'em—72 Corinthian columns designed by
John Russell Pope, architect of the National Gallery and Jefferson Memorial. Each of
the bronze doors weighs 6.5 tons (don't try slamming these!). Trivia fact: Because the
building was constructed on Tiber Creek, which ran through the city, more than 8,500
pilings had to be driven into the ground before construction could begin.

The main attraction here is the **Charters of Freedom,** an exhibit that contains
some of the most precious paper in the country: the 1297 version of the Magna Carta,
the Declaration of Independence, four pages of the Constitution, and the Bill of
Rights. Each night these priceless documents, already sealed in helium-filled bronze-
and-glass cases, are lowered 22 feet into a bombproof and fireproof 55-ton steel-and-
concrete vault. During the day, armed guards keep an eye on things.

The **Record of America** section in the central corridor shows the effects of time
and technology on recordkeeping, from early Native American treaties to presidential

websites. The intention is that each visitor will leave with a better understanding of his or her personal connection to the records housed in this building.

The National Archives is also the storehouse for 5 million photos (including Mathew Brady's Civil War snapshots); nearly 12 million maps, charts, and aerial photographs; and 91 million feet of motion-picture film. And talk about odd couples: The Archives has a photo of Elvis Presley and Richard Nixon at the White House in 1970. Thousands of old newsreels can be screened in the motion-picture, sound, and video branch on the ground floor, but you have to make an appointment first.

Alex Haley began searching for his *Roots* here. So can you! Researchers must be at least 14, have a valid photo ID, and be accompanied by an adult. Call first for details and hours. Research and microfilm rooms are open Monday through Saturday. Use the Pennsylvania Avenue entrance and stop in Room 400 for advice before you begin your quest. Books and souvenirs are sold in the lobby museum shop.

Constitution Ave. and 8th St. NW. © **202/501-5000** for information on exhibits and films, or 202/501-5402 for research information. www.archives.gov. Free admission. Day after Labor Day to Mar 31 daily 10am–5:30pm; Apr to Labor Day daily 10am–8 or 9pm. Closed Dec 25 and Federal holidays. Metro: Archives.

ART

See section 1, "The Smithsonian Institution," of this chapter for listings of the following art museums: the Freer Gallery of Art, the Hirshhorn Museum and Sculpture Garden, the National Museum of African Art, the Renwick Gallery, and the Arthur M. Sackler Gallery of Asian and Near Eastern Art.

Corcoran Gallery of Art ⚑ **Ages 8 and up.** Washington's oldest private museum is best known for its permanent collections of American 19th-century landscapes and Impressionist art, as well as its special exhibitions of contemporary art and photography. Exhibits change frequently but run the gamut from Andy Warhol to Mary Cassat. The first-floor double atrium and imposing marble staircase will probably impress your little ones more than what's hanging on the walls. When you enter, ask at the information desk for a brochure aimed at 6- to 12-year-olds intended to arouse their interest in specific artworks.

The free **Sunday Traditions Workshops** (© **202/638-3211,** ext. 321), usually held from 3 to 4:30pm (not every Sun), introduce children from 5 to 12 years old to various aspects of the museum's architecture and contents. A typical program sends participants searching for different styles of columns and other distinguishing features of the museum's Beaux Arts facade. The budding Frank Lloyd Wrights then return to the classroom to create and embellish their own buildings out of cardboard and glue.

Tours are held Wednesday through Sunday at noon, plus Thursday at 7:30pm, Saturday and Sunday at 2:30pm. (The museum is closed Monday and Tuesday.) The Corcoran School of Art offers a 4-year program to students of the fine arts and photography, and offers studio classes for children of all ages. Inquire at the information desk or call for a catalog about the Children's Workshops and Young People's Program.

In the gift shop, you'll find children's books and educational trinkets, as well as art books for all. For information on special and family events, as well as on group tours, call the education department.

The cafe is open Wednesday, Friday, and Saturday 11am to 2pm, and Thursday 11am to 3pm. The popular Sunday Gospel Brunch is 10:30am to 2pm ($25 adults, $12 kids under 12).

500 17th St. NW, at New York Ave. © **202/639-1700.** www.corcoran.org. Admission $8 adults, $6 seniors, $4 students with current ID, free for kids under 11. Special "twofer" deals may be available. Open Wed, Fri, Sat, Sun

166CHAPTER 6 · EXPLORING WASHINGTON, D.C. WITH YOUR KIDS

Break Time

When I'm downtown and draggin', I head for the picturesque **Pavilion Cafe** ★★★ in the National Gallery Sculpture Garden (9th Street and Constitution Avenue; ✆ 202/289-3360; www.guestservices.com) to unwind and refuel. Glass walls overlook the fountain, reflecting pool, and flowering shrubs. How can you not like it? On warm days, you can dine (or write postcards) outdoors. Personal pizzas, large salads such as the make-your-own Caesar, paninis, and wraps are tasty and satisfying. Most items are $6 to $8. Desserts cost $1.50 to $6. A wide selection of beverages, including wine and beer, is available. Hours are Monday to Thursday and Saturday from 10am to 7pm in summer (until 5pm rest of year), Friday 10am to 9pm, and Sunday 11am to 7pm in summer (5pm rest of year). Friday jazz evenings are from 5 to 9pm and a special light menu is served.

10am–5pm; Thurs 10am–9pm. Closed Mon, Tues, Dec 25, and Jan 1. Open Mon holidays (Labor Day, Columbus Day, and so on). Metro: Farragut West or Farragut North.

National Gallery of Art (East and West buildings) and Sculpture Garden ★★★

Ages 4 and up. Let's dispense with the details first. The East and West buildings are connected by an underground concourse with a moving walkway. You can enter the West Building from the Mall (Madison Dr.) or Constitution Avenue at 6th Street; you also can enter at 4th or 7th street between Constitution Avenue and Madison Drive. The only above-ground entrance to the East Building is on 4th Street. Strollers are available at each entrance. The buildings are least crowded weekdays before noon.

The National Gallery consistently tops the list of the 10 most popular art museums in the United States, attracting more than six million visitors annually. The classically inspired **West Building,** another John Russell Pope creation, houses 12th- to 20th-century sculpture and paintings within its 500,000-square-foot interior. Industrialist Andrew Mellon's collection formed the nucleus, augmented by the sizable collections of Samuel H. Kress, Joseph Widener, Chester Dale, and numerous individual donors.

Here are a few suggestions in the West Building that might appeal to your children: the Byzantine *Madonna and Child,* Giotto's *Madonna and Child,* Filippino Lippi's and/or Botticelli's *Portrait of a Youth,* Raphael's *St. George and the Dragon,* anything by El Greco (kids think he's "weird"), Holbein's portrait *Edward VI as a Child,* Fragonard's *Young Girl Reading,* Renoir's *A Girl with a Watering Can,* Copley's *Watson and the Shark,* and the Degas sculptures.

Do show them the bronze statue of Mercury on top of the fountain in the rotunda and then head for either of the lovely colonnaded garden courts. Under arched skylights, with comfortable upholstered chairs overlooking putti fountains, these courts provide sublime settings for resting museum-weary feet (and children).

Given its size and the breadth of its exhibitions, the West Building can be overpowering and bewildering to an adult. It'd be better to show the kids a few things here and then hightail it over to the less intimidating **East Building.**

Before you enter, walk around to the corner of 3rd Street and Pennsylvania Avenue, and aim your peepers at Frank Stella's 30-foot aluminum-and-fiberglass *Mr. Homburg.* It landed here (and resembles a hard-edged spaceship) because it was too large for the National Gallery Sculpture Garden. Steel cables set in concrete anchor it to terra firma, but it still moves in the wind. Neat!

I think of the East Building as a breath of fresh air. If your kids see nothing more than the soaring ground-level central court with its three-story-high Calder mobile, returned in June 2005 after a year of restoration, and vibrant (much too large for the living room) Miró tapestry, *Woman,* you will have accomplished something. Ask the kids if they can identify the shape of the building. It's a trapezoid, which architect I. M. Pei ingeniously divided into two interconnected triangles.

Pick up a colorful self-guided tour booklet for children and their families, and inquire about family programs. Kids are usually drawn to Mondrian's neat grids and/or Motherwell's sloppy splotches. See what they make of the latter's inkblot, *Reconciliation Elegy.* Their answers should make for interesting conversation. Roy Lichtenstein's *Look Mickey* will strike a familiar chord, while Matisse's *Large Composition with Masks* enchants all ages.

Break Time

Any time is a good time to head for the National Gallery of Art's **Cascade Café** (✆ **202/737-4215**), open from 11am to 3pm Monday through Saturday and 11am to 4pm Sundays. The line moves quickly in this bright and cheery space, with seating for 450. It's located in the East building on the Concourse level. At lunch, create your own salad or choose a premade sandwich or one with hand-sliced deli meats from the carvery, a wood-fired pizza, or a hot main dish (prices range from $6–$10). The hot dogs, burgers, and fries are passable. Kids can make their own sundaes from frozen yogurt and varied toppings. Try to snag a table near the ersatz waterfall. Next to the Cascade Café is a full espresso and gelato bar that also offers sandwiches, salads, and sorbets. Most entrees cost $7 to $8. The espresso bar is open Monday through Saturday from 10am to 4:30pm, and Sunday from 11am to 5:30pm, usually with extended hours in summer. High chairs are available.

The Garden Café (✆ **202/216-2480**) is located on the ground floor of the museum's West Building next to the museum shop. Come here to reflect, cool your heels, and have dessert ($6.75) or sample one of the chef's seasonal offerings amid the ferns and marble. This is probably the most "adult" of the Mall museum eateries and offers sit-down service. It's also the priciest, and reservations are recommended, so you may want to savor it sometime without the kids. Main courses (soups, salads, sandwiches, a deluxe buffet, and desserts) range from $6 to $16. It's open Monday through Saturday from 11:30am to 3pm, and Sunday from noon to 4pm for a la carte dining. Sundays between October and June, it stays open until 6:30pm to feed those attending the gallery's concert series. High chairs are available, but I'd think twice about filling one, if you get my drift.

The Terrace Café (✆ **202/789-3201**) is found on the upper level of the museum's East Building, overlooking Calder's mobile and the atrium. It's open Sundays from 11am to 3pm for light fare, including salads, sandwiches, and desserts.

All of the National Gallery eateries accept American Express, Diners Club, Discover, MasterCard, and Visa.

From the upper level, climb the spiral staircase (it's only 25 steps) to the Tower level, where special works are hung. Getting there is half the fun, and kids enjoy discovering this "secret" place.

Before you leave, check out the Concourse level. Some kids can spend days on the moving walkway and investigating the origin of the waterfall (overflow from street-level fountains) next to the Cascade Buffet.

Information on Audio Tours for adults and kids (ages 7–12), Postcard Tours for Families (all ages), the Children's Film Program (ages 7 and up), special exhibitions, tours, lectures, films, and concerts is available at the art information desks in the West Building and the ground floor of the East Building. If you can, before your visit, check the website for the latest on Family Weekends (for kids 4 and up), Family Workshops (Saturday or Sunday for kids 8–12 and their parents or adult companion); Stories in Art (Sundays at 11:30am and 1pm), and the Children's Film Program (first Saturday and Sunday morning of each month). These programs complement the exhibitions and expose children to the fine arts (*C* **202/842-6249**). Of course, once you arrive, you can always inquire at an information desk.

Aside from all the family-focused activities, one of the nicest aspects, to my mind, for families is the museum's **Sculpture Garden** 🌸🌸🌸, 9th Street and Constitution Avenue NW, open in summer Monday through Thursday and Saturday from 10am to 7pm and Friday from 10am to 9pm; Sunday, it's open from 11am to 7pm. During the fall and winter seasons, the garden closes at dusk. My grandkids love coming here. It sparks their imaginations, and they can roam more freely than in a museum. For those reasons, younger kids will find this a heck of a lot more interesting than what's indoors. Amid indigenous plantings and trees, and a fountain that, I am told, could become an ice rink, are about two dozen 20th-century sculptures. Wait until they see the giant *Typewriter Eraser,* Claes Oldenburg's *House,* headless figures by Polish-born Magdalena Bakanowicz, whimsical *Thinker on a Rock* (a rabbit), and concrete-block *Four-Sided Pyramid.* Your kids might not "get" the inscrutable Noguchi work *Great Rock of Inner Seeking,* but they're sure to flip over *Six-Part Seating.*

On the north side of the Mall between 3rd and 7th sts. NW (entrances at 6th St. and Constitution Ave. or Madison Dr.). *C* 202/737-4215. www.nga.gov. Free admission. Mon–Sat 10am–5pm; Sun 11am–6pm. Summer hours are frequently extended. Closed Dec 25 and Jan 1. Metro: Archives or Judiciary Square.

National Museum of American Art and National Portrait Gallery   These two Smithsonian museums are housed in the Old Patent Office Building at 8th and G streets NW, which is closed for renovation until July 2006 (they say). See the "Old Patent Office to Reopen" box, earlier in this chapter. *C* **202/357-2700.**

National Museum of Women in the Arts   **Ages 8 and up.** This museum celebrates, and is a showcase for, "the contribution of women to the history of art." It opened in 1987 in this striking Renaissance Revival building, formerly the Masonic Grand Lodge. There are more than 1,200 paintings, prints, and sculptures by 400 women. In 1982, the museum's founders, Wallace and Wilhelmina Holladay, donated their collection and library—a cornucopia of artworks by women spanning 5 centuries. Come for the permanent collection, featuring artists such as Mary Cassatt, Frida Kahlo, Georgia O'Keeffe, Helen Frankenthaler, Elaine de Kooning, Käthe Kollwitz, and Judy Chicago, as well as special exhibits and programs, and kids' events requiring reservations (*C* **202/783-7370**).

Works with special appeal for young people include *Noah's Ark* in the mezzanine members' lounge and the story quilts by Faith Ringgold. A snappy self-guided tour workbook for 7- to 12-year-olds, "Artventure," is free at the information desk. Kids are invited to find decorative elements on the mezzanine, distinguish faux marble from the real thing, and examine portraits for the sitter's mood and occupation. At the information desk, unearth the latest museum doings: storytellers, hands-on activities, and folksingers. Family Programs are held the first Sunday of the month during the school year. Kids 6 to 12, accompanied by an adult, are invited to take part in art projects, view performances, and do hands-on activities. The museum's Elizabeth A. Kasser Wing, just east of the preexisting museum, has a museum shop and two upstairs galleries, one dedicated to female artists displaying their works for the first time and the other devoted to sculpture. The **Mezzanine Café** is open for lunch and light fare Monday through Friday from 11:30am to 2:30pm (© **202/628-1068**). Or grab a bite at nearby **A.V.** (p. 91) or **Capitol City Brewing Co.** (p. 92).

1250 New York Ave. © 202/783-5000. www.nmwa.org. Admission $8 adults, $6 seniors (60 and over) and students with ID, NMWA members and children 18 and under are free. Additional fees for selected exhibitions. Guided tours are additional and must be scheduled in advance at © 202/783-7996. Mon–Sat 10am–5pm; Sun noon–5pm. Closed Thanksgiving Day, Dec 25, Jan 1. Metro: Metro Center.

Phillips Collection ⭐⭐ (Finds)   **Ages 6 and up.** The new Phillips addition is slated to open in spring 2006, with more gallery space, an enlarged museum shop and cafe, sculpture courtyard, 180-seat auditorium, activities room, and improved research and library facilities. I can't wait to see the enhancements to this awesome collection of Impressionist, post-Impressionist, and 20th-century American and European art.

Children seem to take to the museum off Dupont Circle because it is homey (maybe not like your home, but homey nonetheless), with elegant furniture, polished floors, and Asian rugs. Most kids react favorably to the playfulness of Klee's works, the sunny colors and good feeling of Renoir's *The Luncheon of the Boating Party* and other Impressionist works, and the large color canvases of Mark Rothko. I'll bet they'll have something to say about Alexander Calder's *Only, Only Bird,* constructed of aluminum beer and coffee cans.

When you enter, pick up a free family guide tied to one or more of the exhibits. With the opening of the new space, the museum's education department promises plenty of programs and activities for families with kids between the ages of 6 and 12 to ignite their interest in art. In the works are **Art at Home,** which asks children to write a poem or story about a painting to enhance their critical thinking about a particular work of art. In **Observation and Imagination,** they're encouraged to express themselves through various media. The programs are offered Tuesday through Sunday for groups of 5 to 20 and must be prearranged (© **202/387-2151**). If your family is small, hook up with another to meet the quota. The Phillips also sponsors family workshops throughout the year. Call to be put on a mailing list (© **202/387-2151,** ext. 247). Although it's inappropriate for younger children, every Thursday from 5 to 8:30pm, the **Artful Evenings** program includes a musical performance or gallery talk ($5). Free introductory tours are offered Saturday at 2pm. In-depth guided tours of the museum's special exhibitions are offered Tuesday and Thursday, by reservation, at 10 and 11:30am. You can grab a light bite or dessert Tuesday through Sunday in the small cafeteria-style cafe. The museum shop carries posters, postcards, and art books.

1600 21st St. NW, at Q St. © 202/387-2151. www.phillipscollection.org. Free admission weekdays, contributions are suggested. Weekends $8 adults, $6 full-time students and seniors over 62, free for age 18 and under and museum members; additional charge ($8) for special exhibitions. Tues–Sat 10am–5pm; Thurs 10am–8:30pm; Sun noon–7pm Labor Day to Memorial Day; noon–5pm Memorial Day–Labor Day. Closed Mon, July 4th, Thanksgiving, Dec 25, and Jan 1. Metro: Dupont Circle, Q St. exit.

HISTORY

See also section 1 for individual listings on the Smithsonian Building, the National Museum of American History, and the Anacostia Museum and Center for African-American History and Culture; all of section 2; all of section 3; the Octagon in "Architecture," earlier in this section; and the Folger Shakespeare Library and the National Archives in "Archives & Libraries," earlier in this section.

Frederick Douglass National Historic Site (Cedar Hill)   **Ages 10 and up.**
Please note: All the furniture and artifacts are in storage until late 2006 or early 2007 while repairs are made to Cedar Hill. You can still visit, however, and park rangers continue to conduct tours. Here's a golden opportunity for your kids to exercise their imaginations and visualize while the ranger describes the (stored) memorabilia and talks of Douglass.

Abolitionist and orator Frederick Douglass purchased Cedar Hill, the 20-room Victorian home on the Anacostia, in 1877 after living on Capitol Hill for 5 years. While the furniture is in storage, large images of the rooms as they appear when furnished, as well as historic photos of the home, are on view so you can visualize the space as it will appear when everything is in place.

A short film detailing Douglass's early years as a slave, his subsequent escape to the North, and lifetime achievements is shown in the visitor center. Self-educated, this civic leader, writer, publisher, and orator carved a significant niche in American history as a spokesman for the downtrodden and oppressed.

During February, which is Black History Month, films and special programs honor this unique individual. February 14, Douglass's birthday, is marked by a wreath-laying ceremony.

From the hill leading to Cedar Hill, you can enjoy a sweeping panorama of the Anacostia River, Washington Navy Yard, the Washington Monument, and the Capitol.

1411 W St. SE. © 202/426-5961. www.nps.gov/frdo. Reservations required for groups of 5 or more; encouraged for 4 or fewer (© 800/967-2283). Reservation fee $2 per person for advance group reservations. Mid-Apr–mid-Oct daily 9am–5pm; mid-Oct–mid-Apr daily 9am–4pm. Closed Thanksgiving, Dec 25, and Jan 1. Metro: Anacostia and then B-2/Mt. Rainier bus (8 blocks). By car (from the Mall): South on 9th St. to I-395 north, to I-295 south across bridge; exit onto Martin Luther King, Jr. Ave., and turn left on W St. SE. Go 3 blocks to visitor-center lot.

Ford's Theatre and Lincoln Museum ✸✸   **Ages 6 and up.** On April 14, 1865, President Abraham Lincoln was shot by John Wilkes Booth while attending a performance of *Our American Cousin* at Ford's. Lincoln was carried to the house of William Petersen across the street, and the president died there the next morning. The incident was anything but good for business, and Ford's wasn't used again as a theater until 1968. In the interim, it was a records-processing site and Army Medical Museum before Congress coughed up the funds to restore the theater to its 1865 appearance.

A 15-minute presentation is given hourly in the theater; visitors are then free to tour on their own. Among the Lincoln memorabilia in the basement museum are the clothes Lincoln wore the night he was assassinated and the Derringer pistol used by Booth. Two of the more eerie items in the exhibit are the Lincoln life mask and plaster casts of his hands. Audiovisual displays describe Lincoln's early life, political experiences, and presidential years.

Several shows have gone on to Broadway after premiering at Ford's, and every December Dickens's *A Christmas Carol* is revived. Catch a performance at this historic theater, if time permits. Sometimes students with an ID get reduced-price tickets half an hour before curtain time. The theater is closed to visitors during rehearsals and performances.

To round out your picture of the events surrounding Lincoln's assassination, visit the **Petersen House** ("The House Where Lincoln Died") at 526 10th St. (© **202/ 426-6924**). It gives me the willies, but kids love it. Because the bed in the ground-floor bedroom was too short for his lanky frame, Lincoln was laid diagonally across it. The original blood-stained pillow makes a powerful impression on kids (and adults, too). In the front parlor, the clock is stopped at 7:22am, the time of Lincoln's death. In 1896, the government bought the house for $30,000; it's maintained by the National Park Service.

511 10th St. NW, between E and F sts. © 202/426-6924 for historic site or 202/347-4833 for box-office information. www.nps.gov/foth. Free admission. Museum and Petersen House daily 9am–5pm; theater portion of museum closed during matinees and rehearsals; box office daily 10am–6pm. Closed Dec 25. Metro: Metro Center or Gallery Place.

International Spy Museum ⊀ **Ages 8 and up.** The word is out on the street, and it's anything but covert. That explains why visitors have been filling the once-ramshackle historic F Street building since the museum's opening in June 2002. Granted, the admission is steep, but not compared to amusement-park fees. The Spy Museum is every bit as amusing and won't nauseate you. Across the street from the Old Patent Office building, and near the MCI Center and Convention Center, the Spy Museum is dedicated to espionage and the technology that fuels it. For the most part, it's a valentine to the characters and technology that contributed to the dissolution of the Cold War. Kids over 8 or 10 will lap up the sugar-coated, spoon-fed history that approaches sensory overload with all the strong visuals, interactives, spoken narrative, and canned music. On view until sometime in 2006 (or beyond) is the exhibit **Spy Treasures of Hollywood.** Your kids may be too young, but surely you or their grandparents will recall the gear carried by famous TV and movie spies such as Maxwell Smart's (Don Adams, aka Agent 86) shoe phone, James Bond's Walther PPK handgun, and the model tarantula featured in *Dr. No.* Among the highlights in the permanent collection are a camera-carrying pigeon, a carved Great Seal of the United States with hidden microphone (a gift from Russia, no less), vintage lock-picking tools, a World War II German encoding device, and a replica of James Bond's Aston Martin. Can his martini stirrer be far behind? The museum has taken certain, um, liberties, using props in some instances instead of the real things. Big deal. Your kids won't notice. Just park your disbelief with your packages at the door. This isn't the Smithsonian. For most, it's a *hoo-ha,* rather than a *ho-hum,* experience.

On site are a large gift shop with a super selection of T-shirts, puzzles, books, and games, and the **Spy City Cafe** (© **202/654-0999**), with salads, sandwiches, wraps, seven varieties of hot dogs, and photos of D.C. spy drop-off points, of which there are *many.* Most items are under $6.50, and there is seating for 50. The formal restaurant, **Zola** (as in Emile), is for fine dining and not suitable for youngsters (reservations recommended; © **202/654-0999**). Pick up same-day tickets at the museum, or to avoid long lines and/or disappointment, purchase tickets in advance at Ticketmaster, Hecht's, 12th and G St. NW (© **800/551-SEAT** or 202/432-SEAT; www.ticketmaster. com). A little closer, please, while I whisper a secret. From April to October, when the museum is open until 8pm, I suggest an early-evening visit. (Oops! Guess it's no longer Top Secret information.)

Past special activities included a KidSpyCamp for kids 9 to 13, in which participants donned disguises, assumed aliases, and learned the fine points of creating cover stories, all for $75 (lunch included).

800 F St. NW. ℂ 202/393-7798. www.spymuseum.org. Admission $14 adults (12–64), $13 seniors (65 and older), $11 kids 5–11, free 4 and under; $5 surcharge for special shows. Open daily April–Oct 10am–8pm; Nov–Mar 10am–6pm. Closed Thanksgiving, Dec 25, and Jan 1. Metro: Gallery Place/Chinatown.

Old Stone House   Ages 4 and up. Kids feel comfortable in this modest pre-Revolutionary War house in Georgetown, probably because it's small like they are. Sometimes in summer, concerts are held in the garden, where you may picnic (as long as you clean up when you're through). Saturday and Sunday, the park rangers give talks and lead tours to local sites, such as Montrose Park. A candlelight tour is held around Christmas. An America's National Parks Bookstore opened here in late 2005, and a welcome addition it is, with goods representative of the 17th and 18th century—stoneware, hand-blown glass, pottery, toys and games—as well as books on Washington, D.C.

3051 M St. NW. ℂ 202/426-6851. www.nps.gov/rocr/oldstonehouse. Free admission. Wed–Sun noon–4pm, until 5pm in summer. House closed Mon, Tues, Thanksgiving, Dec 25, Jan 1, and other federal holidays. Gardens open daily. Metro: Foggy Bottom and then a 15-min. walk, or take Georgetown Connection shuttle or any no. 30 bus from Pennsylvania Ave.

U.S. Holocaust Memorial Museum 𝄞𝄞𝄞   **Ages 10 and up.** When this museum opened in April 1993, I was among the skeptics who were certain that it could not possibly measure up to the advance media hype. I was wrong. The architecture and contents evoke a visceral reaction among visitors, regardless of religious or ethnic background. In fact, officials who track such things say that 80% of the museum's visitors are non-Jews. It would be easy to spend the better part of a day here. But I don't advise it. My personal limit is about 2½ hours before I crave fresh air and daylight.

Nearly two million visitors per year of all ages and backgrounds cross the cobblestones, once part of the Warsaw ghetto, to gaze at the photographs of those who perished. The museum planners' intended purpose has been masterfully and powerfully realized. I strongly recommend a visit here, but with some reservations: Do not bring very young children, and discuss the Holocaust with older kids before visiting. A reading list and suggested answers to typically asked questions are available at the information desk and at www.ushmm.org/education.

Mature 8 year-olds on up can, and should, see the first-floor exhibit **"Remember the Children: Daniel's Story."** Pick up a free family guide at the information desk, along with a list of the day's events and times for the 15-minute orientation video (suitable for all ages). Daniel's Story details a fictional but historically accurate German youth's odyssey from a comfortable and secure home in 1930s Frankfurt, to a 1941 ghetto, to the gates of Auschwitz. Visitors walk Daniel's path, literally and emotionally. While the experience is sobering and unsettling, it stops well short of horrific. At the end, a short film reinforces the tragic message of a family's demise due to genocide. Young visitors are encouraged to express their reactions by recording their thoughts (markers and paper provided) and posting them in a museum mailbox. Also of note: **The Children's Tile Wall** 𝄞, on the lower level, consists of 3,300 tiles painted by American schoolchildren as a memorial to the more than one million children who died in the Holocaust. Taken as a whole, it is decorative and lovely in its simplicity. On closer inspection, it is a poignant reminder of the museum's mission. If you wish, you may light memorial candles in the **Hall of Remembrance.**

Break Time

The itty-bitty, cafeteria-style **U.S. Holocaust Museum Café** is located in a separate light-filled annex, off the museum's west entrance plaza (Raoul Wallenberg Plaza). The limited all-vegetarian menu is not kosher and includes bagels, muffins, knishes, roasted vegetable salads, matzoh ball soup, PB&J, fruit, desserts, and drinks—ideal for a between-meal pick-me-up or light lunch. Security screens all who enter because of the administrative offices upstairs. Prices range from $2 to $8. Reservations are not accepted. It's open daily from 8:30am to 4:30pm; April through mid-June, extended Tuesday and Thursday hours, from 8:30am to 6:30pm. High chairs and boosters are available.

The permanent exhibition is housed on the second, third, and fourth floors. The museum's planners, educators, and child psychologists concur that youngsters 10 or 11 can handle the experience. I agree, but you know best what might or might not upset your kids. Along the way, 4-foot 10-inch walls shield young visitors from the most "difficult" exhibitions. Visitors entering the permanent collection receive an identity card with the name and family history of a Holocaust victim whose fate can be traced during the tour.

After entering the **Hall of Witness,** visitors ride to the fourth floor to begin the tour. (The fifth floor, with its library and archives, is devoted to scholarly pursuits. High-school students are welcome to do research here between 10am and 5:30pm. Help is provided by library staff.) The fourth floor deals with the rise of Nazism from 1933 to 1939; the third floor focuses on the persecution of minorities, ghetto life, and the death camps from 1940 to 1944. The second floor details the liberation of the camps and refugees' resettling efforts. Young people take note: Also on the second floor is the **Wexner Language Center,** where you can learn about the Holocaust at your own pace through the user-friendly interactive computer system, which uses photographs, videos, and oral histories.

After several visits, I still find the most powerful exhibits to be the huge photograph of American soldiers liberating a camp; the *Nazi Rise to Power* and other historical films; the "Tower of Faces," photos of more than 100 shtetl families taken between 1890 and 1941 near Vilna (now Lithuania); the Anne Frank exhibit; a railcar that once stood on the tracks near Treblinka; "Voices from Auschwitz" (memories of survivors); thousands of shoes from death-camp victims; and artwork by children in Auschwitz. Whenever I visit, it is solemnly yet appropriately quiet in the Holocaust Museum.

At 10am the day of your visit, pick up free timed-entry passes to view the Permanent Exhibitions. You may also call ahead (© **800/400-9373;** www.tickets.com). Be prepared for the $1.75 per pass "convenience fee." Passes are not required for Daniel's Story or the Children's Tile Wall. However, if your kids are over 10, I urge you to secure passes and see the permanent exhibitions.

Wednesdays at 1pm, March through August, Holocaust survivors speak in the Rubinstein Auditorium. Suitable for mature 12-year-olds.

The museum shop contains books on the Holocaust, personal narratives, CDs, audio- and videotapes, and several shelves of titles for young readers. From April to mid-June, the shop stays open Tuesday and Thursday until 6:30pm.

100 Raoul Wallenberg Place (15th St. SW). 🕐 202/488-0400. www.ushmm.org. Free same-day timed passes (often gone by 10:30am) at museum box office for permanent exhibits. For advance tickets, call Tickets.com (🕐 800/400-9373; service charge of $1.75 per ticket). Daily 10am–5:30pm. Closed on Yom Kippur and Dec. 25. Metro: Smithsonian (Independence Ave. exit).

Woodrow Wilson House Museum 🏛🏛 *Finds*   **Ages 8 and up.** The handsome Georgian Revival mansion built in 1915 is just off Embassy Row in Kalorama—the only former president's residence in the District open to the public. It's also one of my favorite museums. It will turn on kids with an interest in American history. Wilson, our 28th president, lived in this stately residence for 3 years after his second term, and his widow, Edith, resided here until her death in 1961. Since then, the National Trust has maintained it.

Visitors are surprised to learn that, despite his stern appearance and demeanor, the former scholar and university president was just a regular guy—a movie buff who was a fan of Tom Mix (an early cowboy movie star) and who subscribed to *Photoplay* movie magazine. On a more sublime level, you can see Wilson's inaugural Bible, the casing of the first shell fired in World War I, a White House Cabinet chair, and a vintage 1915 elevator. The 45-minute guided tour, Tuesday through Sunday between 10am and 4pm, offers insight into the private life of the man behind the wire-rimmed spectacles. Programs for school groups are available during the school year.

The Friends of the Wilson House is part of a consortium that sponsors the popular **Kalorama House and Embassy Tour,** which includes a stop at one or more ambassadors' private residences. The annual event is usually the second Sunday of September. For more information and to make reservations, call 🕐 **202/387-4062,** ext. 18.

2340 S St. NW. 🕐 202/387-4062. www.woodrowwilsonhouse.org. Admission $5 adults, $4 seniors, $2.50 students, free 6 and under. Tues–Sun 10am–4pm. Closed Mon, Thanksgiving, Dec. 25, and federal holidays. Metro: Dupont Circle, Q St. exit; then walk north on Massachusetts Ave. for 5 blocks to right at 24th St. and right at S St. half a block.

SPECIAL CHILDREN'S MUSEUMS

DAR Museum 🏛   **Ages 4–10.** Do not pass Go, do not collect $200, just head for the **New Hampshire Toy Attic** on the third floor to see 18th- and 19th-century children's furniture, toys, and dolls. Dollhouse aficionados will delight in the miniature furniture and accessories. To introduce young ones to early American history, 1-hour "Colonial Adventure" tours for 5- to 7-year-olds are held the first and third Saturdays, September through May, 1:30 to 2:30pm and 3 to 4pm. Reservations are required (🕐 **202/879-3240**). Kids don colonial-style garb and visit a reproduction of a one-room house where they may scribble on a chalkboard, card wool, have a make-believe tea party, and imagine what it would be like to sleep in a trundle bed right beside their parents.

The "Touch of Independence" exhibit is filled with touchable kid-size period furniture and old-style toys and dolls. Guided tours of furnished period rooms are offered Monday through Friday from 10am to 2pm. Just show up. Tours are self-guided from 8:30am to 4pm. Call for special exhibition information.

1776 D St. NW. 🕐 202/879-3241. www.dar.org/museum. Free admission. Mon–Fri 8:30am–4pm; Sun 1–5pm. Closed Sat., national holidays, and during DAR's annual meeting in Apr. Metro: Farragut West or Farragut North.

4 For Kids with Special Interests

AIRPORTS

Due to heightened security following the September 11, 2001, terrorist attacks and the war in Iraq, airport tours could be suspended. Call before you go.

Washington Dulles International Airport   **Ages 6–10.** Visitors are welcome to stroll around Eero Saarinen's soaring masterpiece (recently renovated to twice its original size). Pick up information for a self-guided tour at the information desk inside the main terminal. The drive alone is worthwhile, especially at dawn or dusk but never during rush hour, to view this stunning example of avian architecture.

Chantilly, VA. *C* 703/572-2700. www.mwaa.com. Daily 24 hours. Directions: Constitution Ave. to Theodore Roosevelt Bridge, Rte. 66 west. Bear left, and follow signs to Dulles Airport only. From Key Bridge, take Rte. 29 to Rte. 66, and follow the signs.

College Park Aviation Museum   **Ages 6–10.** This Smithsonian-affiliated museum is on the site of the world's oldest continuously operating airport, which opened its doors—make that field—in 1909. Remember Wilbur and Orville? Well, they taught the first two army officers to fly here the year the field opened. Other firsts include the first testing of a bomb dropped from a plane (1911) and the first U.S. Air Mail service (1918). Wing it on your own, and visit the historic airport (*C* **301/864-3029**). Tours are self-guided except the last Saturday of the month at 11am and 1pm. Group tours are available for 10 or more. Pack a picnic to eat on the grounds, or walk a short distance to the **94th Aerosquadron,** 5240 Paint Branch Parkway, College Park (*C* **301/699-9400**). Kids love this restaurant. It's decorated to resemble a war-torn French farmhouse from around World War I and faces the runway. Out front are replicas of World War II fighter planes. Every September, the airport hosts a weekend Air Fair with airplane, helicopter, and hot-air balloon rides, as well as displays and children's entertainment. Preschoolers can join the Peter Pan Club (story time and activities) the second and fourth Thursday of the month, 10:30 to 11:30am. No extra charge.

1985 Cpl. Frank Scott Dr., College Park, MD. *C* 301/864-6029. www.pgparks.com. Admission $4 adults, $3 seniors, $2 kids 2–18, free 1 and under. Daily 10am–5pm. Closed Easter, July 4, Thanksgiving, Dec 25, Jan 1. Groups must call at least 1 week ahead to schedule a tour. Metro: College Park and then walk 2 blocks.

THE MILITARY

See section 2 of this chapter for individual listings on Arlington National Cemetery, the World War II, Korean War, and Vietnam War memorials. Due to heightened security following the September 11, 2001, terrorist attacks and the war in Iraq, tours of these military museums could be suspended. Call before you go.

Navy Museum   **Ages 6 and up.** This museum chronicles the history of the U.S. Navy from the Revolutionary War to the present. Exhibits include "200 Years of the Washington Navy Yard" and "The Navy in the Korean War." Kids gravitate to the model ships and weaponry. They can turn a sub periscope, climb on cannons, and work the barrels of antiaircraft weapons. When they tire of war games, they can board the 1950s destroyer USS *Barry* berthed outside. *Note:* Due to heightened security, visitor access, as of late 2005, was limited to "government employees, active-duty and retired military personnel and their dependents." If you don't qualify, call to make an appointment to visit.

805 Kidder Breese SE, Washington Navy Yard. *C* 202/433-6897. www.history.navy.mil. Free admission. Mon–Fri 9am–4pm; weekends and holidays 10am–5pm. Metro: Eastern Market or Navy Yard and then N22 bus to museum or 25-min. walk. Limited free parking.

MODEL TRAINS

All aboard! As you probably know, model trains are not just for Christmas anymore. With your little cabooses in tow, try trainspotting at the following locations. See also the review of the **Baltimore and Ohio Railroad Museum** (p. 276), in Baltimore, Maryland.

B&O Railroad Station Museum (Ellicott City) **Ages 4 and up.** About an hour's drive from downtown D.C., this museum is housed in an old railroad station. Catch a glimpse of life in the 19th century at several seasonal exhibits: May to October (early railroad history), December to January (holiday model train display), and February to May (Civil War history in Maryland). My money is on the annual holiday event. On permanent display is an HO-scale model replica of the first 13 miles of the Baltimore & Ohio Railroad, the nation's first. When it opened in 1827, it ran from Baltimore to Ellicott City. Train and history buffs will want to stop in the museum store for hats, shirts, books, and other choo-choo–related souvenirs. You'll need a car to get here. If you want to stay longer to explore more of quaint Ellicott City, park in one of the several metered lots within walking distance.

2711 Maryland Ave. (Main St. and Maryland Ave.) Ellicott City, MD. ✆ 410/461-1944. www.ecbo.org. Admission $5 adults, $4 seniors and students, $3 children 2–12, free under 2. Open Fri–Sat 11am–4pm, Sun noon–5pm. Take Colesville Rd. (Rte. 29/Old Columbia Pike) north from I-495 to Rte. 144 east (Old Frederick Road–Main St.). Follow signs to Historic District and museum. Short-term parking on the street and nearby lots.

U.S. Navy Memorial & Visitor Center

There's more here than first meets the eye. After taking a family picture with Stanley Bleifeld's statue *The Lone Sailor* on the plaza, enter the below-ground visitor center, which is unmistakably shiplike. *The Homecoming*, another work by Bleifeld, welcomes visitors at the entrance. Throughout the Gallery Deck are interactive video kiosks. Push a button and learn about Navy history, or retrieve information on naval ships and aircraft. If you have friends or relatives who've served in the navy, see if they're registered in the Navy Memorial Log. If they're not, pick up an enrollment form.

At Sea, a lively, moving, action-packed half-hour movie, is shown March through October, Monday through Saturday at noon; November through February, Tuesday through Saturday at noon. Sometimes the show is canceled in favor of a Guard Drill Team performance or concert by the U.S. Navy Band. Admission is free.

Check out the **"Wave Wall,"** where 200 years of naval history are depicted in 13 panels, before picking up souvenirs in the Ship's Store, full of nautical gifts and memorabilia.

From Memorial Day to Labor Day, you might want to take in at least one of the armed forces' 8pm concerts in the outdoor amphitheater (weather permitting). Tickets are not required. Call ✆ 202/737-2300, ext. 768.

The center is at 701 Pennsylvania Ave. NW, between 7th and 9th streets (✆ 202/737-2300). Admission is free. Hours March through October are Monday through Saturday from 9:30am to 5pm; November through February, Tuesday through Saturday, same hours. Closed on major holidays.

Fairfax Station Railroad Museum   **Ages 4 and up.** Visitors lay tracks for the N-gauge model train displays the third Sunday of every month. But every Sunday, the public is invited to check out the quaint train depot filled with Civil War and Red Cross memorabilia (Clara Barton nursed wounded soldiers at the original site after the second Battle of Manassas). The caboose houses a permanent model train exhibit. The museum serves as a staging area for lectures, workshops, and craft shows. With a little planning, children can celebrate their birthdays with a caboose party. A small gift shop features railroad and Civil War souvenirs.

11200 Fairfax Station Rd., Fairfax Station, VA. ℂ **703/425-9225.** www.fairfax-station.org. Suggested donation $2 adults, $1 children 4–10, free 3 and under. Sun 1–4pm (permanent exhibit in caboose); model trains run 3rd Sun of every month. Directions: Rte. 123 South of George Mason University to Fairfax Station Rd., ¼ mile to museum. Free parking.

SCIENCE & NATURE

See section 1 in this chapter for listings on the following science museums: the National Museum of Natural History, the National Zoological Park, and the National Air and Space Museum.

Albert Einstein Planetarium   **Ages 4 and up.** Exciting out-of-this-world experiences await you in the first-floor planetarium of the Air and Space Museum. Children over 8 and those with longer attention spans will enjoy the breathtaking photography of a trip through the Solar System, "Infinity Express," narrated by Laurence Fishburne. The show runs daily on the half-hour 10:30am to 4:30pm (extra 5pm show Sunday, Monday, and Wednesday). Cost is $8 adults, $6.50 children 2 to 12, and $7 seniors 60 and older. "The Stars Tonight" shows what the night sky looks like during the season of your visit. It airs at 5pm Tuesday, Thursday, and Saturday only. And it's free! Order tickets online at www.si.edu/imax, or call ℂ **202/633-4629.** Both charge a $2-per-ticket service fee. Ask about monthly lectures (no charge). If you want more, listen to the "Skywatcher's Report," a brief but interesting message about stargazing conditions, focusing on which planets and stars your family will be able to see in the current week (ℂ **202/357-2000**).

National Air and Space Museum, 7th St. and Independence Ave. SW. ℂ **202/633-4629.** www.nasm.si.edu or www.smithsonian.org/IMAX. Admission $5–$8. Shows daily 10:30am–5pm; museum 10am–5:30pm. Closed Dec 25. Metro: L'Enfant Plaza.

Discovery Creek   **Ages 6 months and up.** Families are invited to drop in for science- and nature-related activities (hikes, crafts, discussions, stories, guest speakers) Saturday and Sunday, 10am to 3pm. Discovery Creek is in Glen Echo Park's former stables. Every month there's a different theme. Discovery Creek also has satellite locations in the area—the best known is the historic schoolhouse on MacArthur Boulevard where Discover Creek had its start several years ago. (The schoolhouse is also available for private birthday parties.) Most of Discovery Creek's weekday programs are open to school groups only (ℂ **202/337-5111**). The cost for the weekend programs is nominal: $5 for ages 2 to 64, $3 for 65 and older, free for kids under 2. D.C. area residents, take note: Discovery Creek has programs that introduce infants, toddlers, and preschoolers to the wonders of nature. The fee for Toddler Treehouse, for example (four sessions, each 1½ hours), is $65. On your way in or out of the park, ride the beautifully restored 1921 Dentzel carousel (75¢ admission). Glen Echo is also the site for performances by the Puppet Co. and Adventure Theatre. In fact, visitors with Puppet Co. and Adventure Theatre ticket stubs get $1 off. Both offer professional productions that are well worth seeing (see chapter 10). You could spend the better part of a day at this historic former amusement park.

Stables at Glen Echo Park, 7300 MacArthur Blvd., at Goldsboro Road, Glen Echo, MD. © 202/337-5111. www.discoverycreek.org. Open to public Sat and Sun 10am–3pm. $5 adults and kids 2–64, $3 seniors 65 and older, free kids under 2. Closed Thanksgiving weekend, Dec 25, Jan 1, and government holidays. Metro: Friendship Heights and then Metrobus #29. Driving: Massachusetts Ave. to end at Goldsboro Rd., left to MacArthur Blvd., right at MacArthur, left into park, park, and then cross footbridge.

Goddard Space Flight Center Visitor Center   Ages 6 and up.

You can reach the stars just a half-hour from downtown in beautiful Greenbelt, Maryland. Kids are drawn to the hands-on interactive displays in the visitor center and space-age souvenirs in the gift shop. Step outside to the rocket garden, with actual rockets and some mockups. The model-rocket launches have been popular with local families for many moons and are held the first Sunday of every month (weather permitting) at 1pm.

Greenbelt, MD. © 301/286-8981. www.nasa.gov/goddard. Free admission. Tues–Fri 9am–5pm; Sat–Sun noon–4pm. Closed Thanksgiving, Dec 25, Jan 1. Directions: Take New York Ave. to I-295 north (Baltimore–Washington Pkwy.); turn left on Greenbelt Rd. (Rte. 193), turn left at Soil Conservation Rd., and then turn left at the first gate.

National Aquarium   Ages 1 and up.

More than 1,000 specimens are contained in 50 tanks at the oldest public aquarium in the nation. Assorted salt- and freshwater fish, including sharks, an eel, an alligator, and Japanese carp, get along swimmingly. The piranhas—you'll be happy to learn—have their own tank. Feedings are at 2pm: sharks, Monday, Wednesday, and Saturday; alligators, Friday; piranhas, Tuesday, Thursday, and Sunday. In the touch tank, kids can get their hands wet examining horseshoe crabs and other noncarnivorous beach-dwellers. This is an especially good option for toddler and elementary school–age kids; older children may become bored quickly. Families can reserve a room here for birthday parties.

Note: A large multilevel aquarium in Baltimore is also known as the National Aquarium, but the two are oceans apart in content and scope. See the Baltimore entry on p. 280.

Department of Commerce (lower level), 14th St. between Pennsylvania Ave. and Constitution Ave. NW. © 202/482-2825. www.nationalaquarium.com. Admission (cash only) $5 adults, $4 seniors and military, $2 ages 2–10, free under 2. Daily 9am–5pm. Closed Thanksgiving and Dec 25. Metro: Federal Triangle.

National Geographic Society's Explorers Hall ℛ *Finds*   Ages 8 and up.

Before entering Explorers Hall, watch the short introductory videotape on the 16-panel screen to familiarize young trailblazers with the National Geographic Society's mission of "increasing and diffusing geographic knowledge." Permanent exhibits focus on dinosaurs, undersea exploration, and natural history, such as the 3-D models of the vastly different Chesapeake Bay, Mt. Everest, and the Grand Canyon. Temporary exhibits (changing every few months) focus on discoveries by National Geographic researchers and works by National Geographic photographers. Some exhibits may be too sophisticated for kids under 8, but older children enjoy **Explorers Hall** for its relatively intimate size. Here, complex geographic information is explained at a level that they can readily understand and appreciate through the many interactive exhibits and videos, such as "Where Did We Come From?" (evolution) and "What's Shaky and Quaky?" (volcanoes). The fascinating geochron—world time map to the uninitiated—is shaded to show daylight and night. Look up to the 3-D model of the Grand Canyon plastered to the ceiling.

At the **Mammals Kiosk,** the touch screen reveals pictures of 700 animals and 155 vocalizations. Visitors are encouraged to "touch, play, and learn" while testing their trivial pursuit of geophysical knowledge in "Geographica," where you can also feel a tornado and walk beneath a flying dinosaur. Experience orbital flight with loved ones in **Earth Station One,** an amphitheater that several times an hour simulates an orbital flight 23,000 miles above Earth's surface. *Note:* Large groups are advised to call ahead (✆ **202/857-7689**).

Your kids might have to drag you away from **Global Access,** an educational, fun-to-play video game. After picking a country you'd like to know more about, choose specific topics (history, culture, flora, and fauna) from the menu. Voilà! Press a button, and the living atlas tells all. In the **Television Room,** you can watch scenes from the society's enormously popular and instructive TV series.

Wouldn't your kids like to be on the cover of *National Geographic* magazine? Sure they would! Outside the TV Room are two photo booths where they can choose to have their face plastered on a postcard-size cover.

Gaze at the Washington sky overhead in the small planetarium and then take a gander at a nearly 4-billion-year-old moon rock. Pick up past and current copies of *National Geographic* magazine, a wide and interesting selection of beautifully photographed books for the whole family, maps, globes, and souvenirs in the gift shop.

17th and M sts. NW. ✆ 202/857-7588. www.nationalgeographic.com. Free admission. Mon–Sat and holidays 9am–5pm; Sun 10am–5pm. Closed Dec 25. Metro: Farragut North (Connecticut Ave. and L St. exit) or Farragut West.

National Museum of Health and Medicine   **Ages 10 and up.** A multiyear effort had been under way to move this hard-to-find museum (part of the Armed Forces Institute of Pathology) back to the Mall, its original site before moving uptown in 1972. Now, with Walter Reed slated to close, who knows where the museum will be in a few years?

Older kids with a strong stomach and interest in medicine or pathology won't want to miss this. Don't bring young children; they might have trouble sleeping afterward. The museum has numerous exhibits of diseased, injured, and defective body parts—some famous, such as Lincoln's skull bone and President Garfield's spine.

Permanent exhibitions include "Medicine During the Civil War," "Evolution of the Microscope," and "Human Body, Human Being," which features preserved, um, body parts (stomachs, brains, lungs, kidney stones, and so on). Show your kids the smoker's and coal miner's lungs (a far better deterrent than media ads and your nagging about the effects of smoking). The first Saturday of the month, the museum has a health-awareness program from 11am to 2pm. Information on drugs and AIDS is also exhibited. Call about group tours (✆ **202/782-2201**). *Please note:* This is a military site, and the rules for admission to the grounds are strict and many. Most Metrobuses are not allowed on the grounds, so you could be dropped the equivalent of several blocks away. Call or check the website before heading there.

Walter Reed Army Medical Center, Building 54, 6900 Georgia Ave. at Elder St. NW. ✆ 202/782-2200. http://nmhm.washingtondc.museum. Free admission. Daily 10am–5:30pm. Closed Dec 25. Metro: Silver Spring or Takoma Park and then take a bus or taxi 1½ miles to the museum. Free parking.

Rock Creek Nature Center   **Ages 4 and up.** The nature center has exhibitions, a Discovery Room, a library, and an active beehive, connected by a tube to the outdoors. Gather here for guided walks and to explore the self-guided trail on your own. A free planetarium show, "The Night Sky," takes place Wednesday at 4pm and Sundays at 1pm for kids 4 to 7 and their parents/adult companions. Saturday at 4pm, a planetarium show is geared to those 7 and older. Free tickets are distributed half an hour before each show. Themed nature programs are Sundays and Fridays at 4pm (for kids 7 and older). "Exploring the Sky," a stargazing session cosponsored by the National Park Service and the National Capital Astronomers, is held one evening a month from April through November at Picnic Grove No. 13, near the Nature Center, Military and Glover roads NW. Because the time varies from month to month, call ahead.

See the section on "Parks, Gardens & Other Wide-Open Spaces," in chapter 8 for more information on the park itself.

5200 Glover Rd. NW. © 202/426-6829. www.nps.gov/rocr/planetarium. Free admission. Wed–Sun 9am–5pm. Directions: North on Connecticut Ave., turn right onto Military Rd., and then turn right onto Glover Rd.

U.S. Naval Observatory *Finds*   **Ages 8 and up.** On a clear night, you can see forever at the Naval Observatory. Weather permitting, you'll have stars in your eyes after peering through the 12-inch Alvan Clark refractor at celestial bodies 25,000 light-years away. Gates open most Mondays at 8pm for the 8:30pm 1½-hour tour. Wear sturdy shoes, as the tour is on hilly terrain. Leave backpacks, bulky items, and bags behind. Cameras are okay. Here's the catch: Requests must be made at the number below or online 4 to 6 weeks in advance. Include the names in your party, dates of birth, daytime phone, and/or e-mail address. Because this is military property, according to the website, tours "may be suspended at any time." There is some on-street parking. The closest Metro (Dupont Circle) is not so close. The N2 and N4 Metrobuses pass by, but you might miss the show because the buses are less than punctual after 7pm. If you don't have a car, I'd take a taxi.

Massachusetts Ave. at 34th St. NW (enter the South Gate). © 202/762-1438. www.usno.navy.mil. Free admission. Selected Mon at 8:30pm. Closed federal holidays.

MEDIA
Voice of America   **Ages 12 and up.** Between the Air and Space Museum and the Capitol, the world's largest radio station welcomes visitors to the downtown facility, where programs are broadcast worldwide on 26 channels in 42 languages! During the 45-minute tour, you will see the control room, hear part of a feature show, view a short film, and perhaps catch the evening news in Russian. Foreign visitors, who outnumber Americans by a wide margin, are excited when they recognize broadcasters that they listen to at home. The large mural, *The Meaning of Social Security,* was done for the WPA in 1940 by Ben Shahn. Windows to studios are high, so don't bring kids much under 12 (they'll be bored anyway). Reserve by phone or online (© **202/619-3919;** www.voanews.com) or e-mail: tickets@voanews.com.

330 Independence Ave. SW (enter on C St. only). © 202/619-3919. www.voa.gov. Free admission. Tours Mon–Fri 11:45am. Call for reservations. Metro: L'Enfant Plaza or Federal Center SW.

The Washington Post   **Ages 11 and older.** Groups *only* (10–30 people, reservations made in advance) may tour the newsroom, composing room, and press room of this Washington daily. The 1-hour tours are given Mondays only in response to a written request between 2 and 6 weeks in advance. Request must include date and time your group wants the tour, name of organization, number of participants, and name of contact person with day and evening phone numbers. Fax to 202/334-4963. Don't expect to see the presses running. Because the *Post* is a morning paper, that action takes place while you're fast asleep.

1150 15th St. NW. (📞 202/334-7969. www.washingtonpost.com. Free admission, reservations required. Tours by reservation only Mon between 10am and 3pm. Metro: Farragut North or McPherson Square.

5 Organized Tours

For an easy way to see D.C.'s major attractions, or when you're looking for something to do without wearing out the troops, take a guided tour. Ride one of the National Park Service's **Tourmobile** trams (📞 202/554-5100; www.tourmobile.com) and get off as often as you like—or not at all! This is the area's largest sightseeing operation and the only one licensed to make stops at attractions on the Mall. See "Getting Around," in chapter 3 for more information on different tours available.

You can also make tracks for an **Old Town Trolley Tour** (📞 301/985-3020), which has the advantage of pickup and drop-off service at many D.C. hotels but the disadvantage of not stopping along the Mall. Again, see "Getting Around" in chapter 3 for more information on tour options.

Gray Line Sightseeing Tours (📞 202/289-1995) offers several tours—from 3 hours to 2 days—in and around D.C. and to destinations as far as Williamsburg and Charlottesville, Virginia. Gray Line departs from convenient Union Station and picks up passengers at some hotels. I wouldn't try an all-day trip with preschoolers, who might view the confinement as an invitation to riot. Also beware of kids who get nauseous on busses. The "Washington After Dark" tour, for my money, is the best; I love every minute of it. The bus stops at each presidential memorial and major monument for about 20 minutes so that you can take pictures, buy a souvenir, or stop and stare. My favorite moments were spent on the steps of the Lincoln and Jefferson memorials, taking in the scene. Gray Line driver/guide Harold Chavetz, a history buff with 16 years' experience, is extremely knowledgeable. He barely comes up for air. While I think this a memorable D.C. experience, children under 9 or 10 will have a major meltdown. Or fall asleep. You must walk from the drop-off point to the monument (sometimes the equivalent of several blocks). And the tour ends between 10:30 and 11pm. Last time I rode with Harold, we grownups were plenty tired at tour's end. A word to the wise: Eat first, or carry a snack; all the monument concessions close early in the evening. I didn't and would have sold my mother for a bag of pretzels. Gray Line also offers a multilingual tour of Washington, departing from the tour company's Union Station terminal. Advance reservations are required (📞 202/289-1995).

The guides at **Tour D.C.** (📞 301/588-8999; www.tourdc.com) are experts at peppering their narrative with spicy scandals. History buffs, groupies, and teens might enjoy "Women, Love, and Property," a tour of Georgetown, where many influential women, such as Pamela Harriman, Jacqueline Kennedy, and Katharine Graham resided, and "John and Jackie in Georgetown," tracing the years the Kennedys lived there. Tours are spring through fall but never in July and August. Too hot! The cost varies, depending on the tour. Kids 18 and under with a parent/guardian are free. Good deal! And Tour D.C. will craft a tour that fits your group like a glove.

Tour de Force (📞 703/525-2948; www.atourdeforce.com), through owner/guide/historian Jeanne Fogle, creates motor-coach and walking tours mainly for incoming groups but also arranges individual guides for families who prefer a private tour. Fogle is a maven: A guide since 1984 and the author of two books on D.C.'s history, she's a native whose family has resided in the District for 150 years.

Washington Walks (📞 202/484-1565; www.washingtonwalks.com) offers numerous walking tours of the District's neighborhoods as well as private themed tours. How about this: The "Moveable Feast" walk takes participants on the Metro to sample snacks at local eateries. Sounds delicious to me! "In Fala's Footsteps," for kids 4 to 9, is but one of the popular family tours. (Fala was FDR's beloved Scottish terrier.) The licensed guides will tailor craft a tour to your liking, but give them a couple of days to plan. Tours are held April through October daily, rain or shine. You must reserve at least 48 hours in advance. Call or check the website for more on scheduled tours and arranging private tours. Private tours (for small groups like families) are $250 for 3 hours; 48 hours' notice required. Independent guide **Anita Allingham** ⚜ (© **301/493-8568;** anitadctours@earthlink.net) leads a walking "Illuminated Night Tour" that includes stops at the Lincoln Memorial with its unobstructed view of the eternal flame marking John F. Kennedy's grave, the steps of the Jefferson Memorial to ogle the White House and Washington Monument, and the Kennedy Center rooftop for an unequaled panorama of downtown and beyond. She charges $30 to $35 per hour with a 4-hour minimum per family (up to four people). Her tour to the National Zoo includes a stop to see the pandas at feeding time. Anita is a seasoned pro, a D.C. native who has been guiding tourists around the nation's capital since 1976. She'll modify the evening tour to suit you and is also available for tailor-made walking tours (using Metro and/or taxi) and as a guide to Baltimore, Annapolis, and beyond.

A word of caution: If you're considering a small, lesser-known tour company, make sure that the tour guides are licensed. You don't want to hear about Washington from someone recently arrived from Minnesota who makes up commentary along the way. When in doubt, call the **Guild of Professional Tour Guides,** known hereabouts as "the Guild" (© **202/298-1474;** www.washingtondctourguides.com). This association of more than 200 licensed guides with 10 or more years of experience will steer you toward a guide or company meeting your specific needs.

Neighborhood Strolls

Walking is the best way to see Washington. L'Enfant laid out the city on a grid. Wasn't he clever? It's easy to find your way around (see chapter 3), and once you get the hang of subdividing the District, you'll blaze your own trails. Although the shortest distance between two points might be a Metro ride, you'll shortchange your kids and yourselves, missing some of D.C.'s charm and beauty, if you fail to explore on foot.

WALKING TOUR 1	GEORGETOWN

Start: Old Stone House.

Finish: Foggy Bottom Metro.

Time: 2 to 5 hours (2 hrs. if you don't eat or shop; up to 5 hrs. or more if you want to shop, eat, ride the canal boat, or take a cruise to Alexandria).

Best Times: Weekdays.

Worst Times: Weekends, year-round. If you go on a weekend, start early and wind down before the thundering hordes arrive.

Georgetown is the ideal neighborhood for strolling. Kids of all ages take to the unique hodgepodge of old and new. Remnants of the past invite exploration—the C&O Canal, historic buildings and homes, and lush parks. On the flip side, scores of up-to-date shops and restaurants—and no less than four ice cream shops—line Wisconsin Avenue and M Street, and fill The Shops at Georgetown Park (hereinafter, "Georgetown Park"), a three-tiered enclosed mall.

Wisconsin Avenue and M Street is Washington's oldest intersection. Pierre L'Enfant and George Washington set out from this crossroad one frosty October morning in 1791 and traveled east to establish the boundaries of the future District of Columbia. During the 1870s, more than 500 canal boats brought limestone, coal, flour, and other raw goods to the mills, factories, and blacksmiths headquartered along the waterfront of the Port of Georgetown. Consider the history as you browse about 500 shoe stores (only a slight exaggeration).

On weekends from spring through fall, Georgetown's permanent population of 11,000—an interesting mix of government bureaucrats, students, merchants, and bluebloods—swells threefold, making it a primo spot for people-watching. Given that the 272-block parcel in the city's west end boasts more than 100 restaurants and bars, you'll never be more than a hop, skip, or a jump away from sustenance—everything from a bagel or burger to the haughtiest haute cuisine.

Copies of the **"Georgetown Visitors Guide and Map"** and brochures are free at the White House Visitor Center, 1450 Pennsylvania Ave. NW; the concierge desk in the Georgetown Park mall, 3222 M St. NW at Wisconsin Avenue; the Visitor's Center, 3242 M St. next to Clyde's; and most Georgetown hotels, shops, and restaurants.

Take a map and wear comfortable shoes; the area is hilly, and some sections are paved with brick or cobblestone. Your kids will be so tired at the end of the walk that they'll sleep for 48 hours. If you begin at the Foggy Bottom Metro station at 23rd and I streets NW, it's about a 20-minute stroll to Georgetown. To save time and your stamina, grab a transfer from the machine near the escalator before you exit Metro; then hop on the Georgetown Metro Connection shuttle (hereinafter, "Georgetown Shuttle"). When you exit the Metro on 23rd Street, go right half a block and look for the sign. The fare is 35¢ with a transfer, $1 without. (See chapter 3 for more details.) If you choose to walk, go north on 23rd Street toward Pennsylvania Avenue. Bear left at Washington Circle to Pennsylvania Avenue. Continue on Pennsylvania to where it dead-ends at M Street and continue on M Street. The Old Stone House is at 3051 M Street.

---

❶ Old Stone House

The only pre-Revolutionary War building still standing in D.C. was built in 1765, and the five rooms are furnished with items typical of the late 18th and early 19th centuries. It is open Wednesday through Sunday from noon to 4pm (usually until 5pm in summer). Kids can run up and down the hilly lawn (no pesticides are used on the grass), and everyone can enjoy the magnificent flowers that bloom from early spring into October. The garden spills over with picnickers in warm weather.

When you leave, cross M Street (watch the traffic!) to Thomas Jefferson Street, where film buffs will enjoy browsing for posters and other memorabilia at Movie Madness (1083 Thomas Jefferson Street). Then head down the hill toward the river. On your left, you'll see:

❷ *The Georgetown*

One-hour cruises on this working canal boat depart several times a day between mid-April and late October. Stop at the National Park Service office in the Foundry Mall, 1055 Thomas Jefferson Street, for tickets and information. You might prefer to detour along the canal towpath, a lovely place to stroll. The water's odor can get a mite strong in summer, but most of the time it's tolerable.

When you reach the end of Thomas Jefferson Street, you've arrived at:

❸ Washington Harbour

This is a large complex of offices, private residences, restaurants, and shops fronting the Potomac River.

TAKE A BREAK
You could do worse than to fall into the splashy **Sequoia** restaurant at 3000 K Street (© **202/944-4200**). Reservations are a necessity at peak times and for highly desirable outdoor seating (spring through October, weather permitting). There's no kids' menu, but burgers and pizza are always available. Sequoia may be a tourist draw, but it is also top drawer! Nearby, **Cafe Cantina** sells wraps, burritos, and pizza by the slice. **Bangkok Joe's** specializes in dumplings. The adjacent Washington Harbour Park is a splendid picnic site (no tables, but plenty of benches).

Walk toward the river and you'll arrive at the:

❹ Scenic Promenade

Walk along the promenade and, if you face the water, you'll see Theodore Roosevelt Island straight ahead. The infamous Watergate and the Kennedy Center are to the left. Key Bridge, to the right, connects Arlington, Virginia, to Georgetown. At the far right of the promenade is Washington Harbour Park.

Walking Tour: Georgetown

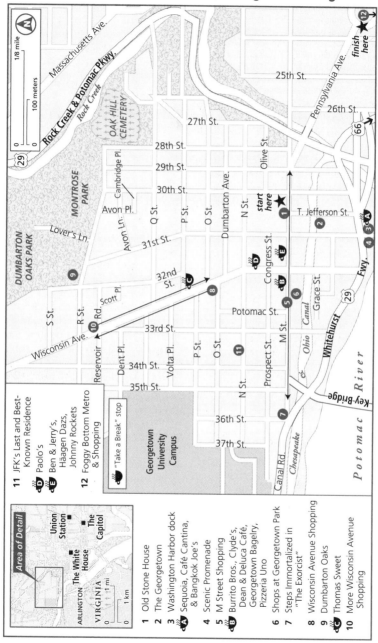

1 Old Stone House
2 The Georgetown
3 Washington Harbor dock
A Sequoia, Café Cantina, & Bangkok Joe's
4 Scenic Promenade
5 M Street Shopping
B Burrito Bros., Clyde's, Dean & Deluca Café, Georgetown Bagelry, Pizzeria Uno
6 Shops at Georgetown Park
7 Steps Immortalized in "The Exorcist"
8 Wisconsin Avenue Shopping
9 Dumbarton Oaks
C Thomas Sweet
10 More Wisconsin Avenue Shopping
11 JFK's Last and Best-Known Residence
D Paolo's
E Ben & Jerry's, Häagen Dazs, Johnny Rockets
12 Foggy Bottom Metro & Shopping

"Take a Break" stop

Exit the area onto K Street (under the Whitehurst Freeway) and walk up 31st Street (it runs parallel to Wisconsin Ave.). Go 1 short block and left at South Street. Measure your fitness level as you climb the steep hill with attached homes banked on the right. On the left is the Ritz-Carlton Hotel Georgetown. Historic Grace Church is on the corner at Wisconsin Avenue. Turn right here. This is the southern end of M Street.

❺ M Street Shopping

A few doors below M Street at 1075 Wisconsin is Georgetown Tees, which sells souvenir shirts. Across the street, Banana Republic at 3200 M Street sells stylish and pricey casual wear in adult sizes. Diagonally across this busy intersection is Benetton's two-story shop at 1200 Wisconsin Ave.

TAKE A BREAK
Burrito Bros. (3273 M St.), Clyde's (3236 M St.), Dean & Deluca Café (3276 M St. NW), Georgetown Bagelry (3245 M St. NW), and Pizzeria Uno (3211 M St.) are all within 2 blocks of Wisconsin Avenue and M Street.

Serious shoppers will want to inspect:

❻ Shops at Georgetown Park

Georgetown Park, at Wisconsin Avenue and M Street, is a multilevel mall with 75 shops, including H&M department store, with reasonably priced trendy clothing; Fit to a Tee, with the zaniest collection of shirts ever assembled in one place; Zerododici and Benetton Kids, for stylish kids' togs in sizes 0 to 12; The Sharper Image; Waldenbooks; and good old Mrs. Field's. If it's been more than 20 minutes since you've eaten, there are a number of restaurants and cafes. If your dogs are dragging, buy your tickets for the Old Town Trolley here (not to be confused with Old Town Alexandria).

If you detour a few blocks and continue walking west on M Street to 36th Street, to your right, you'll see the:

❼ Steps Immortalized in *The Exorcist*

These steps have been immortalized in both the film and book versions of *The Exorcist*.

Get back on track and continue your uphill exploration of:

❽ Wisconsin Avenue Shopping

Walk along the west (left) side of the street. At 1208, check out Abercrombie & Fitch for stylish, durable sportswear. American Eagle Outfitters (1220) has jeans, tees, and the like for teens and adults (but the XS will fit big kids). At 1258 is Gap—adult sizes only; Gap Kids is across the street (1267). Near the corner of P Street, the inimitable Commander Salamander has leatherwear, way-out fashions, irreverent T-shirts, and jewelry. On cobblestone P Street, west of Wisconsin Avenue, remnants of the city's 1890 electric streetcar lines are visible. See what the stars have in store or have your palm read by Mrs. Natalie (1500). Hungry? Cafe Bonaparte (1522) serves authentic French onion soup and mouthwatering crepes (with a dozen fillings, half of them sweet).

Cross Wisconsin at Q Street for the downhill walk on Wisconsin Avenue's east side. Turn right at R Street to:

❾ Dumbarton Oaks

Located between 31st and 32nd streets, Dumbarton Oaks was the site of the 1944 Peace Conferences. The small museum of pre-Colombian art and magnificent grounds never disappoints. Robert Woods Bliss and his wife, Mildred, avid collectors of pre-Colombian and Byzantine art, used Dumbarton Oaks as a country retreat between 1920 and 1940. They donated their collection and the property to Harvard University, which housed the art in eight glass pavilions designed by Philip Johnson.

All ages enjoy the formal gardens and grassy expanses on the 10-acre site. It's especially beautiful spring through fall, when a riot of seasonal flowers blooms behind rows of boxwood hedges. Game time: See if your kids can locate the 10 reflecting pools, 9 fountains, Roman-style amphitheater, and orangery among the broad terraces and twisting paths. (See "Parks, Gardens & Other Wide-Open Spaces," in chapter 8 for more information.)

> **TAKE A BREAK**
> Anchoring the southeast corner at Wisconsin Avenue and P Street is **Thomas Sweet,** an ideal spot to take a break at an institution that's on the endangered species list (an old-fashioned ice cream parlor). You can also get designer coffees (lattes, cappuccino, and so on), soup, or sandwiches.

Head back to Wisconsin Ave., and head up the east side of the street for:

⑩ More Wisconsin Avenue Shopping

On the east side of the street, Piccolo Piggies (1533) sells attractive, distinctive children's clothing. Comic-book lovers will want to browse Beyond Comics at 1419. Appalachian Spring (1415) has kaleidoscopes, finger puppets, wooden toys, and baby gifts among its stunning collection of American crafts. At 1319 Wisconsin, Betsey Johnson draws well-heeled teens and their fashion-conscious moms for au courant duds. Farther on Wisconsin, you'll come across Gap Kids and Baby Gap (1267), and Wet Seal (1225), filled with well-priced fashions for preteen and teen girls.

Head south on Wisconsin to N street. Turn right on N, and go to no. 3307:

⑪ John F. Kennedy's Last and Best-Known Residence

JFK resided at seven Georgetown addresses between 1947 and his presidency. He met his future wife at a Georgetown dinner party in 1951. 3307 N St. NW was home to the Kennedys from shortly after Caroline's birth in 1957 until JFK's inauguration and move into the White House on January 20,

1961. After her husband's assassination, Mrs. Kennedy returned to the house at 31st and O streets, owned by her parents.

> **TAKE A BREAK**
> Ready to take another break? Stop for a plate of pasta, chicken, salad, or pizza at the trendy **Paolo's** (1303 Wisconsin Ave., at N St.), or try one of the places mentioned above.

When you've had enough, you can catch the Georgetown Shuttle on Wisconsin Avenue or any no. 30 Metrobus (Shipley Terrace or Congress Heights) along Wisconsin Avenue or M Street back to the:

⑫ Foggy Bottom Metro & Shopping

If you'd like to fit in a little more shopping, retrace your steps east across M Street to the Metro. Local teens flock to Urban Outfitters (3111), which has on-the-fringe and off-the-wall clothing and home furnishings. Get a makeover or replace tired cosmetics at Sephora (3065). A few doors down at 3005 is Déjà Blue, with thousands of pairs of broken-in (okay, they're secondhand) jeans. CD Warehouse (3001) sells new, used, and imported CDs and DVDs. On the south side of M Street, you'll find a large Barnes & Noble bookstore at 3040 M (at Thomas Jefferson St). The megastore has a large children's section and cafe.

> **TAKE A BREAK**
> As you're winding down your tour of Georgetown, satisfy your sweet-tooth cravings with a takeout sundae in a cone at **Ben & Jerry's** ice cream (3135 M St.). Or cross the street if you are a **Häagen-Dazs** fan. Next door to Ben & Jerry's is **Johnny Rockets** for diner-style burgers, fries and shakes, and '50s music.

Continue on M Street to Washington Circle, bear right to 23rd Street, and then turn right at 23rd to the Metro. Enjoy your nap!

WALKING TOUR 2	MONUMENTS

Start:	Washington Monument.
Finish:	Constitution Gardens.
Time:	4 hours or more. Take snacks or sandwiches, as you will be limited to vendor fast food unless you deviate several blocks to a food court or sit-down restaurant. Take a stroller for children under 5. There are benches and grassy knolls along the way, but with kids under 8 or 9, you may want to carve this into smaller pieces.
Best Times:	Any time during daylight hours is the right time. Start in the morning if you want to ride to the top of the Washington Monument.
Worst Times:	Evenings are the worst times to go.

Start on the monument grounds between 15th and 17th streets NW, between Constitution and Independence avenues (behind the White House and Ellipse). Walk toward the humongous obelisk, one of the most instantly recognizable edifices in the world. If you've arrived on a nice day—and Washington has many throughout the year, but especially between April and November—get outdoors and enjoy this loopy trail of the monuments and memorials.

❶ Washington Monument

Pick up free timed-entry passes in the morning (see listing in chapter 6, p. 145). Weather permitting, hand the kids the camera, ask them to lie on their backs, and shoot up. (If you try it, you may not get up.)

Walk west toward the Lincoln Memorial, and cross 17th Street to the:

❷ World War II Memorial

You'll find it at the east end of the Reflecting Pool (that's the end nearest the U.S. Capitol). Ask your kids what they think of the Field of Stars and Memorial Plaza. Who's got the camera?

Walk south and cross Independence Avenue to:

❸ The Tidal Basin

Pretty, huh? Even without the cherry blossoms it's a sight for sore eyes. Photo op!

If this were a clock, you'd be standing at 12 o'clock. Straight ahead is the Jefferson Memorial at 6 o'clock. Walk clockwise (south) and around the perimeter of this glorified pond to the:

❹ Boat House

Here you can rent a paddleboat March through September, weather permitting. Fuel up with ice cream or a snack from one of the vendors here.

Continue clockwise toward 6 o'clock and over the Outlet Bridge to the:

❺ Jefferson Memorial

This is my personal favorite of all the presidential monuments and memorials. Go in to the memorial itself to read the inscriptions, take pictures of ol' TJ, and take a look in the bookshop, especially inviting to history buffs. Spend some quiet time lolling on the steps, admiring the view—and taking pictures, of course.

Continue around the "clock" path that hugs the Tidal Basin, across the Inlet Bridge to the:

❻ Franklin Delano Roosevelt Memorial

The planners designated this as the exit, but they won't consider you disrespectful or un-American if you see it in reverse, beginning at the south end. Because the bookshop is here, stop to inspect the interesting history books and FDR memorabilia so you don't have to backtrack. Take some photos of the magnificent fountains, granite walls, and 3-foot sculpture of Fala, FDR's beloved Scottie. Let the kids run around. There is nothing to break. Grab a snack and make a pit stop before you leave.

Walking Tour: Monuments

1 Washington Monument
2 World War II Memorial
3 The Tidal Basin
4 Boat House
5 Jefferson Memorial
6 FDR Memorial
7 Korean War Veterans Memorial
8 Lincoln Memorial
9 Vietnam Veterans Memorial
10 Vietnam Women's Memorial
11 Constitution Gardens

Exit at the north entrance heading north through West Potomac Park until you reach Independence Avenue. Cross Independence Avenue to the:

❼ Korean War Veterans Memorial

Are your kids impressed by the steel statues of 19 soldiers on the march? One can hope.

Walk a short distance to the Greek temple lookalike, where a very large man sits brooding. You've arrived at the:

❽ Lincoln Memorial

After looking around inside, rest on the steps and aim your camera across the National Mall toward the Capitol. Not a bad view, eh? If you're here at dusk, walk around to the back of the memorial to watch the sunset.

Walk down the steps, and head left to the:

❾ Vietnam Veterans Memorial

People from all over the world pay their respects at the low-slung black granite walls honoring the nearly 60,000 soldiers who died in the Vietnam War. The victims' names are inscribed chronologically from the first casualty in 1959 to the last in 1975. Since opening in 1983, it remains one of the most-visited sites in Washington.

Walk toward the Reflecting Pool and the nearby:

❿ Vietnam Women's Memorial

Small but poignant, it is dedicated to the 7,500 women who served in the Vietnam War.

Head east toward 17th Street and the pond in this parklike parcel known as:

⑪ Constitution Gardens

With any luck, you'll see some turtles and frogs. In spring, you may see some baby ducklings, along with Mom and Dad.

The closest Metro is Smithsonian, about a 10-minute walk west.

WALKING TOUR 3 DUPONT CIRCLE

Start:	Dupont Circle Metro.
Finish:	Kramerbooks and Afterwords Café (1517 Conn. Ave. NW between Dupont Circle and Q St.).
Time:	2 hours or more. As always, bring snacks or sandwiches and water. There are numerous restaurants near the Metro—both formal and casual—but not along the route.
Best Times:	Anytime during daylight hours is good. If you've spent a busy morning sightseeing, this is a pleasant way to wind down in the afternoon. Finish with a snack or meal and shopping.
Worst Times:	Evenings are the worst time for this tour.

This is a good choice any time of the year. Just be sure to dress for the weather. Because some of this route is uphill, I suggest bringing a stroller if your child is 5 or under. It won't be fun if you have to schlep your kid piggyback-style, and you can always use the stroller for shopping bags and snacks. Start at the Dupont Circle Metro and take the escalator (or elevator) to the street. After getting your bearings, head for the:

---

❶ Fountain (in Dupont Circle)

Take pictures of one another and/or the colorful characters who hang out in this city park. The fountain was designed by Daniel Chester French, the same dude who sculpted Lincoln's statue at the Lincoln Memorial. Exit the south end of the park.

Look both ways; then cross the traffic circle onto New Hampshire Avenue. Walk south 1 block to 1307 New Hampshire Ave. and the:

❷ Heurich Mansion

Nice piece of Romanesque Revival real estate, huh? The former home of local brewer Christian Heurich is command central for the Historical Society of Washington, D.C.

Cross New Hampshire Avenue, make an immediate right at 20th Street, go half a block, and then turn left at O Street, past Victorian-style row houses. Go right at 21st Street to Mass Avenue to ogle the:

❸ Walsh-McLean House

The Indonesian Embassy at 2020 Massachusetts Avenue was formerly the family

home of Evalyn Walsh-McLean, the society hostess and owner of the cursed Hope Diamond (for more, see chapter 6, p. 133).

Head north on Massachusetts Avenue 2 blocks and then west on Q Street to 23rd Street and the:

❹ Bison Bridge

Kids like the four humongous bronze beasts at this bridge (officially, the Dumbarton Bridge) spanning Rock Creek Park. According to the Smithsonian (and who am I to question?), it was bison that roamed the West, not buffalo, which are indigenous to Africa and Asia.

If you're feeling ambitious, continue on Q Street for several blocks into Georgetown. Otherwise, walk north on 23rd Street 1 block to Sheridan Circle; then turn left around the circle to Massachusetts Avenue. Go 2 long blocks and bear right at S Street. Pass the statue of Irish patriot Robert Emmet to 2340 S Street and the:

❺ Woodrow Wilson House

The 28th president is the only U.S. president buried in D.C. (at the National Cathedral) and the only one to live in

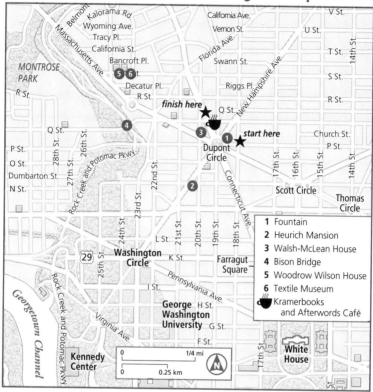

Washington after vacating the White House. Put that in your trivia pipe and smoke it! Stop here with older kids, especially those with an interest in history. It's open Tuesday through Sunday.

Next door, at 2320 S St., is the:

6 Textile Museum

Stop here, if the spirit moves you, for the extensive collection of historic and contemporary rugs and textiles.

Retrace your steps back to Massachusetts Avenue, head south to Dupont Circle, and turn left 1 short block around the circle to Connecticut Avenue. Go left (north) to 1517 Connecticut Ave. and:

 KRAMERBOOKS & AFTERWORDS CAFÉ At this Washington, D.C. institution, you can browse the books to your heart's content and have dessert or a meal.

From here, it's only a block to the Metro.

8

For the Active Family

Museums are marvelous mind-expanders, but little people (and big people, too) grow restless after too much hard-core enrichment. To prevent fatigue and brain strain, stagger periods of sightseeing with visits to places where kids can romp, roam, and let off steam. (We all know what happens to steam when it isn't allowed to escape.) You won't have far to look for these kinds of places, because downtown and its environs are chock full of parks, open spaces, playgrounds, and recreational areas. And the largest front lawn in the neighborhood—the National Mall—is just a Frisbee toss away from many downtown attractions.

1 Parks, Gardens & Other Wide-Open Spaces

GARDENS & PARKS

Battery–Kemble Park   In a residential area not far from the C&O (Chesapeake and Ohio) Canal, this mile-long park boasts flowering dogwood trees in spring, a beautiful fall display of autumn leaves, and good sledding and cross-country skiing in winter. You can fly a kite; take a nature walk; picnic; and play football, baseball, or soccer on one of the fields.

Chain Bridge Rd., between Nebraska Ave. and MacArthur Blvd. NW. (✆) 202-426-6841. Free admission. Daily dawn–dusk. Directions: Take Canal Rd., turn right onto MacArthur Blvd., and then turn right onto Chain Bridge Rd. The entrance and small parking area are about midway between MacArthur Blvd. and Nebraska Ave. Additional parking on side streets.

Brookside Gardens ℛ   A visit here is like a trip to the country. In addition to formal and natural-style landscaping on 50 acres (part of Maryland's park system), Brookside is known for its azaleas, roses, 11 types of gardens, and other seasonal displays. If you're in the area between May and September, don't miss the annual butterfly show in the Conservatory where more than 30 species flit around, sometimes landing on visitors. The experience is like no other, and admission of $4.50 for adults, $3.50 for kids (3–12), is well worth it. Even babies take to the winged beauties, but you'll have to carry your little ones, as strollers are not allowed in the Conservatory. The theme for the **Children's Garden** changes periodically. Children's programs for kids 3 and up include Saturday Morning Story Time in the Visitor Center, with nature stories and related crafts projects. As part of the Weekend Discoveries program, youngsters are invited to take part in projects rooted around various plants and flowers. Call for information on these and other special events (✆ **301/962-1400**). The **Spaceship Earth Garden** has playground equipment resembling planets.

Take your kids into the **Japanese Tea House** and through the **Mosaic Dragon Garden and Conservatories,** filled with exotic plants, a wooden bridge, and a waterfall ending in a tiny stream that they can tiptoe across. Pick up the coloring book/brochure with games and information for the youngsters. Many of the 2,000 volumes in the horticultural library are geared to young people, but these must be used on site.

The **Visitors Center** has classrooms, a library, workshops for schoolchildren and adults, and a 125-seat theater. The light sandstone building was made possible through a bequest from Elizabeth Turner, a Silver Spring secretary who loved to visit Brookside Gardens. The site, which received 30,000 visitors when it opened in 1969, now welcomes more than 300,000 a year. Do visit, if time permits, but leave pets, food, and drinks behind.

1800 Glenallan Ave., Wheaton, MD. © 301-962-1400 Fax 301/949-0571. www.brooksidegardens.org. Free admission. Daily sunrise–sunset. Conservatories open daily 10am–5pm; visitors center 9am–5pm; gift shop 10am–4pm. Closed Dec 25. Metro: Glenmont; then taxi. Directions: Take Georgia Ave. north from the Beltway, and turn right on Randolph Rd.; after 2 blocks, turn right at Glenallan Ave. On-site parking.

C&O Canal National Historic Park *(Finds)*

If you have a car, this park is well worth the half-hour or so drive from most downtown locales. Go during the week or early on weekends, bring a brown-bag lunch, and plan to spend the better part of a day. Orient yourselves at the **Great Falls Tavern Museum,** a short walk from the entrance. Join a nature walk with a park ranger. The Park Service also conducts special programs, including hiking and bird-watching. The cliffs attract rock climbers, and the river is a favorite for kayaking and fishing.

Enjoy Mother Nature on foot or bike along the towpaths that extend along the old C&O Canal, from Georgetown for 185 miles to Cumberland, Maryland. Imagine the canal in its heyday, when boats traveled through 74 lift locks to reach western Maryland. The original plan, which called for a waterway all the way to Pittsburgh, was not completed, and the canal closed after a flood in 1924. Be sure to cross the footbridges that lead to the Olmsted Island overlook. After Hurricane Agnes wiped out the area in 1972, the footbridges were restored and reopened, but the job took 20 years. The view is spectacular, and it's a great photo op. *Be forewarned:* No pets, bikes, or picnics on the bridges. As we went to press, the park's mule-drawn boat was out of commission, so you'll have to go to Georgetown (see "Rides for Children," later in this chapter) for that experience.

Don't even think of wading in the water. Even when it looks calm, it is rocky and turbulent below the surface. Several people drown annually because they ignore warning signs. Please, please *watch your little ones near the canal locks,* and practice hand-holding with your junior trailblazers. Leashed dogs are permitted in the park (but not on the bridges), and there's a refreshment stand.

MacArthur Blvd. and Falls Rd., Potomac, MD. © 301/299-3613. www.nps.gov/choh. Admission $5 per car; $3 walkins and bikers. Daily sunrise–sunset. Directions: Take MacArthur Blvd. into Maryland and continue 4 miles beyond the Beltway. Park entrance is at intersection of MacArthur Blvd. and Falls Rd.

Constitution Gardens *(Kids) (Finds)*

Baby ducks hatch annually between April and June in this park's small lake. Your little ducklings are invited to feed them, along with the turtles, fish, and the occasional frog. The park also features walks, bike paths, and a landscaped island reached by a footbridge. Kids can sail small boats, but no swimming is allowed. Have a picnic on the 14 acres and see the monument memorializing the 56 signers of the Declaration of Independence. The Vietnam War, Korean War Veterans, and World War II memorials are in the western corner of the park (p. 149).

W. Potomac Park, Constitution Ave., between the Washington Monument and Lincoln Memorial. © 202/485-9880. www.nps.gov/coga/index.htm. Free admission. Daily dawn–dark. Metro: Smithsonian. Limited free parking on Constitution Ave.

Washington, D.C. Gardens & Parks

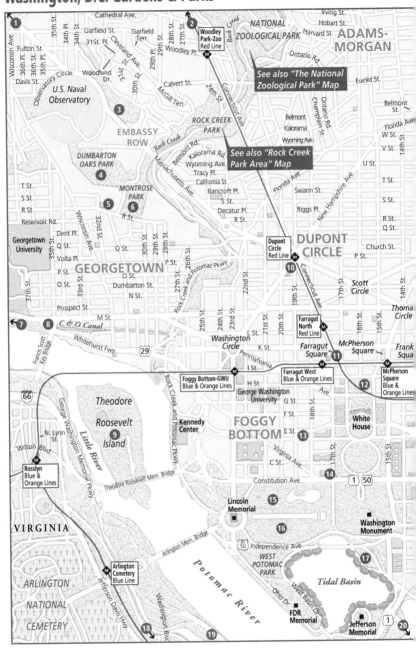

Cathedral Ave.

Irving St.
Hobart St.
Harvard St.

ADAMS-MORGAN

Wisconsin Ave.
Fulton St.
36th St.
35th St.
35th St.
36th St.

35th St.
34th Pl.
34th St.
31St. Pl.
Garfield St.
Garfield Terr.
Cleveland Ave.
31st St.
30th St.
29th St.
28th St.
27th St.
Woodley Pl.
Woodley Rd.

Woodley Park-Zoo
Red Line

NATIONAL ZOOLOGICAL PARK

Ontario Rd.
Euclid St.

See also "The National Zoological Park" Map

Observatory Circle
Davis St.
Woodland Dr.

U.S. Naval Observatory

Calvert St.
McGill Terr.

24th St.
Connecticut Ave.

ROCK CREEK PARK

Belmont
Kalorama
Wyoming Ave.

Belmont St.
Florida Ave.
W St.
V St.
14th St.

EMBASSY ROW

Rock Creek

DUMBARTON OAKS PARK

Belmont Rd.
Kalorama Rd.
Wyoming Ave.
Tracy Pl.
California St.
Bancroft Pl.
S St.
Decatur Pl.
R St.

See also "Rock Creek Park Area" Map

Florida Ave.
New Hampshire Ave.

U St.

Swann St.

Riggs Pl.

T St.
S St.
R St.
Q St.

T St.
S St.
R St.

Massachusetts Ave.

MONTROSE PARK

R St.

Reservoir Rd.

Georgetown University

Dent Pl.
Volta Pl.
Q St.
P St.
O St.

37th St.
33rd St.
32nd St.
31st St.
30th St.
29th St.
28th St.

GEORGETOWN

O St.
Dumbarton St.
N St.

27th St.
26th St.
Rock Creek and Potomac Pkwy

22nd St.

Dupont Circle
Red Line

DUPONT CIRCLE

Connecticut Ave.

Church St.

P St.

Scott Circle

Thomas Circle

14th St.
15th St.
16th St.
17th St.
19th St.
20th St.
21st St.
23rd St.
24th St.
25th St.

Prospect St.

M St.

C & O Canal

Whitehurst Fwy.
29

Washington Circle

Pennsylvania

Farragut North
Red Line

L St.
K St.
I St.

Farragut Square

McPherson Square

Frank Square

Francis Scott Key Bridge

66

Foggy Bottom-GWU
Blue & Orange Lines

Farragut West
Blue & Orange Lines

McPherson Square
Blue & Orange Lines

Rosslyn
Blue & Orange Lines

N. Lynn St.
Wilson Blvd.

Theodore Roosevelt Island

Little River

Rock Creek and Potomac Pkwy

Kennedy Center

H St.
G St.
F St.
E St.

George Washington University

FOGGY BOTTOM

18th St.

White House

15th St.
17th St.

Virginia Ave.
C St.

1 50

George Washington Memorial Parkway

Theodore Roosevelt Mem. Bridge

Constitution Ave.

Lincoln Memorial

Washington Monument

VIRGINIA

Arlington Mem. Bridge

50 Independence Ave.

WEST POTOMAC PARK

Tidal Basin

17

Arlington Cemetery
Blue Line

Jefferson Davis Hwy

Washington Blvd.

Potomac River

West Basin Dr.
Ohio Dr.

ARLINGTON NATIONAL CEMETERY

18

19

FDR Memorial

Jefferson Memorial

1

20

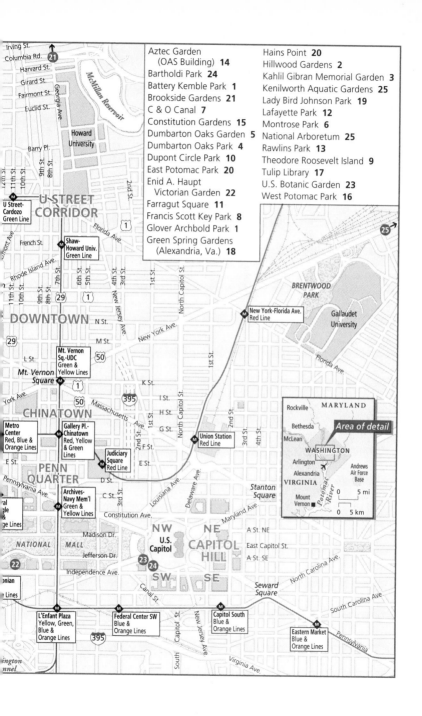

Aztec Garden
  (OAS Building) **14**
Bartholdi Park **24**
Battery Kemble Park **1**
Brookside Gardens **21**
C & O Canal **7**
Constitution Gardens **15**
Dumbarton Oaks Garden **5**
Dumbarton Oaks Park **4**
Dupont Circle Park **10**
East Potomac Park **20**
Enid A. Haupt
  Victorian Garden **22**
Farragut Square **11**
Francis Scott Key Park **8**
Glover Archbold Park **1**
Green Spring Gardens
  (Alexandria, Va.) **18**

Hains Point **20**
Hillwood Gardens **2**
Kahlil Gibran Memorial Garden **3**
Kenilworth Aquatic Gardens **25**
Lady Bird Johnson Park **19**
Lafayette Park **12**
Montrose Park **6**
National Arboretum **25**
Rawlins Park **13**
Theodore Roosevelt Island **9**
Tulip Library **17**
U.S. Botanic Garden **23**
West Potomac Park **16**

Dumbarton Oaks Garden 🖈🖈 *(Moments)*   Restless feet love to explore every inch of these 16-acre, formally designed gardens in Georgetown. The winding brick paths lend themselves to spirited games of hide-and-seek. Spring is glorious when forsythia, narcissus, tulips, daffodils, and flowering trees bloom. The roses and wisteria flower in late spring and summer, and fall brings forth a showy display of foliage and chrysanthemums. Strollers are allowed but could be more of a hindrance due to the gardens' many steps and levels. No visitor to Washington should leave the city without stopping here.

1703 32nd St. NW (garden entrance on R St. between 31st and 32nd sts.). *C* **202/339-6401.** Fax 202/339-6419. www.doaks.org. Admission $7 adults, $5 seniors and age 12 and under Mar 15–Oct; free Nov–mid-March. Daily 2–6pm mid-Mar–Oct 2–5pm Nov–mid-Mar. Metrobuses 30, 32, 34, 36, D2, D4, all stop within 2 blocks of entrance. Directions: Foggy Bottom Metro is more than 2 miles away. Limited 2-hr. on-street parking on R, S, and 32nd sts. weekdays. No time limit on weekends, but you may have trouble finding a space.

Dupont Circle Park   Sit, sun, or stalk the pigeons at Washington's largest circular park, or pick up food from one of the many nearby takeout places and picnic on a bench. There's plenty of entertainment—intended and unintended—particularly on weekends. Some mighty serious chess games are played here, and you're welcome to watch as long as you don't interrupt.

Dupont Circle (intersection of Connecticut, Massachusetts, and New Hampshire aves.) NW. Free admission. Daily dawn–dark. Metro: Dupont Circle.

East Potomac Park 🖈   A one-way road outlines the 300-plus acres of manmade peninsula between the Potomac River and the Washington Channel. Depending on who's counting, 1,200 to 1,300 **cherry trees** 🖈🖈 bloom in late March or early April. The blossoms usually last 7 to 12 days, less if it's windy or if there is a freeze. Most of the trees you see have been added over the years—fewer than 200 of the original trees survive. You can find out more at the cherry trees' very own website: www.nps.gov/nacc/cherry. The original trees—Yoshinos—have single white flowers in clusters and are marked by bronze plaques. A well-equipped playground at Hains Point attracts kids with its colorful climbing apparatus. The imposing statue of a half-buried figure known as *The Awakening* also fascinates most children. The park is perfect for strolling, biking, or fishing, and also has picnic grounds, a public **swimming pool** (*C* 202/727-6523), 24 **tennis courts** (*C* 202/554-5962; www.eastpotomactennis.com), as well as one 18-hole and two 9-hole **golf courses** (*C* 202/554-7660; www.golfdc. com). Call for information on the permit you'll need to use the tennis courts. No permit is needed for playing golf.

Ohio Dr. SW. Park located between the Potomac River and the Washington Channel. *C* **202/426-6841.** Free admission. Daily dawn–dark. Free and ample parking; it's best, however, to arrive by taxi, because streets are hard to navigate.

Enid A. Haupt Victorian Garden   Named for its philanthropic donor, this 4-acre minipark covers the underground complex housing the Sackler Gallery and Museum of African Art. Seasonal flowers brighten the beds and spill from baskets hanging from the iron lampposts. In summer, the tea roses and saucer magnolias are spectacular.

An ideal rest stop when your family is museumed out, the Haupt Garden is for admiring, not stomping on. I found out the hard way when ordered by a uniformed gent to "Kindly get off the grass." There are benches, however, for relaxing. Maybe your kids will be so impressed by the neatness of the 19th-century embroidery parterre that they'll take the concept home and apply it to their rooms.

A handmade brass sundial was built by David Shayt and David Todd, two National Museum of American History staffers. At the dial's corners, the four seasons appear as weather symbols. Can your offspring identify summer? (It's the Smithsonian sunburst logo.) If you're smart enough to read a sundial, whip out your protractor, and make sure that the gnomon is set at approximately 40°, Washington, D.C.'s latitude.

Between the Freer Gallery and Arts and Industries Building, 1000 Independence Ave. SW (also accessible from the Sackler Gallery). © 202/357-2700. Free admission. Daily dawn–dusk. Metro: Smithsonian (Mall or Independence Ave. exit).

Farragut Square   Noontime concerts are held some summer weekdays in this pretty park in the heart of D.C.'s business district. Brown-bag it on a nice day and watch the power bunch lunch.

912 17th St. NW. Free admission. Daily dawn–dusk. Metro: Farragut West or Farragut North.

Francis Scott Key Park   Key Park fills a once-vacant eyesore of a lot just east of the Georgetown side of Key Bridge, which connects D.C. and Rosslyn (Arlington), Virginia. Featuring a wisteria-covered pergola as well as a bronze bust of Key by sculptor Betty Dunston, it is capped by a flag with 15 stars and stripes—similar to the one that inspired Key to write *The Star-Spangled Banner.* A walkway and bike path from the C&O Canal are carefully integrated into the hilltop setting, which has a commanding view of the Potomac River.

35th and M sts. NW, Georgetown. Free admission. Daily dawn–dusk. Metro: Rosslyn, then cross Key Bridge on foot. Directions: Drive to Georgetown, park on street (good luck!) or in garage at Shops at Georgetown Park (Wisconsin Ave. and M St. NW), and walk west on M St. to 34th St.

Glover Archbold Park   The mix of towering trees, a bird sanctuary, and colorful wildflowers makes this long and slender 183-acre park, which stretches south from Massachusetts Avenue to Canal Road, a popular destination for families. A 2-mile nature trail begins at 44th Street and Reservoir Road. There are several others, and plenty of picnic areas, too, sprinkled throughout this park.

MacArthur Blvd. and Canal Rd. to Van Ness St. and Wisconsin Ave. © 202/282-1063. gloverpark.org. Free admission. Daily dawn–dusk. Directions: Take Wisconsin Ave. north; turn left on Cathedral Ave.; then turn left on New Mexico Ave. Park on New Mexico.

Green Spring Gardens Park ⚘⚘   The children's garden has a bathtub filled with a water garden. A pumpkin-shaped form supports vines with turtle-shaped rocks in the center. Check out the enchanting flower bed frame. (Get it? Flower bed?) Elsewhere on the grounds are two ponds with frogs and fish and an occasional blue heron. Canadian geese and ducks visit frequently. Budding horticulturists can learn the basics of gardening in classes geared to two age groups—Garden Sprouts (3–5) and Family Fun Programs (6–9). Adults can sign up for classes, too. The 27-acre public park is filled with native plants, vegetable and herb gardens, and blooming and fruit-bearing trees. Permanent plant displays are housed in the greenhouse in the Horticulture Center. Generous parents take note: You can rent the gazebo outside the 1760 manor house for your child's next birthday party.

4603 Green Spring Rd., Alexandria, VA. © 703/642-5173. www.greenspring.org. Free admission, but reservations and fees required for classes. Park: Daily dawn–dusk. Horticulture Center: Mon–Sat 9am–4:30pm; Sun noon–4:30pm. Directions: From D.C., take I-395 south to Duke St. west. Go about 1 mile to right at Green Spring (between Jerry's Ford and Salvation Army Thrift Shop) and then 2 blocks into parking lot.

Kahlil Gibran Memorial Garden This quiet, reflective garden honors the Lebanese-born mystical poet who spent much of his life in the United States. Here he wrote thoughtful phrases that have been devoured for decades by college kids in search of the truth and themselves. Some of Gibran's pithier musings are inscribed in the benches near the main fountain. The bronze bust of Gibran is by Washington sculptor Gordon Kray. Make your pilgrimage on foot or by taxi; neighborhood parking is sparse, and there's no Metro close by.

3100 Massachusetts Ave. NW, opposite the British embassy. Free admission. Daily dawn–dusk. Metro: Dupont Circle, then bus north on Massachusetts Ave. Directions: Drive north on Massachusetts Ave. about 1 mile past Dupont Circle. If you reach Wisconsin, you've gone too far. (*Note:* Parking is scarce.)

Kenilworth Park and Aquatic Gardens When was the last time you saw an Egyptian lotus (said to be Cleopatra's favorite flower)? Well, it is just one of the more than 100,000 water plants growing on 11 acres of ponds in this sanctuary. About 75 varieties of water lilies and sand lotuses bloom from May through August. The annual Waterlily and Founders Day, held the second or third Saturday in July, showcases these exotic beauties. Except in the dead of winter, kids will see turtles, frogs, and small fish. Bring binoculars in spring; migrating waterfowl and songbirds are frequent visitors. If you come in the morning, you'll see the night-blooming tropicals, which usually close by 10am. There are picnic tables and a playground, and tours are conducted Saturday and Sunday at 9 and 11am and 1pm.

Kenilworth Ave. and Douglas St. NE. ℂ 202/426-6905. Free admission. Daily 7am–4pm (park); visitor center closes at 4pm. Plenty of on-site parking. Metro: Deanwood; then take a taxi. Directions: Take the V2 bus to Kenilworth Ave. and Polk St., and walk 1 block to gardens. (*Note:* This is not a good neighborhood to walk through, so you might want to take a taxi.)

Lady Bird Johnson Park Although considered part of D.C., the former Columbia Island is accessible only by footbridge from the Virginia side of the Potomac River. I don't suggest it because it's so close to the highway. The best way to enjoy the sight— a must in spring—is to drive or be driven. The park was dedicated to Mrs. Johnson in 1968 to recognize her efforts at beautifying the city and the nation. More than 2,500 dogwoods and 1 million daffodils create a gorgeous blanket of gold in the spring. At the south end of the park, there is a 15-acre grove of white pines, azaleas, and rhododendrons, designated as the Lyndon Baines Johnson Memorial Grove.

Adjacent to G. W. Memorial Parkway, VA. Free admission. Daily dawn–dusk. Directions: From D.C., drive over the Arlington Memorial Bridge, take the G. W. Memorial Pkwy. south to and through National Airport, and continue north on the parkway to Memorial Bridge and D.C.

Lafayette Park Check out the statues of Andrew Jackson and Lafayette, whose heads are favorite roosting spots. Protesters, pigeon lovers and haters, bureaucrats, and people-watchers fill the benches and sprawl on the grass at all hours of the day and night. Depending on their ages, your kids might enjoy talking to the protesters or feeding some of the tamest squirrels in the area.

Between Pennsylvania Ave. and H St. NW, across from the White House. Free admission. Daily dawn–dusk. Metro: McPherson Square.

Montrose Park Come here to picnic, commune with nature, or ramble through the heavily wooded terrain. Lover's Lane (off R Street), which forms the western boundary of the park, is a cobblestone path that led to Baltimore in the 18th century. I don't recommend your trying to reach Charm City in this manner.

R St. at Avon Place NW, Georgetown. Free admission. Daily dawn–dusk. Directions from Georgetown: From M St., go north on 29th St., and turn left on R St.

National Arboretum 🏛️🏛️ *(Moments)* Visitors are *tree*-ted to one breathtaking sensory experience after another at this 444-acre haven in northeast D.C., established by an act of Congress in 1927 to educate the public and do research on trees and shrubs. The arboretum is a special place, and the staff is excellent, so most children, regardless of age, will enjoy a visit here. The *koi* (Japanese carp) that live in the pool outside the information center approach Brobdingnagian proportions, reaching nearly 3 feet in length and weighing in at 30 pounds. For 25¢ a handful, visitors can feed the fish. The lily pads are said to be sturdy enough to support a small child, but please don't try it—those koi have big appetites.

Worth a visit at any time of year, the arboretum is most popular from late March through October. In late April and May, the azalea display (about 70,000, at last count) draws large crowds. Kids can sniff the contents of the Herb Garden or become intoxicated in June and July, when 100 fragrant varieties of roses perfume the air. The medicinal, dye, Native American, beverage, and fragrance gardens are of special interest to young people, as is the knot garden with its dwarf evergreens. Some of the specimens in the **National Bonsai Collection**—a gift from Japan to mark our bicentennial—are more than 300 years old! More than 150 species are housed in three pavilions. Don't leave without seeing the **national Capitol columns** 🏛️🏛️, from the Capitol's East Portico, the only things salvaged from the Capitol's original facade after renovation of the central portion in 1959. You might think that you've wandered onto Washington, D.C.'s version of Stonehenge. There are a picnic area, a water fountain, and restrooms near the state trees (pick up a map at the administration building).

Note: This place is huge, so if you didn't drive (and this is one of the few places in D.C. where a car comes in handy), seriously consider the 40-minute guided tram tour, with several departures *weekends only* April to October. Buy same-day tickets at the tram kiosk outside the administration building. The fare is $4 for adults, $2 for seniors, free up to age 16, but you "must share a seat with an adult if the tram is full."

3501 New York Ave. NE. ⓒ 202/245-2726. Fax 202/245-4575. www.usna.usda.gov. Admission to grounds free; fee for tram. Grounds open daily 8am–5pm; bonsai collection and Japanese garden daily 10am–3:30pm; gift shop Mon–Fri 10am–3:30pm, Sat–Sun 10am–5pm. Closed Dec 25. Metro: Union Station; then taxi; or Stadium-Armory; then take a B2 bus to Bladensburg Rd. and R St. Walk east 300 yards to the R St. gate. Weekends only: X-6 bus from Union Station (departs from fountain, outside Mass. Ave. entrance); 1st bus 7:55am and then every 40 min. Last bus leaves Arboretum 4:52pm. Directions: New York Ave. (east) and enter the service road immediately after crossing Bladensburg Rd. Plenty of free parking.

OAS Building/Aztec Garden Introduce your kids to the exotic banana, coffee, palm, and rubber trees growing on the Tropical Patio at the headquarters of the world's oldest organization of nations. Epitomizing the mission of the Organization of American States (OAS) is the Peace Tree, planted by President William Howard Taft in 1910. Walk to the back of the building for a display of seasonal plants around the dazzling blue-tiled pool. The fellow overseeing this lush scene is the Aztec god of flowers, Xochipilli. Before you go, let your kids know that this garden is for looking, not for running around. Those 16 and older must show photo ID to the guard.

OAS Building, 17th St. and Constitution Ave. NW. Free admission. Mon–Fri 9:30am–5pm. Metro: Farragut West.

Rawlins Park This urban pocket park near the Corcoran Gallery gets passing grades most of the year, but when the **magnolias bloom** 🏛️🏛️🏛️ in April to May

(depending on the weather), it rates an A+. The park's statue is of Civil War Gen. John A. Rawlins.

E St., between 18th and 19th sts. NW. Free admission. Daily dawn–dusk. Metro: McPherson Square or Farragut North or West.

Rock Creek Park ✸✸✸   The leader of Washington parks is more than a century old. The 4-mile-long, 1,800-acre parcel fills the center of northwest D.C. longitudinally. (See the "Rock Creek Park" map on p. 201.) And it is nothing short of fantastic. If you have the time, I urge you to introduce your kids to some of its many wonders during your stay (but not after dark).

Nature Center and Planetarium   If time allows only one stop at Rock Creek Park, make it this one, at 5200 Glover Rd. NW (𝒞 **202/426-6829**), where kids will find exhibits pertaining to the park's natural history and wildlife, and can meet a few of the latter. **Guided nature walks** and **self-guided trails** begin and end here. The center is open year-round Wednesday through Sunday from 9am to 5pm; it's closed holidays. Special hikes, activities, and talks geared to young trailblazers take place every month.

Stargazing   This dazzling activity is held once a month from April through November (Apr–May at 8:30pm, June–Aug at 9pm, Sept at 8pm, Oct at 7:30pm, Nov at 7pm), cosponsored by the National Park Service and the National Capital Astronomers. Meet at Picnic Grove No. 13, at Military and Glover roads NW. To receive the upcoming month's activity calendar, "Kiosk," call 𝒞 **202/426-6829.** The Park Service does a dynamite job with this program.

Pierce Mill and Barn   The historic mill, near the intersection of Beach Drive and Tilden Street NW (𝒞 **202/426-6828**), is, unfortunately, closed due to internal damage to the mill (powered by a waterwheel). Plans to rebuild it are in the works, but it will probably take a couple of years. In the meantime, you can visit the Pierce Barn across the parking lot from the mill. A park ranger is usually on site to answer questions. The barn is open Saturday and Sunday from noon to 4pm. Weekday group tours are given by reservation.

Thompson's Boat Center ✸   Across from the Kennedy Center and Watergate, you can rent a boat here and paddle or row along the Potomac. Or hop on a bike, also available at Thompson's, to explore nearby Theodore Roosevelt Island (see listing below).

Candy Cane City (Meadowbrook Recreation Center) ✸   This playground, located at 7901 Meadowbrook Lane (off East–West Hwy.), lies across the border in Chevy Chase, Maryland, and is maintained by the Maryland National–Capital Park and Planning Commission. It's a favorite family destination and ideal picnic spot. Little ones can climb, swing, and slide on the playground equipment while older kids and parents play softball, tennis, or basketball (𝒞 **301/650-2600**).

Other Attractions   Here are a handful of the park's other attractions (call or write for more information and an indispensable map). A 1½-mile **exercise course** for fitness enthusiasts and joggers begins near Calvert Street and Connecticut Avenue NW. You can rent a horse, take riding lessons, or blaze 11 miles of bridle trails at the **Rock Creek Horse Center** (𝒞 **202/362-0117**). There is also a **golf course** off Rittenhouse Street (𝒞 **202/882-7332**). Fulfill your day's exercise quota, and hike or bike your way

Rock Creek Park

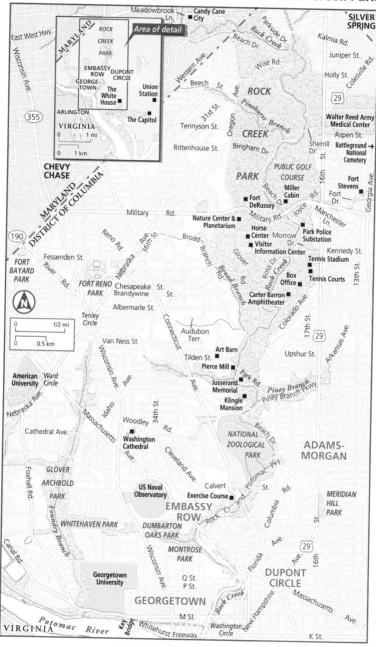

SILVER SPRING

Meadowbrook Ln.

Candy Cane City

Parkside Dr.

Rock Creek

East West Hwy.

MARYLAND

ROCK CREEK PARK

Area of detail

Beach Dr.

Kalmia Rd.

Juniper St.

Western Ave.

Wise Rd.

Holly St.

Wisconsin Ave.

Beech St.

Oregon Ave.

ROCK

Colesville Rd.

EMBASSY ROW

DUPONT CIRCLE

31st St.

29

GEORGE-TOWN

Tennyson St.

Bingham Dr.

CREEK

Walter Reed Army Medical Center

The White House

Union Station

Rittenhouse St.

Pinehurst Branch

Aspen St.

ARLINGTON

355

The Capitol

Sherrill Dr.

Battleground National Cemetery

VIRGINIA

0   1 mi

PUBLIC GOLF COURSE

0   1 km

PARK

Georgia Ave.

CHEVY CHASE

Beach Dr.

Miller Cabin

16th Rd.

Fort Stevens

Fort Dr.

MARYLAND

DISTRICT OF COLUMBIA

Military   Rd.

Fort DeRussey

Military Rd.

190

Reno Rd.

Nebraska Ave.

36th St.

Broad

Nature Center & Planetarium

Horse Center

Morrow Dr.

Joyce Rd.

Manchester Ln.

Park Police Substation

Kennedy St.

FORT BAYARD PARK

Fessenden St.

River Rd.

Branch

Glover Rd.

Visitor Information Center

Ross Dr.

Rock Creek

Tennis Stadium

13th St.

FORT RENO PARK

Chesapeake St.

Broad Branch Rd.

Box Office

Tennis Courts

Brandywine

St.

Albermarle St.

Carter Barron Amphitheater

Colorado Ave.

Tenley Circle

Van Ness St.

Connecticut

Audubon Terr.

17th St.

Upshur St.

29

Arkansas Ave.

0   1/2 mi

Tilden St.

Art Barn

0   0.5 km

Wisconsin Ave.

Ave.

Pierce Mill

Park Rd.

Piney Branch

American University

Ward Circle

Idaho Ave.

34th St.

Jusserand Memorial

Klingle Mansion

Piney Branch Pkwy.

Nebraska Ave.

Massachusetts

Rd.

Beach Dr.

Cathedral Ave.

Woodley

NATIONAL ZOOLOGICAL PARK

ADAMS-MORGAN

GLOVER ARCHBOLD PARK

Washington Cathedral

Cleveland Ave.

Rock Cr. and Potomac Pkwy.

Foxhall Rd.

US Naval Observatory

Calvert

MERIDIAN HILL PARK

WHITEHAVEN PARK

Foundry Branch

EMBASSY ROW

Exercise Course

St.

Columbia Ave.

Canal Rd.

DUMBARTON OAKS PARK

Florida

29

MONTROSE PARK

DUPONT CIRCLE

16th

Georgetown University

Wisconsin Ave.

Q St.

P St.

Rock Creek

Massachusetts Ave.

New Hampshire

GEORGETOWN

M St.

VIRGINIA

Potomac   River

Key Bridge

Whitehurst Freeway

Washington Circle

K St.

through the park. Much of the signposted **bike route** running from the Lincoln Memorial through the park and into Maryland is paved and separate from traffic. On Saturday, Sunday, and holidays, Beach Drive is closed to traffic between Joyce and Broad Branch roads and Sherrill and West Beach drives. **Picnic areas** abound—some can be reserved; others require permits (🕐 **202/673-7646**). **Tennis courts** at 16th and Kennedy streets NW must be reserved from April to November (🕐 **202/722-5949**). Take kids to see **Fort DeRussey, Fort Reno,** or **Fort Bayard,** among the 68 forts built to protect Washington during the Civil War.

5000 Glover Rd. NW (visitor information center). 🕐 202-895-6070. www.nps.gov/rocr/home.htm. Free admission. Open to vehicular traffic around the clock; on foot, dawn–dusk. Directions: Connecticut Ave. north to right on Nebraska Ave. Go 6 blocks into park's entrance and right at Glover Rd. (traffic light). Ample parking throughout park.

Theodore Roosevelt Island ★★ *Moments*   Except for the incessant roar of jets overhead, these 88 acres of forest, swamp, and marsh, outlined by a rocky shore, are pristine and Waldenlike. Hike along the 2½ miles of nature trails of this preserve, which was once inhabited by Native Americans and now memorializes the conservation efforts of President Theodore Roosevelt. A bronze statue of the 26th U.S. president by Paul Manship and Roosevelt's prophetic words inscribed on granite stones can be found in the north-central portion of the island. Rabbits, foxes, muskrats, and groundhogs live in the woods, and you might spot a raccoon or two in the swamp. Bird-watchers have a field day, and so do the mosquitoes in summer—so bring plenty of insect repellent. You can also fish, but you can't picnic on the island, only on the grounds nearby. Depending on staff availability, there are guided tours on weekends, by appointment. You can't bike on the island. However, you may get to and from the island via the Mount Vernon trail and leave your wheels in the bike rack on the parking-lot side of the island. If you row over, be forewarned that your boat may "disappear." Sad but true. A handicapped-accessible fishing area is located near the island's entrance.

Off G. W. Memorial Parkway, between Key and Roosevelt bridges on the Virginia side of the Potomac River. 🕐 703-289-2500. Free admission. Daily 9:30am–dusk. Metro: Rosslyn (VA), walk 2 blocks to the footbridge at Rosslyn Circle, or, if driving, take the Theodore Roosevelt Bridge to the G.W. Memorial Pkwy. north, park on the right, and walk over the footbridge. Or arrive by rented canoe or rowboat from Thompson's Boat Center (see "Boating," later in this chapter). Ample parking.

Tulip Library   If you're in town in April and you like tulips, don't miss this dazzling display—it's more colorful than the Fourth of July fireworks and doesn't make any noise. Park Service gardeners *hand-plant* 10,000 tulip bulbs from Holland every fall. Pick up a brochure from the wooden stand near the beds to help in your identification (about 100 cultivars annually) so that you can add your favorites to your home garden. When the tulips fade, the beds are planted with annuals, making this an enjoyable spot year-round.

Near the Tidal Basin between the Washington Monument and the Jefferson Memorial. Free admission. Daily during daylight hours. Metro: Smithsonian.

U.S. Botanic Garden ★★★   A visit to the Garden (at the foot of Capitol Hill) is as refreshing as lemonade on a sultry summer day. Two wings, east and west, showcase a tropical rainforest, the centerpiece of the 80-foot-high Conservatory. If I could, I'd unfold a cot and spend a week or two.

The former orangerie, inside the Maryland Avenue entrance, has been transformed into the **visitor information desk,** a departure point for docent tours, and a gardening store.

The **west wing** focuses on plants and their relationships to humans, with many rare and endangered species. Among them is a Golden Barrel Cactus from Mexico, resembling a large, prickly globe. You'll also find plants of historic note and some genetically engineered specimens. In the medicinal garden, where plants are grouped by continent, I was astounded to learn that the Madagascar Periwinkle (like the vinca in many gardens) is used in treating leukemia.

The many species of orchids are not only beautiful, but also fragrant, most pleasantly. An exception is the giant titan arum *(Amorphophallus titanum)* indigenous to Sumatra, which smells like rotting garbage when it blooms. My advice: Stay upwind of it. The good news is that it blooms only every 2 years, the last time in July 2005.

The **east wing** zeroes in on the interrelationship of plants and their environment. The plants in the desert display required 20 years of painstaking care before taking root here. According to Native American beliefs, the Saguaro cactus, indigenous to Arizona, is inhabited by spirits. The Garden Primeval replicates a dinosaur landscape of 150 million years ago. See if your kids can locate the fern "pups," or offshoots. Some moss resembles spruce.

The jungle is what we used to call "a real looker," with giant palms, flowering banana trees, Diacorisandra (electric purple lilaclike blooms), and an Asian shrimp plant with gold conical flowers resembling paper cutouts.

Be sure to ask about kid- and family-oriented programs, which have included workshops on making stained-glass mosaic stepping-stones and herbal soap. Lucky locals with preschoolers can sign up for Sprouts: the 1-month sessions (four different programs) are Wednesday, 10:30 to 11:30am, during which 3- to 5-year-olds (with a parent or guardian) get their hands dirty with plant-related activities. Make reservations by phone or at the Web site. When you enter or exit, note the environmental sensor, looking like a microphone, suspended from the ceiling. It reads the light, humidity, and temperature of the building and transmits that data to a computer in the basement.Free tours of the highlights are loosey-goosey, so ask at the visitor information desk when you arrive. Free 45-minute guided tours of the conservatory are by reservation only, at least 3 weeks in advance (© **202/226-4082**). Be sure to cross the street to Bartholdi Park. Rest on a bench, close your eyes, and inhale the rose fragrance. Some Tuesdays at noon, USBG staff conducts a free tour where you can learn about the garden and pick up gardening tips. Frederic Auguste Bartholdi designed the fountain. Sound familiar? He is better known for sculpting the Statue of Liberty.

1st St. and Maryland Ave. SW (foot of Capitol Hill). Entrances at Maryland and Independence aves. © **202/225-8333.** www.usbg.gov. Free admission. Daily 10am–5pm. Metro: Federal Center SW or Capitol South; also near the U.S. Capitol Tourmobile stop.

West Potomac Park

Ask 10 D.C. residents where West Potomac Park is, and I'll bet at least 9 won't know, even though the park takes in the Lincoln and Jefferson memorials, the Korean War and Vietnam War Veterans memorials, the Constitution Gardens, and the Tidal Basin. Cherry trees are the park's main claim to fame, especially during the 2-week **National Cherry Blossom Festival** that runs from late March into April. You can write ahead for a schedule of events: National Cherry Blossom Festival, P.O. Box 33224, Washington, DC 20033-0224, or call the hot line (© **202/547-1500;** www.nps.gov).

Of the original 3,000 Yoshino trees, a gift from Japan in 1912, only about 200 survive. They've been supplemented over the years and now about 1,400 Yoshinos bloom at the Tidal Basin. Most are near the 300-year-old Japanese stone lantern. While the delicate white- and pale pink–blossomed Yoshinos predominate, they now mingle with Akebonos (single pale pink flowers), the Kwanzan variety (double pompomlike blossoms of deeper pink), and Weeping Higans (single or double layers of petals from white to dark pink). Blossoms last up to 2 weeks if Mother Nature is being kind. A total of about 3,700 trees bloom in East and West Potomac Parks. Start counting! My favorite time is dusk, when the fading light creates an otherworldly scene. Also, it's usually the least crowded time.

Approximate boundaries: Constitution Ave. to the north, Jefferson Memorial to the south, Potomac River to the west, Washington Monument to the east. ℂ **202/547-1500.** Free admission. Daily dawn–dusk. Metro: Smithsonian; then a 10- 15-min. walk.

NATURE CENTERS
Audubon Naturalist Society (Woodend) ⚐   Kids can explore self-guided nature trails in this 40-acre wildlife sanctuary and learn about conservation and the environment in special programs. Activities are geared to children 4 and up, with day and weekend family programs, classes, and field trips. For the latest stirrings, call the Voice of the Naturalist recording, updated weekly (ℂ **301/652-1088**).

8940 Jones Mill Rd., Chevy Chase, MD. ℂ **301/652-9188.** Fax 301/951-7179. www.audubonnaturalist.org. Free admission. Nature sanctuary open daily dawn–dusk; building open Mon–Fri 9am–5pm; bookstore/gift shop open Mon–Fri 10am–5pm, Sat 9am–5pm, Sun noon–5pm. Closed holidays. Directions: Drive north on Connecticut Ave.; turn right onto Jones Bridge Rd.; then turn left at Jones Mill Rd.

Discovery Creek Children's Museum of Washington   See chapter 6 for more information.

Rock Creek Nature Center ⚐⚐   Plenty of self-guided nature trails and hands-on activities distinguish this facility in the District's largest park. Guided nature walks, films, planetarium shows, and live animal presentations are scheduled throughout the year. Call ahead for specifics, and see "Parks, Gardens & Other Wide-Open Spaces," earlier in this chapter. See chapter 6 for info on planetarium shows.

Rock Creek Park, 5200 Glover Rd. NW. ℂ **202/426-6829.** www.nps.gov/rocr. Free admission. Daily in summer 9am–5pm, after Labor Day Wed–Sun 9am–5pm. Directions: North on Connecticut Ave.; turn right onto Military Rd.; then turn right onto Glover Rd.

OUTDOOR SCULPTURE
More than 370 outdoor sculptures decorate the D.C. landscape. Here are a handful with special appeal for kids.

National Gallery of Art Sculpture Garden ⚐⚐⚐   This 6-acre sculpture garden on the Mall lies west of the museum's West Building, between 7th and 9th streets, Constitution Avenue, and Madison Drive NW. I urge you to spend at least a few minutes here during your Mall crawl.

(*Fun Fact* **Did You Know?**
As you view Washington's many equestrian statues, note the positions of the horses' legs. Both front legs in the air means the rider died in battle. If one front leg is raised, the rider died as a result of his wounds. If all four legs are on the ground, he died of natural causes.

Native shade trees and curvilinear benches encircle a fountain pool (no swimming allowed). The plantings are lovely, and this heavy metal won't hurt your hearing. (For information on the sculptures, see chapter 6; for a great kids introduction to the sculpture garden, visit www.nga.gov/kids.)

Albert Einstein   Nestled in the gardens of the National Academy of Sciences at 2101 Constitution Ave. NW, Einstein's ample lap invites little ones to climb up and rest a while.

The Awakening   Located at Hains Point in East Potomac Park (see earlier in this chapter), this is a sort of scary giant struggling to free himself from the ground.

In 1993, after a car ran into the statue, the 17-foot arm had to be reattached. Doctor/sculptor Seward Johnson performed the extensive surgery. In September 2003, the statue was nearly washed away by tropical storm Isabel. Clearly, it has nine lives.

Equestrian Statue of Ulysses S. Grant   Get out your camera. Outside the West facade of the U.S. Capitol, with its sweeping view of the National Mall, horse-drawn caissons flank an imposing statue of Grant.

The Lansburgh Eagle   No relation to the bald eagle, *The Lansburgh Eagle,* all 800 pounds, landed with the help of a crane at 8th and E streets NW in March 1992. At last report, it was still resting comfortably in the Pennsylvania Quarter's courtyard.

The Lone Sailor   The windblown sailor stands in the plaza at the U.S. Navy Memorial and Visitor Center at Market Square, Pennsylvania Avenue and 7th Street NW, where military bands give concerts on summer evenings.

Lunchbreak   Located at Washington Harbor, 30th and K streets NW in Georgetown is a realistic workman in overalls enjoying lunch on a park bench.

Man Controlling Trade   If I had sculpted this, I would have called it *Whoa, Horsey.* Michael Lantz's two massive equestrian works mirror each other on the east end of the Federal Trade Commission Building at Pennsylvania Avenue and 6th Street NW (the point of the Federal Triangle). One faces Constitution Avenue; the other faces Pennsylvania Avenue.

National Law Enforcement Officers Memorial   The bronze lions by Washington sculptor Ray Kaskey are grouped majestically around the Judiciary Square memorial to officers who died on duty from 1794 to the present. The memorial is in the vicinity of the National Building Museum, 4th and F streets NW.

FARMS

Claude Moore Colonial Farm at Turkey Run *(Finds)*   If your kids are like most, complaining that they have it rough, take them to see how their colonial forebears lived. Watch a poor colonial family (Park Service staff in period dress) split logs, make clothes, and tend livestock. The one-room house is a real eye-opener. Kids can help the farmer harvest tobacco in August. Go on a weekday, if possible. Special events are ongoing throughout the year, such as 18th-century market fairs in May, July, and October. If you live in the area, ask about the volunteer program for kids 10 and older.

6310 Georgetown Pike, McLean, VA. ☎ **703/442-7557.** www.1771.org. Admission $3 adults, $2 ages 3–12 and seniors. Large groups should call ahead. Apr–mid-Dec Wed–Sun 10am–4:30pm. Closed mid-Dec–Mar, Thanksgiving, and rainy days. Directions: Beltway to Exit 44 (Rte. 193 east), and go 2½ miles to the marked access road on the left to the farm, or take the G. W. Pkwy. to Rte. 123 south, go 1 mile, turn right on Rte. 193, and then turn right into the marked access road to the farm.

Oxon Hill Farm ✯   Activities abound at this working farm from around 1900, operated by the Park Service. It's not every day that kids can help gather eggs, feed chickens, and milk cows. So as not to disappoint, call ahead for the times of these special activities. Pet the animals and learn about farm life by watching seasonal demonstrations of cider pressing, corn harvesting, and sheep shearing. A cow-milking demonstration takes place two or three times a day. A highlight of the self-guided nature walk is the view of the Potomac River, Washington, and Virginia. You may also bike, hike, and picnic on the grounds. For group reservations, call weekdays between 2:30 and 4pm.

Oxon Cove Park, 6411 Oxon Hill Rd., Oxon Hill, MD. © **301/839-1176.** www.nps.gov/oxhi. Free admission. Daily 8am–4:30pm. Directions: Beltway to Exit 3A (Indian Head Hwy. south); turn right at first intersection and right onto Oxon Hill Rd., and follow it to the farm on the right.

2 Outdoor Activities

BIKING
The area abounds with off-road bike paths. The 7-mile **Capital Crescent Trail** between Georgetown and Bethesda, Maryland, is paved and follows an old railroad right-of-way through scenic wooded areas. On weekends the trail is heavily congested. For more information, call © **202/234-4874** (www.cctrail.org). Other major trails include the **C&O Canal Towpath,** 23 miles from Georgetown to Seneca, Maryland; the **George Washington Memorial Parkway** ✯, from the Virginia side of Memorial Bridge through downtown Alexandria, ending at Mount Vernon (with the flattest terrain of all listed); and **Rock Creek Park,** north from the infamous Watergate through northwest D.C., past the zoo, and along Beach Drive into Maryland. Parts of the route along Beach Drive are closed to traffic on weekends (see the entry on Rock Creek Park, earlier in this chapter).

Bookstores and bicycle shops stock maps of local trails, or you can try the **Washington Area Bicyclist Association** (WABA; 733 15th St. NW, #1030 Washington, DC 20005-2112; © **202/628/4141;** www.waba.org). A helpful site for biking in D.C. is www.bikewashington.org. Experienced cyclists who want to tackle the entire C&O Canal (which takes about 3 days, averaging 61 miles a day) can write to C&O Canal, National Historic Parks, P.O. Box 4, Sharpsburg, MD 21782 (© **301/739-4200**) or go to www.nps.gov/choh.

Bike the Sites ✯ (© **202/842/BIKE;** www.bikethesites.com) offers participants professionally guided bike tours on Trek 21-speed hybrid bikes, from March through November. Bike the Sites provides helmets, water bottles, and a handlebar bag. In the **Capital Sites Ride** ✯✯, cyclists visit 55 landmarks on an 8-mile circuit that takes around 3 hours. In summer, an early morning tour departs at 7am, leaving the rest of the day for visiting air-conditioned museums and restaurants. Most of the terrain is flat on paved and gravel trails. Along the way, guides will feed you information. Children between 5 and 14 must be accompanied by an adult. Younger kids ride in trail-a-bikes attached to Mom or Dad's wheels. If you're feeling skittish, you should know that families make up more than half of Bike the Sites business, and a majority of the adult riders haven't been on a bike in years. The tours, which depart across from 1100 Pennsylvania Ave. NW (Metro: Federal Triangle), take around 3 hours and cost $40 for adults and $30 for kids 12 and under.

If you prefer going it alone, bike rentals vary. **Big Wheel Bikes** has three locations: 1034 33rd St. NW in Georgetown (© **202/337-0254**); 2 Prince St., Alexandria, Virginia

(© **703/739-2300**); and 6917 Arlington Rd., Bethesda, Maryland (© **301/652-0192**), where they rent hybrids, mountain bikes, 12-speeds, or tandems. The rental is $25 per day. **Fletcher's Boat House,** 4940 Canal Rd. NW (© **202/244-0461**), rents fixed-gear bikes *only* for $12 per day, $8 for 2 hours (yeah, you read it right!). The towpath is mostly flat, so this shouldn't present a problem. Fletcher's is about a mile west of the Georgetown side of Key Bridge. The nearest restaurants are in Georgetown and on MacArthur Boulevard, which runs parallel to Canal Road. While there is a snack bar at Fletcher's, I prefer to play it safe and tote snacks or a brown-bag lunch to enjoy at Fletcher's picnic area. Another place to rent bikes is **Thompson's,** 2900 Virginia Ave. at Rock Creek Parkway NW (© **202/333-9543**). Fixed-gear bikes are $15 per day, $4 per hour; multispeed $25 a day, $8 per hour.

If your kids are too young to pedal on their own, consider renting a bike child seat or trailer, but know that experts recommend that a second cyclist follow behind a bike with a child seat or trailer. Practice with the equipment before venturing out, stay on smooth surfaces away from traffic, and always give kids helmets. The equipment rents for about $15 to $20 a day at area bike stores.

BOATING

On a mild day between late March and late November, there are at least four good reasons why you should rent a boat: (1) Kids love being on the water. (2) Your brood will gain a new perspective of the city. (3) They'll paddle while you relax. (4) Everyone will sleep like a baby afterward. Prices average $8 to $10 per hour or $20 to $22 per day. Most places are open from 9 or 10am to 5 or 6pm weekdays, with extended weekend and summer hours. Call first, because hours change seasonally. Arrive early on weekends.

Fletcher's Boat House, 4940 Canal Rd. NW (© **202/244-0461;** www.fletchers boathouse.com), rents canoes, rowing shells, small sailboats, rowboats, and bicycles. There's a large picnic area and snack bar, too. Anglers can purchase a D.C. fishing license here. **Jack's Boats,** 3500 K St. NW in Georgetown (© **202/337-9642;** www. jacksboats.com), rents canoes, kayaks, and rowboats. **Thompson's Boat Center,** 2900 Virginia Avenue NW, at Rock Creek Parkway (© **202/333-9543**), rents canoes, rowboats, rowing shells, kayaks, and bikes. (**Note:** You must be certified to rent a kayak or rowing shell.) At the **Tidal Basin,** Ohio Drive and Tidal Basin (near the Jefferson Memorial, roughly 15th St. and Maine Ave. SW; © **202/479-2426**), rent a pedal boat March through September; prices are $8 per hour for a 2-seater, $16 for a 4-seater. Farther afield (or, in this case, astream), if your kids are 7 or older, they can learn to paddle their own canoes summer evenings on the C&O Canal. Bless the **National Park Service!** It offers free evening classes during the summer (although there's a nominal fee to rent equipment) at Fletcher's Boat House and Swain's Lock, off River Road, west of Potomac, Maryland. Younger kids can ride with their parents, but the rule is three to a canoe. Picnic tables are available at both sites for a light supper before the 6:30pm class begins. Call © **301/299-9006** for boat-rental and class prices.

Kayaking has taken off in the past few years as a pleasurable, affordable water sport. If you're considering whitewater kayaking, you'll need some land-based training before heading out. The Potomac can be unpredictable and treacherous—no place for a wanna-be lacking experience. **Atlantic Kayak,** 1201 North Royal St., Alexandria, Virginia (© **703/838-9072;** www.atlantickayak.com), rents canoes and kayaks, and also offers kayaking classes and tours. **Potomac Paddlesports,** 11001 MacArthur Blvd.,

Potomac, MD (© **877/529-2542**; www.potomacpaddlesports.com); and **Valley Mill Kayak School,** 15101 Seneca Rd., Darnestown, MD (© **301/840-7388;** www.valleymill.com), all offer classes for beginners.

FISHING

Thanks to the Clean Water Act, there are fish—live fish—in the waters in and around the D.C. area. Every Friday, see the "On the Move," section of *The Washington Post's* "Weekend" magazine for a listing of what fish are running and biting where. Local anglers tell me that mid-March until July is prime fishing time. Nonetheless, you'll probably catch *something* from late February through October. Cast your line for catfish, bass, and stripers from the wall along the Washington Channel at **Hains Point** or **Pentagon Lagoon,** anywhere near **Chain Bridge,** or at the seawall north of the **Wilson Bridge** in Alexandria, Virginia.

If you want to sink your line in the **Chesapeake Bay,** board a head boat for a half or full day of fishing. Several head boats leave from the **Rod 'N Reel,** Route 261 and Mears Avenue in Chesapeake Beach, Maryland (© **800/233-2080**). It's about a 45-minute drive from D.C., and kids of all ages are welcome as long as someone is watching them. Prices are $45 for all ages, with a $3 discount for kids on weekdays. Most boats go out, weather permitting, once a day at 8am. Although some add a second night-fishing trip at 6pm. You can rent a rod for about $5. Oh, yes, a dozen blood-worms are included with the boarding fee. Use them for best results. (My dad taught me how to fish with bologna as bait—we caught an old shoe once.)

Be sure to wear nonskid shoes for the slippery decks. Take plenty of sunblock, a windbreaker or foul-weather jacket, and two coolers—one for all the fish you'll catch, and one for lunch and drinks. If you're toting your own fishing gear, leave light tackle at home. Those prone to motion sickness should take an appropriate medication a half-hour before boarding.

Many area fishers favor casting off from **Fletcher's Boat House** at the intersection of Reservoir and Canal roads NW (© **202/244-0461;** www.fletchersboathouse.com). Fletcher's sells bait and tackle, rents boats, and has a snack bar. With younger kids, I'd stick to the canal here. Conveniently, you can also pick up a fishing license at Fletcher's. The cost is $7 for residents and $10 for nonresidents, and is good for the day you purchase it through the rest of the calendar year. Short-term visitors will be better served by the $4 license, good for 14 consecutive days. For more information, call the D.C. Department of Health, Fisheries and Wildlife Division, at © **202/535-2260.**

Please be careful when you fish the Potomac. Every year, several people drown in its unforgiving waters, which are especially treacherous and turbulent after heavy rains. Heed warning signs; they're posted for a reason. And be particularly cautious of slippery rocks along the shoreline.

HIKING

Many city and suburban parks have hiking trails (see the "Parks, Gardens & Other Wide-Open Spaces" section, earlier in this chapter), and portions of the **Blue Ridge Mountains** and **Appalachian Trail** are well within reach for a day trip. Some of the best local hiking for families is along the **C&O Canal, Theodore Roosevelt Island, Rock Creek Park,** and the **U.S. National Arboretum.** On the Maryland side of Great Falls Park, 11710 MacArthur Blvd., Potomac (© **301/767-3714**), open from 9am to 4pm daily, the 4-mile **Billy Goat Trail** is a family favorite. The trail's entrance is off a towpath less than 2 miles south of the park's entrance. Section A, the first stretch, is 1.6 miles one-way and the most difficult. Tired? Return to the falls via the flatter and less challenging towpath. Just turn off at the "Emergency Exit" sign. Brave-hearts can continue to Sections B and C. Nobody said you have to do the entire trail on your first try. A snack bar is open near the visitor center weekends until about 6pm.

ICE SKATING

Every few years, Washington endures a severe winter (most recently the record-break-ing 2002–03 one). One of the few pleasant aspects of this phenomenon is that the **C&O Canal** (© **301/767-3707;** www.nps.gov/choh) freezes over for skating. It's a scene straight from Currier and Ives, and one that your family won't want to miss. Skating is allowed only when the "Skate at Your Own Risk" signs are posted; other-wise, forget it!

The ice-skating rink in the **National Gallery of Art Sculpture Garden,** 7th Street and Constitution Ave. (© **202/289-3360;** www.nga.gov), is my fave because of the setting. It is usually open from mid-November until mid-March, and hours are 10am to 11pm Monday through Saturday and 11am to 9pm Sunday. Admission is $7 for adults, $6 for those 12 and younger and seniors. You can rent skates for $3. All ses-sions run about 2 hours. Snacks are sold at the refreshment stand. The smaller **Persh-ing Park Ice Rink,** 14th Street and Pennsylvania Avenue NW (© **202/737-6938;** www.pershingparkicerink.com), is open December through February. The rink is usu-ally less crowded than the sculpture-garden rink, so it's a good choice with very young children. It is open daily from December through February, with varying hours, and is only 3 blocks from Metro Center (12th and F sts. exit). Two-hour sessions are $6.50 for adults, $5.50 for kids 12 and under. Figure-skate rentals are $2.50, and sizes range from toddler size 8 to men's 14.

In the suburbs, the **Fairfax Ice Arena,** 3779 Pickett Rd., Fairfax, Virginia (© **703/323-1132;** www.fairfaxicearena.com), is open year-round and offers skate rentals, les-sons, and a pro shop. Don't be surprised if you run into a few Olympic hopefuls in training. In Maryland, there's an outdoor skating rink at **Bethesda Metro Center,** Wisconsin Avenue and Old Georgetown Road, outside the Hyatt Regency Hotel. Parking is free for 3 hours with ice-rink validation (© **301/656-0588**). Two covered outdoor rinks—**Cabin John Ice Rink,** 10610 Westlake Dr., Rockville, MD (© **301/365-0585**), and **Wheaton Ice Rink,** at Arcola and Orebaugh avenues, Wheaton, Maryland (© **301/649-3640**)—attract scores of families. Both offer skate rentals and lessons. Cabin John has lockers and a snack bar, and is open year-round.

IN-LINE SKATING

In-line skating is a hot fitness trend for all ages. Local shops rent skates for about $15 to $20 per day (including elbow, knee, and wrist pads) and also sponsor clinics. Try **Metropolis Bicycles,** 709 8th St. SE, near Eastern Market (© **202/543-8900**); or **Caravan Skate Shop,** 10766 Tucker St., Beltsville, Maryland (© **301/937-0066**). Several others are listed under "Skating Equipment and Supplies" in the local Yellow Pages.

The best skating sites are Rock Creek Park (when Beach Drive is closed to traffic Sat–Sun) and the C&O Canal trail between Georgetown and Fletcher's Boat House (about 1½ miles). Seasoned skaters only might want to head for the pebbly walkways on the Mall. But please don't try to blade through the museums, and always, always wear a helmet and pads.

KITE FLYING

Spring and fall are the best kite-flying seasons in the capital area. In summer, a breeze is unusual enough to attract media attention, and in winter, it's usually too chilly to enjoy kite flying. Look no farther than the Mall for the optimum kite-flying space with no overhead impediments. Otherwise, head for the nearest schoolyard or playground. The **Air and Space Museum's gift shop,** at 6th Street and Independence Avenue SW, has a mind-boggling selection of kites.

In late March, the Smithsonian sponsors an annual **kite festival** on the west side of the Washington Monument (© 202/357-3030). There are two hitches: The kite has to be homemade, and it's supposed to remain airborne for at least 1 minute at an altitude of 100 feet or more. Ribbons are awarded to winners in different age groups, and trophies are given in several categories. If you're in town, try to catch it.

MINIATURE GOLF

Here is one game that junior and senior tour hopefuls (and hopeless) can enjoy strictly for fun. It doesn't cost an arm and a leg to swing a club in the scenic surroundings of Hains Point in East Potomac Park. The **Circus Mini Golf Putt-4-Fun,** Ohio Drive SW (© 202/488-8087), is open daily March to November, 8am to 9pm, weather permitting. It's $4.50 per game for all ages on weekends, $4 during the week. Outside the district, try **Upton Hill Regional Park Mini Golf** in Arlington, Virginia (© 703/534-3437).

SAILING

The **Mariner Sailing School,** Belle Haven Marina, south of Alexandria, Virginia (© 703/768-0018; www.saildc.com), rents Windsurfers, Sunfish, and larger sailboats to experienced sailors, and offers weekend and evening classes on 19-foot sailboats. Canoes and kayaks are also available. During the summer months, kids 8 to 15 can take a 5-day sailing course or windsurfing lessons: Make reservations to ensure your spot. The **Washington Sailing Marina,** Dangerfield Island off the George Washington Memorial Parkway (1½ miles south of Reagan National Airport), Alexandria, Virginia (© 703/548-9027; www.washingtonsailingmarina.com), rents sailboats ($10–$19 per hour) and runs several week-long youth sailing camps for ages 10 to 16. The WSM fleet includes 14-foot, 17-foot, and 19-foot boats. Week-long courses (for different skill levels) are held from June to mid-August, Monday to Friday, 9:30am to 4pm, rain or shine. The *average* price is $200. For information on sailing instruction on the Chesapeake Bay in Annapolis, Maryland (about 35 miles from downtown), see the "Annapolis" entry in chapter 11.

SWIMMING

For the location of the public pool nearest you, call the **D.C. Department of Recreation Aquatic Programs** (© 202/673-7647). Most public pools are open from mid-June through Labor Day. Frankly, they're very crowded, and most are in D.C.'s less-than-premier neighborhoods. I strongly suggest staying in a hotel with a pool or leaving your bathing suits at home.

If you live in the District or are visiting for an extended period, consider lapping up a family membership at one of the following outdoor hotel pools: **Washington Hilton,** 1919 Connecticut Ave. NW (© 202/483-4100); **Omni Shoreham,** 2500 Calvert St. NW (© 202/234-0700); **Loews L'Enfant Plaza** (indoor/outdoor), L'Enfant Plaza SW (© 202/646-4450); or **Quality Hotel Central,** 1900 Connecticut Ave. NW (© 202/332-9300). *Mar-co, Po-lo!*

TENNIS

In **Rock Creek Park,** the free tennis courts at 16th and Kennedy streets NW are open Monday through Friday from 7am to 11pm, and Saturday and Sunday from 7am to 10pm. Courts must be reserved from April to November (© **202/722-5949**). Or swing your racquet at 1 of the 24 courts (indoor, outdoor, lighted, and clay) in **East Potomac Park,** 1090 Ohio Dr. SW (© **202/554-5962**). They're open spring through fall, Monday through Friday from 7am to 10pm, and Saturday and Sunday from 7am to 8pm—with extended winter hours. Court time is $8 to $17 per hour, depending on the type of court surface.

WINDSURFING

See "Sailing," above.

3 Rides for Children

BALLOON RIDES

Go up, up, and away at several locations outside the Beltway (as if there's not already enough hot air in Washington). A balloon ride does not come cheaply and is appropriate only for kids at least 8 or older, but if you're prepared to cough up the bucks, call one of the following: **Aeronaut Masters** (© **301/869-2FLY**) charges $200 for a 1½-hour ride; **Balloons Unlimited** (© **703/281-2300**) charges $165 per hour for adults, $85 for children 12 and under.

BOAT RIDES

During the warm-weather months, take advantage of Washington's waterfront setting and enjoy the city from offshore with your kids: I'll bet they rate a boat ride as one of the high watermarks of their visit. Rent a pedal boat on the Tidal Basin, or a canoe or rowboat on the C&O Canal or Potomac River. For details on several D.C. boating centers, see the "Boating" and "Sailing" entries in this chapter. Also see the "Annapolis" entry in chapter 11. When boating, make sure there are life vests onboard for each family member, and be sure to put them on before you leave the dock.

CANAL BOAT RIDES ON THE C&O CANAL

Park Service guides in period dress from around 1870 will regale you with 19th-century canal lore and river songs as the mule-drawn boat makes its way slowly along the historic waterway. The *Georgetown* ✹✹, berthed in the heart of Georgetown on the canal between 30th and Thomas Jefferson streets NW (© **202/653-5844**; www.nps.gov/choh), operates mid-April through October, Wednesday through Sunday. During peak season (mid-June to mid-Sept), cruises depart three times a day on weekdays, four times a day on weekends; in spring and fall, there are two cruises a day Wednesday through Friday and three a day on Saturday and Sunday.

The *Georgetown* might look like a barge, but it is actually a boat, the Park Service told me, because it is steerable. The mules are the engine! A true barge has to be pulled and pushed; it cannot be steered. Live and learn. Anyway, the delightful and informative rides are an hour long. Leave it to the Park Service—rangers carry boxes filled with old-fashioned toys for restless little girls and boys. The cost for the ride is $8 adults, $6 seniors 62 and older, $5 kids 4 to 14, free 3 and under. Buy tickets at the Visitor Center, 1057 Thomas Jefferson St. NW, open Wednesday through Sunday 9:30am to 5pm. Reservations are not needed. Times vary, so be sure to call in advance.

CRUISES

Because two sides of the Washington "diamond" are bordered by rivers—the Potomac and Anacostia—you should cast off from terra firma and see the city from the water at least once during your stay. Please note that the prices and schedules for the cruises below change frequently; call or visit the website for the most up-to-date information.

The 150-year-old steel riverboat *Nightingale II* (© 800/405-5511) leaves from the Washington Harbor dock in Georgetown, 31st Street and the river, for a 50-minute narrated cruise departing hourly from noon to 9pm, April through October. The fare is $10 for adults and $5 for kids 3 to 12, and there's a snack bar onboard. Feel free to BYO (lunch) if you like.

The luxurious 510-passenger *Spirit of Washington* (© 202/554-8000 or 866/211-3811; www.spiritcruises.com) offers lunch, brunch, dinner, and moonlight cruises to Mount Vernon from Pier 4, 6th and Water streets SW. However, you should probably forget the dinner and moonlight cruises with kids—it's likely that the cruises will be too long, too expensive, and too boring for them to enjoy. The 2-hour lunch cruise (in the Washington Channel) aboard the carpeted, climate-controlled ship is fine if your kids will do justice to the copious buffet and dessert. Live music and a show are included in the ticket price. Lunch cruises range from $30 to $44; dinner cruises from $54 to $83. For all cruises, reservations are a must (© 202/554-8000, or 202/554-8013 for groups of 20 or more).

If food is secondary, and you want to spend a fun-filled half-day on the water visiting a major sight, board the *Spirit of Mount Vernon* ⊕ (© 202/554-8000). The cruise down the Potomac to George Washington's beautiful estate is pleasing to all ages. Trips depart Tuesday through Sunday March to October (Friday to Sunday only, September 9 to October 16) at 8:30am and return midafternoon. Tickets are $35 for adults, $33 for seniors, $29 for ages 6 to 11, and free for children 5 and under. Admission to Mount Vernon is included in the ticket price. You'll have ample time to look around Mount Vernon before the return voyage. You may not bring food aboard, but there's a concession stand selling all the drinks and fast food that kids' tummies can hold. There's also a restaurant at Mount Vernon. Arrive at the dock 1 hour before departure time. Sightseeing cruises aboard *Potomac Spirit* depart the Mount Vernon dock April through September, Tuesday through Sunday, and in October, Thursday through Sunday. Cruises depart at 10:30 and 11:30am and 12:30pm for the 45-minute ride. The fare is $8 for adults, $4 for kids 6 to 11, and free for 5 and under (© 703/548-9000).

Glide by presidential monuments and the Iwo Jima Memorial, the Kennedy Center, and Georgetown on the *Matthew Hayes* ⊕, which runs several times daily from May until early September, and weekends only April, September, and October. There are two departure points: Georgetown (Washington Harbor dock, 31st St. NW and the river) and Old Town Alexandria (adjacent to the Torpedo Factory). The round-trip fare is $20 for adults, $17 for seniors, and $10 for kids 2 to 12.

The *Miss Christin* cruises the Potomac from Old Town Alexandria to Mount Vernon from April through October (weekends only April, Sept, Oct; Tues through Sun the other months). The cruise departs Old Town two or three times in the morning and leaves Mount Vernon the same number of times in the afternoon. Fare (including admission to Mt. Vernon) is $30 for adults, $28 for seniors, and $17 for children 6 to 10.

Potomac Riverboat Company (© 703/548-9000), based in Alexandria, Virginia, runs both the *Miss Christin* and the *Matthew Hayes.*

In the tradition of the Parisian *bateaux mouche* on the Seine, the riverboat–restaurants **Dandy** and **Nina's Dandy** (© **703/683-6076;** www.dandydinnerboat.com) ply the waters of the Potomac several times a week. Luncheon and dinner cruises depart Old Town Alexandria for a leisurely run up the Potomac past historic monuments and memorials, the Kennedy Center, Watergate, Rosslyn (Virginia), and Georgetown before heading back to port. Kids 10 and older with the palate and patience for a three-course lunch or five-course dinner with mostly adults will enjoy this cruise. I found the food on the dinner cruise plentiful but uninspired. The magnificent scenery doesn't come cheap: Prices range from $37 for the weekday lunch cruise to $45 for the Sunday champagne brunch, to $85 for the Saturday dinner cruise (weeknights cost less). Drinks cost extra. For all cruises except those on Saturday nights and holidays, knock $10 off adult prices for kids 12 and under. Chicken fingers, not on the regular menu, are available for kids. Lasagna and pasta primavera are other kid-friendly choices. Reservations are a must (© **703/683-6076**).

Now here's a cruise worth diving for: **D.C. Ducks** ⚓ (© **202/966-DUCK;** www.dcducks.com) utilizes amphibious vehicles, which transported troops and supplies during World War II, to ferry 30 visitors at a time around several downtown sights before dipping into the Virginia side of the Potomac at the Columbia Island Marina. After a short swim, the Duck waddles ashore at Gravelly Point across from National Airport's main runway and heads back to Union Station over paved roads. The keels-on-wheels tours depart from Union Station, 50 Massachusetts Ave. NE, daily from mid-March to November, every hour on the hour from 10am to 4pm, and more frequently at peak times. The narrated 90-minute ride (60 on land, 30 afloat) costs $30 for adults, $15 for seniors 65 and older and children 4 to 12. Children under 4 are free. There's a 10% discount if you book your ticket online.

Resembling a humongous floating graham cracker, the **Odyssey** (© **202/488-6010;** www.odysseycruises.com) is docked at the Gangplank Marina, 600 Water St. SW. Designed to squeeze under the bridges spanning the Potomac, the glassed-in vessel accommodates 1,800 passengers. Boarding for the dinner cruise (actually, the first hour is spent tied up at the dock) on Sunday through Thursday begins at 5:45pm, and Friday and Saturday at 7pm. There's something going on every day and night of the week, from weekday lunch cruises ($39) to Saturday dinner ($94). Save some money and take the dinner cruise Monday through Thursday or Sunday ($81). In between are several other choices. All include a full-course meal, coffee, tea (soda and juice for the kiddies), and music. A delightful way to celebrate the weekend is the Saturday and Sunday Jazz Brunch ($52). Kids always pay "full fare" at dinner, but children 3–11 get a 50% discount on the brunch and lunch cruises. Kids 2 and under are always free. Bear in mind that alcoholic beverages and an 18% service charge are added to the cruise price. You might want to try it if you're celebrating a special event or just won the lottery. For the same money, I'd rather take a no-frills boat tour and eat in a first-rate restaurant.

FERRY RIDES

About 30 miles northwest of the District of Columbia, the **Gen. Jubal A. Early,** an old cable ferry named after an even older Confederate general, leaves from White's Ferry (© **301/349-5200**) on the Maryland shore to just north of Leesburg, Virginia. The first ferries began crossing here in 1828. Kids of all ages adore the *Jubal Early,* which operates daily from 5am to 11pm, weather permitting. The ferry makes several trips per hour. The ride is 5 to 15 minutes long, depending on the current and weather. You can take your car on the ferry or go on foot ($3 one-way, $5 round-trip, 50¢ for foot passengers). There's a convenience store on the Maryland side. For $1.50, you can use one of the picnic tables. Take the Capital Beltway to I-270 to the Route 28 west exit and then continue on Route 28 west; at Dawsonville, take Route 107 and follow the signs.

If you have the time, consider a visit to **Leesburg,** Virginia, before returning to the Maryland side of the Potomac. The town oozes charm and history. Market and Loudon streets run east and west, transversed by King Street (north and south). Stop at the Loudon Museum, 14 Loudon St. SW (© **703/777-7427**), for information, and browse the historic district with its brick sidewalks. Antique shops and restaurants abound in this gentle place, which is especially beautiful when the fall foliage flames in late October. At the **Leesburg Animal Park,** 19270 James Monroe Highway (© **703/433-0002;** www.leesburganimalpark.com), kids can feed and pet the exotic animals Friday 10am to 3pm, Saturday and Sunday 10am to 5pm. Admission is $8.95 adults, and $6.95 ages 2 to 12 and seniors.

CAROUSELS

Families who enjoy going around together will want to take a ride on an antique carousel. Few excursions are as much fun or cost as little as these—only $2 or less per ride. The **Carousel on the Mall** ⚓, 1000 Jefferson Dr. SW., in front of the Smithsonian Castle (© **202/357-2700**), operates, weather permitting, from 10am to 6pm March through September 6, and 11am to 5pm September 7 through February 28. The 1940s carousel, designed by Allan Herschell, sports 58 horses, 2 chariots, a sea dragon, and no partridge in a pear tree.

Burke Lake Park, 7315 Ox Road, Fairfax Station, Virginia (© **703/323-6600**), is open the first 3 weeks of May weekends only 11am to 6pm; late May until Labor Day daily, 11am to 6pm; and after Labor Day weekends only through the end of October, 11am to 6pm.

Glen Echo Park Dentzel Carousel ⚓, 7300 MacArthur Blvd at Goldsboro Road, Glen Echo, Maryland (© **301/492-6229;** www.glenechopark.org), has a classic 1921 Dentzel carousel. It's been my favorite since I took my kids for their first ride in the 1970s. Now they're taking their kids! Ablaze with more than 1,200 lights, the carousel has 52 carved wood figures and a 165-band Würlitzer organ. It operates from May through September on weekends from noon to 6pm, and Wednesday and Thursday from 10am to 2pm. A park ranger gives a half-hour talk on the carousel's history Saturday at 10:30am.

Lake Fairfax Carousel, 1400 Lake Fairfax Driver, Reston, Virginia (© **703/471-5415**), is open Memorial Day weekend to Labor Day, 7 days a week, 11am to 7pm; from Labor Day through September, weekends only, 11am to 5pm.

Lee District Park Carousel, 6601 Telegraph Road, Alexandria, Virginia (© **703/922-9841**), is open Memorial Day to the day before Labor Day, Saturday 10am to 6pm and Sunday from noon to 6pm.

HAYRIDES

If you're visiting in the fall, especially around Halloween, treat your kids to a hayride at a nearby farm. Afterward, stock up on apples, pumpkins, and fresh-pressed cider while you pick the hay out of each oother's hair. Call for hours and special kids' activities.

Two close-to-D.C. orchards, offering hayrides as part of their all-out Halloween celebration, are **Butler's Orchard** ✸, 22200 Davis Mill Road, Germantown, Maryland
(✆ **301/972-3299**); and **Krop's Crops,** 11110 Georgetown Pike, Great Falls, Virginia
(✆ **703/430-8955**). Check the Maryland and Virginia phone books for bushels more.

TRAIN RIDES

If your youngsters have never been on a big choo-choo, board a northbound **Amtrak**
train at Union Station, 50 Massachusetts Ave. NE (✆ **800/USA-RAIL**), and take a
ride to New Carrollton, Maryland, one stop away. Because it's only a 20-minute hop,
they won't have time to raid the snack car. Trains operate frequently throughout the
day. Unfortunately, there isn't much to see or do in New Carrollton, so once you dis-
embark you'll want to hop on the next train back. But if you'd like to make a day of
it, go to Baltimore (only a 40-min. ride from Union Station), where there are plenty
of kid-pleasing things to do. A one-way unreserved (off-peak) seat on Amtrak, Union
Station to New Carrollton, is $14 for adults and $7 for kids 2 to 15. A one-way unreserved (off-peak) ticket from Union Station to Baltimore's Penn Station is $17 for
adults and $8.50 for kids age 2 to 15 riding with an adult (each adult can bring 2 chil-
dren at the reduced fare). Reserved seats, business class, and the Metroliner and Acela
Express cost more, as does travel at peak times (Fri, Sun, and holidays 11am–11pm).

Less cushy than Amtrak, and also less costly, the MARC commuter train's Penn
Line (✆ **800/325-RAIL;** www.mtamaryland.com) runs from (Washington) Union
Station to Baltimore Penn Station, from 5am to midnight, Monday through Friday
only. The trip is about 45 minutes, and the fare is $7 one-way, regardless of age.

Toddlers and preschoolers delight in riding the small-scale trains in the following
regional parks: **Burke Lake Park** ✸, 7315 Ox Road, Fairfax Station, Virginia (✆ **703/
323-6600**); **Cabin John Regional Park** ✸, 7400 Tuckerman Lane, Rockville, Maryland (✆ **301/469-7835**); and **Wheaton Regional Park** ✸, 2000 Shorefield Rd.,
Wheaton, Maryland (✆ **301/946-6396**).

9

Shopping for the Whole Family

Once upon a time, Washington, D.C. residents had to go to New York and other more worldly cities to find what they wanted. Not anymore! Now even the most seriously addicted shopaholics can feed their habit in the nation's capital. Flashy multilevel malls, dependable department stores, and trendy boutiques are as much a part of the D.C. scene as cherry blossoms and government red tape. In the past decade, numerous discount stores have moved into the area, giving the full-price standbys a run for their money.

If your kids are like most, they break out in hives at the mere mention of clothes shopping. But they probably love browsing books, toys, electronics, nature-related items, and sports gear. For the kind of shopping they'll enjoy, visit one of the specialty stores, museum shops, or enclosed malls listed in this chapter.

1 The Shopping Scene

In 2006, **Macy's** took over **Hecht's** department store, which stood guard for many years over Washington's downtown shopping area near Metro Center (13th and F streets NW). Swedish retailer **H&M** (for Hennes & Mauritz) is a hip international chain with a downtown branch at 11th and F streets NW and a store in the Georgetown Park mall. Less than a mile from Metro Center, along the Connecticut Avenue and K Street business corridor, branches of upscale national chains and specialty shops nudge one another for elbow room. Most of these stores are geared to adults, because this is the heart of D.C.'s private business sector (as opposed to the federal government). Due north, the neighborhood known as **Dupont Circle** attracts browsers and buyers with its many galleries and one-of-a-kind, sometimes left-of-center retail establishments. Dupont Circle and nearby Adams–Morgan (whose hub is 18th Street and Columbia Road) have the most individualized shops. Head to either for shopping as entertainment.

Georgetown fans out from Wisconsin Avenue and M Street NW. It has always been a haven for shopping mavens and an in-place for teenagers to congregate. While their parents drop green in the fashionable clothing and houseware boutiques, kids can shop for affordable souvenir T-shirts and cool clothing at Urban Outfitters on M Street and H&M, among the 75 voguish stores at the **Shops at Georgetown Park.** While many mourn the proliferation of souvenir, record, and chain stores such as American Eagle Outfitters, Gap, and Banana Republic that have eclipsed the old-time establishments, young people lap it up. Some things haven't changed, however. Georgetown is still a numero-uno draw for local and visiting teenagers, especially on weekends.

STORE HOURS   Most stores in the D.C. area open Monday through Saturday at 9:30 or 10am. Closing hours are harder to pinpoint, however. Most stores are also open on Sunday and have extended hours one or more evenings during the week. Hours can change at the manager's whim (and often do). Before setting out for a particular destination, you should always call ahead to make sure it'll be open.

SALES TAX   The sales tax on all merchandise (including clothing) in D.C. is 5.75%.

2 Shopping A to Z
ARTS & CRAFTS

Indian Craft Shop *(Finds)*   Although not widely known, this is an excellent source (since 1938!) for authentic, top-quality Native American arts and crafts. It is also educational. Shop for weavings, sand paintings, kachinas, fetish carvings, and elaborate basketry and jewelry from the more than 45 tribal groups within the United States that this shop represents. Don't miss the section that's devoted to the Artist of the Month. Then stop at the Department of the Interior Museum across the hall (p. 159) or look around the building at the many murals adorning the walls. To gain entrance to the building, you need photo ID—a passport, government ID, or driver's license. Kids need no ID, just an adult with them. Prices start at $3.50 for a beaded pin. Beaded necklaces start at $6.50. Of interest to young shoppers are books, dolls, and small stone carvings. A cafeteria on the lower level is open for breakfast and lunch. If you don't want to walk here, take a taxi; street parking is limited. Open Monday through Friday from 8:30am to 4:30pm and on the third Saturday of the month, 10am to 4pm. Closed federal holidays. Department of the Interior, 18th and C sts. NW, Room 1023. © 202/208-4056. www.indiancraftshop.com. Metro: Farragut West and then south 6 blocks on 18th St. to C St. entrance.

Pearl   Billed as the "world's largest discount art supplier," Pearl is a gem, with materials for craft projects, art supplies, and art kits for children. We're talking paints, easels, canvas, felt squares, gold leaf, glitter, chenille stems, staple and glue guns, and everything in between for creative people. The hours are Monday through Saturday from 10am to 8pm and Sunday from 11am to 6pm. Pearl has a second location in Federal Plaza, 12266 Rockville Pike, Rockville, Maryland (© **301/816-2900**). 5695 Telegraph Rd., Alexandria, VA. © **703/960-3900**. www.pearlpaint.com. Metro: Huntington and then a 5-min. walk.

Plaza Artist Materials   Plaza Artist Materials has "everything your art desires," with a wide array of fine art, drawing, and drafting supplies and children's art kits. This is doodlers' paradise—hundreds of marking pens in enough colors to make a rainbow blush. Open Monday through Friday from 9am to 6:30pm, Saturday 9am to 5pm, and Sunday from noon to 5pm. Branch stores are located in Silver Spring, Bethesda, Rockville, Baltimore, and Towson, Maryland, as well as in Fairfax and Richmond, Virginia. 1990 K St. NW. On the 2nd level. © **202/331-7090**. www.pla-za.com. Metro: Farragut West and then a 3-block walk.

Sullivan's Art Supplies *(Finds)*   Sullivan's draws dabblers and professionals alike. The well-stocked space adjacent to Sullivan's Toy Store (p. 235) has all the basic oils, acrylics, watercolors, canvasses, and brushes that a mini-Picasso or Cassatt could desire, plus craft materials. Open Monday, Tuesday, Thursday, and Saturday from 10am to 6pm; Wednesday and Friday from 10am to 7pm; and Sunday noon to 5pm. 3412 Wisconsin Ave. NW. © **202/362-1343**. Metro: Tenleytown and then walk or take any no. 30 bus 1 mile south.

Washington, D.C. Shopping

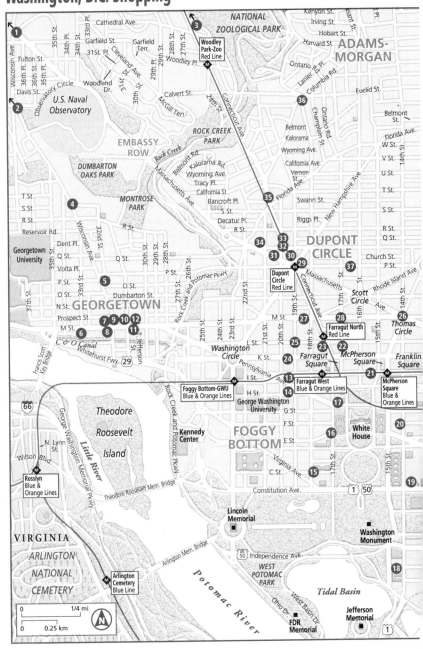

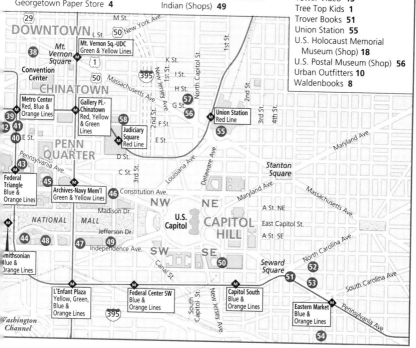

Torpedo Factory Art Center   Kids enjoy watching the potters, sculptors, stained-glass artisans, and other craftspeople do their thing in 84 working studios at this renovated World War I munitions plant. One-of-a-kind items are priced fairly (some would say that many are underpriced). Open daily (except for major holidays) from 10am to 5pm and the second Thursday of each month from 6 to 9pm. 105 N. Union St., Alexandria, VA. (C) 703/838-4565. www.torpedofactory.org. Metro: King St. and then walk 1½ miles, or take the DASH bus ($1) to King and Fairfax and then walk 2 blocks east on King (toward river) and left 1 block to Cameron.

BALLOONS

The Georgetown Paper Store   Blow up a plain or stamped balloon, or save your breath and let the Paper Store fill it with helium. The store also carries a variety of plain and decorated Mylars, as well as the biggest selection of party supplies and favors in the neighborhood. Between 8 and 9am Monday through Saturday, the store gives a 10% discount on all merchandise. Open Monday through Saturday 8am to 8pm, Sunday 10am to 6pm. 1803 Wisconsin Ave. NW. at S St. (C) 202/333-3200. Metro: Foggy Bottom and then take the Georgetown Shuttle to Wisconsin Ave. and M St.; walk 1 block north on Wisconsin.

BOOKS

Although the stores listed below have a wonderful selection of children's books, don't overlook the following chains, some of which also host story hours: **Barnes & Noble,** 3040 M St. NW (corner of Thomas Jefferson St.; (C) 202/965-9880); a smaller B&N store is at 12th and E sts., NW ((C) 202/347-0176); **B. Dalton,** 50 Massachusetts Ave. NE, in Union Station ((C) 202/289-1750); **Borders,** at 600 14th St. NW ((C) 202/737-1385) and 1801 K St. NW ((C) 202/466-4999); **Trover Shop,** 221 Pennsylvania Ave. SE ((C) 202/547-2665); and **Waldenbooks,** Shops at Georgetown Park, 3222 M St. NW ((C) 202/333-8033).

A Likely Story Children's Bookstore   More than 20,000 titles are shelved in this 2,000-square-foot, award-winning children's bookstore, just 2 blocks from the King Street Metro stop. Special programs include story times (Tues at 11am for kids up to 2 years, Wed at 11am for kids 2 and up, Sat at 11am for kids 3 and up; reservations urged), workshops, almost-daily special summer events (book discussions, craft projects, and author visits), and weekend author appearances. There's a play area for younger kids so that older siblings can take their time making selections. Call to be placed on the mailing list for the store's newsletter, showcasing new titles and upcoming events. Open Monday through Wednesday and Friday and Saturday from 10am to 6pm, Thursday from 10am to 8pm, and Sunday from 1 to 5pm. 1555 King St., between Harvard and Peyton sts., Alexandria, VA. (C) 703/836-2498. www.alikelystorybooks.com. Metro: King St. and then walk 2 blocks east (toward Potomac River).

Audubon Sanctuary Shop   Located at the Woodend Nature Center on the site of the headquarters of the Audubon Naturalist Society (p. 204), this shop is just a wing-beat away from a nature preserve where youngsters can search for their favorite feathered friends. There's even a toy-filled room for your fledglings. Prices range from $1 to $30 for bird books (geared to different age groups), DVDs, animal puppets, puzzles, plush animals, and birds. It's open Monday through Friday from 10am to 5pm, Saturday 9am to 5pm, and Sunday from noon to 5pm. 8940 Jones Mill Rd., Chevy Chase, MD. (C) 301/652-3606. www.audubonnaturalist.org.

Borders for Kids (in Borders) *(Finds)*   This popular bookstore within a bookstore has a large play and performance area and an expanded program of children's events, making it a popular family destination. Storytelling takes place most Saturdays at 11am and 1:30pm. The glass-enclosed coffee bar is the perfect place to unwind with a new book and an espresso while the children are occupied. The hours are Monday through Saturday from 9am to 11pm, and Sunday from 9am to 9pm. White Flint Mall, 11301 Rockville Pike, North Bethesda, MD. © 301/816-1067. www.borders.com. Metro: White Flint.

Discovery Channel Store   I double-dare you to walk out of one of these attractive, made-for-browsing stores (part of a national chain) without buying at least one exquisitely photographed nature volume to be enjoyed by the entire family. Open Monday through Saturday from 10am to 9pm and Sunday from noon to 6pm. Other branches are located at the Fashion Centre at Pentagon City, 1100 S. Hayes St., Arlington, Virginia (© 703/413-3425), and Tysons Corner Center, Vienna, Virginia (© 703/748-0980). Union Station, 50 Massachusetts Ave. NE. © 202/842-3700. www.discovery channelstore.com. Metro: Union Station.

Fairy Godmother *(Finds)*   This shoebox-size toys-and-books store on Capitol Hill is often overlooked, unfortunately. Stop in before or after you tour the Hill or grab a bite at Eastern Market, a few doors away. In addition to a wide selection of kids' books (infants through young adults), the shop carries story tapes, toys, hand and finger puppets, and crafts. Inquire about story time and other special events. Hours are Monday noon to 6pm (even fairy godmothers need a rest once in a while), Tuesday through Friday 11am to 6pm, and Saturday 10am to 5pm. Open Sunday seasonally. Ask about extended pre-Christmas hours. 319 7th St. SE. © 202/547-5474. Metro: Eastern Market.

Government Printing Office Bookstore   Perhaps you didn't know it, but the world's largest printer is right in the heart of little ole D.C. No matter how weird or way-out your kids' hobbies are, or whether they're researching a term paper or trying to decide which CD player to buy, they can probably find a book or pamphlet on the subject here. With more than 17,000 titles currently in print, the GPO is a browser's heaven and also sells photographs, prints, lithographs, and posters. Open Monday through Friday from 8am to 4:30pm. 710 N. Capitol St. NW, at H St. © 202/512-0132. http://bookstore.gpo.gov. Metro: Union Station.

Kramerbooks & Afterwords   At this ever-popular Washington institution, you don't have to wait to get back to your hotel room to begin reading. Just step into the cafe at the rear of the bookstore ("Afterwords"—get it?) for a meal or a snack, and sink your teeth into a juicy new book. Kramerbooks stocks a respectable selection of children's books, as well as quality paperbacks and major foreign works. Kids love this place. You will, too. Open Monday through Thursday from 7:30am to 1am and 'round the clock Friday morning until 1am Monday. 1517 Connecticut Ave. NW, between Q St. and Dupont Circle. © 202/387-1400. www.kramers.com. Metro: Dupont Circle.

National Zoo Store   Before or after visiting your family's favorite beasties in the zoo, browse the many animal-specific books for toddlers on up. Surely you will want at least one panda book as a souvenir. Then try to resist plush toys, caps, T-shirts, scarves, posters, tree ornaments, and jewelry. Located near the zoo's main entrance, it's open every day but Christmas from 9am to 5pm. Visitor Center, Education Building, 3001 Connecticut Ave. NW. © 202/633-4800. http://nationalzoo.si.edu. Metro: Woodley Park–Zoo/Adams–Morgan or Cleveland Park and then walk ⅓ mile uphill, or take northbound L2 or L4 bus.

Olsson's Books & Records   Olsson's is a class act. The knowledgeable staff and background classical music contribute to the soothing, nurturing atmosphere. Olsson's has an excellent selection of kids' books, including several shelves of classics. All recommendations are tagged. Open Monday through Saturday from 10am to 10pm and Sunday from noon to 7pm.

Additional locations include 1200 F St. at Metro Center (② 202/393-1853 for records, or 202/347-3686 for books); 418 7th St. NW in the Lansburgh building (② 202/638-7610); Bethesda, Maryland (② 301/652-3336); Arlington, Virginia (② 703/525-4227 books, 703/525-3507 records); Old Town Alexandria, Virginia (② 703/684-0077 books, 703/684-0030 records), and Reagan National Airport (② 703/417-1087). All locations are open daily; call for hours. 1307 19th St. NW, just off Dupont Circle. ② **202/785-2662** for records or **202/785-1133** for books. www.olssons.com. Metro: Dupont Circle.

Politics and Prose *(Finds)*   Browse through the bestsellers and nonfiction at this true book-lover's haunt while Junior selects something suitable for bedtime reading from the children's department. Besides an extensive collection of titles for kids of all ages, Politics and Prose hosts visits by children's book authors and has story time for preschoolers, most Mondays at 10:30am. The shop also fills mail and phone orders promptly. Open Sunday from 10am to 8pm, Monday to Thursday 9am to 10pm, and Friday and Saturday 9am to 11pm. 5015 Connecticut Ave. NW (between Fessenden St. and Nebraska Ave.). ② **202/364-1919.** www.politics-prose.com. Metro: Van Ness and then take L2 or L4 bus north ¾ mile.

Tree Top Kids   Not just a toy store, Tree Top hosts many kid-pleasing events to complement the well-stocked shelves. Throughout the year, children's authors and costumed storybook characters pay a visit, and the store hosts story time for preschoolers. Books fill more than 2,000 square feet of space. No home with children should be without Tree Top's book catalog. Hours are Monday through Saturday from 9:30am to 5:30pm. Other locations in Arlington, Fairfax Corner, and McLean, Virginia. 3301 New Mexico Ave. (Foxhall Square) NW. ② **202/244-3500.** www.treetopkids.com. Directions: North on Massachusetts Ave. to Ward Circle, three-quarters way around circle to Nebraska Ave., left at New Mexico Ave. Metro: Tenleytown and then take A.U. (American University) shuttle bus to campus. Cross Nebraska Ave. to Foxhall Square at New Mexico Ave.

COMIC BOOKS

Beyond Comics   If comic books are your kids' idea of the classics, step into Beyond Comics in Georgetown, where you'll also find comic T-shirts and games. A recorded phone message lists all the new comics stocked since the previous week. Open Monday and Tuesday 11am to 8pm, Wednesday 10am to 9pm, Thursday and Friday from 11am to 9pm, Saturday 10:30am to 9pm, and Sunday from 11am to 6pm. 1419 Wisconsin Ave. ② **202/333-8650** or 202/333-8651. www.beyondcomics.com. Metro: Foggy Bottom and then take Georgetown Shuttle to 30th and M sts.

Big Planet Comics   Big Planet carries the latest X-Men, Disney, and Archie comics, along with vintage Nancy-and-Sluggo and Popeye for Mom and Dad. Comic cards are also available in Big Planet's quarters on one floor of a row house. Open Monday, Tuesday, Thursday, and Friday from 11am to 7pm; Wednesday 11am to 8pm; Saturday from 11am to 6pm; and Sunday from noon to 5pm. Big Planet has branches at 4908 Fairmont Ave., Bethesda, Maryland (② **301/654-6856**), and 426 Maple Ave., Vienna, Virginia (② **703/242-9412**). 3145 Dumbarton Ave. NW. ② **202/342-1961.** www.bigplanetcomics.com. Metro: Foggy Bottom and then take Georgetown shuttle.

DEPARTMENT STORES

One department store *not* in D.C. is still worth noting: **Nordstrom** (at the Galleria at Tysons II, 2255 International Dr., McLean, Virginia, ✆ **703/761-1121;** Pentagon City, 1400 S. Hayes St., Arlington, Virginia, ✆ **703/415-1121;** and Montgomery Mall, Bethesda, Maryland, ✆ **301/365-4111**).

IN D.C.

H&M   H&M (Hennes & Mauritz), the Swedish retailer with stores in New York, Philadelphia, and Delaware (and maybe Mars by the time you read this), is known for its hip and reasonably priced merchandise under its own labels. H&M employs about 100 designers and buys in bulk to keep costs down. The merchandise in the downtown, F Street location is geared to kids up to 14 years old and their families. Office wear geared to D.C.'s sartorially conservative workforce is in abundance, and the store has a maternity department. The (smaller) Georgetown store, at the Shops at Georgetown Park (✆ **202/298-6792**), has more stylish gear and caters to area teens and college students. There's also a branch at Tysons Corner Center (✆ **703/556-8120**). Hours at the F St. (downtown) store are Monday through Saturday 10am to 8pm, Sunday from noon to 6pm. 1025 F St. NW (at 11th st.). ✆ **202/347-3306.** www.hm.com. Metro: Metro Center or Federal Triangle.

Macy's   By the time you read this, Hecht's, a Washington shopping institution, will be Macy's. But the merchandise will remain the same. In this five-story store, the salespeople are friendly and accommodating, and the selection of children's clothing is abundant and moderately priced for all age groups. If you forgot to pack something, you will find it here and not get ripped off in the process. A Ticketmaster outlet is at this store, conveniently located at Metro Center. Just take the escalator upstairs. Open Monday through Saturday from 10am to 8pm, and Sunday from noon to 6pm. 1201 G St. NW (at 12th St.) ✆ **202/628-6661.** www.macys.com. Metro: Metro Center.

Lord & Taylor   This smaller version of New York's famous Fifth Avenue store is located 1 block from the Friendship Heights Metro stop near Chevy Chase, Maryland. You'll find high-quality children's merchandise, and most is fairly priced. Lord & Taylor's frequent sales are legendary. Open Monday through Thursday from 10am to 9:30pm, Friday 10am to 10pm, Saturday 10am to 9:30pm, and Sunday from 11am to 7pm. There are stores in the Maryland and Virginia suburbs too. 5225 Western Ave. NW. ✆ **202/362-9600.** www.lordantaylor.com. Metro: Friendship Heights.

Neiman Marcus   People with deep pockets shop for their kids' and grandkids' clothes at Neiman's. They also feed them USDA prime sirloin steak rather than hamburger. What can I say? Sometimes I go here and pretend I'm rich. The children's departments tend to be low on merchandise and high on prices. Be forewarned: The store does not accept MasterCard or Visa. Open Monday through Friday from 10am to 8pm, Saturday from 10am to 7pm, and Sunday from noon to 6pm. There are 2 hours of free parking in the underground garage and limited street parking. There is also a Neiman Marcus branch at the Galleria at Tysons II in McLean, Virginia (✆ **703/761-1600**). Mazza Gallerie, 5300 Wisconsin Ave. NW. ✆ **202/966-9700.** www.neimanmarcus.com. Metro: Friendship Heights.

IN THE SUBURBS

Bloomingdale's   A Bloomie's is a Bloomie's is a Bloomie's. Taking a cue from their famous trendsetting mother in New York, these two suburban offspring do their best to satisfy the buying appetites of material girls and boys. If you're unfamiliar with the store, I think you'll be pleasantly surprised. Sure, there's plenty of over-the-top (in design and price) imports, but most of the styles and prices are competitive. Open Monday through Saturday from 10am to 9:30pm and Sunday from noon to 6pm. There is a second location at Tysons Corner, McLean, Virginia (© **703/556-4600**). White Flint Mall, North Bethesda, MD. © 301/984-4600. www.bloomingdales.com. Metro: White Flint.

Saks Fifth Avenue   When my kids were little, I loved to shop for them at Saks, but I had to stop when their duds began costing more than mine. If yours tolerate your taste, and you can tolerate the stiff prices, head for Saks. The Metro is a short walk, and there's plenty of parking, free when you remember to validate the ticket in the store. (***Note:*** If Dad is feeling left out, just down the street is Saks' men's store, at Mazza Gallerie, 5300 Wisconsin Ave. NW, © **202/363-2059**.) Open Monday through Wednesday and Friday from 10am to 7pm, Thursday from 10am to 8pm, Saturday from 10am to 6pm, and Sunday from noon to 6pm. 5555 Wisconsin Ave., Chevy Chase, MD. © 301/657-9000. www.saksfifthavenue.com. Metro: Friendship Heights.

FARMERS' MARKETS
Since they were young, my kids have liked to wander through the outdoor markets in D.C. that sell seasonal produce, plants and flowers, homemade foodstuffs, baked goods, crafts, and secondhand stuff. Now they take their kids. And if I promise to behave, they take me, too. It's a great way to get a taste of the country without leaving the city. Here are a few of our favorites.

Adams–Morgan Market   Locally grown produce, as well as homemade baked goods and crafts, are featured at this market. Go early for the best selection. Open May through late December, Saturday only, from 8am to 1pm. Columbia Rd. and 18th St. NW. Metro: Dupont Circle or Woodley Park–Zoo/Adams–Morgan and then a 15- to 20-min. walk.

Eastern Market Farmers Market   In the historic building, the atmosphere is part bazaar, part neighborhood happening. You'll find everything from hog jowls and oxtails, prepared foods to go, farm-fresh produce and baked goods to plants and flowers, aged beef and seafood. Most kids like the action. Outdoors on weekends, kids over 4 or so seem to gravitate to the tables laid out with secondhand clothes and home accessories, crafts, knickknacks, and funky jewelry. On summer weekends, when farmers' stalls line the street, there is often music and other entertainment. If you don't mind the wait, have breakfast or lunch inside at Market Lunch (p. 87). Open Tuesday through Sunday from 8am to 5pm. 225 7th St. SE, between North Carolina Ave. and C St. © 202/543-7793. Metro: Eastern Market.

FreshFarm Farmers Market   Every Sunday, about 30 regional farmers sell at this Dupont Circle location what they themselves have grown or made: vegetables, fruits, herbs, eggs, cheeses, flowers, and baked goods. No middlemen here! You can even pick up fragrant handcrafted soap. For info on other FreshFarm Markets (Foggy Bottom, H Street, the Penn Quarter, and Silver Spring, Maryland), call or check the website. Open Sundays year-round. Late March to mid-December from 9am to 1pm; January through March from 10am to 1pm. 1500 block of 20th St. between Massachusetts Ave. and Q St. © 202/362-8889. www.freshfarmmarket.org. Metro: Dupont Circle (Q St./north entrance).

FASHIONS
Benetton Kids   The Italian-based company sells comfortable, trendsetting clothing through its franchise stores all over the world. Chances are, your teenage daughters are

familiar with it already. This shop is devoted to kids from 6 months to 12 years. Hours are Monday through Saturday from 9:30am to 9pm, and Sunday from noon to 6pm. A second Benetton is at 1666 Connecticut Ave., at R St. NW (☎ **202/232-1770**). 3222 M St. (in Georgetown Park). ☎ 202/333-4140. www.benetton.com. Metro: Foggy Bottom and then a 20-min. walk or the Georgetown Connection shuttle.

Full of Beans   Full of Beans is full of garb for girls and boys (in infant sizes to size 16). The charming neighborhood shop, which draws customers from other D.C. neighborhoods and the 'burbs, carries its own line of cotton clothing that's durable, attractive, and moderately priced. You'll also find unusual gifts—one-of-a-kind items not found in the average toy store. Full of Beans is near Ramer's Shoes (see "Shoes," later in this chapter), on upper Connecticut Avenue, so you should check out both stores before leaving the area. "Beans" is open Monday through Saturday from 10am to 5:30pm. Call about seasonal Sunday hours, usually from 11am to 3pm. 5502 Connecticut Ave. NW. ☎ 202/362-8566. Metro: Friendship Heights and then a 10-min. walk.

Gap Kids and Baby Gap   The same classic denim and casual wear made famous by the "senior" Gap is in D.C. for babies (newborn–24 months) and kids (sizes 2–12). If your hometown doesn't have a Gap Kids, stock up on everything from denim diaper covers to tough-wearing jeans. Open Monday through Friday from 10am to 8pm, Saturday from 10am to 6pm, and Sunday from noon to 5pm. There are other Gap Kids locations at 5430 Wisconsin Ave., Chevy Chase, Maryland (☎ **301/718-0886**), and at 1267 Wisconsin Ave. NW (☎ **202/333-2411**), as well as several more in suburban malls. 2000 Pennsylvania Ave. NW. ☎ 202/429-8711. www.gap.com. Metro: Foggy Bottom.

KBaby   This is one of those service-oriented boutiques that offers monogramming, a gift registry, and gift wrapping—a welcome change from most kids-apparel stores, where they hand you a box and maybe a piece of tissue so you can do it yourself. Come here for layette and nursery-related items, not-your-run-of-the-mill infant and toddler clothing, and special gifts for babies and new moms. It's open Monday through Saturday 11am to 7pm, Sunday noon to 5pm. 3112 M St. NW. ☎ 202/333-3939. www.kbaby.com. Metro: Foggy Bottom and then a 15-min. walk or Georgetown Connection shuttle.

Kid's Closet *(Finds*   I love this shop. It's full of durable, attractive, well-priced kids' wear for boys and girls (Carter's, Osh Kosh, and Absorba, for example) in sizes from 3 months 1 year. Best of all, a salesperson offers help immediately. Reminds me of the good old days. The store also carries accessories and must-haves, such as colorful jewelry and ballet costumes for little girls, and has lots of cute gifts, too. Open Monday through Friday from 10am to 6pm, and Saturday from 11am to 5pm. 1226 Connecticut Ave. NW. ☎ 202/429-9247. Metro: Farragut North or Dupont Circle.

Urban Outfitters   Attention, all teens (and their parents): If you like trendy, stylish clothing and funky but functional accessories for your room, all priced so they won't eat up next year's allowance, you'll love Urban Outfitters, which has women's and men's clothing and shoes. Check out the "renewal" section—a money-saving rather than a religious experience. Open Monday through Saturday from 10am to 10pm, and Sunday from noon to 9pm. A second location is at 737 7th St. NW (between G and H sts.; ☎ **202/737-0259**). 3111 M St. NW. ☎ 202/342-1012. www.urbanoutfitters.com. Metro: Foggy Bottom and then a 15- to 20-min. walk, or the Georgetown Connection shuttle or any no. 30 bus from Pennsylvania Ave.

Why Not? *(Finds*   Why not, indeed! Be sure to include this upbeat shop in your visit to Old Town Alexandria. In business for close to 30 years, Why Not? stocks infant to size-14 clothing for girls, and infant through size 7 clothes for boys. But it doesn't end there. A wide range of colorful and creatively displayed toys and books fills the two-story space. No wonder Why Not? continues to draw shoppers from around the Belt-way. Open Monday through Thursday from 10am to 5:30pm, Friday and Saturday from 10am to 9pm, and Sunday from noon to 5pm (shorter hours in winter). 200 King St., Alexandria, VA. ✆ **703/548-2080.** Metro: King St. and then bus for 1½ miles to King and Fairfax sts.; walk 1 block east toward river.

FURNITURE & ACCESSORIES

In addition to the specialty stores below, try **IKEA,** with stores at 10100 Baltimore Ave., College Park, Maryland (✆ 301/345-6552), and 2901 Potomac Mills Circle, Woodbridge, Virginia (✆ 703/494-4532); any of the nine **Burlington Coat Factory** locations in Maryland and Virginia; or **e.a. kids** (part of Ethan Allen), in Rockville, Maryland (✆ 301/984-4360; www.ethanallen.com), and Vienna, Virginia (✆ 703/356-6405). There's also **Great Beginnings,** Gaithersburg, Maryland (✆ 301/417-9702; www.greatbeginnings.net); and **Kids' Habitat,** Rockville, Maryland (✆ 301/231-6039; www.kidshabitat.com), and Fairfax, Virginia (✆ 703/803-9451).

Bellini Juvenile Designer Furniture They're not kidding about the designer part. Bellini sells top-of-the-line, European-crafted cribs, bunk beds, trundles, and bedding accessories to furnish little princes and princesses with beautiful beginnings. Open Monday through Saturday from 10am to 6pm, and Sunday from noon to 5pm. 12113 Rockville Pike, Rockville, MD. ✆ **301/770-3944.** www.bellini.com. Metro: Twinbrook.

Buy Buy Baby This is nirvana for parents-to-be, new moms and dads, and doting grandparents. On two floors, you'll find everything, and I mean everything, for your bundle from heaven: layette items, strollers, cribs, diapers, clothing, toys, books, and then some. It's positively addictive. There's also a location in Springfield Plaza, Springfield, Virginia (✆ **703/923-9797**). Open Monday through Saturday from 9:30am to 9:30pm, and Sunday from 11am to 6pm. 1683 Rockville Pike (South Congressional Plaza), Rockville, MD. ✆ **301/984-1122.** www.buybuybaby.com. Metro: Twinbrook (½ mile from the store).

HAIRCUTS

Cartoon Cuts One memory I'd like to erase: taking my kids for haircuts. They screamed and carried on like they were undergoing open-heart surgery without anesthesia. At Cartoon Cuts, today's tots get trimmed while glued to the video monitors at each station. Elephant faucets have rinsing hoses for trunks so that shampooing becomes an event instead of a dreaded chore. The shops also host birthday and karaoke parties where little snippets can be made over into their favorite rock stars. Haircuts cost $16 (entertainment included). Hours vary according to branch. Four locations are in suburban Maryland, and six locations are in northern Virginia. Check the Yellow Pages or website. Tysons Corner Center, McLean, VA. ✆ **703/748-CUTS.** www.cartooncuts.com. Metro: West Falls Church and then bus no. 28A or 28B.

Hair Cuttery For a walk-in cut, wash, and blow-dry—$16 (wet), $24 with blow dry—you can't beat it. For kids 8 and under. it's $10 wet, $14 with blow-dry. Anyone (male, female, androgynous) with extra-long hair may have to pay a little more. Men, women, and children are equally welcome. Besides the one D.C. location, there are several in the Maryland and Virginia suburbs. 1645 Connecticut Ave. NW. ✆ **202/232-9685.** www.haircuttery.com. Metro: Dupont Circle.

JEWELRY & BEADS

Beadazzled   There are plenty of baubles, bangles, and beads, plus everything in beadwork supplies and classes to keep you and yours from getting strung out. I love this place. It's great for browsing and shopping. The staff is incredibly good-natured and helpful. You may also purchase earrings, necklaces, and crafts that others have labored over. Open Monday through Saturday from 10am to 8pm, and Sunday from 11am to 6pm. A second store is located at Tysons Corner Center in Virginia (© **703/ 848-2323**). 1507 Connecticut Ave. NW. © **202/265-BEAD (2323)**. www.beadazzled.net. Metro: Dupont Circle.

KITES

Air and Space Museum Store   Your kids will walk on air when they see the selection of kites ($4–$70) sold here. Kites are color coded according to degree of difficulty. Mine ("for 7-year-olds") is a breeze to fly. Launch your purchase on the Mall just outside the museum. Open daily from 10am to 5:30pm, with extended summer hours. 6th St. and Independence Ave. SW. © **202/357-1387**. www.smithsonianstore.com. Metro: L'Enfant Plaza.

MALLS

What did kids do before malls? I have vague recollections of hopscotch, marbles, and stickball, but hanging out at malls is the no. 1 pastime of today's youth. You'll have no trouble keeping your little mall rats satisfied in the D.C. area—just bring lots of money. Besides these listings, there are countless malls in suburban Maryland and Virginia. (Maybe you'll want to keep this bit of information to yourself.)

The Chevy Chase Pavilion   Just a block away from the Friendship Heights Metro station, this bright and compact three-tiered mall is geared more to adults than children at the moment; however, there are some noted exceptions. There's a branch of Sam Goody for tapes and CDs, B. Dalton, J. Crew, Rainbow Hair Designers, Simply Wireless, Talbots and Talbots Petites, Sunglass Hut, and several upper-end shops carrying women's and men's fashions. You'll also find a branch of the Pottery Barn and Georgette Klinger if you want to disappear for a massage, haircut, or makeover. Stein Mart carries brand-name, upscale apparel for the whole family.

Betweenthe Cheesecake Factory (free parking with validation) and the Atrium Cafes–Food Court (Jay's Ice Cream & Deli, Panama Rice Bowl, Sbarro, Starbucks coffee, Truffles Belgian Chocolates, and Café Panini), you have no excuse to leave here hungry. Hours are Monday through Saturday from 10am to 8pm, and Sunday from noon to 5pm. 5335 Wisconsin Ave. NW, at Military Rd. © **202/686-5335**. www.ccpavilion.com. Metro: Friendship Heights.

Fashion Centre at Pentagon City   My Virginia relatives and friends swear by the Fashion Centre (and I know some big-time shoppers on the other side of the Potomac). **Macy's** and **Nordstrom** are the anchors in this three-level mall, which boasts more than 160 stores. You'll find upscalers such as Abercrombie & Fitch, Britches of Georgetown, the Custom Shop, the Museum Company, the Coach Store, Georgetown Leather Design, and Joan and David. One of the few area Scribner's bookstores is here, as is Brentano's.

Of special interest to the *kinder* are the Athlete's Foot, Champs Sports, Foot Locker, The Children's Place, the Game Keeper, Baby Gap, Gap Kids and Gap, Gymboree, Kay-Bee Toys, The Limited Too, America!, the Disney Store, Sony Theatres (count 'em, 6!), Sunglass Hut, and the Sweet Factory.

When you need a break or wear out your wallet, stop for a light bite in the Food Court, with a lucky 13 selections to choose from, or relax at one of the mall's seven restaurants. Johnny Rocket's is always a family favorite with burgers, shakes, and other nutritious offerings that make America great. The Grill at the Ritz-Carlton holds up the high end of the spectrum. Several cafes, L and N Seafood Grill, and Ruby Tuesday—all serving moderately priced fare—fall in between. Hours are Monday through Saturday from 10am to 9:30pm and Sunday from 11am to 6pm, with extended hours during the Christmas season. 1100 South Hayes St., Arlington, VA. ✆ **703/415-2400**. Metro: Pentagon City.

Mazza Gallerie   While **Neiman Marcus, Saks Men's Store,** and most of the bou-tiquey shops at this trés chic four-level mall will be out of reach for little people's tastes and allowances, there are some exceptions, such as **Filene's Basement** (for kids who fit into adult sizes) and a Foot Locker store. f.y.e. sells music, movies, CDs, and DVDs. Slip into McDonald's when a Big Mac attack hits.

The Old Post Office Pavilion   It's nearly 200 feet straight up from the floor to the skylit canopy of this three-level complex of retail shops and restaurants housed in a 100-year-old office building. Don't expect to do serious shopping here, but there are some novelty and souvenir shops that your kids might enjoy.

Ride the glass elevator to the tower observation deck (at the 270-ft. level) for a spec-tacular 360° view of downtown and the environs, and then inspect the 10 massive bells (a bicentennial gift from England) that are rung on state occasions. **TICKET-place** is the place to buy half-price theater tickets to many of the performances in the D.C. area. When it's time for a bite to eat, you can choose from the Bagel Express, Georgetown Deli, Greek Taverna, Enrico's Pizza, Indian Delight, Market Chicken, Quick Pita, and Pavilion Burrito. And if your blood sugar is running low, stop at one of the ice-cream or yogurt stands for a pick-me-up.

Free entertainment—puppet shows, music, mime, singing, and dancing—is pre-sented daily in the West Atrium. The shops are open March through August Monday through Saturday from 10am to 8pm, and Sunday from noon to 7pm; and Septem-ber through February Monday through Saturday from 10am to 7pm, and Sunday from noon to 6pm. The restaurants usually stay open an hour or two later than the retail shops. There are three entrances: 10th and 12th streets NW, and Pennsylvania Avenue (at 11th St.). 1100 Pennsylvania Ave. NW. ✆ **202/289-4224**. www.oldpostofficedc.com. Metro: Federal Triangle.

Potomac Mills   The Potomac Mills discount shopping mall is the top tourist attrac-tion in Virginia. Honest. Not even Mr. Jefferson's Monticello, Mount Vernon, or Para-mount's King's Dominion draws the numbers that PM does. It's not unusual for more than 30,000 salivating shoppers, credit cards in hand, to lighten their wallets in the 1.2-million-square-foot mall daily. In addition to discount outlets for many nationally known department stores, you'll find about 250 specialty shops and the warehouse-size **IKEA** for attractive, well-priced furniture (some assembly required), toys, and housewares. A caveat: Know ahead of time the average retail prices of the items you seek. It's not all bargains here, and some of the merchandise is out of season or irreg-ular. Hours are Monday through Saturday from 10am to 9:30pm, and Sunday from 11am to 7pm. Off I-95 at 2700 Potomac Mills Circle, Prince William, VA. ✆ **703/643-1770**. www. potomacmills.com. Directions: Drive south on I-95 into Virginia, and take Dale City Exit 156.

The Shops at Georgetown Park   This handsome multilevel complex (complete with a stylish brick Victorian interior with skylights, fountains, chandeliers, and plantings) has more than 75 upscale shops. For apparel, teens dig H&M, Express, and J. Crew. Benet-ton Kids and Zerododici of Benetton, Mrs. Field's Cookies, The Magical Animal, Fit to a Tee, The Sharper Image, Sunglass Hut, lilthingamajigs (toys and games), and Walden-books will please the kids most. Have a snack or meal from the Canal Walk Food Court or Dean & Deluca. Open Monday through Saturday from 10am to 9pm and Sunday from noon to 6pm. Discounted garage parking with a $10 purchase. 3222 M St. NW., at Wisconsin Ave. 🕐 202/298-5577. Metro: Foggy Bottom.

The Shops at National Place   When you're following the Inaugural Parade route along Pennsylvania Avenue or sightseeing on the Mall, you can take a small shopping break at this complex attached to the J. W. Marriott Hotel and the National Press Building. Look for some of those "must-have" souvenirs, or stop at Eat at National Place, a food court with Five Guys (hamburgers, hot dogs, fries), Kabuki (Japanese), Quizno's (sandwiches), Slice of Italy (pizza), Naan and Beyond (Indian), and Mei Wah Express (Chinese). Shops are open Monday through Saturday from 10am to 7pm, and Sunday from noon to 5pm. Food court is open Monday through Saturday from 11am to 7pm, closed Sunday. 529 14th St. NW. 🕐 202/783-9090. Metro: Metro Center. Entrance on F St. NW, between 13th and 14th sts., or via the J. W. Marriott.

Tysons Corner Center   This well-known mall is about 30 minutes from D.C. in Vienna, Virginia. The latest expansion opened in September 2005 (as if it were not large enough before). Among the 230 shops here are five major anchor stores: **Bloomingdale's, Nordstrom, Lord & Taylor, L.L. Bean,** and **Macy's.** Other notable empo-ria of interest to kids include the Discovery Channel Store, H&M, Build-A-Bear, Disney Store, Banana Republic, and Gap. The more than 30 restaurants, which run the gamut from Rainforest Café to California Pizza Kitchen, and eight movie theaters make this a good choice for an afternoon shopping spree followed by a relaxing fam-ily dinner and a film. There's free parking for more than 10,000 cars. Open Monday through Sunday from 10am to 9pm. 1961 Chain Bridge Rd., at Rte. 7, Vienna, VA. 🕐 703/893-9400. Metro: West Falls Church and then bus no. 28A or 28B (runs every half-hour on the hour/half-hour).

Union Station   Union Station is a top tourist draw for area and visiting families, not just a departure/arrival spot for Amtrak travelers. I still marvel at the magnificent architecture, inspired by the Baths of Diocletian that were built in third-century Rome. When you're done admiring the marble and gilt, hunker down for something good to eat at Au Bon Pain, Café Renee, Corner Bakery Café, America, and Johnny Rockets, or at one or more of the nearly three dozen eateries in the lower-level Food Court; or one of the stand-alone, table-service restaurants in or near the Main Hall. Do leave room for Vaccaro's pastries. (Love those chocolate-filled cannoli!) Nearly 75 shops are scattered between two levels. Of particular note: Alamo Flags (state, inter-national, and novelty flags), America's Finest (armed services souvenirs), America's Spirit (souvenirs, political memorabilia), Appalachian Spring (wooden toys, blocks and games; soft toys and baby gifts among the beautiful handcrafted items for the home), Destination D.C. (souvenirs), B. Dalton (general and local-interest books), Echo Gallery (expensive handmade dolls), Flights of Fancy (toys), Brookstone (gadg-ets, electronics), Lids (hats), and Out of Left Field (local team clothing and souvenirs).

Still have time to kill? Buy tickets for Tourmobile, the Old Town Trolley, or a Grayline sightseeing tour. Catch nine different movies in the cinema complex. Open Monday through Saturday from 10am to 9pm, and Sunday from noon to 6pm. 50 Massachusetts Ave. NE. 🕐 202/371-9441. www.unionstationdc.com. Metro: Union Station.

Museum Stores

Museum stores are prime sources for educational books, gift items, crafts, and souvenirs (nothing tacky here—this is quality stuff) from all over the world. The Smithsonian museum stores are usually open daily from 10am to 5:30pm, sometimes with extended hours. You can get a sense of Smithsonian museum-store merchandise at its website: www.smithsonianstore.com. Independent museum and gallery shops have varying hours, so call ahead.

Anacostia Museum, 1901 Fort Place SE (© **202/287-3414**). Books about Africa, and African-inspired toys, dolls, textiles, and crafts.

Arthur M. Sackler and Freer Galleries, 1050 Independence Ave. SW (© **202/357-4880**). Asian and African art reproductions, crafts, gifts, and books.

Arts and Industries Building, 900 Jefferson Dr. SW (© **202/357-1369**). Victoriana, miniatures, wooden toys, and Smithsonian gift catalog.

Corcoran Gallery of Art, 500 17th St. NW (© **202/639-1790**). Art books, posters, and jewelry.

Hirshhorn Museum, Independence Avenue and 7th Street SW (© **202/357-1429**). Contemporary art books and monographs, toys, jewelry, and some art supplies.

John F. Kennedy Center for the Performing Arts, 2700 F St. NW (© **202/416-8346**). Posters, videos, and performing-arts memorabilia.

Library of Congress, 1st Street SE, between Independence Avenue and C Street (© **202/707-0204**). Books, books, and more books, as well as specialized library-oriented items.

National Air and Space Museum, Independence Avenue and 7th Street SW (© **202/357-1387**). Flying toys (including kites); space-, flight-, and science-related books; videos; memorabilia; and freeze-dried ice cream.

National Archives, 7th Street and Pennsylvania Avenue NW (© **202/501-5235**). Books on genealogy, campaign buttons, and famous documents (replicas only!).

Westfield Shoppingtown Montgomery   For those of us who shopped here 20 and 30 years ago, it will always be Montgomery Mall. Smaller than some of the mega-malls, you don't need an atlas to find your way around. The mall is chock full of family-oriented stores that sell quality merchandise at (usually) bearable prices. And there's a **Nordstrom,** which needs no introduction, that has a "Mothers' Room" with a changing table and diaper vending machine.

Of interest to little people are The Children's Place, Gap Kids, Spencer's Gifts, Talbot Kids, the Discovery Channel Store, Kay-Bee Toys, Gymboree (kids' wear), The Limited Too (for girls sizes 4–16), Stride Rite, B. Dalton, and Waldenbooks.

Take your pick of about a dozen eateries in the Boulevard Cafés and five sit-down restaurants, including California Pizza Kitchen, Slade's, Burger King, and Legal Sea Foods. You can also catch a flick at one of the three P & G Cinemas. The mall is open Monday through Saturday from 10am to 9:30pm, and Sunday from 11am to 6pm. 7101 Democracy Blvd., Bethesda, MD. © **301/469-6025.** Metro: Grosvenor and then take the no. 47 bus.

National Building Museum, 401 F St. NW (✆ **202/272-7706**). Architectural toys, crafts, books, desktop accessories, and graphics.

National Gallery of Art, 4th and 6th streets at Constitution Avenue NW (✆ **202/737-4215**). Posters, art books, games, stationery, and journals.

National Geographic Society, 17th and M streets NW (✆ **202/857-7588**). Maps, toys, globes, DVDs, and back issues of *National Geographic* magazine.

National Museum of African Art, 950 Independence Ave. SW (✆ **202/786-2147**). African-inspired accessories, crafts, toys, and tapes.

National Museum of American Art, 8th and G streets NW (✆ **202/357-1545**). *Masterpieces of American Art* coloring book, picture frames, and jewelry.

National Museum of American History, 14th Street and Constitution Avenue NW (✆ **202/357-1527**). Americana, contemporary crafts, books, games, toys, and videos.

National Museum of Natural History, 10th Street and Constitution Avenue NW (✆ **202/357-1537**). Ethnic crafts, gems and minerals, dinosaur toys, clothing, jewelry, and books.

National Museum of Women in the Arts, 1250 New York Ave. NW (✆ **202/783-7994**). Notepaper, books, and calendars.

National Postal Museum, 2 Massachusetts Ave. NE. (✆ **202/633-8181**). Postal-history merchandise and stamps for collectors.

National Zoo, 3001 Connecticut Ave. NW (✆ **202/673-4800**). Animal-inspired books, toys, clothing, and crafts.

Phillips Collection, 1600 21st St. NW (✆ **202/667-6106**). Art books, toys, and jewelry.

Renwick Gallery, 17th Street and Pennsylvania Avenue NW (✆ **202/357-1445**). Crafts, jewelry, and how-to books.

U.S. Holocaust Memorial Museum, 100 Raoul Wallenberg Pl. (15th St.) SW (✆ **202/488-0400**). Books, tapes, and Judaica.

MAPS

ADC Map & Travel Center   The center of the local cartophiles' universe for more than 40 years, the former Map Store (remodeled and renamed in 1998) has something for all age levels: wood puzzles of the continents and the United States; inflatable and traditional globes; atlases, road and street maps; and even a world wastebasket for those who want to learn some geography while filing trash. Open Monday through Thursday from 9am to 6:30pm, Friday from 9am to 5:30pm, and Saturday from 11am to 5pm. 1636 I St. NW. ✆ 202/628-2608. Metro: Farragut North or Farragut West.

National Geographic Store   Here you'll find the society's distinctive and finely detailed maps, as well as all National Geographic publications. You can also purchase globes, toys, games, puzzles, videos, DVDs, and back issues of *National Geographic* magazine. Open Monday through Saturday from 9am to 5pm, and Sunday from 10am to 5pm. Closed Dec. 25. 17th and M sts. NW. ✆ 202/857-7588. www.nationalgeographic. com. Metro: Farragut North.

NATURE TREASURES

Discovery Channel Store   See the listing under "Books," earlier in this chapter.

National Museum of Natural History Gift Shops   Many locals shop at this museum store for their holiday gifts. This is one of my personal favorites. You'll find an interesting collection of books—many geared to young people—on natural history and anthropology, as well as fossil reproduction kits; shells; minerals; and attractive and distinctive clothing, crafts, and jewelry. On the ground floor is a much smaller store with puppets, activity books, puzzles, and plush animals. Open daily from 10am to 5:30pm, except December 25. Extended summer hours are determined annually. 10th St. and Constitution Ave. NW. © 202/357-1535. Metro: Federal Triangle.

NEWSPAPERS & MAGAZINES

Newsroom   Still going strong after more than 20 years, the Newsroom is a mainstay of the Dupont Circle area. Come here for more than 200 domestic and foreign newspapers and numerous magazines in 20 languages. The foreign-language department has books and tapes for kids who want to learn other languages. Open daily from 7am to 9pm. 1803 Connecticut Ave. NW. © 202/332-1489. Metro: Dupont Circle.

Satellite Newspapers   This Dutch firm has kiosks at several hotels (currently, the Latham, Omni Shoreham, Marriott Wardman Park, and Hamilton Crowne Plaza) that allow you to access and print many foreign newspapers. Using the touch screen, merely scroll to the paper of your choice, insert your credit card, and—voila!—2 minutes later, the paper will print. Magic! For more info, go to www.pepcworldwide.com.

PERFORMING-ARTS SUPPLIES

Backstage   Kids with an interest in the performing arts should take a cue from Washington thespians, musicians, and dancers and go to Backstage. Under one roof is everything that professionals and amateurs need to get their act together: an award-winning selection of scripts and books, costumes, dancewear, makeup, sheet music, and books. I've enjoyed browsing Backstage since my college days. Open Monday through Saturday from 11am to 7pm (extended pre-Halloween hours). 545 8th St. SE (at G St.). © 202/544-5744. www.backstagebooks.com. Metro: Eastern Market.

POSTERS

Movie Madness   Whether they're looking for a poster of their all-time favorite movie or pop singing group to decorate a bedroom wall, kids will find it at Movie Madness. In this little basement shop are several hundred *original* posters (some mounted or framed), reprints, life-size standups, and movie and rock-star postcards, as well as plenty of oldie-but-goodie posters to accompany Mom and Dad down Memory Lane. Open Monday and Thursday noon to 8pm, Wednesday 3pm to 8pm, Friday and Saturday noon to 9pm, and Sunday noon to 6pm. Closed Tuesday. 1083 Thomas Jefferson Ave. (at M St.) NW. © 202/337-7064. Metro: Foggy Bottom and then a 15-min. walk or the Georgetown Connection shuttle.

SHOES

Georgetown has a lot of shoe stores that your teenagers will especially love. When you're in other neighborhoods, try the stores listed below.

Fleet Feet   Adams–Morgan's total sports/fitness shop carries all the top names for fleet-footed kids and adults, beginning with size 2. Open Monday through Friday from 10am to 8pm, Saturday from 10am to 7pm, and Sunday from noon to 4pm. Limited street parking. 1841 Columbia Rd. NW. 🄯 202/387-3888. www.dcnet.com/fleetfeet. Metro: Woodley Park–Zoo/Adams–Morgan and then walk ½ mile across Calvert Street Bridge, or take bus no. 42.

Kids Foot Locker   It's never too early to pick up a wee-size Redskins jacket, sweats, T-shirt, or shorts along with kids' shoes from newborn to size 6. Some clothing to size 20 is also featured. Because there aren't any of these in D.C., you'll have to hotfoot it to Tysons Corner Center in Virginia, or Prince George's Plaza, St. Charles Towne Center, or Laurel Centre Mall in Maryland. The Tysons, Virginia, store is open Monday through Saturday from 10am to 9:30pm, and Sunday from 10am to 6:30pm. 1961 Chain Bridge Rd., at Rte. 7, Vienna, VA. 🄯 703/506-9020. Metro: West Falls Church and then bus no. 28A or 28B (runs every half-hour on the hour/half-hour).

Ramer's Shoes *(Finds)*   Ramer's, the friendly neighborhood shoe store, is 1 block below Chevy Chase Circle. Come here for Keds, Little Capezio, Sebago's, Sperry's, Stride Rite, and more in sizes 0 to 4½, widths AA to EEE. Then drop in at Full of Beans for kids' duds, 2 blocks south (see the description under "Fashions"). Open Monday through Friday from 9:30am to 6pm, and Saturday from 9:30am to 5:30pm. 3810 Northampton St. NW, off Connecticut Ave. 🄯 202/244-2288. Metro: Friendship Heights, and then a 10-min. walk east on Western Ave. to Chevy Chase Circle (Conn. Ave.); right 1 block and right on Northampton (store is half a block off Conn. Ave.).

SPORTS GEAR

Big Wheel Bikes   Rent a hybrid, mountain bike, 12-speed, or tandem by the hour or day at Big Wheel's original location in Georgetown. Then pedal on the nearby C&O Canal towpath. In business since 1971, Big Wheel also sells recreational, touring, and racing bikes, and a full line of children's bikes. Open Monday through Friday from 11am to 7pm, and Saturday and Sunday from 10am to 6pm. Other locations are Arlington, Virginia (🄯 703/522-1110); Old Town, Alexandria, Virginia (🄯 703/739-2300); and Bethesda, Maryland (🄯 301/652-0192). 1034 33rd St. NW in Georgetown. 🄯 202/337-0254. www.bigwheelbikes.com. Metro: Foggy Bottom and then a 15-min. walk or Georgetown Connection shuttle to 33rd St.

Drilling Tennis and Golf Shop   This shop is owned by Fred Drilling, Washington Tennis Patrons' Hall of Famer, and the staff will see that your youngster comes out swinging the right racket from the store's selection for 2- to 12-year-olds. There's no kids' clothing here, but you'll find plenty of accessories. Open Monday through Friday from 9:30am to 6pm, and Saturday from 10am to 4pm. 1040 17th St. NW. 🄯 202/737-1100. Metro: Farragut North or Farragut West.

Hudson Trail Outfitters   Hudson Trail is a magnet for teens who are into hiking, biking, camping, and other outdoor activities. Quality gear, clothing, and accessories fill the rustic shop, and the youthful, healthy-looking salespeople are helpful and laid back. Open Monday through Saturday from 10am to 9pm, and Sunday from 11am to 6pm. Locations in Maryland and Virginia, too. 4530 Wisconsin Ave. NW. 🄯 202/363-9810. www.hudsontrail.com. Metro: Tenleytown and then 1 block south.

National Diving Center   Even the youngest snorkeler can be outfitted here. The manager says that kids can snorkel as soon as they can swim, but potential scuba divers must be 12. Kids train alongside adults; there are no special kids-only classes. Besides stocking snorkeling and diving gear, the shop offers lessons (with open-water checkouts in Pennsylvania rock quarries) and diving trips off the Atlantic coast and in the

Caribbean. Open Tuesday through Friday from 11am to 7pm, and Saturday 11am to 6pm; closed on Sunday. Call for specific details and schedules. 4932 Wisconsin Ave. NW. ℂ 202/363-6123. www.dcdivers.com. Metro: Friendship Heights and then walk 4 blocks south.

Ski Center   Schuss down to the oldest ski shop in the area. The Ski Center has had an edge on ski stuff in the D.C. area since 1959 and can outfit all the younger members of your ski team with equipment and clothing. You can also buy or rent in-line skates here. Call for seasonal details. Open Monday through Wednesday and Friday from 11am to 6pm, Thursday until 8pm, Saturday from 10am to 5:30pm, and Sunday from noon to 5pm (extended hours around Christmas). 4300 Fordham Rd. (at Massachusetts Ave. and 49th St. NW). ℂ 202/966-4474. www.skicenter.com. Metro: Dupont Circle and then northbound N-4 bus on Mass. Ave. to 49th St.

TAPES, RECORDS & CDS

Olsson's Books & Records *Finds*   It isn't called Olsson's Books & Records for nothing. Most kids head straight for the neon ROCK ROOM sign, where there's always someone to give assistance. If your kids dig classical music, Olsson's has one of the best selections in the city—and if the store doesn't have something, it'll order it. For hard-to-get items, Olsson's mail-order department is open from 9:30am to 7pm (ℂ **800/ 989-8084**). Open Monday through Wednesday from 10am to 10pm, Thursday through Saturday from 10am to 10:30pm, and Sunday from noon to 8pm. See listing under "Books," earlier in this chapter, for additional locations. 1307 19th St. NW, off Dupont Circle. ℂ 202/785-2662. www.olssons.com. Metro: Dupont Circle.

Sam Goody   An offshoot of the long-popular New York record store, Sam Goody has numerous stores in and around D.C. Come here for CDs, DVDs, movies, and games. Open Monday through Saturday from 10am to 9pm, and Sunday from 10am to 6pm. There are other locations at the Chevy Chase Pavilion (call for hours; ℂ **202/ 364-1957**) and in numerous suburban locations. Union Station, 50 Massachusetts Ave. NE. ℂ 202/289-1405. www.samgoody.com. Metro: Union Station.

Tower Records   "Awesome" is my son's succinct appraisal of Tower Records. And it is—a two-story, 18,000-square-foot supermarket of records, tapes, and CDs in Foggy Bottom on the campus of George Washington University. Tower carries standard Barney, Sesame Street, and Disney fare, plus several hundred kid-oriented selections for its discerning junior clientele. Open Monday through Saturday from 9am to midnight and on Sunday from 10am to 10pm. 2000 Pennsylvania Ave. NW. ℂ 202/331-2400. www.tower.com. Metro: Foggy Bottom or Farragut West.

TOYS

Barston's Child's Play   Child's Play carries Playmobil, Lego, Lundby dollhouse furniture, and Gund stuffed animals. The software, book, and art sections have been expanded in recent years. This place is fun to visit. Many of the displayed toys invite touching—and you don't have to be under 3 feet tall to appreciate them. There's free parking behind the shop. Open Monday through Wednesday and Friday from 9:30am to 7pm, Thursday from 9:30am to 8pm, Saturday from 9:30am to 6pm, and Sunday from noon to 5pm. 5536 Connecticut Ave. NW. ℂ 202/244-3602. Metro: Friendship Heights and then a 10-min. walk.

Fairy Godmother   See entry under "Books," earlier in this chapter.

Sullivan's Toy Store *(Finds)*   If a film crew were scouting for a typical neighborhood toy store, Sullivan's would be the ideal. A feeling of comfortable disarray pervades this Cleveland Park shop. Kids of all ages will find plenty to toy with on the well-stocked shelves. There's a huge selection of art supplies, too. The most fun can be had up front, where 60 glass jars are filled with 99¢ toys. Open Monday and Tuesday 10am to 6pm, Wednesday through Friday from 10am to 7pm, Saturday from 10am to 6pm, and Sunday from noon to 5pm. 3412 Wisconsin Ave. NW. ℂ 202/362-1343. Metro: Tenleytown and then take any no. 30 bus south.

Toys "R" Us   Santa's Workshop doesn't hold a candle to this megastore of toys, games, seasonal sports gear and outdoor equipment, juvenile furniture, and party supplies. Shop early or late unless you have nerves of steel and can withstand hundreds of tiny voices whining "I want!" a cappella. Open Monday through Saturday from 9am to 10pm, and Sunday from 10am to 6pm. There are 11 other branches in suburban Maryland and Virginia. 11810 Rockville Pike, at Old Georgetown Rd., Rockville, MD. ℂ 301/770-3376. www.toysrus.com. Metro: Twinbrook and then a 10-min. walk south on Rockville Pike.

Tree Top Kids *(Finds)*   This charming shop, near the campus of American University, is known for its large selection of imported French dolls and baby toys, but you'll find everything from infants' crib toys to big kids' games and models stocked here. Besides toys, Tree Top sells books and clothes (in sizes 0–6). Ask for a copy of the shop's colorful toy and book catalogs. Kids who enroll in the Birthday Club are entitled to free balloons and 20% off their favorite item on their special day. Open Monday through Saturday from 9:30am to 5:30pm. One-hour free parking with validation in garage. There are other locations in suburban Virginia, at the Langley Shopping Center, 1382 Chain Bridge Rd., McLean, Virginia (ℂ 703/356-1400); Arlington, and Fairfax Corner. 3301 New Mexico Ave. NW. ℂ 202/244-3500. www.treetopkids.com. Metro: Tenleytown and then A.U. (American University) shuttle bus to campus (Nebraska and New Mexico aves. intersection).

T-SHIRTS
For a souvenir or gift T-shirt, check out the museum shops for top-quality shirts that wear like iron. Also check out the numerous vendors blanketing the area around the National Mall. Sometimes you can bargain with them, especially if you buy two or more. The shirts make good bargain souvenirs, but don't leave them in the dryer too long.

Fit to a Tee   This shop is crammed with oodles of souvenir and funny-message shirts for kids of all ages, in sizes infant through XXX large. If you're in a bad mood, a visit here will cheer you up. Open Monday through Saturday from 10am to 9pm, and Sunday from 11am to 6pm. Shops at Georgetown Park, 3222 M St. NW. ℂ 202/965-3650. Metro: Foggy Bottom and then 15-min. walk or the Georgetown Connection shuttle to Wisconsin and M sts.

Souvenir City   Check out the shirts, books, paperweights, mugs, and other D.C.-inspired tchotchkes when you're downtown near the Convention Center/FBI/Ford's Theatre/MCI Center. The kids are bound to go wild over all the merchandise, so you may want to give them an "allowance" up front. This place is definitely souvenir central. Open daily 10am to 7pm (usually extended hours Apr–Sept). 1001 K St. NW (between 10th and 11th sts.). ℂ 202/638-1836. Metro: Gallery Place-Chinatown and then a 3-block walk.

VIDEOS
Videotapes might be the next best thing to a babysitter—an ideal way to calm the kids after a frenetic day of sightseeing and buy a bit of quiet time for yourself. Before you run out to a video store, ask the front desk if they have videos to loan.

Blockbuster's   This chain has come on like, well, blockbusters in the last decade, and there seems to be no stopping it. All the branches have a special kids' section. You can rent VCRs that attach easily to a TV for around $20 for 3 nights (plus a $100 deposit). Call the desired branch for hours and directions. Other locations include 1639 P St. NW, Dupont Circle (𝄞 **202/232-2682**); 3519 Connecticut Ave. NW, Van Ness (𝄞 **202/363-9500**); and 410 8th St. SE, Capitol Hill (𝄞 **202/546-4044**). 2332 Wisconsin Ave. NW, Georgetown. 𝄞 **202/625-6200**. www.blockbuster.com. Metro: Foggy Bottom or Dupont Circle and then the Georgetown Connection shuttle to Wisconsin Ave. and Calvert St.

Tower Video   In the heart of Foggy Bottom, just 4 blocks from the White House, Tower rents and sells hundreds of children's videos, one of the largest selections in the city. Open Monday through Saturday from 9am to midnight and Sunday from 10am to 10pm. 2000 Pennsylvania Ave. NW, 20th St. entrance. 𝄞 **202/223-3900**. Metro: Foggy Bottom.

10

Entertainment for the Whole Family

Children's tastes in entertainment are as varied as their parents'. Some kids like watching the pros shoot hoops; others enjoy seeing lions and tigers jump through them. *Swan Lake* might transport some junior culture vultures, while their middle-brow siblings think it's far duckier to yuk it up in a comedy club. Whether your family's musical appetite runs to Beethoven, big bands, or the Backstreet Boys, you won't leave the table hungry after sampling Washington's cultural smorgasbord.

Once a sleepy southern town that shut down when the last government workers left their cubicles—around 9pm (on a good night!)—D.C. now hosts so many events that you'll be hard-pressed to choose from among them. We're second only to New York in the quality and quantity of our theatrical productions, musical offerings, and dance performances, which is why we try harder!

GETTING TICKETS

Depending on availability, you can pick up half-price tickets to many events the day of the performance *only* at **TICKETplace** (© **202/TICKETS;** www.ticketplace.org), on the mezzanine of the Old Post Office Pavilion at 12th Street and Pennsylvania Avenue NW (easily accessible by Metro from the Federal Triangle station 1 block away). A 12% service charge on the full face value of the ticket is added (so a $20 ticket costs $22.40—$20 plus a $2.40 fee). It's first come, first served. You can also purchase full-price tickets to future performances at the walk-up counter. Order tickets online at www.ticketplace.org, and you'll pay a 17% service fee, so the same $20 ticket will be $23.40 ($20 plus $3.40 service fee). More than 60 institutions participate in this service, sponsored by *The Washington Post* and the Cultural Alliance of Greater Washington. Cash, travelers checks, American Express, Discover, MasterCard, and Visa are accepted. TICKETplace is open Tuesday through Friday from 11am to 6pm, Saturday from 10am to 5pm. Tickets for Sunday and Monday events are sold on Saturday.

Full-price tickets to most performances and sporting events are also sold through **Ticketmaster** (© **202/432-SEAT;** www.ticketmaster.com), which also has outlets at all Hecht's department stores. Hecht's (which may be Macy's by the time you read this) flagship store is at 12th and G streets NW (Metro: Metro Center). If you know before you leave home that there's something special you want to see, you should call ahead to ensure that you get tickets.

Always ask about discounts for full-time students, persons with disabilities, and seniors. When you can't get the tickets you want through ordinary channels, there are several ticket brokers in town. They don't like being called "brokers," but that's what they are: They buy blocks of premium seats and resell them, usually with a hefty service charge attached. One that has been around a long time and is centrally located, just 4 blocks from the White House and near the Foggy Bottom Metro, is **Top Centre Ticket Service** at 2000 Pennsylvania Ave. (© **202/452-9040**). Also try **Great Seats** (© **301/985-6250;** www.greatseatsusa.com). Check the Yellow Pages and *Washington Post* classified ads for others.

The **MCI Center,** 601 F St. NW, at 7th and F streets (© **202/628-3200;** www. MCICenter.com), hosts sports events, family entertainment, and concerts by megastars. Britney, Sting, the Rolling Stones, and U2, to name-drop just a few, have played this giant 20,000-seat arena. MCI, occupying an entire city block between 6th and 7th, F and G streets, is responsible, in large part, for the blossoming of this once-seedy neighborhood that has gone decidedly upscale with new office space, condos, shops, and restaurants.

Buy tickets at the box office (open Mon–Sat 10am–5:30pm, Sun only when there is an event) or order online (www.mcicenter.com), where you'll pay a service fee. You may also purchase tickets (with a service fee) at **Ticketmaster** (© **202/432-SEAT;** www.ticketmaster.com). Seats at the 200 level have the best sight lines.

Arrive an hour early to allow for security checks, a pit stop (family restrooms are on every level), and finding your seat. I suggest leaving a few minutes before the closing buzzer. (***Insider's tip:*** Head for handicap-access doors, which are open to everyone.) Dress in layers, as some performers stipulate no air-conditioning in their contracts. Also, it can feel like a giant igloo during Caps hockey games. The food is pricey but

Freebies!

As part of the Kennedy Center's **Millennium Stage** project, free performances—by vocalists, musicians, actors, dancers, mimes, and performance artists—take place daily at 6pm, unless otherwise noted, in the Kennedy Center Grand Foyer (© 202/467-4600). I'm not talking amateur night! One evening I heard Melissa Manchester. Another time I caught NYC cabaret chanteuse Jaymie Meyer. Whenever I have tickets to a Ken Cen performance, I arrive early to enjoy the talent. (Sometimes it's better than what's in the theaters.) Kennedy Center for the Performing Arts, at the southern end of New Hampshire Ave. NW and Rock Creek Pkwy., © 800/444-1234 or 202/467-4600.

Daily from mid-June through early September, between noon and 1:30pm, catch a free concert at the Ronald Reagan Building. The series, known as **Live! on Woodrow Wilson Plaza** (between Constitution and Pennsylvania aves.), has featured such greats as jazz-funk vibraphonist Roy Ayers, the late, great jazz bassist Keter Betts, and blues singer Mary Lou Redmon. Also featured are performances by D.C. dance groups, comedians, and youth talent. Ronald Reagan Building and International Trade Center, 13th Street and Pennsylvania Ave. NW, © 202/312-1300; www.itcdc.com.

For more free entertainment, see "Military Band Concerts," and "The Old Post Office Pavilion," later in this chapter.

> **Tips Rest the Troops**
>
> If you have tickets to an evening event, consider ending your sightseeing in the midafternoon and enforcing a rest period—with extra points for napping—so that everyone will be "up" for a night on the town. To find out what's going on around town, check *The Washington Post* "Style" section Monday through Saturday, "Children's Events" in the *Weekend* magazine on Friday, and the "Show" section on Sunday. *Washingtonian* magazine and the *City Paper* are other good sources for entertainment listings.

adequate. Although there are concessions in the center, families are much better served by the neighborhood restaurants, where there is better value and more to choose from. If you want to eat before or after an event and have ample time, head for Chinatown (7th and H is the crossroads of D.C.'s miniscule Chinatown), or check out the slew of restaurants on 7th Street within a few blocks of the center. **Fuddruckers** (p. 93) is always a safe bet with kids.

1 Theater

The **John F. Kennedy Center for the Performing Arts** (© 800/444-1324 or 202/467-4600; www.kennedy-center.org) and the Washington Performing Arts Society (see below) have the highest visibility as presenters of family events, but numerous other cultural organizations and independent producers excel at delivering high-caliber entertainment suitable for young people and should not be overlooked. The Kennedy Center, Arena Stage, National Theatre, and Shakespeare Theatre offer student discounts. (It wouldn't hurt to ask other presenters about student tickets when you call—ticket policies have been known to change faster than the weather.)

The **Washington Performing Arts Society** (© 202/785-9727; www.wpas.org) has been presenting world-class performances in D.C. since 1965. Think of a top recording artist, musician, choral group, or dance company, and chances are good that they have performed in Washington under the auspices of the WPAS. Many of the hundreds of WPAS-sponsored performances are suitable for families. Recent family-friendly performances have included The Salzburg Marionettes and the Children of the Gospel Mass Choir.

From time to time, some D.C. area theaters offer **backstage tours,** where visitors can do things like enter rehearsal studios and dressing rooms, enjoy a demonstration of the sound and lighting equipment, and watch the hand-cranked fly lines raise and lower scenery. For youngsters, a behind-the-scenes tour is, in many instances, more fascinating than a live performance. Don't be surprised if, during your tour, the curtain goes up and your family is hogging the center-stage spotlight! At the Kennedy Center, hour-long tours of the theaters and public spaces are offered weekdays every 15 minutes between 10am and 5pm, Saturday and Sunday from 10am to 1pm (© 202/416-8341). To tour the National Theatre, you must have a group of 10 or more and call ahead (© 202/783-6854). Some of the theaters listed below offer tours and occasionally escort visitors backstage by special arrangement. Call the theaters directly for more information.

Adventure Theatre *(Finds)* A mix of original and familiar children's plays for 4- to 12-year-olds is presented year-round Saturday and Sunday at 1:30 and 3:30pm and weekdays between Christmas and New Years. The seven annual productions include original works and classics such as *The Lion, the Witch and the Wardrobe, Ferdinand the Bull,* and *The Wizard of Oz.*

Box-office hours are Monday through Friday from 9am to 5pm, and Saturday and Sunday from 10am to 4pm. Call to reserve tickets to individual performances. The distinctive theater with stadium-style seating was once a penny arcade on the grounds of a former amusement park. Cap the afternoon off with a ride on the Dentzel carousel, across from the theater. Glen Echo Park, MacArthur Blvd. at Goldsboro Rd., Glen Echo, MD. *C* **301/320-5331.** www.adventuretheatre.org. All seats $7. Directions: Take Massachusetts Ave. north into Maryland. Left at Goldsboro Rd. Left at MacArthur (park located at this intersection). Follow signs to parking. From suburbs: I-495/95 to Exit 39 (River Rd.) east (toward D.C.). Right at 5th traffic light (Goldsboro Rd.) to end. Right at MacArthur, and follow signs to Glen Echo Park parking. Closest Metro: Friendship Heights and then take taxi (much faster) or no. 29 Metrobus to stop at MacArthur Blvd. and Goldsboro Rd.

Alden Theatre The Alden offers a potpourri of kid-pleasing events and productions for children 3 and older by professional actors from September to June in the state-of-the-art Alden Theatre. Plays, puppet shows, music, and dance are performed various weekends during the school year, and the theater is only a 20-minute ride from downtown (in non–rush-hour traffic) with plenty of on-site parking. Call for specific show times and directions. McLean Community Center, 1234 Ingleside Ave., McLean, VA. *C* **703/790-9223.** www.mcleancenter.org. Box office open Tues–Sat. Prices vary with performance; student discounts. Free parking in the Community Center lot. Metro: West Falls Church (3½ miles away) and then taxi.

Arena Stage Many hit plays make it big at Arena Stage before moving to Broadway, and a roster of Arena "graduates" reads like a who's who of American theater. In one of his first roles, James Earl Jones starred here in the original production of *The Great White Hope.* If you want to introduce older children to drama at its finest, you don't have to look any further. Some productions are not suitable for young people, so call the theater for an educated opinion, and check the reviews in local papers before going with your children.

Under Arena's discount ticket program, "FiveTwentyFive," you may purchase $10 tickets to any performance (subject to availability) up to 5:25pm the day of the performance (for matinees, 5:25pm the day before). Tickets for students with a valid ID (except Sat evenings) are 35% off (one ticket per valid ID). One evening performance per production is designated as "College Night," when college students can purchase a ticket for $10. Seniors 60 and older always get 15% off. Box-office hours are 10am to 7pm. Maine Ave. and 6th St. SW. *C* **202/488-3300.** www.arenastage.org. Tickets $40–$68. Metro: Waterfront Station and then a 5-min. walk.

Capitol Steps Kids 10 and older who are politically savvy may enjoy this irreverent comedy troupe. (I love 'em, but I haven't seen 10 in a while.) With rapier wit, they skewer presidents, politicos, and Washington's weird bureaucratic mentality. Performances are Friday and Saturday at 7:30pm in the amphitheater of the Ronald Reagan Building and International Trade Center. Tickets can be purchased at the D.C. Visitor Information Center on the ground level of the building or through Ticketmaster. 1300 Pennsylvania Ave. NW *C* **202/312-1555.** www.capsteps.com. Tickets $34 main and mezzanine levels, $32 balcony. Metro: Federal Triangle.

Children's Theatre of Arlington Four plays *for* and *by* children are staged annually by this community theater group. *Narnia* (based on *The Lion, the Witch and the Wardrobe*) and *Sleeping Beauty* are examples of past productions. CTA also offers summer workshops for kids of all ages and classes during the school year. Thomas Jefferson Community Theatre, 125 S. Old Glebe Rd., Arlington, VA. (near Rte. 50 and Glebe Rd.). ℂ **703/548-1154.** Adults $10, seniors and kids, $8. Call for prices and directions.

Folger Theatre (at the Folger Shakespeare Library) All the world's a stage in this intimate 243-seat Elizabethan-style theater (celebrating its 75th birthday in 2007) in the shadow of the U.S. Capitol. Want your kids to ham it up with Hamlet? Then bring them to the three (a season) "Shake Up Your Saturdays" performance workshops (drama and improv) for kids 8 to 14 and their parents, offered on select Saturdays from 10am to noon (ℂ **202/544-7077**).

Full-scale renditions of Shakespeare's plays are among the offerings. Lectures, poetry and fiction readings, and family and education programs also fill the playbill at the Folger. This is home to The Folger Consort chamber ensemble and the annual Pen–Faulkner Awards for literature. Frolic at the Bard's birthday party open house, held annually the Sunday closest to April 23rd. Enjoy music, song, dance, storytelling, jugglers, and excerpts from the Bard's plays by local schoolchildren. Arrive early: The birthday cake, in the shape of the Globe Theater, serves only 1,000.

The gift shop sells *Shakespeare for Kids* and other versions of the classics, as well as tapes, CDs, videos, and posters. During the daily tours at 11am, you can peek in the theater. Otherwise, you have to attend a performance. The box office is open from 10am to 5pm. 201 E. Capitol St. SE. ℂ **202/544-7077**. www.folger.edu. Tickets $10–$40; student discounts available. Metro: Capitol South or Union Station.

Ford's Theatre From late November to early January, Ford's Theatre is the site of Dickens's *A Christmas Carol*. Many of the productions staged throughout the rest of the year are also suitable for families, with well-behaved kids 6 and older, but you should always check before going. John Astin and Charlotte Rae in *Leading Ladies* and the musical *Shenandoah* were among the shows during a recent season. Box-office hours are Monday 10am to 6pm, Tuesday to Friday 10am to 8pm, and Saturday and Sunday noon to 8pm. 511 10th St. NW, between E and F sts. ℂ **202/347-4833**. www.fordstheatre.org. Tickets $36–$52 orchestra, lower elsewhere; ask about student and senior discounts. Metro: Metro Center.

Imagination Stage Imagination Stage occupies a 40,000-square-foot, state-of-the-art facility with a 700-seat theater. The high quality of the hour-long shows (musicals and plays) by professionals for young audiences, 4 and older, every weekend (year-round) and holidays has held my grandkids' attention (and mine) several times. Seating on cushions for 60 kids is available at the front of the stage. Kudos to Bonnie Fogel, founder and executive director, who began the program in 1979 as a performing opportunity for kids in her neighborhood. Imagination Stage also offers acting classes, workshops, summer programs in the performing arts, and classes for children with special needs. A shop with theater-themed gifts and souvenirs and a cafe are open daily. Performances are Saturday and Sunday during the school year, every day but Monday in summer. 4908 Auburn Ave., Bethesda, MD. ℂ **301/280-1660**. www.imaginationstage.org. Tickets $10–$15; 5-play subscription $50–$80. Metro: Bethesda and then Ride-On bus no. 47 (toward Rockville) to corner Old Georgetown Rd. and Auburn Ave., right half a block; or walk 5 blocks north on Old Georgetown Rd., right at Auburn Ave. Driving: Wisconsin Ave. north to Bethesda, left at Old Georgetown Rd, go 5 blocks to right Auburn Ave. Parking in garage adjacent to theater is free on weekends.

Youth and Family Programs at the Kennedy Center   These include puppet shows, storytelling, and plays for kids 3 and up. Whoopi Goldberg's *Alice,* based on her book, was a sellout in 2005. Some performances are free (!), such as the kid-pleasing Chinese National Acrobatic Troupe in 2005. The hour-long performances are held throughout the year in the Terrace Theater and Theater Lab. Call for a current brochure, or check the website.

Through the Performance Plus series (talks, interviews, activities, and demos that enhance a performance), held before or immediately following regular Kennedy Center performances (© **202/416-8500**), series subscribers can travel backstage in "From Page to Stage" and learn how productions are developed. There is an additional cost for attending Performance Plus activities.

Box-office hours are Monday through Saturday from 10am to 9pm, and Sunday and holidays from noon to 9pm. Kennedy Center for the Performing Arts, at the southern end of New Hampshire Ave. NW and Rock Creek Pkwy. © **800/444-1324** or 202/467-4600; www.kennedy-center. org. Family Series tickets $48 (4-performance series); individual tickets vary. Youth and Family Programs tickets $5–$20. Metro: Foggy Bottom and then free Kennedy Center shuttle bus.

Mount Vernon Children's Community Theatre   Three major performances are presented annually by this noted ensemble in Virginia's Mount Vernon area. Classes and workshops are offered also. *Treasure Island* opened the 25th anniversary 2005–06 season. Reservations are advised a week or two in advance. Heritage Presbyterian Church, 8503 Fort Hunt Rd., Alexandria, VA. © **703/360-0686.** Prices $10 adults, $8 seniors and kids.

Now This! *Finds*   Every Saturday afternoon, families fill the historic Blair Mansion Inn for a delightful spin-off of the adult dinner-theater concept. Now This! includes lunch or dessert and interactive musical entertainment, so audience participation is key. A musical-comedy improv group performs the show, which is especially suited to young people. Kids' birthdays are their specialty. Reservations are a must. Show up by 1pm if you're lunching or by 1:30pm if you're having dessert. Plenty of on-site parking is available. Blair Mansion Inn, 7711 Eastern Ave., Silver Spring, MD. © **202/364-8292.** www.now thisimprov.com. Tickets (includes tax and tip) $18 lunch and show, $14 birthday cake and show, $11 dessert and show. Metro: Takoma or Silver Spring and then taxi.

The Old Post Office Pavilion   There's family entertainment weekdays during lunch and weekends 1–4 or 2–5pm as choirs, acting groups, clowns, jugglers, musicians, puppets, and dancers do their thing. Seating is limited. While you're here, enjoy lunch or dinner from the Food Court, and visit the clock tower on the 12th floor of this historic building. September through February hours are Monday through Saturday from 10am to 7pm, Sunday from noon to 6pm; March 1 through August 31 hours are Monday through Saturday from 10am to 9pm, Sundays from noon to 7pm. 1100 Pennsylvania Ave. NW. © **202/289-4224.** www.oldpostofficedc.com. Free admission. Metro: Federal Triangle.

Round House Theatre   Round House has two homes: the newer Bethesda facility, at the corner of the East–West Highway and Waverly Street, just a block from the Bethesda Metro (behind the building at 7501 Wisconsin Ave.), and in Silver Spring at 8641 Colesville Road next to the AFI Theatre. Call to see if the current show is appropriate for youngsters. The annual production of *A Broadway Christmas Carol,* a parody of the Dickens holiday classic, draws families by the sleighful. The show runs for 10 days beginning in mid-December. Special student matinees and related activities are offered for school groups. The Round House Theatre School has classes and workshops for kids from first grade through high school and a teen touring company. Ask about discounted student tickets. Box 30688, Bethesda, MD, 20824. ℂ **240/644-1100.** www.round-house. org. Tickets: Bethesda $40–$45; Silver Spring $30. Metro: Bethesda and then walk 1 block. Metro: Silver Spring and then walk 1½ blocks.)

Saturday Morning at the National *(Finds)*   October through April, two free shows are given Saturday at 9:30 and 11am. The well-attended series, begun in 1980, is as good as kids' entertainment gets. Past seasons featured puppet shows, presentations by naturalists and their animals, magicians, and celebrity readings of classic children's stories. I suggest arriving at 8:30am for the 9:30am show. If you don't make the cut, you should be good to go for the 11am show. Tickets are handed out a half-hour before the performance, and it's strictly first come, first seated. National Theatre, 1321 E St. NW, at Pennsylvania Ave. NW. ℂ **202/783-3372.** www.nationaltheatre.org. Free admission. Metro: Federal Triangle.

Shakespeare Theatre   Introduce your kids 10 and over to a play by Shakespeare or one of his contemporaries, as well as other cultural events, in the 447-seat venue in the Lansburgh Building. At a free open house every September, kids can see what goes on behind the scenes. Of course, the Shakespeare Theatre will be a major player in the citywide festival "Shakespeare in Washington" from January through June 2007. Artistic director Michael Kahn spearheaded the festival and serves as its curator. Participants include museums, opera, dance, and other theater companies. See the Kennedy Center website, www.kennedy-center.org, for schedules and ticket info. The free summertime **Shakespeare Free for All** productions (usually running 2–3 weeks, starting around Memorial Day) are always a big hit at the Carter Barron Amphitheater in Rock Creek Park, near the intersection of 16th Street and Colorado Avenue NW. Close to 4,000 tickets to each performance are available the day of the performance at the Shakespeare Theatre box office, *The Washington Post* (1150 15th St. NW), and the Carter Barron box office. For the latest, call the information hotline, ℂ **202/334-4790.** The amphitheater is a 15- to 20-minute taxi ride from the White House. Or take the S-2 or S-4 bus that runs on 16th Street (catch it near the White House); get off at Colorado Avenue, and walk 2 blocks. After a performance here, your kids might be hooked on the Bard. 450 7th St. NW. ℂ **202/547-1122.** www.shakespearetheatre.org. Tickets $15–$60; seniors 20% off; students 50% off 1 hour before curtain. Metro: Archives.

Wolf Trap Farm Park for the Performing Arts *(Finds)*   The best in musicals, groups, star performers, opera, and dance play on the stage of the sylvan 6,900-seat **Filene Center II** during the summer. *Riverdance, Rent,* Miami City Ballet, Garrison Keillor, Seal, and numerous pop, jazz, and country stars have all performed at Wolf Trap (the country's only national park devoted to the performing arts) in recent years. A large percentage of the music and dance events are suitable for those with kids in tow; use your judgment. Many families pack a picnic and blanket, and opt for the less expensive lawn seats, where small children are better tolerated.

Children's Theatre in the Woods has been entertaining youths in July and August with plays, stories, puppet shows, and clowning for more than 30 years. Two acts appear each week. Shows are at 10 and 11:15am on Tuesday through Saturday. The performer from the 10am program gives a hands-on workshop for kids 4 and older on Tuesday, Thursday, and Saturday at 11am. Tickets are a nominal $5 for everyone 3 and older, $8 for both shows on the same day. Reservations are required for all shows and workshops (ℂ **703/255-1827**). Food is not allowed in the theater, but plenty of tables and grassy hillsides accommodate picnickers. I suggest bringing bug spray for the mosquitoes.

The Wolf Trap box office is open Monday through Friday from 10am to 6pm, and weekends and holidays from noon to 6pm. Everyone, regardless of age, must have a ticket. 1624 Trap Rd., Vienna, VA. ✆ **703/255-1868.** Fax 703/255-1916. www.wolftrap.org. Tickets usually $15–$60; some events are free. Metro: West Falls Church (Virginia), then Wolf Trap Express Shuttle bus ($3 round-trip, summer only), which runs every 20 min. starting 2 hours before the performance for all events, except opera. The last bus leaves Wolf Trap at 11pm or 20 min. after the last performance. By car: I-495 to Exit 45 (old Exit 12B/Dulles Toll Road); stay on the local exit road, and then take Route 267 west to Exit 6 until you come to Wolf Trap. Limited free on-site parking available.

2 Dance

Washington draws the top modern, folk, professional ballet, and ethnic dance companies from all over the world. The Kennedy Center and Washington Performing Arts Society are leading presenters. In addition, the acclaimed Washington Ballet Company, as well as numerous modern and postmodern dance groups and several student companies—many of which are springboards for tomorrow's professionals—are headquartered here. All perform regularly in the area. Tickets for performances by local groups are usually nominally priced, often below $20. Most of the local performing groups are also affiliated with schools that offer a wide range of children's dance classes and workshops.

Dance Place *(Finds* Under executive and artistic director Carla Perlo's guiding light, Dance Place has been D.C.'s leading presenter of contemporary and ethnic dance for more than 25 years. Dance Place pulsates year-round with performances, classes, and workshops. Kids feel comfortable in the informal atmosphere of the performance space and are especially welcome at the six Sunday afternoon Family Series performances. The June weeklong Dance Africa D.C. Festival is a multisensory treat celebrating African culture through food, crafts, music, dance, and master classes. Other highlights include the January Tap Dance Festival, performances by Carla's Kids (Dance Place's junior company), and the Youth Festival, showcasing local talent. Box-office hours are Monday through Saturday from noon to 5pm. 3225 8th St. NE. ✆ **202/269-1600.** Fax 202/269-4103. www.danceplace.org. Tickets $7 kids 2–17, $15 students, $20 adults; kids free at Family Series performances. Metro: Brookland.

Fairfax Ballet The Fairfax Ballet, directed by Ilona and Thomas Russell, performs in the spring and during the Christmas season, when it presents *The Nutcracker* annually. The Russells are former professional dancers who established the company's affiliated school, the Russell School of Ballet, more than 30 years ago. Performance sites and ticket prices vary. 14119-Sullyfield Circle Ste. O, Chantilly, VA. ✆ **703/803-1055.** www.fairfax ballet.com.

Glen Echo Park Check out the Contra, Salsa, Swing, or Waltz classes Friday evenings year-round in the old Spanish Ballroom and Bumper Car Pavilion. Teens are welcome to join in the fun; younger kids can watch. Glen Echo Park, 7300 MacArthur Blvd., at Goldsboro Rd., Glen Echo, MD. ✆ **301/229-6022.** $8. Metro: Friendship Heights and then take no. 29 bus to stop at MacArthur Blvd. and Goldsboro Rd.

Maryland Youth Ballet *(Finds* The MYB, under the direction of Hortensia Fonseca and Michelle Lees, presents a superb family concert series twice a year (*The Nutcracker* in Dec and a wildcard in the spring) that features advanced ballet students, many of whom have gone on to successful professional careers. Performances are at the Montgomery College Performing Arts Center in Rockville, Maryland. Get your tickets early for its spirited production of *The Nutcracker,* suitable for kids 3 and older. Box-office hours are 9:30am to 7:30pm. 7702 Woodmont Ave., Bethesda, MD. © 301/652-2232. $22 adults, $16 students and seniors, reserved in advance. Metro: Bethesda for the studio Rockville for performances.

Metropolitan Ballet Theatre   Former New York City Ballet ballerina Suzanne Erlon established the MBT 13 years ago. Many of the young dancers are students at Erlon's North Potomac Ballet Academy and appear with visiting guest artists in *The Nutcracker* and other seasonal performances throughout the year. Children will enjoy the abundance of kids in the show as well as the colorful settings and spirited dancing. Performances are held at the Performing Arts Center of Montgomery College, Rockville Campus, Manakkee Street (off Rte. 355/Rockville Pike). Box-office hours are Monday through Friday from 10am to 6pm. 10076 Darnestown Rd., Rockville, MD. © 301/762-1757. www.metropolitanballettheatre.com. Tickets $18. Metro: Rockville Metro Center and then Ride-On Bus no. 46 or no. 55 to Performing Arts Center.

Virginia Ballet Company   For more than 30 years, the Virginia Ballet has been a fixture on the local dance scene. The company performs *The Nutcracker* annually at Northern Virginia Community College's Ernst Cultural Center in Annandale and a spring concert (two performances) one weekend in May. Classes are ongoing at the Springfield studio. Artistic directors and co-founders Oleg Tupine and Tania Rousseau are well-respected former dancers who run the company's school. 8001 Forbes Place, Springfield, VA. © 703/249-8227. www.virginiaballet.org. Prices $15–$25. Call for directions.

Washington Ballet   Washington's resident professional ballet company, directed by Septime Webre, presents a fall, winter, and spring series at the Kennedy Center's Eisenhower Theater. Tickets are $50 and up. In its 2005–06 season, the company presented Balanchine's *Serenade,* Twyla Tharp's *Nine Sinatra Songs,* Lars Lubovitch's *Othello,* and works by artistic director Webre. Programs are suitable for children over 8 (strictly my subjective opinion). The Family Series of three performances (including *The Nutcracker*) is $184 for front orchestra. Prices elsewhere are lower. *The Nutcracker,* a holiday staple, is presented at George Mason Center for the Arts in suburban Virginia and at D.C.'s Warner Theatre each December. 3515 Wisconsin Ave. NW. © 202/362-3606. www.washingtonballet.org. Prices vary with the performance; discounts for groups of 10 or more.

3 Music

CLASSICAL MUSIC

Washington is home to the National Symphony Orchestra, the Washington Opera, and numerous first-rate chamber orchestras and choral groups that give family and children's performances throughout the area. Guest artists also appear year-round at many sites in and around the city. Consult *The Washington Post* and *Washington Times* or call the individual presenters for performance dates, times, and ticket prices, which vary widely. Family performances, especially around holidays, are often free.

D.C. Youth Orchestra   This excellent youth orchestra sounds as harmonious as many professional ensembles. The spirited and talented group of young people (5–19 years old) has toured 15 countries and played for six U.S. presidents since its founding in 1960. Free concerts are every fifth or sixth Sunday. Call for dates. Coolidge High School, 5th and Sheridan sts. NW. © 202/723-1612. www.dcyop.org. Free. Take a taxi here.

Fairfax Choral Society   The youth 65-voice chorus, as well as the "parent" groups—an 80-voice chorus and 25-voice chorale—always draw an admiring crowd to performances at several Fairfax County sites. Box-office hours are 10am to 2pm. 4028 Hummer Rd., Annandale, VA. ℂ **703/642-3277.** www.fairfaxchoralsociety.org. Tickets $15–$28. Call for directions.

National Symphony Orchestra (NSO) *Finds*   The NSO presents about 200 concerts annually. Choose from several series geared to different age groups. At $45 for three performances of live orchestral music, it's almost too good to pass up. The availability of tickets for individual concerts varies. The **Family Concert Series** falls under the Kennedy Center umbrella, **Imagination Celebration.** The **Kinderkonzerts** (for kids 4 and up) introduce youngest family members to the basic ingredients of a symphony orchestra through classics such as *Peter and the Wolf,* and new works. During the summer, NSO treats families to free concerts on Memorial Day weekend, the Fourth of July, and Labor Day on the West Lawn of the U.S. Capitol. You can also catch them at Wolf Trap's Filene Center in Virginia (p. 243) and the Carter Barron Amphitheatre, 16th Street and Colorado Avenue NW, in the summer. No cameras or recording devices are permitted at Carter Barron. The amphitheater is a 15- to 20-minute taxi ride from the White House. Or take the S-2 or S-4 Metrobus that runs on 16th Street (catch it near the White House); get off at Colorado Avenue, and walk 2 blocks. Kennedy Center for the Performing Arts, at the southern end of New Hampshire Ave. NW and Rock Creek Pkwy. ℂ **800/444-1324** or 202/467-4600. www.kennedy-center.org/nso. Metro: Foggy Bottom and then free Kennedy Center shuttle.

Washington National Opera's Opera Camp for Kids   This 4-week summer camp, where children 10 to 14 receive vocal training and study the ins and outs of opera, culminates in several performances in mid-August at the Round House Theatre, 4545 East-West Highway, Bethesda, Maryland, and at the Kennedy Center's Millennium stage. Tickets are free, but reservations are required. ℂ **202/448-3465.** www.dc-opera.org.

Washington Performing Arts Society (WPAS)   Washington's first presenter of cultural events—concerts by internationally acclaimed orchestras, soloists, chamber groups, and dance companies—also co-presents with about two dozen other arts presenters at numerous venues throughout the city. Performances by jazz and gospel singers and musicians, and contemporary dance companies usually appeal to youngsters more than solo concerts or chamber music. The annual **Children's Concert** (usually held in January) by D.C.'s own jazz/gospel group, Sweet Honey in the Rock, rocks! Ticket prices for the Children's Concert are $15; for other concerts, from $15 to $85 (for Yo-Yo Ma). Box-office hours are Monday through Friday from 9:30am to 5pm. 2000 L St. NW. ℂ **202/785-9727.** www.wpas.org. Call for directions.

MILITARY BAND CONCERTS

One of the perks of visiting Washington in the summer is enjoying the free band concerts held at several downtown venues. Call first to double-check times, because scheduling varies. During the rest of the year, watch local newspapers for information on military band concerts.

Marine Corps Friday Evening Parades *Finds*   Dress parades, Friday evenings from mid-May through August, get under way at 2045 hours (8:45pm). Reservations are required via e-mail; there is no phone. If you pass muster, arrive by 7:30pm. Arrive after 8pm, and it's likely you'll be turned away—reservation or not. Check the website for restrictions. U.S. Marine Barracks, 8th and I sts. SE. C 202/433-6060. www.mbw.usmc.mil/parades. Metro: Eastern Market and then a 10-min. walk.

Military Band Summer Concert Series   Attend a free outdoor concert by a U.S. military band Tuesday at the Ellipse (behind the White House) or Thursday at the U.S. Capitol (West Terrace), beginning at 8pm from Memorial Day through August. In past years, you could catch a concert almost nightly, but call first or check the website. Things can change faster than an *About face!* U.S. Capitol (West Terrace), the Ellipse (behind the White House). C 703/696-3399. www.army.mil/armyband. Free. Metro (to U.S. Capitol): Capitol South, and then a 10-min. walk. Metro (to Ellipse): Federal Triangle and then a 10-min. walk.

Carillon Concerts   Enjoy a free concert at Arlington National Cemetery on Saturday and holidays in April, May, and September from 2 to 4pm. June through August, the concerts are usually held Saturday from 6:30 to 8:30pm at the Marine Corps War Memorial (Iwo Jima Monument). Bring something to sit on. C 202/433-2927. www.drumcorps.mbw.usmc.mil. Free. Metro: Arlington Cemetery and then free shuttle buses.

Sunset Parade   It's first come, first served for lawn seats at the Marine Corps War Memorial, where you'll hear the 80-member Marine Drum and Bugle Corps and see precision drills Tuesday evening at 7pm from early June to mid-August. Shuttle buses run from the visitor center at Arlington Cemetery (a short walk from the Arlington Cemetery Metro stop), starting at 6pm. Iwo Jima Memorial, north end of Arlington Cemetery. C 202/433-2927. www.drumcorps.mbw.usmc.mil. Free. Metro: Arlington Cemetery and then shuttle.

Twilight Tattoo   Enjoy intricate military drills and precision marching along with selections by the U.S. Army Band on Wednesdays from mid-July to mid-August at 7pm. Arrive early to get a good seat. The Ellipse, south of the White House. C 202/685-3611. www.mdw.army.mil. Free. Metro: Federal Triangle and then a 10-min. walk.

BLUES, COUNTRY, FOLK & JAZZ

The Barns of Wolf Trap   Jazz, pop, country, folk, and bluegrass predominate from October to May on the grounds of this cozy center for the performing arts. The 200-year-old restored barn is not a place to bring babies, but the Barns invites school-agers to come with their parents and soak up a little history with the music, dance, and performance art in this charming, rustic setting. 1624 Trap Rd., Vienna, VA. C 703/938-2404, or 703/218-6500 to charge tickets. www.wolftrap.org. Tickets $18–$30; kids pay full price. Free parking. Metro: West Falls Church station, and then Wolf Trap Shuttle Bus (every 20 min. beginning 2 hours before show to 20 min. after; $5 round-trip).

Blues Alley   Washington's first and foremost jazz club for more than a quarter of a century has reverberated to Charlie Byrd, Eartha Kitt, Nancy Wilson, Wynton and Branford Marsalis, Maynard Ferguson, Joshua Redman, and hundreds of other jazz greats. There are two shows (8 and 10pm) weeknights and sometimes three on Friday and Saturday. Reservations are taken up to 2 months in advance, and seating is first come, first served. Box-office hours are noon to 10pm. Anyone well behaved over the age of 8 is welcome.

Dinner begins at 6pm, and you'll have no trouble gobbling up the $9 food or drink minimum. Blues Alley is smoke free. 1073 Wisconsin Ave. NW, in an alley behind M St. C 202/337-4141. www.bluesalley.com. Tickets $28–$35 (students pay half Sun–Thurs 10pm show), plus $9 food or drink minimum and a $2.25 surcharge for the Blues Alley Music Society. Metro: Foggy Bottom and then Georgetown Metro Connection shuttle or taxi.

Dubliner *(Finds)* The Dubliner is so fond of kids that it even has highchairs so that wee leprechauns can enjoy the spirited Irish music and classic pub food (but not the Guinness) along with Mom and Dad at this Capitol Hill fixture in the Phoenix Park Hotel. At night, come early. Things can get rowdy later on. The "For the Wee Folk" menu has grilled cheese, hot dog, hamburger, and chicken nuggets for $4.95. 4 F St. NW. © 202/737-3773. www.dublinerdc.com. No cover charge or minimum; entrees $7–$18 at dinner. Metro: Union Station and then a 2-min. walk.

4 Films

The Johnson IMAX Theater at the Natural History Museum *(Finds)* See beautifully photographed large-scale movies about the natural world, all in 3D! *T. Rex— Back to the Cretaceous* is for dinosaur lovers. *Into the Deep* is an awesome underwater journey. *Wild Safari: A South Africa Adventure* is as close to lions, leopards, and rhinos as you can get without traveling halfway around the world. There is a service charge if you order tickets by phone or on the Internet. Johnson IMAX Theater, 10th St. and Constitution Ave. NW. © 202/633-IMAX. www.smithsonian.org/IMAX. Tickets $8 adults, $6.50 2–11, $7 60 and older. Metro: Smithsonian or Federal Triangle.

The Langley IMAX Theater at the Air and Space Museum *(Finds)* If you're visiting the museum, stop at the box office first, preferably when it opens around 9:45am. The breathtaking films shown on the five-story IMAX screen frequently sell out, and after you've seen one, you'll know why. Tickets may be purchased up to 2 weeks in advance. *To Fly,* the first Langley Theater presentation, debuted in 1976 and still fills the house. The aerial shots, from an 1800s-era hot-air balloon, barnstormer, hang glider, and a Saturn-bound rocket, are guaranteed to knock your socks off. *Space Station 3D,* narrated by Tom Cruise, shows a space station 20 miles above Earth, the collaborative effort of 16 countries. *Fighter Pilot* documents the high-tech acrobatics of an F15-E. *Magnificent Desolation: Walking on the Moon* is an aerial valentine to the lunar landscape. With younger kids I'd opt for *To Fly,* with a running time of a half-hour; the other two are about 45 minutes each. There is a service charge if you order tickets by phone or on the Internet. Langley IMAX Theater, Independence Ave. and 7th St. SW. © 202/357-1686 or 202/357-1675. www. smithsonian.org/IMAX. Tickets $8 adults, $6.50 2–11 -year-olds and $7 60 and older. Metro: L'Enfant Plaza.

National Museum of African Art Call or check the website for a schedule of films and other events related to daily life, folktales, politics, and the art of Africa's rich and diverse culture. Films are 30 to 60 minutes long and suitable for older kids and their families. They are usually shown one or two Sundays a month at 2pm in the Learning Center Lecture Hall on the second level. 950 Independence Ave. SW. © 202/357-2700. www.nmafa.si.edu. Free admission. Metro: Smithsonian.

Screen on the Green *(Finds)* The National Mall, between 4th and 7th streets, is the site of summer movie nights suitable for kids old enough to enjoy the classics and not wander off into the perspiring sea of humanity. For five Monday evenings in July and August, vintage films—*The Big Sleep, Treasure of the Sierra Madre, The Way We Were, Citizen Kane, Singin' in the Rain,* and *Jailhouse Rock* among them—play at sunset (8–8:30pm) on a 20-by-40-foot screen. It's great fun, with movie buffs of all ages cheering their favorite lines or speaking them along with the actors. People start setting up camp as early as 5:30pm, so get here by 7:30pm, or you'll be out of luck and tripping over bodies. Bring a low lawn chair or a blanket and a picnic, if you like. And remember bug spray. Cold drinks and ice cream are sold. National Mall, between 4th and 7th streets NW. (℃ **877/262-5866** (toll-free). Free. Metro: L'Enfant Plaza or Archives–Navy Memorial.

5 Puppet Shows

Puppet shows are given throughout the year, most frequently by the Puppet Co. (at the Puppet Co. Playhouse in Glen Echo Park) as well as by various presenters in the Smithsonian's Discovery Theater and through the Kennedy Center's Theater for Young People. See "Theater," earlier in this chapter, for addresses and phone numbers. For a current listing of performances, check the Friday "Weekend" section of *The Washington Post.*

Most performances are timed for 45 minutes or less, just the right length for restless tykes. Like standup comedians, the puppeteers warm up their audiences first. Some perform cloaked in black in the Bunraku style. Call the following puppeteers to see if they'll be presenting a show during your visit. No strings attached.

For kids who would like to learn more about this ancient craft, puppet-making classes are offered by the Puppet Co. at Glen Echo Park (℃ **301/320-6668**), Bethesda Academy of Performing Arts (℃ **301/320-2550**), the Kennedy Center's Adventures in the Arts program (℃ **202/416-8810**), and the Smithsonian Residents Associates (℃ **202/357-3255**).

Blue Sky Puppet Theatre   Blue Sky has been pulling strings since 1974 and performs hundreds of times a year at venues in and around the city. Wolf Trap Park for the Performing Arts usually hosts them at least once in the summer. Call for dates and locations, which vary from year to year. 4301 Van Buren St., University Park, MD. (℃ **301/927-5599**. www.blueskypuppets.com.

The Puppet Co. *(Finds)*   Try to sandwich in a performance by the Puppet Co. in the Puppet Co. Playhouse, a new 250-seat theater in Glen Echo Park. Award-winning codirectors Christopher Piper and Allen Stevens and their troupe produce shows that win fans from 2 to 102. Each show runs about 6 weeks. Performances are Wednesday through Sunday. Times vary. Call to reserve tickets. The Puppet Co. Playhouse, Glen Echo Park, 7300 MacArthur Blvd., Glen Echo, MD. (℃ **301/320-6668**. www.thepuppetco.org. Tickets $6. From Washington: Massachusetts Ave. north into Maryland. Left at Goldsboro Rd. Left at MacArthur Blvd. and park entrance. Follow signs to parking. From suburbs: I-495/95 to Exit 39 (River Rd.) east (toward D.C.). Right at 5th traffic light (Goldsboro Rd.) to end. Right at MacArthur, and follow signs to Glen Echo Park parking. Closest Metro: Friendship Heights and then take a taxi (much faster) or the no. 29 Metrobus to stop at MacArthur Blvd. and Goldsboro Rd.

6 Story Hours

Story hours at the public library or area bookstores are fun and quiet times for preschoolers and young scholars—and their parents.

Visiting authors speak, from time to time, at the following children's bookstores, which also have story hours: **A Likely Story,** 1555 King St., Alexandria, Virginia (℃ **703/836-2498**); **Borders,** 1800 L St. NW (℃ **202/466-4999**); **Borders for Kids,** White Flint Mall, North Bethesda, Maryland (℃ **301/816-1067**); **Fairy Godmother,** 319 7th St. SE (℃ **202/547-5474**); and **Tree Top Kids,** 3301 New Mexico Ave. NW

(℡ **202/244-3500**). Many of the **Discovery Channel** stores also have story hours for different age groups. Call the individual stores for details (see the "Books," section in chapter 9). Check the monthly literary calendar that appears the third or fourth Sunday of every month in the *Book World* magazine of the Sunday *Washington Post.*

7 Spectator Sports

Washington, D.C. is a happening sports town, with teams in everything from professional soccer to Major League Baseball. If tickets are available (which may be an impossibility for football) they're usually sold at both the sports facility and by **Ticketmaster** (℡ **202/397-7328** or 800/527-6384; www.ticketmaster.com).

Washington Redskins   D.C.'s best-known team is the NFL's (National Football League) **Washington Redskins.** Home games are played Sunday afternoons, with the occasional Sunday- or Monday-night game at FedEx Field. That's the good news. Now the bad: Except in rare instances, you cannot buy individual tickets; they are all purchased by season-ticket holders. The occasional ticket is available through the ticket office (℡ **301/276-6060**) or from a ticket broker (see the Yellow Pages). Expect to pay a premium from a broker. Also try *Washington Post* classified ads. FedEx Field, 1600 Raljohn Rd., Landover, Md. ℡ **301/276-6000.** www.redskins.com. Metro: Landover station and then a shuttle bus ($5). Do not drive.

Baltimore Ravens   The NFL's Baltimore Ravens also have a 16-game schedule. Games are played at M & T Bank Stadium. Buses and MARC trains run from one or more D.C. locations. Single-game tickets range from $40 all the way up to $325. M & T Bank Stadium, 1101 Russell St., Baltimore, Md. ℡ **410/261-7283.** www.baltimoreravens.com or www.mtamaryland.com.

The Washington Capitals   DC's pro hockey team plays at the MCI Center. The fast-skating regular-season action runs from early October through April, and ticket prices range from $10 to $90. MCI Center, 601 F St. NW. ℡ **202-/628-3200.** www.washington caps.com or www.capstickets.com. Metro: Gallery Place/Chinatown.

Washington Wizards   The NBA's (National Basketball Association) Washington Wizards preseason starts in early October. Close to 40 regular season games start early November and run through April. Games are played at the MCI Center (see earlier for details). It's easy to get here by Metro or car from anywhere in the D.C. area. Just hop on a train to Gallery Place/Chinatown, and walk a block. Individual tickets run from $40 to $100. www.nba.com/wizards.

DC United   Soccer fans from around the world applaud our MLS (Major League Soccer) DC United soccer team. The season runs from early April to mid-October, with home games at RFK Stadium. Tickets are mostly in the $16 to $40 range. Whatever the

Washington, D.C. Professional Sports Teams

Factoid: Washington, D.C. was without a baseball team for more than 30 years. The Senators left in 1974 to the consternation of many. Someone finally heard the long-ignored war cry of persevering fans to "Bring Baseball Back to Washington!" In 2005, the Washington Nationals played their first season at RFK. Guess it's true: Slow but steady wins the race.

outcome, the games are fun and high-spirited. RFK Memorial Stadium, 2400 E. Capitol St. SE. © **202/547-9077** or ticket office 202/587-5000. www.dcunited.com. Metro: Stadium/Armory and then a short walk.

Washington Nationals   After more than 30 years without a Major League Baseball team, fans have been cheering (since 2005) the Washington Nationals. The regular season goes from early April until late September. A new stadium is in the works along the Anacostia River, near the Navy Yard. Until the president or another dignitary pitches the first ball there, catch the action at RFK Memorial Stadium. Tickets are $7 to $45. RFK Memorial Stadium, 2400 E. Capitol St. SE. © 202/349-0400. washington.nationals.mlb.com.

Baltimore Orioles   Many D.C. fans, hungry for baseball when the city was without a team, became and continue to be diehard fans of the MLB's Baltimore Orioles. If you're a Birds fan or plan to be in Baltimore during your stay, catch the O's, from early April to October, at Oriole Park at Camden Yards. Most tickets are $8 to $45. Camden Yards, 333 W. Camden St., Baltimore. © **888-848-BIRD**. www.baltimore.orioles.mlb.com. Weekdays: MARC train/Camden Line or 701 Express Bus from Union Station to Camden Yards. Weekends and holidays: No. 703 bus from Greenbelt Metro station.

11

Side Trips from Washington, D.C.

If time permits, you might want to plan a side trip to one or more of the attractions listed below. Using your hotel as a base, you can visit most of the following in a day and be back in D.C. for the late-night news on TV.

1 Theme-Park Thrills

Your idea of a good time may not include losing your lunch on a giant roller coaster, but kids take a different view. Just remember, if they're under a certain height or age restriction, you'll have to ride the roller coaster with them. *A word of warning:* Amusement parks depend on food, beverage, games, and souvenir sales for half their revenues. Although you're a captive audience once you arrive, with a little planning, you don't have to feel like a human ATM machine once you've paid the staggering admission. One solution is to pack a cooler with drinks and snacks, and picnic outside the parks—*after* the roller coaster, of course.

Six Flags America ⍟ **Ages 2 and up.** Only 12 miles from D.C., Six Flags features many water-based rides and one of the world's largest wave pools. Comprised of several miniparks—all with rides, games, and food stands, many with shows—on a 115-acre site in Prince George's County, Maryland, Six Flags is just 15 minutes from the Beltway. The park has a reputation for satisfying visitors' thrill-seeking needs and different tolerances for water saturation and motion. Lines form early, especially on weekends, for the roller coasters. Younger kids are more comfortable with the rides in Looney Tunes Movie Town, where they'll meet their favorite cartoon characters.

A new water park, **Hurricane Harbor,** opened in 2005 with both wave and kiddies' pools. Hearts and stomachs flip flop on the park's **Two Face: The Flip Side.** (Who comes up with these names?) Among the park's other coasters, **Superman, Ride of Steel** flies on steel tracks at speeds up to 70 mph, with a 200-foot drop. Lucky folks on **The Batwing Coaster** ride at a 30° angle, facing heaven, and scream their way through various twists and corkscrews. On 10-acre **Skull Island,** the big draw is the **Typhoon Sea Coaster.** Waiting an hour to ride the wet-and-wild roller coaster is not unheard of, so if at all possible, visit on a weekday, and arrive early. Bathing suits are required for the water slides and pool, but you can stow your dry duds in rental lockers so that you don't have to stay in a wet bathing suit all day.

The **Paradise Island Water Park** has more than a dozen water slides. For younger kids (accompanied by an adult), **Kids' Cove** is on its own lagoon, with an octopus water slide and other tamer fare. The more adventurous head for **Crocodile Cal's**

Outback Beach House, a five-story tower of geysers, waterfalls, and slides. You must be 54 inches tall to board the wilder rides, including the Rainbow Falls, Black Hole, and Bonzai Pipeline. **A Day at the Circus** has 13 rides geared to smaller kids; among them are the Aerial Elephant, Kiddie Bumper Boats, and a Circus Train, along with two shows several times a day. The **Moroccan Village** features the infamous **Python** vertical-looping roller coaster, the **Wild One** (an old-fashioned wooden roller coaster), games, and a private picnic area for large groups only. (You must call first to reserve.) **Pirates Cove** is home of the popular **Shipwreck Falls,** a thriller of a ride that leaves a wall of water in its wake.

An entertaining **Wild West** stunt demonstration show takes place several times a day in Coyote Creek. There, you'll also find oldies but goodies such as bumper cars and a Tilt-a-Whirl.

13710 Central Ave., Largo, MD. ✆ **301/249-1500.** www.sixflags.com. Admission adults $40; seniors (62 and older), adults with disabilities, and kids 48 inches and under $30; free for kids 3 and under. Weekends only May and Oct; daily Memorial Day to Labor Day. Hours vary. Metro: Addison Rd. (not a great neighborhood) and then taxi. Directions: Take I-495/I-95 to Exit 15A (Rte. 214 east). The park is 5 miles on the left. Parking $9.

Paramount's Kings Dominion ⚡⚡   **Ages 4 and up.** Farther afield, near Richmond, Virginia, about a 75-minute drive from the District, this theme park could keep your family busy for a fortnight or two, with its 12 roller coasters, close to 40 other rides in six theme areas, water park, numerous shows, shops, and attractions. The new-in-'05 thrill ride is **Tomb Raider: Firefall.** I can only imagine.

If you are still reading, knock yourselves out and visit **KidZville,** inhabited by Hanna-Barbera characters, or explore **Yogi's Cave** and ride the **Taxi Jam Coaster** (billed as "a child's first coaster"). Youngsters can romp in the Kidz Construction Company, a huge play area, and "drive" a dump truck or cement mixer. Eat in the cutesy **Busytown Café,** decorated with characters from the pen of popular kids' author Richard Scarry.

A word of caution: Don't ride the **Drop Zone Stunt Tower** roller coaster after a full meal. This coaster descends 272 feet at 72 mph and has the dubious distinction of simulating the sensation of sky diving. Thrill seekers still pack the **Avalanche, Anaconda, Grizzly, Rebel Yell, Hypersonic XLC,** and **Volcano** coasters. It's not a bad idea to take a motion-sickness pill half an hour before boarding. (Factoid to stash in your box of caramel corn: The Grizzly was modeled after Coney Island's famous Wildcat.)

At WaterWorks, which opens at noon daily, dip into **Big Wave Bay,** a gigantic wave pool, or swim over to the **Surf City Splash House,** with more than 50 ways to get soaked.

Those prone to motion sickness, and those with kids old enough to ride alone, can pass the time in one of the air-conditioned shows or shops, selling mostly ho-hum, overpriced souvenirs. Lines for rides can be incredibly long on weekends and holidays, so you might want to plan around these times. *Note:* No refunds are given for inclement weather.

Doswell, VA (about 80 miles south of D.C.). ✆ **804/876-5000.** www.kingsdominion.com. Admission $46 ages 7 and older, $40 seniors (55 and older), $32 ages 3–6 or under 48″, free for children 2 and under. **Note:** Coupons for reduced admission are sometimes available at area supermarkets. Late March–Memorial Day and Sept–Oct weekends only; Memorial Day–Labor Day open daily; hours vary. Directions: Take I-95 south to Exit 98 (Doswell). You can't miss it from there. Parking $8.

2 Mount Vernon ⓕ

16 miles S of Washington, D.C.

George Washington's home, just 16 miles from the District, has been lovingly restored to its original appearance, down to the paint colors on the walls. If you're visiting Washington, D.C. for more than a couple of days, this should be at or near the top of your must-see list. GW's estate and final resting place is owned and maintained by the **Mount Vernon Ladies' Association** (ⓒ **703/780-2000;** www.mountvernon.org). The site is open daily April through August from 8am to 5pm; March, September, and October from 9am to 5pm; and November through February from 9am to 4pm. Admission is $11 for adults, $10.50 for seniors 62 and older, $5 for ages 6 to 11, and free for children 5 and under. For a brochure, write to Mount Vernon Ladies Association, Mount Vernon, VA 22121, or go to www.mountvernon.org.

GETTING THERE

BY CAR   Take any of the bridges over the Potomac into Virginia to the George Washington Memorial Parkway going south. The parkway ends at Mount Vernon. If you end up in Richmond (overshooting Mount Vernon by an hour!), turn around and head north.

BY TOURMOBILE   Tourmobile buses (ⓒ **202/554-5100**) depart daily (mid-June–Labor Day) from Arlington National Cemetery and the Washington Monument. Round-trip fare is $25 for adults, $12 for children 3 to 11, and free for kids 2 and under. The fare includes admission to Mount Vernon. Payment is in cash or traveler's checks *only.* Call ahead for departure hours.

BY RIVERBOAT   If you want to make a full day of it, the *Spirit of Mount Vernon* riverboat travels down the Potomac from Pier 4, at 6th and Water streets SW (ⓒ **202/554-8000**), March through October, Tuesday through Sunday, departing 8:15am, returning midafternoon. There is a snack bar on board. Round-trip fares are $35 for adults, $33 for senior citizens, $29 for ages 6 to 11, and free for children 5 and under. Fares include admission to Mount Vernon. Sightseeing cruises aboard *Potomac Spirit* depart the Mount Vernon dock April through September, Tuesday through Sunday and in October, Thursday through Sunday. Call for departure times. The 45-minute ride is a pleasant way to break up a visit and catch some cool breezes off the water. The fare is $8 for adults, $4 for kids 6 to 11, and free for 5 and under (ⓒ **703/548-9000**).

EXPLORING MOUNT VERNON

Ever wonder how an aristocratic 18th-century American family lived? Minus the air-conditioning, you've come to the right place to find out. (Before air-conditioning was added about 10 years ago to cool this hot attraction, the upstairs bedrooms often reached a sweltering 100°F [38°C]. Poor George must have spent many a sleepless night.) Some of the furnishings are original, and the rooms are arranged as if George still lived there. About 500 of the original 8,000 acres still exist as part of the estate, and 30 are yours to explore. The plantation dates from 1674, when the land was granted to Washington's great-grandfather. Washington spent 2 years in retirement here before he died in 1799.

As you tour at your own pace, let the docents answer your queries. They take pride and a personal interest in Mount Vernon's story and are extremely knowledgeable, so don't be bashful with your questions. Children are usually less interested in the period furnishings than in the family kitchen and outbuildings, where everyday tasks—baking, weaving, and washing—took place.

In summer in the **Hands-on-History tent** (next to the mansion), children take part in such activities as carding and spinning wool, trying on colonial clothing, playing corncob darts, and rolling hoops. Also ask about special family programs on weekends from Memorial Day through Labor Day.

April through October, head to **George Washington: Pioneer Farmer,** the working farm site down by the riverside. Depending on the season, kids can watch sheep shearing, ride in a wagon, or even assist in harvesting. Let's not forget that George was, first and foremost, a farmer who planted new crops and experimented with new farming techniques at Mount Vernon. Ask at the barn for an Activity Pack, a guide to the hands-on activities available.

A short walk from the mansion is the tomb where George, Martha, and other family members are buried. On the third Monday of February, a memorial service commemorating Washington's birthday, open to the public, is held at the estate.

Also of interest are the slave burial ground and 30-minute walking tour describing slave life in Mount Vernon. The tour is available April through October at 10am, noon, 2pm, and 4pm. Tours of the gardens are given April through October at 11am, 1pm, and 3pm. In the museum, you can view the family's personal possessions. Allow time for a stroll through the grounds and gardens. Wait until you see the view from the front lawn. Talk about prime waterfront property!

Every December, the mansion is decorated for Christmas. During the two Friday and Saturday evenings preceding Christmas, a candlelight tour is held from 5 to 8pm. The tour begins with gingersnaps and cider on the grounds. The actors/docents are superb. I heartily recommend it for families with kids 8 and older. Show up by 5pm for a good parking spot, and be forewarned—you'll do a lot of walking.

The Shops at Mount Vernon is rather Disneyesque, but you can pick up reproductions of GW's riding boots and Martha's wedding slippers, books on Washington (the largest collection in the nation, I hear), china and other Mount Vernon–inspired housewares and crafts, and a cherry-flavored hatchet. If you're desperate (desperately hungry, that is), there is a food court here. Just outside the main gate is the **Mount Vernon Inn** restaurant, open daily except Christmas. Lunch is served every day from 11am to 3:30pm; dinner is Monday through Saturday from 5 to 9pm (© **703/780-0011**). Reservations are a must at the Inn. Picnic, if you like, 1 mile north of Mount Vernon at scenic Riverside Park, or on your way back to D.C., stop in Old Town Alexandria (see below), where there are scores of restaurants. If you choose the *Spirit of Mount Vernon* (see above) as your mode of travel, you can eat at the onboard snack bar.

3 Old Town Alexandria ★

6 miles S of Washington, D.C.

Everyone enjoys a visit to Old Town, the once-thriving colonial port on the western shore of the Potomac River. About 6 miles south of D.C., it's a picturesque parcel that invites walking, browsing, and people-watching. The area is steeped in history, with many fine restorations of 18th- and 19th-century buildings dotting its cobblestone streets. If possible, plan your visit for midweek. Some attractions are closed Monday, and weekends, the crowds are everywhere.

George Washington was a teenage surveyor's assistant when Alexandria became a city in 1749. The original 60 acres now comprise Old Town. During your visit, allow time to explore the waterfront and board a tall ship, watch artisans at work in the **Torpedo Factory Art Center,** and shop for up-to-date merchandise in old-style buildings.

The easiest way to get to Old Town is via Metro to the King Street station. On weekends, there's a free DASH shuttle bus (𝄐 **703/370-3274;** www.dashbus.com), which runs every 15 minutes from the King Street station to Market Square. The bus runs Saturday from 10am to midnight and Sunday from 11am to 7pm January through March; Friday from 7pm to midnight, Saturday from 10am to midnight, and Sunday from 11am to 10pm April through December. Weekdays, the fare is 35¢ if you remembered to pick up a rail-to-bus transfer in the Metro station; otherwise, it is $1. Kids 4 and under are free with a paying adult. Of course, you can walk the 15 blocks, too.

It's only about a 6-mile trip by car. In rush hour, however, those 6 miles will feel like 60. Old Town's narrow streets become traffic-choked on weekends, and you won't need your car to sweep through the neighborhood anyway. *Most* of the sights are contained within 36 square blocks. But if you insist, take the Arlington Memorial or 14th Street Bridge to George Washington Memorial Parkway (which becomes Washington St.). Take a left at King Street, and continue 4 blocks to Ramsay House Visitor Center for a parking permit (good for 2 hrs. at meters).

Make the **Ramsay House Visitors Center,** 221 King St. (𝄐 **703/838-4200;** www. funside.com), your first stop. A faithful reconstruction of Alexandria's first house, it is open every day but Thanksgiving, December 25, and January 1 from 9am to 5pm. Pick up a brochure (available in several languages) and **Discovery Sheets,** outlining self-guided walking tours for families with kids in three age groups. If your kids are old enough to appreciate such things, you can purchase admission tickets to historic homes and sights here. The **Liberty Pass** is a combo ticket that includes (1) a water shuttle from Old Town to Washington Harbour in Georgetown and return on the *Matthew Hayes* or *Miss Mallory,* (2) a ticket for the Lil' Red Trolley sightseeing tour from Washington Harbour to several monuments and museums (get on and off as often as you like), and (3) admission to three historic Alexandria attractions. Passes are $43 for adults and $21 for children 11 through 17. Call for kids-under-11 prices. The pass represents a savings of nearly 30% based on individual admission prices. Also available are a Potomac and VIP (patriot) Pass. Passes are also available at the Potomac Riverboat Company ticket booth (Alexandria City Marina, behind the Torpedo Factory); Washington Harbour, 31st and K streets NW; or Virginia Welcome Center, 1629 K St. NW, between 16th and 17th streets (𝄐 **888/738-2764;** www.funside.com).

Alexandria Colonial Tours (𝄐 **703/548-0100;** http://alexcolonialtours.com) offers several family-friendly tours. How's this for fun? Self-guided **Scavenger Hunts** take kids on **themed tours** through Old Town, lasting about an hour each. **Trail of the Pirates' Treasure** is geared to kids 4 to 7 (and an adult companion). Reservations are a must. The hour-long **Ghost & Graveyard Tour** is offered Wednesday through Sunday evenings and is suitable for kids 10 and older. Call for prices and seasonal hours. From the Ramsay House Visitors Center, Old Town extends approximately 5 blocks north and south, and 3 blocks west and east (to the waterfront).

SPECIAL EVENTS

Inquire about special events, some of which require tickets, at the visitor center, or call the Alexandria Convention & Visitors Association ("The Fun Side of the Potomac") (𝄐 **703/838-4200;** www.funside.com). Additional contact info for a few events is listed below.

Old Town Alexandria

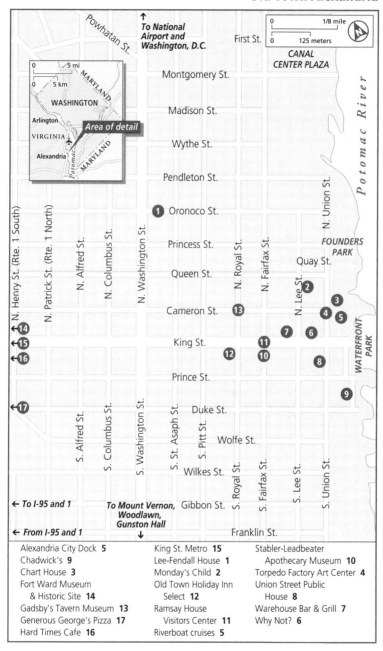

JANUARY   The **birthdays of Robert E. Lee** and his father, **"Light Horse Harry" Lee,** are celebrated with house tours, music, and refreshments.

FEBRUARY   Festivities marking **George Washington's birthday** include the nation's largest George Washington Day parade, a 10km race, and special tours in honor of Alexandria's most famous former resident.

MARCH   Alexandria's origin might be Scottish, but you wouldn't know it when **St. Patrick's Day** rolls around. The town grows greener than a field of shamrocks, and there's a parade and plenty of entertainment.

APRIL   Tours of historic homes and gardens are featured during **Historic Garden Week.**

MAY   From May to September, narrated **Lantern Tours** leave from the visitor center on Saturday at 8pm. Purchase your tickets right before the tour. The anecdotal narration about Alexandria's history interests most kids 8 and up.

JUNE   Don't miss the **Red Cross Waterfront Festival,** an outstanding family event held the second week of June. Boat rides and races, historic tall ships, children's games, entertainment, and food are featured at the harbor. The event draws around 100,000 people. For information, call © **703/549-8300.**

Drive or taxi over to **Fort Ward** (see listing below) on selected days for Civil War drills, concerts, and lectures.

JULY   Alexandria's Scottish heritage is celebrated with **Virginia Scottish Games** the fourth weekend of the month. Athletic competitions, a parade of tartan-clad clans, Highland dancing, and storytelling are some of the events.

AUGUST   An 18th-century tavern is the scene for music, entertainment, and food—1700s style—during **August Tavern Days. Union Army Garrison Day** features authentically dressed military units in drills. Call Fort Ward Museum and Historic Site (© **703/838-4848;** http://oha.ci.alexandria.va.us).

SEPTEMBER   Storytellers, jugglers, crafts, and people in period dress are featured at the **Colonial Fair.** Kids especially like the glassblowing demonstration.

OCTOBER   The competition is stiff at the **War Between the States Chili Cookoff** in Waterfront Park. For a small admission fee, you can sample all the entries, and enjoy fiddling contests and country music (www.waphc.com).

Take your ghouls and boys (over the age of 10, please) to the 1-hour **Ghost & Graveyard Tours,** conducted Friday, Saturday, and Sunday evenings.

NOVEMBER   Your older kids might accompany you willingly to the **Historic Alexandria Antiques Show** (© **703/549-5811**), with dozens of dealers from several states showing their wares.

DECEMBER   The **Annual Scottish Christmas Walk** heralds the holiday season with bagpipers, a parade of the clans, puppet and magic shows, children's games, and, of course, food.

Visit historic Alexandria homes and a tavern, decked with holly and other seasonal decorations, during the **Old Town Christmas Candlelight Tour,** usually the second week of the month. **First Night Alexandria** is a family-focused, alcohol-free celebration held December 31, similar to those in cities across the country. About 50 acts perform on three dozen stages in and around Old Town. Admission for kids 12 and under is free; for adults, $15. Midnight fireworks at the pyramidal Masonic Temple welcome the new year. Afterward, free shuttle buses take revelers to area garages where parking is also free (provided you sport a 1st Night badge; www.firstnightalexandria.org).

EXPLORING OLD TOWN

Take younger children to Waterfront Park, where they can run loose, feed the pigeons, and look at the boats. Board the 125-foot schooner *Alexandria,* a classic Scandinavian cargo vessel berthed here. Tour the decks, the main salon, and a stateroom of this tall ship Saturday and Sunday from noon to 5pm. The tour is free, but donations are appreciated.

Bring your lunch, if you wish, and take a narrated cruise of the Alexandria Waterfront and beyond aboard the Potomac Riverboat Co.'s fleet (© **703/548-9000; www.potomacriverboatco.com**). The *Admiral Tilp* cruises for 40 minutes along the Alexandria waterfront. The fare is $10 for adults, $8 for seniors, and $5 for kids 2 to 12. The *Miss Christin* cruises from Old Town to Mount Vernon. The fare, which includes admission to Mount Vernon, is $30 for adults, $28 for seniors, and $17 for kids 6 to 10. Cruises cast off from the Alexandria City Marina, Union and Cameron streets, behind the Torpedo Factory. Departures are several times daily from May until early September, and weekends only in April, most of September, and all of October. Also see "Cruises," in chapter 8.

Everyone enjoys a stroll through Old Town's quaint streets to browse the area's enticing shops. Of special interest to kids are **Why Not?**, 200 King Street, with children's clothing, some toys, books, and gift items; and **Monday's Child,** 218 N. Lee Street, with fancy kids' clothing, shoes, and toys. *Note:* Some properties are closed on Monday.

Fort Ward Museum and Historic Site   Ages 2 and up. This 45-acre park, a short drive from Old Town, boasts an extensive Civil War research library and is the site of one of the forts erected to defend Washington during the Civil War. Explore the fort, six mounted guns, and reproduction of an officer's hut. Civil War weapons and other war-related exhibits are displayed in the museum. Picnic areas surround the fort, and outdoor concerts are given every Thursday during the summer. Every year during **Living History Day** (usually the hottest day in August), visitors flock to the Civil War encampment, where uniformed regiments perform drills. Tell the kids—no battles allowed.

4301 W. Braddock Rd. © **703/838-4848**. www.fortward.org. Free admission; donations appreciated. Museum Tues–Sat 9am–4pm (sometimes until 5pm in summer); Sun noon–5pm. Park open daily 8am in summer; 9am rest of year–sunset. Directions: I-395 south to Seminary Road exit. Left at 4th light (Alexandria Hospital/North Howard St.), and right at West Braddock Rd. to entrance on left. Free parking next to museum. Metro: King Street or Braddock Road.

Gadsby's Tavern Museum 🍴   **Ages 10 and up.** For a meaningful Old Town experience, especially for history buffs, I suggest a stop at this tavern, visited by Washington, Madison, and Jefferson (but not recently), which is now a museum of colonial furnishings and artifacts.

Notice that there are two buildings. The first was built around 1770 and operated as a tavern run by Mary Hawkins. The second building was built around 1792. John Gadsby took it over in 1796 and ran it as the City Hotel. In 1802, Gadsby took over the lease of the first building and turned it into a coffeehouse. Gadsby hosted two birthnight (birthday) balls for George Washington and his date, Martha, in 1798 and 1799. Contrary to popular opinion, GW never slept here. Today the ballroom is used for weddings and historic reenactments.

Half-hour tours are conducted 15 minutes before and after the hour. October through March, the first tour is at 11:15am and the last is at 3:15pm. April through September, the first tour is at 10:15am, and the last is at 4:15pm. Sunday tours are between 1:15 and 4:15pm year-round.

In the dormer room in the 1770 section of the museum, kids can try out the straw mattresses and rope beds. Very lumpy and scratchy! Gadsby's Tavern, on the newer building's first floor, is open for lunch and dinner, and offers half-price children's portions of some entrees. Strolling musicians entertain evenings and during Sunday brunch.

134 N. Royal St. ✆ 703/838-4242. www.gadsbystavern.org. Admission $4 adults, $2 ages 11–17, free for children 10 and under with paying adult. Apr–Oct Tues–Sat 10am–5pm, Sun–Mon 1–5pm; Nov–Mar Wed–Sat 11am–4pm, Sun 1–4pm.

Lee–Fendall House   Ages 8 and up.
Many Lees have called this home over the years, but Robert E. never hung his clothes in the closet. Alexandria's only Victorian house museum was built in 1785. The original structure was renovated in 1850. It is currently undergoing renovation but is remaining open. Younger kids will probably like the antique dollhouse collection and boxwood garden better than the home, which serves as a museum of Lee furniture and memorabilia. The half-hour tour paints an impressionistic picture of family life in the Victorian age. Take time to enjoy the garden and lovely grounds. Lectures, educational programs, and special events are ongoing throughout the year. In February, families can learn about Valentine's Day in the 19th century. Call for information on other special events; reservations are required.

614 Oronoco St. ✆ 703/548-1789. www.leefendallhouse.org. Admission $4 adults, $2 ages 11–17, free for children 10 and under. Tues–Sat 10am–4pm; Sun 1–4pm. Metro: King Street and then DASH bus or a mile-plus walk.

Stabler–Leadbeater Apothecary Museum ⚘ (Finds)   Ages 8 and up.
The second floor was once the site of a large wholesale drug (no, not that kind) operation that processed herbs and medicines for 500 other apothecary shops. View the hand-blown medicine bottles, medicinal herbs and potions, and bloodletting paraphernalia in the first-floor museum, and pick up a souvenir or two in the gift shop.

105–107 S. Fairfax St. ✆ 703/836-3713. www.apothecarymuseum.org. Admission $2.50 adults 18 and older, $2 ages 11–17, free for children 10 and under. Mon–Sat 10am–4pm; Sun 1–5pm. Metro: King Street and then DASH bus or a mile-plus walk.

Torpedo Factory Art Center ⚘⚘⚘ (Finds)   Ages 4 and up.
This is a must-see for all ages, and there's a lot of history here, too. The Torpedo Factory was just that—a navy-built torpedo shell–case factory, around World War I. These days, the only thing fired up is the clay. Observe sculptors, painters, weavers, potters, and numerous other craftspeople and artisans doing their thing. You also get to talk to the artisans and buy their wares. Because most items are priced reasonably, it's an excellent opportunity to stock up on one-of-a-kind gifts. Kids seem most fascinated watching clay take shape on the potter's wheel. Self-guided tours, available at the information desk, will help you structure your visit. Alexandria Archaeology, in Studio 327 on the third floor, showcases many artifacts from Alexandria's 10,000-year history.

105 N. Union St. ✆ 703/838-4565. www.torpedofactory.org. Free admission. Torpedo Factory: Daily 10am–5pm. Alexandria Archaeology and Research Lab: Tues–Fri 10am–3pm; Sat 10am–5pm; Sun 1–5pm. Closed Thanksgiving, Dec 25, Jan 1, Easter, July 4th. Metro: King Street and then DASH bus or a mile-plus walk.

WHERE TO STAY
EXPENSIVE

Old Town Holiday Inn Select ⚐   If you want to stay overnight in Old Town, you can't get any closer than this. It's the only hotel inside the historic district. Besides its location, another plus is a large indoor pool open year-round. And kids 12 and under stay free (in same room as parents) and eat breakfast free in **The 101** (as in 101 Royal St.; the hotel is at the corner of King and Royal) restaurant, serving breakfast, lunch, and dinner. Try **Annabelle's Lounge** for a snack or quick bite. During happy hour, from 5 to 8pm, there are specially priced drinks. Complimentary coffee and Danish in the morning and afternoon tea are included in the room rate Monday through Friday. Cocktails and hors d'oeuvres are gratis at the manager's reception Wednesday from 5:30 to 6:30pm.

480 King St., Alexandria, VA 22314. ✆ **703/549-6080.** www.holiday-inn.com. 227 units. $159–$269; ask about specials, based on availability. Crib free; rollaway $15 per night. AE, DISC, MC, V. Metro: King Street and then DASH bus or a mile-plus walk. Pets (under 40 lb.) accepted. **Amenities:** 2 restaurants; indoor pool. *In room:* A/C, TV, minibar, high-speed Internet access.

WHERE TO DINE
EXPENSIVE TO VERY EXPENSIVE

Chart House ⚐ SEAFOOD/BEEF   What distinguishes this Chart House is its prime waterfront location—almost like dining on a luxury yacht. Though expensive, the food is consistent, and the servers are professional and attentive. An ideal setting for a special-occasion dinner, the Chart House welcomes kids of all ages, although I don't want to dine there with anybody's kids who are under 6 or so; also make sure that any older children you bring here are well behaved.

The fried coconut shrimp is sensational, and the Chart House also turns out tasty, if uninspired, fish and beef. Unlimited trips to the copious salad bar, with about 40 items, and bread are included in the main-course price. Or make a meal of salad for $13. The kids' menu includes chicken fingers, hamburgers, shrimp, and spaghetti.

1 Cameron St. ✆ **703/684-5080.** www.chart-house.com. High chairs, booster seats, kids' menu. Reservations recommended. Main dishes lunch $5–$14, dinner $13–$35; kids menu items $6–$8; Sun brunch $25. AE, DC, DISC, MC, V. Lunch Mon–Sat 11:30am–3pm; brunch Sun 10:45am–2:15pm; dinner Mon–Thurs 5–10pm, Fri–Sat 5–11pm, Sun 4–10pm. Metro: King Street and then DASH bus or a mile-plus walk.

MODERATE

Union Street Public House AMERICAN   Try the burger topped with cheddar on toasted rye, ribs, hero, or Nawlins-style po' boy at this lively and inviting pub known for consistently good food and service. More adventurous? Try the New Orleans–style fare (Creole chicken, gumbo, jambalaya, and the like) or one of the nightly specials. Sample one of the local beers while you're here. Little ones can order from the kids' menu, with six items from $3 (bow-tie pasta and cheese) to $3.95 (fish and chips).

121 S. Union St. ✆ **703/548-1785.** www.usphalexandria.com. High chairs, booster seats, kids' menu. Reservations not accepted. Soups, salads, and sandwiches $7–$10; entrees $11–$19. Kids' menu items under $4. AE, DISC, MC, V. Mon–Thurs 11:30am–10:30pm; Fri–Sat 11:30am–11:30pm; Sun 11am–10:30pm (brunch 11am–3pm). Metro: King Street and then DASH bus or a mile-plus walk.

Warehouse Bar & Grill SEAFOOD/CAJUN   This popular steak and seafood house, with its warm mahogany bar and cozy ambience, is known mainly for its seafood and Cajun cuisine. Often, it combines the two effectively, as in the crawfish and shrimp beignets (dinner appetizer for $7.95). Nobody's stopping you from getting two orders in lieu of an entrée. The pecan-crusted rockfish, crab cakes, and seafood sampler are highly recommended by friends living in Old Town. If you have room, dip into the bread pudding for dessert. Reasonably priced, surprisingly good steaks are on the menu too. The kids' menu ($5.95) features pint-size portions of pasta, chicken nuggets, or fish nuggets.

214 King St. ⓒ **703/683-6868.** High chairs, booster seats, kids' menu. Reservations recommended. Lunch $6.95–$17; dinner main courses $7.95–$26; kids menu $5.95. AE, DISC, MC, V. Mon–Thurs 11am–10:30pm; Fri 11am–11pm; Sat 8:30am–11pm; Sun 10am–9:30pm (brunch 10am–4pm). Metro: King Street and then DASH bus or a mile-plus walk.

INEXPENSIVE

Chadwick's AMERICAN   Eat in or carry out at good old reliable Chadwick's, a stylish pub opposite the waterfront, between Duke and Prince streets. The salads, burgers, homemade soups, and Sunday brunch—served until 4pm—are all standouts, and kids always receive VIP treatment. This isn't fine dining, but the food is above average and served with a smile. The servers are usually friendly and accommodating. Diners 10 and under can order from their own menu, which includes hamburger/ cheeseburger, pizza, grilled cheese, chicken tenders, spaghetti, and PB&J. Kudos to Chadwick's for fighting inflation—the prices have changed little over the years. There's some street parking, and a pay lot ($5) is across the street.

203 S. Strand St. ⓒ **703/836-4442.** High chairs, booster seats, kids' menu. Reservations accepted. Main courses $6.95–$22 (most under $17); kids menu items $2.95. AE, DISC, MC, V. Mon–Thurs 11:30am–midnight; Fri–Sat 11:30am–1am; Sun 10am–midnight (Sun brunch 10am–4pm). Metro: King Street and then DASH bus or a mile-plus walk.

Generous George's Pizza ⭐⭐ PIZZA/PASTA   Although 2 miles from Old Town, GG's is a destination in and of itself that has been doing right by families for more than 25 years. No wonder it is consistently voted one of the best family restaurants in the metropolitan area. A foursome can enjoy superior pizza and a beverage in a supercasual, funky 1950s setting and escape for $30. And you won't have to "shush" your little pepperonis. If you're adventurous, try George's ingenious (and tasty) Specialty Pizzas, such as BBQ chicken or taco style ($10.99 for personal size, $15.99 for regular, $17.99 large). There is also a selection of sandwiches/subs, pasta dishes, and salads. The kids' menu, for children 11 and under, includes a personal pizza with two topping (kids can make it themselves weekdays only), chicken dinosaurs (shaped chicken nuggets), and mac and cheese. All items are $3.99 to $4.99. A clown entertains Tuesdays at dinner.

3006 Duke St., Alexandria, VA (2 miles from Old Town). ⓒ **703/370-4303.** www.generousgeorge.com. High chairs, booster seats, crayons, balloons. Reservations accepted for groups of 20 or more (call 24 hr. ahead). Most items $10–$18. AE, DISC, MC, V. Sun 11:30am–10pm; Mon–Thurs 11am–10pm; Fri–Sat 11am–midnight. Call for directions.

Hard Times Cafe *Value* AMERICAN   One could live on Hard Times' onion rings, but it'd be a shame not to leave room for the chili. Kids usually prefer the milder, tomatoey Cincinnati variety (with a hint of cinnamon) to the spicy, mostly meat Texas style. Or they can order PB&J, hot dogs, a burger, or spaghetti off the kids' menu There's also vegetarian chili and Terlingua Red Chili (Texas-style with a kick). The chili burger is sensational. Hard Times does a lot of to-go orders, too. There's some metered street parking, as well as free evening and weekend parking in the rear lot. Don't forget the Hard Times when in Herndon, Arlington, or Clarendon, Virginia; or Bethesda, Rockville, Laurel, Columbia, or College Park, Maryland.

1404 King St. at West St. ⓒ **703/837-0050.** www.hardtimes.com. High chairs, booster seats, kids' menu. Reservations for 10 or more. Main courses $5.95–$8. Kids menu items $3–$4. AE, MC, V. Sun–Thurs 11am–11 pm; Fri–Sat 11am–midnight. Metro: King Street and then DASH bus or walk.

4 Annapolis

35 miles NE of Washington, D.C.

Set off with your crew for Annapolis, the jewel of the Chesapeake. Annapolis is less than an hour's drive—as the gull flies—from downtown D.C. (except at rush hour!). Judging by the upturn in the number of tourists the past several years, it's clear that the secret is out. Explore the many facets of this friendly, charming 18th-century seaport on the Severn River, dubbed "the sailing capital of the United States." Annapolis is home to the U.S. Naval Academy, the Maryland State House, St. John's College, beautifully maintained historic homes, fine shops and restaurants, and about 30,000 pleasure boats.

GETTING THERE

BY BUS   Monday through Friday only, bus transport is available via Dillon's Bus Service (© **410/647-2321;** www.mtamaryland.com). It's not much help to visitors, because the buses carry commuters from Annapolis to D.C. in the morning and make return trips between 3 to 7pm. But if you can figure a way to utilize this service, do so. It's a bargain. The no. 921 bus travels between Annapolis and the New Carrollton Metro station. The no. 922 carries passengers from Annapolis to several stops in D.C. One-way fare is $4.25. Call for departure times and to find the most convenient departure point.

BY CAR   Annapolis is easily reached from D.C. (in non-rush-hour traffic) in about 40 minutes by car via U.S. 50, an eastern extension of New York Avenue. If you leave D.C. after 4pm on a weekday, you'll be in the thick of commuter traffic. Don't make the trip on Friday after 3pm, mid-May to September—beach traffic is horrendous. Take the Rowe (rhymes with *cow*) Boulevard exit off U.S. 50, and follow the signs to Annapolis.

PARKING   If you can't find a metered spot near City Dock, or if you want to avoid the hassle of looking, try the Hillman Garage (closest to the downtown action), with entrances on Duke of Gloucester Street and Main Street, or Gott's Court Garage, Northwest Street off Church Circle (behind the visitor center on West St.). Both cost $1 an hour. If you strike out, head back to the Navy–Marine Corps Stadium (Rowe Blvd. and Taylor Ave.), where all-day parking costs $4 ($5 during special events). The shuttle to downtown is 75¢ (paid one-way only). The lot is open between 10am and 9pm (extended hours during special events).

BY METRO   Take the Metro Orange line to New Carrollton or MARC commuter train from Union Station (Mon–Fri only) and then take a cab (about $40).

INFORMATION

Stock up on brochures at the **Visitor Information Center** booth at City Dock in the heart of town. It's open daily from 9am to 5pm. More comprehensive information is available from the walk-in **Visitors Center** at 26 West Street, off Church Circle, open daily from 9am to 5pm (© **410/280-0445**). A touch-screen video guide there dispenses information about sights and special events.

For information on events, lodging, and restaurants, write to the Annapolis Visitor Center, 26 West St., Annapolis, MD 21401, or visit www.visit-annapolis.org. Another helpful site is www.annapolis.com. To see Annapolis from the Chesapeake Bay, stop at City Dock or call for information on Watermark Cruises (© **410/268-7600**).

Annapolis

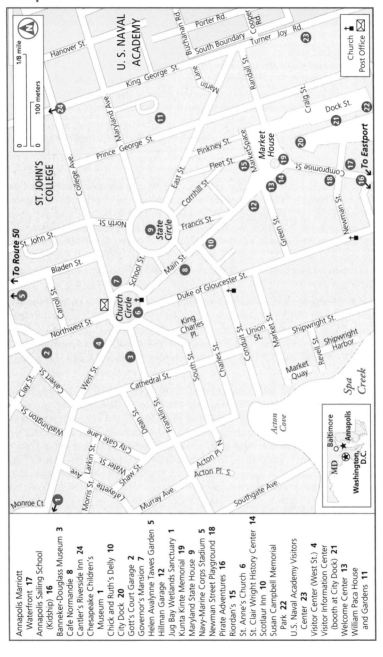

U. S. NAVAL ACADEMY

ST. JOHN'S COLLEGE

State Circle

Church Circle

Market House

Acton Cove

Spa Creek

To Route 50

To Eastport

1/8 mile

100 meters

Church

Post Office

Hanover St.
Porter Rd.
Cooper Rd.
Buchanan Rd.
South Boundary
Turner Joy Rd.
King George St.
Martin Lane
Randall St.
Prince George St.
Craig St.
Dock St.
Maryland Ave.
College Ave.
Pinkney St.
East St.
Fleet St.
MarketSpace
Compromise St.
Newman St.
Cornhill St.
Francis St.
North St.
St. John St.
Main St.
Bladen St.
Green St.
Carroll St.
School St.
Duke of Gloucester St.
Northwest St.
King Charles Pl.
Conduit St.
Union St.
Market St.
Shipwright St.
Shipwright Harbor
West St.
South St.
Charles St.
Revell St.
Market Quay
Cathedral St.
Calvert St.
Clay St.
Washington St.
Franklin St.
Dean St.
City Gate Lane
Acton Pl. N.
Acton Pl. S.
Lafayette Ave.
Larkin St.
Morris St.
Water St.
Shaw St.
Monroe Ct.
Murray Ave.
Southgate Ave.

Baltimore
Annapolis
MD
Washington, D.C.

264

Annapolis Marriott Waterfront **17**
Annapolis Sailing School (Kidship) **16**
Banneker-Douglass Museum **3**
Cafe Normandie **8**
Cantler's Riverside Inn **24**
Chesapeake Children's Museum **1**
Chick and Ruth's Delly **10**
City Dock **20**
Gott's Court Garage **2**
Governor's Mansion **7**
Helen Avalynne Tawes Garden **5**
Hillman Garage **12**
Jug Bay Wetlands Sanctuary **1**
Kunta Kinte Memorial **19**
Maryland State House **9**
Navy-Marine Corps Stadium **5**
Newman Street Playground **18**
Pirate Adventures **16**
Riordan's **15**
St. Anne's Church **6**
St. Clair Wright History Center **14**
Scotlaur Inn **10**
Susan Campbell Memorial Park **22**
U.S. Naval Academy Visitors Center **23**
Visitor Center (West St.) **4**
Visitor Information Center (booth at City Dock) **21**
Welcome Center **13**
William Paca House and Gardens **11**

Hint: To see Annapolis at its least crowded, plan on arriving before noon, especially on weekends and June through September.

SPECIAL EVENTS

JANUARY Kids 10 and older (with a parent) can attend Opening Day of the **Maryland General Assembly** at the State House on State Circle (✆ **410/841-3810**).

APRIL The Ballet Theatre of Maryland presents its spring **Dance Concert** at this time of the year (✆ **410/263-8289**).

MAY The **Waterfront Festival** (✆ **410/268-8828**) features short sailing lessons, Chesapeake Bay retriever obedience demonstrations, sea chanteys, crafts, and food booths galore. The **Clyde Beatty–Cole Brothers Circus** pitches its tents for several days at the Navy–Marine Corps Memorial Stadium on Rowe Boulevard (✆ **410/268-TOUR**). During Commissioning Week in late May at the Naval Academy, the public is invited to dress parades and a stunning air show by the Blue Angels, celebrating the graduation of the Naval Academy's first class (seniors, to us civvies). Walk tall and bring bottled water, because it's usually hot (✆ **410/263-6933**). A festive **Memorial Day Parade** wends its musical way through the streets of the Historic District to the City Dock (✆ **410/280-0445**).

JULY Bring lawn chairs or sit on cement, and enjoy the waterfront **Summer Serenade Concert Series** at City Dock, most Tuesday evenings at 7:30pm through mid-August (✆ **410/280-0445**). A **Fourth of July Celebration** with oodles of family fun takes place at City Dock and the Naval Academy. At 9:15pm, fireworks over the Severn River cap the Fourth. The Ship and Soldier Shop's semiannual **Toy Soldier Show** convenes at Loews Hotel on West Street one weekend this month, with more than 150 tables of miniatures, representing dealers from all over the country (✆ **410/268-1141**).

AUGUST Crab pickers by the bushel scuttle over to the **Rotary Crab Feast** (it's the world's largest crab feast), usually the first Friday night of the month, at the Navy–Marine Corps Stadium (✆ **410/841-2841;** www.annapolisrotary.com). The **Maryland Renaissance Festival** kicks off at the Anne Arundel County Fairgrounds in Crownsville (20 min. from downtown Annapolis) and runs through October (✆ **410/266-7304** or 800/296-7304). At the annual **Kunta Kinte Festival,** held the second weekend of the month at the Anne Arundel County Fairgrounds in Crownsville, the life of this African slave (1 of 98 to arrive in Annapolis in 1767 and the inspiration for his descendant Alex Haley's *Roots*) and African-American culture are celebrated with music, crafts, storytelling, and a family workshop or two. Artists paint kids' faces with tribal markings, a griot (African storyteller) tells stories about slave life, and dancers and musicians perform African-inspired works (✆ **410/923-3400**).

SEPTEMBER **Navy football** kicks off this month in the Navy–Marine Corps Stadium. Even when navy loses, the games and halftime shows are colorful and inspiring. Your kids are sure to enjoy the march-on by the Brigade of Midshipmen before the game and the precision drills and entertainment at halftime (✆ **410/268-6060**). Come to the **Anne Arundel County Fair** at the county fairgrounds in Crownsville. Kids 10 and under are admitted free with a paying adult (✆ **410/923-3400**).

OCTOBER The **U.S. Sailboat and Powerboat Shows** draw boating enthusiasts from all over the world to City Dock on succeeding weeks (usually the 2nd and 3rd weeks, Thurs–Mon). It's not for tiny tots, and strollers are discouraged (✆ **410/268-8828**). The **Ballet Theatre of Maryland,** a regional professional company, presents its annual fall performance at Maryland Hall for the Creative Arts (© **410/263-8289**). The **Annapolis Symphony Orchestra Youth Concert** features works accessible to young people. Before the performance, players from the brass, wind, string, and percussion sections demonstrate the range of their instruments for little ears (© **410/263-0907**). The annual **Halloween Concert,** hosted by the Naval Academy, invites kids and adults to come in costume for a Halloween sampling of spooky organ selections and a light show at the Naval Academy Chapel (© **410/293-7766**).

NOVEMBER The Saturday of Thanksgiving weekend, **Santa Claus** arrives (by boat, of course) at City Dock (© **410/280-0445**).

DECEMBER Treat your kids to a performance of *The Nutcracker* by the Ballet Theatre of Maryland (© 410/263-8289) or *The Messiah* by the Annapolis Chorale (© 410/263-4309), both at Maryland Hall for the Creative Arts. A light and festive production of *A Christmas Carol* is presented annually by the Colonial Players (© 410/268-7373). March up West Street to the Annapolis **Christmas Toy Soldier Show** at the Annapolis National Guard Armory (© 410/267-7619). Enjoy a **Child's Colonial Christmas** at the London Town Publik House and Gardens in Edgewater (© 410/222-1919). Take part in the **Grand Illumination** at City Dock, where the community Christmas tree is lit and carolers do their holiday thing (© 410/280-0445). Bundle up and go early to the **Christmas Lights Parade,** usually the second Saturday of the month, sponsored by the Eastport Yacht Club and visible from several spots in and around City Dock. Scores of local boaters spend months festooning their rigs with lights, greenery, and costumed mates (© 410/267-8986). Bid adieu to the old year and welcome the new one at the alcohol-free, family-oriented **First Night Annapolis** celebration, featuring performances by musicians, mimes, choral groups, and dancers in storefronts and public buildings throughout downtown, at the Naval Academy, and at St. John's College. Special kids' entertainment starts at 4pm on New Year's Eve, and at midnight, fireworks light up the harbor (© 410/974-9332; www.firstnightannapolis.org).

EXPLORING ANNAPOLIS

Weekends and holidays, bench seats are scarce at **Susan Campbell Memorial Park,** fronting Ego Alley, Spa Creek, and the Chesapeake Bay. Even so, it's a great place to stroll and enjoy the panoramic view of the harbor and beyond. Plan your day as pleasure craft parade up Ego Alley. A ceremony commemorating the arrival of *Roots* author Alex Haley's ancestor, Kunta Kinte, aboard the slave ship *Lord Ligonier* on September 29, 1767, is held annually at City Dock, where there's a life-size statue of Mr. Haley reading a book to three children. Along the adjacent seawall, plaques contain quotes from *Roots.* Take a minute or two and read the powerful messages.

Despite a small-town population of 35,000, Annapolis encompasses 16 miles of waterfront. Not surprisingly, the views from the water are awesome, so board one of the **cruise boats** or water taxis berthed at the dock; or **learn to sail**—it's a breeze at one of the area's sailing schools. Sightseeing, shopping, and restaurants are all an easy walk from the heart of the historic district.

For an introduction to this East Coast "City by the Bay," **Discover Annapolis Tours** offers visitors 350 years of history and architecture in an hour-long tour aboard minibuses with big windows. With little ones (and old ones), this is an easy way to view the sights. Bring your camera for the stop at Governor Richie Overlook, with its sweeping views of the Severn River and Naval Academy. Tours depart from the Visitors Center, 26 West

Street (half a block from St. Anne's Church), several times a day. The cost is $15 for adults, $7 for kids 11 to 15, $3 for kids 3 to 10, and free for kids 2 and under. Call for departure times (© **410/626-6000;** www.discover-annapolis.com).

Take an **audio tour** (lasting about 1 hr. and 15 min.), narrated by Walter Cronkite, from the **Welcome Center** at 77 Main Street (© **410/ 268-5576**). You also can take an **African-American Heritage** tour, with narrative about the African-American experience in Annapolis. For a **guided walking tour** of the historic district, State House, U.S. Naval Academy, and St. John's College, led by knowledgeable tour leaders in period dress, call the **Historic Annapolis Foundation** (© 410/267-7619) or **Three Centuries Tours** (© 410/263-5401).

Hike up **Main Street** from City Dock to Church Circle. Regrettably, national chains have moved in with a vengeance, forcing many mom-and-pop stores to bite the dust. Stop at the **St. Clair Wright History Center,** opening spring/summer 2006 at 99 Main Street. The exhibits in the restored 1790s building showcase the history, architecture, and cultural attractions of Maryland's state capital.

At 194 Green Street is the **Bowie Toy Co.**—open daily and a must with youngsters. It reminds me of the toy stores of my youth—baseball cards, soap bubbles, books, plush toys, puzzles, games, and even candy cigarettes. **A. L. Goodies** is still at 100 Main Street for souvenirs, T-shirts, fudge (skip the cookies—they look better than they taste), and a large and entertaining greeting-card selection (on the second floor). **Avoca Handweavers,** at 141 Main Street, stocks beautiful woolens and gifts from the British Isles for the whole family. The clan plaid trousers and kilts for kids are hard to resist. **Snyder's Bootery,** facing Conduit Street, has a huge selection of boat shoes (or it will order your size). Across from Snyder's is **Chick and Ruth's Delly,** an Annapolis institution since the 1950s and open nearly 'round the clock (see "Where to Dine," later in this section).

Encircling the Maryland State House on **State Circle** are some of the town's premier shops and galleries, often overlooked by visitors. At **Annapolis Pottery,** where browsers can catch potters at work, a dazzling assortment of attractive, well-priced dishes and accessories is for sale, and special orders are taken. Another gem is the **Maryland Federation of Art Gallery,** housed in a restored building dating from 1840, at 18 State Circle. Solo and small-group exhibits of multimedia works change every 4 weeks and include three national shows per year.

Maryland Avenue, with its many home-design and accessory boutiques, antique shops, and galleries, is more reminiscent of "old" Annapolis and, therefore, worthy of investigation. The commercial section runs from State Circle to Prince George Street.

KidShip Sailing School   Ages 5 and up.
Before you go overboard for sailing, this is a good place to start. KidShip is part of the Annapolis Sailing School (in business for more than 40 years and the largest sailing school in the country). In 2 days of concentrated instruction, alternating between the classroom and the school's fleet of 24-foot Rainbow sloops, families can learn enough to skipper a small boat. May through August, **KidShip** offers sailing instruction—basic, intermediate, and advanced—for kids 8 to 15 in weekend ($235) and 5-day ($465) sessions. A half-day summer course for kids 5 to 7 ($235) is offered June to August.

601 6th St. © **800/638-9192** or 410/267-7205. www.annapolissailing.com. Packages with hotel room available. Late Mar–Oct.

Banneker–Douglass Museum **Ages 8 and up.** This little-known museum, housed in a Victorian Gothic church built in 1874 by former slaves, is located off Church Circle. Anyone interested in American history and the black American experience should take a few minutes to visit the edifice, named for Frederick Douglass (a leader in the abolition movement) and Benjamin Banneker (1731–1806), an astronomer, farmer, surveyor, almanac writer, and mathematician who is best known for assisting Maj. Andrew Ellicott, the surveyor chosen by President George Washington, to establish the boundaries of the District of Columbia in 1791. A new permanent exhibit with interactive displays showcases the contributions of Maryland's most important African Americans: Banneker, Douglass, Harriet Tubman, and Thurgood Marshall. Changing exhibits are devoted to African-American history in Maryland.

84 Franklin St. (C) 410/974-2893. Free admission. Tues–Sat 10am–4pm.

Chesapeake Children's Museum **Ages 2–10.** I hate to be the one to drag your family away from the waterfront, but this hands-on museum, the brainchild of executive director Debbie Wood several years ago, is a worthwhile detour for those traveling with young children, especially preschoolers. The building is on 5½ acres of parkland and lies on Spa Creek Trail. Nature walks make use of the woodland and wetland habitats.

Indoors, youngsters try on foul-weather gear and climb aboard an anchored mini-tug, peer into an osprey nest, fashion clay molds of duck tracks, try on costumes, or grab an instrument and entertain on a pint-size stage. Many are content to watch and touch the diamondback terrapins or role-play in the dental office.

The Minnows room, for infants and toddlers, is filled with soft, safe playthings. The museum holds story times, special events, classes in art and movement, and talks for parents on child-related topics. *Note:* Children must be accompanied by an adult.

25 Silopanna Rd. (C) 410/266-0677. www.theccm.org. Admission $3, free for children under 1. Thurs–Tues 10am–5pm June–Labor Day, 10am–4pm rest of the year; Wed for groups only. Directions: Rte. 50 east to Exit 22/Aris T. Allen Blvd./Rte. 665, which flows into Forest Dr.; go left at 4th light, Hilltop Lane. Turn left at next light, Spa Rd. Go right at Silopanna Rd. and left at stop sign into lot.

Watermark Cruises **Ages 2 and up.** If you're first-timers, the 40-minute narrated cruise on the double-decked *Harbour Queen* provides a pleasing introduction to the waterfront sights, including the Bay Bridge and Naval Academy. The cruise operates late March through November (weather permitting) with several departures daily, more on weekends. The *Miss Anne* (actually, there are two *Miss Annes!*) tours Spa Creek from April through November, with several departures daily at quarter of and quarter after the hour. Drinks and snacks are available on board all boats.

When time permits, you might want to take a 90-minute cruise or an all-day trip to historic and scenic St. Michael's on the Eastern Shore, but reservations are required. Watermark also arranges private parties.

City Dock. (C) 410/268-7600. www.watermarkcruises.com. $8 adults, $4 kids 3–11, free 2 and under. Daily April–Oct morning–dusk; March and Nov–Dec, weather permitting.

Jug Bay Wetlands Sanctuary *(Finds* **Ages 4 and up.** This is an incredible spot for anyone with an interest in the natural world and/or Chesapeake Bay ecology. It's about a half-hour from Annapolis, but it's well worth the ride. At seven environmentally themed workstations in the visitor-friendly laboratory, hands-on activities encourage youngsters to learn about the wetlands ecosystem.

Most weekends, Jug Bay offers seasonal outdoor workshops—hiking, birding, and such—on 7 miles of wetlands paths. Nature lectures (many of which are appropriate for kids with their families) are also given most Saturdays and Sundays. Special summer kids' programs are always well attended. Please note that Jug Bay is open on a limited basis by reservation only. No reservation is required to hike the Glendening Nature Preserve, open Saturday 9am to 5pm.

1361 Wrighton Rd., Lothian. ℂ 410/741-9330. www.jugbay.org. Admission $3 adults, $2 seniors and under age 18. Year-round by reservation only, Wed, Sat, Sun (never on Sun Dec–Feb) 9am–5pm. Directions from D.C.: Take the Beltway to Rte. 4 east/south, 10½ miles to right at Plummer Lane, and go right on Wrighton Rd. Go half a mile to entrance on left. Call or check the website for directions from Annapolis. Free on-site parking.

Maryland Hall for the Creative Arts   **Ages 6 and up.** Maryland Hall, which offers year-round workshops in the fine arts as well as demonstrations, exhibits, and performances, is less than a 10-minute ride from downtown Annapolis. The Annapolis Symphony (ℂ **410/269-1132**), Ballet Theatre of Maryland, and Annapolis Youth Orchestra (once a school) all make their home here. You can catch each of them several times annually.

801 Chase St. ℂ **410/263-5544.** www.mdhallarts.org. Admission varies. Directions: Rte. 50 east to Rowe Blvd. exit. Right at bottom of ramp. Right at 2nd light (Taylor Ave.), proceed to traffic circle (West St.), and go ⅓ way around. Turn right on Spa Rd., 1st left (Greenfield).

Maryland State House   **Ages 8 and up.** The oldest state capitol in continuous legislative use served as the nation's capitol from November 1783 to June 1784. In this building, George Washington resigned his commission in 1783, and the Treaty of Paris was ratified. The stained-glass skylights are by Louis Comfort Tiffany. Guided half-hour tours are scheduled between 9am and 5pm daily.

State Circle. ℂ **410/260-6401.** www.mdarchives.state.md.us. Free admission. Daily 9am–5pm.

Newman Street Playground ⛱ **Ages 2 and up.** Local school kids helped plan these humongous wooden play structures. You can picnic here or seek shade and rest during your tour of Annapolis. Weekdays, September to June, during school hours, the park fills with students from the elementary school that backs onto the park.

Newman and Compromise sts. (Marriott side of City Dock). Free admission. Daily during daylight hours.

William Paca House and Gardens *(Moments*   **Ages 6 and up.** William Paca, a signer of the Declaration of Independence and governor of Maryland during the Revolution, built this five-part Georgian mansion between 1763 and 1765. In the early 1900s, the house became a hostelry for legislators and visitors to the U.S. Naval Academy. When the wrecker's ball threatened in 1965, the Historic Annapolis Foundation stepped in and restored the house and 2-acre garden to their former grandeur. Older kids generally find the house of interest, and *everyone* delights in the garden, with its intricate terraces and waterway. The flower enclosure is abloom from March to November. A self-guided audio tour costs $1. Or join a guided tour, several times a day. Metered street parking is nearby; a garage is within walking distance.

186 Prince George St. ℂ **410/267-7619.** www.annapolis.org. Adults $8, seniors $7, kids 6–17 $6, 5 and under free. Mon–Sat 10am–5pm; Sun noon–5pm. Closed Mon–Thurs mid-Jan–mid-March. Closed Thanksgiving, Dec 24–25.

Pirate Adventures on the Chesapeake   **Ages 2 and up.** Pirate "Ruby" or a substitute welcomes kids boarding the 35-foot *Sea Gypsy IV* with a booming "Hello, mates!" All summer and weekends spring and fall, the 75-minute "pirate" cruise plies

Annapolis Harbor several times daily, weather permitting. Kids dress up in pirate garb, listen to seafaring songs, and search for treasure buried beneath a well-marked buoy. The highlight for most is an encounter with "Pirate Pete," who pulls alongside the *Sea Gypsy* in a small powerboat. That's when the little tars get to fire the hydraulic water cannons. Without even knowing it, children learn something about map-reading, local ecology, pirates, and commerce on the Chesapeake. Preschoolers through third graders especially go overboard for this splashy cruise.

Annapolis City Marina, Severn Ave. (behind Carrol's Creek restaurant). C 410/263-0002. www.chesapeakepirates.com. $17 for 3 and over, $8.50 2 and under. Discounts for groups of 30 or more. Reservations required. Directions: From downtown Annapolis, cross Spa Creek bridge. Left at Severn Ave. Go 1 block and left into Annapolis City Marina parking lot. Walk to water behind restaurant/office complex.

Helen Avalynne Tawes Garden ♣   All ages. This delightful 6-acre garden depicts Maryland's varied landscape, from the Appalachians in the western part of the state to the ocean beaches of the Eastern Shore. It reminds us of the necessity to value and conserve our precious natural resources.

Weekdays, pick up a booklet at the garden display in the lobby, and check out the great blue heron and Baltimore oriole (the state bird, not a baseball player) before beginning your walk. More than likely, the most interesting thing to younger kids will be the Texture, Taste, and Fragrance Garden, which invites visitors to "taste and see if you can identify" certain herbs. I'm partial to the gazebo and nearby pond. Monday to Friday, the gift shop is open 9am to 3pm, and the cafeteria is open 7:30am to 3pm.

Behind Department of Natural Resources, 580 Taylor Ave., at Rowe Blvd. (across from the stadium). C 410/260-8189. www.dnr.state.md.us/publiclands/tawesgarden.html. Free admission. Garden daily sunrise–sunset. Lobby exhibits Mon–Fri 8am–5pm (closed holidays).

U.S. Naval Academy ♣   Ages 6 and up. Before visiting, check security restrictions via phone or online. It's only a 5-minute walk from City Dock in downtown Annapolis to the Naval Academy, founded in 1845. Hours change seasonally for the hour-long guided walking tour that departs from the Armel-Leftwich Visitor Center adjacent to the Halsey Field House inside Gate 1.

Try to see the short film *To Lead and to Serve* before you begin your tour. The interactive exhibits and displays will give you and your kids a sense of Naval Academy life. The gift shop bears checking out, as does the view of downtown from the riverfront promenade behind the building. Depending on security restrictions, you may be able to visit several buildings on your own. In **Lejeune Hall,** across from the visitor center, you'll find cases of trophies and photographs of the academy's athletic achievements, and maybe catch some action in the Olympic-size pool. Close by is **Dahlgren Hall,** where a chrome yellow biplane "flies" from the ceiling. The navy's ice hockey team plays here. Pick up a hockey schedule, along with a snack, at the Dry Dock Restaurant. It's a hop, skip, and jump across the Yard, as the academy grounds are called, to the awesome **Navy Chapel** and **John Paul Jones's crypt.** Nearby is the Naval Academy Museum, **Preble Hall** (C 410/293-2108), filled with 200 years of naval art and artifacts. The ground-floor **Gallery of Ships** delights all ages. Many of the ships are original builder's models. The museum is open Monday to Saturday, 9am to 5pm; Sunday 11am to 5pm. From the seawall at the **Robert Crown Sailing Center,** you might see boatloads of plebes learning to sail. Most will never board a sailboat at any other time in their lives, yet they are all required to learn the basics.

Bancroft Hall is the "dormitory" for all 4,000 midshipmen. If you're touring on your own, arrive at Bancroft Hall a few minutes before noon (weather permitting) for

noon meal formation (about 12:10pm weekdays, 12:20pm weekends)—in my mind, the highlight of an academy visit. Would your kids be willing to line up like this for their lunch? There's usually plenty of activity in the afternoon on the fields behind Bancroft. Stroll the beautiful grounds, and walk along the **Dewey seawall** for a wide-angle view of the Chesapeake Bay. In season, catch a band concert in the gazebo. After **Commissioning Week,** in late May or early June, it's fun to watch the procession of weddings (one an hour!) from the lawn opposite the chapel.

Many athletic events are free and open to the public. For information and tickets, call the Naval Academy Athletic Association (© **800/US-4-NAVY;** www.navysports.com).

Please note that everyone 16 and over must have a photo ID to be admitted to the U.S. Naval Academy grounds.

Visitor Gate at foot of King George St. © 410/263-6933. www.usna.edu. Visitor Center www.navyonline.com. Free self-guided tour; guided tour $7.50 adults, $6.50 seniors (62 and older), $5.50 for children in 1st–12th grades, free for children under 1st grade. Visitor center daily Mar–Dec 9am–5pm; Jan–Feb 9am–4pm. Tour hours vary seasonally. Call ahead. Closed Thanksgiving, Dec 25, Jan 1. Group tours by appointment year-round. Directions: Rte. 50 east to Rowe Blvd. exit. Proceed on Rowe about 1 mile to left at College Ave., and right at King George St. to Gate 1. Limited parking behind USNA Visitor Center.

WHERE TO STAY

If you're planning an overnight stay, take your pick of historic inns, B&Bs, and luxury hotels. Hotels outside the historic district often offer complimentary shuttle service. For a brochure describing B&Bs in Annapolis, write the **Annapolis Association of Licensed Bed and Breakfast Owners,** P.O. Box 744, Annapolis, MD 21404, or check out the **Annapolis, Maryland Bed and Breakfasts** website, www.azinet.com/annaarea.html.

EXPENSIVE

Annapolis Marriott Waterfront Overlooking the harbor and Spa Creek, the Marriott enjoys a prime downtown location, as does **Pusser's Landing** restaurant and dockside bar/lounge. A children's menu at lunch and dinner offers a handful of reasonably priced items, or the kids can fill up on one of the light-fare offerings. Scores of Annapolis eateries (not to mention shopping and sightseeing) are within a few blocks. Room service is available, and the hotel has an exercise room with fitness equipment. The second floor is a smoking floor. All other floors are nonsmoking. Two rooms and the top-floor suite have Jacuzzis. Regrettably, the hotel paved over the swimming pool several years ago to gain parking. When there are big doings at the Naval Academy and during October's boat shows, this place is booked a year ahead.

80 Compromise St., Annapolis, MD 21401. © 800/336-0072 or 410/268-7555. www.annapolismarriott.com. 150 units. $159–$329 (waterfront suite) single or double. Cribs and rollaways free. AE, DISC, MC, V. Ask about special packages and promotions. Valet parking $15 per 24-hour period. **Amenities:** Restaurant; 2 bars; basic fitness center; concierge (weekends only); room service (breakfast and dinner only); laundry service; dry-cleaning service. *In room:* A/C, TV, hair dryer, iron.

MODERATE

Scotlaur Inn Roll out of bed onto Main Street—literally! Stay at what could be the world's only "Bed and Bagel," and enjoy a full complimentary breakfast in **Chick and Ruth's Delly** downstairs. The 10 distinctive rooms in the family-owned and operated establishment all have private bathrooms (some with shower only, so be sure to ask if you must have a tub) and modem hookups. The rooms are small, but the Victorian furnishings, antique bookcases and books, and dynamite location more than compensate.

They haven't built structures with such thick walls in many moons. When you go downstairs for breakfast, ask Ted to do magic tricks for your kids. You won't have to ask twice.

165 Main St., Annapolis, MD 21401. © 410/268-5665. www.scotlaurinn.com. 10 units. $90–$140 per room (slightly higher during special events). Cribs free, rollaways $15 per night. Ask about special winter rates. MC, V. Garage parking $10 per night. Pets accepted, with advance notice. **Amenities:** Restaurant. *In room:* A/C, TV/VCR, hair dryer.

WHERE TO DINE
MODERATE

Cafe Normandie COUNTRY FRENCH   I would have no problem dining at this cozy, plant-filled bistro several times a week. Don't try all these at one sitting, but I can personally recommend the cream of crab soup, Caesar salad (with grilled chicken or blackened fish), veal and fish main courses, sautéed soft-shell crabs, and crepes (seafood or ratatouille). Wrap up with a fruit- or ice cream–filled crepe. If your kids are finicky, they're bound to dig the crepes.

185 Main St. © 410/280-6470. High chairs, booster seats. Reservations recommended. Lunch and dinner main courses $6.95–$26. AE, MC, V. Sun–Thurs 8am–10pm; Fri–Sat 8am–11pm.

Cantler's Riverside Inn 🦀🦀 SEAFOOD   You can't visit Annapolis and not go to Cantler's. It'd be a crime not to dig into the local delicacy, steamed Maryland blue crabs (in season May–Oct), at this down-home restaurant on Mill Creek. Be prepared: The harvest the past few years has approached pitiful, and prices rose to $60 a dozen for jumbos in 2005. When they're that expensive, I order the lump crab cake. Grab a seat on the deck, covered patio, or inside. Get here early on the weekends—that means by noon for lunch and before 5pm for dinner if you don't want a horrible wait. The crabs and steamed clams (when available) are the best around. I also recommend the crab–vegetable soup, soft-shell or crab-cake sandwich, or broiled fish of the day. There's fried chicken and steak for non–crab eaters, as well as hot dogs, hamburgers, chicken, fried or steamed shrimp, or crab-cake sandwiches for the kids. *Note:* The steamed crabs are heavily doused with Old Bay seasoning. You may want to scrape some off before the little ones dig in.

Take the kids underneath the restaurant for a peek into the shedding boxes. This is where the Maryland blue crabs do their striptease (with no privacy) to become the sought-after delicacy, soft-shell crabs. Call for directions—about a 10-minute ride from downtown Annapolis.

458 Forest Beach Rd. © 410/757-1311. High chairs, booster seats. Reservations not accepted Fri–Sun; accepted for groups of 10 or more Mon–Thurs. Most items $5–$24 (not including crabs). AE, DC, MC, V. Sun–Thurs 11am–11pm; Fri–Sat 11am–midnight.

INEXPENSIVE

Chick and Ruth's Delly *Finds* DELI/AMERICAN   The **Dellyland Delight kids' menu** (for those 7 and under) offers breakfast fare and sandwiches with potato chips or french fries. Of course, you'll treat them to one of the oversize sodas or shakes that they won't be able to finish (that's where you come in). I love the well-seasoned "delly" (home) fries on the breakfast platters, which are served all day. The 44 tasty sandwiches (try the Main Street, if you can't decide) are named for Maryland pols and locals. You can also get everything from a hot dog or hamburger to a Caesar salad and homemade vegetable crab soup. You gotta love the funky decor, fountain treats, and cheeky waitresses at this friendly eatery that has served four generations of Annapolitans. And the servers don't seem to mind cleaning up after little ones. Join the locals reciting the Pledge of Allegiance weekdays at 8:30am and weekends at 9:30am.

165 Main St. ℂ **410/269-6737**. High chairs, booster seats, kids menu. Reservations not accepted. Most items $3–$8; kids' menu items $3–$4. No credit cards. Daily 24 hr. Closed Thanksgiving and 4pm Dec 25–4pm Dec. 31.

Riordan's AMERICAN   Picture a neighborhood saloon—lots of wood and brass, tchotchkes on the walls, and locals and tourists bellied up to the bar. That's Riordan's. Annapolitans introduce their children early on to the potato skins with the works, burgers, and sandwiches. Try the French dip (roast beef), the Reuben, or the soup of the day (the chowders and vegetable crab soup are a cut above). The food is consistently good, and the friendly servers know how to hustle. Sunday brunch (entrees $7.95–$9.95; kids $4.50) is an Annapolis tradition and includes a Mimosa (champagne and OJ) or flute of champagne. The kids' menu has hot dogs, burgers, chicken tenders, and penne pasta for lunch and dinner.

26 Market Space. ℂ **410/263-5449**. High chairs, booster seats, kids' menu. Reservations not accepted. Main dishes (dinner) $9–$16; sandwiches $8–$9.50; kids menu $5–$7. AE, DC, MC, V. Mon–Sat 11am–1:30am, Sun 10am–1:30am. Brunch Sun 10am–1pm.

5 Baltimore

38 miles NE of Washington, D.C.

Where to start? Only an hour's drive or 40-minute train ride from D.C., Charm City offers families an abundance of sights and experiences. You could easily spend several days in Baltimore and leave begging for more. Birthplace of Babe Ruth, H. L. Mencken, Cal Ripken, and our national anthem, the city is enlivened by its rich ethnic heritage. Baltimore is also a big sports town, supporting both the Baltimore Ravens (NFL football) and Orioles baseball.

A myriad of activities are centered at the **Inner Harbor,** a revitalized complex of businesses, sightseeing attractions, shops, restaurants, and hotels built around the city's natural harbor. The Baltimore Orioles play in Oriole Park at Camden Yards (see "Exploring Baltimore," later in this section), frequently to sellout crowds. The Baltimore Ravens play at PSI Stadium next to Oriole Park.

Not the least of Baltimore's claims to fame are steamed blue crabs, harvested spring through fall from the Chesapeake Bay. When the local pickin's are slim, they're brought in from the Carolinas and Gulf states. Baltimore also boasts the best corned beef between New York City and Miami Beach.

GETTING THERE

BY BUS   Greyhound (ℂ **800/231-2222**) provides frequent service between the Washington bus terminal at 1st and L streets NE and 2110 W. Fayette St. in Baltimore. The current fare Monday through Thursday is $11 one-way and $22 round-trip; Friday through Sunday $12.50 one-way, $24 round-trip. Children 2 through 11 pay half price (one child per paying adult).

BY CAR   To get to Baltimore from D.C., take I-95 to I-395 north to Pratt Street; make a right and another right at President Street. You'll find many parking lots near the harbor.

BY TRAIN   Frequent daily train service via Amtrak (ℂ **800/USA-RAIL**) is available between Washington and Baltimore. Fare for a family of 4 (2 adults and 2 kids 2–15) is $78 round-trip, reserved coach. The trip takes about 40 minutes and links D.C.'s Union Station and Baltimore's Penn Station, about 15 blocks or a short taxi ride from the Inner Harbor.

Less expensive than Amtrak is the **MARC commuter train, Penn Line** (© 800/ 325-RAIL; www.mtamaryland.com). It's a glorified subway car, but the price recommends it. The fare from D.C.'s Union Station to Baltimore's Penn Station is only $7 per adult one-way, free for up to two kids 5 and under with each paying adult (additional children pay full fare), but bear in mind that it operates weekdays only.

INFORMATION

For maps and information on sightseeing and walking tours, contact the **Baltimore Convention and Visitor Association,** 100 Light St., Baltimore, MD 21201 (© 888/ BALTIMORE or 410/837-4636; www.baltimore.org). A **visitor center** is located at the Inner Harbor opposite the Pratt Street Pavilion, near the USS *Constellation*. Unless otherwise noted below, you can find out about all special events and festivals at © 410/837-4636 or www.baltimoreevents.org.

Getting around the harbor (the National Aquarium, Fells Point, Fort McHenry, the American Visionary Art Museum, Federal Hill, Port Discovery, and Little Italy), is easily done by water taxi. The 11 blue-and-white boats crisscross the harbor on several routes year-round, weather permitting. May through September, boats stop at landings every 15 to 18 minutes. Tickets ($8 adults, $4 kids 10 and under) are good for unlimited, all-day use. For more information, call © **800/658-8947** or 410/536-3901; www.thewatertaxi.com.

SPECIAL EVENTS

Note: For event information, call ©800/HARBOR-1 unless otherwise noted.

JANUARY Ring in the New Year at the Inner Harbor, where you'll be dazzled by a stunning pyrotechnic display at midnight. For a chilling experience, watch ice carvers create spectacular sculptures.

FEBRUARY Bring older kids to the **Baltimore Craft Show.** More than 500 artisans sell their wares in Festival Hall at one of the largest and most prestigious craft shows in the country (© **410/649-7000**).

MARCH Musicians and other performers entertain at Harborplace around **St. Patrick's Day.**

APRIL Enjoy contemporary band music at the **Easter Sunday Music Fest** in the Harborplace Amphitheatre. The Easter Bunny greets children throughout Harborplace and the Gallery on Easter Sunday afternoon.

MAY The **Preakness** horse race (part of the Triple Crown) is celebrated with concerts, parades, and balloon festivals the third week of May preceding the race at Pimlico (© **410/542-9400**).

JUNE **Summer ethnic festivals** take place June to September, but not every weekend. Admission is free, but bring your wallet and appetite. Call the visitor center for the dates of the Polish, German, Italian, and other festivals. Enjoy music Friday, Saturday, and Sunday all summer at the Harborplace Amphitheatre's **Summer Concert Series.** Head for **Citysand** in the Harborplace Amphitheatre, where architects work with kids to sculpt elaborate sand creations. Pay tribute to the Stars and Stripes on **Flag Day** (June 14) at **Fort McHenry** (© **410/962-4290**).

BALTIMORE 275

JULY Baltimoreans celebrate the **Fourth of July** in grand style with daytime entertainment and a dazzling fireworks display at the Inner Harbor. A summer concert series takes place every Friday, Saturday, and Sunday night in the amphitheater. As part of Baltimore's Festival of the Arts, **Artscape** is usually held the third weekend of the month along Mount Royal Avenue. Artwork by youngsters as well as visual arts-and-craft exhibits are displayed at this happening, enlivened by jugglers, mimes, music makers, and street theater.

AUGUST Who can resist the free entertainment dished out by fire eaters, unicyclists, jugglers, and clowns at the **Inner Harbor?** Look for them daily at lunchtime or on weekends in summer.

SEPTEMBER Bookworms from several states wriggle over to meet and greet local authors, attend workshops, and listen to speakers at the annual **Baltimore Book Festival,** held one weekend at Mount Vernon Place (www.baltimorebookfestival.com).

OCTOBER The **Fells Point Funfest** (first weekend) attracts kids of all ages to its colorful street festival. Clowns, jugglers, and musicians entertain, and children's games, tempting snacks, and crafts are always within easy reach. Celebrate Baltimore's rich maritime history at **Kids on the Bay,** held at the Inner Harbor as part of the 2-week Baltimore on the Bay festival. Plenty of kid-pleasing activities will delight your little swabs (℡ **410/675-8756**).

NOVEMBER What would Thanksgiving be without a parade? Follow the floats and cartoon characters from Camden Yards to Market Place on the Saturday before Turkey Day for the **Thanksgiving Parade.**

DECEMBER The **Annual Lighted Boat Parade** illuminates the harbor as more than 50 boats in holiday finery file past. In a **Merry Tuba Christmas,** traditional carols are played by an orchestra of tubas and euphoniums in the Harborplace Amphitheatre. The **New Year's Eve Extravaganza** at the Baltimore Convention Center is a perfect way for the entire family to bid adieu to the old year: no booze and plenty of entertainment, with fireworks at midnight over the Inner Harbor (℡ **800/282-6632**).

EXPLORING BALTIMORE

American Visionary Art Museum ✺ **Ages 6 and up.** There's some really weird stuff going on here, and it's utterly captivating. I imagine that if Hieronymous Bosch and Monty Python joined forces to create an art museum, this is what it would look like. Most of the self-taught artists are outsiders—jailbirds, religious visionaries, and certifiable wackos. Because most of the paintings, drawings, sculptures, and assemblages are so off center that they're in the next galaxy, they grab children with their stripped-bare honesty and lack of pretension. No climbing, please, on the 55-foot whirligig in the outdoor plaza.

The July 4th "Big Kabooooooom!" family day features a pet parade, pie-eating contest, and activities such as the Mr. Potato Head Beauty Contest—only $1 admission. Check out the museum shop for stuff that you won't find in the Smithsonian. Atop the museum, the **Joy America Café,** with indoor and outdoor seating on a covered patio, has wonderful views of the harbor, a kids' menu, and an eclectic, organic-fare menu. For reservations, call ℡ **410/244-6500.**

800 Key Hwy. ℡ **410/244-1900.** www.avam.org. Admission $11 adults, $7 students age 5 and older (through grad school with ID) and seniors, free for children 4 and under. MC, V. Tues–Sun 10am–6pm. Closed Mon, Thanksgiving, Dec 25. Directions: Take I-95 north to Exit 55, and turn left onto Key Hwy. Continue 1½ miles to Covington St. Park across from main entrance ($3 all day).

Baltimore and Ohio Railroad Museum **Ages 2 and up.** The museum is on the site of the country's first train station, Mount Clare, where the first passenger ticket was issued in 1830. Check out the HO gauge (between regular size and miniature) train display on the second floor: The detail is astounding. In the roundhouse, you can wander through the locomotives, freight and passenger cars, and cabooses. The comprehensive exhibits are a must-see for little toots who get steamed up over trains and railroad history. In the backyard, train rides on the diesel Montclair Express are offered Saturday, Sunday, and holidays. Half-hour movies on railroad history run on weekends, and a museum stores stocks books, train memorabilia, clothing, and whistles. All aboard!

901 W. Pratt St. (at Poppleton). © 410/752-2490. www.borail.org. Admission $11 adults, $10 seniors, $8 ages 2–12, free for children under 2. Daily 10am–5pm. Directions from D.C.: Take New York Ave. east to I-295 north, to I-95 north, to I-395 north (Martin Luther King, Jr. Blvd.); go left at Lombard, and go 3 blocks to left at Poppleton to free museum parking. Directions from Pratt St. (Baltimore Inner Harbor): Go north 1 block to Lombard St., cross MLK Blvd. (do not get on MLK), proceed 3 blocks to 1st light, and turn left (Poppleton) to free museum parking.

Baltimore Maritime Museum **Ages 4 and up.** Kids will get an idea of how sailors live and work on a guided tour of the lightship *Chesapeake,* the submarine USS *Torsk,* the 327-foot Coast Guard cutter *Taney,* and the 7-foot Knoll Lighthouse, which once stood at the mouth of the Patapsco River. All are docked at/near Pier 3.

Pier 3, Inner Harbor, Pratt and Gay sts. © 410/396-3453. Admission Admiral (60 and older) $6, Captain (15–59) $7, Petty officer (6–14) $4, stowaway (5 and under) free. Daily summer 10am–6pm; winter 10:30am–5pm. Closed major holidays. Directions: Take I-95 north and follow signs to Inner Harbor.

Baltimore Museum of Art 🅐🅐 **Ages 8 and up.** Maryland's largest art museum is noted for its decorative arts, furniture, and paintings. The Cone Collection is one of the world's outstanding modern-art collections, with works by Matisse, Picasso, Cézanne, Van Gogh, and Gauguin. The Levi and Wurtzburger outdoor sculpture gardens brim with contemporary pieces.

The modern-art wing houses a prestigious collection of 20th-century art in 16 galleries. Changing exhibitions augment the permanent collection. **Gertrude's,** the on-site restaurant, has seating indoors and on the terrace (© **410/889-3399**). Summer jazz performances take place in the sculpture garden, where picnicking is welcome (© **410/396-6314**). Special family programs are ongoing. The museum store is worth a stop.

Art Museum Dr., at North Charles and 31st sts. © 410/396-7100. www.artbma.org. Admission $10 adults, $8 seniors 65 and older, $6 college students with ID, free for age 18 and under; free admission 1st Thurs of month. Wed–Fri 11am–5pm; Sat–Sun 11am–6pm. Closed Mon and Tues, major holidays. Directions: Rte. I-295 north to Russell St. exit. Right at Pratt, and left on Charles to Art Museum Dr.

Baltimore Museum of Industry 🅐 *(Finds* **Ages 4 and up.** This museum is dedicated to the industrial history of Baltimore and is housed in the former Platt Oyster Cannery on the Inner Harbor. Weekends in the Children's Motorworks section, youngsters as young as 5 turn out cardboard vans on an assembly line. Kids 10 and up can punch a clock at the Oyster Cannery and become workers in an 1883 Baltimore cannery for an hour. The young shuckers use real oyster shells with white clay oysters before moving on to a skilled task such as making or labeling cans. Kids are paid with brass tokens that they can then use in the company store. Children gravitate to the turn-of-the-century drugstore, a replica of George Bunting's apothecary (he invented Noxzema, in case you didn't know), complete with a soda fountain. In other parts of the museum, visitors encounter a meat-packing exhibit and a 1920s garment loft workshop.

Baltimore

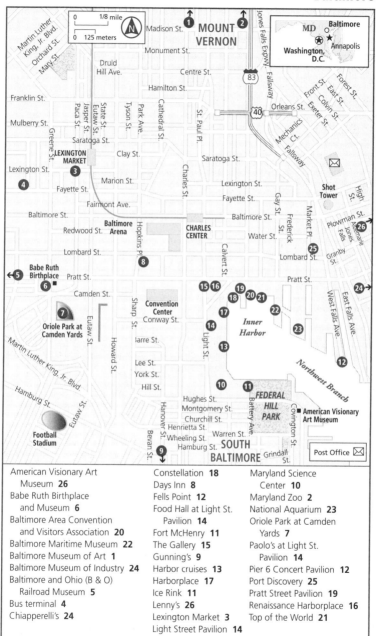

Tickets can be purchased at the door for the Cannery ($3.50) Saturday at 11am and 2pm, and Sunday at 2:30pm; and the Children's Motorworks ($2) Saturday and Sunday at 1pm. (It's advisable to call ahead to avoid disappointment.)

1415 Key Hwy. ⓒ 410/727-4808. www.thebmi.org. Admission $10 adults, $6 seniors, students, children 5 and older; free for children 4 and under. Workshops extra. Tues–Sat 10am–5pm; Wed 6–9pm; Sun noon–5pm. Directions: I-95 to Ft. McHenry exit and then follow signs to Key Highway.

The Maryland Zoo 🅚🅚 **Ages 2 and up.** Come see why this is rated the nation's no. 1 children's zoo. The Maryland Zoo has long been an innovator in trading cages for natural habitats. Animal lovers benefit by coming face to face (well, almost) with their favorite creatures. With fewer barriers, kids leave with a greater appreciation of the interdependence of *all* living things.

Be a voyeur and watch from the underwater viewing station at Polar Bear Watch as Alaska and Magnet (polar bears) go through their aquatic antics.

More than 100 species inhabit the **Maryland Wilderness** section of the Children's Zoo. Visitors learn about the bog's role in the overall "health" of the Chesapeake Bay. Your little bipeds can climb into a huge oriole's nest, scale a tree, or crawl through an acrylic tunnel under a dam. In the **Maryland Farmyard,** kids are invited to ride a pony, pet a sheep, breeze down the silo slide, or watch a cow-milking demonstration. Lunch with the Kodiak bears at 2pm, or watch the African black-footed penguins dive for raw fish at 3pm.

In the **Chimpanzee Forest,** designed as part of a species-survival plan, you and your little monkeys can watch the chimps swing from a firehose vine and frolic in their very own play area. The well-placed observation platforms allow visitors to feel almost at one with the chimps. Year-round, the zoo typically has free activity booklets and special family events. Be sure to ask about these and summer programs. Cap your visit with a ride on the antique carousel and Zoochoo Train.

Druid Hill Park. ⓒ 410/366-LION or 410/396-6165 for group rates. www.marylandzoo.org. Admission $15 adults 12–64, $10 ages 2–11, $12 seniors 65 and over, free for children under 2. Mon–Fri 10am–4pm; Sat–Sun 10am–5:30pm (6:30pm in summer). Directions: Take I-95 north to I-695 west (toward Towson) to I-83 south (Jones Falls Expressway). Exit 7 west off the expressway to Druid Park Lake Dr., and follow signs to the zoo. Plenty of free parking.

Fort McHenry National Monument and Historic Shrine 🅚 **Ages 4 and up.** Francis Scott Key was so moved on the night of September 11, 1814, as the British fired on Fort McHenry (missing their target repeatedly, I might add) that he wrote a poem that became our national anthem in 1931. Visit the spot where the bombs were "bursting in air" while Key was waxing poetic from a boat in the harbor. A 16-minute orientation film plays on the half-hour from 9am to 4pm. The flag change is at 9:30am and 4:30pm. Pretty stirring, I think. The gun collection and underground dungeons are of special interest to most kids. The waterfront park is an idyllic spot for watching Old Glory snapping in the breeze and boat traffic on the Patapsco River and Chesapeake Bay. The first or second weekend in September, the annual Defenders' Day event features marching troops, military encampments, and fireworks. Keep an eye out for the two ghosts in War of 1812 uniforms that reportedly haunt the fort.

East Fort Ave. (at the very end). ⓒ 410/563-3524. www.nps.gov/fomc. Free admission to the grounds; admission to Star Fort $5 age 17 and over, free for age 16 and under. Daily 8am–5pm (enter before 4:45pm). Ask about extended summer hours. Directions: Take I-95 north to Exit 55/Fort McHenry (before the tunnel), to left on Lawrence St., turn left on Fort Ave. Continue 1 mile to park.

The Gallery   All ages. During your visit to the Inner Harbor, browse The Gallery, a pleasing, four-level mélange of shops and restaurants that is part of Harborplace (see below). Unlike many malls, with their claustrophobic, tomblike ambience, The Gallery has a soaring, light-filled atrium that evokes the outdoors. The big draws for families are Brookstone (electronics and gadgets), Sam Goody (CDs, DVDs), Suncoast Motion Picture Co. (videos and movie memorabilia), and Gap and Gap Kids for stylish, durable clothing.

When hunger strikes, head for the fourth-level food court, where the Ocean City fries and burgers are sure kid-pleasers. You'll also find Bain's Deli, Steak Escape, Salad Creations, Sbarro, and China City. Bourbon Street Café has New Orleans–style fare. Donna's Coffee Bar & Café (2nd level) serves soups, salads, sandwiches, and pizza. For dessert, dip into some rich and creamy Ben & Jerry's. Or cross the street to the Pratt and Light Street Pavilions for more choices.

200 E. Pratt St.; Pratt, Light, and Calvert sts. at the Inner Harbor. ✆ 800/HARBOR-1 or 410/332-4191. www.harbor place.com. Mon–Sat 10am–9pm; Sun 11am–7pm; some extended summer hours. Directions: Take I-95 north and follow signs to Inner Harbor.

Harborplace 🍴 **All ages.** Baltimore's top tourist draw at the Inner Harbor consists of two pavilions (Light and Pratt streets) and a mall (the Gallery) that do their seductive best to lure visitors into their shops, restaurants, and food stalls. The **Light Street Pavilion** is primarily food-oriented. Kids love the second-floor Food Hall, which boasts a wide array of American-style and ethnic fast food. Weather permitting, chow down on a bench overlooking the harbor. For sit-down service, try Capitol City Brewing Co., Johnny Rockets (1950s-style diner), or Paolo's. Lee's Ice Cream is made locally. Check out the Discovery Channel Store (nature-related items), Flag Shop, and Baltimore Zoo Store (animal-inspired souvenirs, gifts). At the information kiosk, find out about special events, which in the past have included rowing regattas, band concerts, and crab races.

Shoppers head for the **Pratt Street Pavilion,** filled with big-name retail stores, one-of-a-kind boutiques, and more restaurants. Check out Dapy for wacky electronic playthings. Pig out at the following sit-down restaurants: California Pizza Kitchen, Pizzeria Uno, the Cheesecake Factory, Five Guys (burgers, fries and shakes), Tex Mex Grill, or Wayne's Bar-B-Que. Even on nonholidays, the air is festive around Harborplace. Without spending a cent, you can have a rich time watching the other tourists, strolling the waterfront promenades, and window shopping.

Pratt, Light, and Calvert sts. ✆ 410/332-4191. Shops and Food Hall: Mon–Sat 10am–9pm; Sun 11am–7pm (extended weekend hours in summer); restaurants with separate entrances stay open later. Directions: Take I-95 north and follow signs to Harborplace.

Baltimore Ice Rink at Harbor Point   Ages 3 and up. Skate daily from December through early March at this outdoor rink with the Inner Harbor as a backdrop to the north. The view is particularly stunning after dark. Skate rentals are available for kids 3 years and older. Don't forget hats and gloves for the kiddies, and keep a tight rein on youngsters under 5.

Rash Field, 201 Key Hwy., Inner Harbor. ✆ 410/837-4636. www.bop.org. Admission $5; skate rentals $3. Hours vary. Directions: Take I-95 north to I-395 north. Right at Conway Street (Oriole Park on left), right at Charles St., left on Key Highway (Maryland Science Center), to Rash Field and Ice Rink on left.

Lexington Market 🍴🍴 *(Finds*   **All ages.** Skip breakfast; it's pig-out time! The former open-air market, named for the Revolution's first battle, opened in 1782. Back then, farmers arrived with produce, game, fowl, and dairy goods. The first shed was raised in 1803, and the market grew in fits and starts. Fire destroyed it in 1949. Two brick buildings opened in 1952. Today, about 130 merchants hawk produce, seafood, poultry, and a variety of prepared foods and baked goods from row upon row of stalls in two buildings. An information kiosk is located in the center of the Arcade, the site of entertainment and special events such as the annual chocolate and ice cream festivals. Seating for 500 is available on the Arcade's second level. Free concerts take place Friday and Saturday noon to 2pm.

Recommendations (diligently researched over many years) include Polock Johnny's sausage sandwiches (with the works), Barron's Deli for corned beef, Faidley's for seafood, Utz potato chips, and Berger's for doughnuts and the best cookies in the area.

West Lexington St. (between Paca and Eutaw). ℂ 410/685-6169. www.lexingtonmarket.com. Mon–Sat 8:30am–6pm. Directions: Take I-95 north to Russell St. exit. Russell runs into Paca; continue 5 blocks. Ample garage and lot parking; limited street parking.

Maryland Science Center 🅐🅐 **Ages 2 and up.** Time passes quickly in this facility, established by the Maryland Academy of Sciences. Scores of hands-on exhibits invite kids of all ages to touch, explore, and learn. Enter a distorted room, make friends with a computer, and delve into physics, geology, and the human mind.

The third-floor **Kids' Room** features a jungle gym and slide, plant and animal specimens, and a dress-up corner. It's open daily from 12:30 to 4:30pm. See (reconstructed) dinosaurs that once called Maryland home in the new Dinosaur and Earth Sciences Hall. Kids can try their hand at digging for archaeological finds in the Dark Pit.

Watch a movie on the five-story-high **IMAX** screen, or reach for the stars in the **Davis Planetarium.** Both are recommended for kids 4 and over. Several movies alternate in the IMAX theater, and planetarium shows air twice a day on weekdays and numerous times on weekends. Thursday and Friday at 7:30pm, a double feature is shown in the IMAX. Timed tickets are sold at the box office.

Admission includes all exhibits, one IMAX movie, and a planetarium show. (*Note:* Sometimes timed tickets are required for special exhibits, at an additional cost.) Strollers are allowed in the museum but not in the theaters.

Weather permitting, you can ride the carousel next to the science center weekends throughout the year. The figures on this 1912 Herschell–Spillman creation include horses, dogs, pigs, and roosters. Rides cost $1.25

Inner Harbor, 601 Light St. (at Key Hwy.). ℂ 410/685-5225. www.mdsci.org. General admission to museum, planetarium, and Demo Stage: Adults $14.40, kids 3–12 $10, seniors (60 and older) $13.50. Tues–Fri 10am–5pm; Sat–Sun 10am–6pm. Closed Mon. Extended summer hours. Closed Thanksgiving and Dec 25. Directions: Take I-95 north and follow signs.

National Aquarium 🅐🅐 **Ages 2 and up.** Enter this multistory aquarium towering over the harbor via the dramatic pavilion entry. A 35-foot waterfall flows through pools with turtles and frogs, representing the water that cascades from the Allegheny Mountains in western Maryland to the Chesapeake Bay. Set aside at least 2½ to 3 hours, preferably *early or late in the day,* to do justice to the main Aquarium Building and Marine Mammal Pavilion. Admission is by timed-entry tickets. Whenever possible, steer clear of midday (about 11am–3pm) and weekend crowds. To avoid disappointment, always order tickets ahead (see information below). The new Australia exhibit should be open by spring 2006. When it is, cockatoos, lorikeets, and flying foxes (a type of fruit bat) will accompany you through a rock-gorge habitat like those in the Northern Territory. The freshwater crocs will be at a safe distance.

Moving ramps and escalators transport visitors through various aquatic habitats. The various ring tanks contain rays, tropical fish, and sharks. The **"Maryland Exhibit"** follows a raindrop from pond to ocean. Kids like to hunt for protectively colored species in **"Surviving Through Adaptation"** and to inspect horseshoe crabs and sea stars in the touch pool in the **Children's Cove.** The steamy and exotic South American **Rain Forest,** where small animals and tropical birds roam freely, is still a highlight. Visit the puffins next to the rainforest. The **Atlantic Coral Reef** has more than 800 species. The coral is plastic, but the fish don't mind.

Very young kids who might be bored in the main aquarium will wake up in the **Marine Mammal Pavilion,** with its many interactive displays. One allows you to mimic whale sounds. Bottlenose dolphins cavort several times a day during entertaining half-hour shows in the 1,300-seat pavilion with two multiscreen video monitors.

The seals are fed several times a day outside the main aquarium. Call for feeding times, because they are not "sealed" in stone. Check the sign over the lobby information desk to find out when the sharks dine.

Pier 3, 501 E. Pratt St. (adjacent to Harborplace). *©* **410/576-3800.** www.aqua.org. Timed-entry tickets required. Admission $19.50 adults, $18.50 seniors 60 and over, $13.50 ages 3–11, free for children 2 and under. Purchase advance tickets after 3pm a day ahead through www.aqua.org. Or order tickets up to 3 months ahead through Ticketmaster (*©* **202/432-SEAT** or 410/481-7328). Sat–Thurs 9am–5pm; Fri 9am–8pm. Closed Thanksgiving and Dec 25. Directions: Take I-95 north and follow signs to Inner Harbor. Garage across the street.

Oriole Park at Camden Yards   Ages 6 and up. Take them out to an Orioles ball game, *if* your young ones are old enough to sit still through nine or more innings. Even when the game is lackluster, it is a thrill to be in this magnificent structure where Cal Ripken, Jr. broke records and played his last game in 2001. For my money, the view of downtown Baltimore, perfectly framed beyond the outfield, beats an O's ninth-inning home run with the bases loaded. If the game is boring, check out the overflow memorabilia from the Babe Ruth Museum (see entry below).

You could do worse than to patronize the numerous and varied food concessions, but as always, the food is pricey, although surprisingly tasty. Pack a picnic, and enjoy it pregame at one of the tables provided for such purposes on the Eutaw Street corridor, between the warehouse and the ballpark. Seats at the park are roomy, and best of all, restrooms are abundant. Tickets are a hot commodity, so order early. Ask about special events and promotional giveaways, many of which are geared to young people. You can purchase tickets over the phone or at the O's website (see below) or the Orioles Washington, D.C. store, open in season at 925 17th St. NW (*©* **202/296-2473**). There is plenty of parking in nearby lots on game days. However, since the terrorist attacks against the United States on September 11, 2001, you should allow extra time to park and get through the stadium's security. Feel free to bring plastic bags of food and plastic drink bottles. However, no coolers or backpacks are allowed in the stadium.

Main gate at 333 W. Camden St. *©* **888-848-BIRD.** www.theorioles.com. Admission $8–$45 (SRO on day of game, if a sellout); several tiers of medium-priced seats up to $45 (club box); free for children 2 and under. Tours of the stadium offered daily when there's an evening game. Call for times, which vary (*©* 410/685-9800). To charge tickets in D.C., call *©* 202/432-SEAT. Early Apr–early Oct (later, if the O's make the playoffs). Directions: Take I-95 north to Rte. 395/Downtown or I-295 north. Follow signs to stadium. For information on public transportation to the games, call *©* 800/543-9809 or 410/539-5000.

Babe Ruth Birthplace and Museum and Sports Legends at Camden   Ages 4–14. Stand in the very room where George Herman Ruth, Jr. drew his first breath in 1895. The Sultan of Swat's career record of 714 homers remained unbroken for

more than 40 years, until Hank Aaron settled the score in 1974. Displays in this downtown row house chronicle the Babe's life. Don't miss the photo of 3-year-old slugger Babe Ruth playing ball. Lots more stuff is displayed 3 blocks east (just follow the baseballs painted on the sidewalks) at the 22,000-square-foot Sports Legends museum at historic Camden Yards at Oriole Park, 301 W. Camden Street.. My staff of experts tells me this is one of the top sports museums in the country, folks. Among the exhibits and interactives, you'll find plenty of Orioles memorabilia, too, like Cal Ripken's last home-run ball (Sept. 23, 2001). At the **Second Saturdays** programs (second Sat of each month), special guests regale visitors with baseball stories and reminiscences.

216 Emory St. ℂ 410/727-1539. www.baberuthmuseum.com; www.sportslegendsatcamdenyards.com. Admission Birthplace (Babe Ruth Museum) only: $6 adults, $4 seniors, $4 kids 3–12; Sports Legends $10 adults, $8 seniors, $6.50 kids 3–12. Combined ticket: $14 adults, $11 seniors, $9 kids 3–12. Apr–Oct daily 10am–6pm (until 7pm on Oriole home-game days). Nov–Mar, Tues–Sun 10am–5pm. Closed Thanksgiving, Dec 25, Jan 1. Directions: Take I-95 north to Rte. 395/Downtown. At fork, take Martin Luther King, Jr. Blvd. Turn right on Pratt, go 2 blocks, and turn right on Emory. Go 1 block to museum. Limited free parking; also street parking.

Passport: Voyages of Discovery   Ages 8–14.
This multisensory theater experience asks you to choose between a moving roller-coaster-type seat (***Note:*** must be 3 years old and 40" or taller) or immovable seat. Two or more movies, each 45 minutes long, alternate throughout the day. In late 2005, the choices were ***Oceanarium,*** an underwater adventure, or ***Time Elevator America,*** which accompanies a family from the American Revolution to the present. Call before your visit to see if new titles are playing. Three huge wraparound screens and special effects (fog, wind, mist) add thrills and chills. Next to the aquarium and just a few doors from the Power Plant building (Hard Rock Cafe, Barnes & Noble, ESPN Zone).

Pier IV Building (near National Aquarium), 621 E. Pratt St. ℂ 410-468-0700. www.passportvoyages.com. Admission: Adults $17, kids 3–12 $13. Open daily. Time of last shows varies. If you're anywhere at the Inner Harbour, you can walk. Ample parking lots and garages.

Port Discovery ★★ (Finds   Ages 2–10.
Trace your kids against the "magic" wall of a glass booth, help them fly a virtual plane, watch them climb the Empire State Building, and cheer them on as they explore Kid Works, a maze full of opportunities for climbing, jumping, and sliding. Families also applaud The Dreamlab, Sensation Station, and other innovative interactives at this "kid-powered" museum. There's some new stuff for kids 2 to 5. The best, in my opinion, is The Diner, an authentic '50s-style hash house where kids can pretend to cook and serve their parents. The first Saturday of the month a local chef does a cooking demo. Kids between 2 and 10 seem to get the most from a visit, but it's not unusual for older siblings and parents to get involved. Occupying a former fish market, Port Discovery is stimulating, educational, and, most of all, fun. Show up when it opens on weekends and during school vacations. Even then, the ticket line moves slowly. You may want to order tickets ahead at Ticketmaster (ℂ 800/551-7238). There's a McDonald's on the first-floor atrium level, and half a dozen sit-down restaurants are a stone's throw away at Market Place.

35 Market Place (at Lombard St.). ℂ 410/727-8120. www.portdiscovery.org. Admission $11 adults, $10 seniors, $8.50 kids 3–12, free for kids 2 and under. Mon–Sat 10am–5pm; Sun noon–5. Directions from D.C.: Take I-95 north to I-395 and turn right at Pratt. Follow signs. Plenty of garage parking at Discovery Park Garage, entrance Lombard St. at Market Place.

Star-Spangled Banner Flag House   Ages 4–14.
Almost everyone has heard of Francis Scott Key. But how many of you know who Mary Pickersgill was? It seems

that the commander of Fort McHenry during the War of 1812 entrusted Mary with creating a garrison flag 30 by 42 feet. Not just any flag would do. The order was for a flag that the British would have no trouble seeing from a distance. When the flag outgrew Mary's bedroom, she pieced it on the floor of a nearby malt house. Mary delivered the goods in about 6 weeks, and it inspired Key to write our national anthem in 1814. Stroll down Pratt from the Inner Harbor to this brick row house, built in 1793, to see many of Mary's personal possessions and view a video in the adjacent museum building. Call about special programs, held monthly (such as Flag Day in June). If you want to see the flag itself, you'll have to go to the Smithsonian's National Museum of American History.

844 E. Pratt St. (at Albemarle St.). ✆ 410/837-1793. www.flaghouse.org. Admission $6 adults, $5 seniors and military (with ID), $4 ages 3–18 and students (with ID), free for kids 2 and under; all kids free (with paying adult) 2nd Sun of month. Group rates. Tues–Sat 10am–4pm; Sun noon–5pm.

Top of the World Observation Level   **Ages 4 and up.** On a clear day you can see forever—well, almost. Would you settle for the harbor, the O's stadium, and north to Towson 13 miles away?

Inner Harbor, 27th floor of World Trade Center, 401 E. Pratt St. ✆ 410/837-VIEW. www.bop.org. Admission $5 adults, $4 seniors, $3 kids 3–16, free 2 and under. Sept–Memorial Day Wed–Sun 10am–6pm; Memorial Day–Labor Day 10am–9pm daily. Directions: Take I-95 north and follow signs to Inner Harbor (next to National Aquarium).

USS Constellation   **Ages 4 and up.** The USS *Constellation* sailed to its Inner Harbor berth in 1999 amid friendly cannon fire after 3 years of refurbishment. Built in 1854 and retired in 1945, it was the last navy ship powered entirely by sail. The crew grants landlubbers permission to come aboard and tour the majestic sloop of war (handicap accessible). Special activities take place on weekends.

Inner Harbor. Pier 1, Pratt and Light sts. ✆ 410/539-1797. www.constellation.org. Admission $7.50 adults, $6 seniors, $3.50 kids 6–14, free for kids 5 and under. Daily June–Aug 10am–6pm; Sept–Apr 10am–4:30pm. *(Note: Last tickets sold half-hour before closing.)* Closed major holidays.

CRUISES

Of the numerous cruise boats plying the Inner Harbor during the warm-weather months, here are a few that are particularly appealing to tiny tars.

Harbor Cruises   **Ages 2 and up.** Harbor Cruises offers 1½ hour Kids' Day cruises around the Inner Harbor every Friday, May through August from 10 to 11:30am. The cruise includes lunch (hot dog, potato chips, cookie, and soft drink). With older kids, you may want to take one of the numerous 3-hour and longer cruises (with food, entertainment, and holiday themes) on the *Lady Baltimore* or *Bay Lady,* offered year-round.

Inner Harbor, corner of Light and Lee sts. ✆ 800/695-BOAT or 410/347-5552. www.harborcruises.com. Kids' cruise $14.50; other cruises vary. Year-round; more cruises April–Oct. Directions: I-295 north to right at Pratt, right at Light St., right at Lee St., and right into Harbor Court (hotel) garage. Big boats are just across the street.

WHERE TO STAY
EXPENSIVE
Renaissance Harborplace ★★   Any closer to the harbor, and you'd be swimming. The Renaissance's location is prime, and rooms are spacious and well appointed. The rooms received a major facelift in 2003–04 and are very cushy and comfy. Suites and parlor suites are available, at a higher rate, of course. **Windows,** the hotel's restaurant and lounge overlooking the harbor, welcomes families, but it seems a bit formal for

kids. The hotel is attached to the Gallery, a multilevel mall with scores of shops, restaurants, and food stands. Harborplace is just across Pratt Street and is reachable by a skywalk from the hotel. The concierge will secure tickets for local attractions and help you plan your sightseeing activities. If you can, opt for a room with a view of the harbor. Always ask about special packages and discounted rates.

202 E. Pratt St., Baltimore, MD 21202. © 800/535-1201 or 410/547-1200. www.renaissancehotels.com. 622 units. Weekdays $299–$344 double; weekends from $209. Children 17 and under stay free in parent's room. Cribs and roll-aways free. AE, DC, DISC, MC, V. Self-parking $18, valet parking $25. **Amenities:** 2 restaurants (formal, coffee shop); lounge/bar; indoor pool; health club; sauna; concierge; business center; 24-hour room service; laundry/dry cleaning. *In room:* AC, TV, minibar, coffeemaker, hair dryer, iron.

MODERATE
Days Inn *Kids Value*   Just 3 blocks from the Inner Harbor, 2 blocks from Oriole Park at Camden Yards, and 4 blocks from the aquarium, the Days Inn is a good buy for families, especially if you're able to take advantage of one of several special packages usually offered on weekends.

A free refrigerator is available upon request to cut down on the cost of snacking and eating out. **Hopkins Bar and Grill,** the hotel's restaurant, features Maryland crab cakes and American fare. It's open for breakfast, lunch, and dinner weekdays, and breakfast and dinner on weekends. Kids 12 and under eat free with a paying adult. An outdoor heated pool is open from Memorial Day to Labor Day.

100 Hopkins Place, Baltimore, MD 21201. © 800/325-2525 or 410/576-1000. www.daysinnerharbor.com. 250 units. $114–$199 double. Age 18 and under stay free in parent's room; age 12 and under eat free with paying adult. Cribs free, rollaways $10 per night. Ask about special family and weekend packages. AE, DISC, MC, V. Self-parking $12. **Amenities:** Restaurant; bar; outdoor pool; fitness center (nearby); concierge; room service (7am–11pm). *In room:* A/C, TV, coffeemaker, hair dryer, iron.

WHERE TO DINE
EXPENSIVE
Chiapparelli's *Kids* ITALIAN   Bring the bambinos for heartily sauced pastas (nothing subtle or bland here), seafood, and veal (such as veal Neapolitan) at this Little Italy fixture, still going strong since 1940. Create a meal from fried calamari or clams casino and Italian wedding soup (with spinach, pasta, and meatballs). Be warned: The portions are huge, especially the pasta. The large house salad, deliciously drenched in a creamy garlicky dressing, is meal sized. Force yourselves to try the homemade bread. Pizzas and subs (cold cuts, sausage and pepper, meatball) are available at lunch. The children's menu has pasta with tomato or meat sauce and chicken fingers and such.

237 S. High St. © 410/837-0309. www.chiapparellis.com. High chairs, booster seats, kids' menu. Reservations recommended. Most lunch main courses $7–$11; most dinner main courses $12–$21; kids' menu items $6–$8. AE, DC, MC, V. Mon–Thurs 11am–10pm; Fri–Sat 11am–midnight; Sun 11am–10pm.

MODERATE
Gunning's Seafood Restaurant SEAFOOD   This is Brooklyn, Maryland (not to be confused with Brooklyn, New York), and it's hard-shell crab territory, so roll up your sleeves and dig into a pile of steamed crabs while the waitresses "Hon" you to death. If picking crabs seems too much like work, try Gunning's award-winning crab cakes or one of several other seafood offerings. Gunning's is also known for its fried green pepper rings. Try 'em (you'll thank me). A kids' menu features hamburgers, hot dogs, chicken tenders, a side dish, and ice cream for dessert. Eat in one of the dining rooms, the large enclosed "garden" room, or outdoors in the crab garden when the

weather cooperates. Crabs are also available for carryout. *Tip:* Buy the largest crabs—less work and more meat.

3901 S. Hanover St. © 410/712-9404. High chairs, booster seats, kids' menu. Reservations required for 8 or more. Main courses lunch $6–$11, dinner $13–$28; crabs $40 and up a dozen, depending on size; kids' menu items $4.95. AE, DISC, MC, V. Daily noon–10pm. Directions from D.C.: I-95 or I-295 to I-695/Glen Burnie, Exit 6A/N Linthicum; go 3.5 miles to 2nd traffic light, and turn and left (Hanover), 1 block to restaurant.

Paolo's ✦ ITALIAN/AMERICAN   This place has plenty going for it: atmosphere, friendly service, reasonable prices, and very good food to boot. Children are given crayons while waiting for pizza, spaghetti, grilled chicken, or chicken fingers from the kids' menu. You won't go wrong with pizza, pasta, seafood, or a giant salad, but the chicken (grilled or oven roasted), served with grilled vegetables and roast potatoes, is really special. Some of us like the shrimp scampi served on capellini (very skinny spaghetti). Not too hungry? Order from the appetizer menu. Come for brunch on Saturday and Sunday.

Light St. Pavilion at Harborplace, Pratt and Light sts. © **410/539-7060.** www.paolosristorante.com. High chairs, booster seats, kids' menu. Reservations not accepted. Most main courses $12–$24; kids' menu items average $3.95. AE, MC, V. Mon–Thurs 11:30am–10pm; Fri 11:30am–11pm; Sat 11am–11pm; Sun 11am–10pm.

INEXPENSIVE

Lenny's Deli DELI   Lenny's location might leave something to be desired, but such a minor irritation disappears with the first bite into a corned-beef sandwich. The pastrami is as good as it gets. Don't forget a pickle—half done or well done (sour)—to go with your corned beef. Lenny's also offers a selection of sandwiches, subs, chicken (rotisserie and fried), hot turkey or roast beef platter, and more than a dozen side dishes—from mashed potatoes and macaroni and cheese to knishes and Kosher pickles. It's strictly cafeteria style and no frills. Come here to drool over the corned beef or pastrami, not the decor. The original Lenny's is still thriving in Owings Mills.

1150 E. Lombard St. © **410/327-1177.** www.lennysdeli.com. Reservations not accepted. Most items $6. AE, DISC, MC, V. Mon–Sat 7:30am–6pm; Sun 8am–5pm.

Appendix:
For International Visitors

Whether it's your 1st visit or your 10th, a trip to the United States may require advance planning. This chapter will provide you with essential information, helpful tips, and advice on the most common problems that international visitors may encounter while vacationing in Washington, D.C.

1 Preparing for Your Trip

ENTRY REQUIREMENTS

Check at any U.S. embassy or consulate for current information and requirements. You can also obtain a visa application and other information online at the **U.S. State Department's** website at **www.travel.state.gov**.

VISAS The U.S. State Department has a **Visa Waiver Program** allowing citizens of the following countries (at press time) to enter the United States without a visa for stays of up to 90 days: Andorra, Australia, Austria, Belgium, Brunei, Denmark, Finland, France, Germany, Iceland, Ireland, Italy, Japan, Liechtenstein, Luxembourg, Monaco, the Netherlands, New Zealand, Norway, Portugal, San Marino, Singapore, Slovenia, Spain, Sweden, Switzerland, and the United Kingdom. Citizens of these nations need only a valid passport and a round-trip air or cruise ticket upon arrival. If they first enter the United States, they may also visit Mexico, Canada, Bermuda, and/or the Caribbean islands and return to the United States without a visa. Further information is available from any U.S. embassy or consulate. Canadian citizens may enter the United States without visas; they need only proof of residence.

Citizens of all other countries must have (1) a valid passport that expires at least 6 months later than the scheduled end of their visit to the United States, and (2) a tourist visa, which may be obtained without charge from any U.S. consulate.

To obtain a visa, the traveler must submit a completed application form, with a 1½-inch-square photo, and demonstrate binding ties to a residence abroad. Usually, you can obtain a visa at once or within 24 hours, but it may take longer during the summer rush from June through August. If you cannot go in person, ask the nearest U.S. embassy or consulate about applying by mail. Your travel agent or airline office may also be able to provide you visa applications and instructions. The U.S. consulate or embassy that issues your visa will determine whether you will be issued a multiple- or single-entry visa and any restrictions regarding the length of your stay.

British subjects can obtain up-to-date visa information by calling the **U.S. Embassy Visa Information Line** (© **0891/200-290**) or by visiting the "Visas to the U.S." section of the American Embassy London's website at www.usembassy.org.uk.

Irish citizens can obtain up-to-date visa information through the **Embassy of the U.S. Dublin,** 42 Elgin Rd., Dublin 4, Ireland (© **353/1-668-8777**), or by checking the "Consular Services" section of the website at http://dublin.usembassy.gov.

Australian citizens can obtain up-to-date visa information from the **U.S. Embassy Canberra,** Moonah Place, Yarralumla, ACT 2600 (✆ **02/6214-5600**), or by checking the U.S. Diplomatic Mission's website at http://usembassy-australia.state. gov/consular.

Citizens of **New Zealand** can obtain up-to-date visa information by contacting the **U.S. Embassy New Zealand,** 29 Fitzherbert Terrace, Thorndon, Wellington (✆ **644/472-2068**), or get the information directly from the "For New Zealanders" section of the website at http:// usembassy.org.nz.

MEDICAL REQUIREMENTS Unless you're arriving from an area known to be suffering from an epidemic (particularly cholera or yellow fever), inoculations or vaccinations are not required for entry into the United States. If you have a medical condition that requires **syringe-administered medications,** carry a valid signed prescription from your physician—the Federal Aviation Administration (FAA) no longer allows airline passengers to pack syringes in their carry-on baggage without documented proof of medical need. If you have a disease that requires treatment with **narcotics,** you should also carry documented proof with you—smuggling narcotics aboard a plane is a serious offense that carries severe penalties in the United States.

DRIVER'S LICENSES Foreign driver's licenses are usually recognized in the United States, but you should get an international one if your home license is not in English.

PASSPORT INFORMATION

Safeguard your passport in an inconspicuous, inaccessible place, such as a money belt. Make a copy of the critical pages, including the passport number, and store it in a safe place separate from the passport itself. If you lose your passport, visit the nearest consulate of your native country as soon as possible for a replacement. Passport applications are downloadable from the websites listed below.

Note: The International Civil Aviation Organization has recommended a policy requiring that *every* individual who travels by air have a passport. Many countries are now requiring that even children have their own passports to travel internationally.

FOR RESIDENTS OF CANADA

You can pick up a passport application at any of 28 regional passport offices or most travel agencies. Canadian children who travel must have their own passport. However, if you hold a valid Canadian passport issued before December 11, 2001, that bears the name of your child, the passport remains valid for you and your child until it expires. Passports cost C$87 for those 16 years and older (valid 5 years), C$37 children 3 to 15 (valid 5 years), and C$22, children under 3 (valid 3 years). Applications, which must be accompanied by two identical passport-size photographs and proof of Canadian citizenship, are available at travel agencies throughout Canada or from the central **Passport Office,** Department of Foreign Affairs and International Trade, Ottawa, ON K1A 0G3 (✆ **800/567-6868;** www. dfait-maeci.gc.ca/passport). Processing takes 5 to 10 days if you apply in person or about 3 weeks by mail.

FOR RESIDENTS OF THE UNITED KINGDOM

To pick up an application for a standard 10-year passport (5-year passport for children under 16), visit the nearest passport office, major post office, or travel agency. You can also contact the **United Kingdom Passport Service** at ✆ **0870/571-0410** or visit its website at www.passport. gov.uk. Passports are £42 for adults and £25 for children under 16, with another £30 fee if you apply in person at a passport office. Processing takes about 2 weeks (1 week if you apply at the passport office).

FOR RESIDENTS OF IRELAND

You can apply for a 10-year passport (€57) at the **Passport Office,** Setanta Centre, Molesworth Street, Dublin 2 (ℂ **01/671-1633;** www.irlgov.ie/iveagh). Those under age 18 and over 65 must apply for a €12 3-year passport. You can also apply at 1A South Mall, Cork (ℂ **021/272525**) or over the counter at most main post offices.

FOR RESIDENTS OF AUSTRALIA

You can get an application from your local post office or any branch of Passports Australia, but you must schedule an interview at the passport office to present your application materials. Call the **Australian Passport Information Service** at ℂ **131-232** or visit the government website at www.passports.gov.au. Passports for adults are A$150, and passports for those under 18 are A$75.

FOR RESIDENTS OF NEW ZEALAND

You can pick up a passport application at any New Zealand Passports Office or download it from its website. Contact the **Passports Office** at ℂ **0800/225-050** in New Zealand or 04/474-8100, or log on to www.passports.govt.nz. Passports for adults are NZ$71, and passports for children under 16 are NZ$36.

CUSTOMS
WHAT YOU CAN BRING IN

Every visitor more than 21 years of age may bring in, free of duty, the following: (1) 1 liter of wine or hard liquor; (2) 200 cigarettes, 100 cigars (but not from Cuba), or 3 pounds of smoking tobacco; and (3) $100 worth of gifts. These exemptions are offered to travelers who spend at least 72 hours in the United States and who have not claimed them within the preceding 6 months. It is altogether forbidden to bring into the country foodstuffs (particularly fruit, cooked meats, and canned goods)

and plants (vegetables, seeds, tropical plants, and the like). Foreign tourists may carry in or out up to $10,000 in U.S. or foreign currency with no formalities; larger sums must be declared to U.S. Customs on entering or leaving, which includes filing Form CM 4790. For details regarding U.S. Customs and Border Protection, consult your nearest U.S. embassy or consulate, or **U.S. Customs** (ℂ **202/927-1770;** www.customs.ustreas.gov).

WHAT YOU CAN TAKE HOME

U.K. citizens returning from a non-EU country have a customs allowance of 200 cigarettes, *or* 100 cigarillos, *or* 50 cigars, *or* 250g of smoking tobacco; 2 liters of still table wine; 1 liter of spirits or strong liqueurs (over 22% volume), *or* 2 liters of fortified wine, sparkling wine, or other liqueurs; 60cc (ml) of perfume; 250cc (ml) of toilet water; and £145 worth of all other goods, including gifts and souvenirs. People under 17 cannot have the tobacco or alcohol allowance. For more information, consult **HM Customs & Excise** at ℂ **0845/010-9000** (from outside the U.K., 020/8929-0152) or http://customs.hmrc.gov.uk.

For a clear summary of **Canadian** rules, request the booklet *I Declare,* from the **Canada Customs and Revenue Agency** (ℂ **800/461-9999** in Canada, or 204/983-3500; www.cbsa-asfc.gc.ca/E/pub/cp/rc4044/). Canada allows its citizens a C$750 exemption, and you're allowed to bring back duty free 200 cigarettes, 50 cigars or cigarillos, 200 tobacco sticks, and 200g manufactured tobacco; and 53 imperial ounces of wine, *or* 40 imperial ounces of liquor, *or* 8.5 liters of beer or ale. Canadian citizens under 18 or 19, depending on their province, cannot have the tobacco or alcohol allowance. In addition, you're allowed to mail gifts to Canada valued at less than C$60 a day if they're unsolicited and don't contain alcohol or tobacco (write on the package

"Unsolicited gift, under $60 value"). All valuables should be declared on the Y-38 form before departure from Canada, including serial numbers of valuables you already own, such as expensive foreign cameras. *Note:* The C$750 exemption can be used only once a year and only after an absence of 7 days.

The duty-free allowance in **Australia** is A$900 or, for those under 18, A$450. Citizens age 18 and over can bring in 250 cigarettes *or* 250 grams of loose tobacco and 2.25 liters of alcohol. If you're returning with valuables you already own, such as foreign-made cameras, you should file Form B263. A helpful brochure available from Australian consulates or Customs offices is *Know Before You Go.* For details, consult the **Australian Customs Service** at *©* **1300/363-263** or www.customs.gov.au.

The duty-free allowance for **New Zealand** is NZ$700. Citizens over 17 can bring in 200 cigarettes, *or* 50 cigars, *or* 250 grams of tobacco (or a mixture of all three if their combined weight doesn't exceed 250g), plus 4.5 liters of wine or beer and 1.125 liters of liquor. New Zealand currency does not carry import or export restrictions. Fill out a certificate of export, listing the valuables you are taking out of the country; that way, you can bring them back without paying duty. Most questions are answered in a free pamphlet available at New Zealand consulates and Customs offices: *New Zealand Customs Guide for Travellers, Notice no. 4.* For more information, contact **New Zealand Customs,** The Customhouse, 17–21 Whitmore St., Box 2218, Wellington (*©* **0800/428-786** or 04/473-6099; www.customs.govt.nz).

HEALTH INSURANCE

Although it's not required of travelers, health insurance is highly recommended. Unlike many European countries, the United States doesn't usually offer free or low-cost medical care to its citizens or visitors. Doctors and hospitals are expensive, and in most cases, they require advance payment or proof of coverage before they render their services. Policies cover everything from the loss or theft of your baggage and trip cancellation to the guarantee of bail in case you're arrested. Good policies will also cover the costs of an accident, repatriation, or death. Packages such as **Europ Assistance's "Worldwide Healthcare Plan"** are sold by European automobile clubs and travel agencies at attractive rates. **Worldwide Assistance Services, Inc.** (*©* **800/777-8710;** www.worldwideassistance.com) is the agent for Europ Assistance in the United States.

INSURANCE FOR BRITISH TRAVELERS   Most big travel agents offer their own insurance and will probably try to sell you their package when you book a holiday. Think before you sign. **Britain's Consumers' Association** recommends that you insist on seeing the policy and reading the fine print before buying travel insurance. **The Association of British Insurers** (*©* **020/7600-3333;** www.abi.org.uk) gives advice by phone and publishes *Holiday Insurance,* a free guide to policy provisions and prices. You might also shop around for better deals: Try **Columbus Direct** (*©* **0870/033-9988;** www.columbusdirect.net).

INSURANCE FOR CANADIAN TRAVELERS   Canadians should check with their provincial health plan offices or call **Health Canada** (*©* **866/225-0709;** www.hc-sc.gc.ca) to find out the extent of their coverage and what documentation and receipts they must take home in case they are treated in the United States.

MONEY

CURRENCY   The U.S. monetary system is very simple: The most common **bills** are the $1 (a "buck"), $5, $10, and $20 denominations. There are also $2 bills (seldom encountered), $50 bills, and $100 bills (the last two are usually not welcome as payment for small purchases). All the paper money was recently redesigned, making the faces on them disproportionately large, but the old-style bills are still legal tender.

Coins come in seven denominations: 1¢ (1 cent, or a penny); 5¢ (5 cents, or a nickel); 10¢ (10 cents, or a dime); 25¢ (25 cents, or a quarter); 50¢ (50 cents, or a half dollar); the gold-colored Sacagawea coin, worth $1; and the rare silver dollar.

Note: The "foreign-exchange bureaus" so common in Europe are rare even at airports in the United States and nonexistent outside major cities.

TRAVELER'S CHECKS Traveler's checks are widely accepted, but make sure that they're denominated in U.S. dollars; foreign-currency checks are often difficult to exchange. The three traveler's checks that are most widely recognized—and least likely to be denied—are **Visa, American Express,** and **Thomas Cook.** Be sure to record the numbers of the checks, and keep that information in a separate place in case they get lost or stolen. Most D.C. businesses are pretty good about taking traveler's checks, but you're better off cashing them in at a bank (in small amounts, of course) and paying in cash. Remember: You'll need identification, such as a driver's license or passport, to change a traveler's check.

CREDIT CARDS & ATMs Credit cards are the most widely used form of payment in the United States: **Visa** (Barclaycard in Britain), **MasterCard** (Euro-Card in Europe, Access in Britain, Chargex in Canada), **American Express, Diners Club,** and **Discover.** There are, however, a handful of stores and restaurants in D.C. that do not take credit cards, so be sure to ask in advance. Most businesses display a sticker near their entrance to let you know which cards

they accept. (***Note:*** Businesses may require a minimum purchase, usually around $10, to use a credit card.)

It's highly recommended that you bring at least one major credit card. You must have one to rent a car, and hotels and airlines usually require a credit card imprint as a deposit against expenses.

You'll find automated teller machines (ATMs) in just about every part of D.C. Some ATMs will allow you to draw U.S. currency against your bank and credit cards. Check with your bank before leaving home, and remember that you will need your personal identification number (PIN) to do so. Most accept Visa, Master-Card, and American Express, as well as ATM cards from other U.S. banks. Expect to be charged up to $3 per transaction, however, if you're not using your own bank's ATM.

One way around these fees is to ask for "cash back" at grocery stores that accept ATM cards and don't charge usage fees. Of course, you'll have to purchase something first. The same is true at most U.S. post offices.

ATM cards with major credit card backing, known as "debit cards," are now a commonly acceptable form of payment in most stores and restaurants. Debit cards draw money directly from your checking account. Some stores enable you to receive "cash back" on your debit-card purchases as well.

SAFETY

GENERAL SUGGESTIONS If you're in doubt about which neighborhoods in D.C. are safe, don't hesitate to make inquiries with the hotel front-desk staff or the local tourist office. Avoid deserted areas, especially at night, and don't go into public parks after dark unless there's a concert or similar occasion that will attract a crowd.

Avoid carrying valuables with you on the street, and keep expensive cameras or electronic equipment bagged up or covered when not in use. If you're using a map, try to consult it inconspicuously—or, better yet, study it before you leave your room. Always lock your room door—don't assume that once you're inside the hotel, you are automatically safe and no longer need to be aware of your surroundings.

DRIVING SAFETY   Driving safety is important, too, and carjacking is not unprecedented. Question your rental agency about personal safety, and ask for a traveler-safety brochure when you pick up your car. Obtain written directions—or a map with the route clearly marked—from the agency showing how to get to your destination. (Many agencies now offer the option of renting a cellphone for the duration of your car rental; check with the rental agent when you pick up the car. Otherwise, contact **InTouch USA** at ✆ **800/872-7626** or www.intouchusa. com for short-term cellphone rental.)

And, if possible, arrive and depart during daylight hours.

If you drive off a highway and end up in a dodgy-looking neighborhood, leave the area as quickly as possible. If you have an accident, even on the highway, stay in your car with the doors locked until you assess the situation or until the police arrive. If you're bumped from behind on the street or are involved in a minor accident with no injuries, and the situation appears to be suspicious, motion to the other driver to follow you. Never get out of your car in such situations. Go directly to the nearest police precinct, well-lit service station, or 24-hour store.

Park in well-lit, busy areas when possible. Always keep your car doors locked, even if the vehicle is attended. Never leave any packages or valuables in sight. If someone attempts to rob you or steal your car, don't try to resist the thief/carjacker. Report the incident to the police department immediately by calling ✆ **911.**

2 Getting to the U.S.

Most international flights to the Washington, D.C. area land at Washington Dulles International Airport, with Baltimore–Washington International Airport handling some, and Ronald Reagan Washington National Airport offering service to only one international carrier. Specific information follows.

The one international airline with scheduled flights into Ronald Reagan Washington National Airport is **Air Canada** (✆ 888/247-2262; www.air canada.ca).

International airlines with scheduled flights into Baltimore–Washington International airport include **Air Canada** (see above), **British Airways** (✆ 0870/850 9850 in the U.K., or 800/247-9297; www. british-airways.com), and **Aer Lingus** (✆ 800/474-7424; www.aerlingus.com).

International airlines with scheduled flights into Washington Dulles International Airport include **Aeroflot** (✆ 888/ 340-6400; www.aeroflot.com), **Air Canada** (see above), **Air France** (✆ 800/321-4538; www.airfrance.com), **Alitalia** (✆ 800/223-5730; www.allitalia.com), **ANA Airways** (✆ 800/235-9262; www. svc.ana.co.jp), **British Airways** (see above), **KLM** (✆ 800/225-2525; www. klm.com), **Lufthansa** (✆ 800/645-3880; www.lufthansa.com), **Saudi Arabian Airlines** (✆ 800/472-8342; www.saudi airlines.com), and **Virgin Atlantic** (✆ 0870 380 2007 in the U.K., or 800/ 862-8621 in the U.S.; www.virgin-atlantic. com).

AIRLINE DISCOUNTS   The smart traveler can find numerous ways to reduce the price of a plane ticket simply by taking

> ### ⌒*Tips* Prepare to Be Fingerprinted
>
> As of January 2004, many international visitors traveling on visas to the United States will be photographed and fingerprinted at Customs in a new program created by the Department of Homeland Security called **US-VISIT**. Non–U.S. citizens arriving at airports and on cruise ships must undergo an instant background check as part of the government's efforts to deter terrorism by verifying the identities of incoming and outgoing visitors. Exempt from the extra scrutiny are visitors entering by land and those who don't require a visa for short-term visits (mostly from Europe; see p. 286). For more information, go to the Homeland Security website at **www.dhs.gov/dhspublic**.

time to shop around. For example, overseas visitors can take advantage of the APEX (Advance Purchase Excursion) reductions offered by all major U.S. and European carriers. For more money-saving airline advice, see "Getting There," in chapter 2. For the best rates, compare fares, and be flexible with the dates and times of travel.

3 Getting Around the U.S.

BY PLANE Some large airlines offer transatlantic or transpacific passengers special discount tickets under the name **Visit USA,** which allows mostly one-way travel from one U.S. destination to another at very low prices. Unavailable in the United States, these discount tickets must be purchased abroad in conjunction with your international fare. This system is the easiest, fastest, cheapest way to see the country. Obtain information well in advance from your travel agent or the airline, because the conditions attached to these discount tickets can be changed without notice.

BY TRAIN International visitors (excluding Canadians) can also buy a **USA Rail Pass,** good for 15 or 30 days of unlimited travel on **Amtrak** (© **800/ USA-RAIL;** www.amtrak.com). The pass is available through many overseas travel agents. Prices valid for travel across the United States in 2005 for a 15-day pass were $295 off peak, $440 peak; a 30-day pass costs $385 off peak, $550 peak. Fares are significantly cheaper, however, within particular regions. See Amtrak's website for the cost of travel within the western, eastern, or northwestern United States. With a foreign passport, you can also buy passes directly from some Amtrak locations, including San Francisco, Los Angeles, Chicago, New York, Miami, Boston, and Washington, D.C. Reservations are generally required and should be made as early as possible. Regional rail passes are also available.

BY BUS Bus travel is often the most economical form of public transit for short hops between U.S. cities, but it can also be slow and uncomfortable—certainly not an option for everyone (particularly when Amtrak, which is far more luxurious, offers similar rates). **Greyhound/ Trailways** (© **800/231-2222;** www. greyhound.com), the sole nationwide bus line, offers an **International Ameripass** that must be purchased before coming to the United States or by phone through the Greyhound International Office at the Port Authority Bus Terminal in New York City (© **212/971-0492**). The pass can be obtained from foreign travel agents or through Greyhound's website (order at least 21 days before your departure to the U.S.) and costs less than the domestic version. Passes cost as follows in 2005: 4 days ($179), 7 days ($239), 10 days ($289), 15 days ($349), 21 days ($419), 30 days ($479), 45 days ($529), and 60 days ($639). You can get more info on the pass at the website or by calling ☎ **402/330-8552.** In addition, special rates are available for seniors, students, and children.

BY CAR   The most cost-effective way to travel the United States—including day trips from the D.C. area—is by car.

The interstate highway system connects cities and towns all over the country, with an extensive network of federal, state, and local highways and roads as well. Some of the national car-rental companies with offices in D.C. include **Alamo** (☎ 800/462-5266; www.alamo.com), **Avis** (☎ 800/230-4898; www.avis.com), **Budget** (☎ 800/527-0700; www.budget.com), **Dollar** (☎ 800/800-3665; www.dollar.com), **Hertz** (☎ 800/654-3131; www.hertz.com), and **National** (☎ 800/227-7368; www.nationalcar.com).

FAST FACTS: For the International Traveler

Automobile Organizations   Auto clubs will supply maps, suggested routes, guidebooks, accident and bail-bond insurance, and emergency road service. The **American Automobile Association (AAA)** is the major auto club in the United States. If you belong to an auto club in your home country, inquire about AAA reciprocity before you leave. You may be able to join AAA even if you're not a member of a reciprocal club; to inquire, call AAA (☎ **800/222-4357**). AAA is actually an organization of regional auto clubs, so look under "AAA Automobile Club" in the White Pages of the telephone directory. AAA has a nationwide emergency road service telephone number (☎ 800/AAA-HELP).

Business Hours   Offices are usually open weekdays from 9am to 5pm. Banks are open weekdays from 9am to 3pm or later and sometimes Saturday mornings. Stores typically open between 9 and 10am and close between 5 and 6pm Monday through Saturday. Stores in shopping complexes or malls tend to stay open late—until about 9pm on weekdays and weekends—and many malls and larger department stores are open on Sundays.

Currency & Currency Exchange   See "Entry Requirements" and "Money" under "Preparing for Your Trip," earlier in this chapter.

Drinking Laws   The legal age for purchase and consumption of alcoholic beverages is 21; proof of age is required and often requested at bars, nightclubs, and restaurants, so it's always a good idea to bring ID when you go out. Supermarkets and convenience stores in D.C. sell beer, wine, and liquor.

Electricity   Like Canada, the United States uses 110 to 120 volts AC (60 cycles), compared to 220 to 240 volts AC (50 cycles) in most of Europe, Australia, and New Zealand. If your small appliances use 220 to 240 volts, you'll need a 110-volt transformer and a plug adapter with two flat parallel pins to operate them here. Downward converters that change 220 to 240 volts to 110 to 120 volts are difficult to find in the United States, so bring one with you.

Embassies & Consulates All embassies are located in the nation's capital, Washington, D.C. Some consulates are located in major U.S. cities, and most nations have a mission to the United Nations in New York City. If your country isn't listed below, call for directory information in Washington, D.C. (© **202/555-1212**), or log on to **www.embassy.org/embassies**.

The embassy of **Australia** is at 1601 Massachusetts Ave. NW, Washington, DC 20036 (© **202/797-3000**; www.austemb.org). There are consulates in New York, Honolulu, Houston, Los Angeles, and San Francisco.

The embassy of **Canada** is at 501 Pennsylvania Ave. NW, Washington, DC 20001 (© **202/682-1740**; www.canadianembassy.org). Other Canadian consulates are in Buffalo (New York), Detroit, Los Angeles, New York, and Seattle.

The embassy of **Ireland** is at 2234 Massachusetts Ave. NW, Washington, DC 20008 (© **202/462-3939**; www.irelandemb.org). Irish consulates are located in Boston, Chicago, New York, San Francisco, and other cities. See the website for a complete listing.

The embassy of **Japan** is at 2520 Massachusetts Ave. NW, Washington, DC 20008 (© **202/238-6700**; www.embjapan.org). Japanese consulates are located in many cities, including Atlanta, Boston, Detroit, New York, San Francisco, and Seattle.

The embassy of **New Zealand** is at 37 Observatory Circle NW, Washington, DC 20008 (© **202/328-4800**; www.nzemb.org). New Zealand consulates are found in Los Angeles, Salt Lake City, San Francisco, and Seattle.

The embassy of the **United Kingdom** is at 3100 Massachusetts Ave. NW, Washington, DC 20008 (© **202/588-7800**; www.britainusa.com). Other British consulates are available in Atlanta, Boston, Chicago, Cleveland, Houston, Los Angeles, New York, San Francisco, and Seattle.

Emergencies Call © **911** to report a fire, call the police, or get an ambulance anywhere in the United States. This is a toll-free call. (No coins are required at public telephones.)

If you encounter serious problems, contact the **Traveler's Aid Society International** (© **202/546-1127**; www.travelersaid.org), a nationwide, nonprofit, social-service organization geared to helping travelers in difficult straits, from reuniting families separated while traveling, to providing food and/or shelter to people stranded without cash, to emotional counseling. Traveler's Aid operates help desks at Washington Dulles International Airport (© **703/572-8296**), Ronald Reagan Washington National Airport (© **703/417-3975**), and Union Station (© **202/371-1937**).

Gasoline (Petrol) Petrol is known as gasoline (or simply gas) in the United States, and petrol stations are known as both gas stations and service stations. At press time, the cost of gasoline in the United States is abnormally high ($3 a gallon) and fluctuating drastically, on the rise. Taxes are already included in the printed price. One U.S. gallon equals 3.8 liters or .85 imperial gallon.

Holidays Banks; government offices; post offices; and many stores, restaurants, and museums are closed on the following legal national holidays: January 1 (New Year's Day), the third Monday in January (Martin Luther King, Jr. Day), the third Monday in February (Presidents' Day), the last Monday in May (Memorial

Day), July 4 (Independence Day), the first Monday in September (Labor Day), the second Monday in October (Columbus Day), November 11 (Veterans' Day/Armistice Day), the fourth Thursday in November (Thanksgiving Day), and December 25 (Christmas). The Tuesday after the first Monday in November is Election Day, a federal government holiday in presidential-election years (held every 4 years, and next in 2008).

Legal Aid If you are "pulled over" for a minor infraction (such as speeding), never attempt to pay the fine directly to a police officer; this could be construed as attempted bribery, a much more serious crime. Pay fines by mail or directly into the hands of the clerk of the court. If you are accused of a more serious offense, say and do nothing before consulting a lawyer. Here the burden is on the state to prove a person's guilt beyond a reasonable doubt, and everyone has the right to remain silent, whether he or she is suspected of a crime or actually arrested. Once arrested, a person can make one telephone call to a party of his or her choice. Call your embassy or consulate.

Mail If you aren't sure what your address will be in the United States, mail can be sent to you, in your name, c/o General Delivery at the main post office of the city or region where you expect to be. (Call © **800/275-8777** for information on the nearest post office.) The addressee must pick up mail in person and must produce proof of identity (driver's license, passport, etc.). Most post offices will hold your mail for up to 1 month and are open Monday to Friday from 8am to 6pm and Saturday from 9am to 3pm.

Generally found at intersections, mailboxes are blue with a red-and-white stripe and carry the inscription U.S. MAIL. If your mail is addressed to a U.S. destination, don't forget to add the five-digit postal code (or zip code) after the two-letter abbreviation of the state to which the mail is addressed. This is essential for prompt delivery.

At press time, domestic postage rates were 24¢ for a postcard and 39¢ for a letter. For international mail, a first-class letter of up to ½ ounce costs 80¢ (60¢ to Canada and Mexico); a first-class postcard costs 70¢ (50¢ to Canada and Mexico); and a preprinted postal aerogramme costs 70¢. For more information, see http://pe.usps.gov.

Measurements See the chart on the inside front cover of this book for details on converting metric measurements to U.S. equivalents.

Smoking Smoking is legal in most bars and restaurants throughout the city.

Taxes The United States has no value-added tax (VAT) or other indirect tax at the national level. Every state, county, and city may levy its own local tax on all purchases, including hotel and restaurant checks and airline tickets. These taxes will not appear on price tags.

The sales tax on merchandise is 5.75% in the District, 5% in Maryland, and 4.5% in Virginia. The tax on restaurant meals is 10% in the District, 5% in Maryland, and 4.5% in Virginia.

In the District, you pay 14.5% hotel tax. The hotel tax in Maryland varies by county by 5% to 8%. The hotel tax in Virginia also varies by county, averaging about 9.75%.

Telephone, Telegraph, Telex & Fax Private corporations run the telephone system in the United States, so rates can vary widely, especially for long-distance service and operator-assisted calls. Generally, hotel surcharges on long-distance and local calls are astronomical, so you're better off using a **public pay telephone,** which you'll find clearly marked in most public buildings and private establishments, as well as on the street. Convenience grocery stores and gas stations almost always have them. Many convenience groceries and packaging services sell **prepaid calling cards** in denominations up to $50; these can be the least expensive way to call home. Many public phones at airports now accept American Express, MasterCard, and Visa credit cards. **Local calls** made from public pay phones in most locales cost either 25¢ or 35¢. Pay phones do not accept pennies, and few will take anything larger than a quarter.

You may want to look into leasing a cellphone for the duration of your trip.

Most long-distance and international calls can be dialed directly from any phone. **For calls within the United States and to Canada,** dial 1 followed by the area code and the seven-digit number. **For other international calls,** dial 011 followed by the country code, city code, and the number you are calling.

Calls to area codes **800, 888, 877,** and **866** are toll free. However, calls to area codes **700** and **900** (chat lines, bulletin boards, "dating" services, and so on) can be very expensive—usually, there's a charge of 95¢ to $3 or more per minute, and they sometimes have minimum charges that can run as high as $15 or more.

For **reversed-charge or collect calls** and for person-to-person calls, dial the number 0 and then the area code and number; an operator will come on the line, and you should specify whether you are calling collect, person-to-person, or both. If your operator-assisted call is international, ask for the overseas operator.

For **local directory assistance** ("information"), dial 411; for long-distance information, dial 1, followed by the appropriate area code and 555-1212.

Telegraph and telex services are provided primarily by Western Union. You can bring your telegram to the nearest Western Union office or dictate it by phone (© **800/325-6000**). You can also telegraph money, or have it telegraphed to you, very quickly over the Western Union system, but this service can cost as much as 15% to 20% of the amount sent.

Most hotels have **fax machines** available for guest use (be sure to ask about the charge to use it). Many hotel rooms are even wired for guests' fax machines. A less expensive way to send and receive faxes may be at stores such as **The UPS Store** (formerly Mail Boxes Etc.), a national chain of retail packing service shops. (Look in the Yellow Pages directory under "Packing Services.")

The United States has two kinds of telephone directories. The **White Pages** list private households and business subscribers in alphabetical order. The inside front cover lists emergency numbers for police, fire, ambulance, poison-control center, crime-victims hot line, and so on. The first few pages will tell you how to make long-distance and international calls, complete with country codes and area codes. Government numbers are usually printed on blue paper within the White Pages. Printed on yellow paper, the so-called **Yellow Pages** list all local services, businesses, industries, and houses of worship according to activity with an index at the front or back. (Drugstores/pharmacies and restaurants are also listed by geographic location.) The Yellow Pages also include city plans or detailed area maps, postal ZIP codes, and public-transportation routes.

Time The continental United States is divided into **four time zones:** Eastern Standard Time (EST), Central Standard Time (CST), Mountain Standard Time (MST), and Pacific Standard Time (PST). Alaska and Hawaii have their own zones. For example, noon in Washington, D.C. (EST) is 11am in Chicago (CST), 10am in Denver (MST), 9am in Los Angeles (PST), 8am in Anchorage (AST), and 7am in Honolulu (HST).

Daylight saving time takes effect at 2am the first Sunday in April until 2am the last Sunday in October, except in Arizona, Hawaii, the U.S. Virgin Islands, and Puerto Rico. (Indiana is expected to begin observing daylight saving time in April 2006.) Daylight saving moves the clock 1 hour ahead of standard time. (A new law will extend daylight saving time in 2007; clocks will change the second Sunday in March and the first Sunday in November.)

Tipping Tips are a very important part of certain workers' income, and gratuities are the standard way of showing appreciation for services provided. (Tipping is certainly not compulsory if the service is poor!) In hotels, tip **bellhops** at least $1 per bag ($2–$3 if you have a lot of luggage), and tip the **chamber staff** $1 to $2 per day (more if you've left a disaster area for him or her to clean up). Tip the **doorman** or **concierge** only if he or she has provided you some specific service (for example, calling a cab for you or obtaining difficult-to-get theater tickets). Tip the **valet-parking attendant** $1 every time you get your car.

In restaurants, bars, and nightclubs, tip **service staff** 15% to 20% of the check, tip **bartenders** 10% to 15%, tip **checkroom attendants** $1 per garment, and tip **valet-parking attendants** $1 per vehicle.

As for other service personnel, tip **cab drivers** 15% of the fare; tip **skycaps** at airports at least $1 per bag ($2–$3 if you have a lot of luggage); and tip **hairdressers** and **barbers** 15% to 20%.

Toilets You won't find public toilets or "restrooms" on the streets in most U.S. cities, but they can be found in hotel lobbies, bars, restaurants, museums, department stores, railway and bus stations, and service stations. Large hotels and fast-food restaurants are often the best bet for clean facilities. If possible, avoid the toilets at parks and beaches, which tend to be dirty; some may be unsafe. Restaurants and bars in resorts or heavily visited areas may reserve their restrooms for patrons. Some establishments display a notice indicating this. You can ignore this sign or, better yet, avoid arguments by paying for a cup of coffee or a soft drink, which will qualify you as a patron.

Index

See also Accommodations and Restaurant indexes, below.

A Guide for Every Type of Traveler

FROMMER'S® COMPLETE GUIDES

For independent leisure or business travelers who value complete coverage, candid advice, and lots of choices in all price ranges.

These are the most complete, up-to-date guides you can buy. Count on Frommer's for exact prices, savvy trip planning, sightseeing advice, dozens of detailed maps, and candid reviews of hotels and restaurants in every price range. All Complete Guides offer special icons to point you to great finds, excellent values, and more. Every hotel, restaurant, and attraction is rated from zero to three stars to help you make the best choices.

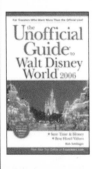

UNOFFICIAL GUIDES®

For honeymooners, families, business travelers, and anyone else who values no-nonsense, *Consumer Reports*–style advice.

Unofficial Guides are ideal for those who want to know the pros and cons of the places they are visiting and make informed decisions. The guides rank and rate every hotel, restaurant, and attraction, with evaluations based on reader surveys and critiques compiled by a team of unbiased inspectors.

FROMMER'S® IRREVERENT GUIDES

For experienced, sophisticated travelers looking for a fresh, candid perspective on a destination.

This unique series is perfect for anyone who wants a cutting-edge perspective on the hottest destinations. Covering all major cities around the globe, these guides are unabashedly honest and downright hilarious. Decked out with a retro-savvy feel, each book features new photos, maps, and neighborhood references.

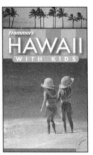

FROMMER'S® WITH KIDS GUIDES

For families traveling with children ages 2 to 14.

Here are the ultimate guides for a successful family vacation. Written by parents, they're packed with information on museums, outdoor activities, attractions, great drives and strolls, incredible parks, the liveliest places to stay and eat, and more.

Visit Frommers.com

Now you know.

ROMMER'S® COMPLETE TRAVEL GUIDES

laska
malfi Coast
merican Southwest
msterdam
rgentina & Chile
rizona
tlanta
ustralia
ustria
ahamas
arcelona
eijing
elgium, Holland & Luxembourg
elize
ermuda
oston
razil
ritish Columbia & the Canadian
   Rockies
russels & Bruges
udapest & the Best of Hungary
uenos Aires
algary
alifornia
anada
ancún, Cozumel & the Yucatán
ape Cod, Nantucket & Martha's
   Vineyard
aribbean
aribbean Ports of Call
arolinas & Georgia
hicago
hina
olorado
osta Rica
roatia
uba
enmark
enver, Boulder & Colorado Springs
dinburgh & Glasgow
ngland
urope
urope by Rail

Florence, Tuscany & Umbria
Florida
France
Germany
Greece
Greek Islands
Hawaii
Hong Kong
Honolulu, Waikiki & Oahu
India
Ireland
Italy
Jamaica
Japan
Kauai
Las Vegas
London
Los Angeles
Los Cabos & Baja
Madrid
Maine Coast
Maryland & Delaware
Maui
Mexico
Montana & Wyoming
Montréal & Québec City
Moscow & St. Petersburg
Munich & the Bavarian Alps
Nashville & Memphis
New England
Newfoundland & Labrador
New Mexico
New Orleans
New York City
New York State
New Zealand
Northern Italy
Norway
Nova Scotia, New Brunswick &
   Prince Edward Island
Oregon
Paris
Peru

Philadelphia & the Amish Country
Portugal
Prague & the Best of the Czech
   Republic
Provence & the Riviera
Puerto Rico
Rome
San Antonio & Austin
San Diego
San Francisco
Santa Fe, Taos & Albuquerque
Scandinavia
Scotland
Seattle
Seville, Granada & the Best of
   Andalusia
Shanghai
Sicily
Singapore & Malaysia
South Africa
South America
South Florida
South Pacific
Southeast Asia
Spain
Sweden
Switzerland
Texas
Thailand
Tokyo
Toronto
Turkey
USA
Utah
Vancouver & Victoria
Vermont, New Hampshire & Maine
Vienna & the Danube Valley
Vietnam
Virgin Islands
Virginia
Walt Disney World® & Orlando
Washington, D.C.
Washington State

ROMMER'S® DOLLAR-A-DAY GUIDES

ustralia from $60 a Day
alifornia from $70 a Day
ngland from $75 a Day
urope from $85 a Day
orida from $70 a Day

Hawaii from $80 a Day
Ireland from $90 a Day
Italy from $90 a Day
London from $95 a Day

New York City from $90 a Day
Paris from $95 a Day
San Francisco from $70 a Day
Washington, D.C. from $80 a Day

ROMMER'S® PORTABLE GUIDES

capulco, Ixtapa & Zihuatanejo
msterdam
uba
ustralia's Great Barrier Reef
ahamas
erlin
g Island of Hawaii
oston
alifornia Wine Country
ancún
ayman Islands
harleston
hicago

Disneyland®
Dominican Republic
Dublin
Florence
Las Vegas
Las Vegas for Non-Gamblers
London
Los Angeles
Maui
Nantucket & Martha's Vineyard
New Orleans
New York City
Paris

Portland
Puerto Rico
Puerto Vallarta, Manzanillo &
   Guadalajara
Rio de Janeiro
San Diego
San Francisco
Savannah
Vancouver
Venice
Virgin Islands
Washington, D.C.
Whistler

ROMMER'S® CRUISE GUIDES

laska Cruises & Ports of Call

Cruises & Ports of Call

European Cruises & Ports of Call

FROMMER'S® DAY BY DAY GUIDES

Amsterdam
Chicago
Florence & Tuscany

London
New York City
Paris

Rome
San Francisco
Venice

FROMMER'S® NATIONAL PARK GUIDES

Algonquin Provincial Park
Banff & Jasper
Grand Canyon

National Parks of the American West
Rocky Mountain
Yellowstone & Grand Teton

Yosemite and Sequoia & Kings
 Canyon
Zion & Bryce Canyon

FROMMER'S® MEMORABLE WALKS

Chicago
London

New York
Paris

Rome
San Francisco

FROMMER'S® WITH KIDS GUIDES

Chicago
Hawaii
Las Vegas
London

National Parks
New York City
San Francisco

Toronto
Walt Disney World® & Orlando
Washington, D.C.

SUZY GERSHMAN'S BORN TO SHOP GUIDES

Born to Shop: France
Born to Shop: Hong Kong, Shanghai
 & Beijing

Born to Shop: Italy
Born to Shop: London

Born to Shop: New York
Born to Shop: Paris

FROMMER'S® IRREVERENT GUIDES

Amsterdam
Boston
Chicago
Las Vegas
London

Los Angeles
Manhattan
New Orleans
Paris

Rome
San Francisco
Walt Disney World®
Washington, D.C.

FROMMER'S® BEST-LOVED DRIVING TOURS

Austria
Britain
California
France

Germany
Ireland
Italy
New England

Northern Italy
Scotland
Spain
Tuscany & Umbria

THE UNOFFICIAL GUIDES®

Adventure Travel in Alaska
Beyond Disney
California with Kids
Central Italy
Chicago
Cruises
Disneyland®
England
Florida
Florida with Kids

Hawaii
Ireland
Las Vegas
London
Maui
Mexico's Best Beach Resorts
Mini Las Vegas
Mini Mickey
New Orleans
New York City

Paris
San Francisco
South Florida including Miami &
 the Keys
Walt Disney World®
Walt Disney World® for
 Grown-ups
Walt Disney World® with Kids
Washington, D.C.

SPECIAL-INTEREST TITLES

Athens Past & Present
Cities Ranked & Rated
Frommer's Best Day Trips from London
Frommer's Best RV & Tent Campgrounds
 in the U.S.A.

Frommer's Exploring America by RV
Frommer's NYC Free & Dirt Cheap
Frommer's Road Atlas Europe
Frommer's Road Atlas Ireland
Retirement Places Rated

FROMMER'S® PHRASEFINDER DICTIONARY GUIDES

French

Italian

Spanish